Warfare in History

THE BATTLE OF CRÉCY, 1346

Warfare in History
ISSN 1358–779X

Editorial Board
Matthew Bennett, Royal Military Academy, Sandhurst
David Parrott, University of Oxford
Hew Strachan, University of Oxford

This series aims to provide a wide-ranging and scholarly approach to military history, offering both individual studies of topics or wars, and volumes giving a selection of contemporary and later accounts of particular battles; its scope ranges from the early medieval to the modern period.

New proposals for the series are welcomed; they should be sent to the publisher at the address below.

Boydell & Brewer Limited, PO Box 9, Woodbridge, Suffolk, IP12 2DF

*Previously published volumes in this series
are listed at the back of this book*

THE BATTLE OF CRÉCY, 1346

Andrew Ayton and Sir Philip Preston Bart.

with additional contributions from
Françoise Autrand
Christophe Piel
Michael Prestwich
Bertrand Schnerb

THE BOYDELL PRESS

First published 2005
The Boydell Press, Woodbridge

ISBN 1 84383 115 5

The Boydell Press is an imprint of Boydell & Brewer Ltd
PO Box 9, Woodbridge, Suffolk IP12 3DF, UK
and of Boydell & Brewer Inc.
668 Mt Hope Avenue, Rochester, NY 14620, USA
website: www.boydellandbrewer.com

A CIP catalogue record for this book is available
from the British Library

Library of Congress Cataloging-in-Publication Data
Ayton, Andrew, 1959–
    The Battle of Crécy, 1346 / Andrew Ayton and Sir Philip Preston ; with
additional contributions from Françoise Autrand, Michael Prestwich,
Bertrand Schnerb.
        p. cm. – (Warfare in history, ISSN 1358–779X)
    Summary: "First large-scale study of Crécy and its context, bringing out its
full significance in English and French history" – Provided by publisher.
    Includes index.
    ISBN 1–84383–115–5 (hardback : alk. paper)
    1. Crécy, Battle of, Crécy-en-Ponthieu, France, 1346.   2. Hundred Years War,
1339–1453 – Campaigns – France.   3. France – History, Military – 1328–1589.
4. Great Britain – History, Military – 1066–1485.   I. Preston, Sir Philip, 1946–
II. Autrand, Françoise.   III. Prestwich, Michael.   IV. Schnerb, Bertrand.
V. Title.   VI. Series.
DC98.5.C8A98 2005
944'.02542'0944262 – dc22   2004024033

This publication is printed on acid-free paper

Typeset by Pru Harrison, Hacheston, Suffolk
Printed in Great Britain by
The Cromwell Press, Trowbridge, Wiltshire.

Contents

List of Illustrations

Preface and Acknowledgements

In October 1998 the Battlefields Trust held their first overseas residential conference at Crécy-en-Ponthieu, with the battles of Crécy and Agincourt as its twin foci and with invited speakers from the United Kingdom and France. This book owes its inspiration to that occasion, and in particular to the conference dinner, during which, as strangers, we struck up a conversation on some of the perennial questions that surround the campaign and battle of Crécy. It quickly became apparent that we shared the belief that a substantial, multi-faceted study devoted to the battle of Crécy was long overdue; and in the light of the new evidence and fresh interpretations that had emerged during the conference, it was clear to us that the time was ripe for such a project. That it has taken flight has been owing to the enthusiastic – and patient – support of Boydell & Brewer, who have been everything that authors could wish for in a publisher.

Several of those who spoke at the Crécy conference in 1998 have been kind enough to submit their papers as chapters for this book. For their contributions, we are most grateful to Professor Bertrand Schnerb, of the Université de Lille; to Professor Michael Prestwich, of the University of Durham; and to Dr Christophe Piel, of the Paris Sorbonne. Although inspired by the Crécy conference, this book is by no means a straightforward collection of the papers that were given on that occasion. The original lecture on the English army has been greatly expanded to form Chapter 5. (This represents the first major output from a project on Edward III's armies supported by the Arts and Humanities Research Board: RLS: APN 13143 / AN 8490.) There were some important gaps to fill, and we have taken it upon ourselves to supply the greater part of this new material (Chapters 1, 2, 3, 9 and 10). However, for Chapter 8, on the political repercussions in France following the battle, we are particularly grateful to Madame Françoise Autrand of the École Normale Supérieure. We should also like to thank Dan Smith for his assistance in the translation of this paper.

We are pleased to acknowledge the expert assistance of Professor Jean Sommé, of the Laboratoire de Géomorphologie et d'Étude du Quaternaire at the Université de Lille, who provided an opinion on a significant element of the topography of the battlefield; and Robert Hardy, who offered technical guidance concerning the longbow. Similarly, we are grateful to Dr Paul Adamthwaite of the Archives and Collections Society, who compiled a report on the tides in the Somme estuary on 24 August 1346 (see http://www.aandc.org/research/tides.html). We would like to thank Monsieur Eric Balandra, of the History Society of Crécy, whose formidable academic and local knowledge has frequently been of assistance to us. For advice and encouraging words at various stages of our research, thanks are also due to Professor John Palmer, Professor David Crouch, Dr Julian Haseldine and Dr Richard Gorski – all of the History Department at the University of Hull. Richard Gorski is also responsible for the

Battle of Crécy Trust website, where a range of source materials relating to the battle may be consulted (http://www.hull.ac.uk/history/dept/crecytrust.htm). The staff of the Bibliothèque municipale d'Abbeville kindly assisted in the interpretation of nineteenth-century maps of the battlefield of Crécy. For the conference that inspired us, we would like to acknowledge the co-operation of the Battlefields Trust, and in particular their Secretary, Chris Scott; the logistical help of Jean-Claude Brasseur and Roger Brechet of L'Association Crécy la Bataille; and the support of the Mayor of Crécy, who allowed the use of both the cinema and the Salle des Fêtes. Our gratitude goes also to Miss Monica Harper, British Consul General in Lille, whose presence brought the occasion official recognition.

We should like to take this opportunity to remember the late General Sir Martin Farndale KCB, who was present at the 1998 conference in his capacity as President of the Battle of Crécy Trust, and to whom this book is dedicated. As a past Master Gunner at St James's Park, General Farndale's interest in Crécy was not only in his unceasing efforts to help in the creation of a Battle Centre, but also for the fact that it was at Crécy that the forerunners of his regiment, The Royal Artillery, first used guns.

This book has been some years in the making and, like Michelangelo, we have been asked many times when we would be finished. We leave it to others to decide whether it satisfies 'in its artistic details'. That it has been brought to completion is due in no small part to our wives, Agnes and Kirsi, who have been faithful and patient supporters, and sources of much good sense, throughout the years that we have spent talking about the battle of Crécy.

Andrew Ayton   Sir Philip Preston Bart.
Shugborough   Crécy-en-Ponthieu
Staffordshire

Abbreviations

Acta Bellicosa, ed. Moisant	'Acta Bellicosa Edwardi Tertii', in J. Moisant, *Le Prince Noir en Aquitaine, 1355–6, 1362–70* (Paris, 1894)
Acts of War, ed. Barber	'The acts of war of Edward III (1346)', *The Life and Campaigns of the Black Prince*, ed. and trans. R. Barber (Woodbridge, 1986), pp. 26–40
Anonimalle	*The Anonimalle Chronicle, 1333–1381*, ed. V.H. Galbraith (Manchester, 1927)
Avesbury	Adam Murimuth, *Continuatio chronicarum* and Robert de Avesbury, *De gestis mirabilibus regis Edwardi Tertii*, ed. E.M. Thompson, Rolls Ser. (London, 1889)
Baker	*Chronicon Galfridi le Baker de Swynebroke (1303–56)*, ed. E.M. Thompson (Oxford, 1889)
BIHR	*Bulletin of the Institute of Historical Research*
BL	British Library
Black Prince Register	*Register of Edward the Black Prince*, ed. M.C.B. Dawes, 4 vols (London, 1930–3)
Brut, ed. Brie	*The Brut*, ed. F.W.D. Brie, 2 parts, Early English Text Society, cxxxi and cxxxvi (1906–8)
Canterbury	*Chronica Johannis de Reading et anonymi Cantuariensis 1346–1367*, ed. J. Tait (Manchester, 1914)
CCR	*Calendar of Close Rolls*
CFR	*Calendar of Fine Rolls*
Chandos Herald, ed. Tyson	*La vie du Prince Noir by Chandos Herald*, ed. D.B. Tyson (Tübingen, 1975)
Chronique de Flandre	*Istore et croniques de Flandres d'après les textes de divers manuscrits*, 2 vols (Brussels, 1879–80), ii, pp. 27–45, 56–71 [short continuation of the *Chronique de Flandre*]
Chronique des quatre premiers Valois	*Chronique des quatre premiers Valois (1327–1393)*, ed. S. Luce (Paris, 1862)
Chronique Normande	*Chronique Normande du xive siècle*, ed. A. and E. Molinier (Paris, 1882)
Chronographia	*Chronographia regum Francorum*, ed. H. Moranville, 2 vols (Paris, 1891–7)
CIPM	*Calendar of Inquisitions Post Mortem*
Complete Peerage	*The Complete Peerage*, ed. G.E. Cokayne, revised edn, 12 vols in 13 (London, 1910–57)
CPR	*Calendar of Patent Rolls*
EHR	*English Historical Review*
Eulogium	*Eulogium historiarum sive temporis*, ed. F.S. Haydon, Rolls Ser., 3 vols (London, 1858–63)
Foedera	*Foedera, conventiones, litterae etc.*, ed. T. Rymer, revised edn by A. Clarke, F. Holbrooke and J. Coley, 4 vols in 7 parts (Record Comm., 1816–69)

Fowler, 'News from the front'	K. Fowler, 'News from the front: letters and despatches of the fourteenth century', in P. Contamine, C. Giry-Deloison, M. Keen, eds, *Guerre et société en France, en Angleterre et en Bourgogne, xive–xve siècle* (Lille, 1991), pp. 63–92
Froissart: Amiens	Froissart, *Chroniques, Livre 1. Le manuscrit d'Amiens*, ed. G.T. Diller, 3 vols (Geneva, 1991–2)
Froissart: Rome	Froissart, *Chroniques. Début du premier livre. Edition du manuscrit de Rome Reg. lat. 869*, ed. G.T. Diller (Geneva, 1972)
Froissart, ed. Lettenhove	*Oeuvres de Froissart*, ed. K. de Lettenhove, 28 vols (Brussels, 1867–77)
Froissart, ed. Luce	Jean Froissart, *Chroniques*, ed. S. Luce et al. (Paris, 1869–1957)
Gilles le Muisit	*Chronique et annales de Gilles le Muisit, abbé de Saint-Martin de Tournai (1272–1353)*, ed. H. Lemaître (Paris, 1906)
Grandes chroniques	*Grandes chroniques de France*, ed. J. Viard (Paris, 1920–53)
Historia Roffensis	BL, Cotton MSS, Faustina, B. V [*Historia Roffensis* or Rochester chronicle]
Jean de Venette, ed. Newhall	*The Chronicle of Jean de Venette*, trans. J. Birdsall, ed. R.A. Newhall (New York, 1953)
Jean le Bel	*Chronique de Jean le Bel*, ed. J. Viard and E. Déprez, 2 vols (Paris, 1904–5)
John of Reading	*Chronica Johannis de Reading et anonymi Cantuariensis 1346–1367*, ed. J. Tait (Manchester, 1914)
Knighton, ed. Martin	*Knighton's Chronicle, 1337–1396*, ed. G.H. Martin (Oxford, 1995)
Lanercost, ed. Stevenson	*Chronicon de Lanercost*, ed. J. Stevenson (Edinburgh, 1839)
Le Prince Noir, ed. Michel	*Le Prince Noir. Poème du heraut d'armes Chandos*, ed. F. Michel (London and Paris, 1883)
Melsa	*Chronicon monasterii de Melsa*, ed. E.A. Bond, 3 vols, Rolls Ser. (London, 1866–68)
Murimuth	Murimuth, Adam, *Continuatio chronicarum* and Robert de Avesbury, *De gestis mirabilibus regis Edwardi Tertii*, ed. E.M. Thompson, Rolls Ser. (London, 1889)
Norwell	*The Wardrobe Book of William de Norwell, 12 July 1338 to 27 May 1340*, ed. M. Lyon, B. Lyon, H.S. Lucas and J. de Sturler (Brussells, 1983)
PRO	Public Record Office
RDP	*Reports . . . Touching the Dignity of a Peer*, 5 vols (London, 1820–9)
Récits	*Récits d'un bourgeois de Valenciennes*, ed. K. de Lettenhove (Louvain, 1877)
Rogers, *War Cruel and Sharp*	C.J. Rogers, *War Cruel and Sharp: English Strategy under Edward III, 1327–1360* (Woodbridge, 2000)
Rot. Parl.	*Rotuli Parliamentorum*, ed. J. Strachey et al., 6 vols (London, 1767–83)
Rotuli Scotiae	*Rotuli Scotiae*, ed. D. Macpherson et al., 2 vols (Record Comm., 1814)
Scrope and Grosvenor	*The Scrope and Grosvenor Controversy*, ed. N.H. Nicolas, 2 vols (London, 1832)

St Omer chronicle Paris, Bibliothèque Nationale, MS Fr. 693, fos 248r–279v

Sumption, *Trial* J. Sumption, *The Hundred Years War: Trial by Battle* (London,
  by Battle 1990)

Tout, *Chapters* T.F. Tout, *Chapters in the Administrative History of Medieval
  England. The Wardrobe, the Chamber and the Small Seals*, 6
  vols (Manchester, 1920–33)

Treaty Rolls, *Treaty Rolls, ii, 1337–1339*, ed. J. Ferguson (London, 1972)
  1337–39

TRHS *Transactions of the Royal Historical Society*

Villani *Chronica di Giovanni Villani*, ed. M.L. Ridotta (Florence,
  1823)

Wrottesley, *Crecy* G. Wrottesley, ed., *Crecy and Calais from the Original
  and Calais* Records in the Public Record Office* (London, 1898)

Documents cited in the notes by class number alone are to be found in the National
Archives (formerly known as the Public Record Office), Kew.

This book is dedicated to the memory of
General Sir Martin Farndale KCB
late President of the Battle of Crécy Trust

1

The Battle of Crécy: Context and Significance

ANDREW AYTON

At dawn on 12 July 1346, a vast armada of ships appeared off the coast of Normandy. Their destination was St Vaast-la-Hougue, a small port on the north-eastern corner of the Cotentin peninsula. The size of the fleet and the presence of ships bearing the quartered leopards and lilies of the royal arms of England indicated that this was no mere raid. In fact, it was to be the largest amphibious operation of the Hundred Years War, and it had achieved complete surprise. The consternation of the local population can easily be appreciated. Robert Bertran, Marshal of France and commander on the spot, was able to muster a few hundred men. But since, according to an English narrative, a force of five hundred Genoese crossbowmen, their pay in arrears, had withdrawn from the area a few days previously, it is small wonder that the English met only light resistance as they landed and moved inland.[1] It took several days to disembark the horses and supplies, during which time flying columns ranged across the Cotentin peninsula. Barfleur, a town 'as good and large as Sandwich', was burnt.[2] 'The men-at-arms of the region have withdrawn into the castles and fortified towns,' noted Bartholomew Burgherssh in his report of 17 July. 'There is no one left in the surrounding countryside for twenty miles around who is offering resistance,' added Thomas Bradwardine in his letter of the same day. It had been an auspicious opening for the English, and on Tuesday, 18 July Edward III and his army set out from La Hougue and began the campaign proper. The king's intention, reported Burgherssh, was 'to secure his rights by conquest'.[3]

---

[1] *Acts of War*, ed. Barber, p. 28; St Omer chronicle, fo. 259r; *Chronique de Flandre*, ii, p. 39. Cf. *Récits*, pp. 215–16; *Canterbury*, p. 187.

[2] Michael Northburgh's newsletter of 27 July: *Murimuth*, pp. 212–14; *Avesbury*, pp. 358–60. This is one of eight newsletters to survive from the Crécy campaign. The others are: Bartholomew Burgherssh, 17 July and 29 July (*Murimuth*, pp. 200; 202–3); Thomas Bradwardine, the chancellor of St Paul's (*Murimuth*, pp. 201–2); Michael Northburgh, 4 September (*Avesbury*, pp. 367–9); Richard Wynkeley, 2 September (*Murimuth*, pp. 215–17; *Avesbury*, pp. 362–3); Edward III, 29 July (C81/314, no 17803, printed in Fowler, 'News from the front', pp. 83–4) and 3 September (Bodleian Library, MS Ashmole 789, fos 148r–148v; printed in *Le Prince Noir*, ed. Michel, pp. 308–11). All except the king's letter of 29 July are reproduced in English translation in R. Barber, *Life and Campaigns of the Black Prince* (Woodbridge, 1986), pp. 13–25. On the newsletters arising from the Crécy campaign, see G. Martin, 'John the Blind: the English narrative sources', *Johann der Blinde, Graf von Luxemburg, König von Böhmen 1296–1346*, ed. M. Pauly (Luxembourg, 1997), pp. 83–92 (at pp. 86–9); and Fowler, 'News from the front', pp. 76–80, 83–4.

[3] 'le roy ou soun hoste chivache avant en la terre pur conqerer soun dreit'. *Murimuth*, p. 200.

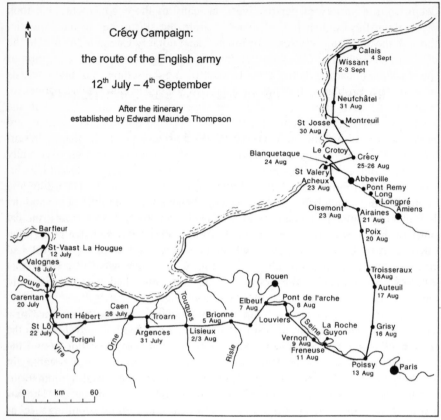

Map 1

A good deal is known about the six-week campaign that followed. An itinerary for Edward III's march across Normandy can be established from a combination of administrative records and fourteenth-century narratives.[4] (See Map
1.) Eyewitness accounts and contemporary secondary sources provide much

---

[4] Sources: (1) William Retford's financial account for the king's kitchen (E101/390/11):
arranged as a journal, it records the names of the places where this department of the royal
household lodged on each day of the campaign. See *Baker*, pp. 252–3; Tout, *Chapters*, iv, p.
115 and n. 5. (2) A contemporary itinerary, surviving in a fifteenth-century copy: BL, Cotton
MS, Cleopatra D. VII, fo. 179, printed in *Baker*, pp. 253–5. (3) The *Acta Bellicosa*, a campaign
diary apparently written by a member of Edward III's army. It survives in a single, incomplete,
late fourteenth-century copy, which narrates events up to 28 July, resuming on 11 August to
continue the story to 20 August. Cambridge, Corpus Christi College, MS 370; imperfectly
printed in J. Moisant, *Le Prince Noir en Aquitaine, 1355–6, 1362–70* (Paris, 1894); translated
in Barber, *Life and Campaigns of the Black Prince*, pp. 26–40. (4) Geoffrey Baker's account of
the campaign, which is clearly based on another contemporary itinerary (*Baker*, pp. 79–86).
(5) The English newsletters: see n. 2 above. E.M. Thompson reconstructed Edward III's itinerary based upon (1), (2) and (4): see *Baker*, pp. 255–7. As he noted, the 'discrepancies' in detail
that are evident when these texts are compared are no doubt the consequence of the texts
having been 'written independently by persons marching with different divisions of the army'.
For amendments to Thompson's interpretation of the place-names in Retford's kitchen
journal, see H. Belloc, 'Crécy', *Six British Battles* (Bristol, 1931), pp. 15ff.

detail, from a variety of perspectives, on many of the engagements that took place along the English line of march – from the skirmishes in the Cotentin, through the storming of a series of towns, most notably Caen on 26 July, to the climactic encounter at Crécy-en-Ponthieu on 26 August. With the exception of the week or so leading up to Crécy, reconstructing the sequence of major events presents few problems. For the most part, we seem to know what happened, where and when. However, difficulties arise when attention is turned to the *interpretation* of these events, for in this respect the documentary sources are both less revealing and less consistent in their testimony. In these circumstances, it is easy to see how historians seeking to discover what was really happening during this campaign, and why, have come to very different conclusions. Did the English march from La Hougue to Crécy proceed according to a strategic plan, which had anticipated the necessity of crossing the Seine and the Somme, and which had a battlefield confrontation with Philip VI as its principal aim? Or was this, in the main, an improvised operation, responsive rather than purposeful: a great chevauchée, which by the second week of August had become 'a very dangerous adventure',[5] and which culminated in a battle that Edward, having been closely pursued by his adversary, had been compelled to fight?

At first glance, the Crécy campaign does indeed have the appearance of a great 'chivalrous adventure'.[6] It was punctuated by dramatic *coups de main*: the assault on Caen, the seizure of a bridgehead over the Seine at Poissy and the crossing of the Somme at Blanquetaque. The campaign is also notable for smaller-scale feats of arms, which contributed much to the chivalric reputations of those involved but little to Edward's purpose. Take, for example, Sir Thomas Holland's reckless ride onto the bridge at Rouen – 'une emprise oultrageuse' as one chronicler characterised it; or Sir Robert Ferrers's audacious amphibious raid across the Seine to attack the castle of La Roche Guyon.[7] The chroniclers delighted in reporting such displays of knightly prowess, but for all the bravado, there was a darker side to this campaign. A central feature of the English march from La Hougue to Crécy that is not readily conveyed by a line drawn on a map is the ravaging of the countryside and the plundering of towns that accompanied the progress of the army. The extent of the devastation wreaked is emphasised by contemporary writers, whether of continental or English provenance. Eye-witnesses recorded that ravaging was undertaken on a broad front – about fifteen to twenty miles around the line of march.[8] If anything, the sacking and burning of towns along the route was still more damaging, since 'the greatest concentrations of wealth in the medieval world were to be found' in such places.[9] As Jean

---

5   As characterised by Charles Oman: *A History of the Art of War in the Middle Ages*, 2nd edn, 2 vols (London, 1924), ii, p. 132.
6   Oman, *A History of the Art of War in the Middle Ages*, ii, p. 131.
7   *Récits*, p. 220; *Acts of War*, ed. Barber, p. 35.
8   *Murimuth*, p. 215; *Avesbury*, p. 358. See also C.J. Rogers, 'By fire and sword: *bellum hostile* and "civilians" in the Hundred Years War', *Civilians in the Path of War*, ed. M. Grimsley and C.J. Rogers (Lincoln, Nebraska, 2002), pp. 33–78: map 2.1 (p. 38) provides some indication of the extent of devastation along chevauchée routes.
9   Rogers, 'By fire and sword', pp. 45–7 and n. 62.

le Bel observed, 'no man alive could imagine or believe . . . the riches that were gained and robbed' in the great mercantile town of St Lô.[10] Few historians would now doubt that such extensive devastation of town and country was, in the main, calculated and purposeful, the very essence of the 'practice of war', intended (in addition to the gathering of supplies) to destroy economic resources and challenge the authority and honour of the Valois king and his nobility.[11] Taking the argument a stage further, Clifford Rogers has recently found a 'definite strategic rationale' in this destruction. This was to 'to put [Philip VI] in a lose–lose situation', in which he either accepted battle, in all likelihood in unfavourable circumstances, or failed 'visibly and unequivocally . . . in the foremost duty of kingship: to protect (or at least to avenge) the subjects of the realm'.[12]

Edward III's chivalric mentality, centred as it was on the enhancement of his martial reputation and on the vindication of his honour, especially with regard to his claim to the French throne, was the driving force in his 'just quarrel' with Philip VI. The chivalric code to which he subscribed was flexible enough to accommodate the practical requirements of the English way of war. Thus, for Edward, the two faces of the Crécy campaign, the chivalric and pragmatic, coexisted comfortably and without contradiction. In the first place, we may be sure that neither he nor indeed his peers in the aristocratic elite of Christendom would have been troubled by the hardship caused by the systematic ravaging of town and country. Such activities were legitimate in a just war, and the guiding principles of chivalry were, in any case, little concerned with the welfare of the peasantry.[13]

Secondly, from the outset of the campaign, political calculation was tightly woven into the chivalric ceremonial that was an essential part of the martial ritual of the king's army. Immediately upon landing at La Hougue, 'the king and his army . . . in a group made their way to a high hill near the shore', where the Prince of Wales and other noblemen were knighted by the king.[14] The dubbing ceremony formed part of a spectacle that was charged with political symbolism. Much emphasis was given to Edward's claim to the French throne, as demonstrated by Godfrey de Harcourt's homage for his lands in Normandy and symbolised by the prominently displayed Garter, bearing the uncompromising motto 'Hony soit q' mal y pense'.[15] And the whole event was witnessed by a sizeable proportion of England's political elite, headed by six of the eight earls who were militarily active at the time. The ritual was repeated before the climactic battle began at Crécy. According to Froissart (here, as usual,

---

[10] *Jean le Bel*, ii, pp. 77–8.

[11] The classic study of this subject is H.J. Hewitt, *The Organisation of War under Edward III* (Manchester, 1966), ch. 5: 'War'.

[12] Rogers, 'By fire and sword', pp. 56–7; C.J. Rogers, *War Cruel and Sharp: English Strategy under Edward III* (Woodbridge, 2000), *passim*. Hewitt noticed the 'battle provocation' argument, but was unconvinced by it: *Organisation of War*, pp. 99–100, 116–17.

[13] See Rogers, 'By fire and sword', pp. 54–5, and references cited there.

[14] *Acts of War*, ed. Barber, pp. 27–8.

[15] Harcourt: *Acts of War*, ed. Barber, p. 29. The argument that the Garter was 'an integral part' of Edward's Norman campaign from the outset draws upon Juliet Vale's convincing interpretation in *Edward III and Chivalry* (Woodbridge, 1982), pp. 77–82.

elaborating upon Jean le Bel, but perhaps based upon independent eyewitness testimony), Edward toured the ranks of his army mounted on a white palfrey and carrying a white baton.[16] The Monk of Malmesbury notes that 50 men were elevated to knighthood, some of whom can be identified in the Chancery records.[17] Edward was fully aware that 'ritual preparation . . . was vital for a medieval army'. As Michael K. Jones has observed: 'The effectiveness of ritual could determine the way men fought and how battle might unfold. A force inspired by a shared cause that all could understand and believe in would have greater cohesion and unity.'[18]

Political calculation might also lead to the partial suspension of the chivalric code that regulated the behaviour and treatment of knightly combatants during and after battle. This can be seen in Edward's attitude towards French prisoners of war. During the aftermath of the English assault on Caen, a group of French noblemen, including the count of Eu and the lord of Tancarville, expecting no quarter from the common soldiery, were greatly relieved to see Sir Thomas Holland, with whom they had served 'in Prussia, Grenada and elsewhere' and to whom they could now surrender. Needless to say, Holland was delighted to oblige. Jean le Bel's story reminds us that the aristocratic protagonists in 1346 were members of a wider, international knightly community and that, at another time and place, they had been comrades in arms.[19] The count of Eu may have hoped for parole and early release in return for a ransom, in accordance with the norms of chivalric convention, but Edward III had other ideas. As Burgherssh notes in his newsletter, the king ordered the prisoners' immediate despatch to England, 'without being released for ransom or by any other means, until he shall have accomplished more by his war'.[20] The count of Eu was constable of France, and removing such a figure from the political and military equation would weaken the French war effort. Indeed, such 'great' prisoners could bring other benefits. Froissart states that in order to obtain his release, the count agreed to sell to the English king his county and castle of Guines – a strategic location close to Calais, which if true would explain the count's execution for treason on his eventual return to France in 1350.[21]

[16] Jean le Bel mentions the king's tour of the ranks; Froissart adds the description of his appearance. *Jean le Bel*, ii, p. 106; *Froissart*, ed. Luce, iii, p. 170; *Froissart: Rome*, p. 719. It was usual practice for Edward to engage with his men in this fashion on the eve of battle: see M. Prestwich, *Armies and Warfare in the Middle Ages: The English Experience* (New Haven and London, 1996), p. 313.

[17] *Eulogium*, iii, p. 211; *CPR, 1345–8*, p. 474.

[18] M.K. Jones, *Bosworth, 1485. Psychology of a Battle* (Stroud, 2002), pp. 157–8; see also, M.K. Jones, 'The battle of Verneuil (17 August 1424): towards a history of courage', *War in History*, ix (2002), pp. 375–411 (at pp. 400–3), for the duke of Bedford's ceremonial review of his army outside Ivry in August 1324.

[19] *Jean le Bel*, ii, pp. 81–3; see notes to these pages for Raoul de Brienne, count of Eu and Jean de Melun, lord of Tancarville and chamberlain of Normandy.

[20] *Murimuth*, p. 203. Sir Thomas Holland did, however, become a rich man through the release of his prisoner to the king. The sum agreed was 20,000 marks, payable over a three-year period from the customs duties on wool. *CPR, 1345–8*, pp. 337, 538–9, 550–1.

[21] C. Given-Wilson and F. Bériac, 'Edward III's prisoners of war: the battle of Poitiers and its context', *EHR*, cxvi (2001), pp. 802–33 (for the count of Eu, see pp. 821–2).

At Crécy, all regard for the bonds of an international chivalric brotherhood were set aside in the single-minded pursuit of a crushing victory. At the end of the fight the field was littered with the corpses of French (and allied) noblemen. There were few prisoners and certainly none of note.[22] The 'Vallée des Clercs' (as it became known) had become a killing ground through the employment of devastating archery, the enforcement of a severe disciplinary regime, and the effective exploitation of terrain. Whether or not it had been known about in advance (perhaps even regarded as a potential battle site from the outset of the campaign), the ground at Crécy had been well selected and the English army's tactical deployment carefully prepared. A moment's contemplation upon the events that unfolded in the Vallée des Clercs, a veritable valley of death, appears to dispel any notion that this had been a 'chivalric' encounter. We seem very far away from the world of the knightly feat of arms, as epitomised by Sir Thomas Colville's amicable joust with a French knight on the banks of the Somme just two days earlier. [23] And yet chivalry was as relevant to what happened at Crécy as to any battle during the later middle ages. For Edward III, the overwhelming need to vindicate his honour had brought him to this climactic encounter. It has been well observed that the concept of honour in the chivalric context is inherently aggressive: 'the honourable man must demonstrate his honour continually before his peers, and this in turn often involves challenging the honour of others'.[24] Yet Edward's aggression was controlled, and it was founded upon recognition that the prevailing mentality of the European aristocratic military elite could be turned to his advantage. On the one hand, an appeal to the martial mentality of his own nobility ensured that they became participants in his 'just quarrel'; on the other, an appreciation that, quite as much as himself, his adversary was susceptible to the demands of honour was to have a considerable influence on the shaping of his campaign strategy. Whereas for Edward the focused aggression that was fuelled by his chivalric ideals was a source of strength, for Philip VI the need to defend his honour was potentially his Achilles heel. For if the Valois king was to be provoked into making a tactical mistake that could lead to military disaster it would in all likelihood involve a situation in which he, in the midst of his assembled nobility, had been driven, in unfavourable circumstances, to defend his honour as anointed king of France. Thus the significance of Edward's choice of battleground at Crécy was not simply that it was a site that maximised his army's strengths, while neutralising those of his opponents: it was ground upon which his opponent felt compelled to fight. As we shall see, the fact that the site lay in Ponthieu may well provide the key to understanding the battle of Crécy.

In the sense that it was a point of honour for both (in fact, all five participant) kings to fight at Crécy, Edward's campaign could indeed be described as a

---

22 Given-Wilson and Bériac, 'Edward III's prisoners of war', pp. 804–5.

23 *Anonimalle chronicle*, pp. 22, 160; *Eulogium*, iii, p. 210.

24 J. Barnie, *War in Medieval English Society. Social Values and the Hundred Years War, 1337–99* (New York, 1974), p. 75, which draws on J. Pitt-Rivers, 'Honour and social status', in J.G. Peristiany, ed., *Honour and Shame: The Values of Mediterranean Society* (London, 1965).

'chivalric adventure'. But for Edward it was an adventure that had been founded upon careful preparation, rather than improvisation: Crécy was a battle that he had planned to fight, not one that he had been forced to accept while seeking to escape the clutches of his adversary. This is surely the most important of the implications of the killing fields at Crécy, and it is a conclusion that is reinforced by re-examination of other aspects of the campaign. Thus, while some historians have regarded the landing in Normandy as the result of a last-minute change of plan, a fresh look at the evidence suggests that a descent upon the Cotentin coast, at La Hougue, was planned well in advance of embarkation, and that this was intended as the principal thrust of a multi-front strategy. Similarly, while the dramatic river crossings at Poissy and Blanquetaque may have the appearance of lucky escapes from 'a very dangerous adventure', there is reason to believe that each had been anticipated before the campaign began and that each was as much a triumph of planning as of prowess. These ideas will be developed in detail in Chapter 2. For the moment, it is sufficient to conclude that there was a good deal more to the English march from La Hougue to Crécy than first meets the eye, that this has indeed been a 'much studied, but much misunderstood' campaign.[25]

Edward III's six-week campaign in northern France in July–August 1346 was much more than the audacious adventure that has been portrayed by many historians. It certainly left an extensive zone of destruction in its wake. Yet what made this campaign memorable, what gave it lasting significance, was the great battle that was fought at its climax. Edward had led three previous expeditions into France and on each occasion the field operations ended in an anti-climactic withdrawal after a tense stand-off. As a consequence, apart from the maritime engagement at Sluys (the prelude to the second of these expeditions), Edward III's early French campaigns are today little remembered outside specialised historical works. The campaign of July–August 1346 was concluded very differently from its predecessors. Indeed, the battle of Crécy can be viewed as a turning point in Edward III's struggle with his Valois adversary, and in many ways a momentous event for the continent of Europe as a whole. It witnessed the defeat of the greatest power in Christendom, of a major army led by the French king in person, by an expeditionary force raised by a kingdom that at that time was not renowned for its military prowess. It was not the first occasion that a king of England had triumphed over a king of France in the field;[26] but the scale of the victory in 1346 was unprecedented. By the standards of the period, the armies that fought the battle were large and the casualties suffered by the French nobility crippling. Philip VI's military reputation was irredeemably damaged, while Edward III's, and that of the English as a whole, soared. Without Crécy and its consequences, it would be difficult to conceive of a 'Hundred Years War': Edward III's war effort would probably have fizzled out. Yet despite its importance, the battle of Crécy has not attracted the academic attention that it

---

[25] Rogers, *War Cruel and Sharp*, p. 219.
[26] At Brémule in 1119, Henry I had defeated Louis VI.

deserves,[27] and thanks largely to Shakespeare it is Agincourt that has engaged the popular imagination.[28] The present collaborative volume, a response to this neglect, has been planned on a scale appropriate to its subject, with the hope of filling a notable lacuna in the historiography of the Hundred Years War. It would probably be naïve to imagine that the deeds of Edward III and his lieutenants may yet be raised to a level of popular awareness comparable to that occupied by Henry V's 'band of brothers'. But if this book succeeds in casting new light on the events of 26 August 1346 and in demonstrating the wider significance of those events, it will have fulfilled its primary purpose.

In seeking to understand the battle of Crécy we are confronted by a fundamental problem. How are we to reconstruct what happened on that late summer's evening in Ponthieu? On the one hand, we are constrained by the limitations of our narrative sources. The eyewitness accounts are few in number and brief in their comments on the battle. The second-hand narratives are more numerous and some are more substantial, but they are selective in their coverage, raise as many questions as they answer, and often contradict each other. No doubt some of these weaknesses arose from the fact that the battle began in the evening twilight and continued into the night. As a consequence, the testimony of eyewitnesses, when passed on to chroniclers, may have been more than usually fragmentary and imprecise. For the latter, the temptation to 'fill the gaps' would have been hard to resist, as can be seen to have happened with Geoffrey Baker, author of one of the most famous contemporary accounts of the battle.[29] Yet, it seems that few fourteenth-century chroniclers of the battle attempted to construct a detailed narrative that takes the reader from the beginning of the battle to the end. (An exception is Giovanni Villani, but his version of events, distinctive as it is in a number of respects, has been largely ignored in the English-language historiography of the battle.) Most accounts are brief and insubstantial, but even the longer ones, such as those composed by Jean Froissart, lack a clear, continuous narrative line. Froissart relied heavily on Jean

---

[27] The most carefully researched modern studies of the campaign and battle of Crécy appear as sections in more general works: R. Barber, *Edward Prince of Wales and Aquitaine* (Woodbridge, 1978), chapter 3; J. Sumption, *The Hundred Years War: Trial by Battle* (London, 1990), chapter 14; K. DeVries, *Infantry Warfare in the Early Fourteenth Century* (Woodbridge, 1996), chapter 13; Rogers, *War Cruel and Sharp*, chapters 10 and 11. There have been only two volumes devoted to Crécy in modern times: Henri de Wailly, *Crécy 1346: Anatomy of a Battle* (Poole, 1987) and D. Nicolle, *Crécy 1346* (Oxford, 2000). De Wailly offers some intriguing material on the archaeology of the campaign, but is dependent on a very limited range of sources. Nicolle's book is intended for a popular audience, but displays the author's breadth of knowledge concerning medieval warfare. The recent reprinting of A.H. Burne, *The Crecy War* (London, 1954) will no doubt find a fresh crop of readers for this entertaining if rather dated volume. Prior to de Wailly, the most substantial study by a French scholar was written in the 1920s: J. Viard, 'La campagne de juillet–août 1346 et la bataille de Crécy', *Le moyen âge*, 2nd ser., xxvii (1926), pp. 1–84. The historiography of Crécy is discussed in greater depth in Chapters 3 and 9 of this book; see also, Rogers, *War Cruel and Sharp*, pp. 230–7.

[28] Shakespeare's Edward III is little known outside academic circles: E. Sams, ed., *Shakespeare's Edward III* (New Haven and London, 1996).

[29] Geoffrey Baker and the other chroniclers discussed here are examined in detail in Chapter 9.

le Bel's version of events, but the latter's tale takes an unusual approach, recounting the story first from the French point of view, then (more selectively) from the English perspective. His battle narrative stops abruptly after the defeat of the first French cavalry onslaught, and all Froissart could do by way of continuation was to append a series of chivalric episodes, assembled it seems from a variety of eyewitness sources.

Added to the difficulties presented by the narrative sources – indeed, partly responsible for those difficulties – is the distinctive nature of the events that they describe. It is the complexity of a battle that is so difficult to recapture: the swirl of simultaneous movements by thousands of participants, and beyond the physical level, the psychological dimension of combat, the frame of mind and emotional responses of those engaged. It is small wonder, as John Keegan memorably demonstrated in his classic study *The Face of Battle*, that the writing of convincing 'battle pieces', for whatever period of history, is exceedingly difficult.[30] Peter Paret's suggestion, while reviewing a book on the Napoleonic Wars, that 'all passages dealing with combat be printed in a different colour so that readers would know at once that they were entering treacherous territory' might well be applied to studies of medieval warfare.[31] It is clear, therefore, that 'reconstructing' Crécy must present a major challenge to the historian. Indeed, such is the challenge that it is impossible to piece together a detailed and convincing sequence of events, a narrative line, from the chronicle accounts alone, still less a series of parallel or concurrent sequences that would stand as a more accurate representation of what actually happened. Six and a half centuries after the events of 1346, we are no better placed than Froissart to construct a composite narrative of Crécy from documentary sources of diverse provenance and reliability.

An alternative approach is required, which combines the testimony of as wide a range of sources as possible with a measure of historical imagination. The narrative sources require particularly careful handling. Contrary to the 'cherry-picking' approach that is all too often encountered, these texts must be used in a way that is consistent with their purpose and sensitive to the circumstances that gave them life. We must also make the most of their strengths, including the rich vein of eyewitness testimony that runs through many of them. Some historians would stress the limitations of such testimony. After all, owing to a restricted field of vision and an overriding preoccupation with self-preservation, no single participant in a battle could have been able to take in more than a fraction of the action. But while eyewitness testimony may contribute little to the construction of a battle narrative or to the elucidation of a commander's tactics (the usual preoccupations of the military historian), it can convey a powerful impression of what mattered to those involved and what was passing through their minds, as well as offering vivid snapshots of what was really happening in the battle. For it is from eyewitnesses, mediated through the pens of chroniclers, that we see the crucial role played by chivalric ritual and

---

[30] J. Keegan, *The Face of Battle* (Harmondsworth, 1978).
[31] P. Paret, *Understanding War. Essays on Clausewitz and the History of Military Power* (Princeton, 1992), p. 85.

inspirational leadership, of 'prowese'.[32] We learn too of small-group collaborative combat techniques, of 'micro-tactics'. We see standards functioning as
rallying points; we hear war cries; and we witness the crippling effect of missile
weapons on horseflesh. We also gain an impression of 'the mental outlook of
the participants' and how that shaped their actions. Thus, something of the
essence of the battle of Crécy, together with some of its landmark events, can be
found in the chronicles.

That is as far as some scholars are prepared to go, but there is really no necessity to break off the chase once the chronicles have been scoured for evidence.
The historian should have other strings to his bow. Admittedly, even with the
benefit of additional sources and methodologies, it is impossible to construct an
evenly paced narrative of the battle. But if we can recapture something of its
general character, including some of its critical moments, we may yet fashion an
account that is as satisfying for our time as Froissart's was for his. There are a
number of methodological possibilities. For example, the evidence of the narrative sources can be combined with an understanding of combat psychology and
a grasp of the practical limitations of fourteenth-century weapons technology.
The topography of the battlefield is also of particular importance. Here it should
be noted that while most historians have accepted that the battle took place on
the 'traditional' site, centred on the Vallée des Clercs, few have subjected that
piece of ground to close inspection. As a consequence, the true significance of
the topography of the site has gone unrecognised in all modern accounts of the
battle. Time and again historians have proposed a narrative that, in some of its
essential features, could not have been permitted by the lie of the ground. This
book looks at the ground afresh and considers how the topography of the field
may have shaped not only the course of the battle, but also the strategy of the
campaign.

There is a further category of source material that has been underutilised in
modern accounts of the battle of Crécy: the administrative records that illuminate the structure and composition of the armies. The potential offered by these
records should require no emphasis, and yet how the personnel (their past military experience and their relationships) and the organisation of the armies may
have contributed to the outcome of the battle has never before been investigated
beyond a superficial level. What is needed is a systematic prosopographical
investigation of the combatants, combined with a reconstruction of the social
networks that underpinned the recruitment and functioning of the armies. That
would be a challenging research project. In this book, we offer a methodological
template and some preliminary findings, which not only cast new light on the
battle of Crécy but may also serve as an example for the investigation of other
Edwardian battles.

---

[32] This paragraph owes much to the work of Michael K. Jones who has argued that historians
would do well to take greater note of 'the role of chivalric ritual' that occurred within medieval armies before and during battle; and to recognise the importance of individual courage
and inspirational leadership rather than tactics. See his article 'The battle of Verneuil (17
August 1424): towards a history of courage', and his book *Bosworth, 1485. Psychology of a
Battle*.

*

The six contributors to this book have approached the battle of Crécy from a variety of directions. Yet underlying these contributions can be identified three fundamental questions: Firstly, why did the battle of Crécy take place? Secondly, how was it that the English won? Thirdly, how significant an event was it? To take the second of these questions first: one of the few undisputed facts about the battle of Crécy is that the English emerged victorious, but how is this outcome to be explained? In Chapter 4, Michael Prestwich reviews the available evidence for the course of the battle, including an important new interpretation of the topography of the traditional site, which Sir Philip Preston presents in Chapter 3. Views on why the English won are also to be found in the chapters dedicated to the two armies (Chapters 5 and 7). Following, in Chapter 9, an examination of the narrative sources for the battle and the problems of interpretation that they present, the concluding chapter of the book offers further thoughts on how the English achieved such an astounding victory.

Formulating answers to the first and third of the questions posed above – 'why did the battle take place?' and 'how significant an event was it?' – is the primary concern of the opening part of this book. We turn to the problem of why a major battle took place at Crécy in August 1346 in Chapter 2; but first we must consider the significance of the battle. To examine the aftermath and consequences of the battle before we have tackled what happened on the field – and why – may appear to be putting the cart before the horse. But as we shall see, the 'significance' of Crécy, as of all major battles, involves not only the consequences that flowed from it, but also the event itself – the battle. Thus, in assessing the significance of Crécy, we begin by examining the part played by battles in medieval warfare, and in particular their role in commanders' strategic thinking. Then, we consider the magnitude of the military and political encounter that occurred in northern France during the summer of 1346. Lastly, and most substantially, we look beyond the strictly military issues, such as the scale of the mobilisation and casualties, to examine what may be termed the 'chivalric politics' of the armies and the social networks that underpinned them. An understanding of these phenomena helps us to reconstruct what took place on the battlefield, while serving to emphasise the impact that the battle must have had in England and France. It also contributes to a more satisfying explanation of why the battle took place.

* * *

There was a time when studies of medieval warfare focused predominantly on battles. For an example of this approach one need only think of the work of Charles Oman.[33] More recently it has been argued that the amount of attention given to battles in the past was 'disproportionate',[34] since such engagements were actually not all that common. John Gillingham has summed up this view

---

[33] Oman, *A History of the Art of War in the Middle Ages*. Similar, in this respect, are the books of A.H. Burne: *The Crecy War* (London, 1955); *The Agincourt War* (London, 1956).
[34] R.C. Smail, *Crusading Warfare (1097–1193)* (Cambridge, repr., 1976), p. 165. Smail's pioneering work was first published in 1956.

succinctly (and provocatively): 'In European medieval history as a whole battles are rare and making war did not normally involve seeking battle.'[35] Medieval commanders were reluctant to give battle because the risks usually far outweighed the likelihood of achieving a decisive outcome. This was the advice of Vegetius's *De Re Militari*, a 'late Roman handbook on war', which (it has been supposed) was widely consulted.[36] Taking the spotlight off such exceptional events as battles would allow us to see more clearly that medieval warfare was typically concerned with destructive raids and sieges. This, it has been emphasised, is not an 'attempt to deny the significance of battle itself, but rather to contextualise it'.[37] Nevertheless, perhaps inevitably, there has been a tendency to play down battles 'for fear of falling into a "decisive battle" approach which can obscure the realities of warfare'.[38]

It is tempting to place J.F. Verbruggen at the head of a very different school of thought, since his major work on *The Art of Warfare in Western Europe during the Middle Ages*, first issued in 1954 and recently republished in English, is primarily concerned with what happened on the battlefield, and as he notes (surely indisputably) 'a great deal can be learnt about medieval warfare from the study of battles'.[39] Yet when we read his next sentence we realise that Verbruggen's view of warfare is not so very different: 'We can enquire why battle was so often avoided, why the pursuit could not be carried very far, why wars were so seldom decisive.' Another influential commentator on this subject, Philippe Contamine, has offered a further 'contextualisation' of battle. He notes the infrequency of pitched battles, and the tendency among medieval commanders to avoid them, yet adds: 'for all that, it remains the case that the pitched battle was conceived as the culminating point of a war, the major event which made sense of a campaign, the chief episode which, although limited in area and concentrated in time, was the object of all fears, expectations and hopes'.[40]

35 J. Gillingham, 'Richard I and the science of war in the Middle Ages', *Anglo-Norman Warfare*, ed. M. Strickland (Woodbridge, 1992), pp. 194–207 (at p. 207). He added the important qualification that 'victory in battle normally offered rewards sufficient to offset the risks involved only in those societies where the science of fortification was relatively poorly developed' (p. 206).

36 Gillingham, 'Richard I and the science of war in the Middle Ages', p. 198. Vegetius had advised that a commander should avoid battle unless the odds were heavily – overwhelmingly – stacked in his favour. Many medieval manuscripts of *De Re Militari* (including in the vernacular) survive, but just how influential Vegetius was has been disputed. See, for example, S. Morillo, *Warfare under the Anglo-Norman Kings, 1066–1135* (Woodbridge, 1994), p. 118 n. 89; Prestwich, *Armies and Warfare in the Middle Ages*, pp. 186–7.

37 M. Strickland, 'Introduction', *Anglo-Norman Warfare*, ed. Strickland, p. xx. As demonstrated by J. Bradbury, 'Battles in England and Normandy, 1066–1154', *Anglo-Norman Warfare*, ed. Strickland, pp. 182–93.

38 M. Bennett, 'General Preface' to J.F. Verbruggen, *The Art of Warfare in Western Europe during the Middle Ages* (Woodbridge, 1997), p. x.

39 Verbruggen, *The Art of Warfare in Western Europe during the Middle Ages*, p. 9. Verbruggen is also the author of *The Battle of the Golden Spurs: Courtrai, 11 July 1302*, ed. K. DeVries, trans. D.R. Ferguson (Woodbridge, 2002). First published in Dutch in 1952, this penetrating examination of the sources, the battleground and the armies is a model of its kind.

40 P. Contamine, *War in the Middle Ages*, trans. M. Jones (London, 1985), pp. 219–37 (at pp. 228–9).

Battles are not to be consigned to the margins of later medieval military history, even if we are inclined to believe that the 'realities of warfare' were rooted in less dramatic events. On a number of levels, battles 'bore an importance out of all proportion with their frequency'.[41] But were they really such rare phenomena in the fourteenth century? Did commanders usually display Vegetian caution in their strategy? Conditions no doubt varied throughout Europe, and an investigation of these variations has yet to be undertaken. However, two recent contributions have offered some useful thoughts on this subject. Clifford Rogers has explored the 'many sound reasons why a medieval commander might want to fight a battle',[42] while Stephen Morillo has devised a theoretical framework for the study of medieval strategy, within which battle occupies a prominent place.[43] As far as the English experience of warfare is concerned, doubt has recently been cast (as Michael Prestwich has noted) on the universal application of the 'new orthodoxy . . . that medieval commanders sought to avoid battle wherever possible'.[44] Michael K. Jones's brilliant re-examination of the battle of Verneuil (17 August 1424) provides a case in point, for here we see both army commanders, for different reasons, actively seeking a battlefield contest.[45] What is clear is that command decisions prior to that battle involved not just tactical calculation, but also the 'chivalric element', honour and courage.

These issues are directly relevant to our present task, for understanding why the kings of England and France finally came to blows at Crécy, after a sequence of inconclusive 'stand-offs' in earlier campaigns, is one of the central problems of the opening part of this book. Of the protagonists of 1346, Philip VI does indeed display all the characteristics of a commander of Vegetian caution. We shall examine his frame of mind later in this chapter. What of Edward III? It is

---

[41] C.J. Rogers, 'The Vegetian "science of warfare" in the middle ages', *The Journal of Medieval Military History*, i (2002), pp. 1–19 (at p. 19).

[42] Rogers concludes that 'the commander of the side pursuing aggressive war aims typically wanted a battle'. Those 'fighting on the strategic defensive . . . did often prefer to avoid pitched battle, but even that generalisation has many exceptions'. Rogers, 'The Vegetian "science of warfare" in the middle ages', p. 19.

[43] Morillo concludes that 'the Vegetian paradigm, modified to recognize a regular place for battle, does describe much medieval European warfare'; and that where 'Vegetian strategy had no role to play' (campaigns waged by steppe nomads; warfare 'within a closed cultural or political world that in one way or another established rules that governed the meaning and practice of conflict'), battle-seeking strategies were dominant. S. Morillo, 'Battle seeking: the contexts and limits of Vegetian strategy', *The Journal of Medieval Military History*, i (2002), pp. 21–41.

[44] 'There is no doubt that battle was sought on many occasions, and its part in the structure of warfare should not be dismissed, as some recent commentators have tended to do.' Prestwich, *Armies and Warfare in the Middle Ages*, p. 11.

[45] The French, planning to unleash their secret weapon, a powerful contingent of heavily armoured horsemen from Lombardy, had selected a suitable, open site and awaited the English. Angered by the last-minute withdrawal of the French from a pre-arranged battle (or 'journée') outside Ivry on 15 August (on a site that suited the English), John, duke of Bedford felt honour bound to confront the French at Verneuil, despite having to accept an engagement on unfavourable ground and against a numerically superior opponent. Jones, 'The battle of Verneuil', pp. 377–88.

undeniable that he had managed only two set-piece battles before the Crécy campaign (Halidon Hill, 1333; Sluys, 1340),[46] but this was not for want of trying. Examination of Edward's Scottish campaigns suggests that he and his lieutenants had actively sought to bring their elusive adversaries to battle. In July 1336 he narrowly missed catching Andrew Murray, the guardian of Scotland, as he was besieging Lochindorb castle.[47] In a revealing aside, a northern captain, probably Sir William Felton, writing to the king in 1340, noted than 'a certain secret matter' could have 'as great an effect on the war as a battle'.[48] Given the heavy casualties that were inflicted on the Scottish nobility at Dupplin Muir and Halidon Hill, and the immediate political consequences of those encounters, that the English should be seeking battle in the north is altogether understandable. What is perhaps more surprising is that Edward maintained this strategic aim in his early French campaigns as well.

The idea that Edward III, far from setting out to avoid battle in France, pursued a consistent policy of seeking battle has recently been presented in a vigorously argued investigation by Clifford Rogers.[49] Edward's battle-seeking strategy was based upon confidence in his army's tactical superiority when fighting on the defensive, combined with the realisation that great political gains could be made on the battlefield. Battles could be decisive and the risks could be minimised. His opponents' reluctance to engage with him on his terms had to be overcome, and he sought to do this by provoking them beyond endurance, principally by extensive devastation of the French countryside, which while destroying wealth challenged the authority and honour of the Valois king and his nobility. That Edward had failed to bring Philip VI's army to battle in 1339 and 1340 (and perhaps early in 1343, though the English king's intentions during the siege of Vannes are less clear) makes an investigation of his success in doing so in 1346 all the more fascinating. What was different about Edward III's methods during July–August 1346, and why did Philip VI respond differently? We shall seek answers to these questions in Chapter 2.

The magnitude of the military and political event that occurred at Crécy can be demonstrated in various ways. The Liègeois chronicler, Jean le Bel, character-

---

46 Of course, there were captains in Edward's army in 1346 who had rather more experience of 'real' battles, as opposed to assaults on fortified positions. Sir Thomas Ughtred, the sub-marshal of the army, had fought at Bannockburn, Byland, Dupplin Muir, Halidon Hill and St Omer. A. Ayton, 'Sir Thomas Ughtred and the Edwardian military revolution', *The Age of Edward III*, ed. J.S. Bothwell (Woodbridge, 2001), pp. 107–32.

47 As reported in a campaign newsletter: H. Ellis, ed., *Original Letters Illustrative of English History*, 3rd ser., 4 vols (London, 1846), i, pp. 33–9. See Rogers, *War Cruel and Sharp*, pp. 117–18.

48 G.G. Simpson and J.D. Galbraith, eds, *Calendar of Documents Relating to Scotland*, vol. 5 (Edinburgh, 1986), no. 809 (p. 269).

49 Rogers, *War Cruel and Sharp*. Rogers's ideas had been given an initial outing in 'Edward III and the dialectics of strategy, 1327–1360', *TRHS*, 6th ser., iv (1994), pp. 83–102. Other historians have proposed that Edward was seeking battle with his Valois adversary during the early campaigns of the French war (see, for example: Sumption, *Trial by Battle*, pp. 281 [siege of Cambrai], 351 [siege of Tournai]), but Rogers was the first to argue that this was the *consistent* strategy of the English king. See also, Morillo, 'Battle seeking: the contexts and limits of Vegetian strategy', p. 40.

ised the battle of Crécy as the triumph of a 'little company' over 'all the power of France'.[50] In truth, although certainly numerically inferior to the French army, the host that Edward III had at his disposal was substantial and potent. Indeed, numbering as many as 14,000 or 15,000 combatants, the army that disembarked at La Hougue in Normandy in July 1346 was the largest English force to be transported to France at one time during the entire middle ages.[51] The king had raised an army of similar overall size at least once before – for the Scottish campaign of 1335.[52] But during the summer of 1346 he faced an altogether more complex and demanding range of military commitments. While the main thrust of his continental war effort was directed towards Normandy, other expeditionary forces were simultaneously operating in Aquitaine, Brittany, Flanders and Ireland.[53] In a letter to David II of Scotland, Philip VI claimed, perhaps not unreasonably, that Edward III's multi-front assault on France must have left his kingdom defenceless, but this was actually far from true.[54] The military community north of the Trent had been excused continental service in order to ensure the security of northern England, a responsibility that they were called upon to perform at Neville's Cross on 17 October.[55] Moreover, garrisons were maintained in the Channel Islands, at Dover and Carisbrooke castles, at Berwick and elsewhere;[56] and close attention was given to the defence of the 'maritime land' in southern and eastern England.[57] In these circumstances,

[50] *Jean le Bel*, ii, p. 107.

[51] For a discussion of the size and composition of the English army, tentatively suggesting 14,000 men, not including non-combatants, see below, Chapter 5. For a slightly higher estimate, see Rogers, *War Cruel and Sharp*, pp. 216, 423–6.

[52] R. Nicholson, *Edward III and the Scots* (Oxford, 1965), pp. 198–200.

[53] For Aquitaine (Henry, earl of Derby), see K. Fowler, *The King's Lieutenant* (London, 1969), pp. 222–4 and references cited there. Brittany (Thomas Dagworth): A. Prince, 'The strength of English armies in the reign of Edward III', *EHR*, xlvi (1931), pp. 364–5; M. Jones, 'Sir Thomas Dagworth et la guerre civile en Bretagne au XIVe siècle: quelques documents inédits', *Annales de Bretagne*, lxxxvii (1980), pp. 621–39 (E101/25/17, 18 and 19). Ireland (Ralph Ufford): R. Frame, 'The justiciarship of Ralph Ufford: warfare and politics in fourteenth-century Ireland', *Studia Hibernica*, xiii (1973), pp. 7–47. According to a pay account, Sir Hugh Hastings's force in Flanders included a company of 237 foot archers (to whom 6 chaplains were assigned), and a personal retinue of 8 men-at-arms and 11 archers (E372/191, m. 49). However, the latter contingent seems small for a captain of his standing and no mention is made of Hastings's colleagues, Sir John Montgomery and Sir John Moleyns (see Wrottesley, *Crecy and Calais*, p. 173; *Knighton*, ed. Martin, pp. 58–9), so we must suspect that we are seeing only part of this army.

[54] Philip VI's letter of 22 July, printed in *Chronicon domini Walter de Hemingburgh*, ed. H.C. Hamilton (London, 1849), pp. 422–3. The idea, mutated in various ways, found its way into a number of chronicles: see D. Rollason and M. Prestwich, eds, *The Battle of Neville's Cross* (Stamford, 1998), pp. 138, 144, 152 (Walter Bower's *Scotichronicon*); *Knighton*, ed. Martin, pp. 68–9.

[55] *Rotuli Scotiae*, i, pp. 668–75; M. Prestwich, 'The English at the battle of Neville's Cross', *The Battle of Neville's Cross*, ed. Rollason and Prestwich, pp. 1–14.

[56] Channel Islands: E101/25/6; E403/336, m. 43 (Castle Cornet, Guernsey, garrison). Dover castle: E101/531/21; E372/191, mm. 49. Carisbrooke castle: E372/191, m. 54. Berwick: *Rotuli Scotiae*, i, pp. 669, 671, 674–5.

[57] E.g., the appointments of keepers in March 1346 (Wrottesley, *Crecy and Calais*, pp. 73–7) and a stream of orders issued to them in July–August (C76/23, mm. 25, 24d, 22, 21d, 20, 19d).

raising an army consisting of as many as 14,000 fighting men for the Normandy campaign was indeed an impressive recruiting achievement.

In some ways still more impressive was the logistical feat required to transport an army of this size across the channel.[58] The shipping of armies to continental Europe was to become so commonplace a feature of the English war effort during the Hundred Years War that we are apt to take for granted the capacity of royal officials to requisition and retain the services of hundreds of merchant ships from ports around the coast of England, and to organise the refitting of many of these vessels to carry horses or to serve as warships. It is also easy to overlook the fact that waging this kind of war represented a new departure in the late 1330s. There was no established tradition of campaigns in France involving armies shipped from England: they had been infrequent events during the preceding hundred years. Few in 1338 could have recalled the expeditions to Gascony and Flanders in the 1290s, and the last army to be transported to France, in 1325, had been carried in only 80 vessels.[59] The naval dimension of the Scottish wars, and in particular the essential task of supplying armies by sea, could involve dozens of vessels, but an all-out concentration on continental warfare, such as we see from the late 1330s, would make altogether greater demands on England's maritime resources. Thus, on three occasions during the early years of his French adventure – in 1338, 1340 and 1342 – Edward III crossed the channel with an army of 4,000 to 5,000 combatants; and a similar number of troops, divided into three separate expeditionary forces, was conveyed to France during the summer of 1345.[60] These armies may not appear large, but they presented a major logistical challenge because a significant proportion of the combatants were accompanied by horses.[61] In 1297 an army of 895 men-at-arms and 7,800 infantry, together with their supplies, had been conveyed to Flanders in 305 ships.[62] In July 1338, only half as many combatants,

---

58 The preparations required for a cross-channel expedition during this period are discussed in Hewitt, *The Organisation of War under Edward III*: see pp. 55–9 for the supply of food-stuffs to the army, essential during its lengthy wait for a favourable wind at the ports and on board ship, and during the early days of the campaign in Normandy. For an analysis of the difficulties encountered in raising a sufficiently large fleet, see R. Kaner, 'The Management of the Mobilization of English Armies: Edward I to Edward III', D.Phil. thesis, University of York, 1999, chap. 7 (at pp. 142–8, 150–1).

59 M. Prestwich, *Edward I* (London, 1988), pp. 381–6; 392–5; Prestwich, *Armies and Warfare in the Middle Ages*, p. 73.

60 A. Ayton, 'Edward III and the English aristocracy at the beginning of the Hundred Years War', *Armies, Chivalry and Warfare in Medieval Britain and France,* ed. M. Strickland (Stamford, 1998), pp. 173–206 (at pp. 179–82); Sumption, *Trial by Battle*, pp. 453–5, 457–61. In both 1338–9 and 1340, Edward's Anglo-Welsh force was substantially supplemented by contingents supplied by his continental allies. In July 1345, the king's small army did not actually disembark, but the forces led by Northampton and Derby conducted operations in Brittany and Aquitaine respectively.

61 Evidence for the horse-carrying capacity of individual ships is not plentiful, but an average of twenty per ship may be about right. See M. Prestwich, *War, Politics and Finance under Edward I* (London, 1972), p. 147 (1303); E101/695/20 (1355).

62 N.B. Lewis, 'The English forces in Flanders, August–November 1297', *Studies in Medieval History Presented to F.M. Powicke*, ed. R.W. Hunt et al. (Oxford, 1948), pp. 310–18; Prestwich, *War, Politics and Finance under Edward I*, p. 142.

but including about 1,400 men-at-arms and 1,200 mounted archers, required a transport fleet of 361 vessels crewed by over 12,500 mariners (twice as many as were needed in 1297).[63] The emergence of armies in which mounted archers served alongside men-at-arms ensured that even secondary expeditions would make heavy demands on the English merchant marine.

If in terms of intensity of maritime involvement, the early campaigns of the French war had marked the beginning of a new chapter in Edwardian warfare, these expeditions were in fact but a modest prelude to the operation that was to be launched in July 1346. Having turned his back on his former strategy, which had involved the recruitment of expensive and unreliable foreign allies (who in 1337 contracted to supply nearly 7,000 men-at-arms), Edward III was now faced with the problem of shipping his entire army from England. That force would need to be large if a battlefield confrontation could seriously be contemplated. Indeed, the army that landed with the king at La Hougue was about three times larger than that which had accompanied him to Brittany in October 1342. And there must have been a great many horses: single mounts for each of the 3,000 or so mounted archers and hobelars, and (on average) several for each of the 2,500–3,000 men-at-arms, not to mention the animals required for the baggage train. Without the original mariners' pay-rolls we cannot be sure of the size of the transport fleet, but it is clear from the chroniclers' comments that it was very large, and it may well have consisted of as many as 1,000 vessels – a veritable 'city on the inconstant billows dancing'.[64] Naturally, gathering a fleet of such proportions had caused considerable problems. There is an air of desperation about the order of 18 March, which directed officials responsible for arresting vessels to include those of as little as 10 or 12 tons burden, excepting only fishing boats.[65] But although, as the king noted in a letter written on board ship off Yarmouth (Isle of Wight) on 7 July, his passage had been much delayed 'pur defaute des niefs',[66] a remarkable maritime mobilisation had indeed been achieved. The armada of vessels assembling in the Solent must have been an awesome sight, stretching (as a contemporary noted) from Yarmouth to the Needles.[67]

A fleet of this size was needed to ship an army that was exceptionally large by

[63] *Norwell*, p. ciii.

[64] For a survey of the chroniclers' estimates, which range from 600 to 1,600 vessels, see J. Viard, 'La campagne de juillet–août 1346 et la bataille de Crécy', *Le moyen âge*, 2nd ser., xxvii (1926), p. 8 n1. In 1345, 443 ships had been assembled to carry the three expeditions. Fowler, *The King's Lieutenant*, p. 49.

[65] Wrottesley, *Crecy and Calais*, p. 70.

[66] Printed in *Jean le Bel*, ii, pp. 337–8. The king was to be held up a few days more by adverse winds. The fleet finally set out across the channel on 11 July, arriving off St Vaast-la-Hougue before dawn on the 12th.

[67] *Acts of War*, ed. R. Barber, p. 27. The author of this account gives some impression of the difficulties involved in bringing together so large a number of vessels in the open water of the Solent. Although the principal initial assembly point for the fleet had been the large natural harbour at Portsmouth (the king's headquarters being at Portchester castle: *CCR, 1346–9*, p. 31), it is clear that other inlets convenient for the Solent were used. For example, the earl of Northampton was based at Beaulieu abbey, his ships presumably anchored in the Beaulieu River: C81/1734, nos 54, 60, 63.

English standards. Despite the attrition of a six-week campaign, Edward III's host was still a formidable force on the day of the battle of Crécy; perhaps all the more formidable for the experience gained during the six weeks since the landing at La Hougue. Yet there can be no doubt that it was heavily outnumbered by Philip VI's army. Admittedly, the French king's troops were not as numerous as they had been in the 'host of Bouvines' in the summer of 1340, when he had well over 20,000 men-at-arms at his disposal.[68] In July 1346 a sizeable French army, plausibly estimated at 15,000 to 20,000 combatants of all kinds, was preoccupied with besieging Aiguillon in Aquitaine. The siege was not abandoned until 20 August – too late for these troops to take part in the battle of Crécy.[69] Nevertheless, King Philip had managed to assemble a imposing array of chivalry in northern France: 'toute la fleur de Crestienneté . . . montée en armes si richement que merveilles',[70] credibly estimated by Edward III at 8,000 knights and esquires among a total of 12,000 mounted men-at-arms.[71] This force of heavy cavalry outnumbered Edward III's men-at-arms by four to one; indeed, it approached the size of the entire English army. And it was supported by several thousand Genoese crossbowmen and a large, though indeterminate number of common infantry, who were so numerous that 'tous les champs en estoient couvers'.[72] It is true that sheer numbers of common soldiery, or indeed heavy cavalry, might not in itself count for much against a well-deployed opponent with effective missile weapons. But it can hardly be denied that disparity of numbers on the field, reflecting the manpower resources available to the protagonist kings, was a powerful indicator of the magnitude of military upset that had occurred at Crécy.

The scale of the French defeat, and its wider significance, is further underlined by another aspect of the composition of the two armies. Substantial contingents had been contributed to Philip VI's host by princes whose lands lay beyond the borders of France but still within the French sphere of influence. The most notable of Philip's foreign allies were John of Luxembourg, king of Bohemia and his son, Charles, who had been elected king of the Romans on

---

68 The financial accounts indicate that there were 22,500 men-at-arms in the army of Bouvines and in the frontier garrisons in this part of France; but several important contingents, including those of the King of Bohemia and the duke of Brittany, are not included in these records. P. Contamine, *Guerre, état et société à la fin du moyen âge* (Paris, 1972), pp. 68–70; P. Contamine, ed., *Histoire militaire de la France. 1: des origines à 1715* (Paris, 1997), pp. 137–8.

69 Sumption, *Trial by Battle*, pp. 484–8, 496–7, 512–13, 519–20. Note, however, that part of the army had been transferred to defence duties in Normandy in late June: *ibid.*, p. 499.

70 *Chronique de Flandre*, ii, p. 43.

71 'plus de xii. mille dez hommes-d'armes, desquelx viii. mille furent de gentil gentz, chevaliers et esquiers': *Le Prince Noir*, ed. Michel, p. 310. Philip Contamine argues that there were fewer than 10,000 men-at-arms, not all of the contingents having arrived in time for the battle: Contamine, ed., *Histoire militaire de la France. 1*, p. 138. The available evidence suggests that Edward III had in the region of 2,800 men-at-arms at the start of the campaign.

72 For the Genoese, see Bertrand Schnerb's comments, below, p. 269. Foot soldiers: St Omer chronicle, fo. 261v. Writing on 2 September, Richard Wynkeley reported that there were 12,000 men-at-arms and 60,000 others in the French army. *Murimuth*, p. 216.

11 July 1346, and was due to be crowned on 27 August.[73] According to the contemporary Florentine chronicler, Giovanni Villani, they arrived at the head of 500 men-at-arms.[74] They were joined by Raoul, duke of Lorraine, the counts of Namur, Salm and Saarbrücken, and a Savoyard contingent, led by Louis de Vaud, regent to the young Amadeus VI of Savoy.[75] Adding still further to the cosmopolitan flavour of the French army was the political exile, Jaime II, king of Majorca. By contrast, Edward III's army was almost entirely Anglo-Welsh in composition. Those 'few Strangers' (as Joshua Barnes termed them)[76] who landed at La Hougue with the English were either disaffected Norman noblemen, like Godfrey de Harcourt, or 'German' soldiers of fortune, like the knights Rasse Maskerel, Adam von Ederein and Gerhard von Wendendorp.[77] But all told there cannot have been more than 150 foreign troops on the English side at Crécy (and that is probably a high estimate), and we should not be surprised to learn that they found English fighting methods difficult to comprehend.[78] It was the chivalry of mainland western Europe – 'toute la fleur de Crestienneté – that was defeated at Crécy.

The scale of the defeat is also indicated by the extraordinarily heavy casualties suffered by the French and allied nobility and their retinues. Most, it seems, fell to archery rather than to the sword, lance or battle-axe. English newsletters, written within days of the battle, noted that over 1,500 noblemen, knights and esquires had been killed during the evening battle on 26 August. The overall total seems to have been at least 2,000, with a disproportionate number of magnates among the slain.[79] In addition to his close ally, King John of Bohemia,

[73] John's relationship by marriage to Philip VI (his daughter, Bonne, was married to Philip's son, John, duke of Normandy) and his staunchly francophile outlook put him firmly in the Valois camp in the Anglo-French war. See P. Contamine, 'Politique, culture et sentiment dans l'Occident de la fin du Moyen Âge: Jean l'Aveugle et la royauté française', *Johann der Blinde. Graf von Luxemburg, König von Böhmen, 1296–1346*, ed. M. Pauly (Luxembourg, 1997), pp. 343–61. For Charles's coronation, see F. Seibt, *Karl IV: ein Kaiser in Europa, 1346–1378* (Munich, 1978), p. 144.

[74] *Villani*, vii, p. 158.

[75] Villani (*ibid.*, vii, pp. 168–9) notes that the duke of Lorraine reached the battlefield late and was killed in the rout on the morning of 27 August. The Savoyard contingent also arrived after the battle but shrewdly marched on to Montreuil and held it for Philip VI. E.L. Cox, *The Green Count of Savoy: Amadeus VI and Transalpine Savoy in the Fourteenth Century* (Princeton, 1967), pp. 59–60.

[76] Joshua Barnes, *The History of that Most Victorious Monarch Edward III* (Cambridge, 1688), p. 340.

[77] At the Tower, on 2 May 1346, they had agreed to serve with a company of twenty men: E101/68/3, no. 64. See Chapter 5, Appendix 2, Table 2, n. 35. Cf. *Jean le Bel*, ii, p. 106; *Froissart: Amiens*, iii, p. 13.

[78] *Chronique de Flandre*, ii, p. 44.

[79] Edward III noted that more than 1,500 'chivalers et esquiers' were killed in the area of the first onslaught (*Le Prince Noir*, ed. Michel, p. 310), while Michael Northburgh stated that 1,542 'bones gentz darmes' fell on the evening of 26 August, and more the following morning (*Avesbury*, p. 369). Northburgh's figure is probably based upon the official enumeration of the dead, which we know took place after the battle. The chronicles of Adam Murimuth (the Nero D. X text) and Henry Knighton both give an overall figure of 2,000 and more knights and esquires killed: *Murimuth*, p. 248; *Knighton*, ed. Martin, pp. 62–3. The Bourgeois of Valenciennes states that, in addition to magnates, 500 bannerets and 1,600 knights fell,

who was arguably the most famous chivalric figure in Europe, Philip VI of France lost his brother, Charles, count of Alençon, and his nephew, Louis de Châtillon, count of Blois. The other leading noblemen cut down in the evening battle included Louis de Nevers, count of Flanders; Jean, count of Harcourt;[80] Louis, count of Sancerre; Simon, count of Salm; and Jean de Chalon, count of Auxerre. The duke of Lorraine fell during the renewed fighting on the morning of 27 August. 'It was said for a long time', wrote Jean le Bel, 'that no one had heard of so many princes killed on a single day, not at Courtrai, nor at Benevento, nor anywhere else.'[81] Such breathtaking losses made Crécy not only a devastating military humiliation but also 'a political catastrophe for the French Crown'.[82] Only the death or capture of Philip VI could have made matters worse.

That is how it must have seemed on the morrow of the battle, but within a year Edward III had indeed made matters worse. He had capitalised on his victory by capturing Calais, thereby securing a base on the continental mainland that proved to be of lasting strategic and economic importance.[83] It is sometimes suggested that the military consequences of Crécy were 'small',[84] but it is clear that the battle created the conditions that allowed the English to prosecute the siege of Calais for nearly a year. The political community in England backed the enterprise with money and manpower, while Philip VI's government, paralysed by a political and financial crisis, was unable to raise an adequate relief army until the summer of 1347. When, towards the end of July, that army did arrive on the heights of Sangatte, it was confronted by an English host so effectively entrenched that Philip VI shied away from risking another battlefield disaster outside the besieged town. Calais fell to the English on 3 August 1347 and, coming so soon after Crécy, and the successes in Aquitaine and at Neville's Cross, it further cemented Edward III's relationship with his Flemish allies and prompted the Wittelsbach group among the Electors of the Holy Roman Empire to offer him the Imperial Crown.[85]

In the aftermath of Crécy, newsletters listing the prominent noblemen who had fallen fighting for Philip VI circulated around Europe.[86] The merits of Vegetian

---

figures that are consistent with his anecdote that over 2,200 heraldic surcoats were collected from the corpse-strewn field. *Récits*, pp. 233, 235. Lists of the principal casualties are to be found in the newsletters and chronicles, though many contain inaccuracies. See, for example, *Baker*, pp. 85, 262.

[80] The elder brother of Godfrey de Harcourt, who fought with Edward III. The count of Harcourt's son, Jean, count of Aumale, was wounded in the battle.

[81] *Jean le Bel*, ii, p. 109. Repeated by *Froissart: Amiens*, iii, p. 26.

[82] Sumption, *Trial by Battle*, p. 532.

[83] For the importance of Calais to the war effort, see C. Richmond, 'The War at Sea', *The Hundred Years War*, ed. K. Fowler (London, 1971), p. 100.

[84] Sumption, *Trial by Battle*, p. 532. For a very different view, see Rogers, *War Cruel and Sharp*, pp. 283–4.

[85] H.S. Offler, 'England and Germany at the beginning of the Hundred Years War', *EHR*, liv (1939), pp. 627–31; Rogers, *War Cruel and Sharp*, p. 284 and n. 61.

[86] See, for example, Johann von Schönfeld's letter to the bishop of Passau: J.F. Böhmer, ed., *Acta Imperii selecta* (Innsbruck, 1870), no. 1055.

caution could hardly have been more forcefully demonstrated. The personal military involvement of the aristocracy, particularly when headed by the king, gave battle such political immediacy that, in any given war, it was likely that *at least one* of the protagonists would seek to avoid coming to blows on the battlefield because the stakes were too high. Military objectives might be achieved by other, less risky means. This had certainly been Philip VI's viewpoint. He had fought only one major battle before the summer of 1346 (Cassel in 1328), and had been unwilling to take the plunge against Edward III at Buironfosse (1339) and Bouvines (1340). King John of Bohemia was among the most experienced of the senior commanders at Crécy, but most of his battles had been fought in his early adulthood – notably Esslingen (1316) and Mühldorf (1322).[87] Since then he had been involved in more than his fair share of 'stand-offs', as in 1331 against Charles I of Hungary, and in 1336, when he and Louis of Bavaria observed each other from adjacent armed camps.[88] And, of particular relevance to Crécy, he had also witnessed the 'batailles manquées' at Buironfosse and Bouvines. King John was one of the foremost chivalric figures in Christendom, yet in a world in which the political elite took up arms in person, he was as aware as anyone that caution was usually the better part of valour. Indeed, on the eve of Crécy, he had received a forceful reminder of the hazards inherent in precipitate action. On 19 July 1346, a few days after Edward III's landing at La Hougue, King John and his son, Charles, had been dismayed spectators of the battle of Vottem, when perhaps 4,000 heavy cavalry had been defeated by an array of Liègeois fighting on foot.[89] This was indeed a 'sauvage aventure',[90] and an ominous prelude to King John's fateful involvement in the Crécy campaign.

'Batailles manquées' occurred so frequently in medieval warfare that it could be argued that they deserve as much attention as the battles that actually took place. Indeed, when viewed as political and chivalric events a case can be made for bracketing the two phenomena together. A royal army was a remarkable political and social organism. A king would rarely, if ever, assemble as large a proportion of the aristocracy of his realm for any other purpose, while the raising of contingents of infantry from among the rural peasantry was itself not without political significance.[91] It would also be a breathtaking spectacle, bewildering to the untutored eye: a sea of armorial bearings, displayed on banners, surcoats and warhorse caparisons, proclaiming the distinctiveness of noble

---

[87] R. Cazelles, *Jean l'Aveugle, comte de Luxembourg, roi de Bohême* (Paris, 1947), pp. 63–4, 111–14. Cazelles argues that King John cannot personally have taken part in the battle of Cassel; but he was involved in the attack on the Lithuanian stronghold of Medvegalis in early 1329: *ibid.*, pp. 157, 170–1; S.C. Rowell, *Lithuania Ascending: A Pagan Empire within East-Central Europe, 1295–1345* (Cambridge, 1994), pp. 239–40.

[88] Cazelles, *Jean l'Aveugle*, pp. 197, 237–8.

[89] C. Gaier, 'La bataille de Vottem, 19 juillet 1346', in C. Gaier, *Armes et combats dans l'univers médiéval* (Brussels, 1995), pp. 27–37; DeVries, *Infantry Warfare in the Early Fourteenth Century*, pp. 150–4.

[90] *Jean le Bel*, ii, p. 141.

[91] See J.R. Maddicott, 'The English peasantry and the demands of the Crown, 1294–1341', *Past and Present, Supplement 1* (1975), p. 45, who concludes that 'The more frequent assembling of large armies [during the Edwardian period] may also have served to widen the political consciousness of the peasantry'.

lineages.[92] Yet this was not simply a crowd of individuals; nor, if we visualise an army as a form of social network, was it a network of random associations. In addition to family and retaining ties, there would be a regional or tenurial basis to much of the recruitment in the banneret-led retinues and even in some of the large 'battles' or divisions that formed the main organisational units of the army.[93] If the bannerets were foci for relatively small clusters of knights and esquires, perhaps a few dozen men, the king's principal lieutenants, at the head of the 'battles' under whose organisational umbrella the bannerets were grouped, were the principal 'hubs' in the network.[94] Moreover, the lieutenants were linked by ties of shared status, and particularly by their shared access to the king. In this way, the social and institutional network of the army, resting upon that of the political elite itself, offered clear channels of communication whereby the opinions of the nobility, including their views concerning immediate military matters as well as broader political issues, could be distributed among themselves and transmitted directly to the king. Viewed in this way, an army was a forum for debate, particularly between individuals and groups who would otherwise have little opportunity for communication and the exchange of ideas. This characteristic of medieval armies, notable in the case of those raised by the king of England, was especially significant in France, for this was a kingdom of huge territorial extent and distinctive provincial character, whose armies customarily included contingents supplied by foreign princes. When Philip VI mustered a royal host he was gathering what would have been regarded by contemporaries as the most powerful fighting force in Christendom, but he must also have been aware that, in some senses, he was opening Pandora's box. His actions, the strategy he adopted for the campaign, and the tone of his leadership would be closely watched and discussed.

It can be seen that when two major royal armies met in the field, whether or not they actually came to blows, it was an event that could have far-reaching political consequences, of which those that resulted from defeat in battle were merely the most obvious. Here was the dilemma facing Philip VI in 1346. Having mustered the political elite of his realm, he ran the risk of alienating them if he opted for the militarily prudent course of action and avoided battle when close to his adversary. Caution in the face of the enemy, however sound the reasons underlying it, could carry a political price. A prolonged stand-off would

[92] The heraldry on such occasions could be 'read' by the heralds attached to each army: indeed, recognising the noblemen in both armies, before and during the battle, was one of their prime functions. For the instructions given in a fifteenth-century heralds' manual, see P. Contamine, 'Batailles, bannières, compagnies: aspects de l'organisation militaire française pendant la première partie de la Guerre de Cent ans', *Les Cahiers Vernonnais,* iv (1964), p. 19.

[93] See, for example, Contamine, *Guerre, état et société à la fin du moyen âge,* pp. 74–85; and Contamine, 'The French Nobility and the War', *The Hundred Years War,* ed. Fowler, pp. 147–9, for an analysis of the composition of the 'bataille' of Raoul de Brienne in the host of Bouvines (1340).

[94] This kind of network has been aptly labelled 'aristocratic'. It is otherwise known as 'scale-free'. See A.-L. Barabasi, *Linked: The New Science of Networks* (Cambridge, Mass., 2002); M. Buchanan, *Nexus: Small Worlds and the Groundbreaking Science of Networks* (New York and London, 2002).

test the strength of the bonds that held together the army. Tensions and rivalries could arise among the nobility, assembled in all their finery and fired-up for action, but frustrated by inactivity.[95] Esquires would be elevated to knighthood yet denied the consummation of battle. On the other hand, the social network that linked an army's personnel provided conduits for the distribution of rumour and dissension. Waiting uneasily in anticipation of a battle that failed to materialise, men would talk, and while we cannot be sure what they said, an understanding of the 'aristocratic' network within the army does offer some indication of how ideas could have spread. An anti-climactic end to the stand-off could be interpreted as dishonourable and would reflect badly on the army leadership. Edward III was only too aware of this: as a boy of fourteen, he had been reduced to tears of frustration by the humiliating conclusion of the Weardale campaign in 1327.[96] Philip VI's prestige had been seriously dented by the 'batailles manquées' of 1339 and 1340. As Jonathan Sumption has observed, '[t]o the knights and noblemen who marched with the army the King's inactivity was a betrayal of instincts which made the pitched battle the highest form of warfare and its avoidance tantamount to defeat. Each of these men took back to his home his own kind of camp-fire dissidence and gossip.'[97] We should not underestimate the effect of these earlier inconclusive encounters on the mentality and actions of the French king and his lieutenants in August 1346.

If the social network within an army's political elite could be a source of instability in the circumstances of an anti-climactic stand-off, that same network provided the essential underpinning for effective combat in battle. It was not unusual for fourteenth-century European wars to reach a climax in a trial of arms between two rival political elites fought at close quarters in a small area. Indeed, there was a certain inevitability about this: medieval kings did not always find it easy to follow Vegetius's advice. Although offering opportunities for individual prowess, the 'knightly' combat that would occur in such an encounter, whether mounted or on foot, was essentially a team activity. Where possible, men-at-arms fought co-operatively in groups, and what counted most were the bonds of mutual trust based perhaps upon a shared locality of origin or, better still, upon longstanding comradeship in arms. The clusters of individual relationships within the social network of the military class were, therefore, the foundation upon which successful battlefield performance could be built. But significant battles rarely involved two evenly matched teams of men-at-arms fighting on a level playing field. Commanders were not seeking a fair fight; they were in pursuit of victory. The network of relationships that gave tactical formations their strength in some combat situations was especially vulnerable to attack by missile weapons. At Crécy, each army attempted to use such weapons to break the cohesion of the other; but in the initial exchange of missiles, Philip VI's crossbowmen were outclassed by Edward III's archers, who were then given a free hand to wreak havoc on the massed formations of French cavalry.

---

[95] For the bitter arguments among the French commanders at Buironfosse, see Rogers, *War Cruel and Sharp*, pp. 171–2.

[96] Nicholson, *Edward III and the Scots*, p. 36.

[97] Sumption, *Trial by Battle*, p. 368. See also Rogers, *War Cruel and Sharp*, p. 173.

As was noted earlier, the losses sustained by the French nobility were extraordinarily heavy: more were killed in this battle than at Courtrai in 1302,[98] with a particularly large proportion of magnates among the dead. It seems that whole groups of knights and esquires, fighting together in retinues, or 'conrois', were destroyed or severely weakened by archery, the survivors left vulnerable and at a grave disadvantage in any close combat that occurred. But what was more damaging to the French army's fortunes was the neutralising of its captains, from bannerets to the commanders of 'battles'. There may have been a couple of hundred leaders of this rank in the army at Crécy.[99] The killing or disabling of so many of them tore the 'hubs' out of the 'aristocratic' network that held the army together, and without its centres of command and control, Philip VI's host fell apart.

'On the morrow of Crécy', the death of King John of Bohemia 'was seen by kings, lords, clerks, knights, and chroniclers as the distinguishing mark of that sanguinary and astonishing day.'[100] Driven by the demands of upholding his dispersed territorial interests, as well as by his enthusiasm for crusading, King John's thirty-year military career had made him a household name throughout Christendom. To contemporaries, he was 'le bon roi', a paladin of chivalry. That he should fall fighting for Philip VI in his war against England ensured that the shock waves from the battle reached the furthest corners of Europe.[101] As was fitting for such a celebrated martial figure, the manner of his death became the stuff of chivalric legend. A variety of chroniclers relate how, although blind, he had himself led into the fray by his loyal knights.[102] Froissart's justly famous version conveys to the reader the vivid image of the fallen king surrounded by

---

98   The proportion who died at Courtrai was higher: 40 to 50 per cent of the 2,500 noblemen who fought in the battle. Verbruggen, *The Art of Warfare in Western Europe during the Middle Ages*, pp. 190–4. Cf. Agincourt, where the losses appear to have been 'proportionately larger' than at Crécy, although this was partly the consequence of the killing of many of the prisoners: A. Curry, *The Battle of Agincourt: Sources and Interpretations* (Woodbridge, 2000), pp. 472–3.

99   An extrapolation from Philippe Contamine's calculations for the well-documented host of Bouvines in 1340: Contamine, 'The French Nobility and the War', *The Hundred Years War*, ed. Fowler, p. 144.

100 Martin, 'John the Blind: the English narrative sources', *Johann der Blinde, Graf von Luxemburg, König von Böhmen, 1296–1346,* ed. Pauly, p. 92.

101 King John heads the schedule of casualties attached to contemporary newsletters. See Johann von Schönfeld's letter to the bishop of Passau: Böhmer, ed., *Acta Imperii selecta*, no. 1055. For an example of the wide interest in King John's death, see the fifteenth-century Polish chronicle, *The Annals of Jan Długosz*, ed. M. Michael (Chichester, 1997), pp. 296–7.

102 *Jean le Bel*, ii, 108; *Chronique de Flandre*, ii, p. 43; St Omer chronicle, fo. 262v; *Jean de Venette*, ed. Newhall, p. 44. J. Viard, 'Henri le Moine de Bale à la bataille de Crécy', *Bibliothèque de l'École des chartes*, lxvii (1906), pp. 489–96. *The Annals of Jan Długosz*, ed. Michael, p. 296. Of the English chroniclers, only Thomas Walsingham offers an account of King John's heroism: *Historia Anglicana, 1272–1422*, ed. H.T. Riley, Rolls Ser., 2 vols (London, 1863–4), i, pp. 268–9; *Chronicon Angliae, 1328–1388*, ed. E.M. Thompson, Rolls Ser. (London, 1874), pp. 22–3. Many of the French chronicles merely note his death, without describing the circumstances.

the bodies of his companions, their horses tied together.[103] This was surely the tightest of the clusters of men-at-arms to be wiped out en masse at Crécy.

The death of King John of Bohemia deprived Philip VI of a loyal friend and an invaluable ally, and it also highlighted his own flight from the field. In fairness to Philip, it should be mentioned that various of the chronicles narrate how he tried to rally his army, that he attempted take part in the battle personally and that it was his attendants, principally Jean of Hainault, who led him from the field.[104] There is also the suggestion that he was unhorsed, even that he was wounded, all of which implies that he did get dangerously close to the action.[105] Moreover, it should be emphasised that retreat was not in itself dishonourable. Geoffrey de Charny's *Livre de chevalerie*, written within a few years of Crécy, suggests that it was perfectly acceptable 'to make a safe and honourable withdrawal, when it is the time to do so'.[106] Yet it would seem that many of Philip VI's noblemen made a different choice on that damp August evening in 1346. Of course, we cannot be sure what was passing through their minds, either individually or collectively; and it is certainly true that Crécy was a particularly merciless battle. The French knightly cavalry were obliged to advance into the teeth of English archery, only to find themselves trapped in a confined combat area in which little or no quarter was given and from which escape was difficult.[107] However, it is not easy to disregard the testimony of the chronicles, much of it no doubt based upon the eyewitness accounts of heralds. And their testimony is clear: once committed to battle, whether owing to their own 'pride and envy' or the king's misjudgement, the flower of French chivalry preferred the likelihood of death or capture to a dishonourable flight. It was just such a principle that was incorporated into King John II of France's Company of the Star in 1351–2. The letter of election to the Company stipulated that knights who fled from battle would be suspended. Jean le Bel, the only chronicler to comment independently on this matter, noted that the knights of John II's 'belle compaignie' took an oath never to flee the field further than four arpents,

---

[103] *Froissart*, ed. Luce, iii, pp. 178–9 (A and B MSS) and *Froissart: Rome*, pp. 730–1, which are expanded versions of *Froissart: Amiens*, p. 19. King John's psychology may well have been more complex than Froissart realised. He would have been aware that 26 August was the anniversary of the battle of Dürnkrut, in which King Ottokar of Bohemia had been killed in 1278 (Seibt, *Karl IV*, p. 147). Indeed, this may account for his reported premonition that he would die on the field at Crécy (*Baker*, p. 82). Moreover, coming within weeks of his withdrawal from the field at Vottem, flight at Crécy would have been unthinkable. Consequently, there is little reason to doubt the chroniclers' testimony that, on hearing that the battle was going badly, he determined to intervene personally, to turn the tide of events or die in the attempt.

[104] See, for example, *Chronique de Flandre*, ii, p. 44; *Grandes chroniques*, ix, p. 283; *Chronique Normande*, pp. 81–2; *Jean le Bel*, ii, p. 103; *Froissart*, ed. Luce, iii, pp. 179–80.

[105] Richard Wynkeley, writing within days of the battle, reported an arrow wound to the face: *Murimuth*, p. 216. See also, Rogers, *War Cruel and Sharp*, p. 269 and n. 176.

[106] *The Book of Chivalry of Geoffroi de Charny*, ed. R.W. Kaeuper and E. Kennedy (Philadelphia, 1996), pp. 102–3.

[107] To discuss in detail the reasons for the heavy French casualties at this stage would anticipate Michael Prestwich's examination of the battle (Chapter 4), as well as the concluding chapter of this book, which investigates the impact that archery and the topography of the site may have had on the engagement.

preferring death or surrender. As a consequence, notes the chronicler, at the battle of Mauron in August 1352, 89 knights fell who might otherwise have saved themselves.[108]

There is no reason to believe that French knights were any less resolute and courageous at Crécy. For, as Edward III observed in his battlefield despatch, 'les ennemiz se porterount moult noblement, et moult sovent se ralierent'.[109] Cool assessment of the situation from an early stage in the battle would surely have brought them to the conclusion that the struggle was hopeless, yet they returned repeatedly to the fray until nightfall. Once again, the network of relationships within the aristocratic elite may have exerted a strong influence on these events. 'When a soldier is . . . known to the men who are around him,' wrote General S.L.A. Marshall in 1947, 'he has . . . reason to fear losing the one thing that he is likely to value more highly than life – his reputation as a man among other men'.[110] Although concerned with a very different military context, Marshall's view of combat psychology is equally relevant to the medieval battlefield; indeed, perhaps especially relevant, given the code of honour that was so important to the chivalric class of Christendom. The dishonour of flight would have been particularly difficult to accept among knights who knew each other well. We are left with the conclusion that the aristocratic social network and the mentality that underpinned it, which were essential for the raising of Philip VI's army, and which made the avoidance of battle a politically damaging course of action, may also have contributed to the destruction of the French host at Crécy.

A few hours' fighting on the 'mont de Cressy' had left the kingdom of France, as Froissart observed, 'much weakened in honour, power and counsel'.[111] The political risks of battle could have no clearer demonstration. Magnates with whom Philip VI was accustomed to consult and upon whom he depended for raising large contingents of troops had disappeared from the scene overnight. The situation was exacerbated by the duke of Normandy's withdrawal from court throughout the winter of 1346–7 and the king's icy relations with the duke of Burgundy. That neither Edward III outside Calais nor Henry of Lancaster in Aquitaine were opposed in the field during the autumn of 1346 was, to some extent, the result of confused military planning and a collapse of royal finances;[112] but there was also a recruiting crisis. Jonathan Sumption has noted

---

[108] *Jean le Bel*, ii, pp. 204–7; D'A. J. D. Boulton, *The Knights of the Crown: The Monarchical Orders of Knighthood in Later Medieval Europe, 1325–1520* (Woodbridge, 1987), chap. 5 (at p. 196). Even if the creation of the Company of the Star, and the 'no flight' stipulation in particular, were intended as a response to the performance of the French nobility (and Philip VI's ignominious retreat) at Crécy, this tells us more about John II's prejudices than about the actual events of that battle. His own military performance in Aquitaine during the summer of 1346 had hardly been impressive, and it may well have long rankled with him that he had been obliged to raise the siege of Aiguillon but had not reached his father's army before it had suffered its disastrous defeat at Crécy.

[109] *Le Prince Noir*, ed. Michel, p. 310.

[110] Cited by John Keegan, *The Face of Battle*, pp. 71–2. For General Marshall's insightful discussion of 'Why men fight', see *Men Against Fire: The Problem of Battle Command in Future War* (repr. Gloucester, Mass., 1978), chapter 10 (modified quotation at p. 153).

[111] *Froissart*, ed. Luce, iii, p. 186.

[112] On the political crisis in France after Crécy, see Françoise Autrand's discussion in

that 'the response of the French military class [to a call to arms in the autumn of 1346] was late and poor', and that the following spring 'recruitment was even slower and patchier than it had been in the previous October'. One reason for this was the impoverishment of the nobility after ten years of war,[113] but we should also recognise that with so many magnates, bannerets and militarily active knights removed at a stroke at Crécy, raising an army capable of challenging Edward III outside Calais was going to be no easy matter. For, as we have seen, the recruitment of the 'military class' in both England and France depended to a considerable degree upon the exploitation of social networks. It is said that Queen Jeanne suggested a return to compulsory, unpaid military service for the nobility and that Philip VI rejected the idea. It way well be that he realised that without supplementing the remaining well-established 'hubs' in the aristocratic social network, recruiting the nobility at large – including those families whose martial role had fallen into abeyance – would be difficult, if not impossible. In fact, the better part of a year had passed before the French king managed to assemble an army powerful enough to challenge Edward III outside Calais.[114]

The loss of counsel and recruiting potential would have been a serious enough consequence of the deaths of so many noblemen at Crécy. But there must also have been major consequences for landholding society and local administration in France (and perhaps also, beyond the frontiers, in those territories that had supplied contingents to the French army). A moment's reflection on the 2,200 heraldic surcoats ('tournicles') which, having been taken from fallen French noblemen, were displayed like trophies in Edward III's pavilion,[115] brings home forcefully the scale of the social and economic impact of the Crécy casualties. The death of a front-rank nobleman would have had wide-ranging consequences, for a magnate 'was not just a warrior and a politician, he also stood at the head of a vast business empire . . . and exercised powers of management over all aspects of his empire'.[116] By its very nature, combat would claim the lives of a disproportionate number of young adult males – men whose heirs were underage or who themselves were heirs to estates. Even when the lordships concerned were small, the sudden loss of the immediate heir could spell the end of a venerable noble line. It has recently been written of Agincourt that 'the many deaths at the battle caused numerous wrangles over wardship and inheritance, and there is also evidence of dislocation to economies and administration of lordships'.[117] Who can doubt that the same occurred after Crécy, affecting the fortunes of hundreds of noble families?[118]

Chapter 8. For a broader view of the political and military situation in France, see Sumption, *Trial by Battle*, pp. 538–50, 554–780.
113 Sumption, *Trial by Battle*, pp. 554, 560, 561–2.
114 According to Villani, the army included 11,000 mounted men-at-arms: Sumption, *Trial by Battle*, p. 578.
115 *Récits*, p. 235.
116 C. Given-Wilson, *The English Nobility in the Late Middle Ages: the Fourteenth-Century Political Community* (London and New York, 1987), p. 87.
117 Curry, *The Battle of Agincourt: Sources and Interpretations*, p. 459. Cf. the 'terrible casualties' suffered at Verneuil and their commemoration: Jones, 'The battle of Verneuil', p. 410.
118 This subject has not to my knowledge been researched. In his examination of the numbers

Such wide ranging socio-economic problems were not experienced in England after the battle of Crécy, for none of Edward III's noble captains was killed and, as far as we can tell, losses among his knights and esquires (and, indeed, the archers) were light. A search of the administrative records and narrative sources has yielded the names of only two fatalities: one knight, Aymer Rokesley, and one esquire, Robert Brente.[119] Those memorials to members of the Edwardian military community that date from this period relate to the more numerous casualties from the siege of Calais.[120] But if the English political elite emerged unscathed from the battle of Crécy they were certainly not unaffected by it. The king and his eldest son had been accompanied to Normandy by many of the great men of the realm, including six of the eight militarily active earls. Of the 54 laymen who had received a personal summons to the last parliament to be held prior to Crécy, in June 1344, more than a quarter disembarked with the king in France in July 1346.[121] When it is recalled that a second expeditionary force, under Henry, earl of Derby, was campaigning simultaneously in Aquitaine and that the northern nobility had remained in England to keep an eye on the Scots, it is clear that the majority of the lay peerage were preoccupied with their military responsibilities during the summer of 1346.[122] Looking beyond the select group of men receiving a personal parliamentary summons, we can see that the more broadly based constituency of lesser noble families were well represented among the 50 or so bannerets who fought at Crécy, as were a great many of the county gentry families by the 600 knights bachelor.[123] Edward III's triumph had been shared by the community of the realm.

On one level, what they had shared was a dramatic military event in which the English, on ground of their choosing, had completely outfought the army of the greatest power in Christendom. They had witnessed the beginning of a new chapter of warfare for the English, though not so much in terms of the organisation and composition of the army – or, indeed, in terms of battlefield tactics – since these facets of the Edwardian military machine had been developing

---

of noblemen in later medieval France, Philippe Contamine notes in passing 'les pertes humaines entraînées par les grandes défaites contre les Anglais, de Crécy à Agincourt et au-delà'. *La noblesse au royaume de France de Philippe le Bel à Louis XII* (Paris, 1997), p. 54.

[119] Rokesley: *Eulogium*, iii, p. 211; *CIPM*, viii, no. 627. Brente: SC1/39, no. 178; cf. Wrottesley, *Crecy and Calais*, pp. 125, 146.

[120] Such as the east window of St Peter's Abbey, Gloucester, which was probably erected by Sir Thomas Bradeston in memory of his friend, Sir Maurice Berkeley; the brass at Elsing, Norfolk, commemorating Sir Hugh Hastings; and its exquisite if more modest counterpart at Wimbush, Essex, a memorial to Sir John Wautone and his wife. For references, see below nn. 130 and 131.

[121] *RDP*, iv, pp. 551–3. It is worthy of note that parliamentary attendance in June 1344 was poor, at which the king 'marvelled greatly'. J.S. Roskell, 'The problem of the attendance of the lords in medieval parliaments', *BIHR*, xxix (1956), pp. 166–7; J.E. Powell and K. Wallis, *The House of Lords in the Middle Ages* (London, 1968), pp. 351–2.

[122] The fact that the parliamentary summons of 30 July 1346 could be issued to only 16 lay peers speaks for itself (*RDP*, iv, p. 559). Several of these 16 men had sons or other family members at Crécy.

[123] These estimates are based on the figures supplied in Chapter 5, Appendix 2, Table 2.

steadily for twenty years.[124] The English had suffered their Crécy at Bannock-burn in 1314, and it had taken several decades of experimentation, and a good many less than successful military enterprises, to devise a winning formula. That formula had been settled upon by the mid-1340s, which witnessed a remarkable series of English triumphs in Aquitaine, Brittany and northern England, as well as in northern France. It involved, on the one hand, the aban-donment of expensive foreign allies and mercenaries and an almost total reli-ance on smaller armies composed of Anglo-Welsh (and, in south-western France, Gascon) personnel; and, on the other, the recruitment of large numbers of archers who were mounted for the march yet fought on foot in close co-operation with dismounted men-at-arms. The organisational ideal was for archers and men-at-arms to be closely integrated at retinue, even company, level. In this respect the Crécy army represents merely a stage in the process of development, for while 'mixed' retinues provided more troops than ever before, perhaps two-thirds of the army's archers (along with Welsh spearmen) were recruited by means of traditional commissions of array. However, the general principles, and indeed the subtle nuances, of successful 'combined arms' tactics had been well worked out prior to Crécy – in Scotland in the early 1330s and in several engagements in the French war. Given this accumulated battlefield experience, there is a strong likelihood that Edward III had planned to fight a battle like Crécy in 1346 and that he expected to win.

Edward III and his lieutenants may not have been altogether surprised by the outcome of the battle, yet Crécy was a landmark event because a well-rehearsed performance had been presented on the grandest of continental stages. It marked a new chapter in warfare for the English principally in terms of the boost that it gave to their reputation and their self-confidence. At the beginning of Edward III's reign, England had not been rated as a military power, but 'At Crécy the fame of England grew', as a patriotic poem put it,[125] and after that battle, rein-forced as it was by the other military successes of the mid-1340s, the English were clearly a force to be reckoned with. Continental writers, like Jean le Bel, a worldly secular clerk from Liège, agreed. Writing in 1358, le Bel presented Crécy as the triumph of a confident, authoritative king at the head of tightly disciplined and highly efficient army; and elsewhere in his chronicle he contrasted the low regard in which the English were held when Edward III became king with the situation in the mid-1350s, when they were the 'plus nobles et les plus frisques combastans qu'on sache'.[126]

The enhanced military reputation of the English ensured that their distinctive

---

[124] See A. Ayton, 'English armies in the fourteenth century', *Arms, Armies and Fortifications in the Hundred Years War*, ed. A. Curry and M. Hughes (Woodbridge, 1994), pp. 21–38.

[125] A.G. Rigg, 'Propaganda of the Hundred Years War: Poems on the Battles of Crécy and Durham (1346): A Critical Edition', *Traditio*, 54 (1999), pp. 169–211 (at p. 185). This poem was originally published by T. Wright as 'An invective against France'; see also, J. Barnie, *War in Medieval English Society: Social Values and the Hundred Years War, 1337–99* (Ithaca, NY, 1974), pp. 8–9, 113–14.

[126] *Jean le Bel*, i, pp. 155–6. This remark is located in the first part of the chronicle, which was completed by March 1356 (*ibid.*, ii, p. xiv).

fighting methods influenced warfare in various parts of Europe. It is well known that the English were much sought after as mercenaries in the Italian peninsula and that their style of fighting also left its mark in Portugal; but it may come as a surprise to learn that English archers were employed by King Louis I of Hungary for garrison duty at his border fortress of Törcsvár.[127] Moreover, in the years after Crécy, the French changed their battlefield tactics in direct response to English methods, and in particular to the devastating effect that archery could have on warhorses. It became usual for the greater part of the French knightly elite to dismount and fight on foot, with only small contingents retained on horseback for attacks on the flanks or rear of their enemy.[128] Some successes were achieved with these tactics, as at Cocherel (1364) and Roosebeke (1382); but, deployed without supporting bowmen and gravely disadvantaged if the terrain was difficult (especially since the onus would usually be on them to attack), dismounted men-at-arms were more often heavily defeated, as at Mauron (1352) and Poitiers (1356). Such tactics were sometimes carried beyond the context of the great Anglo-French conflict. The most notorious occasion was the battle of Nicopolis (1396), where (as the Hungarian chronicler, János Thuróczy, noted) the western European knights 'leaped from their horses, as is their custom, intending to fight on foot', and attacked the enemy who were ranged against them, with disastrous consequences.[129] Thus, if it would be going too far to argue that Crécy marked the opening of a new chapter in European warfare, it can nevertheless be seen that, during the decades after that momentous battle, 'English' methods of fighting had a wide impact on the conduct of war across the continent.

The new-found martial confidence and strong sense of comradeship in arms of the English military community are graphically reflected in some of the notable works of art from this period, including the east window of St Peter's Abbey, Gloucester, which displays the heraldry of some of the captains involved

---

[127] For references, see A. Ayton, *Knights and Warhorses: Military Service and the English Aristocracy under Edward III* (Woodbridge, 1994), p. 21 and nn. 65–7.

[128] T.F. Tout, 'Some neglected fights between Crécy and Poitiers', *EHR*, xx (1905), pp. 726–30; J.F. Verbruggen, 'La tactique de la chevalerie française de 1340 à 1415', *Publications de l'universite de l'etat à Elizabethville*, i (1961), pp. 39–48; M. Bennett, 'The development of battle tactics in the Hundred Years War', *Arms, Armies and Fortifications in the Hundred Years War*, ed. A. Curry and M. Hughes (Woodbridge, 1994), pp. 1–20. As was pointed out by V.H. Galbraith, 'the first time the French men-at-arms followed the new English practice and fought on foot' was probably at the first battle of La Roche Derrien, in Brittany, in June 1346: 'Extracts from the *Historia Aurea* and a French "Brut" (1317–47)', *EHR*, xliii (1928), pp. 206, 213–14; cf. another version of the *Historia Aurea*, printed in M. Jones, 'Sir Thomas Dagworth et la guerre civile en Bretagne au XIVe siècle: quelques documents inédits', *Annales de Bretagne*, lxxxvii (1980), pp. 628–9, 637–8. It would seem that Charles de Blois had learned a lesson from his defeat at Morlaix in 1342, where he launched mounted charges against the English position (I can find no evidence that the French dismounted on this occasion, as suggested by Jim Bradbury). See *Knighton*, ed. Martin, pp. 42–3; T.F. Tout, 'The tactics of the battles of Boroughbridge and Morlaix', *EHR*, xix (1904), pp. 711–15; J. Bradbury, *The Medieval Archer* (Woodbridge, 1985), p. 103.

[129] *Johannes de Thurocz, Chronica Hungarorum*, I. Textus, ed. E. Galántai and G. Kristó (Budapest, 1985), p. 215.

in the campaign of 1346–7;[130] and the magnificent brass at Elsing, Norfolk, which commemorates Sir Hugh Hastings (d. 1347), accompanied by eight noble warriors, identifiable from their arms, who are presented as mourners in the side-shafts.[131] Underlying such artistic representations – indeed, made tangible by them – were the shared mentality and social networks of a military class, which had been forged during the half century or so prior to the outbreak of Edward III's French war. Of particular importance were the protracted wars in Scotland. These made heavy recruiting demands on the country gentry, which could only be met by exploiting and supplementing existing social networks. Moreover, regular service in this challenging campaigning arena resulted in a great many noble and gentry families, including recently established ones, becoming conditioned to the acceptance of an active martial role.[132] This process of militarisation – a complex process whose details have yet to be worked out in detail – reached a peak under Edward III, who took full advantage of it in the prosecution of his continental war. Thus, when veterans of the Scottish wars can be detected on active service during the summer of 1346, what we are seeing are not simply militarily experienced individuals, but men maintaining and building upon family traditions of martial participation established by their immediate forebears, and occupying places in a network of relationships based upon social ties and shared campaign experience. Noble and knightly families from all corners of England were drawn into this process of militarisation. Indeed, it is an essential part of the symbolism of Sir Hugh Hastings's memorial brass. His career seems to have begun in the mid-1330s, but his father and half brother, both named John, had seen much service in Scotland under Edward I and Edward II, the latter John having witnessed the debacle at Bannockburn with his uncle, Aymer de Valence, with whom he served several times thereafter.[133] Many of the knights and esquires who fought in the Normandy–Crécy campaign could boast similar family service records. Sir

[130] J. Kerr, 'The east window of Gloucester cathedral', *Medieval Art and Architecture at Gloucester and Tewkesbury*, British Archaeological Association Conference Transactions, vii (1985 for 1981), pp. 116–29. See also, A.K. McHardy, 'Some reflections on Edward III's use of propaganda', *The Age of Edward III*, ed. J. Bothwell (Woodbridge, 2001), pp. 171–92 (at pp. 186–7).

[131] The most recent contribution to a large body of work on this brass is L. Dennison and N. Rogers, 'The Elsing Brass and its East Anglian Connections', *Fourteenth Century England* I, ed. N. Saul (Woodbridge, 2000), pp. 167–93. Cf. Nigel Saul's analysis of the heraldry of Reginald, lord Cobham's tomb chest in Lingfield church: *Death, Art and Memory in Medieval England* (Oxford, 2001), pp. 149–68.

[132] On the formation of a military elite during the reigns of Edward I and II, and its exploitation by Edward III, see A. Ayton, 'Sir Thomas Ughtred and the Edwardian Military Revolution', *The Age of Edward III*, ed. Bothwell, pp. 111–14.

[133] See A. Ayton, 'Sir Hugh Hastings (c. 1310–1347), *Oxford Dictionary of National Biography*, 2004; *Complete Peerage*, VI, pp. 351–4. Careers of the two John Hastings: C67/14, mm. 7, 14 (1300, 1301); C67/16, mm. 3, 6, 11 (1306, 1307); C71/5, m. 4 (1310); C71/6, mm. 3–5 (1314); C71/7, m. 2; E101/15/6, m. 1 (1315); C71/10, m. 5 (1319); *CPR, 1321–4*, pp. 186, 190 (1322). The sub-marshal of the army at Crécy, Sir Thomas Ughtred, who had himself served at Bannockburn, was the son of Sir Robert, who had founded the family's fortunes in East Yorkshire and established its pattern of military service (Ayton, 'Sir Thomas Ughtred and the Edwardian Military Revolution', pp. 114–16).

James Etchingham was apparently dubbed during the campaign and may have fought only once before (in Brittany in 1342–3), but his family, and especially his father Robert, had been regular participants in the king's wars since the late 1290s.[134]

The gathering of England's political elite who shared Edward III's military triumph at Crécy were participants in an event of great symbolic significance. Victory on that August evening in Ponthieu served, in English eyes, to vindicate Edward III's claim to the French throne, a claim that (Juliet Vale has argued) was symbolised from the start of the Normandy–Crécy campaign by the belt-like Garter, bearing the uncompromising motto 'Hony soit q' mal y pense'.[135] In the euphoric aftermath of the battle, there can have been few among the massed ranks of the English political community who had witnessed the engagement who thought ill of their king's aspirations. Edward took full advantage of these sentiments. In making the Garter the basis of a new order of chivalry, he celebrated the military triumphs of the mid-1340s, while institutionalising the unity of purpose and outlook of his noble comrades in arms.[136] He also ensured that these same warriors took their place in the political arena. As we have seen, more than a quarter of the 54 laymen who had received a personal summons to the last parliament to be held prior to Crécy, in June 1344, participated in the Normandy–Crécy campaign. By the end of 1350 as many as eighteen more 'Crécy men' had received a parliamentary summons. As a consequence, about 40 per cent of the lay peers summoned for the February 1351 session were veterans of the Crécy campaign.[137] Sir John Lisle's career epitomises this development. Elevated to the status of banneret on the day of Crécy, Lisle became a founder knight of the Garter and was summoned to parliament from 1350. But military service remained of central importance; indeed, he died on active service in October 1355.[138]

Given the scale of his triumph, it would have been wholly understandable had Edward III found a means whereby the population at large would be regularly reminded of it; and yet Crécy is not commemorated in the coinage, as the battle

---

134 Sir James: C76/22, mm. 10, 12 (1346); Wrottesley, *Crecy and Calais*, p. 102. For the service of James's father, Robert, and two uncles, see: H. Gough, ed., *Scotland in 1298: Documents Relating to the Campaign of Edward I in that Year* (London, 1888), p. 213; E101/9/23, m. 3 (1301); N. Saul, *Scenes from Provincial Life: Knightly Families in Sussex, 1280–1400* (Oxford, 1986), pp. 4–5, 51–5; C71/6, mm. 1, 5 (1314); C71/8, m. 6 (1315); C71/10, m. 5 (1319); BL, Stowe MS 553, fo. 60v (1322).
135 J. Vale, *Edward III and Chivalry: Chivalric Society and its Context, 1270–1350* (Woodbridge, 1982), pp. 79–82.
136 It was not just Crécy that was being celebrated: three of the prominent founder knights – Henry of Grosmont, Ralph Stafford and the Captal de Buch – were in Aquitaine when that battle was fought. Juliet Vale has also suggested that a consideration in the choice of the founder members was the need to form two balanced tournament teams: Vale, *Edward III and Chivalry*, pp. 86–91.
137 *RDP*, iv, pp. 552, 573–4, 576, 579–80, 588–9. For a differently focused analysis of the recruitment of peers after Crécy, see Powell and Wallis, *The House of Lords in the Middle Ages*, pp. 355–8.
138 *Complete Peerage*, viii, pp. 73–6. A newsletter relates that Lisle was killed 'mult merveilousement' by a crossbow bolt. *Avesbury*, p. 440.

of Sluys seems to have been,[139] nor was the anniversary of the battle earmarked for annual celebration, as 25 October was to be after Agincourt.[140] However, it should not be concluded that the king failed to make the most of his victory back in England. Within days of the battle, four members of his inner circle, Bartholomew Burgherssh senior, John Darcy senior, and Masters John Thoresby and John Carleton, returned to England in order to report to parliament.[141] When they did so on 13 September, they had a remarkable story to tell and those who heard it could have been forgiven for thinking that the story had grown in the telling. Speaking on behalf of his colleagues, Burgherssh announced that 'l'Adversaire de Fraunce' with a great army had been defeated at Crécy, and that 'kings, prelates, dukes, counts, barons, knights and other great men have been killed, captured or despoiled'.[142] The underlying message was clear: the victory had demonstrated divine favour for the king's cause in the war and justified the huge burden that the kingdom had borne in pursuit of it.[143] Moreover, more money was needed, since the king, ever 'en la pursuyte de sa querele', would not return to England until he had made an end to the war. In particular, he was determined to capture Calais. The post-Crécy euphoria made it possible for the king to finance this siege, which lasted nearly a year, involved a massive recruiting and logistical effort and escalated the wages bill for the campaign to over £127,000.[144] It was no doubt widely hoped that one last push might indeed bring an end to the war. In the event, the great chevauchée planned for September 1347, following the capture of Calais, was cancelled,[145] and the arrival of the Black Death in 1348 brought a halt to hostilities.

Nevertheless, during the two years after Crécy, the political community of England granted lay and clerical subsidies that yielded over £200,000, to which should be added about £60,000 p.a. from the wool subsidy, together with other one-off levies, such as the unpopular feudal aid of 1346 and the forced loan of

---

[139] The Meaux chronicle tells us that, following the battle of Sluys (in fact, in 1344), a gold noble was issued to show 'on the one side of it, a ship, the king armed and eager within, circumscribed with the royal name, and on the other side of it, a cross firmly stamped with this circumscription: Jesus autem transiens per medium illorum ibat.' *Melsa*, iii, p. 45. There has been some discussion as to whether this coin design was intended to refer to the battle of Sluys: see Barnie, *War in Medieval English Society*, pp. 113 and 175 (n. 51); P. Grierson, *The Coins of Medieval Europe* (London, 1991), p. 156.

[140] The feast of the translation of St John of Beverley, who had 'demonstrated his special patronage of the English people at Agincourt'. See P. Heath, *Church and Realm, 1272–1461* (London, 1988), p. 281.

[141] *CPR, 1345–8*, p. 474; *Murimuth*, p. 217. Parliament was due to open on Monday, 11 September, but was adjourned until Wednesday, by which time the king's messengers had arrived: *Rot. Parl.*, ii, p. 157.

[142] *Rot. Parl.*, ii, p. 158. If a more detailed account of the battle was offered, it did not find its way into the records of parliament. Burgherssh added that the king was now besieging Calais and that once the town had been taken, he would endeavour to bring the war to an end.

[143] For a calculation of the quantifiable tax burden in 1336–42, which approached £665,000, see W.M. Ormrod, 'The Crown and the English economy, 1290–1348', *Before the Black Death*, ed. B.M.S. Campbell (Manchester, 1991), pp. 149–83 (at pp. 182–3).

[144] R. Brady, *History of England* (London, 1700), ii, appendix, p. 86.

[145] Sumption, *Trial by Battle*, pp. 583–5; Rogers, *War Cruel and Sharp*, pp. 282–3.

20,000 wool sacks in 1347.[146] Although not raised without some grumbling,[147] that such sums could be achieved after ten years of war with France 'is an impressive testimony to the exercise of royal and seigneurial authority in the afterglow of Crécy'.[148] With the king and his realm's military reputation at unprecedented heights, enthusiasm for the war soared. Recruitment was not to pose problems during the 1350s despite the demographic consequences of the Black Death. Moreover, the victories that began with Crécy 'persuaded the higher clergy that the king was fighting a just war, and turned them into enthusiastic supporters of the Crown'.[149] The contrast between political conditions in England and those facing Philip VI and his son in France could hardly be more stark. The very different fortunes of the two monarchies in the aftermath of Crécy found symbolic expression in the history of their respective orders of chivalry, for while the Order of the Star was effectively destroyed on the battlefields of Mauron (1352) and Poitiers (1356), the Order of the Garter went from strength to strength.

[146] W.M. Ormrod, *The Reign of Edward III* (New Haven and London, 1990), pp. 204–5; Ormrod, 'The Crown and the English economy, 1290–1348'; G.L. Harriss, *King, Parliament and Public Finance in Medieval England to 1369* (Oxford, 1975), pp. 410–16, 450–9.
[147] See, for example, the Commons' grievances presented in the September 1346 parliament, within three weeks of the battle of Crécy: *Rot. Parl.*, ii, pp. 159–62.
[148] Harriss, *King, Parliament and Public Finance*, p. 415. Dr Harriss's words, which refer specifically to the raising of the feudal aid, have a more general application.
[149] Ormrod, *The Reign of Edward III*, pp. 20, 132–3.

2

The Crécy Campaign

ANDREW AYTON

From La Hougue to Crécy: The strategic plan

Why did a major pitched battle take place in August 1346 at Crécy-en-Ponthieu? The question has two elements, concerning time and place. The significance of the 'place' of battle, the immediate locality and the region, will be examined later in this chapter; but at this stage it should be noted that, prior to August 1346, Ponthieu had felt little of the impact of the war. The county had been occupied, it seems without resistance, in 1337 when Philip VI confiscated the king of England's continental lands. Since then there had been no land-based operations in this part of France.[1] From 1337 to 1345 English expeditions had been focused on the Low Countries (specifically Flanders, Artois and Hainault), Aquitaine and Brittany. As we have seen, several of those campaigns had witnessed stand-offs, but no pitched battles, between major field armies led by the protagonist kings.[2] In July 1346 the English king returned to the fray and on this occasion Philip VI accepted battle. This prompts a number of questions. What was different about the circumstances of the campaign in July–August 1346? Had Philip simply been forced to accept battle by political pressure that had grown with each successive stand-off? Or did he genuinely believe that he had a decisive advantage in August 1346: an advantage of sufficient proportions to overcome the Vegetian caution that had been a feature of his earlier confrontations with Edward III? Or was his willingness to engage on that fateful August evening due to a loss of sang-froid: had he been outwitted and simply lost control? Was he the prey rather than the hunter? As we shall see, each of these questions is pertinent to an understanding of why the battle took place, but the main emphasis of the discussion that follows will be on the intentions and actions of Edward III. It will be argued that his strategy during the summer of 1346 was innovative in a number of important respects.

One striking difference about the campaign of July–August 1346 concerns the area over which it was fought. King Edward landed in the Cotentin peninsula

---

[1]   In the summer of 1339, Rue was among the coastal locations raided by a maritime force led by Sir Robert Morley: *Knighton*, ed. Martin, pp. 14–17; Sumption, *Trial by Battle*, p. 266.
[2]   This is not to diminish the significance of Sluys, a naval battle in which the French political elite did not participate, still less the earl of Derby's victory at Auberoche in October 1345, which was the result of a well-timed attack on an unsuspecting siege camp.

and marched eastwards across Normandy, a region of France that had witnessed no previous fighting, apart from coastal raids. His search for a crossing of the Seine brought him to within 25 kilometres of Paris, and having reconstructed the bridge at Poissy he marched north towards his 'droit héritage', the county of Ponthieu, where the long-awaited climactic battle with Philip VI took place. Whether all – or indeed any – of this had been planned in advance has long been debated by historians, the wide divergence of opinion arising from the inconsistency of the clues offered by the documentary evidence, as well as from sharply contrasting opinions concerning medieval generalship in general and Edward III's skills as a commander in particular.[3] Here it will be argued that a descent upon the Normandy coast, at La Hougue, was indeed planned well in advance of embarkation; and that it was the first step towards achieving the principal aim of the expedition, namely, to bring Philip VI to battle at a time and a place that were to Edward's advantage. As was noted in Chapter 1, there are grounds for believing that Edward had been in search of a decisive battle with Philip VI since the beginning of the war.[4] The English king was confident in the tactical superiority of his army, but practical exploitation of that advantage depended upon the French accepting battle and taking the offensive. Edward would have welcomed a battle in 1339 and 1340 (1342–3 is less certain), but on each occasion, the Valois king was disinclined to engage. Edward, it seems, concluded that, in order to persuade the French king to fight in 1346, a change of approach was needed.

The first change was the selection of a new theatre of war, which it was hoped would bring about a level of provocation that would draw the French king into accepting battle on Edward's terms. As we shall see, Normandy would have been judged suitable for a number of reasons, but perhaps above all it was its wealth and distinctive political identity that made it an attractive target. Extensive devastation of the countryside and towns of Normandy would seriously affect the level of taxation that could be extracted from the duchy while challenging the authority and honour of the Valois king and his nobility.[5] Perhaps such a strategy would be more effective in Normandy than it had been in the Cambrésis; and if the French king chose to back away, the option was open to march up the Seine valley towards Paris. And, all the while, secondary forces would be mounting holding operations in other regions of France, thereby preventing Philip VI from concentrating all of his military resources against Edward III's army. All things considered, no other point of entry into northern France – Brittany, Flanders or Ponthieu – offered such strategic possibilities as Normandy, and such potential for provocation.[6] It cannot be stressed too forcefully that it was Edward's intention to provoke Philip, to enrage him so that he

---

[3] Edward III's merits as a commander have recently been summarised by Clifford Rogers: 'England's greatest general', *Military History Quarterly*, 14/4 (summer, 2002), pp. 34–45.
[4] Rogers, *War Cruel and Sharp, passim*.
[5] That damaging the Valois king's fiscal resources was central to English strategic thinking is made explicit in Sir John Wingfield's newsletter from Aquitaine, dated 23 December 1355: *Avesbury*, pp. 439–43.
[6] The possibilities offered by Flanders and Brittany had, in any case, been fully explored before.

blundered into a battle that was fought on terms set by the English. That is why Edward would not accept a staged battle outside Paris in response to Philip's challenge.[7] Edward was not averse to taking risks, as is shown, for example, by his military adventures in 1336 and 1350. But in July–August 1346 he was not seeking a chivalrous fair fight. What he wanted was a battle on his terms and on ground of his own choosing. One feature of the battle of Crécy that the narrative sources make abundantly clear is that it was a brutal, bloody, one-sided affair.

To argue that the 1346 campaign had been carefully planned beforehand is not to suggest that Edward's march from La Hougue to Crécy was executed precisely according to a simple blueprint. War is rarely as straightforward as that. After the landing, Edward's strategy must have allowed for several possible courses of action, because much would depend upon the nature of the French reaction to the invasion. He probably expected to receive only limited support from the Norman nobility; but also, in all probability, he anticipated only limited military resistance before reaching Caen. It was, perhaps, less easy to predict with confidence where he would be met by Philip VI and the main French army, or at least those forces that were not already occupied in Aquitaine. His best guess would have been that his opponent would assemble his host at Rouen and that a confrontation would take place west of the Seine. In the days immediately after the capture of Caen it did indeed look as though this would happen. But, not for the first time, Philip lost his nerve and retired back across the Seine, breaking the bridges to prevent the English from following.[8] Such a course of action from Philip could – and would – have been predicted. It was wholly in character, and probably to be expected given the threat from a Flemish army, led by Sir Hugh Hastings, which by this time would have been evident on the march of Flanders. Consequently, although the English progress upstream along the Seine in search of a bridge may have the appearance of what Oman described as 'a very dangerous adventure',[9] the possibility that such a march would be necessary would have been anticipated.

The search for a crossing over the Seine that was intact or repairable involved an element of risk, but not of the magnitude suggested by some commentators. First, there was the problem of how to keep a large army adequately supplied,[10] when foraging would be confined very largely to the left bank of the river and perhaps further restricted by the likelihood of imminent battle. In the event, the freedom of English pillaging and foraging does not appear to have been

[7] Edward's response, 15 August: *CPR, 1345–8*, pp. 516–17.

[8] Sumption, *Trial by Battle*, p. 513.

[9] C. Oman, *A History of the Art of War in the Middle Ages*, 2nd edn, 2 vols (London, 1924), ii, p. 132.

[10] For the first fortnight of the campaign supplies had been plentiful. In addition to victuals brought from England, the army had been able to draw on the resources of the countryside and several well-stocked and ill-prepared towns. Edward was naturally concerned about the unnecessary waste of stores at Carentan, but his army suffered no supply difficulties before the capture of Caen. His letter of 29 July, which orders the urgent provision of men, money and munitions, makes no mention of victuals. *Acts of War*, ed. Barber, p. 30; Fowler, 'News from the front', pp. 83–4. Efficient foraging in Normandy had been made possible by a slow rate of march and effective dispersion of the army: *Baker*, pp. 255–7 (rate of march); *Jean le Bel*, ii, pp. 76–7 (three parallel columns).

interrupted to any significant degree during the first half of August; and in any case the fruits of these activities were supplemented by supplies carried in the army's wagon train, which would have been fully replenished at Caen.[11] Shortage of supplies would only have become a critical problem if the English had settled down to besiege the French capital.

At first glance, the search for a usable crossing over the Seine represented an altogether more formidable challenge, for the river below Paris is wide and deep and the French would surely secure every bridge, by defending it or breaking it. However, the English must have known that the bridges would only be partially dismantled;[12] and they would have trusted their ability to resist any attempt to interfere with the repair teams, if necessary by sending advance parties across the river in boats, as had happened at La Roche Guyon on 11 August.[13] Above all, the English arrived at Poissy well prepared for bridge repair work. A company of forty carpenters had accompanied the army to France, presumably with the likelihood of such work in mind.[14] The resourcefulness of these engineers was shown

---

[11] For the importance of supply trains (wagons and pack animals) 'to supplement [foraging] and serve as a safety net on which the army could rely if local supply proved insufficient', see Yuval Noah Harari, 'Strategy and supply in fourteenth-century western European invasion campaigns', *Journal of Military History*, lxiv (April 2000), pp. 297–334 (at p. 319).

[12] Completely dismantling a stone bridge would take a long time, and would not be considered necessary or desirable. At Rouen (and elsewhere) a stone bridge had a wooden section that could be broken up in times of emergency: see R.A. Newhall's notes in *Jean de Venette*, p. 172 (n. 25). That this is what the English found at Poissy is suggested by the anonymous English diarist, who tells us that the broken section of the bridge could be traversed by a tree trunk sixty feet long (*Acts of War*, ed. Barber, p. 37; *Acta Bellicosa*, ed. Moisant, p. 170). Given the difficulty of laying a single span of this length, and the fact that the repair work was completed so rapidly, we may assume that much of the essential superstructure of the bridge remained in place in the river. Indeed, that is precisely what Froissart reports ('[ils] trouvèrent le pont romput et deffait, mais encores estoient les estaches et les gistes en le rivière': *Froissart*, ed. Luce, iii, pp. 149, 379, 382), though this may be nothing more than his rationalisation of a situation that his principal source, Jean le Bel, had found difficult to explain. The latter regarded the whole episode at Poissy as a 'grand merveille', since (as he asserts) the English achieved the work so quickly and without boats, and the French did not defend the crossing more effectively (*Jean le Bel*, ii, pp. 86–7). If, in his turn, we may detect Jean le Bel's distinctive agenda in his portrayal of these events (the purposeful English king opposed by a weak French one), it is clear that Philip VI had not expected the English to rebuild to bridge at Poissy. This was 'a feat which the French had thought impossible' (*Jean de Venette*, ed. Newhall, p. 42). Small wonder that noblemen at Philip VI's court would not believe the first bearer of the news (*Grandes chroniques*, ix, p. 278).

[13] *Acts of War*, ed. Barber, p. 35; *Acta Bellicosa*, ed. Moisant, p. 167. The *Chronique Normande* (p. 78) states that the bridge at Poissy was repaired under cover of darkness. However, the English accounts relate that a contingent of French troops appeared at the bridgehead in the afternoon of 13 August, soon after the first piece of timber had been thrown across the gap, and the earl of Northampton's archers, dashing across the narrow 'plaunke' (as King Edward calls it), drove the enemy away with heavy loss. *Acts of War*, ed. Barber, p. 37; *Acta Bellicosa*, ed. Moisant, p. 170; *Le Prince Noir*, ed. Michel, p. 309 (Edward III's letter); *Avesbury*, p. 367 (Northburgh's letter); *Murimuth*, p. 216 (Wynkeley's letter). For French losses, as variously estimated, see Rogers, *War Cruel and Sharp*, p. 256 n. 107.

[14] For William of Winchelsea and his company of carpenters, see E101/390/12, fo. 8r; Wrottesley, *Crecy and Calais*, pp. 62, 65, 80. For their work at the Douve and Vire, see *Acts of War*, ed. Barber, p. 30.

early in the campaign, at the crossings of the rivers Douve and Vire; but for William of Winchelsea and his men, repairing the sixty-foot gap in the bridge at Poissy represented their real challenge. According to the *Acta Bellicosa* the search for suitable timber began on the morning of 13 August. We should imagine the dismantling of nearby buildings, the felling of trees and the retrieval of timbers from the river.[15] Then, in the afternoon, the broken section of the bridge, 60 feet across, was repaired for men on foot, and within a few hours a serviceable track-way for horses and carts had been laid down. It was a remarkable feat of engineering efficiency. One French chronicler aptly described the operation as making a bridge and laying it down upon the broken structure.[16] As with other aspects of this campaign, we are driven to the conclusion that the task had been planned for, indeed rehearsed, before the army left England.

There were, therefore, risks involved in the march up the Seine, but they could be minimised by careful planning; and such a march might also serve to bring Philip VI to battle in circumstances favourable to the English. The destruction of the royal palaces at Montjoye and Poissy, and a threat to Paris itself, might be enough to push Philip into an ill-considered military encounter,[17] while the great bends of the Seine would not make it easy for the French king to deploy his forces effectively. Until the duke of Normandy arrived with his army from Aquitaine, Philip's host would not be overwhelmingly superior to Edward III's. The odds were not so heavily stacked against the English as has sometimes been supposed, but time was of the essence. Because of the risk of being caught between two major French armies – the king's and his son's, or even having to fight them both on favourable ground – Edward could not afford to linger in the vicinity of Paris for more than a few days. An attempt to lay siege to the French capital was out of the question. (Such a course of action could not have been supplied in any case.) If Philip were only prepared to accept battle in the Ile de France on his own terms (as actually happened), then the logical plan for Edward would be to march north, away from the duke of Normandy and towards Ponthieu.

The possibility that the campaign would reach a climax in Ponthieu must have been foreseen from the outset, and we may be sure that it was one of the contingencies that had been carefully considered in advance. We know that Edward was anticipating a march towards Ponthieu by 29 July at the latest, because on that day he sent a letter to his council in London requesting that men,

---

[15] The Bourgeois of Valenciennes notes that 'les Englès amassèrent tout quanques qu'ils peurent trouver de bois et de hayes pour faire le pont, et les aultres entrèrent en l'eauwe et trouvèrent sur la rivière de Saine II pièces de bos qu'ils prinrent pour leur pont'. *Récits*, p. 223.

[16] 'Maiz Anglois firent ung pont qu'ilz jetterent sur le pont rompu et passerent oultre.' *Chronique des quatre premiers Valois*, p. 15.

[17] According to Thomas Burton, the destruction of Montjoye was 'in order all the more to provoke Philip to fight': *Melsa*, iii, pp. 56–7. A contemporary author based at St Denis considered the despoliation of the French king's principal residences in the heart of his kingdom as 'plus grant deshonneur au royaume de France', and also as 'traïson evident', since the French nobility made no attempt to prevent it (*Grandes chroniques*, ix, p. 276). See also *Gilles le Muisit*, pp. 155–6; *Jean de Venette*, ed. Newhall, p. 41.

military supplies and money be sent to Le Crotoy, a port at the mouth of the Somme.[18] The clear implication of the letter is that Edward intended to march towards Le Crotoy in order to take advantage of the additional manpower and resources that he expected to arrive there. This letter was despatched before Edward had a clear idea of Philip VI's intentions and before he had begun his search for a crossing point on the Seine. That search involved a major detour, but as soon as he was over the Seine he continued with the plan that can be discerned in his 29 July letter: to march towards Ponthieu. Having failed to provoke Philip into fighting a battle on favourable terms in the vicinity of Paris, Edward turned to another option: to entice Philip into a battle in the county of Ponthieu, the English king's 'droit heritage', which he had acquired from his mother, Queen Isabella.

The 'Ponthieu option' offered a number of practical advantages to the English. As yet largely untouched by the war, this corner of France could be counted on for supplies. In addition to the resources of the countryside and the smaller, unfortified towns, the huge hunting ground of Crécy forest offered the prospect of plentiful game for an army that could boast many expert archers. As it turned out, such opportunities would have been particularly welcome at the end of the march from the Seine to the Somme, during which much of the army's mobile supplies would have been expended.[19] The other attraction of Ponthieu was that it was familiar territory for some of Edward's lieutenants. Indeed, as we shall see, there is good reason to believe that the ground upon which the battle of Crécy was ultimately fought was known to the English in advance. It may even have been earmarked as an ideal site for a defensive battle. If so, this is a consideration that must have weighed heavily with the king and his lieutenants, for one aspect of Edward's battle-seeking strategy that might involve last-minute improvisation was the selection of a suitable battleground: a site that enabled the English to play to their strengths while neutralising those of the enemy. It is conceivable that the battle could have taken place, for example, west of Rouen or in the vicinity of Paris on ground that was not ideal. But from the outset, it is likely that Edward knew that he had at least one excellent site up his sleeve: at Crécy-en-Ponthieu.

How was Edward to lure Philip into fighting a battle on the English king's terms at Crécy when he had failed to do so earlier in the campaign? Since Edward had twice paid homage to Philip for the possession of Ponthieu, to challenge the king of France on this ground was itself a provocative act, a symbolic defiance on the grandest of stages. Moreover, Edward's march north from the

---

[18] Discussed below, pp. 73–7.

[19] Michael Northburgh's comment, in his 4 September newsletter, that 'since we left Caen we have lived off the land with great difficulty and much harm to our men' (*Avesbury*, p. 369), arose from the army's immediate need for supplies for the coming siege of Calais, but also reflects the practical limitations on foraging, and consequent supply shortages, experienced during the rapid march from Poissy to the Somme. Two contemporary continental chroniclers refer to the army's lack of bread and the reliance on meat (*Villani*, vii, p. 162; *Gilles le Muisit*, pp. 158–9), which, if true, may not have been regarded as such hardship by the men. Cf. Harari, 'Strategy and supply in fourteenth-century western European invasion campaigns', p. 309.

Seine would have the outward appearance of a retreat, particularly since it was conducted quite rapidly.[20] If Philip could not be coerced into battle by aggression, perhaps he would be tricked into attacking an opponent who seemed to be running away. That Edward appeared to be retreating towards his Flemish allies was another factor in the equation. Edward must have realised that he could not rely upon meeting up with Sir Hugh Hastings's army, but Philip might nevertheless be tempted into battle in order to prevent such a junction occurring. It is significant that several contemporary observers (followed by some modern historians) thought that the English were indeed marching to join their allies, though such a view can only have been founded upon an interpretation of the situation. There can have been no hard evidence. Moreover, so effective was Edward's 'feigned flight' from the Seine to the Somme, that both the French high command and several chroniclers were indeed fooled into thinking that Philip VI was the hunter and Edward III the prey.

Edward III and Normandy

In offering an interpretation of the campaign that argues that the descent upon the coast of Normandy was planned well in advance of embarkation, we must confront the very different views proposed by other historians. It has been argued by some scholars that the English landing at La Hougue in July 1346 was the result of a change of plan, made within days of departure or even at the last minute. According to this interpretation, Edward III had intended to lead an army to Aquitaine in support of the earl of Derby, and specifically to relieve the English garrison that had been besieged in Aiguillon since April. But he changed his mind, the decision to go to Normandy being made either 'at a secret meeting of the King's closest military advisers on about 20 June', as suggested by Jonathan Sumption;[21] or even later, after the troops had been embarked and were awaiting a favourable wind, as was reported by one of the king's closest advisers, Sir Bartholomew Burgherssh, in a campaign bulletin from La Hougue, dated 17 July.[22] While appearing at first glance to chime with the evidence of the documentary sources, this interpretation raises serious problems. The expedition that landed at La Hougue had involved a massive mobilisation of men, shipping and supplies: no larger army was conveyed to France during the Hundred Years War. King Edward had taken a close personal interest in the preparations for what he seems to have regarded as a climactic encounter with his Valois rival. In these circumstances it would surely be reasonable to assume that he had formulated a clear plan as to where his army was to be deployed and to what purpose.

---

[20] From Poissy to Airaines, over 110 km were covered in six days. Of course, with Ponthieu now Edward's clear goal, he did not want to fight Philip's army on less suitable ground. He had outwitted his adversary at Poissy and gained a head start in his march north: see, for example, *Jean de Venette*, ed. Newhall, pp. 41–2; *Gilles le Muisit*, p. 158.

[21] Sumption, *Trial by Battle*, p. 497. The timing of the change of plan is suggested by the date of Sir Hugh Hastings's appointment as king's lieutenant in Flanders (20 June), the two decisions being 'probably made at the same time': *ibid.*, p. 622 (n. 17).

[22] As accepted by M. Prestwich, *The Three Edwards* (London, 1980), p. 176.

Yet we are asked to believe that the destination and, therefore, the purpose – indeed, the whole strategic thrust of the expedition – were changed within days of the intended departure, perhaps even after the fleet had put to sea.

To be convincing, this interpretation would need to be supported by hard evidence, but there is actually very little to back up the case for a late and complete change of strategy. According to Burgherssh's letter, the plan to sail to Gascony was thwarted by contrary winds and the fleet was carried to the Cotentin peninsula by the hand of providence.[23] In fact, this story appears little more than an elaboration of the message contained in a letter sent by the king to his chancellor and treasurer on 7 July: namely, that the fleet was intending to set out on the next tide and would arrive where God willed and the wind carried them.[24] Neither the king's nor Burgherssh's words are to be taken literally. Indeed, both documents are illustrative of the tight security and fog of disinformation that accompanied preparations for this campaign.[25] It is clear that Edward kept all except his closest advisers in the dark. According to the English chroniclers, the rank and file of the army had no idea where they were bound when they embarked. The ships' masters were instructed simply to follow the course set by the admirals. The Florentine chronicler Giovanni Villani adds, perhaps for effect, that they had sealed orders that were to be opened in the event of the fleet being dispersed by a storm.[26] Anxiety that spies in London might, at the eleventh hour, acquire vital intelligence prompted the king, in his 7 July letter, to prohibit anyone from leaving the kingdom for a period of eight days after his departure. The only exception was to be Sir Hugh Hastings's expedition to Flanders, and his men were to be searched for documents.[27]

The veil of secrecy that shrouded preparations for the campaign of July–August 1346, and that makes the work of twenty-first century historians particularly difficult, is in itself suggestive that the decision to land in Normandy was not taken at the last minute. Edward wanted to keep his adversary guessing for a very good reason. That the French should not learn the precise location of Edward's intended landfall was crucial to the success of his venture. For whereas each of his previous expeditions to France had disembarked in a friendly port, the landing in Normandy would by necessity be made on a stretch of hostile coastline. Serious opposition could lead, at the very least, to the expedition being aborted. It seems that the combination of tight security and the selective release of disinformation was successful. The French government could not be sure where Edward intended to land,[28] and in the absence of

23 *Murimuth*, p. 200.

24 *Jean le Bel*, ii, p. 338.

25 See also, the king's letter, of 6 May, to the bishop of London and various religious orders, requesting that prayers be said for his coming expedition. Although making reference to the earl of Lancaster's military successes in Gascony, the king's destination was not specified, any more than it had been in a propaganda broadsheet, issued for wide distribution on 15 March, which had referred merely to the king's 'speedy passage'. Those coming into contact with these documents were left to interpret them as they wished. *Foedera*, III, i, p. 81. *CCR, 1346–9*, pp. 57–8, 65.

26 *Murimuth*, p. 199; *Baker*, p. 79; *Villani*, vii, p. 156.

27 *Jean le Bel*, ii, p. 338.

28 *Jean le Bel*, ii, p. 68. That much of the English fleet was gathering at Portsmouth would

reliable intelligence, a case could be made for Aquitaine, Brittany or Flanders. Eventually, around the middle of June, attention turned to Normandy: coastal garrisons were hurriedly strengthened, troops being recalled from the siege of Aiguillon for the purpose.[29] But it is unlikely that these measures were prompted by concrete information gathered by agents in England or Flanders. It was more a matter of deduction from known facts: the presence at Edward III's court of the banished Norman nobleman, Godfrey de Harcourt,[30] and its possible implications for English strategy, combined with the (somewhat belated) recognition that Normandy was an attractive, vulnerable and accessible target for an English fleet gathering at Portsmouth. What is certain is that the French did not know precisely where the English would land. They had to watch all the ports and a lengthy stretch of coastline. Although his delayed departure was deeply frustrating for King Edward, anxious as he was that the French would discover his intentions at the very last moment, it proved to be a blessing in disguise. Lack of pay prompted a contingent of five hundred Genoese crossbowmen to withdraw from the area of St Vaast-la-Hougue a few days before Edward's fleet arrived on the morning of 12 July, and the scratch force that the marshal, Robert Bertran, was able to raise was easily dispersed by the English advance guard led in person by the earl of Warwick.[31] Given the vulnerability of the transport fleet during the five days of disembarkation, it was indeed fortunate for the English that the Genoese galleys, which had been contracted to protect the northern coast of France, did not reach the mouth of the Seine until mid-August.[32]

In the absence of clear indications in the administrative records, some historians have assumed that the veil of secrecy concealed changes in the intended destination of the expedition rather than a consistent plan.[33] Indeed, the conventional view has been that, from start to finish, Edward III's conduct of the expedition was based upon, at best, inspired improvisation rather than methodical preparation and strategic single-mindedness.[34] In all fairness, this interpretation has

---

not have provided a clear indication of Edward III's intentions. Fleets bound for Gascony had left from that port in 1294, 1325 and 1337, while in 1345 the Portsmouth fleet sailed to Brittany. Rogers, *War Cruel and Sharp*, p. 224 n. 31; K. Fowler, *The King's Lieutenant* (London, 1969), p. 49.

[29] The constable, Raoul, count of Eu, was recalled from Aiguillon and assigned to the defence of Harfleur and Caen, where he was joined by the count of Flanders. *Jean le Bel*, ii, pp. 68–9 and 68 n. 2; Sumption, *Trial by Battle*, pp. 493–5, 499. For the roll of the constable's retinue, see H. Prentout, *La prise de Caen par Edouard III, 1346* (Caen, 1904), Documents inédits, VIII, pp. 69–72.

[30] Godfrey de Harcourt, a younger son John, count of Harcourt, and lord of Saint-Sauveur-le-Viscomte, had been exiled from Normandy for several years. From Brabant, Harcourt came to England in May 1345. Sumption, *Trial by Battle*, pp. 412–14, 453.

[31] *Acts of War*, ed. Barber, p. 28.

[32] J. Viard, 'La campagne de juillet–août 1346 et la bataille de Crécy', *Le moyen âge*, 2nd ser., xxvii (1926), pp. 4–6; Sumption, *Trial by Battle*, pp. 494–5.

[33] For example: 'Edward himself changed his mind more than once.' Sumption, *Trial by Battle*, p. 493.

[34] For example: the campaign 'finally assumed the character of a chivalrous adventure': Oman, *A History of the Art of War in the Middle Ages*, 2nd edn, ii, p. 131. This was 'a mere

been encouraged not only by Burgherssh's letter, but also by the testimony of several chroniclers. Not, it should be noted, those of English provenance, for they have little to say on the subject of Edward's original intentions or the underlying circumstances of the landing in Normandy.[35] Adam Murimuth admits characteristically that 'no one could know for certain' what Edward's intentions were.[36] Some of his continental counterparts, including a couple writing from the French perspective, do hazard an opinion, but whether their testimony is reliable may be doubted, for they are unlikely to have been better informed than anyone else outside Edward III's inner circle. Consequently, their work can only have been fuelled by rumour and conjecture, and, in the case of the most influential among them – Jean Froissart – by a vivid creative imagination.

Upon closer examination, each of these accounts contains demonstrable factual or chronological errors. The *Chronique Normande* was apparently written by a militarily experienced Norman nobleman, and a participant in the events of 1346. He states that, having heard about Derby's plight, Edward III set out for Gascony but was held up by adverse winds. After a detour to Guernsey, where Castle Cornet was re-captured from the French, the decision was made to land on the Normandy coast. Cherbourg was initially approached but found to be too heavily defended, and so the fleet moved on to La Hougue.[37] The point about Cherbourg is intriguing and unverifiable; but we do know that Castle Cornet had actually been recovered from the French a year earlier. Moreover, as far as we can tell, the Channel Islands played no part in Edward's channel crossing in July 1346. It is curious, therefore, that Jean le Bel, a secular clerk from Liège, writing a little over a decade after the campaign, also relates that it was while on Guernsey that the decision was made to attack Normandy. But, significantly, he adds that this was 'by the counsel and strong encouragement of Godfrey de Harcourt', who knew the country well and spoke eloquently of its wealth.[38] As a consequence, argues le Bel, Edward appointed Harcourt as one of the marshals of the army (the other being the earl of Suffolk), and he played a leading role in the campaign, not least in the ravaging of the countryside.[39]

The most fully developed narrative of the Crécy campaign to attribute an

raid', which 'could accomplish nothing but devastation': J. Ramsay, *Genesis of Lancaster, 1307–99*, 2 vols (Oxford, 1913), i, p. 321. Edward 'was not so much sluggish as apparently without plan. He did not know quite what he was going to do next': H. Belloc, *Six British Battles* (Bristol, 1931), p. 17.

[35] The one exception, Robert Avesbury, appears to have based his account on Burgherssh's bulletin, to which he would have had access as registrar of the court of the archbishop of Canterbury, at Lambeth. He did not include a transcription of this document in his chronicle, preferring Michael Northburgh's account of the early days of the campaign. *Avesbury*, p. 357.

[36] *Murimuth*, p. 199.

[37] *Chronique Normande*, pp. 74–5 (cf. the closely related *Chronographia*, ii, pp. 222–3). The editors of the *Chronique Normande*, Auguste and Emile Molinier, suggested that the author may have served under the count of Eu at Aiguillon and Caen, and so was close to the action in July 1346 (pp. x-xiii).

[38] *Jean le Bel*, ii, pp. 69–70.

[39] In fact the earl of Warwick was the marshal of the army, and Sir Thomas Ughtred the sub-marshal.

influential role to Godfrey de Harcourt was written by Jean Froissart. Several French chroniclers note that Harcourt was the 'guideur, conduiseur et gouverneur de l'ost du dit roy Edouart' and was responsible in particular for the intensity of the pillaging that was undertaken in the duchy;[40] but it was only Froissart who took up Jean le Bel's story that it was the exiled Norman nobleman who was the instigator of the last-minute change of strategy. There are three quite distinct versions of these events in the three major editions of Book 1 of his *Chroniques*.[41] Comparison of these texts, particularly when viewed in the most likely order of composition, reveals Froissart's working methods: his use of sources as a starting point in the creation of a narrative that draws equally heavily on his well-stocked historical imagination; and his employment of dialogue as a literary device to accentuate the drama of the story while conveying ideas that he considers to have been important to the protagonists' thinking and behaviour.

In the Amiens MS, Froissart presents a version of events that has been taken, in most essentials and sometimes verbatim, from Jean le Bel's chronicle. However, the 'change of mind' on Guernsey is more effectively contextualised by introducing a scene, before the army's departure from England, in which Harcourt presents the advantages of a campaign in Normandy to the king, who at this stage is still inclined to lead the expedition to Gascony.[42] The narrative of these events in the A and B MSS of Froissart's Book 1 has been significantly reworked, its dramatic power considerably enhanced. Some aspects of Jean le Bel's story, including the Guernsey interlude, have been dropped and additional material appears to have been garnered from other sources. Now the decision to change direction takes place at sea. The fleet bound for Gascony is held up by contrary winds and driven towards the coast of Cornwall, where it remains at anchor for six days.[43] Harcourt seizes the opportunity to press the case for a campaign in Normandy. Convinced by the argument that it is a rich but poorly defended province, the king orders the fleet to turn towards the Cotentin peninsula.[44] In the last version of his *Chroniques*, the Rome MS, which was begun after 1399, Froissart added further embellishment to the story, including a more extended discussion between Harcourt and the king. Having made an

---

[40] *Chronique des quatre premiers Valois*, pp. 14–15; *Grandes chroniques*, ix, pp. 271, 274. *Jean de Venette*, ed. Newhall, p. 40. Cf. *Récits*, pp. 217, 221, 225, 227. By contrast, English chroniclers devote far less attention to Harcourt.

[41] For a fuller discussion of the texts of Froissart's *Chroniques*, see below, pp. 325–31.

[42] *Froissart: Amiens*, ii, p. 370. Froissart also notes that Philip VI sent Robert Bertran to guard the Cotentin peninsula because he thought it likely that Harcourt, who was lord of St-Sauveur-le-Viscomte, would lead the English there (*ibid.*, p. 371). Froissart follows Jean le Bel in making Harcourt and Suffolk the marshals of the army, but later in the campaign Suffolk has been replaced by Warwick (*ibid.*, pp. 374, 387). It would seem that at this stage Froissart had not yet fully reconciled his sources.

[43] 'li vens leur fu tous contraires et les rebouta sus les marces de Cornuaille; si jeurent là à l'ancre six jours' (*Froissart*, ed. Luce, iii, p. 131). This additional point in Froissart's narrative may have been taken from the 'Bourgeois of Valenciennes', who noted that 'le vent les mena en la marche de Cornuaille, et se reposèrent là'. *Récits*, p. 214.

[44] *Froissart*, ed. Luce, iii, pp. 131–2. In this version, Harcourt and Warwick are the two marshals throughout the campaign.

unsuccessful attempt to persuade Edward of the attractions of Normandy before embarkation, Harcourt returns to the subject when at sea. He suggests that God had shown, through the wind, that he wanted King Edward to go to Normandy; and he adds, tellingly, that the most effective way to relieve Aiguillon would be to mount a major campaign in the north. The earls of Warwick and Arundel agree with him, and Edward is won over.[45]

Thus, it can be seen how, in his interpretation of this episode, Froissart has taken Jean le Bel's uneven narrative and transformed it into the first act of a compelling drama. This tale of a last-minute change of direction at sea has not usually been taken at face value,[46] but it has been widely accepted that a major strategy shift did take place shortly before the king's departure from England and that Harcourt played some part in this decision. The influence on modern historiography of Froissart's version of events, not only at the opening of the expedition, but throughout from La Hougue to Crécy, should not be underestimated. The account of the campaign in the A and B MSS of Froissart's Book 1 is without doubt the most widely known by a fourteenth-century author.[47] It has been justly celebrated as an elegantly constructed and stylishly written narrative, a masterpiece of historical imagination, which deviates little from the known chronological framework of the campaign.[48] However, there can be no doubt that at the heart of Froissart's account is a misleading interpretation of the character of the English expedition and of Edward III's generalship in particular.

In Froissart's version of events, Harcourt becomes an almost Svengali-like figure, under whose spell the English king falls. By 1346, Edward III was a seasoned field commander of twenty years' experience; yet for Froissart, he was a man 'in the flower of his youth' who 'paid much attention to the words of Sir Godfrey de Harcourt, whom he called his cousin'.[49] As was appropriate for the 'marshal and director of the army, by whose counsel the king had undertaken the expedition',[50] it is Harcourt who is the source of sound military thinking. Thus, as we have seen, in the Rome MS, Froissart has the exiled Norman nobleman point out, during the course of his shipboard dialogue with the king, that mounting an expedition in northern France 'will cause the siege of Aiguillon to be raised; for all the [French] men-at-arms, wherever they may be, will be sent for to come to meet you and fight with you'.[51] Then, at Caen, when Edward is enraged by the losses that he had sustained in the assault and wishes to put the

---

45 *Froissart: Rome*, pp. 673–5. In this version, the discussion takes place while the fleet is anchored off the Channel Islands.

46 The story has more often been accepted by non-specialists: e.g., Wrottesley, *Crecy and Calais*, p. 11; J.F.C. Fuller, *The Decisive Battles of the Western World* (London, 1965), p. 460. Modern historians favouring a last-minute change of plan include Henri de Wailly, *Crécy 1346: Anatomy of a Battle* (Poole, 1987), pp. 17–18.

47 The B MSS was chosen as the core text in Simeon Luce's edition of the *Chroniques*, and several standard English translations, including Johnes's, are based upon this version of Book 1.

48 Although lacking specific references to dates, the sequence of events in Froissart's narrative fits the itinerary of the English army that can be established from other sources.

49 *Froissart*, ed. Luce, iii, pp. 131–2.

50 *Froissart*, ed. Luce, iii, p. 142.

51 *Froissart: Rome*, p. 675.

townspeople to the sword, Harcourt urges restraint, pointing out that the king should preserve the strength of his army for what may turn out to be a lengthy campaign, particularly since Philip VI would surely soon offer battle.[52] In passing, Harcourt conveys a piece of information that had not previously even been hinted at: that Calais was the ultimate goal of the campaign.[53]

Through Harcourt, Froissart seeks to explain the underlying strategic rationale of the English expedition and in the process bring greater verisimilitude to his narrative. It made such good sense to relieve Aiguillon by invading Normandy that Edward's willingness to overturn his plans at the last minute becomes somewhat more credible. That Calais was the intended goal from early in the campaign helps to explain the English itinerary after Caen. Although plausible enough, the strategic points articulated by Harcourt can only have been the product of Froissart's creative imagination: the former, it seems, being the result of mature reflection on Edward's strategy in 1346; the latter involving the modification of an idea that Froissart had found in Jean le Bel's chronicle.[54] Froissart's rationalisations do not sit comfortably with other parts of his narrative. Indeed, between the chronicler's recognition that the campaign must have had strategic aims and his instincts as a dramatic storyteller there is a tension that is not resolved. For the fact remains, that according to Froissart, the English conduct of the campaign from La Hougue to Crécy rested upon an impulse decision followed by improvisation rather than strategic single-mindedness. The lack of forward planning is exposed when the army reaches the Somme. No one in the army has any idea of the existence, let alone the location, of the Blanquetaque ford.[55] What of the systematic devastation of the French countryside, which has stimulated so much debate among modern historians? As presented by Froissart, there appears to have been no underlying purpose to this activity in July–August 1346, apart from the accumulation of booty and the satisfaction of Harcourt's desire for revenge. There is certainly no indication that Edward was actively seeking battle at any point during the campaign. He finally accepts an engagement at Crécy, which was 'le droit hiretage' of his mother, Queen Isabella; but, according to Froissart, of the two kings it is Philip who was determined to bring his adversary to battle.[56]

If we were to accept Froissart's interpretation of Edward III's most celebrated campaign, it would be difficult to avoid the conclusion that he was indeed a 'capable tactician but a poor strategist'. It is a conclusion that other fourteenth-

---

[52] *Froissart*, ed. Luce, iii, pp. 145–6; *Froissart: Rome*, p. 694. To underline the point, Froissart notes several times subsequently that Edward was concerned to preserve the strength of his army: e.g. *Froissart*, ed. Luce, iii, pp. 152.

[53] 'Vous avez encores à faire un moult grant voiage, ançois que vous soiiés devant Calais, où vous tirés à venir.' *Froissart*, ed. Luce, iii, p. 145. For a discussion of Harcourt's speech and the possibility that Edward 'intended to besiege [Calais] from so early in the campaign', see Rogers, *War Cruel and Sharp*, pp. 247–50.

[54] In Jean le Bel's narrative, it is only during the later stages of the campaign, after the crossing of the Seine, that Calais is said to be Edward's destination: *Jean le Bel*, ii, p. 89.

[55] *Froissart*, ed. Luce, iii, pp. 154–60. In the Rome MS, Froissart has Harcourt offer advice on the likelihood of a crossing point over the Somme below Abbeville: *Froissart: Rome*, p. 704.

[56] *Froissart*, ed. Luce, iii, pp. 137, 150, 156, 165.

century chroniclers do little to undermine, for they offer few reliable indications of what Edward's strategic aims may have been and their judgements are tinged with patriotic bias. Take, for example, the author of the *Grandes chroniques*, who was writing at St Denis soon after Crécy and quite well-informed about the English army's itinerary. He viewed the campaign as a contest between a French king, who was keen for battle but surrounded by traitors and noblemen who were less than ardent for a fight, and his slippery and dishonourable English adversary, who was in no hurry to engage.[57]

Turning to the English chronicles, we naturally find a more positive image of the English king's conduct of the expedition, but only occasional hints concerning his strategy, either at the outset of the campaign or throughout its course. Geoffrey Baker's narrative, the final version of which dates from the later 1350s, is a case in point. His is perhaps the best known of the English accounts, and its most notable feature is a detailed itinerary (though lacking dates) of the English march from La Hougue to Crécy. For this, the author had clearly drawn on a campaign diary, probably similar to that which has been preserved in a fifteenth-century copy in Cotton MS, Cleopatra D. VII.[58] Baker's heavy dependence on this source gives his narrative a 'flat', lifeless quality. It focuses heavily on the English (Philip VI and the main French army are mentioned for the first time at the Somme), yet we do not learn why Edward's army is marching across northern France. Events unfold without interpretation. Towns are attacked, burnt and looted, or by-passed; prior to Poissy, the reader is not told that crossing the Seine had posed a problem to the English;[59] and their passage of the Somme is dealt with in an equally matter-of-fact way. That Baker's account leaves so many questions unanswered serves only to throw Froissart's altogether more richly textured and confident testimony into sharper relief. The most that can be wrung from Baker's narrative are hints that Edward was seeking battle. At Lisieux he rejects the cardinals' peace terms, and after crossing the Somme at Blanquetaque he offers Philip VI an unopposed passage of the ford so that they might fight on a suitable site – an offer that the French king declines.

The idea that Edward was actively seeking battle with his Valois adversary in July–August 1346 receives some support in several other English chronicles, which in turn can be traced back to the eyewitness accounts from the campaign.[60] These consist of a collection of newsletters written by men accompanying the

[57] *Grandes chroniques*, ix, pp. 270–82. Similar in content and emphasis are the chronicle of *Jean de Venette*, ed. Newhall, pp. 40–3 and the *Chronique Normande*, pp. 75–80.

[58] *Baker*, pp. 79–82. Cotton MS, Cleopatra D. VII is printed among the notes of E.M. Thompson's edition of Baker's chronicle (pp. 253–5). Based on a comparison of this text with Baker's account and details provided in Retford's 'kitchen journal' (E101/390/11), Thompson has reconstructed the itinerary of the English march: pp. 255–7.

[59] Cf. Froissart, where the English march from Caen to Poissy is dealt with quite briefly, yet we are told that 'everywhere they found the bridges on the Seine broken down'. *Froissart*, ed. Luce, iii, p. 149.

[60] Many of the Crécy campaign narratives in fourteenth-century English chronicles draw heavily on these eyewitness accounts, and so we should expect to find, here and there, statements of Edward's battle-seeking intent: see, for example, *Anonimalle*, pp. 20–1; *Historia Roffensis*, BL, Cotton MSS, Faustina, B. V, fo. 91v.

English army, including the king himself; and the *Acta Bellicosa*, an unusually detailed (but now incomplete) campaign dairy by an unknown author. Of the three bulletins composed within a few days of the battle of Crécy, the most explicit is the king's newsletter of 3 September.[61] This states that once Philip VI was known to be at Rouen, within striking distance of the English army, Edward became single-minded in his pursuit of a battlefield confrontation with his rival: 'we made our way straight towards him, but when he knew this he broke the bridge at Rouen so that we could not cross'. Philip then shadowed the English march along the Seine from the far bank of the river, but broke or defended all the bridges and refused battle, 'which annoyed us very much'. At Poissy, the English waited for the French king, who was nearby in Paris, and when it was clear that he still did not want to give battle, they laid waste the locality. Perhaps most telling of all, Edward notes that having crossed the Seine, his army marched towards Picardy 'in order further to entice our enemy into battle'.[62]

The king's letter appears to present unequivocal testimony, but we should remember that this is history written by the victor at his moment of triumph. What of the bulletins despatched to England at earlier stages in the expedition, from La Hougue and after the capture of Caen? In the main, they are less explicit about Edward's campaign strategy. The king's letter from Caen, dated 29 July, is cautiously selective in its coverage, narrating events rather than explaining methods or revealing his intentions in detail.[63] Thus, the successful march from La Hougue reaches a climax with the capture of Caen (which was 'larger than any town in England except London' according to Michael Northburgh). This was a triumph that was definitely worthy of celebration in England, as was the destruction of over a hundred ships along the coast from Cherbourg to Ouistreham. But important aspects of the campaign are passed over without comment. While Northburgh's despatch makes much of devastation wreaked on the rural landscape and towns of Normandy, though without commenting on its purpose,[64] the king's mentions only the destruction of the coastal communities and shipping. It seems that Edward was maintaining a prudent silence about his plans while the campaign was in progress. After all,

---

[61] Bodleian Library, MS Ashmole 789, fos 148r–148v. The copy in *Le Prince Noir*, ed. Michel, pp. 308–11, omits a crucial passage. Michael Northburgh's newsletter casts no light on this problem, but Richard Wynkeley's implies that the countryside was devastated by the English in order to provoke Philip VI into crossing the Seine and accepting battle. *Avesbury*, pp. 367–9; *Murimuth*, pp. 215–17.

[62] 'et pour plus attraire notre ennemi à la bataille, nous nous traiames devers Picardie'. Edward says that the sudden arrival of Philip's army at Blanquetaque took him by surprise, but there is no mention of the proposal of battle recorded by Geoffrey Baker.

[63] C81/314/17803; Fowler, 'News from the front', pp. 83–4. The original letter is stored among the files of privy seals at the National Archives, London. For circulated copies, see: *Lanercost*, ed. Stevenson, pp. 342–3; *Registrum Johannis de Trillek, episcopi Herefordensis, 1346–1361*, ed. J.H. Parry, Canterbury and York Society (London, 1912), pp. 280–1; J. Delpit, *Collection générale de documents français qui se trouvent en Angleterre* (Paris, 1847), no. 145 (pp. 71–2). The king's letter of 29 July was reused as the opening section of his post-Crécy despatch, and this explains why the latter reveals nothing about Edward's intentions prior to the capture of Caen.

[64] *Avesbury*, pp. 358–60.

his newsletter was intended for wide circulation and he would wish to keep his opponent guessing. Moreover, he could not be certain that, for all his bellicose intentions, the campaign would not fizzle out into a stalemate. Only in the closing remarks of the letter are we given an indication of the king's strategic intentions: 'by the assent of all our magnates – who have shown themselves to be good, united and of one mind, we have already taken the decision to hasten towards our adversary, wherever he may be from day to day, as far as we are able'.[65]

The same statement of intent, as viewed by one of Edward's 'grantz', can be found in Bartholomew Burgherssh's letter to the archbishop of Canterbury, also dated 29 July.[66] Burgherssh initially characterises the expedition as a chevauchée, with Caen as its first major target. But he closes by paraphrasing the concluding message of the king's letter, noting that once the army had been reprovisioned from the supplies found in Caen, the king 'intends to march directly towards his adversary, to bring matters to whatever end God may have decreed'.[67] It is just possible that the statements with which Edward and Burgherssh conclude their bulletins reflect a change of strategy decided upon while the army rested at Caen. But a simpler explanation would be that word had just reached the English that a major French army was gathering at Rouen and that the French king was expected to join it.[68] Up to this point in the campaign, the English had been opposed by secondary forces; now there was a real prospect of a major confrontation with Philip VI in person. Indeed, according to the Bourgeois of Valenciennes, when Edward heard that Philip VI had arrived at Rouen, 'il luy manda à avoir bataille par pluseurs fois', but Philip declined the offer of battle because he was still assembling his army.[69]

If we turn to the *Acta Bellicosa*, which though incomplete is the most substantial of our eyewitness reports on the campaign, we find no evidence of a shift in strategy at Caen.[70] Indeed, the underlying message that is readily apparent to the reader of this narrative is that the English were seeking battle

---

[65] 'nous ja par l'assent de touz noz grantz qi se moustrent de bone entiere et une volente pris pourpos de nous hastier devers nostre adversaire, queu parte q'il soit de jour en autre, tant come nous purrons'. This statement comes immediately before the 'closed' section of the letter, which was directed to the royal council.

[66] *Murimuth*, pp. 202–3. This despatch was probably intended only for the eyes of the archbishop and other members of the royal council. For although it has an upbeat tone ('our affairs have gone as well as possible'), it conveys a more vivid impression of the tactical confusion that accompanied the attack on the bridge at Caen than would be appropriate for a 'public' news bulletin. It also adds, in a postscript, that the prisoners who were being sent to England were 'not to be released against ransoms or otherwise, until [the king] has made more progress with his war'.

[67] 'le roi . . . pense de sui trere tot dreit devers soun adversere'. Burgherssh's earlier letter, written from La Hougue, ends by stating that Edward intended to 'conqerer soun droit' (*Murimuth*, p. 200), which Rogers translates as 'to win his rights by force of arms': *War Cruel and Sharp*, p. 242 and n. 25.

[68] Philip VI 'reached Rouen on about 31 July': Sumption, *Trial by Battle*, p. 513.

[69] *Récits*, p. 220.

[70] The only changes suggested in this source actually occurred before the army reached Caen, and these concern the leadership's attitude to the devastation of the countryside (see below) and an unspecified amendment to the king's plans on 23 July.

throughout the campaign. For example, having crossed the Vire at Pont-Hébert, the Prince of Wales's division deployed in battle array in preparation for an attack 'which they hoped was imminent'.[71] Of course, this account, like those of the chroniclers – and, indeed, the king's letter of 3 September – may simply have been influenced by knowledge of the outcome of the campaign. It is fortunate, therefore, that we have access to copies of the letters that Philip VI and Edward III exchanged in mid-August, since they do cast some light on Edward's strategy without being influenced by hindsight. On 14 August, Philip wrote to Edward challenging him to fight an open battle on one of two sites on 17, 19, 20 or 22 August. He noted pointedly that 'You who want to conquer this land, if you seek battle as you assert, should not refuse this offer.'[72] Unlike some modern historians, Philip understood all too clearly what Edward's underlying strategic intention was. Edward's reply, versions of which are included in several sources, including the *Acta Bellicosa*, further underlines the message. He states that he had come to France to 'to put an end to the war by battle' and that he had been continually frustrated in this ambition by Philip's avoidance of a direct confrontation. However, Edward closes, he would not accept battle on Philip's terms: 'we shall never be dictated to by you, nor will we accept a day and a place for battle on [your] conditions'.[73] Edward certainly wanted to fight, but only at a time and place that suited him.

Some historians would regard the content of such letters as little more than rhetoric. Yet they bring us as close to Edward's strategic thinking in mid-August 1346 as we are likely to get with any explicit documentary source. It needs always to be borne in mind that Edward III's wars are illuminated by few sources that could be described as 'strategic planning papers'; and, as we have seen, the narrative sources, whether secondary accounts or from eyewitnesses, are able to offer no more than scraps of reliable information on Edward's strategic intentions before or during the campaign. Because the writers of contemporary history in the fourteenth century were no better informed about such matters than anyone else outside Edward's inner circle of advisers, they must by necessity have turned to speculation. For example, it is difficult to see how the suggestion, by Villani and Gilles Le Muisit, that the English march north, after crossing the Seine at Poissy, was prompted by the intention of joining up with their Flemish allies, was anything other than informed guesswork.[74] In the absence of documentary sources providing direct and reliable evidence concerning Edward's strategic thinking prior to and during the Crécy campaign, the historian must look elsewhere. We may not be privy to the king's thoughts

---

[71] *Acts of War*, ed. Barber, p. 30.

[72] Rogers, *War Cruel and Sharp*, pp. 256–7; *Chronicon domini Walter de Hemingburgh*, ed. H.C. Hamilton (London, 1849), pp. 423–5 (at p. 424).

[73] *CPR 1345–8*, pp. 516–17 (original French). The version in the *Acta Bellicosa* (French) omits 'par bataille' (Corpus Christi College, Cambridge, MS 370, fos 102v–103r), but this is included in the Latin version in the *Historia Aurea* (Bodleian MS 240, p. 578; *Chronicon domini Walter de Hemingburgh*, p. 425). The *Historia Roffensis* reports the verbal exchange between Edward III and the French king's messenger: BL, Cotton MSS, Faustina B. V, fo. 91v (discussed in Rogers, *War Cruel and Sharp*, p. 257).

[74] *Villani*, vii, p. 161; *Gilles le Muisit*, p. 159.

and plans during the weeks leading up to embarkation, but some indication of
his intentions for the coming campaign can be gained by examining his preparations, the composition and structure of his army and the deployment of his lieutenants. By drawing on such indirect evidence, a case can be made that Edward
was indeed pursuing a battle-seeking strategy during the summer of 1346, that
the descent upon the Normandy coast had been planned for months before the
actual landing in July, and that the 'Ponthieu option' was one of the strategic
contingencies that were being seriously considered from the start of the
campaign.

Perhaps the most obvious place to look for an indication of what Edward III had
in mind in July–August 1346 is his army. As we have seen, this was the largest
force to be shipped en bloc to France during the later middle ages, and the
product of a massive mobilisation of men, supplies and shipping. It is true that,
unlike the expeditions to Flanders of 1338–40, this campaign would be fought
without substantial military support from continental allies, but the composition
of the army in July 1346 suggests that Edward was preparing for a major
set-piece battle. This was not a compact force of horsemen, which would be
appropriate for a chevauchée. Indeed, with a heavy dependence on foot soldiers
raised by commissions of array in the shires of England and lordships of Wales,
the army had a somewhat old-fashioned (or perhaps hybrid) appearance. But
speed of movement was not a primary consideration, and this was a potent force,
with the all-important combination of archers and men-at-arms, both being in
unusually large numbers. This was an army with which Edward, on suitable
ground, could realistically plan to take on the massed heavy cavalry that he
knew Philip VI would have at his disposal. Edward had drawn the logical
conclusions from his earlier continental campaigns. In 1339 and 1340 he had
been constrained by dependence upon the manpower of his foreign allies, while
in Brittany in 1342–3 he had simply had too few men to risk a pitched battle.

    If Edward III's aim was to 'make an end to this war, either by battle, or by
suitable peace' as the lords in parliament had requested in June 1344[75] – and as
he stated in his reply to Philip VI's challenge – he certainly had the army with
which to do it. But Edward had no desire for a battle against impossible odds.
What he wanted was a battlefield confrontation with Philip VI in person, but
with only part of the mobilised military community of France in attendance. The
prospect of facing a French army as large as that which had assembled in 1340
('l'host Bouvines') with only Anglo-Welsh resources must have given Edward
pause. The answer was a strategy that involved the co-operative deployment of
several expeditionary forces in separate theatres of war, which would cause
French manpower to be divided in order to meet each of the threats.[76] The key to

---

[75] *Rot. Parl.*, ii, p. 148.
[76] Although his view of the 1346 campaign differs in many respects from that offered here,
Yuval Noah Harari's conclusions concerning the co-operative deployment of expeditionary
forces are similar to those expressed in this chapter. Y.N. Harari, 'Inter-frontal co-operation in
the fourteenth century and Edward III's 1346 campaign', *War in History*, vi (1999), pp.
379–95, especially pp. 392–5.

success was to commit just enough men in the provincial theatres and to take full advantage of local support (Gascons, Montfortist Bretons and Flemings) in order to hold the attention of large contingents of the enemy. Meanwhile, Edward at the head of the largest army that could be transported to France would go in search of a decisive showdown with Philip VI.

If Edward's campaign in northern France is viewed as the principal thrust of a multi-front strategy, much of the uncertainty surrounding the events of the summer of 1346 disappears.[77] Seen in this light, it is clear that the king never had any intention of campaigning in Aquitaine in person. Indeed, he expected the Anglo-Gascon forces under the earl of Derby's skilful direction to tie down the duke of Normandy's army. As it turned out, the duke's reluctance to raise the siege of Aiguillon until 20 August meant that the French troops in Aquitaine made no contribution to the Crécy campaign.[78] Sir Thomas Dagworth's role in Brittany was similar, and with his Anglo-Breton forces he kept Charles de Blois fully occupied, even defeating him at the first battle of La Roche Derrien on 9 June.[79] The last of the 'provincial' forces to be despatched was led by Sir Hugh Hastings, who on 20 June was appointed as Edward's lieutenant in Flanders. Like Dagworth, he had only a small force of Englishmen at his disposal – about 250 archers and a personal retinue of men-at-arms; but this was intended as the core of an army that would be contributed mainly by the Flemish towns.[80] Given his disappointments earlier in the war, Edward may well have concluded that this was the most effective way to exploit his Flemish allies. While it has sometimes been argued that Edward was seeking to effect a junction with Hastings and his Flemish forces, it is unlikely that this was ever seriously contemplated. The value of Hastings's contribution was as one element of a co-operative strategy that did not depend upon the physical convergence of forces. Such convergence would have been difficult to bring off;[81] but in any case the essential feature of

[77] Indeed, so central to the English king's strategy was the neutralisation of his Valois rival's huge potential superiority in manpower, that the distraction of French resources may have been the motive behind Edward's diplomatic approaches to King Louis of Hungary in the mid-1340s. Initial contact was made following the murder of Louis's brother, Andrew, in Naples in September 1345. Then, in the spring of 1346, Edward sent a Dominican friar, Walter atte More, as an envoy to Hungary, where he had meetings with both Louis and his mother, Queen Elizabeth. (F. Trautz, 'Die Reise eines englischen Gesandten nach Ungarn im Jahre 1346', *Mitteilungen des Instituts für Österreichische Geschichtforschung*, lx (1952), pp. 359–68, which prints Walter atte More's expenses account, E101/312/22.) Nothing is recorded concerning the negotiations, but we do know that the friar, having hastened back to England, briefed Edward on his mission shortly before the king's departure for Normandy. On 7 July, the king ordered a team of high-ranking churchmen 'de treter et acorder' with the envoys from Spain, Portugal and Hungary, should they arrive during his absence (*Jean le Bel*, ii, p. 338; *CPR, 1345–8*, p. 138). It would seem that the Crécy campaign should be viewed not simply within the context of a multi-front strategy designed to prevent Philip VI from concentrating his military resources, but also as the central element of a wider network of diplomatic relationships that were intended to contribute to the same end.

[78] Raising siege: *Murimuth*, p. 373 (Derby's newsletter).

[79] M. Jones, 'Sir Thomas Dagworth et la guerre civile en Bretagne au XIVe siècle: quelques documents inédits', *Annales de Bretagne*, lxxxvii (1980), pp. 628–9.

[80] For Hastings's expeditionary force, see Chapter 1, n. 53.

[81] Harari, 'Inter-frontal co-operation', pp. 380–3 (practical difficulties preventing close co-

the diversionary actions mounted in secondary theatres of war was that they were *separate* from the king. The independent actions of Derby, Dagworth and Hastings gave the king a better prospect of achieving his aims in Normandy.

Edward was seeking a battle in which the odds were not overwhelmingly stacked against him. The despatch of task forces to the regions of France, where they would combine with local manpower, was an important preparatory step towards this goal. Viewed in this way, a strategic deployment in which his lieutenants were already operating independently in Aquitaine, Brittany and (just before the king's departure) Flanders, seems to indicate that a landing on the Normandy coast had been planned for some time. The problem for the historian lies in establishing how long Edward had been contemplating such a plan and how consistently he pursued it. Jonathan Sumption has argued that the king's expeditionary force that embarked at Sandwich in late June 1345 may actually have been intended for Normandy, only to be diverted to Sluys by the political crisis in Flanders and then, later in July, prevented from reaching its original destination by stormy weather in the channel.[82] No supporting evidence is offered; indeed, as Sumption notes, Edward's 'plans were so completely shrouded in secrecy that not a trace of them can be discovered in the sources or had reached the ears of the French'. Nevertheless, there is some evidence to suggest that plans for a descent upon the coast of Normandy were indeed being formulated during 1345, and that this had become the king's preferred option by early 1346.

In early June 1345, Sir Thomas Ferrers, warden of the Channel Islands, left England for Guernsey. His expenses account reveals how the force of men-at-arms, archers and seamen under his command succeeded in recapturing Castle Cornet from the French. Yet this document also suggests that there may have been more to Ferrers's mission than first meets the eye. Among those on Guernsey during that summer were several of the Normans who were later to play a part in the Crécy campaign.[83] The most notable was Godfrey de Harcourt himself (accompanied by a retinue of five knights and 24 men-at-arms), but also in the king's pay were two members of the Groucy family, William and Nicholas, and Roland de Verdon.[84] We know that these men were in communication with associates in Normandy, since the expenses account shows that their valets

ordination between widely separated theatres of war). Harari concludes (p. 391) that (from Caen) 'it is fairly likely that Edward intended to link up with Hastings, but failed to effect such a juncture due merely to communication problems'.

[82] Sumption, *Trial by Battle*, pp. 459–63. It should be noted that had Edward campaigned in Normandy in July 1345 it would have been with an army much smaller than that with which he eventually arrived the following year.

[83] E101/25/6; printed in M.H. Marett Godfray, 'Documents relatifs aux attaques sur les Iles de la Manche, 1338–1345', *La société Jersiaise pour l'étude de l'histoire,* Bulletin, iii (1877), pp. 11–53 (at pp. 47–53). For the Normans, see below, Chapter 6, nn. 15 and 18.

[84] Harcourt's expenses, totalling £188 2s, were paid for the period from 13 August to 19 November 1345. William de Groucy and Roland de Verdon, with 6 esquires and 8 valets, received financial support during the second half of June. Early in the Crécy campaign, Nicholas de Groucy and Roland de Verdon were given custody of Carentan by Edward III, but they were soon captured and taken to Paris, where they were executed in December. *Grandes chroniques*, ix, p. 271.

were sent to the mainland on no fewer than five occasions to gather news and test the water. We know too, from the same source, that the king was kept informed of these developments as his army prepared for departure from Sandwich. What is not clear is whether Edward's interest in the exiled Normans' cultivation of their mainland contacts had any bearing on his own immediate campaign plans.

It is tempting to see a connection between the king's plans and the monk who, in August 1345, was taken into custody in Ouistreham 'pour senspecon d'estre espié'.[85] Doubtless well aware that Ouistreham, at the mouth of the Orne, could serve as a suitable disembarkation point for the English, Robert Bertran, the captain of the maritime frontier in this area, ordered that the monk be brought to him under secure guard for interrogation. By this time – a year to the day before the battle of Crécy – Edward had begun to issue mobilisation orders for a new expedition. The army was scheduled to set out from Portsmouth on 20 October.[86] To be sure, the departure date was repeatedly postponed, owing to shortages of shipping or bad weather, but the port of embarkation remained unchanged throughout. If this can be taken to indicate consistency of purpose, it must be conceded that we still cannot be certain what that purpose was, for the destination of the expedition is never stated in the administrative records. Our best guess would be that Normandy was already the favoured option, and not simply because this is suggested by the inherent logic of Edward's multi-front strategy and by the opportunities offered by a campaign in this region of France (to which we shall return below). The Norman noblemen who had been so busy with their intrigues during the previous summer were still on the royal pay-roll. Thus, shortly before Christmas 1345, we find issues being made to Godfrey de Harcourt and William de Groucy for the maintenance of their retinues and to several further knights and esquires.[87] Then, in early–mid April 1346, several of these men – most notably Harcourt and Hugh Calkyn – received pay advances for what was to be the Crécy campaign.[88] We cannot be sure how much the Norman exiles knew of Edward's intentions at this time, but their willingness to participate in his new continental campaign was presumably founded upon a belief that Normandy would have some part to play in English strategy.

In fact, there can be little doubt that Edward's sights were indeed firmly set on Normandy by the spring of 1346. Any thoughts about another campaign in Brittany, if such thoughts had ever been seriously entertained, had been abandoned by this time.[89] Apart from keeping his plans secret, the king's principal concern at this stage must have been the gathering of as large and potent an army

---

[85] Prentout, *La prise de Caen par Edouard III, 1346*, Documents inédits, VII, p. 69.

[86] Wrottesley, *Crecy and Calais*, p. 58.

[87] E403/336, m. 21. The 'new names' are: Odard Darrentyn (with two valets), Peter de Hassely, valet of Normandy, and Hugh Calkyn, knight of Normandy.

[88] E403/336, mm. 41, 42, 43; E101/390/12, fos 5v, 6r, 6v, 7r. These payments are included among a huge block of entries recorded under the date '10 April'. It is worth noting that Peter de Hassely is described here as 'valet of Flanders' (E403/336, m. 42).

[89] For Brittany, see Sumption, *Trial by Battle*, pp. 471–3, 493. The author suggests that the plan was abandoned in early 1346, in part because the earl of Northampton had been unable to secure a suitable and accessible port on the north coast of the duchy.

as was logistically practicable for his own expedition. Consequently, the earl of Northampton was recalled from Brittany in March, leaving English interests in the duchy in the capable hands of his brother-in-law, Sir Thomas Dagworth, at the head of a modest force of 80 men-at-arms and 120 archers (plus Breton troops).[90] The earl, together with the other captains who had returned from Brittany, were among the recipients of advance payments of war wages in April. The best available evidence suggests that they contributed over 400 men-at-arms and a similar number of archers – or perhaps 15 per cent of all retinue-based personnel – to the army that landed at La Hougue.[91]

It can only have been after the first instalments of pay for the coming expedition had been distributed to captains that the king learned of the siege of Aiguillon. The siege had begun during the first half of April 1346,[92] and it must have taken at least a fortnight for the information, borne by the earl of Derby's messenger, Simon Simeon, to reach the king.[93] It has often been argued that when Edward heard about the siege he decided to lead his army to Aquitaine.[94] There is, however, no convincing evidence that Edward made any such decision. He was prepared to despatch three hundred Welsh archers as reinforcements,[95] but the suggestion that we find in some of the continental chronicles that Edward intended to go in person to Gascony cannot be relied upon. This is what he wanted his adversary to think, not what he actually proposed to do. It is true that the penultimate clause of Henry, earl of Derby's military contract for service in Aquitaine had stipulated that if he were heavily pressed, the king would rescue him by one means or another, provided that it was expedient to do so.[96] Pressure was certainly building on Derby during the spring of 1346, though he was not personally among the garrison of Anglo-Gascon troops besieged in Aiguillon by the duke of Normandy. However, the terms of Derby's indenture

---

[90] Sumption (*Trial by Battle*, p. 493) states that Northampton was recalled in January, apparently on the strength of Dagworth's appointment as deputy lieutenant in Brittany (indenture dated 28 January: E101/68/3, m. 62). However, on 8 March, the earl's valet, Matthew Redman, having arrived in England with letters from Brittany, was about to return with the king's letters to the earl. E403/336, m. 36. For Dagworth's troops, see E101/25/17, 18 and 19.

[91] The earl of Northampton's principal lieutenants in Brittany had been the earls of Oxford and Devon, John Darcy senior, William Kildesby, Edward Montagu and Michael Poynings. Of these, all except the earl of Devon served from La Hougue to Crécy. E403/336, mm. 22, 41–2. For retinue sizes in 1346, see below, Chapter 5, Appendix 2, Table 2.

[92] The siege began 'between 10 and 15 April': Fowler, *The King's Lieutenant*, p. 66 and n. 48. Cf. Sumption, *Trial by Battle*, p. 485, which places the arrival of the 'van of the French army . . . on about 1 April'.

[93] The date of Simeon's arrival is uncertain, because the issue of expenses to him was included among the host of payments implausibly lumped together under the date '10 April': E403/336, m. 48. For speed of travel from Gascony to London, see Harari, 'Inter-frontal co-operation in the fourteenth century and Edward III's 1346 campaign', p. 382.

[94] For example: Edward decided 'in about April or May 1346 that he would proceed to Gascony'. Sumption, *Trial by Battle*, pp. 493, 497.

[95] E403/336, m. 49; E101/25/9, m. 1.

[96] 'Item, le roi ad grante que s'il aviegne que le dit conte soit assiege ou prisse par si grant force des gentz q'il ne se pourra eider saunz estre rescous par le poair du roi, que le roi soit tenuz de lui rescoure par une voie ou par autre, issint q'il soit rescous convenablement.' Fowler, *The King's Lieutenant*, pp. 230–2.

did not oblige Edward III to campaign in Gascony *in person*; and such a direct military intervention, necessarily involving an attempt to raise the siege of Aiguillon, could only have been conducted at a strategic and tactical disadvantage.[97]

An altogether more effective method of relieving pressure on Derby's troops in Aquitaine would be, as Froissart recognised, to mount a major expedition in the north. As we have seen, in the last version of his *Chroniques*, Froissart has Godfrey de Harcourt draw to the king's attention the advantages offered by such a strategy. Of course, in reality Edward would hardly have needed a tutorial in how to conduct a war. Indeed, it is likely that he would have welcomed the news of the siege of Aiguillon, regarding the preoccupation of the duke of Normandy's forces in Aquitaine as essential to the success of his own expedition in the north, while being sure that the pressure on Derby's troops would be relieved when the English landing in Normandy became known. In the meantime, if the French believed that Edward intended to proceed to Gascony in person, so much the better. The broad principles of the multi-front strategy had no doubt been discussed before Derby's departure for Aquitaine in July 1345, and details of the king's immediate plans would have been conveyed to the earl by Richard Cardoil, who was despatched to Gascony following the arrival in England of the earl's messenger, Simon Simeon.[98]

Normandy was the ideal campaigning ground for the principal thrust of Edward's multi-front strategy. It was a conveniently located and vulnerable entry point to the kingdom of France. With any luck, launching an attack there would take the French by surprise: they would need time to assemble an army, thereby allowing Edward a valuable breathing space.[99] In the meantime, a region whose countryside was 'merveilleusement gras et planteureux' and unscarred by war, as well as militarily ill-prepared, was at his mercy.[100] For his men this meant rich pickings. But if, as the king noted after Caen, 'many of our people have been comforted by the gains they have made', for him campaigning in Normandy served different purposes. One objective was to inflict severe damage on the shipping and coastal communities of the duchy and thereby neutralise, at least temporarily, the maritime threat to southern England. Newsletters report in some detail the tide of destruction that swept along the Norman coast from Cherbourg to Ouistreham at the mouth of the Orne.[101] The threat posed by the duchy was confirmed by the discovery, among the records in Caen, of a detailed plan to

---

[97] On the pros and cons of a campaign in Aquitaine, Flanders or Normandy, see Rogers, *War Cruel and Sharp*, pp. 222–7. See also, N.A.M. Rodger, *The Safeguard of the Sea: a Naval History of Britain, vol. 1, 660–1649* (London, 1997), p. 102.

[98] E403/336, m. 48. That Derby had been informed in advance about Edward's landing in the north is suggested by his brusque response to the duke of Normandy's offer of a truce in mid-August (Fowler, *The King's Lieutenant*, p. 67; Sumption, *Trial by Battle*, p. 519).

[99] The element of surprise is stressed by Clifford Rogers, though as we have seen it seems that, belatedly, the French did become aware of the threat to this previously untouched region.

[100] *Jean le Bel*, ii, p. 70. *Froissart*, ed. Luce, iii, p. 131. The coastal communities of Normandy had felt the impact of war: raids in 1339 and 1340, and the battle of Sluys.

[101] Northburgh: *Avesbury*, pp. 358–60; Burgherssh: *Murimuth*, p. 203; Edward III: *Le Prince Noir*, ed. Michel, pp. 308–9. At La Hougue, 'fourteen ships, well fitted out for an attack on England by the enemy' were destroyed: *Acts of War*, ed. Barber, p. 28.

invade England, which had been drawn up in March 1339 but never acted upon. Publishing the document in London, Archbishop Stratford emphasised that the wasting of Normandy contributed to the security of the realm.[102]

However, by choosing Normandy as the starting point for his own expedition Edward was pursuing a larger goal. A landing on the Norman coast, followed by a destructive march through the duchy, cutting a swathe of devastation, was intended to force Philip VI to accept the pitched battle that he had long been unwilling to fight. Philip had stood by while the Cambrésis and Thiérache were consumed by fire in October 1339, and he could probably be relied upon to do the same if the English entered France via Ponthieu. But it might be different if similar treatment were meted out to Normandy, a province whose wealth made it an important potential source of funds and manpower for the king's war, yet with which the French crown enjoyed a particularly delicate political relationship.[103] We need only examine the invasion scheme of March 1339, or indeed the subsidy granted to the duke of Normandy in 1347, to recognise the significance of the duchy's resources to Philip's war effort. But the Normans' distinctive position, of which the 'charte aux Normands' of 1315 was emblematic, meant that gaining access to those resources could not be counted upon. The Normans' 'generous aid for the purposes of financing an invasion of England' in 1339 had been dependent upon the issue of a new charter 'which made more explicit the limitations on the king's right to proclaim the *arrière-ban* and demand their aid for military ventures'.[104]

The advantages offered by a campaign in Normandy would have been apparent to Edward and his advisers from the beginning of the war, and there is some evidence that the king had wanted to land there in 1337–8.[105] The argument in favour of a Normandy landing became all the greater following the inconclusive end to the campaign in Brittany in January 1343. As Edward and his circle of advisers searched for a more effective strategy with which to pursue the war, the arrival of the Norman exiles in England in 1345 provided an opportunity to explore the 'Normandy option' further. The particular value of Harcourt and his associates lay in their local knowledge. We may assume that they drew attention to St Vaast-la-Hougue as a suitable disembarkation point, offering a stretch of open beach to the south of the port, and a natural harbour to

---

[102] *Froissart*, ed. Lettenhove, xviii, no. 24 (pp. 67–73); *Murimuth*, pp. 205–11; *Avesbury*, pp. 363–7; P. Contamine, 'The Norman "nation" and the French "nation" in the fourteenth and fifteenth centuries', *England and Normandy in the Middle Ages,* ed. D. Bates and Anne Curry (London and Rio Grande, 1994), pp. 216–34 (at pp. 227–8). Edward had presumably learned of the plan from Godfrey de Harcourt, who is named in the agreement, along with many other Norman noblemen.

[103] On this relationship, see Chapter 6.

[104] 'The promise of a vigorous and potentially glorious campaign, not to mention the second Norman charter, had opened the purses of this region's leading inhabitants.' J.B. Henneman, *Royal Taxation in Fourteenth-Century France. The Development of War Financing, 1322–1356* (Princeton, 1971), pp. 139–41 (see also pp. 111, 182–3, 188, 228–9).

[105] W.M. Ormrod, 'England, Normandy and the beginnings of the Hundred Years War, 1259–1360', *England and Normandy in the Middle Ages,* ed. Bates and Curry, pp. 197–213, esp. pp. 198–200; *Froissart*, ed. Lettenhove, xviii, no. 15 (pp. 38–9); Sumption, *Trial by Battle*, pp. 199–200.

the north;[106] and they surely acted as guides to the English army during the march across Normandy. Whether Edward believed that they could carry with them the wider support of the Norman nobility must be doubted. That this region of France offered considerable military potential was indicated in Philip VI's invasion scheme of March 1339, to which the Normans were to contribute 4,000 men-at-arms and 20,000 foot sergeants; and it would be demonstrated during the period 1360–1407, when over a third of prominent military leaders in French royal armies came from Normandy and neighbouring counties.[107] But gaining access to this pool of manpower would require a more extensive network of influence than the exiled younger brother of the count of Harcourt had at his disposal, and despite a tradition of separatism, there was little likelihood of the Norman nobility supporting Edward III's cause in any numbers. As Philippe Contamine has noted, 'Godfrey de Harcourt was far from being typical of the whole of Normandy'.[108] Edward cannot have been unaware of this. The situation in Normandy was quite unlike that which Edward had exploited in Brittany. He would not be backing one side in a succession dispute, a civil war; he was taking advantage of the opportunities offered by a dissident nobleman and his associates.

Edward III's view of the Norman exiles who accompanied him to La Hougue in July 1346 was simple. They were to be encouraged and exploited, and then discarded when they were no longer useful. Froissart's interpretation of the campaign, with its central story of Edward being manipulated by Godfrey de Harcourt, is therefore more than a little misleading. Of course, each tried to take advantage of the other, but in reality it was Edward who was pulling the strings. His experience of Robert d'Artois and the Montfortist Bretons had taught him to be cautious in his dealings with the Normans, suspicious of their motives and doubtful of their reliability. Having received Harcourt's homage at La Hougue,[109] Edward had no compunction in pursuing a course that did not serve the Norman dissidents' interests. For some, their efforts did not go wholly unrewarded. At Caen, on 30 July, William de Groucy, an old servant of Edward's, was granted an annuity of £100 in consideration of the 'les damages et pertes' that he had endured in Edward's service.[110] He remained at the English king's

---

[106] In the enclosed harbour is an extensive wave-cut platform (today used for oyster beds) upon which it would have been possible, at low tide, to beach and unload many ships simultaneously in July 1346. However, it is uncertain whether this was accessible since (according to the Canterbury chronicle) Bertran had closed the entrance of the harbours at La Hougue and Barfleur with stakes: *Canterbury*, p. 187. Removal of these obstacles may explain the five-day disembarkation period. After 1346, La Hougue became a favoured landing point for English expeditions to Normandy (e.g. in 1356 and 1412).

[107] J.B. Henneman, 'The military class and the French monarchy in the late middle ages', *American Historical Review*, lxxxiii (1978), pp. 946–65 (at pp. 953–5, 964).

[108] Contamine, 'The Norman "nation" and the French "nation" in the fourteenth and fifteenth centuries', p. 229.

[109] *Acts of War*, ed. Barber, p. 29. This was a repeat, on Norman soil, of the homage that had been rendered in June 1345, at which time Edward had given Harcourt a variety of assurances, including the promise to restore him to his Norman estates if the English king recovered his 'héritage en Normandie': *Froissart*, ed. Lettenhove, xviii, no. lx (p. 273).

[110] C81/314, no. 17804; *CPR, 1345–8*, pp. 168–9.

side, but for Harcourt it was different. Having found the body of his brother on the battlefield of Crécy, he seems to have recognised that he had been no more than a pawn in a greater power struggle. Soon after, he returned to the Valois camp.[111]

This assessment of Edward's view of the Normans, and what they could offer, has some bearing on an interpretation of the English king's intentions in July 1346 that has found favour recently. According to this view, Edward was seeking to establish a permanent foothold in Normandy, just as he had in Brittany.[112] Jonathan Sumption has argued that there is 'little doubt' that Edward had 'origi-nally intended' to do this. Having messengers proclaim that he came 'not to ravish the land but to take possession of it', Edward had hoped to secure the loyalty of the Normans, but it soon became clear that he was unable to protect them from either the undisciplined looting and violence of his own soldiers or from Valois reprisals once his army had moved on. Consequently, Edward reverted to a conventional strategy of devastation, and so 'what began as a campaign of conquest became a chevauchée'.[113] Although Clifford Rogers differs from Sumption in arguing that the 'primary purpose' of Edward's expedi-tion was to 'seek out his adversary and do battle with him', he concedes that the campaign began with the secondary aim of establishing a 'permanent foothold' in the Cotentin, 'or if possible all of Normandy'. This, he argues, would have made 'an excellent portal into France'. Like Sumption, Rogers believes that 'it was indeed the indiscipline of the troops which foiled Edward's plans to secure a new base area in Normandy'.[114]

There are problems with this interpretation that collectively undermine its credibility. First, there is no compelling evidence that Edward actually took any steps to establish a permanent foothold in the Cotentin in 1346. No attempt was made to put down roots in a defensible coastal town, to establish a 'sally port'. Barfleur and Cherbourg were left in flames. No garrisons of *English* troops were installed in the Cotentin or indeed anywhere else in Normandy in July 1346. Two related French chronicles assert that 1,500 Englishmen were left in Caen, and subsequently overwhelmed,[115] but such a significant event would surely have left a mark on the English sources.[116] It is clear that Edward was only prepared to leave a garrison in the wake of his progress across the duchy if it did

---

[111] For Harcourt's letters of remission, dated 21 December 1346, see Delisle, *Histoire du château et des sires de Saint-Sauveur-le-Vicomte* (Valognes, 1867), Pièces justificatives, no. 79 (pp. 109–11).

[112] This is not a new idea. Charles Oman speculated that Edward 'might have aimed at a conquest of Normandy or some part of it – the projecting part of the Cotentin peninsula perhaps – in order to secure a firm basis of operations for future attacks on France'. Oman, *A History of the Art of War in the Middle Ages*, 2nd edn, ii, p. 131.

[113] Though it is not quite clear when this change is supposed to have occurred, since Sumption accepts that an English garrison was left in Caen, and that it was 'rounded up and killed by the French troops in the citadel'. Sumption, *Trial by Battle*, pp. 532–3.

[114] Rogers, *War Cruel and Sharp*, pp. 226, 238–43, 252.

[115] *Chronique Normande*, p. 77 n. 1; *Chronographia*, ii, pp. 225–6.

[116] The monk of Malmesbury suggests, in a passing remark, that Edward left a few men in Caen (*Eulogium*, iii, p. 207).

not affect the combat strength of his army. Thus, Carentan was left in the hands of Normans allied to Godfrey de Harcourt's cause.[117] Edward needed every available fighting man in his predominantly Anglo-Welsh army for the large-scale battle that he hoped would take place later in the campaign.

There is, therefore, no direct evidence that garrisons of English troops were left in Normandy, and it is doubtful whether Edward would have seriously contemplated doing so. The duchy may well have been judged as the ideal jumping-off point for the pursuit of a battle-seeking strategy, but it was less suitable as the location for a new 'sally port'. Cotentin was an isolated corner of France, a peninsula that could easily be blockaded. If Edward and his advisers did indeed begin the campaign with the intention of establishing a strategically important foothold on the French coast, Calais would have been regarded as altogether more promising, being closer to both Edward's Flemish allies and Paris.[118]

Another consideration concerns the reception that Edward could reasonably have anticipated from the population of Normandy. He cannot have been confident that his arrival would generally be welcomed in the duchy. The Norman exiles on his pay-roll were neither numerous nor decisively influential, even in the Cotentin. Burgherssh's upbeat newsletter from the early days of the campaign does not suggest that the nobility flocked to Edward's standard. 'The men-at-arms of the region have withdrawn into the castles and fortified towns,' he notes.[119] This is hardly surprising given that Philip VI's local commander, one of the marshals, Robert Bertran, was an important landowner in the Cotentin, his caput at Bricquebec being located about ten kilometres to the north-west of Harcourt's at St Sauveur-le-vicomte. Given the mutual antipathy that existed between the maritime communities of southern England and Normandy, fuelled by raids and the losses sustained at Sluys, Edward's arrival would not be welcomed by the coastal towns of the Cotentin. The reaction of the peasantry could also have been predicted: that they would be cowed into submission in the immediate vicinity of the army (as Burgherssh suggests)[120] but defiant elsewhere, giving a hostile reception to messengers bearing the king's conciliatory letters.[121] The fact that Edward was prepared to employ 'local Plantagenet supporters from the Harcourt and Clisson affinities' in this hazardous public relations role does not necessarily indicate that he planned to establish a 'sally port' in the Cotentin.[122] It merely shows him, as an experienced

---

117 *Grandes chroniques,* ix, p. 271.
118 There is no direct evidence that the capture of Calais was an objective from the start of the campaign. As we have seen, Froissart uses Harcourt as a mouthpiece to suggest that this had been decided upon before Caen had been reached, though here Froissart appears to be merely reworking material that he had found in Jean le Bel's chronicle. *Froissart,* ed. Luce, iii, p. 145; *Jean le Bel,* ii, p. 89. See also Rogers, *War Cruel and Sharp,* pp. 247–50.
119 *Murimuth,* p. 200.
120 'les comunes de la terre viengnent tout pleyn al obeissaunce nostre seignur le roy'. *Murimuth,* p. 200.
121 Contamine, 'The Norman "nation" and the French "nation" in the fourteenth and fifteenth centuries', p. 229.
122 Cf. Rogers, *War Cruel and Sharp,* pp. 240–1.

and calculating commander, to be taking advantage of every opportunity to smooth the passage of his army, while disparaging the rule of his Valois adversary.

The argument that Edward initially intended to establish a foothold in the Cotentin relies heavily on the interpretation of an army disciplinary order that was proclaimed on 13 July, the day after the landing at La Hougue. The *Acta Bellicosa* explains that:

> the English king, feeling for the sufferings of the poor people of the country, issued an edict throughout the army, that no town or manor was to be burnt, no church or holy place sacked, and no old people, children or women in his kingdom of France were to be harmed or molested; nor were they to threaten people, or do any kind of wrong, on pain of life and limb. He also ordered that if anyone caught someone in the act of doing these or other criminal acts and brought him to the king, he should have a reward of forty shillings.[123]

No 'official' copy of this proclamation has survived, but a summary of its contents is also to be found in the *Historia Roffensis*, a contemporary chronicle that has been attributed to William of Dene, a clerk in the service of Hamo of Hythe, bishop of Rochester.[124] Consequently, although the proclamation is not mentioned by any other eyewitness or secondary narratives, there is no reason to doubt that standing orders concerned with army discipline were indeed issued at La Hougue. But how should they be interpreted? Sumption and Rogers have argued that by keeping his army under a tight rein and prohibiting looting, burning and violence, Edward hoped to demonstrate to the population at large that he had indeed come 'not to ravish the land but to take possession of it'. Unfortunately for the king's plans, the proclamation was 'a dead letter from the beginning'. The failure of the constable and marshal to 'check the rashness of the troops' and prevent them from running riot throughout the Cotentin forced Edward to abandon the idea of permanent occupation.[125]

Since this interpretation appears in the most scholarly of recent accounts of the campaign, it must be accorded serious consideration. Any interpretation of the 'La Hougue proclamation' must confront the problem that the testimony of our sources is inconsistent, particularly with regard to the intended scope of the restrictions on ravaging. The Rochester chronicler's summary of the procla-

---

[123] *Acts of War*, ed. Barber, pp. 28–9. 'Rex insuper Anglorum mitissimus, augustiis miserabilis ipsius patrie populi multipliciter compaciens, ubique per suum exercitum edictum faciebat, ut nullus villas aut maniera incendere, ecclesias vel loca sacra depredari, senibus, parvulis aut mulieribus quibuscumque regni sui Francie malum seu molestiam inferre presumeret, seu quibuscumque personis aliis, nisi viribus instarent, malefacerent quovismodo, sub pena vite et membrorum. De cetero jubebat quod, si aliquis in premissis seu premissorum aliquo criminosum et actu deprehensum regi adduceret, quadraginta solidos pro merito reportaret.' *Acta Bellicosa*, ed. Moisant, p. 160.

[124] BL, Cotton MSS, Faustina B. V, fo. 91r. See Rogers, *War Cruel and Sharp*, p. 240 n. 6, which first drew attention to this summary. It is not known how the Rochester chronicle, alone among second-hand accounts, had access to this material. A relationship of some kind with a variant copy of the *Acta Bellicosa* or the use by both writers of a common source are two possibilities.

[125] Sumption, *Trial by Battle*, pp. 501, 532–3; Rogers, *War Cruel and Sharp*, pp. 238–43.

mation differs slightly from that given in the *Acta Bellicosa*. The *Historia Roffensis* omits the comprehensive prohibition on the burning of towns and manors and adds those 'who freely enter the king's peace' to the list of persons who, with their property, were to be protected from harm or molestation.[126] That the version of the proclamation reported in the *Acta Bellicosa* may not be wholly reliable is further suggested by close examination of the remainder of that text. It does report a number of instances of 'rashness', of pillaging and burning by the common soldiery in breach of the king's orders. But there are inconsistencies in the testimony. For example, the ravaging of the coast, including such towns as Barfleur, does not receive the censure of our author, and after St Lô, the burning of town and countryside is actively encouraged by the army high command.[127] These and other mismatches with the letter of the proclamation suggest, firstly, that the king's disciplinary orders had been prompted by more complex motives than are allowed for by the *Acta*; and, secondly, that the proclamation in its original form was more subtly worded.

Some indication of what may have been set aside when the proclamation was summarised for inclusion in the narrative sources can be gained by examining the earliest surviving schedules of disciplinary regulations for English royal armies – the ordinances for Richard II's campaign in Scotland in 1385, and for Henry V's in France.[128] That the 1346 proclamation and the later ordinances were concerned with essentially the same problems is shown by the fact that the substance of the proclamation as issued at Le Hougue and repeated later in the campaign[129] is to be found in the second and third clauses (of twenty-six) of the 1385 regulations, which prohibit interference with the holy sacrament and provide immunity from pillage and violence to the clergy, women and unarmed labourers.[130] The Ordinances of 1419 dwell at greater length on the protection afforded to civilians, with two new clauses displaying an understanding that leading an expedition in France demanded subtleties of judgement from a

---

126 'ne quis sacrosancte ecclesie religiosis presbiteris mulieribus parvulis neque alicui alteri se ad Regis pacem reddere volenti de Regno Francie dampnum seu molestiam in personis vel rebus facerent vel inferrent, sub pena et forisfactura membrorum et vite'. BL, Cotton MSS, Faustina B. V, fo. 91r.

127 The latter *may* indicate a change of policy that could be considered consistent with the interpretation offered by Sumption and Rogers. But that interpretation finds little support in the other eyewitness sources.

128 M. Keen, 'Richard II's Ordinances of war of 1385', *Rulers and Ruled in Late Medieval England,* ed. R.E. Archer and S. Walker (London and Rio Grande, 1995), pp. 33–48; M. Prestwich, *Armies and Warfare in the Middle Ages* (New Haven and London, 1996), pp. 179–81. The 1385 Ordinances are printed in *The Black Book of the Admiralty*, ed. T. Twiss, Rolls Ser., 4 vols (London, 1871), i, pp. 453–8. For the ordinance issued at Mantes in 1419, see *ibid.*, pp. 459–72; see also, Sir H. Nicolas, *History of the Battle of Agincourt*, 3rd edn (London, 1833), Appendix VIII, pp. 31–44.

129 At Caen it was proclaimed, as before, that 'no one was to imprison women, children or clergy or [to ransack] churches or religious houses, on the same terms as before'. *Acts of War*, ed. Barber, p. 33; *Acta Bellicosa*, ed. Moisant, p. 166.

130 Moreover, the essence of the first clause of the 1385 Ordinances – that everyone in the army 'shall be obedient to our lord, to his constable and marshal, under penalty of everything they can forfeit in body and goods' – is implicit in the La Hougue proclamation as contextualised in the *Acta Bellicosa*.

commander.[131] In terms reminiscent of the Rochester chronicle's summary of the 1346 proclamation, clause 26 of the 1419 Ordinances extends protection to those who freely enter the king's peace, while clause 37 prohibits burning without the 'comandement speciall of the Kinge'. The latter surely reflects the realities of war: the king would want some locations to be burnt, while sparing others. We can only speculate whether Edward included the same stipulation in his 1346 proclamation, but given what we know about the ravaging that actually occurred and his attitude to it, it seems likely that he did.

Many of the clauses in the ordinances of 1385 are concerned with the implementation of a disciplinary regime designed to ensure the combat effectiveness of the army as well as the smooth performance of such routine but essential tasks as foraging, patrolling and billeting. Indications that these issues were very much preoccupations of Edward III and his lieutenants in 1346 can be found in the *Acta Bellicosa*'s detailed narrative of the campaign. As we shall see, foraging and the management of the army's supplies were matters of central concern to the army's commanders. As for the enforcement of discipline, when the *Acta Bellicosa* notes the appointment of the constable and marshal 'to check the rashness of the troops', we hear an echo of the juridical authority that is so central a feature of the later ordinances.[132] The *Acta* reports that these officials were also responsible for dividing the army into three 'battles', which – as we see in the ordinances – were key features of army organisation on and off the battlefield. Despite structural differences, the armies of 1346 and 1385 were inhabiting similar worlds in terms of their disciplinary regimes. Examination of the *Acta Bellicosa* in the light of the later ordinances suggests that there may have been more to the La Hougue proclamation than first meets the eye.

This conclusion is reinforced if we turn our attention to the other English eyewitness sources. Here we find scarcely a hint that the king had ever prohibited an activity as customary as ravaging, still less that he had done so in order to win the hearts and minds of the Normans. Admittedly, the king's bulletin of 29 July is reticent with regard to the ravaging of the countryside, but this is not in itself significant. He had maintained a similar silence in his newsletter from Brittany in early December 1342. The contrast with his bulletin on the autumn 1339 campaign, which reported with some relish the systematic burning of the Cambrésis, can probably be explained by reference to his formal assumption of the title 'king of France' in January 1340.[133] What the king does mention in his bulletin of 29 July 1346 is the destruction of the coastal communities from Barfleur to the mouth of the Orne (plus Cherbourg), together with more than a hundred ships 'of the enemy'.[134] This was clearly a planned operation against an identifiable threat and Edward was delighted with the results. If we turn to the other newsletters from early in the campaign, we find that they not only celebrate the crippling of the maritime resources of Normandy, they also take for

[131] Clauses 8, 26, 28, 29, 33, 37.
[132] *Acts of War*, ed. Barber, p. 29. However, the suggestion that Northampton and Warwick were appointed to these posts *after* the landing at La Hougue is unconvincing.
[133] *Avesbury*, pp. 304–6, 340–2.
[134] Fowler, 'News from the front', p. 84.

granted the burning of the countryside and the gathering of booty. The only suggestion that such activities were not officially sanctioned is to be found in Michael Northburgh's letter of 27 July, and this is no more than a passing remark. Having noted, without obvious disapproval, that 'several good towns and manors in the surrounding countryside [of the Cotentin] were burnt', he reports that much of Carentan was similarly consumed, 'for all that the king could do'.[135]

The testimony of the newsletter writers, especially when viewed alongside that of the second-hand accounts,[136] leaves us in no doubt that systematic ravaging was central to Edward's strategy in 1346, just as it had been in his earlier campaigns. But it is important to recognise that what he always sought to achieve, in July–August 1346 as on previous occasions, was a programme of devastation that remained firmly under his control. Ravaging was not to be haphazardly pursued or left to the whim of common soldiers: it was to be planned, targeted and purposefully executed. This was surely the underlying rationale of the proclamation of 13 July, and the testimony of our eyewitness sources is wholly consistent with it. From the outset, the coastline of Normandy, its ports and shipping, had been earmarked as a prime target, but inland in the Cotentin, some distinction had to be made between the land of Edward's Norman supporters and those of his enemies. Although we may doubt Harcourt's reputed strategic role as 'guideur, conduiseur et gouverneur de l'ost du dit roy Edouart', we may be sure that he took a close interest in the direction and intensity of the pillaging that was undertaken in the duchy.[137]

Once Edward's army had left the Cotentin peninsula, it was directed single-mindedly in pursuit of his overriding strategic aim: to bring his Valois adversary to battle on ground favourable to the English. Systematic ravaging of the prosperous Norman countryside would, it was hoped, force Philip to accept the confrontation that he had been avoiding for so long. According to the *Acta Bellicosa*, the change of gear occurred after St Lô. Thus, on 24 July, before Caen was reached, Cormolain and the surrounding country were burnt by the English 'so that the enemy should know of their coming'.[138] Ravaging was a strategic device, intended to intimidate the local population and provoke those in political and military authority. It was also good for the army's morale and its collective sense of purpose. So, on 28 July, after Caen had fallen, 'the countryside was set on fire all around, so that at least the men were not idle for lack of work'.[139] Well might Edward note in his letter of 29 July that 'many of our people have been comforted by the profits that they have made'.[140] There is little sign in any of this of the king's supposed concern for the 'sufferings of the poor people of the country', which according to the *Acta Bellicosa* had prompted him to issue the proclamation of 13 July. Those standing orders were intended, above all, to

135 *Avesbury*, pp. 358–60.
136 For example, *Récits*, pp. 217–18.
137 *Chronique des quatre premiers Valois*, pp. 14–15; *Grandes chroniques*, ix, p. 271. *Récits*, p. 217.
138 *Acts of War*, ed. Barber, p. 31.
139 *Acts of War*, ed. Barber, p. 34.
140 Fowler, 'News from the front', p. 84.

ensure that the army remained an effective fighting force while cutting a swathe of destruction through Normandy. For however tactically proficient on the battlefield, an army on the march could be vulnerable, especially when raiding parties were widely dispersed and pillaging was pursued carelessly. Wide dispersal was necessitated by the foraging needs of an army that was unusually large by English standards and by the strategic desirability of ravaging on a broad front: about fifteen to twenty miles around the line of march, according to eyewitnesses.[141] With regard to the need for vigilance while ravaging, the *Acta* relates a telling anecdote. On the road to Caen, 'some of the archers, trusting in their own strength and despite the king's edict, were suffocated when the building which they were sacking was set on fire by enemies lying in wait'.[142] It was not pillaging *per se* that was being criticised, but that it had been pursued without attention to military security.

Edward and his lieutenants were quite as aware as the compilers of the later ordinances that poor discipline on the march could lead at best to a reduction in combat effectiveness and at worst to the army's piecemeal destruction. During the march from Poissy to the Somme, unnecessary assaults on fortified places were prohibited in order to conserve the strength of the army.[143] (Indeed, Edward's offer of excellent terms to Caen – surrender without loss of property – should probably be interpreted in the same light.) In addition to minimising casualties and reducing vulnerability to enemy action on the march, maintaining a firm grip on the army's ravaging of town and countryside was also necessary for logistical reasons. The supply needs of a large army, including (and perhaps especially) the fodder requirements of its horses, demanded that the burning and destruction of villages and barns, fields and orchards, was preceded by thorough and efficient foraging.[144] Discipline was required if valuable pasture was not to be thoughtlessly ruined, and moveable supplies of food and wine were not to be wasted in orgies of destruction and drunkenness. Such logistical preoccupations – an awareness that an army marches on its stomach – are everywhere to be found in our sources. In Brittany in 1342, Edward had been relieved to find that 'the land is sufficiently abundant in cereals and in meat'.[145] With a much larger army under his command in 1346, Edward could not simply rely on the country-side. According to the *Acta Bellicosa*, the English brought across the channel a

---

[141] *Murimuth*, p. 215; *Avesbury*, p. 358. Cf. Jean le Bel's account, which describes the dispersal of the army: *Jean le Bel*, ii, pp. 76–7. See also C.J. Rogers, 'By fire and sword: *bellum hostile* and "civilians" in the Hundred Years War', *Civilians in the Path of War*, ed. M. Grimsley and C.J. Rogers (Lincoln, Nebraska, 2002), pp. 33–78 (at pp. 36–7).

[142] *Acts of War*, ed. Barber, p. 31.

[143] *Acts of War*, ed. Barber, p. 39. Cf. Henry V's 1419 Ordinances, clause 19.

[144] Yuval Noah Harari has shown that an army pursuing an offensive strategy would not depend entirely on living off the land: 'even during raids conducted in summer and in prosperous country, it was often supplemented by other supply methods', specifically a supply train of wagons, pack horses and cattle on the hoof. However, the horses would be dependent on local fodder supplies. Harari, 'Strategy and supply in fourteenth-century western European invasion campaigns' (esp. pp. 313–22). It is noteworthy that a clause in a fifteenth-century set of ordinances explicitly prohibited the destruction of fruit trees and vines: Nicolas, *History of the Battle of Agincourt*, Appendix VIII, p. 42.

[145] *Avesbury*, p. 341.

'mass of supplies for both men and horses'.[146] It is also clear that they employed a supply train, 'whose purpose was not so much to replace local supply, but rather to supplement it and serve as a safety net on which the army could rely if local supply proved insufficient'.[147] It could be replenished from captured food stores, those based in towns being especially important.

Thus, when reporting on the 1346 campaign, the king recalled how several days had been spent at La Hougue unloading the ships and 'provisioning our men'. Similarly, the four days of rest at Caen were necessary 'pour vitailler et frecsher notre host'.[148] Between La Hougue and Caen, the army had progressed from one town to the next. The logistical significance of these centres of commerce and population is made clear in both the *Acta Bellicosa* and Michael Northburgh's newsletter. Northburgh notes that 'an abundance of wine and food' was found at Carentan ('as large as Leicester'), while at St Lô, which 'is larger than Lincoln', there were 'at least a thousand barrels of wine and a great quantity of other goods'. He adds that 'wine, food and other goods and chattels beyond measure were found in [Caen], which is larger than any [town] in England except for London'. In a later letter, Northburgh reports that 'since we left Caen we have lived off the countryside with great difficulty and harm to our men', though he had noted that when Le Crotoy was stormed it was found to be full of provisions.[149] As a member of the king's council beyond the seas, Northburgh's logistical preoccupations were those of Edward's inner circle,[150] and they were shared by the directing mind behind the *Acta Bellicosa*.[151] Characteristically, the latter is highly critical of the foot soldiers who had wasted food stocks at Carentan regardless of 'the harm that it might do to the army'.

It can be seen that the most satisfactory interpretation of the La Hougue proclamation of 13 July is that it was intended to provide the necessary disciplinary underpinning for Edward's policy of controlled devastation, which was important not only for the fulfilment of the army's supply needs but especially for the achievement of the English king's strategic aims in July–August 1346. The problem was not new and neither was the solution. The implementation of standing orders to regulate army discipline can be detected in the military tribunal cases recorded on a plea roll for Edward I's Scottish campaign of 1296.[152] Proclamations laying down specific organisational requirements for armies that were about to muster can also be found in the records relating to

146 *Acta Bellicosa*, ed. Moisant, pp. 159–60.
147 Harari, 'Strategy and supply in fourteenth-century western European invasion campaigns', p. 319.
148 *Le Prince Noir*, ed. Michel, pp. 308–11.
149 *Avesbury*, pp. 358–60; 367–9.
150 Described by Robert Avesbury as a 'mighty clerk', Northburgh had been 'engaged to be of the king's council' on 10 May 1346. Tout, *Chapters*, iv, p. 114 and n. 3.
151 The *Acta Bellicosa* reports that the disciplinary ordinance was repeated at Valognes and Carentan (the latter occasion, specifically in order to preserve food supplies in the town). At St Lô 'there was plenty of food of all kinds', while at Caen, before the attack was launched, the army was 'fed from the abundant stores of meat and drink'. *Acts of War*, ed. Barber, pp. 30–2.
152 C.J. Neville, 'A plea roll of Edward I's army in Scotland, 1296', *Miscellany XI*, Scottish History Society, 5th ser., iii (Edinburgh, 1990), pp. 7–133.

campaigns earlier in the fourteenth century.[153] The disciplinary orders of July 1346 do not, therefore, in themselves represent a new departure for an Edwardian army. Consequently, although the *Acta Bellicosa* reports that the proclamation was issued in direct response to the dispersion of parts of the army in a spree of burning and pillaging, it was almost certainly in the pipeline prior to the landing. Edward and his lieutenants cannot have been unaware that they faced a major problem of 'command and control' as they disembarked at La Hougue.

The distinctive character of Edward's army can only have contributed to the disciplinary challenge facing the constable, the marshal, and their deputies. This was an unusually large army by contemporary English standards, but the difficulties involved in controlling the host were not simply a consequence of its size. Nor, indeed, were they fundamentally the result of its regionally heterogeneous make-up. Of course, bringing men together from all corners of the realm could give rise to tensions. Among the genteel combatants, we know that armorial disputes flared up 'sur les champs' when knights bearing the same heraldic arms came into contact with one another for the first time. Clearly concerned about the effect that these 'chalenges darmes' were having on the army's sense of purpose, Edward ordered the constable and marshal to put a stop to them for the duration of the campaign.[154] Among the common soldiers, there may well have been clashes between the English and the Welsh, as there had been on earlier expeditions,[155] but we do not hear of them. (To be sure, the Welsh attract the attention of eyewitnesses and chroniclers alike, but for different reasons.) The army's operational and disciplinary problems are to be attributed to organisational features more prosaic than its regional heterogeneity.

It has been suggested that armies raised entirely by means of voluntary contracts presented 'special problems of organisation and discipline', to which the ordinances of war of 1385 were a response.[156] However, it could be argued that the constable, the marshal and their deputies faced a more complex situation in 1346. For while a 'contract army' was uniform in structure, the host that landed at La Hougue was a hybrid. Its two main components were 'mixed' retinues of men-at-arms and archers, recruited and managed by captains who had a direct contractual relationship with the king;[157] and arrayed companies of foot soldiers raised in the shires of England and lordships of Wales. It is likely that

---

[153] The orders issued in April 1327, prior to the first campaign of Edward III's reign (*Rotuli Scotiae*, i, p. 208), provide a particularly interesting example, not least because they have the appearance of supplementary regulations, suggesting the existence of a more comprehensive schedule of ordinances 'in the background'.

[154] PRO30/26/69, nos 176, 183, 186. Nicholas Burnell challenged Robert, Lord Morley 'sur les champs' in Normandy, and the case was resolved by the Court of Chivalry during the siege of Calais: see A. Ayton, 'Knights, esquires and military service: the evidence of the armorial cases before the Court of Chivalry', *The Medieval Military Revolution*, ed. A. Ayton and J.L. Price (London and New York, 1995), pp. 81–104.

[155] As in 1296 (Neville, 'A plea roll of Edward I's army in Scotland, 1296', pp. 21–2; nos 111, 121) and 1322 (N. Fryde, 'Welsh troops in the Scottish campaign of 1322', *Bulletin of the Board of Celtic Studies*, xxvi (1974), pp. 82–9, at p. 85).

[156] Keen, 'Richard II's Ordinances of War of 1385', pp. 34–5, 48.

[157] The structure and composition of the English army is examined in detail in Chapter 5. Note that, with one exception, the contractual agreements were not formalised in indentures.

the 'mixed retinues' (which contributed rather less than half of the total manpower of the army) caused fewest headaches to the constable and marshal. Over half of these retinue-based personnel were serving in nine large contingents, and most of the rest were located in retinues attached to the 'household division'. In the main, this section of the army was tightly managed.[158] The retinues were commanded by a team of experienced captains (assisted by their own constables and marshals), who had developed a close relationship with the king. As the *Acta Bellicosa* makes clear, these retinues were organised into three 'battles' or divisions, which were the disciplinary basis of the army's marching order, logistical arrangements and tactical deployment. A clear chain of command down to the individual combatant was created by the internal company structure of each retinue, many of which were composed of men who had served together before. Continuity of service made the bonds that held this section of the army together at company level especially strong.

Our sources suggest that the army's disciplinary problems in 1346 can be traced to its heavy dependence on arrayed foot soldiers raised in the English shires and Welsh lordships. It is tempting to explain this simply by reference to the archers and spearmen themselves. Although not a great deal is known about these men, it is likely that there were more unwilling conscripts and fewer regularly serving combatants among them than we find in the retinues.[159] That their ranks included violent criminals, for whom service at Crécy and Calais would bring a charter of pardon, was also clearly a mixed blessing for the army's commanders. The latter may well have felt the same way about the Welsh contingents, which are accused by our sources of unbridled pillaging, behaving (notes the *Historia Roffensis*) 'as if they were beyond the king's jurisdiction'.[160]

The disorderly conduct of the Welsh and English levies could probably have been contained by a more effective command hierarchy. Maintaining discipline in each of the companies of arrayed troops was the responsibility of its *ductor*, or leader, and his subordinates – the centenars (at the head of groups of one hundred men) and vintenars (leading twenty men). Given that the shire levies contributed at least half of the army's manpower and that individual companies frequently numbered a hundred or more men, their leaders should have been important links in the army's chain of command. However, the links were weak, since these men lacked the social and military status required to carry out their responsibilities effectively. Their authority as leaders was not reinforced by contractual or tenurial ties with their men, as was the case with the retinue captains, nor by social weight, since most were men-at-arms of obscure origins and limited personal means.[161] That a large section of the army had been placed

---

[158] With the possible exception of the chivalric escapades that are reported by our sources (for example, at the bridge at Rouen and at La Roche Guyon) and the attack on Poix on 20 August, which was in breach of the king's repeated orders. *Récits*, p. 220; *Acts of War*, ed. Barber, pp. 35, 39.

[159] See below, Chapter 5, pp. 215–24.

[160] *Historia Roffensis*, fo. 91r. Later, at Lisieux, they stole the horses of the peacemaker cardinals: *Eulogium*, iii, pp. 207–8.

[161] In the Crécy army, we catch only occasional glimpses of these leaders: e.g. Edmund Blount, leading the Norfolk levy, and Thomas Scarle (Kesteven): E403/336, mm. 42–3. The

in the hands of a tier of under-powered leaders represented a significant structural weakness that can only have affected the implementation of orders from the constable and marshal, or from the commanders of the 'battles' to which the shire levies were attached.[162] Unlike his counterparts at the head of the larger 'mixed' retinues, the *ductor* was unable to draw on personal resources, or command any influence, for the benefit of his men. In these circumstances, the arrayed troops could hardly be blamed for believing that they were second-class combatants, which they almost certainly were when supplies were being distributed. Unauthorised foraging, such as the ransacking of the Carentan food stores, should therefore be interpreted as the response of men who had no choice but to fend for themselves.

It is small wonder that, on occasion, Edward's lieutenants failed to maintain a tight grip on sections of his host. Yet, these disciplinary problems should be kept in perspective. First, there is a danger of being misled by the preoccupations of an unusual source. The *Acta Bellicosa* offers by far the most detailed narrative of the campaign from the English perspective, with many compellingly vivid passages. But that it was apparently written from one of the command centres of the army probably explains the prominent attention that it gives to disciplinary matters, a preoccupation that is shared by no other narrative source to the same degree.

Second, it should be recognised that the most significant breaches of the king's standing orders occurred in combat situations that would have severely tested the disciplinary regimes of post-medieval armies. Given the challenge that an amphibious operation against a hostile coastline represented, the immediate aftermath of the landing at La Hougue was always going to be an unstable period for the English army. Nervous energy, bottled up during the long wait at the port of embarkation, followed by days of uncomfortable ship-bound confinement, found release once men set foot in the Cotentin. Only by keeping the army on board ship could complete control be achieved.[163] It was equally difficult to prevent the common soldiers of the army from rampaging through a captured town, wasting valuable food stores in the process. Tempting as it may be to attribute such events to the uncontrollable passions of the 'formless mass of men' that was a medieval army, in reality the sacking of towns by troops whose blood was up (or who, quite simply, were hungry) was not a phenomenon confined to the middle ages.[164] One need only recall the aftermath of the British

king was pleased to learn that Thomas Huscarl, leading the Berkshire contingent, was 'ioesnes homme & le plus suffisant qui soit en dit countee pur menir mesme les archers en notre service' (C81/1332, no. 2). Somewhat more plentiful evidence exists for the August 1346 reinforcements (see, for example, E101/556/30; E101/575/15, m. 11; E101/584/5, m. 1). It is interesting to note that cases of insubordination on the army plea roll of 1296 involve transgressions by centenars and vintenars as well as by ordinary soldiers. Neville, 'A plea roll of Edward I's army in Scotland, 1296', p. 22; nos 13, 17, 116.

162 For practical purposes (for example, supply and control on the march, and tactical deployment), the arrayed companies must have been integrated into the army's structure of three 'battles', though quite how this integration was achieved is not known.

163 *Acts of War*, ed. Barber, p. 28.

164 'Formless mass of men' is how Sumption characterises the English army soon after the landing at La Hougue. According to his judgement, 'without any clear chain of command it

capture of Badajoz in April 1812, or indeed the looting of the Smolensk food stores by the retreating French army later in the same year.[165]

There is a third reason for keeping the disciplinary issue in perspective. As we have seen, from the very outset of the campaign, much of the army's ravaging had been undertaken on Edward's orders. Indeed, what is particularly notable is that so much of the devastation appears systematic and controlled. Take, for example, the operations in the Ile de France in mid-August, which demonstrate the army's capacity for selective and co-ordinated pillaging, and rapid recall. On 14 August, the 'finest palaces of the kingdom of France [in the neighbourhood of Paris] . . . and all the countryside around to within two miles of Paris, were burnt almost at the same time'. Then, that evening, continues the *Acta Bellicosa*: 'The king had it proclaimed throughout the army that no raiding or burning was to be done the next day, because it was the Feast of the Assumption of the Blessed Virgin, on pain of life and limb.'[166] As Clifford Rogers has convincingly argued, Edward had recalled his flying columns in anticipation of a battle on 15 August, for which 'Edward would want his men rested and concentrated, not spread out for twenty miles laying waste the countryside'.[167]

'Rested and concentrated' Edward's men might be, but could they be relied upon to fight in a disciplined fashion? Throughout the campaign there are instances of impetuous attacks on defended positions, but it should not be imagined that these always arose from an inability to control the 'formless mass of men' in the shire levies. For example, although the English were 'unable to restrain themselves' from attacking the fortified bridge at Meulan, and received a bloody nose as a result, this was clearly a small-scale, combined-arms assault that had been decided upon by the Constable and Marshal, Northampton and Warwick.[168] At Caen, a major action, it is clear that the English and Welsh levies did take a particularly prominent part in the mêlée, and according to the newsletters, written soon after the battle, their contribution unfolded in a not altogether planned way.[169] It may be that the leaders of the shire levies simply lost control

was quite impossible for [the Constable and Marshal] to control' them. Sumption, *Trial by Battle*, p. 501.

[165] 'For two days [after the capture of the Badajoz] officers were powerless to prevent every outrage of pillage, drunkenness, violence, brutality and rapine which could be imagined . . . It was the most disgraceful episode in the annals of the Peninsular army.' P.J. Haythornthwaite, *Die Hard: Famous Napoleonic Battles,* repr. (London, 1999), pp. 185–6. At Smolensk: 'Although measures were taken to conserve what was left, the troops – even the Guard – threw over the bonds of discipline and indulged in an orgy of looting and destruction.' D.G. Chandler, *The Campaigns of Napoleon* (London, 1966), p. 827.

[166] *Acts of War*, ed. Barber, p. 37; *Acta Bellicosa*, ed. Moisant, p. 171.

[167] Rogers, *War Cruel and Sharp*, p. 257.

[168] *Acts of War*, ed. Barber, pp. 35–6. The attack on Poix on 20 August was also undertaken by men-at-arms and archers: *ibid.*, pp. 39–40.

[169] Michael Northburgh reports that 'common soldiers from our army ('noz gentz del host'), without leave or array, attacked the bridge, which had been strengthened with a stockade and barriers, and they had a hard fight ('avoient mult affaire'). *Avesbury*, p. 359. Bartholomew Burgherssh relates that the archers began the attack on the bridge with a volley of arrows, but were put under pressure and Edward, fearing losses among his men because they were unsupported by men-at-arms, recalled them. However, when Warwick arrived on the scene, the tide was turning in favour of the archers, who were hotly engaged at the barriers.

of their men as they approached the enemy. But, in truth, 'control' of such an attack would be difficult for the most disciplined of armies, and it appears to have been the elan and resourcefulness of the archers that won the day. Similar boldness and courage were displayed at Poissy, where the archers, sent across the Seine to ward off a French attack, were obliged to negotiate the narrow timbers that had been thrown across the broken section of the bridge.[170] The Welsh may have behaved in the Cotentin 'as if they were beyond the king's jurisdiction'; they may have been more inclined to slit the throat of a French nobleman than ransom him. But, if effectively channelled, their audacity was an invaluable asset. Which other contingent in the army could have swum across the Seine to attack the enemy, 'returning safely and bringing with them some little boats' in order to allow men-at-arms to cross?[171]

The common soldiers, Welsh and English, made a distinctive contribution to Edward's expedition, and we may suspect that he could almost forgive them their excesses in the urban food stores. But when it came to the climax of the campaign, at Crécy, he insisted upon absolute adherence to his disciplinary orders. Jean le Bel tells us that, on the eve of the battle, Edward commanded, on pain of death, that there was to be no breaking ranks for pillaging without his leave.[172] Once again, now in the context of battlefield discipline, we find a pre-echo of the later ordinances of war, which laid down that an unauthorised cry of 'havoc' – a sign to break ranks for the pursuit of personal gain – was punishable by beheading.[173] If Edward's battle-seeking strategy rested squarely upon confidence in his army's tactical superiority, he had to be sure that this battlefield dominance would not be compromised by indiscipline.

Edward III and Ponthieu

It has been argued that the essential aim of Edward III's strategy in 1346 was to bring Philip VI to battle in circumstances that were as favourable as possible to the English. As we have seen, Edward's strategy succeeded not only in that he managed to induce Philip to accept battle, but also in that, at the crucial point of contact, the French king did not have an army of overwhelmingly superior

---

Murimuth, pp. 202–3. According to the *Acta Bellicosa*, the attack was directed by Warwick, Northampton and Talbot, and the reader is left with the impression that the archers and Welshmen played a distinctive *but planned* part in the proceedings. The only suggestion that 'control' of the English foot soldiers slackened concerns their indiscriminate slaughter of noblemen. *Acts of War*, ed. Barber, pp. 32–3; *Acta Bellicosa*, ed. Moisant, pp. 165–6. Planning is also suggested by the *Chronique Normande* (p. 76), which states that the English, having entered the town at several points, attacked the French defenders of the bridge in the rear.

[170] *Acta Bellicosa*, ed. Moisant, p. 170.

[171] Monk of Malmesbury in *Acts of War*, ed. Barber, p. 34; *Eulogium*, iii, p. 208.

[172] *Jean le Bel*, ii, p. 106. Jean le Bel's description of English preparations prior to the battle should be read as part of a wider agenda in which the qualities of the two protagonist kings as war leaders are contrasted, but his comments on Edward's disciplinary regime have the ring of truth.

[173] Keen, 'Richard II's ordinances of war of 1385', p. 43.

numbers at his disposal. Edward's multi-front strategy had ensured that French military resources were divided, while the focus on Normandy for his own assault had probably been the decisive factor in provoking Philip to accept battle. But did the successful execution of the English plan extend to the site upon which the battle was fought? Two questions stem from this. Firstly, and most obviously, did Edward meet his adversary on chosen ground? Secondly, was the location of the site, at Crécy-en-Ponthieu, significant?

In offering answers to these questions, we shall begin with a suggestion made by Kenneth Fowler in a paper published in 1991. Discussing the original copy of the letter that Edward III sent to the royal council from Caen on 29 July 1346, Fowler pointed out that it ordered manpower reinforcements, munitions and money to be sent to Le Crotoy on the north bank of the estuary of the Somme.[174] Not only does this appear to explain the route taken by the English army after bridging the Seine at Poissy, it also suggests, in Fowler's words, that 'from the moment Edward III had arrived in Caen, and in all probability from the time he left England, he had intended to proceed in the direction of Le Crotoy, and in view of the speed with which he took up position after crossing the Somme, the battlefield [of Crécy] must have been reconnoitred in advance'.[175] Since Fowler offered no supporting evidence, some readers of his paper may have felt 'must' to be a little too categorical. However, the apparent purposefulness of Edward's march towards Ponthieu; the efficiency with which his army crossed the Somme at Blanquetaque; and the ease with which a suitable battleground was settled upon does invite further investigation. As we shall see, there are good reasons for believing that a march towards Ponthieu was a strategic option that Edward III and his counsellors had in mind before the army left England, and that it had become the favoured option by the time that Caen had been reached.

The capture of Caen marked the end of the first stage of an expedition that was founded upon one clear objective – to bring Philip VI to battle. From the eyewitness accounts, we can see how, after eight days of marching and its first major engagement, the English army paused at Caen for several days, gathering supplies and making arrangements for the transport of booty and prisoners to England.[176] As we have seen, the *Acta Bellicosa* notes that the countryside was set ablaze 'so that at least the men were not idle for lack of work'. For Edward and his lieutenants, this was a time for discussion, for weighing-up the pre-planned strategic options, as intelligence was gathered on the whereabouts of Philip VI and his army. As we have noted, Edward's statement of intent, echoed by Burgherssh, that he would 'hasten towards our adversary' probably reflects the fact that a major French army, with Philip in attendance, was now known to be gathering at Rouen. This, then, did not mark a major change in Edward's campaign strategy, but rather the refinement of it. Similarly, the evidence suggests that the plan to march towards Ponthieu, which is implicit in

---

174 Fowler, 'News from the front', pp. 78–9, 83–4. This document (C81/314, no. 17803) had been used by Sumption, *Trial by Battle* (London, 1990), pp. 510–11.
175 Fowler, 'News from the front', p. 79.
176 *Murimuth*, p. 203; *Avesbury*, p. 359; *Acts of War*, ed. Barber, p. 34.

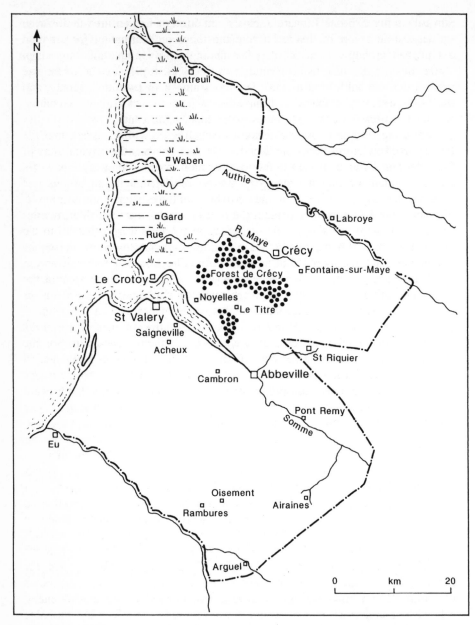

Map 2. The county of Ponthieu in the mid-fourteenth century

Edward's letter of 29 July, was not conceived during a council of war at Caen, but was a strategic option that had been planned before the army left England.[177]

On 26 July, only two weeks after the landing at La Hougue and three days *before* the despatch of Edward's letter from Caen, the royal council in England ordered the array of a total of 1,240 archers from 19 shires and London. They were to be ready to embark for France by 13 August, a date that was subsequently put back a week.[178] It would seem that Edward had arranged for the raising of these reinforcements before leaving England.[179] In his letter of 29 July, the recruitment of troops is taken for granted. The administrative orders in that letter focus principally on the urgent need for money ('our people press us greatly for their wages') and munitions ('to purvey as many bows, arrows and bowstrings as you can'),[180] and on the fact that the ships returning from Normandy with the earl of Huntingdon should be used to convey 'all the money that you can raise' and 'as many men-at-arms and archers as possible' to Le Crotoy. The 'men-at-arms' mentioned in the king's letter included the personnel of a group of retinues that appear to have been in arms in July but which were not shipped to La Hougue. They were detached to form the core of a small army of reinforcements for despatch somewhat later in the summer, the decision perhaps arising from the realisation that there would be insufficient transports to ship the whole army in June/July. This force included the contingents led by Sir William Fraunk (who was appointed constable of the follow-up army), Sir Thomas Haukeston (marshal) and Sir Miles Stapleton, and it was to this group of retinues that the newly recruited companies of archers were attached.[181] Fraunk and Stapleton had received prests on their wages in April,[182] yet the fact

---

[177] Cf. Harari, who argues that 'the idea of marching to Flanders was adopted only at Caen', but the evidence deployed to demonstrate this is anything but conclusive. Harari, 'Inter-frontal co-operation in the fourteenth century and Edward III's 1346 campaign', pp. 389–90.

[178] Wrottesley, *Crecy and Calais*, pp. 101–2. For the sequence of orders sent to the sheriff of Norfolk and Suffolk, see E101/575/15, mm. 1, 2 and 4.

[179] It is possible that the decision was actually made after the king's arrival in Normandy. We know that a letter was sent very early in the campaign (it is alluded to in the king's 29 July despatch), and this would explain why the array orders were issued as late as 26 July. It is conceivable that a request for additional manpower was prompted by the realisation that the expedition would receive less support from the Norman nobility than Edward had been led to believe, though as we have seen it is unlikely that the king would have built an expectation of such support into his strategy.

[180] Apparently prompted by the king's letter, on 1 August orders were issued from Windsor to 15 sheriffs to acquire a total of 2,280 bows and 5,550 sheaves of arrows (or 133,200 shafts) for the king's army (*Foedera*, III, i, pp. 87–9). See below, pp. 359–62 for further discussion of the king's need for munitions so early in the campaign. The king's letter suggests that, if anything, the need for money was more urgent. Many (but not all) captains had received their first instalment of wages in mid-April, and it would seem that the funds to pay the second quarter were not available at the time of embarkation: E403/336, mm. 41–4.

[181] Fraunk and Haukeston were appointed to their posts on 21 August (*Foedera*, III, i, p. 89) and they received prests on their wages on 18 September (E101/390/12, fo. 8v). Naval preparations, from early August: C76/23, m. 15. Much about the army of reinforcements remains uncertain, including its overall size and its date of departure from England. See below, Appendix 1; and Rogers, *War Cruel and Sharp*, p. 425 n. 12.

[182] E403/336, m. 41.

that protections for the men in their retinues were not enrolled in June (as was the case with most of the army that disembarked at La Hougue), but only in August and September, suggests that the decision to leave them behind was not made at the very last minute.[183]

It can be seen that some, if not all, of the reinforcements that were assembling in August 1346 had been planned before the king's departure for La Hougue. Of course, this does not in itself point towards the pursuit of a 'Ponthieu strategy' from the outset. For that we must look for evidence elsewhere. For example, are there any indirect indications, in the orders issued by the council on 26 July, that the reinforcements were indeed intended for Ponthieu? Unfortunately, there is no mention in those orders of the intended port of embarkation: it is only after the king's letter of 29 July that we hear that a transport fleet was being assembled at Winchelsea (an ideal point of departure for Le Crotoy), to which location sheriffs were now ordered to send their arrayed troops.[184] However, some indication that the royal council had been aware all along that the reinforcements would be leaving from a port in the south-east of England is to be found in the list of counties to which they sent array orders. Archers were not requested from the shires of the west and north midlands, as they had been for the army that had embarked at Portsmouth in July.

Why were the reinforcements to be sent to Le Crotoy? The king's despatch states enigmatically that they were 'pour restreindre noz enemis celles parties'; but it is also implicit in his letter that the intention was for them to join forces with his own army, since it is clear that he had need of the money and supplies that would accompany them.[185] The choice of Le Crotoy may have been a matter of convenience, for it made sense to arrange for reinforcements to be sent to a rendezvous point that lay well ahead of the main army's current position. But this port also offered the advantage of being close to the Somme crossing point at Blanquetaque, the existence and importance of which (as we shall see) must surely have been known to Edward and his lieutenants.[186] What is clear is Edward's intention to march towards Ponthieu from the moment he left Caen. The search for a crossing of the Seine caused a major detour, but once the bridge at Poissy had been repaired, the English made directly for Ponthieu and (in all likelihood) the Blanquetaque crossing of the Somme. Moreover, as soon as the estuary had been forded, Hugh Despenser led a flying column to Le Crotoy, evidently to determine whether the reinforcements had arrived from England.[187] The king's letter of 29 July did not include a timetable for the arrival of the troops and supplies, but the urgent tone made it clear that they should be

---

[183] Protections (C76/23, mm. 15, 19): mid–late August (Haukeston); September (Fraunk and Stapleton). Stapleton had received a personal protection in early June (C76/22, m. 14).

[184] C76/23, mm. 15, 21. Additionally, the prince of Wales ordered the best 100 archers from the 300 arrayed in Cheshire and Flint to be sent to Sandwich by 20 August. *Black Prince Register*, i, pp. 13–14.

[185] For a different view, see Harari, 'Inter-frontal co-operation in the fourteenth century and Edward III's 1346 campaign', pp. 387–8.

[186] Seizing Le Crotoy would also provide Edward with a convenient port through which a withdrawal from France could be mounted should the necessity arise.

[187] *Avesbury*, p. 368.

despatched as soon as possible. In the event, when Despenser reached Le Crotoy there was no sign of the fleet, and he had to content himself with the supplies that he found in the port.

We must turn now to consider the Crécy battlefield. Kenneth Fowler suggested that it had been 'reconnoitred in advance' by the English, though he offered no evidence to support his suggestion, apart from the observation that it was settled upon very quickly. Assuming that the traditionally accepted battlefield is indeed the site of the battle, it can be seen that effective exploitation of the ground would have given the English a decisive tactical advantage.[188] As Sir Philip Preston shows in his new investigation of the locality (Chapter 3), the eastern side of the Vallée des Clercs is sharply defined by a steep bank, which would have had a profound influence on the course of the battle. From the French point of view, the bank would have made a broad-front advance across the valley impossible. Indeed, once Philip VI's army had been channelled into the valley bottom through a bottleneck at its southern end, there would have been little space for deployment before approaching, on a narrow front, the English on the western slopes. While the French were unable to make effective use of their superior numbers, especially in heavy cavalry, the English position on a slope punctuated with rideaux (hedged banks) maximised the potential offered by massed archery. This was indeed a perfect site for the employment of Edwardian tactics, particularly so because its strengths would not be immediately apparent to the French. Provided that they were not tipped off before commencing their attack (as had happened at Buironfosse in October 1339),[189] the French would only realise the trap that had been laid for them after they had become irretrievably committed to an engagement.

Provided that Edward and his lieutenants were aware of the distinctive topography of the Crécy–Wadicourt area, they could not fail to appreciate its merits. But is there any evidence that this site had been 'reconnoitred in advance'? Did Edward and his captains have prior knowledge of this area and is it conceivable that they could have planned to fight there? Let us begin with the king himself. While not wishing to suggest that he knew this part of his continental inheritance intimately, it should be recalled that Edward III had visited Ponthieu on at least two earlier occasions in his life.[190] The first had been in 1329, when, at

---

[188] The generally accepted site of the battle rests upon tradition rather than unequivocal documentary evidence. However, when taken as a group, the chronicle references do seem to point to the traditional site. For a detailed discussion, see Chapter 3.

[189] *Avesbury*, pp. 305–6.

[190] It is possible that he stayed, or at least travelled through, the county in 1325–6, but neither his journey to Paris for the ceremony of homage nor his long sojourn in France thereafter are documented in sufficient detail for us to be sure. We are equally unclear about Queen Isabella's movements after November 1325, when her household records dry up: J. Hunter, 'Journal of the mission of Queen Isabella to the court of France, and of her long residence in that country', *Archaeologia*, xxxvi (1855), pp. 242–57; H. Johnstone, 'Two lesser households', in Tout, *Chapters*, v, pp. 245–6. Hilda Johnstone suggested (*ibid.*, pp. 277–8) that Isabella took refuge in Ponthieu (granted to her by Edward II in 1308) when 'she had worn out her welcome at the French court', but offered no supporting evidence. Prince Edward was not necessarily with his mother throughout 1326: 'some accounts state that he went into Guienne' (Hunter, 'Journal of the mission of Queen Isabella to the court of France',

sixteen years of age, he travelled, with great pomp and ceremony, to Amiens to perform simple homage to Philip VI for his lands in France. Then, in 1331, he had passed through en route for a secret meeting with the French king, which had been arranged to resolve the question of Edward's homage. Of these two visits to Ponthieu, the second is the less well documented. Edward travelled incognito, accompanied by only a handful of close attendants, and neither household records nor Chancery records can yield a full itinerary.[191] Fortunately the 1329 mission is more fully documented.[192] A roll that records the daily expenditure of the royal household at this time offers a detailed itinerary of the king's journey to Amiens and back.[193] According to this document, the royal household, en route for Amiens, stayed at *Cressy* on Tuesday, 30 May, and again on Friday, 9 June while travelling back to the coast.[194] This should occasion no surprise, since Crécy was an well-established stopping point for royal visits to France. Edward III's grandfather, father and mother had all stayed there

---

p. 252); and he may have been in Normandy in the late summer of 1326 (N. Fryde, *The Tyranny and Fall of Edward II, 1321–1326* (Cambridge, 1979), pp. 184–5).

[191] For the 1331 visit, see *Murimuth*, p. 63; *Baker*, p. 48. The household remained in England and the roll of daily expenses for this period reveals nothing of the king's movements in France (E101/385/15). An itinerary for the king in 1331 based on the dating clauses of surviving privy seal warrants does not include Crécy. The king crossed from Dover to Wissant on 4 April; he arrived at *Seint Juist*, which Déprez identified as Saint-Just-en-Chaussée, on 7 April and is next seen at Pont-Sainte-Maxence from 13 to 16 April. E. Déprez, *Les préliminaires de la guerre de cent ans* (Paris, 1902), pp. 75–6. He arrived back at Dover on 20 April, 'a heure de none': C81/181, no. 4541. But, as we shall see with the records for 1329, such evidence is not an infallible guide to the king's whereabouts: only a handful of privy seals survive for the period of this visit (five in C81, file 181, excluding no. 4536, dated Eltham, 5 April). Anticipation that some light might be cast on the matter by the receiver of Ponthieu's account book for the period 23 February to 29 September 1331 is not altogether satisfied either, for it contains no more than passing references to the king of England's visit (E101/166/2, fo. 20r).

[192] An apparently authoritative itinerary for Edward's journey from Dover to Amiens and back in late May and early June 1329 was established about a hundred years ago by that pioneer researcher at the Public Record Office, Eugène Déprez. Using the dating clauses of privy seal warrants, correlated with the evidence of narrative sources, Déprez noted that the king crossed from Dover to Wissant on 26 May, was at Boulogne on the 27th, at Montreuil on the 29th and 30th, reaching Amiens by 5 June, for the ceremony in the cathedral on the 6th. He arrived back at Dover on 11 June. There is, therefore, no mention of Crécy. Déprez, *Les préliminaires de la guerre de cent ans*, pp. 42–7. The relevant file of privy seals is C81/162: only six are dated to the period of the king's stay in France.

[193] E101/384/9. This is a fair copy of the 'rough roll' that would have been supplemented daily. The location of the household in the evening of each day (when the account was held) is given in the left-hand margin. J.H. Johnson, 'The king's wardrobe and household', *The English Government at Work, 1327–36*, ed. J.F. Willard and W.A. Morris, 3 vols (Cambridge, Mass., 1940–50), i, pp. 218–19. For Edward III's itinerary for the years 1327 to 1333, see C. Shenton, 'The English court and the restoration of royal prestige, 1327–1345', DPhil thesis, University of Oxford, 1995, appendix IV; for May–June 1329, see p. 284.

[194] The royal household had stopped at Montreuil on 29 May, before arriving at *Cressy* on Tuesday, 30th. Two further stops were made before Amiens was reached on 3 June: St-Riquier, about 15 km to the south of Crécy, on 31 May and 1 June; and Long, on the north bank of the Somme, on 2 June. The return journey from Amiens to the coast was less leisurely, stopping only at Crécy on Friday, 9 June before arriving at Wissant on the 10th.

briefly, while Piers Gaveston had been resident there for rather longer in 1307, during his first exile from England.[195] How the young king and his entourage passed the time during his brief sojourns at Crécy is not recorded, but given his fondness for hunting and hawking, it would not be too fanciful to visualise him riding within the nearby forest and in the open country.[196]

We can do no more than place Edward III at Crécy in his youth. Whether the topography of the locality had a lasting impression on him we cannot say. What is certain is that the English government was taking a close interest in Ponthieu at this time. This was because from 1 December 1330, when the county was surrendered to Edward III by Queen Isabella, until September 1334, when it was restored to her, Ponthieu was administered by officials appointed by the king.[197] As a consequence, much routine business relating to the county was recorded on the Chancery rolls during these years. Further valuable detail is provided by the receiver of Ponthieu's account book for the period 23 February to 29 September 1331. What these records make abundantly clear is how much Ponthieu, and in particular Crécy with its forested environs, were engaging the attention of the English king and his advisers in the early to mid-1330s.[198]

---

[195] Edward I's visits to Ponthieu in 1279 and 1286 (though not 1289) involved overnight stays there. He was at Crécy on 12 and 13 June 1279: *Itinerary of Edward I, part 1, 1272–90*, List and Index Society, ciii (1974), p. 111; for 1286 and 1289, see H. Johnstone, 'The county of Ponthieu, 1279–1307', *EHR*, xxix (1914), p. 446 n. 65; and J.P. Trabut-Cassac, 'Itinéraire d'Edouard 1er en France, 1286–1289', *BIHR*, xxv (1952), pp. 166, 203. Edward II stopped at Crécy for a day or two in May 1313 and in June 1320: *The Itinerary of Edward II and his household, 1307–1328*, ed. E.M. Hallam, List and Index Society, ccxi (1984), pp. 98, 197. Queen Isabella stayed for one night on her journey to Paris in March 1325: Hunter, 'Journal of the mission of Queen Isabella to the court of France', p. 245; *The War of St Sardos*, ed. P. Chaplais, Camden Soc., 3rd ser., lxxxvii (1954), Appendix III: Notes on Queen Isabella's itinerary in France (9 March–14 November 1325), p. 267. For Gaveston's residence at Crécy, see H. Johnstone, *Edward of Carnarvon, 1284–1307* (Manchester, 1946), pp. 124–5; J.S. Hamilton, *Piers Gaveston, Earl of Cornwall, 1307–1312* (Detroit and London, 1988). pp. 35–6.

[196] When travelling in war or peace the Edwardian kings were customarily accompanied by a sizeable staff of huntsmen and falconers. See B. Lyon, 'Coup d'oeil sur l'infrastructure de la chasse au Moyen Âge', *Le Moyen Âge*, civ (1998), pp. 211–27. For Edward III's enthusiasm for hawking, see C. Shenton, 'The English court and the restoration of royal prestige, 1327–45', pp. 180–3.

[197] Surrendered: *CPR, 1330–34*, p. 24; *CFR, 1327–37*, pp. 234, 237. Restored: *CPR, 1334–38*, pp. 24–5, 60. John Vincent of Waltham Cross was appointed receiver of Ponthieu on 1 December 1330 (*CFR, 1327–37*, p. 228); William Borden became controller and surveyor of works on 21 December 1330, and clerk of the turbary on 1 March 1331 (*CPR, 1330–34*, pp. 37, 77). Gerard d'Oron had been seneschal since 20 August 1329 and was reappointed on 22 December 1330 (*CPR, 1327–30*, p. 420; *CPR, 1330–34*, p. 34); for his career, see C.L. Kingsford, 'Sir Otho de Grandson', *TRHS*, 3rd ser., iii (1909), pp. 185–7. On 24 October 1331, d'Oron was replaced as seneschal by Bartholomew Burgherssh, who was still in office in September 1334: *CPR, 1330–34*, p. 188; *CPR, 1334–38*, p. 25. In addition to his fee as seneschal, Burghersh received a bonus payment of £100 sterling *per annum*: *CCR, 1330–33*, pp. 350, 490.

[198] Edwardian Ponthieu has attracted a certain amount of scholarly attention, the most important modern contributions being: H. Johnstone, 'The county of Ponthieu, 1279–1307', *EHR*, xxix (1914), pp. 435–52; E. Déprez, 'Le Ponthieu sous la domination anglaise, 1360–69', *Bulletin société antiquaires de Picardie*, xxxi (1924–5), pp. 200–15; S.B.

On one level, there was the management of the forest of Crécy for its own sake. As Hilda Johnstone pointed out, sales of 'wood played a great part in the annual revenue of the county';[199] and there is plentiful evidence to support this from the 1330s, as there is of gifts of 'vestures' of wood.[200] But the principal function of the forest was as a hunting ground. The main attraction was the resident wild boar, which was 'the beast of this world that is strongest armed, and can sooner slay a man than any other' (as the English translator of Gaston de Foix's *Livre de Chasse* expressed it),[201] and a beast not commonly encountered in England.[202] It is evident that Edward took a close interest in the management of this hunting ground, and of the wild boar within it.[203] It is also notable that Englishmen were appointed to forestry duties at Crécy. English names stand out in the list of sergeants of the forest, while being less prominent in other spheres of county administration, at least in 1331 at the beginning of Edward III's spell of 'personal rule' in Ponthieu.[204]

More seriously, forest matters might figure among those jurisdictional disputes between lord and vassal that were a commonplace of Anglo-French relations, and which had proved to be a catalyst for serious conflict in the past. One such dispute that is visible in the receiver of Ponthieu's account book concerns one Oudinet Filement whom Philip VI had appointed verdier in the forest of Crécy, 'ou providice du droit du Roi dengleterre'.[205] The receiver, John Vincent, spent 15 days in Paris, with Sir William Trussel, in pursuit of this case. He also visited England to hear the deliberations of the council on the matter, one of several cross-channel journeys mentioned in his account. The face-saving compromise that was finally reached involved the revocation of Philip VI's original letters of appointment followed by the reappointment of the same man, Oudinet Filement, to the same post, but this time by Edward III 'at the request'

Storey-Challenger, *L'administration anglaise du Ponthieu après le traité de Brétigny, 1361–69*, trans. R. Petit (Abbeville, 1975); E.H. Shealy, 'The English administration of Ponthieu, 1279–1369', PhD thesis, Emory University, 1975; J.C. Parsons, 'The beginnings of English administration in Ponthieu: an unnoticed document of 1280', *Mediaeval Studies*, 1 (1988), pp. 371–403; E.H. Shealy, 'The persistence of particularism: the county of Ponthieu in the thirteenth and fourteenth centuries', *Essays in Medieval History Presented to George Peddy Cuttino*, ed. J.S. Hamilton and P.J. Bradley (Woodbridge, 1989), pp. 33–47.

199 Johnstone, 'The county of Ponthieu', p. 439 and n. 22.

200 E.g., *CPR, 1330–34*, pp. 187–8, 212, 320, 434.

201 *The Master of Game by Edward, Second Duke of York*, ed. W.A and F. Baillie-Grohman (London, 1909), p. 46.

202 N. Neilson, 'The forests', *The English Government at Work, 1327–1336*, ed. Willard and Morris, i, p. 400.

203 E.g., E101/166/2, fo. 22v; *CPR, 1330–34*, p. 198.

204 E101/166/2, fo. 16r; *CPR, 1330–34*, pp. 211, 214, 215. Those sergeants with the most obviously English names include Stephen Ho, William Morton and William Stedeman. Full lists of officials receiving wages in 1331 are to be found in the receiver's account book: E101/166/2, fos 15r–16v. On the tradition of using 'Frenchmen for the subordinate posts in the county's hierarchy', and the modification of this policy under Edward III, see Shealy, 'The persistence of particularism: the county of Ponthieu in the thirteenth and fourteenth centuries', p. 36; Shealy, 'The English administration of Ponthieu, 1279–1369', chap. 2 (p. 59).

205 E101/166/2, fos 20v, 21v.

of the king of France and on condition that the English king's rights in the forest would not be affected.[206] More common than direct confrontations with the king of France were clashes with his agents, especially the bailli of Amiens (whose responsibility it was to look after the interests of his royal master in Ponthieu),[207] and disputes between the competing claims of comital administration and private individuals or communes in Ponthieu. These were raised to the level of international relations when one of the two parties appealed to the Parlement of Paris.[208] Such suits were less numerous than those arising from Gascony, but nevertheless troublesome for the English government.[209] An example is the long-running and complex case between the king and the Hospital of St John of Jerusalem concerning, among other matters, the rights of the two parties 'in the waste land in the forest of Crécy'.[210] Such disputes ensured that Edward III's proctors in Paris were kept busy;[211] that high-powered commissions would be appointed, as in September 1333 and March 1334, to survey the county of Ponthieu, with the aim of correcting 'any abuses they may find therein';[212] and that the affairs of Ponthieu, and often those of the forest of Crécy, appeared regularly as items on the agenda of meetings of the king's council during the 1330s.

This concern for the internal affairs of Ponthieu was founded, to some extent, upon financial considerations. The county might be expected to yield a net income for the crown of at least £1,000 *per annum*, which was a not insignificant

---

[206] *CPR, 1330–34*, p. 212.

[207] See, for example, *CPR, 1330–34*, p. 434.

[208] 'Bourgeois and by nature litigious, the Pontivans could be just as troublesome to their lord as any Gascon noble': Shealy, 'The persistence of particularism: the county of Ponthieu in the thirteenth and fourteenth centuries', p. 38.

[209] J.A. Kicklighter, 'English-related cases at the Parlement of Paris, 1259–1337', PhD thesis, Emory University, 1973, Appendix III, which lists (p. 264) five separate cases in Edward III's reign prior to 1337, one of which involved an unsuccessful appeal to Parlement by the English crown against a decision of the French bailli of Amiens in a property dispute.

[210] An elaborate agreement was finally arrived at and enrolled on the Patent Rolls in June 1334. In 1336 the Parlement of Paris waived the fine that would normally be payable in such cases of private settlement. *CPR, 1334–38*, pp. 59–60; Kicklighter, 'English-related cases at the Parlement of Paris, 1259–1337', p. 264.

[211] E.g., Master John Hildesley, canon of Chichester, was appointed king's proctor at the court of Philip VI on 3 December 1330: *CPR, 1330–34*, p. 22. On Hildesley's career, see G.P. Cuttino, *English Diplomatic Administration, 1259–1339* (Oxford, 1971), pp. 102–3. Given such sources of tension, it is not surprising that we catch a glimpse in the receiver's account book of Elias Joneston, longstanding Keeper of Processes and Memoranda concerning Gascony and expert in the complexities of Anglo-French relations, staying in Ponthieu 'pur les bosoignez du Roi dengleterre'. E101/166/2, fo. 23. On Joneston's visit, see also Cuttino, *English Diplomatic Administration*, Appendix II: 'The accounts of Elias Joneston', at pp. 202–4.

[212] *CPR, 1330–34*, pp. 465, 534. The commission of March 1334 included John Stratford, archbishop of Canterbury, William Clinton (whose father had been seneschal of Ponthieu in 1306–7), Geoffrey Scrope and John Shoreditch. Nothing amounting to a report from these commissions appears to have survived, although it may be possible to detect its findings in the appointment of a further commission in January 1335, which was instructed 'to survey the king's castles and manors in the county of Ponthieu, which are reported to have fallen greatly into decay before the king granted the county to Queen Isabella'. *CPR, 1334–38*, p. 135.

sum in the context of the king's peacetime revenues.[213] In addition, there was the right to collate to prebends in the collegiate church of St Wulfran, Abbeville, a useful source of patronage. However, the extent to which the revenues from Ponthieu could be dissipated through neglect and peculation had been demonstrated by the report into the state of the county presented to Edward II in 1318.[214] In the months following Edward III's takeover of the county in December 1330, his government issued a stream of orders intended to minimise unnecessary expenditure and maximise revenue. The list of pensions and fees payable from county funds was to be carefully scrutinised. Grants from Queen Isabella's time were to be revoked with a view to demising property 'at farm to the king's greatest advantage'.[215] Then, early in 1334, the receiver, John Vincent, was arrested by the seneschal. 'Nowhere is it stated how he had fallen from grace, but one is led to suspect that peculation was at the root of the whole affair.'[216] When released to allow him to render his account, Vincent went to ground and evaded all attempts to apprehend him. Five years later he was accused of owing £1,500 from his period of office in Ponthieu; and, to make matters worse, he had put himself under the protection of Philip of Valois, the 'self-styled' king of France.[217] With a jolt, we are brought back to the greater issue of Anglo-French relations, which looms ever-present in the background in Edward III's management of his 'droit heritage' of Ponthieu. Thus, the group of commissioners appointed to survey the county in March 1334 were also required, from April, to function 'as the king's proctors to treat of all matters in dispute touching the county of Ponthieu'.[218] And returning to the report compiled in 1318, we find that the last two items, having dwelt on matters that were threatening to damage relations with the king of France,[219] concluded that Queen Isabella should write a 'secret letter' to Philip V 'to know his intention and will'. Ponthieu was much more than a source of revenue; it was one of the potentially explosive points of contact between a lord and a vassal who were both kings in their own right. Indeed, in the autumn of 1334 it was feared that deadlock in the process of Agen would lead to seizure of Ponthieu by the French.[220]

Although we lose sight of the minutiae of Pontivan affairs once the county had been handed back to Queen Isabella in September 1334, there is sufficient evidence, especially from the highly illuminated years during the early 1330s, to

---

[213] Johnstone, 'The queen's household', *The English Government at Work, 1327–1336*, ed. Willard and Morris, i, p. 261; Shealy, 'The English administration of Ponthieu, 1279–1369', pp. 123–36.

[214] *Calendar of Chancery Warrants, 1244–1326* (London, 1927), pp. 482–3.

[215] *CPR, 1330–34*, p. 134; *CCR, 1330–33*, p. 246; *CFR, 1327–37*, p. 234. Characteristic of this period is a document (dated 5 Edward III) that is concerned with the 'Decai de rentes certaines de la contee de Pontif': E101/619/13.

[216] Shealy, 'The English administration of Ponthieu, 1279–1369', pp. 59–63 (at p. 61).

[217] *CPR, 1338–40*, p. 356.

[218] *CPR, 1330–34*, p. 534.

[219] It was doubted whether sufficient knights could be raised to fulfil the count's feudal obligation; and there was real concern about the consequences of the seneschal's brother being an enemy of the king of France: *Calendar of Chancery Warrants, 1244–1326*, p. 483.

[220] Cuttino, *English Diplomatic Administration*, p. 111.

show that until 1337, when it was occupied by the French, the king of England and his advisers were in close and continual contact with Ponthieu. Information about the county flowed steadily across the channel by letter and by word of mouth. Weighty matters, concerning finance and jurisdiction, held the attention of the king and his council, and made work for their agents in Ponthieu and Paris. Given all this activity, we should expect to find men in the English army in July–August 1346 who, like the king, could boast prior knowledge of Ponthieu, and of the Crécy area in particular. And find them we do. Edward III had been accompanied to the homage ceremony at Amiens in June 1329 by a substantial entourage, and we know the names of slightly fewer than a hundred of them.[221] Admittedly, only a handful can be shown to have been at Crécy seventeen years later, but they include men who occupied positions of influence in the army. Most notable among them are Robert Ufford, earl of Suffolk and Richard Talbot, steward of the royal household (together with Talbot's inseparable companion, Philip Buketot);[222] and Reginald Cobham, who (according to Froissart) investigated the ground before the battle and advised the king on the army's dispositions.[223]

Moreover, there were at least two of Edward's companions in arms at Crécy who had acquired a close personal connection with Ponthieu during the previous two decades. One of these was Sir Gawain Corder. A household knight who had probably witnessed the homage ceremony in Amiens cathedral (though we cannot prove it),[224] Corder had been in the service of Queen Isabella and Prince Edward during the summer of 1326, and may have gained first-hand experience of Ponthieu at this time.[225] What is certain is that in July 1327, for good service to the young king and the queen mother, Corder was granted custody of the comital manor of Gard près de Rue,[226] which lies about fifteen kilometres west of Crécy. This was not a remote and insignificant corner of Ponthieu. Indeed,

---

[221] Ten of the most eminent of the English witnesses are mentioned by name in the notarial instrument recording the details of the ceremony on 6 June: P. Chaplais, ed., *English Medieval Diplomatic Practice, Part I: Documents and Interpretation*, 2 vols (London, 1982), i, no. 200. For those who received letters of protection for this journey, see *CPR, 1327–30*, pp. 386, 388–92, 395.

[222] *CPR, 1327–30*, pp. 388, 390. Talbot was a household knight in 1328, and both he and Ufford were household bannerets in 1330: *Calendar of Memoranda Rolls, 1326–1327* (London, 1968), pp. 373, 377.

[223] *Froissart*, ed. Luce, iii, p. 166. Although Froissart's reliability may be questioned, it is interesting to note that, according to Henry Knighton, Cobham performed a similar reconnaissance role before Sluys: *Knighton*, ed. Martin, pp. 28–9.

[224] *Calendar of Memoranda Rolls, 1326–1327*, pp. 373, 377.

[225] In July 1326 he is termed 'an adherent of the enemies and rebels against the king', and he consequently forfeited an annuity paid by Christ Church priory, Canterbury, for which religious house Corder acted as agent in France and at Edward III's court. *CPR, 1324–27*, p. 279; *Literae Cantuarienses: the Letter Books of the Monastery of Christ Church, Canterbury*, ed. J. Brigstocke Sheppard, Rolls Ser., 2 vols (London, 1887–8), i, pp. 184–5, 208–10, 446–7; ii, pp. 24–6, 48–53.

[226] C81/147, no. 1143: privy seal dated Tudhoe, 18 July 1327; ratification in February 1331: *CPR, 1330–34*, p. 80. The moated site of the comital manor at Gard survives to this day: for a (dated) aerial photograph, see S.B. Storey-Challenger, *L'administration anglaise du Ponthieu après le traité de Brétigny, 1361–1369* (Abbeville, 1975), plate 6.

Edward I had stayed at Gard for several days on each of his three visits to the county (1279, 1286, 1289), on the first occasion for four days before moving on to Crécy. The evidence suggests that Corder did indeed draw wages as 'chastelain du Gard', though for how long is uncertain, since he appears to have been pursuing a range of activities during the early–mid-1330s.[227] During the first two decades of Edward III's reign, Corder became one of king's most trusted servants, employed in sensitive diplomatic work as well as administrative duties and soldiering.[228] He fought with a retinue from La Hougue to Crécy in 1346, and his undoubted knowledge of Ponthieu may have proved useful to the king during the closing stages of the campaign.[229]

Corder was not the only man qualified to offer advice on suitable battle sites in Ponthieu. Indeed, in the absence of a former constable of Crécy castle, it is likely that the best informed of Edward's comrades in arms was Sir Bartholomew Burgherssh.[230] Like Corder, Burgherssh had been close to the king since the beginning of the reign. He performed sterling service as diplomat and administrator and – of greatest significance for the present discussion – he held the office of seneschal of Ponthieu from the autumn of 1331 until September 1334.[231] He was also one of the senior captains at Crécy. That he was much more than simply a retinue commander in 1346 can be gauged from the tone of the campaign newsletters that he sent to the archbishop of Canterbury, and from the fact that, soon after the battle, we find him back in England addressing parliament on the progress of the war. If the march towards Ponthieu had indeed been planned from the beginning of the campaign, and if the ground at Crécy had been selected in advance as the ideal place to confront the French army, then Burgherssh was surely one of the key contributors to the plan. It is clear that his

---

227 The receiver's book includes, among those taking wages as keepers of the lord's manors, a man named Sir Gawain de Calleville, who is designated 'chastelain du Gard' and is presumably Corder: E101/166/2, fo. 16r. Corder was constable of Leeds castle in 1331 (*CCR, 1330–33*, p. 256); he was marshal of Princess Eleanor's household at the time of her marriage to the count of Guelders in 1332 (BL, Additional MS 38006); and until 1334 at least, he continued to act on behalf of Christ Church priory, Canterbury.

228 In 1338 Corder was one of four knights of the king's chamber: E101/388/5, m. 17. He had served against the Scots in 1327 (C71/11, m. 6), 1333 (C71/13, m. 28) and 1335 (Roxburgh castle: E101/19/27, mm. 6, 6d, 7). He accompanied the king to Flanders in 1338–40 (*Norwell*, p. 338), led an important diplomatic mission to Brittany in 1341 (E101/23/5), and was involved in two military expeditions to the duchy – in 1342–3 (E36/204, fo. 107r) and 1344 (E101/24/10; E403/331, mm. 29, 30). During the second of these Breton adventures he was taken prisoner and the king contributed 100 marks towards his ransom: E404/5/31; E403/335, m. 36.

229 For his retinue at Crécy and Calais, see BL, Harleian MS 3968, fo. 124v.

230 The only Englishman known to have been constable of Crécy castle during the 1330s was Thomas Saunford, a royal household esquire who was appointed to the post in February 1333 (*CPR, 1330–34*, pp. 409). As a household knight, he later served in Scotland (1338; 1341) and the Low Countries (1338–40; Sluys and Tournai): E101/388/5, mm. 15–16; *Norwell*, p. 337; E101/389/8, mm. 9, 13; E36/204, fo. 89r, 102v. Although a man of that name was an arrayer in Middlesex in 1346, there is no evidence that he actually served on the Crécy campaign (Wrottesley, *Crecy and Calais*, p. 73).

231 *CPR, 1330–34*, pp. 188, 229; *CPR, 1334–38*, p. 25. For Burgherssh's career, see *Complete Peerage*, ii, pp. 426.

work was appreciated by his royal master, for he became the king's chamberlain some months after Crécy,[232] while his son was included among the founder members of the Order of the Garter.

The Somme and beyond: Blanquetaque and the Forest of Crécy

In considering the influence that prior knowledge of Ponthieu may have had on the planning and execution of the campaign of July–August 1346, we should bear in mind not only the choice of the Crécy battlefield, but also the vexed question of how the English located the Somme crossing at Blanquetaque. Most modern accounts of this stage of the campaign present the English king as either wholly unaware of the existence of the ford below Abbeville, or aware of it, but unsure of its precise location.[233] Either way, locating the crossing point depended upon finding a local man willing to act as guide. Jean le Bel tells us that it was a peasant, who had been taken prisoner, to whom Froissart gives the name Gobin Agace.[234] The Bourgeois of Valenciennes relates a different version of events in which one of Wulfart de Ghistelles's esquires informs the king that he had found the ford.[235] Most of the English sources, whether chronicles or newsletters, are reticent about how the king came to know about the crossing. Some imply that a miraculous event, similar to the parting of the Red Sea, took place at Blanquetaque.[236] But one, the Meaux chronicle, offers a more down-to-earth explanation. The author, Thomas Burton, of the Cistercian abbey of Meaux in East Yorkshire, was writing about half a century after the events, but apparently based his account on a lost, local monastic chronicle. He states that a Yorkshireman from Ruston, near Nafferton, who had been living in Ponthieu for sixteen years, showed the English where to cross the Somme at low tide.[237] Residence for sixteen years would bring this East Riding man to

---

[232] *CCR, 1346–49*, p. 249.

[233] Edward wholly unaware: e.g., A.H. Burne, *The Crecy War* (London, 1955), p. 158; Sumption, *Trial by Battle*, p. 523. Edward not sure of location: Wailly, *Crécy 1346*, pp. 30–1. Cf. Rogers, *War Cruel and Sharp*, p. 263 and n. 138; and D. Nicolle, *Crécy 1346* (Oxford, 2000), p. 48.

[234] *Jean le Bel*, ii, p. 96; *Froissart*, ed. Luce, iii, pp. 159–60; *Froissart: Amiens*, iii, pp. 3–4. In the Rome MS, Froissart drops the Gobin Agace story and has Godfrey de Harcourt offer advice on the likelihood of a crossing point below Abbeville: he had heard of such a crossing, but had not used it. *Froissart: Rome*, pp. 704–8.

[235] *Récits*, p. 226. Ghistelles, a knight from Hainault, had been associated with Edward III since at least 1332 (BL, Cotton MS, Galba E. III, fo. 184r) and served in the English king's wars throughout the 1330s and 1340s.

[236] *Murimuth*, p. 216; *Avesbury*, p. 368; *Knighton*, ed. Martin, pp. 60–1.

[237] *Melsa*, iii, p. 57. Antonia Gransden notes 'the possibility that to 1348 Burton used some lost monastic chronicle written at Meaux in the mid-fourteenth century': *Historical Writing in England, vol. ii: c. 1307 to the early sixteenth century* (London and Henley, 1982), pp. 359–60 and n. 112. Of the East Riding men serving in the Crécy army who may have been the source of information for the earlier, lost chronicle, the most likely candidate is Sir Thomas Ughtred, or someone serving with him. As sub-marshal of the army, Ughtred would have been directly involved in the search for the ford. It is notable, moreover, that Ughtred himself appears elsewhere in Thomas Burton's account of Edward III's wars: at Roxburgh Bridge

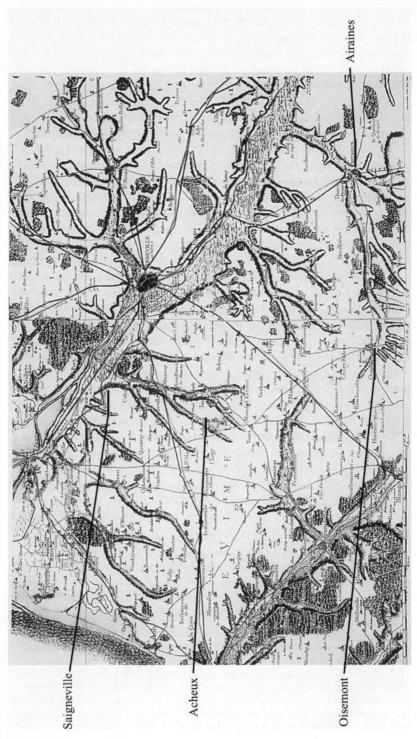

Airaines

Saigneville

Acheux

Oisemont

Map 3. The topography south and west of Abbeville. On 23 August, the main body of the English army marched from Airaines to Acheux, via Oisemont. The remaining short distance to the Blanquetaque ford, near Saigneville, was covered early on the 24th. Map by Cesar-François Cassini de Thury (1714–84), with later amendments. © IGN Paris. Reproduced with permission.

Ponthieu at the time that a group of Englishmen were appointed sergeants in the forest of Crécy. There is, therefore, a possibility that Thomas Burton's Yorkshireman was one of those English foresters who are mentioned in the receiver of Ponthieu's account book and Chancery rolls for 1331.

Edward III may well have welcomed the appearance of a guide with precise local knowledge, but what surely happened was guidance towards a ford that the English knew to exist. For there can be no doubt that Blanquetaque was a well-known crossing point, where (according to the short continuation of the *Chronique de Flandre*) 'les bestes du pays' were accustomed to pass at low tide.[238] The master of every ship engaged in trade with Abbeville would, by necessity, have been aware that the Somme was fordable at low tide; and it is clear that the French high command knew about the crossing, since they posted Godemar du Fay with a contingent of troops to defend it. It is evident that the English knew about it too. King Edward's own newsletter, written a week after Crécy, is very matter-of-fact about the river crossing: 'When we came to the river Somme, we found the bridges broken, so we went towards St Valery to cross at a ford ('ung gué') where the sea rises and falls.'[239] There were a number of men in Edward's army who could – indeed should – have known about Blanquetaque. The *gué* was no further from Gawain Corder's manor at Gard près de Rue than was Crécy, while it is difficult to see how Bartholomew Burgherssh could have failed to have become aware of this important crossing point during his three-year term of office as seneschal of Ponthieu. It should always be borne in mind that Ponthieu is not Aquitaine; it is of about the same area as a middle-sized English county, like Dorset.

Edward's conduct of the Crécy campaign makes a great deal more sense if we accept that he knew of the existence of the Blanquetaque ford from the outset. In ordering reinforcements of men and supplies to be sent to Le Crotoy, the king's letter of 29 July assumes that crossing the Somme would not pose a problem to his army. Seen in this light, his march from Poissy to the Somme no longer appears to be a voyage into the unknown, carrying with it the risk of being caught in a trap – the triangle of land bounded by the sea, the Somme and the approaching French army. That Edward did indeed know where he was going at this stage of the campaign is suggested by the sources that provide detailed information on his itinerary.[240] At first glance there appears to be some conflict between these sources (see table, below).

According to Retford's 'kitchen journal', the royal household arrived at Acheux on 21 August and remained there until (the early morning of) 24 August, when Edward set off for Blanquetaque. But Cleopatra D. VII and Geoffrey Baker's chronicle suggest that the army stayed at Airaines on the nights of 21 and 22 August, only reaching Acheux on the 23rd. To complicate matters still further, several chroniclers, including Jean le Bel (followed by

(1332), where he made an heroic stand against the Scots, and at St Omer (1340). *Melsa*, ii, 366; iii, p. 46.

238 *Chronique de Flandre*, ii, p. 41; St Omer chronicle, fo. 260v.

239 *Le Prince Noir*, ed. Michel, p. 309.

240 For these sources, see above, p. 2 n. 4.

	Kitchen Journal	Cleopatra D. VII	Baker
20 August	Camps-en-Amienois	Camps-en-Amienois	–
21 August	Acheux	Airaines	Airaines
22 August	[unspecific about place]	Airaines	Airaines
23 August	'the same place'	Acheux	Acheux
24 August	'sub foresta de Cressy'	'juste la foreste de Cressy'	[crossing Somme]
25 August	'in foresta de Cressy'	'un altre cost de la forest'	–
26 August	'adhuc sub foresta de Cressy'	'les champs devaunt la ville de Cressy en Pountyf'	[battle of Crécy]
27 August	'in campis sub foresta de Cressy'	'en mesme le champ juste la forest'	[battlefield]

Froissart) and the author of the *Chronique Normande,* tell us that Edward's itinerary took him from Airaines to Oisemont, from where his army marched directly to Blanquetaque.[241] However, these apparent inconsistencies can be reconciled if we interpret the kitchen journal as indicating that part of the army – the king, his headquarters staff and presumably the whole of the household division – rode on to Acheux, well ahead of the rest of the army. Edward was aware of the existence of the ford, but he still needed to locate it precisely and determine the optimum time for a crossing. We should imagine mounted reconnaissance parties questioning local peasants, just as Chandos Herald relates.[242] It may have been Wulfart de Ghistelles's esquire who brought back the essential information. Before embarking on a potentially hazardous crossing of a wide tidal river, Edward would also have wanted to investigate conditions on the far bank. How much resistance could he expect to meet? Where and how would the defenders be deployed and how could their position be turned? Given the width of the Somme estuary at the presumed site of the ford (over two kilometres) such information could only be obtained by sending reconnaissance groups across the river. For men of intrepid stamp, who had already shown themselves capable of river crossings in boats – at Caen and La Roche Guyon, for example – this would not have presented a major problem.[243] We are reminded of the

241 *Jean le Bel,* ii, pp. 91–8; *Froissart,* ed. Luce, iii, 154–62; *Froissart: Rome,* pp. 704–8; *Chronique Normande,* p. 79 (likewise, the closely related *Chronographia,* ii, p. 229). Note, however, that Jean le Bel states that Edward stayed at Airaines for two days. Cf. *Grandes chroniques,* ix, p. 280 and *Gilles le Muisit,* pp. 159–60, which suggest that Edward marched directly from Airaines to Blanquetaque. Had the text of our most valuable campaign diary, the *Acta Bellicosa,* extended right up to the battle of Crécy, there would probably be no need for further discussion, so precisely detailed is this narrative. 'On the 20th', notes the diarist, 'the English crossed at Camps-en-Amienois. The king ended his day's journey there, but the prince stayed at Molliens-Vidame.' Unfortunately the single surviving copy of this text breaks off in the midst of a detailed description of the assault on Poix, which also occurred on 20 August.
242 *Le Prince Noir,* ed. Michel, p. 17.
243 *Acts of War,* ed. Barber, pp. 33, 35.

team of observers that Edward sent 'to reconnoitre and see how the [French] fleet lay' prior to the battle of Sluys in June 1340.[244] For the English king, careful preparation was the key to military success.

While Edward investigated the lower Somme valley, another section of the army explored the river crossings above Abbeville. The English narratives have little to say about these activities: most do no more than allude to them.[245] But Jean le Bel, Froissart and several French chroniclers tell a story of heavy but unsuccessful assaults on a series of crossing points.[246] We should be wary of taking these accounts at face value. For Gilles le Muisit, the defeat of the attack at Pont Remy on 22 August – allegedly led by the English king – was a rare military success to be seized upon and celebrated.[247] For Froissart, the repulse of Warwick and Harcourt's assault on the bridge at Pont Remy – 'très grant . . . et très fort, et qui dura dou matin jusques à prime' – heightened the drama of the army's perilous predicament and its subsequent narrow 'escape' at Blanquetaque. At least, this is how Froissart tells the story in the majority of the manuscripts of his *Chroniques* (A and B MSS and the Amiens text). In the Rome MS, written towards the end of his life, the emphasis was different. Here, Warwick and Harcourt investigate the crossings with a strong mounted force, but finding the bridges heavily defended, move on without a serious fight.[248] This account has the ring of truth about it, and it is unfortunate that it cannot be verified by reference to the *Acta Bellicosa*, our most detailed source for the movements of Edward's army, since the single surviving copy of this text stops abruptly on 20 August. Nevertheless, reading between the lines of the sources that we do have, it is possible to piece together a plausible sequence of events. It would seem that detachments of the English army did indeed probe the defences of the Somme bridges above Abbeville, but their actions were no more than feints, intended to engage the attention of the enemy and throw them off the scent of Edward's real intention, which was to cross below Abbeville rather than above it. Thus, for a couple of days (21 and 22 August), the French army on the right bank of the Somme was kept under surveillance and kept busy, the probing extending as far as Abbeville, while Edward undertook his reconnaissance of the lower reaches of the river.

On 23 August, the main body of Edward's army set out from Airaines for Acheux, a march that they completed in a day. As we have seen, several of the narrative sources state that the English travelled via Oisemont. Although the timing of this march as described in Jean le Bel and Froissart must be erroneous, the route itself makes perfect sense if we take account of the topography of the area and the local road network. (See Map 3.) From Airaines, the English would have followed the natural route up the valley to Oisemont, from there taking the

---

[244] *Knighton*, ed. Martin, pp. 28–9.

[245] The Monk of Malmesbury, who mentions the broken bridge at Long, is unusually explicit: *Eulogium*, iii, p. 209.

[246] *Jean le Bel*, ii, pp. 92–4 (Pont Remy, Long, Longpré); *Froissart*, ed. Luce, iii, pp. 155–6; *Froissart: Amiens*, ii, pp. 392–3 (Pont Remy, Long, Longpré, Picquigny); *Chronique Normande*, p. 79 (Hangest, Pont Remy).

[247] *Gilles le Muisit*, p. 159.

[248] *Froissart: Rome*, pp. 704–5.

road to Acheux – in all, a distance of about 25 kilometres. This was actually the only practical route for an army with supply wagons to take, since to march directly from Airaines to Acheux – or even Blanquetaque – would have involved a cross-country journey cutting across a series of shallow valleys. Once the whole army had concentrated at Acheux on the evening of 23 August, all that remained was a short march of about eight kilometres to the Somme. This could be so timed as to ensure that the army arrived at Blanquetaque at low tide, thereby permitting an immediate crossing and allowing no opportunity for the French defenders of the ford to be reinforced from Abbeville.

The scene that confronted Edward's army when they arrived at Blanquetaque on the morning of 24 August can only be recreated in the imagination, for the landscape and water systems of the Somme valley below Abbeville have undergone major changes since the mid-fourteenth century. Today the Somme enters the sea through the Canal maritime d'Abbeville, which having been under construction for an extended period was finally completed in about 1840. The lower part of the Somme valley continued to be subject to tidal flows until 1911, when construction of a railway embankment a little above St Valery completely closed off the original mouth of the river. Behind the embankment, the former river bed has been transformed by reclamation and peat digging into a landscape of water meadows interspersed with ponds. This is the scene that greets a visitor to the locality today, but what would the English have found in the mid-fourteenth century? It is known that the water-level in the lower Somme valley fluctuated with the ebb and flow of the tides. At high tide, when water spread across the entire valley floor (a width of two kilometres or more), and the river was navigable as far as Abbeville, the lower Somme presented a formidable obstacle. When the sea retreated, the river was fordable: it was 'plate, et pou y avoit d'eaue'.[249]

The precise nature of the crossing point is difficult to establish with certainty from the contemporary source material. Indeed, few of our sources actually describe it. The continental chroniclers all refer to the crossing by name ('Blanquetaque' or something similar), but most note simply that it was a 'gué' or 'passage'. The only detailed description of Blanquetaque by a fourteenth-century author appears in the chronicle of Jean le Bel (Jean Froissart's more famous account is merely a copy of le Bel's work).[250] He tells us that an otherwise impassable river could be crossed twice a day when the tide was out by means of a ford ('gué') with a bed of chalk ('blanche marle fort et dur'), which was firm enough to allow wheeled vehicles to cross and wide enough to permit the passage of twelve men in line abreast, the water reaching no higher than their knees.[251] Le Bel adds that it was the white rock of the ford that gave 'Blanquetaque' its name.[252] Determining the precise location of this causeway

---

[249] *Chronique Normande*, p. 79.

[250] *Jean le Bel*, ii, p. 96. *Villani*, vii, p. 162, refers to a place with 'uno saldo fondo'.

[251] The bed of the ford may have been artificially reinforced with locally quarried chalk. See Belloc, *Six British Battles*, p. 30.

[252] An alternative tradition, of uncertain origin, has it that the name derived from a 'white mark' on the hillside behind the ford on the Ponthieu side of the river. According to Louandre, Blanquetaque, 'c'est-à-dire tache blanche, est le point le plus apparent de la falaise

on the ground today is no easy matter since no trace of it survives on the surface. Several chroniclers offer locational guidance, the most precise being the *Grandes Chroniques*, which notes that it was at Saigneville (on the south bank of the Somme), and the *Chronographia*, the *Récits* of the Bourgeois of Valenciennes, and Geoffrey Baker's chronicle, all of which place it close to Noyelles-sur-Mer (on the north bank).[253] The consensus of current opinion is that the route of Jean le Bel's white-bedded ford is marked today, at its southern end, by a road leading north from Saigneville, and at its northern by a building named Châtelet Gué de Blanchetaque, which is located about three kilometres to the south-east of Noyelles and two kilometres north-west of Port le Grand.[254]

That Jean le Bel's description of the Blanquetaque ford has become one of the anchor-points of the 1346 campaign is largely owing to its reproduction in Jean Froissart's *Chroniques*.[255] Froissart also drew heavily on the Liègeois chronicler for his dramatic account of the English army's river crossing. Consequently the most widely known version of the Blanquetaque affair is, in effect, Jean le Bel's narrative, with embellishments from Froissart's pen.[256] Froissart follows his exemplar in stating that the English arrived at the ford at about sunrise ('environ soleil levant'), but found the water-level too high. They waited 'jusques aprièz prime', by which time Godemar du Fay had deployed a substantial force on the far bank of the river to defend the 'passage'. Both le Bel and Froissart present the English crossing as a hard-fought action, in which the French offered stout resistance. But whereas le Bel's account is concise, Froissart amplifies his source considerably to create one of those vivid dramatic episodes for which his *Chroniques* have become famous. According to Froissart, the English knights and esquires, the best mounted to the fore, rode into the shallow water amid unfurled banners and war cries. Godemar's men advanced to meet them, and the result was a swirl of chivalric combat at the ford. Froissart tells us that Godemar had crossbowmen at his disposal, but it is the English archers who had the greater impact on the outcome of the engagement, and King Edward's men were eventually able to force their way across the river. The French broke and there was much slaughter among the common infantry.

crayeuse qui forme au-dessus de Port une longue bande de colour blanche'. F.-C Louandre, *Histoire d'Abbeville et du comté de Ponthieu jusqu'en 1789*, 3rd edn, 2 vols (Abbeville, 1883), i, p. 197 n. 1.

[253] *Grandes chroniques*, ix, p. 281: 'à Soigneville, au lieu qui est dit Blanche Taque'. *Chronographia*, ii, p. 229: 'non multum distantem a quadam villa nomine Noiella supra Mare'. *Récits*, p. 226: 'd'encoste Noielle'. *Baker*, p. 81. Cf. 'per locum vocatum a le Blanke Take ad duas leucas prope Abeville' (*Gilles le Muisit*, p. 160); 'pres de saint Walery' (St Omer chronicle, fo. 260v). Thomas Burton and the Monk of Malmesbury place the ford between St-Valery and Le Crotoy: *Melsa*, iii, p. 57; *Eulogium*, iii, p. 209.

[254] For an annotated aerial photograph, see Wailly, *Crécy 1346*, p. 32. For a careful discussion of the location of the ford and the circumstances of the English crossing, based upon a survey of the ground before the First World War, see Belloc, *Six British Battles*, pp. 24–35. See also, Viard, 'La campagne de juillet–août 1346 et la bataille de Crécy', p. 61 n. 3.

[255] *Froissart: Amiens*, iii, pp. 3–4; *Froissart*, ed. Luce, iii, pp. 159–60. The Rome MS omits the description of the ford.

[256] *Froissart*, ed. Luce, iii, pp. 160–3; *Froissart: Amiens*, iii, pp. 5–8; *Amiens: Rome*, pp. 706–12. *Jean le Bel*, ii, pp. 96–8.

Froissart (Amiens MS) relates that Godemar du Fay was among those wounded in the battle, this being but one of several points of detail that he adds to Jean le Bel's brief account. However, it is followed by a more significant deviation from his source. Jean le Bel had emphasised that all the English baggage ('chars, charrettes, sommiers') crossed the river without mishap, but Froissart rounds off his account of the Blanquetaque affair in a very different way, by noting that the last English baggage wagons to cross the Somme were cut up by forward units of the French army.

Froissart's embellishment of Jean le Bel's account of the Blanquetaque encounter is the version of events that has captured the imagination of modern writers.[257] But as always with the most celebrated of the chroniclers of chivalry, we should be aware of the possibility that Froissart's additions to Jean le Bel were no more than products of his imagination, inserted with the intention of fleshing out a brief source text and to accentuate the drama of the narrated events. Froissart himself changed his mind on some points. Thus, Godemar's crossbowmen, which are not mentioned by other narrative sources, are 'Genoese' in the Amiens, A and B MSS of the *Chroniques*, while in the latest version of Froissart's work, the Rome MS, they are said to be from local French towns.[258] In fact, the Rome MS offers a considerably reworked account of the whole sequence of events at Blanquetaque. The episodes involving Gobin Agace and the destruction of the baggage at the rear of the English army are both omitted, and the 'bonhommes dou pais', who were supposed to defend the ford, are said to have run away, leaving Godemar's 'gentilhommes' to fight on alone. It is as if Froissart, upon returning to this story long after the earlier redactions of his chronicle had been written, had become aware of the shortcomings of his original account and resolved upon an interpretation that was less highly coloured and more authentic in tone.

In assessing the reliability of the most famous account of the Blanquetaque encounter, it is necessary to look beyond Froissart's embellishments and subject his exemplar, Jean le Bel, to closer scrutiny. The Liègeois chronicler is perhaps best known for his vivid eyewitness account of the Weardale campaign of 1327, but for his narrative of the 1346 expedition, which was written over a decade after the events, he was reliant on the testimony of others. For the battle of Crécy, he claims to have spoken to eyewitnesses from both armies, and it is just possible that this was also the case with Blanquetaque. One aspect of his narrative – the timing of low tide and the English crossing – can be shown to be essentially accurate. He tells us that, having arrived at the Somme at about sunrise (a little after 5.00 a.m.), the English had to wait until after prime (6.00 a.m.) before they could cross. According to calculations made by Dr Paul Adamthwaite of the Archives and Collections Society, the ebbing tide on the morning of 24 August 1346 would have receded below the generally accepted position of the ford at about 7.20 a.m., leaving only the shallow, sluggish flow of

---

[257] E.g., Burne, *The Crecy War*, pp. 158–60; Wailly, *Crécy 1346*, pp. 41–4; Nicolle, *Crécy 1346*, pp. 48–52.

[258] 'les arbalestriers d'Amiens et d'Abbeville, de Saint Riqier et tous les arbalestriers des villes la environ'. *Froissart: Rome*, p. 708.

the Somme to be negotiated.[259] We may safely assume that the English would have begun their crossing while the tidal waters were still retreating.

Should we conclude from the accuracy of Jean le Bel's testimony concerning the timing of the crossing that the remainder of his account is also reliable? Perhaps; but as will become evident when we examine his account of the battle of Crécy, Jean le Bel was not averse to shaping his story according to an underlying interpretative agenda, and there are certainly aspects of his Blanquetaque account that prompt doubts. For example, he suggests that Philip VI himself never actually reached the bank of the Somme. Receiving news of the crossing while on the march from Airaines, the French king was advised to cross the river at Abbeville.[260] To set against this we have convincing testimony, from a variety of other sources, that the main French army arrived soon after the English had completed their crossing, with the result that the two hosts faced each other in a stand-off across the rising waters of the Somme.[261]

The main obstacle to accepting Froissart's version of events at Blanquetaque, and in particular the image of a heroic charge across a narrow, white-rock bedded ford, is that other narrative sources tell different stories. The 'bataille dure et forte', in which it had taken a considerable feat of arms to overcome Godemar du Fay's men, is nowhere to be found in fourteenth-century French chronicles. Those who comment on the encounter state simply that Godemar's men had offered little or no resistance and suffered heavy casualties in their flight.[262] Even when a continental chronicle does describe a contested crossing, as is the case with the *Récits* of the Bourgeois of Valenciennes, what we find is a narrative that has comparatively little in common with Jean le Bel's and Froissart's version of the Blanquetaque affair. The Valenciennes chronicler's account of the campaign as it reached its climax at Crécy is distinctive and independent, and perhaps based upon the recollections of an eyewitness, Wulfart de Ghistelles, a Hainaulter who fought on the English side.[263] Edward III is portrayed as confident and reassuring before the discovery of the Blanquetaque

---

[259] Low water at the entrance of the Somme estuary was at about 10.00 a.m., but the ebb tide would have already receded below the Blanquetaque ford at about 7.20 a.m. (tidal level at the ford had been dropping since high water, at 4.05 a.m.), with theoretical low water at that point at 11.13 a.m. From that time the waters would have begun to rise, reaching their highest point at 4.30 p.m. By the time that the tidal waters had once again retreated below the ford – at about 7.45 p.m. – it was already over an hour after sunset. I am indebted to Dr Adamthwaite for these findings. His full report, including assessments of the accuracy of the timings, can be consulted online at http://www.aandc.org/research/tides.html.

[260] *Jean le Bel*, ii, p. 100; *Froissart: Amiens*, iii, p. 7; *Froissart*, ed. Luce, iii, p. 163; *Froissart: Rome*, pp. 714–15.

[261] For example, Edward III's newsletter (*Le Prince Noir*, ed. Michel, pp. 309–10); *Chronique Normande*, p. 80; *Eulogium*, iii, p. 210.

[262] *Jean de Venette*, ed. Newhall, p. 42; *Gilles le Muisit*, p. 160; *Chronique Normande*, pp. 79–80; *Chronique de Flandre*, ii, p. 41. The nineteenth-century cavalry officer, Joachim Ambert, continued to express the view that 'n'est pas même un combat sérieux': 'Mémoire sur l'expédition anglaise de 1346, et sur la bataille de Crécy', *Le Spectateur Militaire,* xxxix (1845), p. 13.

[263] Ghistelles appears a couple of times in this chronicler's story of the 1346 campaign, and it will be recalled that it was one of his esquires who is credited with having located the Blanquetaque ford (*Récits*, pp. 225–6).

ford, while his men, 'pensant et mélancoliant', murmured among themselves at the prospect of being cornered by the French against the River Somme.[264] It is as if the king knew perfectly well that there was a ford below Abbeville, and it was simply a question of finding its precise location.

The Valenciennes chronicler's description of the actual crossing is one of the fullest that we have, and it leaves the reader in no doubt that it was a hard-fought encounter. But it also differs in a number of respects from the narratives offered by Jean le Bel and Froissart.[265] The English arrived at the river to find that the tide was out and that Godemar du Fay was already in position on the far bank. (This discrepancy may simply reflect the late arrival of the chronicler's witness on the river bank.) Where Jean le Bel merely implies that men-at-arms and archers fought co-operatively during the crossing,[266] the Valenciennes chronicler describes the deployment of the English army with some precision. Archers led the way, closely followed by Welsh spearmen, the latter presumably intended to form a bristling defence in the event of a sudden attack by Godemar du Fay's men. After this infantry force came a large contingent of men-at-arms, headed by Warwick and Harcourt, and then the baggage train. The king, the prince of Wales and a powerful force of men-at-arms – and presumably more archers – brought up the rear. When the English reached the far side of the river, the French mounted a counter-attack, but this was beaten off by archery, and King Edward's men were all able to pass over the ford. Speed was of the essence because Philip VI's army was closing fast behind them. But the latter, having marched more than 13 leagues in the day, arrived at Blanquetaque only after the English had completed their crossing and the waters of the Somme had begun to rise. Despite differences on points of detail, it is tempting to interpret the account of the Blanquetaque affair by the Bourgeois of Valenciennes in the light of Jean le Bel and Froissart, so vivid is the story told by the latter. And yet the Bourgeois's *Récits* do not mention a narrow, white-rock bedded ford. Indeed, if we set aside the dramatic image of a heroic dash across a causeway that is conjured up in particular by Froissart and Chandos Herald,[267] we find that the *Récits* can be interpreted rather differently.

That the crossing of the Somme was more a triumph of sound planning than knightly heroics is suggested by contemporary narrative sources of English provenance. None of these accounts mention 'Blanquetaque' by name, and more importantly, two of our English eyewitness accounts, followed by several chronicles, suggest that the crossing was made on a wide front. Richard Wynkeley's campaign newsletter, dated 2 September, described the crossing 'in the tidal reach between Crotoy and Abbeville':[268]

---

[264] *Récits*, p. 226.

[265] *Récits*, pp. 227–8.

[266] *Jean le Bel*, ii, p. 97.

[267] *Le Prince Noir*, ed. Michel, p. 17: 'Et toutz les cent à une fie/En l'eawe la launce baissie/Se sont feru sur lour coursers/Moult furent vaillantz chivalers.'

[268] *Murimuth*, p. 216; translation in Barber, *The Life and Campaigns of the Black Prince*, p. 19. The English authors refer to the crossing as a 'gué', 'passage' or 'vadum'. The exception is Henry Knighton, who states that the English crossed 'per unum whassum maris ad longitudinem unius leuce': *Knighton*, ed. Martin, p. 60.

here the whole army crossed unharmed at a place which none of the local people knew to be a safe ford except for six to ten people at a time. Our men crossed almost everywhere, as if it were a safe ford, much to the amazement of those who knew the place.

According to the king's newsletter, dated 3 September, 'a thousand men abreast crossed where hitherto only three or four were accustomed to pass, and so we and all our army crossed safely in an hour'.[269] Setting aside the possibility of a miraculous event, what this eyewitness testimony appears to be describing is a mass movement of men across a broad stretch of the Somme that at low tide was easily fordable on foot or on horseback. For the local people, who were used to seeing *individuals* crossing at Blanquetaque, the passage of an army would indeed have been an extraordinary sight.

The nature of the river in the pre-modern period can be deduced from the distinctive topography of this wide, flat-bottomed valley and from the fact that it was necessary, in the nineteenth century, to dig a canal to reopen a navigable channel from Abbeville to the sea.[270] In its lower reaches, below Abbeville, the medieval Somme would have spread across the valley, resulting – when the tide was out – in a shallow, sluggish flow of water. This is exactly the scene that, according to the *Chronique Normande*, confronted the English on the morning of 24 August: 'A cele heure estoit la mer retraite et al riviere plate, et pou y avoit d'eaue.'[271] Such a river, which was altogether different from the Seine at Poissy, did not present a serious obstacle to Edward's army. Once the tide had receded, it would have been passable practically everywhere: men on foot or in the saddle would have been able to pick their way through the water meadows and wade across the deeper channels on a wide front, just as the English sources describe. But Edward's wagon train could not have crossed such soft ground. Wheeled vehicles required a bridge, or a ford with a firm bed. This, then, was the importance of Blanquetaque: it was the only available crossing point for the English baggage. That this hard ford was below the tidal limit and only passable for a few hours twice a day at low water created the drama of Blanquetaque on 24 August 1346.

Drawing on all of the available evidence, it is possible to reconstruct with some confidence what happened at Blanquetaque on St Bartholomew's day

---

[269] *Le Prince Noir*, ed. Michel, pp. 309–10. For a repetition of Edward's words, see *Anonimalle*, p. 21; for close echoes, see *Melsa*, iii, p. 57. Cf. *Avesbury*, p. 368; *Knighton*, ed. Martin, pp. 60–1.

[270] According to George Beltz, in 1839, 'the river [was] now entirely fordable from Port to Noyelles'. G.F. Beltz, 'An inquiry into the existing narratives of the battle of Cressy, with some account of its localities, traditions and remains', *Archaeologia*, xxviii (1840), p. 174. What remained of the water flow after the opening of the canal was investigated in 1860 by G.M. Musgrave, a clergyman and tireless writer of travel books, who recorded his findings in *By-Roads and Battle-fields in Picardy* (London, 1861), chap. 3 (pp. 42–7). He suggested a location for Blanquetaque that is marked, at its northern end, by a 'brick-built archway under the railroad' (about 3 km north-west of Port-le-Grand and 2 km south of Noyelles-sur-Mer; clearly marked on the 1:25000 IGN map, sheet 2107 E), but he offered no substantial evidence and his claim that he crossed the Somme estuary in 700 paces, without apparently encountering the Somme canal, raises serious doubts.

[271] *Chronique Normande*, p. 79.

1346. For the English, careful preparation and good timing were the keys to success. Having monitored the tidal movements over a couple of days, Edward was able to plan his arrival at the ford at low tide (as indeed is suggested by the Bourgeois of Valenciennes and the *Chronique Normande*), sure in the knowledge that he would have until early afternoon to complete his crossing. As we have seen, the tide receded below the presumed position of the ford between 7 and 8 a.m. Once the water confronting the English consisted of no more than the shallow, sluggish flow of the Somme, they advanced across it on a broad front, with only their baggage dependent upon the hard-bottomed ford at Blanquetaque. The detailed testimony of the Valenciennes chronicler reveals the essentials of Edward's tactical plan. The archers led the way, backed up by Welsh spearmen, providing a screen on a wide front, followed by mounted men-at-arms. What followed demonstrated that English knights and esquires had not lost their aptitude for mounted combat, and that skilfully deployed archers could provide valuable support for their knightly comrades in an offensive situation. Softened up by long-range archery, Godemar's defensive line was vulnerable to a coup de grâce delivered by mounted men-at-arms. Lacking effective missile troops of his own, Godemar's only response was to counter-attack with heavy cavalry, but this too was defeated by a combination of sword and arrow.

The French chroniclers were highly critical of Godemar's performance, but in truth his task was far from easy. Firstly, he did not have a large force at his disposal. Michael Northburgh, an eyewitness, noted that the crossing was guarded by 500 men-at-arms and 3,000 armed commons. The *Chronique Normande* gave Godemar only 1,200 men, although an underestimate of the defenders' numbers would be expected from this source.[272] As we have seen, Froissart suggests that Godemar also had crossbowmen, though even if they were present they were probably local townsmen with little or no military experience. Godemar's second problem was finding the most effective deployment for his modest force. Because it was possible for the English to cross on a broad front it was actually very difficult for Godemar to stop them.[273] If he concentrated his defensive line at the 'hard' ford, presumably positioning his men on the firm ground of the river bank rather than the mud of the river bed, he could be taken in the flank and rear. That this is indeed what happened is suggested by Henry Knighton, who notes that the French were 'drawn up where the English ought to have come ashore, but the English burst upon them with skilful daring'.[274] It seems that Godemar's force was surprised by an outflanking

---

[272] *Avesbury*, p. 368; *Knighton*, ed. Martin, p. 60 (3,000); *Chronique Normande*, p. 79. Cf. *Récits*, p. 227 (10,000 men, not including 'ceulx du pays').

[273] Several of the narrative accounts suggest that Godemar shifted the position of his men after the English arrived on the far bank (*Le Prince Noir*, ed. Michel, pp. 309–10; *Jean le Bel*, ii, p. 97). Perhaps this movement was in response to English preparations for a wide-front crossing.

[274] *Knighton*, ed. Martin, pp. 60–1. Henry Knighton's chronicle was written during the last quarter of the fourteenth century, but for the early years of Edward's French war contains much distinctive military detail, which apparently derives from eyewitness testimony of various kinds.

manoeuvre executed by a task force that had crossed the river in advance of, and at a separate location from, the main body.[275]

The Valenciennes chronicler suggests that a heavily armed contingent was the last part of the English army to cross the Somme. No doubt this was close to the 'hard' ford, covering the army's slow-moving baggage. While the bulk of the army may have crossed the river in an hour, as suggested by the English accounts, the wagon train, confined to the hard crossing, would have taken longer. The passage was completed without interference from the forward units of Philip VI's host, but only by a narrow margin. Edward's post-Crécy newsletter picks up the story:

> soon after we had crossed [the river], our adversary with a very large force appeared on the other bank so suddenly that we were not in the least prepared. Consequently, we waited there and took up battle positions.[276]

What Edward does not mention is that the water of the Somme was rising, for as the *Chronique Normande* notes, 'le flot de la mer vint à cele heure, qui engroissa si l'eaue de Somme, que François n'y peurent passer'.[277] According to modern calculations, the rising water level would have become apparent in the early afternoon, with high water being reached at Blanquetaque at about 4.30 p.m. It would be over three hours – an hour after sunset – before the tide had retreated below the ford again.

The only contact that day between elements of the main English and French armies were chivalrous exploits between individuals who, in the early afternoon, were willing to brave the rising waters. Thus, in response to a call from the French lines, Sir Thomas Colville crossed the river 'a graunt perille de sa vie' in order to joust with a French knight. The two men parted as friends, though whether the Frenchman survived the altogether less gentlemanly encounter at Crécy two days later is not recorded.[278] While such chivalric encounters provided some entertainment for the assembled armies, King Edward attended to more practical matters.[279] Having settled the bulk of his army on the right bank of the Somme, he sent Sir Hugh Despenser at the head of a flying column

---

[275] This was probably the 100 men-at-arms and 'some archers', who according to Richard Wynkeley, 'went ahead of the army' under the command of Northampton and Reginald Cobham. *Murimuth*, p. 216.

[276] 'bientost aprez ce que nous estoms passés le eawe, se monstra del autre part l'eau notredict adversaire ou graunt povair dez gentz si soudainement que nous n'estoms de rien grevez: pour quoy nous y demouraims et preins notre place'. *Le Prince Noir*, ed. Michel, p. 310. Cf. *Anonimalle*, p. 22, which substitutes 'garnyez' for 'grevez'.

[277] *Chronique Normande*, p. 80.

[278] The story is told in *Anonimalle*, pp. 22, 160; more briefly by the Monk of Malmesbury (*Eulogium*, iii, p. 210); and with a less amicable outcome by Thomas Walsingham (*Gesta Abbatum Monasterii Sancti Albani*, ed. H.T. Riley, Rolls Ser., 3 vols (London, 1867–9), ii, p. 376).

[279] Edward himself behaved chivalrously towards Catherine, countess of Aumale, whose father, Robert of Artois, had died in the English king's service in Brittany in 1342. Her castle and town of Noyelles, a few kilometres downstream from the ford, were spared the torch. *Jean le Bel*, ii, p. 98 and n. Cf. *Récits*, pp. 228–9.

to Le Crotoy – a distance of about ten kilometres.[280] The purpose of Despenser's mission was twofold: to make contact with the reinforcements and supplies from England that had been ordered by the king's letter of 29 July; and to seize any stores that were to be found in Le Crotoy. There was no sign of the fleet, but following a stiff fight, the town was taken by assault and, according to Northburgh, yielded 'graunt plente du vitailles'.[281]

What exactly Edward and his army were doing during the two days between the successful crossing of the Somme and the commencement of the battle at Crécy has stimulated much inconclusive discussion in the secondary literature. The central problem concerns the route that the English army took from Blanquetaque to Crécy;[282] but there is also some dispute as to when Edward set off from the bank of the Somme. These problems are of more than purely academic interest, for Edward's actions immediately prior to Crécy – whether they were purposeful or responsive – may well cast light on his strategic intentions. The lack of unanimity of opinion in the historical literature arises from the contradictions in the fourteenth-century sources. It would be natural to look to Edward III's post-Crécy newsletter for a clear view of what happened. He tells us that, following his army's successful passage of the Somme and his adversary's sudden appearance on the other bank:

> we remained there and took up position, and waited throughout the day and the next day until vespers. At last, when we saw that [Philip VI] did not wish to cross [the river], but turned towards Abbeville, we marched towards Crécy in order to meet him on the other side of the forest.[283]

The curious aspect of the king's testimony is that it suggests that he and his Valois adversary faced each other across the Somme until the evening of 25

---

[280] Northburgh's newsletter: *Avesbury*, p. 368. Forming part of the rearguard of the army, Despenser's retinue had probably taken little part in the action at Blanquetaque.

[281] See also, *Jean le Bel*, ii, pp. 98–9. According to Geoffrey Baker, the town was defended by over 300 Genoese mercenaries: *Baker*, p. 81. The burning of Le Crotoy is widely recorded in the continental chronicles. In December, Philip VI confirmed the town's charter of privileges, which had been lost in the conflagration. F. Lefils, *Histoire de la ville du Crotoy et de son château,* repr. (Paris, 1996), pp. 76–7.

[282] Nineteenth-century accounts considered a number of routes around the northern or southern perimeters of Crécy forest, or through it. Opinions were confidently expressed, but were rarely securely grounded in documentary sources. See, for example, Beltz, 'An inquiry into the existing narratives of the battle of Cressy, with some account of its localities, traditions and remains', which paraphases Baron Seymour de Constant, 'Bataille de Cressy', *France Littéraire*, 1832, pp. 563–5. The pugnacious Joachim Ambert offered a very precise route north of the forest (Le Crotoy; Rue; Arry; Regnière-Ecluse-Vironchaux; Crécy), which, he argues, minimised the risk of battle on unfavourable ground: 'Mémoire sur l'expédition anglaise de 1346, et sur la bataille de Crécy', pp. 22–3. Least dogmatic is F.-C. Louandre, who offers two alternative routes, the second of which traversed part of the forest by a 'chemin vert': *Histoire d'Abbeville*, 3rd edn, i, p. 199.

[283] 'nous y demouraims et preins notre place, et attendans tout le jour et lendemain tant que al hour de vespre. Et au darain, quant nous voiames qu'il ne vouloit illoeques passer, mez se tourna devers Abbevill, nous nous traiames devers Crescy pour lui encontrer de l'autre part de la forest.' *Le Prince Noir*, ed. Michel, p. 310.

August, whereupon both set off upon their different routes to the field of Crécy, where they met barely a day later. Apart from a near verbatim copy of the king's newsletter in the Anonimalle chronicle, and garbled echoes of it in the chronicles of Henry Knighton and Geoffrey le Baker, there is no corroborative evidence in the English sources for the king's story of a prolonged stand-off at the Somme.[284] Michael Northburgh's newsletter reveals a somewhat different sequence of events:

> And that night [the 24th] the king of England made camp in the forest of Crécy, next to the river, because the French army appeared on the other side after we had crossed; but [the French king] did not wish to cross over to us, and returned towards Abbeville. And the following Friday the king of England camped once more in the forest of Crécy. And on the Saturday morning he set out towards Crécy . . .[285]

Not only does Northburgh's testimony tally precisely with the itinerary embedded in Retford's kitchen journal,[286] it also coexists more comfortably with views of these events – admittedly varied views – that are to be found in the continental chronicles. The *Chronique Normande* and the closely related *Chronographia* are exceptional among accounts written from the French perspective, in that they state that Philip VI arrived at the Somme in person after the English had passed over the river. However, finding that the tide was coming in, Philip and 'tout son ost' marched off to Abbeville in order to cross there. The implication is that this happened on the evening of 24 August.[287] More explicit evidence of Philip's movements is to be found elsewhere. According to the *Grandes Chroniques*, the French king, having pursued the English as far as Airaines on 24 August, returned to Abbeville, where he spent the whole of the 25th celebrating the feast of St Louis.[288] His sojourn there, at the priory of St Peter, is confirmed by the administrative records.[289] This version of events ties

---

[284] According to Knighton, having crossed the Somme, 'King Edward stayed there in the field with his army all that day and night, and the next day up to the hour of compline'. But the French were not in the vicinity; indeed, it is their move towards Crécy that spurred Edward and his men to enter the forest. *Knighton*, ed. Martin, p. 61. In Baker's chronicle, the confrontation between the two kings at Blanquetaque *began* at vespers on 25 August, and although the French king soon withdrew 'to cross the river at another place', Edward 'waited for him throughout the night' and only moved off to Crécy on the morning of 26 August. *Baker*, pp. 81–2.

[285] 'Et cele nuyt herberga le roy Dengleterre en la forest de Cressy, sour mesme leawe, purceo qe lost de France vint de lautre part de la ville [sic] apres nostre passage; mais il ne voudra prendre leawe sour nous, et retournerent vers Abbeville. Et le Vendredy proschein soi herberga le roy Dengleterre en mesme la forest de Cressy. Et la Samady a matin se remua devers Cressy': *Avesbury*, p. 368.

[286] 24 August: 'sub foresta de Cressy'. 25 August: 'in foresta de Cressy'. *Baker*, p. 252.

[287] *Chronique Normande*, p. 80; *Chronographia*, ii, p. 230. Gilles le Muisit's narrative of Philip VI's movements jumps from his arrival at Airaines (24 August) to his crossing of the Somme at Abbeville on the 25th (p. 160).

[288] *Grandes chroniques*, ix, pp. 280–1. The St Denis writer notes that the 'old and feeble' bridges needed to be strengthened to enable the army, which was gathering at Abbeville, to pass.

[289] *Jean le Bel*, ii, p. 100 n. 2.

in well with the testimony of several other chroniclers. Jean le Bel (followed by Froissart in all editions of his *Chroniques*) states that Philip was informed of the English success at Blanquetaque long before he had reached the Somme in person, and accepted the advice of his lieutenants to cross the river by the bridge at Abbeville.[290] The French king (adds the Bourgeois of Valenciennes) stayed in that town 'II jours ou environ'.[291]

In the light of this evidence, if there was indeed a stand-off at the Somme until the evening of 25 August, it can have involved no more than detachments of the two armies. On the night of the 24th, having watched the French army (with or without Philip VI in attendance) withdraw from the far bank towards Abbeville, Edward III and the greater part of the English army settled down in the vicinity of the Somme crossing. This was, in effect, 'close to' or on the edge of the forest of Crécy. (That the forest covered a greater area in the past than at present may be gauged from Cassini's maps.) On the 25th, Edward and the main body of the army moved deeper into the forest, having chosen a route to Crécy that ran through the comital hunting ground rather than around it. This is made clear by sources of all kinds, and most notably by Northburgh's newsletter, Retford's kitchen journal and the campaign diary in Cotton MS, Cleopatra D. VII. The latter, like the kitchen journal, conveys a sense of movement since it distinguishes between the location of the camp on the night of the 24th ('juste la foreste de Cressy') and the place that was occupied the following evening ('un altre cost de la forest').[292]

The route taken by the main column cannot be determined with certainty, but it is likely (as Viard suggests) that it cut across the forest from Forest-l'Abbaye to Crécy, following the course of the 'chemin vert', an ancient trackway that lies a few hundred metres to the east of the current D111.[293] To march through the forest from the Somme to Crécy offered considerable advantages to the English. It is sometimes argued that such a route would have been unthinkable because of the risk of ambush.[294] We are asked to imagine Crécy forest as a hostile wilderness, through which the English army would have been running the gauntlet, ever at risk of being set upon by well-organised and motivated bands of Pontivan 'Robin Hoods'. The reality was very different. The English army was well supplied with men familiar with woodcraft: archers who were foresters or parkers in their 'civilian' lives. Indeed, as we have seen, it would not be too far-fetched to suggest that Edward was guided by men who had been employed as foresters in the comital hunting ground. And we should not forget that, for the genteel element in Edward's army, for whom the chase was a favourite pastime,

---

[290] *Jean le Bel*, ii, p. 100; *Froissart: Amiens*, iii, p. 7; *Froissart*, ed. Luce, iii, p. 163; *Froissart: Rome*, pp. 715–16. Le Bel's chronology is defective in that he omits the day between Blanquetaque and Crécy, but this is corrected in the later versions of Froissart's chronicles.

[291] *Récits*, p. 229. In this account, Philip does arrive at Blanquetaque.

[292] *Baker*, p. 254.

[293] The 'chemin vert', which once carried railway tracks, can still be traced on the ground today. Viard, 'La campagne de juillet–août 1346 et la bataille de Crécy', p. 65. Cf. Seymour de Constant, 'Bataille de Cressy', p. 563; Louandre, *Histoire de Abbeville*, 3rd edn, i, p. 199.

[294] E.g., Beltz, 'An inquiry into the existing narratives of the battle of Cressy', pp. 176–7.

the prospect of entering Crécy forest would not have stirred feelings of dread. The truth of the matter is that at this climactic point in the campaign, Edward exploited the forest and gained a considerable advantage in the psychological game that he had been playing with his Valois adversary. The hunting ground offered a plentiful supply of game for an army well supplied with bowmen, and this combined with the food and wine acquired at Le Crotoy alleviated the army's supply shortages. Jean le Bel (followed by Froissart) records that it was a well-fed English army that won the battle of Crécy, and there is no reason to doubt his words.[295] It might be pointed out that the shortage of water within the forest could pose a logistical problem to an army accompanied by – indeed dependent upon – thousands of horses. Ideally a horse should be allowed at least four gallons of water a day. Yet assuming that adequate preparations were made before entering the forest, and provided that the army pushed on and camped near the Maye on the evening of 25 August, a march of this duration cannot have been regarded as particularly gruelling.[296]

The other advantage that Edward gained when he entered the forest was the strategic initiative. It is not simply that he had secured for his army a breathing space and a measure of security from sudden attack by the French. The forest concealed his movements for a day, and he was now able to dictate when, as well as where, the campaign would reach its climax. It is clear that had he wished to withdraw beyond the reach of his enemy he could have done so after Blanquetaque. But he had no intention of running away. Throughout the campaign, Edward had wanted to fight Philip at a time and a place that were advantageous to the English. Such a place was now close at hand – at Crécy. Indeed, the 'chemin vert', Edward's presumed route through the forest, led straight to this location. Taking the direct route also ensured that he would arrive there first. He could then prepare his position and rest his army, confident that once Philip learned of his whereabouts he would be unable to resist the challenge.

It can seen, therefore, that it made sense for Edward to march through the forest; indeed, it played a part in Edward's strategy of luring Philip to fight on ground chosen by the English. There is, however, another historiographical tradition dating back to the writings of two authors from Valenciennes, the *Récits* of the anonymous 'Bourgeois' and the altogether better-known chronicles of Jean Froissart. These suggest that Edward's army, or at least part it, marched *around* the forest, rather than through it.[297] As we have seen, the Bourgeois of Valenciennes offers a valuable, independent account of the Crécy campaign, which may well be based upon the recollections of a participant on the English side. Consequently, the proposal that Edward's route from Noyelles to Crécy took him via Le Crotoy, Rue and Waben (which were plundered) cannot be

[295] *Jean le Bel*, ii, p. 106. *Froissart*, ed. Luce, iii, p. 168. Froissart's elaboration of le Bel's words indicates, as so often, that he was not unaware of the practicalities of war.
[296] There are no streams within the forest of Crécy today, merely a scatter of *mares* (ponds). There was a well at the 'haute loge' in the forest and others in the peripheral settlements.
[297] Some commentators on the Crécy campaign have accepted this testimony: for example, Wailly, *Crécy 1346*, p. 48 (southerly route); Rogers, *War Cruel and Sharp*, p. 264 n. 147 (northerly route).

dismissed out of hand,[298] particularly as it receives some confirmation from Jean Froissart. As we would expect, Froissart's narratives of the events between Blanquetaque and Crécy are more detailed; and, as before, the problem of assessing the reliability of his work is complicated by the fact that each of the three main versions of Book 1 of his *Chroniques* tells a slightly different story.[299] The earliest of the three redactions, with regard to the Crécy campaign, is the Amiens MS, and this part of the narrative is little more than an elaboration of Jean le Bel's account.[300] Apart from unwittingly inserting an extra day into the sequence of events, Froissart's only real factual addition to le Bel's story is to state where the English set up camp after the Blanquetaque crossing – and after Edward had decided not to occupy Noyelles, out of respect for the countess of Aumale. This was said to be near 'La Broie', an unidentified place that is retained in all three versions of Froissart's work.[301] In the A and B MSS of his *Chroniques*, Froissart departs from his exemplar and offers a fuller account of the English march to Crécy. On the morning of 25 August, the English set off for Crécy by several routes, two of which, circumventing the forest of Crécy, are explicitly described. One column, taking a southerly route, rode up to the gates of Abbeville and then turned towards St Riquier, while the other took a course 'au desous sus le marine' and approached Rue. The various sections of the army reassembled at about midday and the whole host made camp near Crécy.

At first glance, this narrative – the most familiar of Froissart's accounts – appears to conflict with the testimony of the English sources, but reconciling them is actually not difficult, for they are simply focusing on different parts of the English army. Given that the two-pronged advance towards Rue and St Riquier were fast-moving raids – chevauchées – and that 'three battles' reassembled later in the day, it seems that the main body of the army, with most of the baggage, had travelled by a third route. This, as we have seen, was *through* the forest. In the Rome MS, Froissart has woven in a few new details,[302] but overall this is a more concise story, which represents a return to the simpler framework of the Amiens MS. The two-pronged advance around the forest on the 25th is not mentioned: the army simply arrives at Crécy. The raid on Rue now takes place on the evening of the 24th.

How are we to interpret this change of emphasis? If the story of the multi-pronged advance had been derived from a newly encountered informant, why did Froissart discard it in the Rome MS, preferring the framework that Jean le Bel had laid down over four decades earlier? The likelihood is that there was no new informant; rather that our chronicler, seeking to construct a satisfying

298 *Récits*, p. 229.

299 *Froissart: Amiens*, iii, p. 9; *Froissart*, ed. Luce, iii, pp. 164–5; *Froissart: Rome*, p. 713.

300 As is often the case, Froissart's elaborations have the appearance of inventions to improve the flow of le Bel's narrative. Froissart's chronology has been disrupted by his acceptance of le Bel's assertion that Le Crotoy was attacked on the day after the Blanquetaque crossing. This is corrected in Froissart's later editions.

301 The Amiens MS implies that 'la Broie' was beyond Noyelles. In the A and B MSS, the fruits of the raid on Le Crotoy are brought back to the army 'qui estoit logiés à deux petites liewes de là'. On the possible locations of 'la Broie', see Wailly, *Crécy 1346*, pp. 45–6.

302 For example, the raid on Le Crotoy burns the town but fails to take the castle.

prelude to the climactic battle of Crécy, and with incomplete and ambiguous materials at his disposal, plumped for different narrative solutions at different stages of his writing career. All that can be said by way of corroboration of Froissart is that the 'northern' arm of the two-pronged advance outlined in the A and B MSS agrees with the route suggested by the Bourgeois of Valenciennes, and that the burning of Rue is noted by other sources.[303] Perhaps Despenser's contingent, having raided Le Crotoy (and with the supplies despatched to the king), pushed on towards Crécy along this northerly route, rejoining the main body on 25 August.

Such indications as there are in the sources indicate that Edward's reassembled army made camp on the edge of the forest near to Crécy and moved into the fields, on what was to become the battle site, on the morning of the 26th.[304] Jean le Bel describes the preparations that were made on the morning of the battle. This principally involved the creation of an enclosure ('ung grand parc') of carts, which – according to the French and Italian chronicles – was to be an important feature of the English defensive position in the coming battle.[305] Froissart had a different narrative agenda, which is reflected in his elaboration of le Bel's story. He tells us that, while scouts were sent towards Abbeville to establish whether Philip was already on the move, Edward III's marshals went in search of suitable ground for the battle.[306] It is a credit to Froissart's historical judgement as well as his literary skill that all of this rings true. But if our assumptions are correct – that Edward and his lieutenants had indeed been aware of the potential of the site at Crécy from the start of the campaign – Froissart's reconnaissance of the locality involved not so much a search for suitable ground as the verification of it.

The forest had shielded the movements of the English army from the French king, who consequently remained in Abbeville throughout 25 August, awaiting news of his adversary's whereabouts and allowing his army to assemble. At this stage, Philip cannot have been sure of Edward's intentions. The favoured opinion will have been that the English would beat a hasty retreat in the direction of their Flemish allies. Thus, although Edward's emergence from the forest at a point near Crécy could have been predicted, they would have a head start on the road north. Philip had to accept that his enemy would escape his grasp. Then, on the evening of 25 August, or early the following morning, he received news that the English had indeed resurfaced in the vicinity of Crécy and were showing no sign of hastening away. Perhaps they might still be caught. After hearing mass on the 26th, Philip set his army on the road to march the twenty kilometres

---

[303] *Chronographia,* ii, p. 230.

[304] *Récits,* p. 229; *Jean le Bel,* ii, p. 105; *Le Prince Noir,* ed. Michel, p. 310; *Avesbury,* p. 368; *Baker,* pp. 252–4. We cannot be sure about the precise location of the English camp on the night of 25 August. Precision would in any case be inappropriate given the size of the army and the likelihood that the forest in 1346 covered a greater area than it does today. It would seem that part of the army occupied the forest margin, while another part erected 'ses pavylions et ses tentes en pleyn chaump' (*Anonimalle,* p. 22). To overcome the shortage of water in the forest, the army must have made camp within easy reach of the Maye.

[305] *Jean le Bel,* ii, p. 105. For a discussion of this enclosure, see Chapter 10, pp. 359–60.

[306] *Froissart,* ed. Luce, iii, p. 166.

to Crécy. He was fired up for the fight and wanted to rush on ahead.[307] But he was leading his army, in some disorder, to an engagement that he would begin at a grave disadvantage and which within a short time had spiralled irretrievably out of control.

According to a contemporary English chronicler, on the eve of the battle of Crécy Edward III was in a lighted-hearted and jocular mood at the prospect of meeting his adversary in the field.[308] The reasons for the king's positive frame of mind are not difficult to fathom. It can only have been with a profound sense of satisfaction that he settled down with his army in the vicinity of the forest of Crécy. As we have seen, the forest had been the cause of considerable tension in Anglo-French relations; it was now to be the site of a dramatic confrontation. Indeed, for Edward III, where better than Crécy-en-Ponthieu to confront his Valois rival? Jean le Bel, followed by Froissart, has Edward III observe before Crécy that he was making his stand on his 'droit heritage', his rightful inheritance, which had been given to his mother on her marriage.[309] And it was near to this inheritance in northern France that he had been obliged to subordinate himself, in humiliating circumstances, in two meetings with Philip VI.[310] The significance of Edward's stand at Crécy was not that he was seeking to defend the *territory* of his 'droit heritage', for as was seen in 1337, and again in 1369, defending Ponthieu against a Valois invasion was not a serious option.[311] In Ponthieu, Edward lacked a network of fortified places in favourable terrain and the support of the local nobility – factors that made the defence of Gascony possible; and as far as we can tell, he made no attempt to occupy any part of Ponthieu in the aftermath of Crécy.[312] It was the symbolism of Edward's stand in

---

[307] This would appear to be the most plausible interpretation of Philip's stay in Abbeville throughout the 25th and his sudden march towards Crécy on the morning of the 26th. The continental chroniclers present several slightly different views of this sequence of events: *Grandes chroniques*, ix, pp. 281–2; *Jean le Bel*, ii, pp. 100–1; *Froissart: Amiens*, iii, p. 10–11, 14–16; *Froissart*, ed. Luce, iii, pp. 167–8, 171–4; *Froissart: Rome*, pp. 715–16, 721–5; *Récits*, p. 230; *Chronique de Flandre*, ii, p. 42; St Omer chronicle, fos 261–261v. Drawing on local tradition that the road from Abbeville to Noyelles is called 'Chemin de Valois', some historians have argued that Philip marched for two leagues towards Noyelles, before receiving news that the English were at Crécy (Louandre, *Histoire d'Abbeville*, 3rd edn, i, p. 205; Siméon Luce's notes in *Froissart*, ed. Luce, iii, p. xlix n. 2; interpretation accepted by some modern writers, including Wailly, *Crécy, 1346*, pp. 54–5; Nicolle, *Crécy 1346*, pp. 55–6). This version of events finds no support in the narrative sources.

[308] The variant text of Adam Murimuth's chronicle in BL, Cotton MS, Nero D. X: *Murimuth* p. 246. The king's cheerful confidence is also reported by *Jean le Bel*, ii, p. 106.

[309] 'il estoit sur son droit heritage, qui fut donné à madame sa mere à mariage': *Jean le Bel*, ii, pp. 99, 105. *Froissart*, ed. Luce, iii, pp. 165, 402.

[310] He had also performed homage to Charles IV at Vincennes in September 1325. Philip VI was inclined to remind Edward of the liege homage that he had performed, as in his reply to Edward's challenge, dated 30 July 1340: *Murimuth*, pp. 112–14.

[311] For the French occupation of the county in 1369, despite some refortification, especially at Le Crotoy, see Déprez, 'Le Ponthieu sous la domination anglaise, 1360–69', pp. 206–15; and Storey-Challenger, *L'administration anglaise du Ponthieu après le traité de Brétigny, 1361–69*, pp. 196–205.

[312] Drawing on the work of the nineteenth-century historian, Florentin Lefils, E. Howard

Ponthieu that was important. He was on 'home ground', for which he had paid homage to Philip VI and on which he now challenged him to fight.

If it was a point of honour for Edward to challenge Philip in Ponthieu, from the French king's perspective, to do so made the breach of homage all the more brazen. The fact that the counsel of caution was disregarded on 26 August 1346, when such Vegetian restraint had prevailed in 1339, 1340 and 1343, can in large part be attributed to the degree to which Edward had provoked his rival beyond the point that could be endured. Having witnessed the devastation of Normandy, the Ile de France and Picardy, Philip felt that he had been tricked outside Paris by an opponent who appeared to be beating a retreat towards his Flemish allies. Then, after Blanquetaque, despairing of catching up with his enemy, he found that Edward had thrown down the gauntlet in Ponthieu. Keen to take advantage of this renewed opportunity for revenge, Philip hastily left Abbeville 'sans arroy', his blood up. Froissart's assessment of Philip's frame of mind is surely accurate. For having accepted the advice of a reconnaissance party to postpone the battle until the following morning, Philip is then overcome by his hatred for the English when they come into view.[313] And he would have been surrounded by men who shared his outrage, for the homage ceremony at Amiens in June 1329 had been witnessed by the flower of the French nobility, an 'army of princes', as Eugene Déprez put it.[314] It is small wonder, then, that Philip agreed with the hotheads, threw caution to the wind and ordered the Oriflamme to be unfurled, thereby indicating that this was to be *guerre mortelle*.[315] Rather than avoiding battle on 26 August, outflanking the English position to the north and blocking the line of march towards their Flemish allies, the French rushed head-long into a battle that could only be fought at a disadvantage. 'Par hastiveté et desarroy furent les François desconfiz,' noted one chronicler.[316]

It was no accident, therefore, that Edward and Philip finally came to blows in Ponthieu in August 1346. Honour dictated that both kings would be willing to

Shealy argued that 'an English garrison remained in the fortress of Le Crotoy, which was turned into "un petit Gibraltar" ' ('The English administration of Ponthieu, 1279–1369', pp. 39, 138). However, the present writer has found no evidence of such a garrison. Cf. F. Lefils, *Histoire de la ville du Crotoy et de son château* (Paris, 1996: facsimile of 1860 edition), pp. 76–7, where it is argued that the English moved on after burning the town.

[313] *Froissart*, ed. Luce, iii, p. 175. This represents a deviation from Jean le Bel's narrative, which has the French king agree to a postponement but then lose control of his army. Froissart's interpretation is corroborated by French chronicles.

[314] Déprez, *Les préliminaires de la guerre de cent ans*, pp. 43–4. For the witnesses to the ceremony, see Chaplais, ed., *English Medieval Diplomatic Practice. Part I*, i, no. 200. Probably with an eye to the events of July–August 1346, Froissart has the kings of Bohemia, Majorca and Navarre witnessing the event: *Froissart: Rome*, pp. 188–9. The attitude of the count of Flanders and the king of Majorca, both exiles in 1346, may easily be guessed. The same applies to John of Bohemia and his son, Charles. On 18 June they had witnessed the battle of Vottem, which had been the bloody climax of the city of Liège's rebellion against its bishop.

[315] *Gilles le Muisit*, pp. 161, 163–7; *Grandes chroniques*, ix, p. 282; *Chronique de Flandre*, ii, p. 43; St Omer chronicle, fo. 262r. Also *Jean de Venette*, ed. Newhall, p. 43. Rogers, *War Cruel and Sharp*, p. 267 and n. 166. The St Omer chronicle notes that Philip's decision was 'contrary to the wishes of those experienced in war'.

[316] *Chronique des quatre premiers Valois*, p. 16.

fight at Crécy. This was a drama shot through with powerful emotions, but while Philip lost his sang-froid, rapidly followed by his grip on events, Edward remained in control throughout. Indeed, one aspect of the latter's conduct of the Crécy campaign that has not received the recognition that it deserves is Edward's shrewd understanding of his rival's psychology and his capacity to exploit it. Edward was aware that if Philip was to be provoked into committing a tactical blunder anywhere, it would be in Ponthieu, especially if he had been made to endure, by turns, humiliation and frustration in the preceding campaign. This may well be the key to understanding the planning and execution of the campaign that culminated at Crécy. For, as we have seen, the evidence suggests that one of the strategic options that Edward had in mind at the outset of the campaign, an option that had become central by the time his army had reached Caen, was to cut a swathe of destruction across Normandy to Ponthieu in the hope of forcing Philip VI to accept battle on terms favourable to the English, perhaps even on a site that had been pre-planned. The king's order of 29 July, that reinforcements of manpower and supplies should be sent to Le Crotoy, reveals that he planned to march in that direction. It also implies that Edward and his lieutenants knew about the tidal crossing at Blanquetaque and were familiar with the land that lay beyond. That they did possess such knowledge can scarcely be doubted. Several of Edward's captains in 1346, and an indeterminate number of his men, were well acquainted with Ponthieu. Some had accompanied the king to the county in 1329 and 1331; others were old Ponthieu hands, having served there as royal servants and administrators during the period of 'direct' royal rule in the early and mid-1330s.

Whether such knowledge extended as far as appreciating the tactical possibilities offered by the distinctive topography to the east of Crécy cannot be known for certain. As one of the principal centres of comital power, this vicinity would have been as familiar as any part of the county for those who had served in Ponthieu before. Edward himself had become acquainted with the area during his impressionable teenage years: we should imagine him staying in Crécy and hunting and hawking in the surrounding woods and fields during his brief visits in 1329 and 1331.[317] It is possible that, having arrived in the area on the morning of 26 August, the king and his lieutenants chanced upon the site no more than a few hours before the battle commenced, rather in the fashion suggested by Jean Froissart. If so, it was indeed a stroke of good fortune to find ground so perfectly suited to maximising the strengths of the English army, heavily dependent as it was on archery, while neutralising those of the French and in particular their abundance of heavy cavalry. The alternative interpretation, that the English were already aware of the ground at Crécy and fully realised its potential, appears more plausible. Appreciation of the possibilities of this site would have made the

---

[317] The comital residence was Crécy castle, the remains of which are thought to be incorporated in the 'Chateau Fort', a moated site located, opposite the school, on the Place du 8 mai. This is only a few hundred metres from 'le Moulin Edouard III', overlooking the 'traditional' battlefield. Detailed accounts for the refurbishment of Crécy castle in the early fourteenth century may be consulted at the National Archives, London: E101/156/14; E101/157/26.

argument in favour of the 'Ponthieu option' especially compelling. And, once the Somme had been traversed, prior knowledge of the destination would explain the purposefulness and timing of the English march to Crécy.

It is not difficult for us to imagine the thoughts of the vanquished and the victors during the hours that followed the decisive and sanguinary evening's work in the fields near to Crécy. Philip VI must have been in the darkest of depressions, for he had lost a brother, a nephew and his friend and confidant, King John of Bohemia, as well as many members of the French nobility. As he passed what was no doubt a sleepless night, first at La Broye and then on the road to Amiens (even assuming that the English reports that he had been wounded were inaccurate), and as he reflected upon events during the following weeks, one question must have returned to his mind repeatedly. How could a disaster of such magnitude have befallen his army?

The aftermath of the battle was spent very differently by the English commanders. Jean le Bel tells us that on the night of the battle, Edward III invited the great men of his army to dine with him. Everything had gone according to plan and there must have been a good deal of mutual congratulation, given that 'such a small company had resisted and held the field against all the power of France'.[318] For Edward III, Crécy marked a triumphant pinnacle of military achievement, which could hardly have seemed possible at the beginning of his reign, nearly twenty years earlier. He may well have recalled on that August evening in 1346 how his first experience of campaigning, in July–August 1327, had culminated in a humiliating stand-off with the Scots at Stanhope Park. Aged only fourteen, Edward had experienced bitter disappointment when he discovered that his Scottish adversaries had quietly slipped away, having previously, in a daring moonlight raid, bloodied his army's nose and cut the guy-ropes of the royal pavilion.[319] Twenty years later, on the morrow of Crécy, Edward's world appeared very different. He was already a respected chivalric figure in western Europe, but through the scale of the slaughter meted out to his opponents, 'toute la fleur de Crestienneté', England's international reputation as a military power was established in an evening's hard fighting on a hillside in Ponthieu.

Some people of the Crécy district regarded the battle as the fulfilment of an old prophecy that foretold that five kings would fight on the field of 'Buscamps'.[320] Edward III may even have been aware of the prophecy as he selected the ground upon which to fight. But he more than anyone knew that there had been more to the campaign and battle of Crécy than the inexorable workings of fate. In this chapter, an attempt has been made to uncover the strategic plan that led, through its successful implementation, to the battle at Crécy-en-Ponthieu in late August 1346. We must now turn our attention to the problem of how the outcome of the battle is to be explained.

---

[318] *Jean le Bel*, ii, p. 107.
[319] R. Nicholson, *Edward III and the Scots* (Oxford, 1965), pp. 35–6.
[320] *Chronique de Flandre*, ii, p. 45; *St Omer Chronicle*, fo. 263r; Louandre, *Histoire d'Abbeville*, 3rd edn, i, pp. 219–20. Louandre notes (p. 220 n. 1) that Buscamps was 'ancien nom de la Vallée des Clercs'.

3

The Traditional Battlefield of Crécy[1]

SIR PHILIP PRESTON Bart.

The precise geographical placement of many battlefields is anchored by tradition rather than established fact, there being no more than anecdotal evidence, and perhaps an association with existing place names, to 'authenticate' their location. Such is the case with the traditional site of the battle of Crécy. That the battle certainly occurred close by Crécy is supported not only by the adoption of the name of the village, but also by accounts and letters written very shortly after the battle.[2] However, attempts through documentary research to pinpoint the battlefield run headlong into the vagaries of chroniclers who offer no precision; and, as we shall see later in this chapter, neither such references as do exist, nor the small amount of archaeological research that has been undertaken, do much to add or subtract from the likelihood that the traditional site is indeed where the actual battle took place. In the absence of hard evidence, therefore, tradition remains the compulsive indicator, and those who have hitherto offered an interpretation of the battle have perhaps understandably found no need, or indeed no means, to challenge the belief that tradition is a continuum of the truth. As a result, the most respected accounts of the battle that we have refer generally to a landscape and topography that we see today. Indeed, the landscape

---

[1] Throughout this chapter I have referred to the battlefield as 'the battlefield', because in the context of a book on the battle of Crécy this term is naturally appropriate. It may, however, be of interest to readers to know that the British Government's advisory committee on battlefields, The Battlefield Commission of English Heritage, makes a distinction between 'battlefields' and 'battle sites'. The term 'battlefield' is used where members of the commission feel they are, in a court of law, able to assert that a certain piece of land was the actual location of a battle. The term 'battle site' is reserved for locations where circumstantial evidence suggests that in all probability a battle took place, but insufficient proof exists for this claim to be substantiated under oath. By these standards we should consider the traditionally accepted site of the battle of Crécy to be the Crécy battle site.

[2] Johann von Schönfeld's letter, dated Bruges 12 September 1346, describes the pitched battle 'iuxta unam dietam sancti Georii iuxta villam, que vocat4eur Kersy': J.F. Böhmer, ed., *Acta Imperii selecta* (Innsbruck, 1870), no. 1055. Richard Wynkeley's letter, dated 2 September 1346, notes that 'our lord the King went towards Crécy [*versus Cressi*] where his adversary came up with him in the fields' (*Murimuth*, p. 216); and Edward III's letter, dated 3 September, reports that, on 26 August, 'à notre venue à Cresci . . . nous arraimez nos batailles' (*Le Prince Noir*, ed. Michel, p. 310). Also, Bradwardine's sermon, Calais, October 1346: 'in bello . . . de Cresy'. H.S. Offler, 'Thomas Bradwardine's "Victory Sermon" in 1346', *Church and Crown in the Fourteenth Century*, ed. A.I. Doyle (Aldershot, 2000), XIII, p. 24.

The Battle of Crécy, 1346

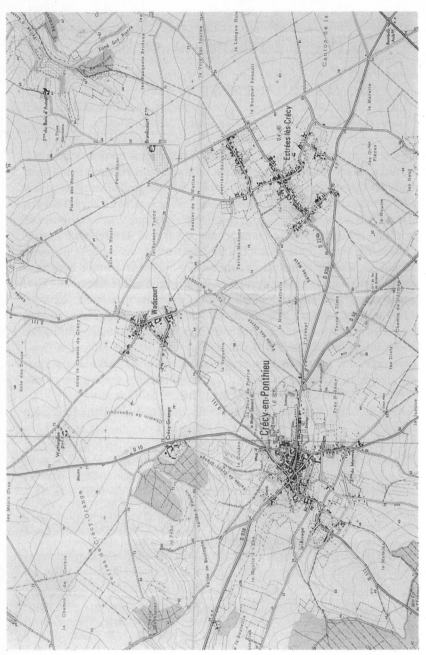

Map 4.   The traditional battlefield of Crécy. The steep bank is marked on the eastern side of the 'Vallée des Clercs' (centre of map). Note also Wattéglise, a farm located on the northern edge of the map. Reproduced, with permission, from Carte IGN 1:25000 no. 2206 O. © IGN Paris 1999. Autorisation no. 60.2187

and topography are essential ingredients in these historians' military analyses, in their telling of the story of the battle of Crécy. However, a recent and more detailed look at the traditional battlefield suggests that at least some of these interpretations are not comfortably consistent with the existing topography. It is not the purpose of the present author to challenge the authenticity of the traditional site, nor to propose that the battle was fought elsewhere. It is, however, his intention to identify physical features of the battlefield that deserve specific – and in some cases perhaps revised – military explanations as to how the battle was arranged and fought.

The potential influence of a battlefield on the strategy, tactics and course of a battle, and thereafter on history itself, is emphatic. Just as military commanders consider the selection of a battle ground of primary importance, so military historians who follow place equal importance on these choices in their interpretation and analysis of warfare. In the case of Crécy, about which much has been written and upon which so much history resides, little published work has dwelt upon the provenance of the traditional site. Nor, where the battlefield has been accepted, has the site itself always been thoroughly examined. In the absence of certainty, the acceptance by historians of the traditional Crécy battle site is perhaps justifiable. Tradition does not lightly attach itself to a battlefield, and in cases where it remains the principal or only witness, time has allowed both truth and deception an equal opportunity to assert themselves. For Crécy, no rival battleground exists, and such doubts as there are concern specific locations rather than the general site.[3] This is not to suggest that tradition is without corruption. Recent studies of the authenticity of sixty English battlefields by the Battlefields Committee of English Heritage[4] revealed that four or five of those battlefields examined had been falsely attributed. Although this statistic does not give tradition a clean bill of health, it suggests a notable inclination towards integrity, and tends to support the acceptance of an unchallenged site.

A closer look at the reasoning behind the identification of a battlefield such as Crécy can offer more than the reward of reaffirmation. It can provide the opportunity to look more closely at a terrain specifically selected to make battle, where the potential risks were not only of life and limb, but also the loss of military and national reputations, and even kingdoms. With so much at stake, a commander's choice of battlefield, when choice is possible, provides an intimate insight into the workings of a military mind, and in this respect Crécy is no exception. Furthermore, those who hold that Edward had always intended to make battle in his campaign of July–August 1346 imply that he and his lieutenants had formed a plan of how such a battle should be fought, with a predetermined notion of the kind of terrain best suited for it. Indeed, Edward's warrior apprenticeship in Scotland had demonstrated to him the critical role of terrain.

---

[3] An alternative site, straddling the Chaussée Brunehaut, which runs to the east of Estrées-lès-Crécy, was proposed by Joachim Ambert in *Le Spectateur Militaire*, vols xxxviii–xxxix, in 1845 ('Mémoire sur l'expédition anglaise de 1346, et sur la bataille de Crécy'). Ambert, a serving cavalry officer, applied a form of 'inherent military probability' to the problem of the battlefield, but his account, resting heavily upon a particular reading of Froissart, is unconvincing and has had no impact on subsequent writing on the battle (*ibid.*, xxxix, pp. 34ff.).
[4] Until recently under the chairmanship of the late General Sir Martin Farndale KCB.

Too strong a defensive position could dissuade an enemy from attack, while too frail a position could cause the failure of defensive tactics. If the decision to give battle was itself a gamble with the very highest stakes, then equal to the risk was the importance of choice of field.

The popular description of the Crécy battlefield as a 'little valley' does it less than justice,[5] nor does such a description confer great strategic and tactical credit on Edward III and his lieutenants. His was a particularly critical choice. In the deployment of a numerically inferior army against a great force of heavy cavalry, every advantage that landscape and topography could provide would be vital and would surely be sought. If, as seems to have been the case, Edward had the luxury of choice of battleground, then the choice that was finally made surely deserves greater examination. Before looking in detail at the traditional battlefield, it may be useful to attempt to answer two questions. How, in the absence of certainty, did the present site become accepted as the Crécy battlefield? What evidence exists either to reinforce its claim or to give rise to doubt?

Lieutenant Colonel Alfred Burne and the Baron Seymour de Constant

Few modern works on the battle of Crécy fail to make, either in passing or in detail, some reference to A.H. Burne's classic work, *The Crecy War*.[6] Indeed, it is to his lasting credit that his audience includes both the academic and the lay historian, all of whom acknowledge some debt to the manner in which he brought the battle of Crécy into their lives. It is perhaps fitting, therefore, that Burne and his account of the battle should become a starting point in a search for the provenance of the battlefield.

Burne did not extend his brief to examining the evidence for the traditional battlefield. In giving his sources, he singles out two nineteenth-century French historians – F.-C. Louandre and Baron Seymour de Constant – acknowledging the former for his topographical observations and the latter for locating the battlefield.[7] It would appear likely from these references that Burne was relying on material available to him in the British Library, and was thus unaware of the first edition of Louandre (1834), and more significantly (not least for preceding it by two years) Seymour de Constant's first published work on the 'battle of Cressy'.[8] Although, in passing, he acknowledges de Constant for establishing

---

5   A.H. Burne, *The Crecy War* (London, 1955), p. 170. Cf., recently, D. Nicolle, *Crécy 1346* (Oxford, 2000), p. 52: 'the Vallée des Clercs was little more than a dip in the prevailing high ground'.

6   E.g., M. Bennett, 'The development of battle tactics in the Hundred Years War', *Arms, Armies and Fortifications in The Hundred Years War*, ed. A. Curry and M. Hughes (Woodbridge, 1994), p. 1: 'Burne [is] still the most well-known military historian of the Hundred Years War'.

7   Burne, *The Crecy War*, p. 190. Burne writes: 'In 1844 F.C. Louandre wrote *L'Histoire d'Abbeville*, containing a fund of useful information, topographical and local . . . Two years later . . . the Baron Seymour de Constant established the exact site of the battle.'

8   F.-C. Louandre, *Histoire d'Abbeville et du comté de Ponthieu jusqu'en 1789* (Abbeville, 1834); Baron Seymour de Constant, 'Bataille de Cressy', *France Littéraire*, 1832, pp. 559–75.

the battlefield, it is perhaps regrettable that Burne found no space to pay de Constant closer attention. He and many military historians before and after him have accepted de Constant's battlefield without either a glance at an alternative, or a salute for his reasoning. As we shall see when looking at the battlefield in more detail, this was most probably their loss.

Although tradition, anecdote, legend, the French Academie,[9] and patriotic English pilgrims, had got there before him, de Constant brought reasoned military analysis to the popular acceptance of the traditional battlefield. If this is what Burne meant when stating that de Constant *established* the battlefield, he was perhaps justified. In what appears to be his first article on the 'battle of Cressy', de Constant examines alternative sites and scenarios, and, reminiscent of Burne's 'inherent military probability', concludes with his endorsement of the French Academie's marking of the Vallée des Clercs as the authentic site of the battle. In looking at alternative sites, de Constant focuses on the high ground to the south of Crécy, immediately to the north of the forest. A visit to this ridge today reveals why for some this had become an attractive contender. High above the village, with its back to the west, it is the mirror version of the traditional battlefield. Such a position would allow an army to anchor its right by the forest, and its left by the modest River Maye. Arranged like this, the English would have been well placed to meet a French army arriving from Abbeville via Marcheville, obliging the French to turn west at the north of the forest, without crossing the Maye. However, as de Constant points out, such a position, if tactically sound, contained strategic difficulties. With the Maye to his north, Edward would have limited his means of retreat to the west or the south, either of which could have ultimately trapped him with his back to the sea. Furthermore, had Philip wished, he could have taken the high ground to the north of Crécy, as Edward did, and stolen the defensive element from Edward's battle plan. Having dismissed this option, de Constant examines the traditional battlefield. Here, he observes that this site offers similar protection at either flank, has its back to the west, allows for retreat, 'stands on a height with difficult access and dominates a ravine with a gentle slope, called the Vallée des Clercs'.[10]

While de Constant's analysis of potential choices of battlefield close to Crécy satisfied Burne, it is based almost exclusively on a military analysis of the topography, and clearly falls short of certainty. Notably absent is any reference to supporting evidence, and while his conclusions, founded on a thorough examination of the ground, are well reasoned and persuasive, we should look for other indicators.

---

[9] Seymour de Constant ('Bataille de Cressy', p. 573) may be referring to an article on the battle of Crécy written by a member of the Académie Française, M. de Pongerville: 'Guerre de 1346 Édouard – Philippe de Valois'. Undated copy in Bibliothèque municipale d'Abbeville, ref. 63.819.

[10] Seymour de Constant, 'Bataille de Cressy', p. 566: 'occupant des hauteurs d'un accès difficile, . . . et dominant dans son front un ravin en pente douce, nommé la Vallée des Clercs'.

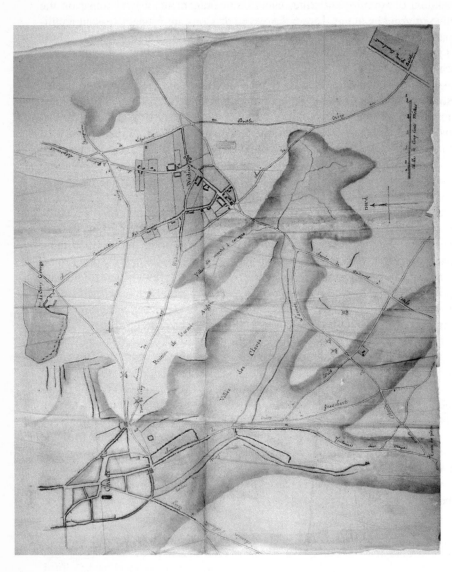

Plate 1. A survey drawing of the traditional battlefield of Crécy (c. 1825), perhaps the work of Baron Seymour de Constant. Bibliothèque municipale d'Abbeville, Collection Delignières de Saint Amand et de Bommy. Reproduced with permission

Toponymic evidence

That not a few toponyms associated with the battlefield exist should come as little surprise. Until the arrival of Napoleonic land registration and its systematic designation of parcel numbering, everyday management of land relied on the labelling of land by name. Toponyms were the essential currency of land identification, and more often than not such names would reflect ownership, a physical feature possessed by land, or an occurrence associated with it. In cultures of rural illiteracy, it was the logical means of geo-reference, and later as history developed a social and geographic significance, and literacy emerged to record them, toponyms acquired a commemorative and romantic value. Unfortunately, in the absence of records, the dating of the emergence of such names is almost impossible. A few may have been carried forward for centuries by word of mouth, many will have sprung up more recently. These may have been inspired by a need to celebrate persons or activities that hitherto had been considered unimportant, perhaps inspired by a desire for a greater sense of attachment to local history, perhaps simply by ever-increasing land use.

Potentially a rich source for toponymic research, the archival notary records of land registration and ownership transactions in and around Crécy were destroyed in the aerial incendiary bombardment of Abbeville in 1940. The earliest maps of the area, notably that of Ponthieu by Cassini in 1750, are far too general to carry more than the names of principal towns and villages. The map included in the books by Seymour de Constant is intended only to indicate the route taken by both armies towards Crécy. However, an original and detailed survey drawing of the traditional battlefield, reproduced in lithograph and dating from perhaps 1825, and possibly the work of de Constant, carries several 'battle toponyms', indicating that some were in use at least one hundred and fifty years ago (Plate 1).[11]

Those toponyms that remain and are likely in an age of records now to endure are: *Le Chemin de l'Armée* – traditionally the way by which the French approached and arrived in Crécy; *La Vallée des Clercs* – traditionally the valley into which the clerks of Crécy Grange descended to count the dead; *Le Croix de Bohéme* – traditionally the place at which the blind king of Luxembourg died after the battle; *Le Moulin Edouard III* – traditionally the site of the windmill from which Edward directed his battle; and *Le Marché à Carognes* – said to be where the dead horses were buried. In addition to these names, the legend

---

[11] For the original undated and unsigned drawing on tracing, see Bibliothèque municipale d'Abbeville, Collection Delignières de Saint Amand et de Bommy. It is possible that the original drawing is by Seymour de Constant, the result of his detailed studies of the battlefield. His first published work on the battle appeared as an article in 1832 (see note 8). This was subsequently published in book form (undated), with a map of the approaches to Crécy dated 1831. This implies that he had been working on the battlefield before the 1830s. The same collection in Abbeville library contains several lithographs almost certainly based on the original drawing. They are also undated, but attributed to de Langlumé, suggesting to the librarian they were published c. 1825. The author has found no published work containing these lithographs.

persists at *Crécy Grange* that this was where many wounded were taken, and where many were subsequently buried, within a parcel of land that to this day is not cultivated. All of these toponyms appear on the map attributed to de Langlumé. Another potential echo of military activities around the traditional site is the name *le Guidon*, allocated to a field immediately behind the windmill site.[12] Further from the battlefield by distance, but as close by association are, *La Chapelle de Trois Cents Corps* – said to be the site of the burial place of three hundred French knights; the *Chapelle Forest L'Abbaye* – said to be a burial site of English dead; and the spring of a stream at Duchy, known as *La Source de Pleureurs* – so named after the weeping French wives of the dead. What, if anything, can these tell us about the authenticity of the battlefield? Certainly the sheer number of associations suggests a persuasive body of circumstantial evidence. If they are deceits, what might have inspired them?

One contender is the Grand Tour and its triggering of interest in cultural visits to places of historical repute. Certainly in the early nineteenth century English interest in the battlefield had reached a level worthy of observation by the French.[13] Just as today, a story-less history would have had little appeal, and both visitor and guide would have been better rewarded by a story – hitherto with only a beginning and an end – if it were now given a middle. One can imagine an enthusiastic Crécy guide interweaving windmills, valleys, marl pits and ancient calvaires into an intriguing account of the battle, so that by the time of the first modern cartographic surveys, it may have been these romanticised names that found their way onto the maps of today. An example of likely romantic association is La Croix de Bohéme. The authenticity of the association of this Celtic-like cross with the death of the blind king is dismissed by the respected local historian M. Eric Balandra, as the attachment of legend to the site of a boundary marker, which almost certainly pre-dated the battle.[14] But if such an association should be discounted, its deception has perhaps been in claiming to mark a specific event, rather than indicating a general area as it yet may do. And it is perhaps in a general geographic sense that the integrity of many of these toponyms should be regarded. Observing their position on a map, and their disposition around and about the traditional battlefield, it is hard to accept that even an honestly misplaced battle site would propagate such a collection. Although it is impossible to prove the authenticity of the relationship of these features with the battle, it is perhaps worth looking briefly at one of them in more detail to see if logic and tradition are comfortable companions.

Let us take, for example, the claim that Edward commanded his battle from atop or by the side of, a windmill, and that this site is that which now is known as Moulin Edouard III.[15] For this to have foundation, we need not only to be

---

12 The author is grateful to M. Emmanuel Tonetti for pointing this out.
13 Baron Seymour de Constant, *Bataille de Cressy* (1851 edn), p. 74: 'c'est surtout depuis 1814 epoque d'ou datent leur pilerinages au champ de bataille de Crécy'.
14 J.-P. Legrand, 'La Forêt de Crécy', *Bulletin Société Linnéenne Nord-Picardie*, viii (1990), pp. 13–20.
15 'le roy qui se tenoit plus amont, sus le mote d'un moulin à vent': *Froissart*, ed. Luce, iii, p. 182. That the first battle of the English army was deployed 'vers les champs pres dun moulin' is mentioned in the narratives originating from St Omer: St Omer chronicle, fo. 262r;

satisfied that a windmill stood at the brow of the valley at the time of the battle, but that this windmill had greater credentials than those of any other available to Edward as a command post above his battlefield. That this was a site of wind-mills, at least in the late nineteenth century, we can be sure. The Victorian travel writer G.M. Musgrave records that he counted nine windmills on the rising ground beyond Crécy.[16] Though he remains imprecise about where these were, early photographs and lithographs show one or more windmills in this location, and pen and ink plans of the battlefield produced around 1850 indicate two windmills on the Crécy–Wadicourt ridge, one in approximately the place of the Moulin Edouard III, and another to the west. Indeed, local inhabitants of Crécy record with confidence that the stones of a mill on the site of the present viewing tower now form the garden wall of a particular house in the village. But what of the fourteenth century? Wind-generated power appeared in France in the middle of the twelfth century, principally in the west and in areas of Flanders, and in regions such as Champagne just before the thirteen-hundreds. The earliest mills – post mills of timber construction turned into the wind by hand – gave way during and after the fourteenth century to tower mills – stone towers topped with a rotating wooden structure – the remains of several of which still stand today in Picardie. The proliferation of mills coincided with the 'painification' of France, and there can be no doubt that in areas like Picardie, and therefore like Crécy-en-Ponthieu, windmills were a common feature with perhaps several in each community. How then can one narrow the field? Of the points of high ground above and surrounding the village of Crécy, there are three that when judged by height appear to be ideal locations for windmills. On two of these we can be sure that in recent history such structures stood, their presence being signalled both by modern-day toponyms[17] and by notation on nineteenth-century plans of the battlefield.

Before looking at these two particular sites, we should perhaps at least consider the other (de Constant's main) contender – Mont Crinquet. Although Mont Crinquet, at 81 metres, is the highest point around Crécy, neither modern maps nor those of the mid-nineteenth century provide any clues to it having been the site of a windmill. One explanation for this is its location immediately north of the Forest of Crécy. Although its height rises above that of the forest, perhaps sufficiently to avoid serious attenuation, its proximity to it today – no more than five hundred metres – must raise the suspicion that at the time of the battle this distance could have been significantly less. If this were the case, the combina-tion of its juxtaposition to the forest and the distance from an immediate community may have outweighed the benefits of its height. But in addition to height, Edward required a mill that commanded a view over his battlefield and provided warning of the oncoming enemy and their disposition. In these respects Mont Crinquet fails. As a watch tower for an approaching army, its views would

Chronique de Flandre, ii, p. 42. The receiver of Ponthieu's account book for 1331 reveals that there were three seigneurial mills in Crécy, one windmill and two watermills. Unfortu-nately, the location of the 'molin a vent' is not mentioned. E101/166/2, fos 7r, 17r, 18r.

[16] G.M. Musgrave, *By-Roads and Battle-fields in Picardy* (London, 1861), p. 141.

[17] See IGN série bleue 2206 O.

have been limited, allowing sight of Philip and his army only as they emerged from behind the eastern fringe of the forest at Marcheville. And, as Seymour de Constant pointed out, as a battlefield it would have presented serious drawbacks for Edward. Situated between the forest and the Maye, it would have obliged the French to place themselves between the English and the north. This would not only have left Edward with the forest and the inhospitable south towards Abbeville as a direction of urgent retreat; it would also have allowed the French to occupy the Crécy ridge, permitting them the advantage of awaiting a break-out by the English towards what would then have been French defensive positions.[18]

A second high point, actually known as 'Moulin Rathuile', lies directly to the east of the village and in the path of the Chemin de l'Armée. In addition to the toponym, drawings indicate that in the nineteenth century this was the location of at least two mills. Standing at approximately 72 metres, on the outskirts of Estrées, and surrounded by farmland, this is a natural site for a mill and would have provided excellent views of any enemy approach from Abbeville. But as a command post for a battlefield it has serious flaws that could not have escaped the notice of a competent military commander. Directly to the west is the steep bank of the La Vallée des Clercs: hardly the kind of natural feature that an army would wish to have at its immediate rear. Furthermore, had the English archers been aligned beneath a mill at this place, they would have been looking into the afternoon sun, something which, regardless of Froissart,[19] was no doubt as unwelcome to a medieval archer as it is to a batsman today. However, the view from its summit would have been useful to Edward in at least one respect. Any military observer noting the bank of the La Vallée des Clercs would have recognised the advantages of placing this valley between himself and the enemy, and could not have failed to notice other windmills conveniently stationed on its other side, one of which being that now known as Moulin Edouard III.

Of the three high points around Crécy, therefore, only one combines those qualities required both by the miller and the military commander,[20] so that if we keep faith with the windmill tradition, logic both agricultural and military favours the site known as Moulin Edouard III. Only here do we combine sure evidence that this was the site of recent windmills (and thus quite reasonably such a site in earlier times) with the presence of a topography suitable, even ideal, for the defensive battle that Edward was obliged to fight. But if this conclusion should suggest too great a reliance upon land beneath the mill as an ideal battlefield, perhaps we should briefly consider the process by which it was chosen.

We should not imagine the choice of battlefield to have been a carefree affair. Indeed, in Chapter 2 it was argued that there was a strong possibility that

[18] For a detailed discussion on the disadvantages of this site, see Seymour de Constant, 'Bataille de Cressy'.

[19] *Froissart*, ed. Luce, iii, p. 176.

[20] An opinion shared by C. Oman, *A History of the Art of War in the Middle Ages*, 2nd edn, 2 vols (London, 1924), ii, p. 138 n. 1: 'Walking carefully over the field, I found no spot commanding such a good general view as that where lie the foundations of the ruined mill . . . Local tradition still calls it Moulin d'Edouard.'

Edward and his lieutenants had been aware of the potential offered by the ground at Crécy from the start of the campaign.[21] Thus, although Froissart tells us that the site was selected with great care on the morning of the battle,[22] it may well be that this reconnaissance involved not so much a 'from scratch' search for a suitable battlefield as the inspection of a known piece of ground, with a view to deciding upon the most effective deployment of the army's men-at-arms and archers. We should not overlook the skills that Edward's marshals brought to this task: the medieval military eye would have been better attuned to judge topography than its counterpart today. The combination of rural sporting pursuits, the dependence upon nature and the overwhelming extent of it would have produced a fine eye for the lie of the land. If we cannot be certain *when* the ground at Crécy was selected, we may be sure of the criteria that informed the selection. Not just any valley or hillside would suffice. Edward would have been seeking ground that maximised the strengths of his army, heavily dependent as it was on archery, while neutralising those of the French and in particular their abundance of heavy cavalry. The narrow valley to the east of Crécy, in the path of the French, with limited entry and means of escape was ideal. While other sites offered high ground and ridges, and looked down upon slopes from which an enemy would have to make his assault, none so restricted the enemy's direction of attack, nor would have constricted his subsequent manoeuvres. If Edward's strategy has often been questioned, by contrast his tactical abilities have been admired. Unless this is another myth of history, it seems highly improbable that Edward, as we shall see from a closer look at the battlefield, would not have appreciated that the Vallée des Clercs and its windmill was the perfect site for his battle.

Archaeological evidence

The phrase 'archaeological evidence' needs immediately to be qualified. Little archaeology has been applied to the site, and that which has been undertaken either falls outside the pure definition of the science or has provided nothing upon which certainty, one way or the other, can be reasonably based. The earliest, and indeed only, record that the author has found of any archaeological work being done on the site is that of an excavation apparently carried out in the early nineteenth century by the Comte de Foulenelle.[23] The subject of this excavation is said to have been a burial pit, apparently still visible (presumably from higher ground nearby) in 1840, situated just to the north of the mouth of the Vallée des Clercs, above what is now a transport depot, and close by the 'great sprawling

---

[21] There is, of course, no direct evidence that the military potential of the ground at Crécy had been noted in the past by Edward and/or his advisers. But, as was shown in Chapter 2, both Edward himself and several of his captains were familiar with the area; and much of Edward's strategy in July–August 1346 makes sense if we accept that the environs of Crécy, at the heart of his 'droit heritage', had been earmarked as an ideal site for the climactic confrontation with Philip VI.

[22] *Froissart*, ed. Luce, iii, p. 166.

[23] See Bibliothèque municipale d'Abbeville, Collection Macqueron.

beet factory' mentioned by Burne.[24] This excavation is noted by Louandre,[25] but no records of the results nor any findings appear to have survived. Perhaps, therefore, the only significance that can be attributed to this reported dig is the implication that some evidence must have existed, at least one hundred and fifty years ago, to suggest that such an excavation was worthwhile.[26]

A similar burial story concerns the village of Brailly Cornehotte, some 7 km to the south of Crécy. A minor historical rumour speaks of several French knights from the battle being buried in a now lost chapel. This misty story has very recently been resuscitated by the discovery, during ploughing, of human bones in a field on the edge of the village. This occurred at the time of writing, in the autumn of 1999. Apart from confirming that two of the bones are human tibia, my friend and local archaeologist, Roget Brechet, has yet to establish whether funds are available to allow the area to be excavated. It is perhaps the moment to observe that in an area steeped in history, local medieval archaeology is in the careful but financially neglected hands of a very small band of volunteers.

In his book on the battle of Crécy, the French historian Henri de Wailly includes an aerial photograph of the battlefield and identifies various circular shadings as being the vestiges of ancient burial pits.[27] Although he acknowledges that their provenance has not been established, he suggests that two of these to the north-east of the battlefield, close to the place called the 'Marché à Carognes' (or 'carcass market'), are 'probably the burial place of hundreds of horse carcasses'. That the same photograph shows no trace of the burial pit mentioned by Louandre can perhaps be explained by the fact that this ground was covered over earlier this century by waste soil from sugar-beet processing. Although no evidence remains to support the existence of burial pits, it is certain that, following a battle in high summer, rapid burial of both men and horses would not only have been a priority, but, where status allowed, would logically have taken place as close to the dead as was practically possible. In this respect, the suggestion that burial pits are situated at the northern and southern extremes of the valley has an attractive logic. That the battlefield contains any traces of what appear to be pits is also consistent with the fact that in Picardie the practice of excavating marl pits was established some time before the battle of Crécy. When viewed from the air, both types of in-filled pit would present similar signatures. A convenient conclusion would be that marl pits were employed for the burial of men and horses, though until they are excavated, their true purpose may never be known.

It should perhaps come as no surprise that the number of artefacts claimed to have been found on or about the battlefield, or indeed to have originated from the battle, greatly exceed those that survive, and entirely exceed those that are proven.[28] That such precious claims are supported by so few objects is both a

---

24 Burne, *The Crecy War*, p. 190.
25 Louandre noted that the burial pits ('fosses') 'are still visible today'. F.-C. Louandre, *Histoire d'Abbeville et du comté de Ponthieu* (Abbeville, 1844), i, p. 247.
26 Seymour de Constant speaks of bones always being found here, but this is unsubstantiated.
27 H. de Wailly, *Crécy 1346: autopsie d'une bataille* (Paris, 1985), pp. 73–5.
28 M.A. Francqueville, 'Armes de fouilles découvertes aux environs de Crécy', *Bulletin Antiquitaires de Picardie*, xxxii (1926), pp. 15–20.

sadness and a mystery, though perhaps their tragic association and the turmoils of more recent times can excuse their loss. Those that seem to have disappeared completely from history's reach include a collection of items illustrated in 1881: 'trois pommeaux d'épées', 'deux crochets de guerre', 'deux éperons' and 'un fer de lance'.[29] Those that remain for examination include a bassinet, now on display at the Musée de l'Armée; a sword said to have been found between the battlefield and Estrées lès Crécy; the occasional horseshoe and one or more cannon balls. Of all these discoveries, only that of a cannon ball is recorded,[30] a record that neither justifies its attribution to the battle of Crécy nor frustratingly does more than generally locate its discovery. The single cannon ball found by a Monsieur Douvergne is that stated as having been found 'entre la Vallée des Clercs et le Croix de Bohéme'. The closest distance to the likely English position that such vagueness allows is approximately 700 metres, while the maximum distance is in excess of 1,800. Both these are somewhat excessive by modern estimates of the range of primitive guns, and the general direction is wide of the battlefield. However, journalism that accepted the traditional site perhaps saw no need to pin-point the place of discovery, so that it could yet have been unearthed closer to the battlefield than the report leads us to believe.

The most recent work, and to some extent perhaps the most systematic, was a survey of a part of the battlefield using metal detectors. This survey was carried out in 1995 with the authority of the Department for Archaeology in the Somme, and organised and supervised by the author. The survey took as its geographical limits an area available and accessible to the survey equipment as dictated by crop conditions, and one that, according to traditional accounts of the battle, was considered an area of 'high expectation'. The survey was intended as a rapid and non-invasive means of sampling the upper twelve inches of top soil for the existence of metal objects that might be related directly to the battle. The area covered was immediately south and south-west of the existing viewing tower. Prior to the survey, estimates had ranged from between half and one million metal objects that might have been present at the battle. These estimates included not only arrow heads, but horse harnesses, objects of protection, clothing, horseshoes, their fixings etc.

The survey uncovered over 500 metallic objects held in the shallow top soil over the chalk substrate. Although a few of the recovered objects were found to pre-date the battle of Crécy – most being coins and all being non-ferrous – nothing was discovered that could directly be attributed to the battle.[31] This somewhat negative result can perhaps be explained in several ways. The most obvious conclusion is that the area under survey was not where the battle took place. Alternatively, the soil conditions may have since eroded all trace of iron objects. Lastly, since the gleaning of battlefields was a scrupulous art, much if not most of the detritus of battle may have been recovered either directly after the event or in the subsequent years of labour-intensive agriculture.

[29] In an edition of Froissart's *Chroniques*, seemingly privately published by Mme de Witt: Hachette, Paris, 1881.
[30] Bibliothèque municipale d'Abbeville, *Courrier de la Somme*, 5 Sept. 1850.
[31] This survey is unpublished, but may be inspected in the premises of Emhisarc, the local Crécy archaeological society.

Although the survey was non-productive in terms of association with the battle, perhaps few conclusions should be drawn from the results. Most of the battlefield remains to be surveyed, particularly (it must be said) those parts which, since the time of the metal detector survey, might now be considered as nearer the centres of action. The field above the mouth of the valley, where the French dead are said to be buried – and thus an area of potential interest – is unfortunately all 'new ground'. Before the arrival of the transport company on the modest industrial zone, a sugar-beet factory occupied the site. Part of the production process included the removal of soil from the beet in large brick basins. The residual soil that collected at the bottom of these basins was subsequently carted away by tractor to be spread on the field to the north. The current owner of this field, Monsieur Olivier Griffoin, estimates that at least 40 cm of top soil has arrived this way: too deep for a survey by metal detection and sufficient to obscure any trace of the Louandre burial pit from aerial detection.

From a perusal of the evidence, I am persuaded that in the case of the Crécy battlefield, tradition's claim that this is where the great battle took place deserves to remain intact. That such a conclusion is based as much on the circumstantial evidence *for*, as on the lack of evidence *against*, is acknowledged as imperfect. Yet in addition to the balance of probability there remains one further factor that personally dispels doubt. Although the scant and localised archaeological surveys have offered us little in its support, I would suggest that the battlefield, if looked at as a whole, as Seymour de Constant did in the early nineteenth century, has a persuasive voice and a contribution to make in its own support. Hitherto, the battle of Crécy has been commonly described as having been fought across a shallow valley:[32] a description that brings to mind an innocuous and commonplace feature of landscape, a feature that suggests little inherent tactical advantage to one protagonist or the other, and modest, if any, strategic discernment in its pre-selection. A detailed look at the site, however, reveals that this is not the case at all. It suggests that the choice of battlefield was likely to have been a more astute and specific judgement, more suited to Edward and his plan of battle than he has been credited with, and potentially providing some explanation as to why Crécy was the extraordinary victory it was.

The battlefield[33]

The traditional battlefield lies north-east of the village of Crécy-en-Ponthieu, and consists of the gentle western slope and flat-bottomed bed of the valley known as La Vallée des Clercs. Its length from north to south is almost two

---

[32] Burne, *The Crecy War*, p. 170: 'a little valley . . . scooped out of the prevailing high ground'. Oman, *A History of the Art of War in the Middle Ages*, 2nd edn, ii, p. 135: 'The little valley . . . on each side of it a gentle ascent rises to the main level of the downs.' H. Belloc, *Six British Battles* (Bristol, 1931), p. 42: 'this shallow depression . . . on either side . . . lift the soft and inconspicuous slopes that bound it'.

[33] The longitudinal axis of the Vallée des Clercs, and thus effectively the battlefield, runs almost precisely north-east/south-west. However, to spare the reader the hyphens of compass

kilometres, and its width on the floor of the valley at mid-point, is about 200 metres. The width diminishes to approximately 100 metres at either end. Topographically the valley is well defined, though neither a map nor always a cursory visit in person will necessarily do it justice. Its western limit is a ridge (75 metres) running from Crécy at its south to Wadicourt to the north. Its northern limit (65 metres), and diametrically opposed to the traditionally accepted direction of the advancing French army, is the narrowing head of the valley beneath Wadicourt. Its southern limit (35 metres), defined to the west by the rising ground towards Crécy and the sloping side of the valley to the east, is the mouth of the valley where it sweeps down to join the valley of the River Maye. Finally, and critically, its eastern limit is the eastern side of the valley itself, a distinct topographic feature consisting of a tall, steep and almost sheer bank running the full two kilometres of the length of the valley. Generally the height of this bank is between 2.5 and 5.5 metres above the valley floor.

The significance of this bank requires particular emphasis, and the reader is referred to the photograph taken from the southern end of the valley (Plate 2). Figure 1 provides some of its dimensions. This impressive topographic feature, hitherto either ignored or unobserved, would have been a potentially fatal barrier to massed cavalry attempting to charge into and across the valley from the east. No less significantly, to those within the valley, the bank would have presented an obstacle to retreat or escape. While similar obstacles feature in equestrian eventing, descent of this particular bank by literally thousands of horses and armoured men, in the heat of attack, as proposed in a frontal advance of the French cavalry across the valley towards the English lines, would surely have ended in awful disaster.[34] Indeed, it seems reasonable to suggest that the presence of this feature transforms the reputation of the battlefield: from being a shallow or innocuous valley it has become a potential topographic trap. With restricted access into the valley from the east, the principal lines of attack open to the French would have been from the mouth of the valley at the south or, by means of a wider sweep, into the head of the valley from the north. Of these, the most direct approach for a predatory army arriving from Abbeville, particularly as defined by the Chemin de l'Armée, would have been to enter the valley from the south. In both cases, however, these relatively narrow approaches, limited by the width of the valley and perhaps further reduced by missile fire, would have made it impossible for the French to form up on the six or even eight hundred-yard front as has been so often proposed.[35]

It must remain a curiosity why this crucial topographic element of the battlefield has been discussed by neither modern historians nor, indeed, by those

---

bearings, descriptions of the battlefield refer to this axis as being simply north/south. Figures in brackets are heights above sea level.

[34] Almost without exception this is the picture modern historians have provided of the French attack, most of whom support this with plans showing the French cavalry assembled to the east of the valley.

[35] For examples of the frequently accepted French formation and attacking approach, see Bennett, 'The development of battle tactics in the Hundred Years War', p. 9; Burne, *The Crecy War*, p. 179; Sumption, *Trial by Battle*, p. 527; K. DeVries, *Infantry Warfare in the Early Fourteenth Century* (Woodbridge, 1996), p. 165.

writing earlier. That the bank existed, and was observable to nineteenth-century visitors to the battlefield, is evident from a survey drawing made of the battlefield in the first half of that century (Plate 1). Albeit that this plan was drawn nearly five hundred years after the event, it is of particular value to us in two respects. First, the specific topographic features that it records are suggestive of an author who understood the military significance of terrain. Second, it provides a detailed topographic insight into the battlefield before the coming of the sugar-beet factory, the college buildings, or indeed the railway.[36] Unlike the graphically elegant topographic drawing of the battlefield provided by Ramsay,[37] in which the Vallée des Clercs and a southern bank are somewhat lost by the inclusion of Estrées lès Crécy and Fontaine-sur-Maye, the draughtsman of the earlier rendering restricts himself to recording only the principal topographic features of the valley. Free from the 'background interference' of a wider landscape, the militarily significant topography of the battlefield is revealed. Notable is the distinctly marked eastern bank of the valley, indicated by strong banking lines running the full length of the Vallée des Clercs from its mouth to the 'Fond de Wadicourt' at the north. Of equal interest is the recording of several other sections of banking or terracing on the English side of the valley. Prominent among these for its isolation, halfway down the 'English' slope and midway along the valley side, is an arrow-shaped terrace, which juts forward to form a small escarpment pointing towards the eastern bank. Seen on the plan at the centre of the western slope, it almost divides the English side of the battlefield into Crécy and Wadicourt wings. Also shown clearly are a cluster of four lengths of terracing immediately to the east of Crécy, stepping down parallel with the Maye from the traditional windmill site. The ground between this series of terraces and the arrow-shaped bank forms a crescent-shaped rim above a 'bowl' of ground that is the mouth of the valley. Standing there today, beneath a prolific wild apple tree, it is impossible to reject the thought that ringed with archers, and in perfect bow shot, this bowl would have become a deadly cauldron. Finally, at the foot of the English slope, at the northern end of the valley beneath Wadicourt, the plan records a short section of bank, reminiscent of Burne's reference to a 'slight ravine' striking north near Wadicourt.[38]

Almost a solitary voice appearing to recognise the eastern bank and its potential effect upon the battle is that of George Frederick Beltz, who presented a paper to the Society of Antiquaries of London in January 1839. Drawing openly on the work of Louandre, Beltz fixes the English position, 'on the high ground near Cressy . . . its front commanding a ravine on a gentle slope'. He adds tellingly that 'this excellent position attests so much more the military talent of Edward, as it deprived Philip of Valois of the power of employing his cavalry with success, except on his right'.[39] This last and surprisingly specific remark

---

[36] Until removed in the 1950s, a railway ran up the valley, on a small embankment, between Crécy and Dompierre. The embankment remains and is certainly the 'bump towards the bottom of the slope' [of the valley], referred to by Nicolle, *Crécy 1346*, p. 52.

[37] J. Ramsay, *Genesis of Lancaster, 1307–99*, 2 vols (Oxford, 1913), i, between pp. 328 and 329. Note that this was Burne's preferred map of the battlefield (*The Crecy War*, p. 191).

[38] Burne, *The Crecy War*, p. 191.

[39] G.F. Beltz 'An inquiry into the existing narratives of the battle of Cressy, with some

Plate 2. The traditional battlefield of Crécy: view of the bank on the eastern
side of the Vallée des Clercs, looking north

clearly implies impedimenta to a frontal attack consistent with a recognition of
the tactical importance of the 'ravine' or bank opposite the English position, a
recognition that can be attributed directly to Louandre, or perhaps more appro-
priately to the earlier work of Seymour de Constant.[40] That fifty or more years
later Oman should have described the valley as having 'on each side of it a
gentle ascent [rising] to the main level of the downs' is not only mysterious.[41]
An essential element of his description is its erroneous suggestion of a
symmetry of slope between the western and eastern sides of the valley. That
Oman considered this to be the case, and thus for the eastern descent into the
valley to be as accessible as that from the west, is made explicit by his use of 'on
each side' and 'to right or left'. Such a description was not only as misleading
then as is evident now, but it permitted – if not encouraged – Oman to base his
account of the battle on an approach of the French from 'the Estrées plateau'.[42]
Had he recognised the presence of the bank, his observation that the 'main stress
seems to have fallen on the southern "battle" . . . because the enemy emerging
from the Fontaine–Abbeville road made haste to strike at the nearest foe' would

account of its localities, traditions and remains', *Archaeologia*, xxviii (1840), p. 178. Cf.
F.-C. Louandre, *Histoire d'Abbeville* (Abbeville, 1834), p. 429: on the English position:
'devant son front, un ravin en pente douce'.
[40] Baron Seymour de Constant 'Bataille de Cressy', *France Littéraire*, 1832, p. 566, '. . . et
dominant dans son front un ravin en pente douce'.
[41] He adds, more suggestive of personal experience, that 'when this ascent is climbed, to
right or left, the pedestrian finds himself on an undulating plateau'. Oman, *A History of the
Art of War in the Middles Ages*, 2nd edn, ii, p. 135.
[42] Oman, *A History of the Art of War in the Middles Ages*, 2nd edn, ii, p. 141.

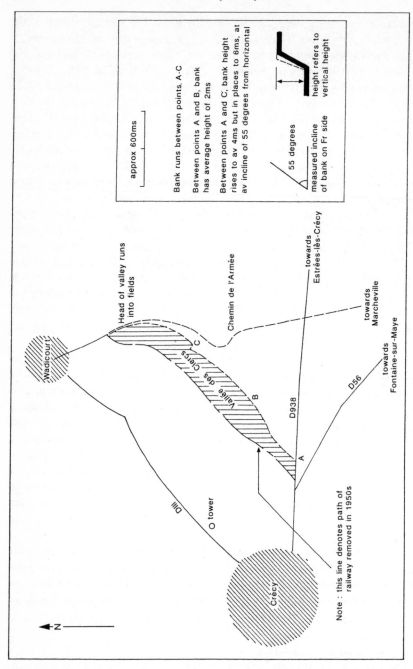

Figure 1. The traditional battlefield of Crécy: survey of the bank

perhaps have been even more logical.[43] Belloc goes even further, stating of the eastern bank that it 'is much easier and more gentle even than its counterpart'.[44]

Oman and Belloc should not be singled out. The extent of the obscurity that the eastern bank still enjoys is demonstrated in a recent book by Kelly DeVries, in which the reader is referred to Burne for 'good modern descriptions of the battlefield'.[45] That students of the battle of Crécy should be referred to Burne is understandable, and not least for this reason; but because his descriptions of the battlefield continue to impress military historians, it is essential to take a closer look at the actual battlefield that Burne describes. The description of the Vallée des Clercs that rewards the reader of Burne is 'a little valley . . . scooped out of the prevailing high ground'.[46] In his account of the battle no reference is made to the imposing eastern side of the valley, despite the inclusion in his appendix chapter of a passing mention, perhaps in respect to Louandre, of a slight ravine at the northern end of the valley.[47] Clearly, however, Burne attached no importance to this ravine, since, as he notes of Edward's position, 'the left had merely the small village of Wadicourt as protection, with open country beyond'.[48] That Burne should have ignored the bank on the eastern side of the valley is made more remarkable when one observes his drawing of a view from the English line looking down into the Vallée des Clercs. Here one can clearly see the dark outline of the formidable bank, but, flowing over it in three places, his arrowed lines indicate the advance of the French army.

The reason why Burne (and others) have omitted to mention this bank may never be known, but there could be two explanations. The first, and perhaps the most likely, is that he failed to observe it. From a distance, this can be excusable. When seen from the road on the English side, almost exactly one kilometre away, the bank frequently appears as no more than a thin line, resembling that of a hedge. Depending upon crop conditions there can be even greater deception. In high summer, when both valley and the field beyond are in the stubble of wheat, the wild grass of the bank takes on an identical colour, so that the two fields merge. Indeed the greater shock, as the author can testify, can be to approach the bank from the Estrées side. Descending towards the valley from the east, the presence of the bank can become apparent only a few metres from its edge.

A second, though (in the absence of published discussion) less probable explanation for the neglect of this imposing physical feature is that it has been observed by historians but considered to be man-made, post-dating the battle of Crécy and therefore irrelevant. While the sheer physical presence and scale of

---

43 Oman, *A History of the Art of War in the Middles Ages*, 2nd edn, ii, p. 144.

44 Belloc, *Six British Battles*, pp. 42–3.

45 DeVries, *Infantry Warfare in the Early Fourteenth Century*, p. 160 n. 23. Cf. Bennett, 'The development of battle tactics in the Hundred Years War', pp. 1–2: '[Burne] deserves credit for the work he did in exploring battlefields and his observations may be perceptive'.

46 Burne, *The Crecy War*, p. 170.

47 Burne, *The Crecy War*, p. 191: 'Of the grave-pits . . . the other high up the Vallées aux Clercs where a slight ravine strikes north to Wadicourt.' Cf. Louandre and de Constant: above, notes 39 and 40.

48 Burne, *The Crecy War*, p. 170.

such an impressive bank may seem to deserve no such suspicion, for two reasons this possibility needs to be addressed. The first is simply the fundamental consequences of the existence of the bank on the interpretation of the battle. The second is the assertion by some archaeologists that similar though generally lesser banks are the result of early agricultural practices and are thus man-made.[49] For this reason and because traces of smaller banks remain visible on the western slope of the valley and thus may have offered potential defensive elements for the English, these features deserve closer consideration.

These terraced banks, or *rideaux*,[50] have been attributed to the action of early agricultural cultivation of long, narrow fields across the slope of a valley. Their formation derives from such fields being typically delimited by either hedges, ditches or stones, which in the course of time arrest the gradual downhill erosion of topsoil destabilised by the action of ploughing and harrowing. The result is long strips of level field forming terraced steps or lynchets parallel to the contours of a valley. In northern Europe, agricultural systems in which lynchets were a feature have been dated back to the early Bronze Age of three thousand years ago.

Although the bank forming the eastern side of the valley is significantly larger than a typical lynchet, its potential impact on the dynamics of the battle require that its provenance be established. The author is very grateful, therefore, to have received an opinion from Professor Jean Sommé of Lille University.[51] While acknowledging that the origins of these *rideaux* are still occasionally discussed as being either natural or man-made, in his judgement they should be considered to be ancient topographic features. As such, we should regard the eastern bank of the valley to have been an element of the landscape at the time of the battle. As corroborative evidence for the age of the bank, Jean Sommé observes that the boundary line between the adjacent communes of Crécy-en-Ponthieu and Estrées-lès-Crécy follows the direct line of the bank for the length of the valley.[52] This is consistent with the medieval preference for boundary lines to be associated with banks and, as he adds further, suggests an origin in an ancient agricultural regime.

If we can be confident, therefore, about the authenticity and antiquity of the bank forming the east side of the valley, what of the western slope and its *rideaux*? The clearest picture we can have of this part of the battlefield, from at least more than one hundred and sixty years ago, is the early survey drawing of the battlefield. This clearly records the jutting *rideau* in the centre of the English slope, a further rideau to the north by Wadicourt, and the cluster of *rideaux* directly to the east of Crécy, stepping down parallel to the River Maye. If the

---

[49] For a general article on such banks, see E. Balandra, 'Les "rideaux" ou "royons" picards aux xiii et xiv siècles', *Bulletin de la Société d'Emulation Abbeville*, xxiv/5 (1980), pp. 757–63.

[50] Called 'linches' or 'lynchets' in English and 'royons' in Picard, they are referred to as 'raidillons' by Burne and Hardy. Burne, *The Crecy War*, p. 171; R. Hardy, *The Longbow* (Sparkford, 1976, repr. 1998), p. 66.

[51] Professor Jean Sommé, Professor of Geomorphology, Faculty of Science and Technology, Lille University (Laboratoire de Géomorphologie et d'Étude du Quaternaire).

[52] See IGN map 1/25000 Hesdin 5–6.

existence of the eastern bank may have obliged the French to enter the valley from the south and north, the existence of the *rideaux* on the western slope of the valley, not least those above the mouth of the valley, may gain in significance. What, therefore, can be said of the reliability of the record of these *rideaux*, and their age? That the early plan has an inherent reliability (greater, indeed, than those of subsequent plans) can be attested by a visit to the existing east bank. Indeed, a comparison of the plan with a modern topographic map of the battlefield demonstrates a reliable correlation between the *rideaux* it records and those shown today. With little exception, these are banks of two or more metres in height. This supports the supposition that the early plan records only features of topographic significance, as well as underlining their potential military significance.[53] As far as the existence of these *rideaux* at the time of the battle is concerned, the author is again grateful to have received an opinion from Professor Jean Sommé. In his view these, like the eastern bank, are likely to have been present on the day of the battle.

The full extent of these *rideaux* in the fourteenth century is difficult to estimate now, not least at the south-western end of the battlefield, which has suffered most from man's recent interference. As has been pointed out earlier, the level of the land to the west of the mouth of the valley has been built up by at least 40 cm by the spreading of reject soil from the old sugar-beet factory, while further up the slope towards the ridge, the ground has been significantly disturbed by the building of a college and its recreation ground. Despite both this and modern farming practices, surprisingly good examples of the *rideaux* shown on the early plan remain intact.

A further insight into the battlefield that our early plan provides is its omission of any record of a bank at the base of the western slope. Seen today, this is initially surprising, because at the point where the western slope meets the valley floor a substantial track runs the full length of the valley, raised on a small embankment reminiscent of a typical *rideau*.[54] Reference, however, to an earlier IGN map reveals that this was the sleeper bed of a small-gauge railway line,[55] running northwards from Crécy to Wadicourt, and removed in the 1950s. (It will be of interest later to note here that this line emerged from the valley to the south of Wadicourt, and continued north towards the valley of the Authie.) Some reliance can be placed on there not having been a *rideau* at the base of the western slope of the valley from the fact that at the extreme northern end, to the south of Wadicourt, the early plan shows only one distinct length of *rideau*, which does not continue southwards. To the west of this feature, towards the Wadicourt ridge, modern maps show a length of terracing that is still evident today. Curiously, despite detailing many of the buildings in and around Wadicourt itself, our early map does not record it. One explanation might be drawn from a unique feature of this terrace: that the ground beneath its slope is markedly dished. Such sunken forms can be the result of an underground collapse of the substrate, as in

---

[53] For those who wish to judge the defensive qualities of these *rideaux*, they are typically of two metres in height and have a forward slope of 55 degrees from the horizontal.

[54] See photo of the track with a bus on it in Hardy, *The Longbow*, p. 67.

[55] Referred to in Oman, *A History of the Art of War in the Middles Ages*, 2nd edn, ii, p. 135.

the formation of 'sink holes', collapses that in certain areas of local farmland still occur today. It does, however, meet one criterion of a 'rideau', namely that it lies parallel to contour lines. Without excavation, we should perhaps treat this banking with particular caution.

Finally, while dwelling on the upper reaches of the valley, it is worth noting that its northern extreme, known now as the 'Fond de Wadicourt', sees an end to the stark eastern bank. Here the floor of the valley rises up to meet that part of the plain that lies between Wadicourt and the Forêt de Labroye, allowing the (now dismantled) railway to have continued towards Dompierre to the north. Indeed, it is instructive to note that a line drawn along the north/south axis of the valley leads almost directly to Labroye. This, and the impassability of the eastern bank of the valley appear to have eluded Burne entirely – so much so that he states of Philip's flight to Labroye that it was 'an extraordinary direction to take . . . instead of to the rear'.[56] This is a telling remark, not least with its emphasis, because the truth is, of course, that 'the rear' referred to and defined by Burne's illustration of the battle was simply not available as a means of retreat. Indeed, the further one ventures up the valley the greater the obstacle the bank becomes, so much so that for the greater part of its length it would have been suicide for man and war horse in urgent and perhaps poor repair even to consider an attempt to scale it.[57] Furthermore, if it is reasonable to imagine the mouth of the valley becoming choked with dead,[58] then its northern end, pointing towards Labroye, may have offered one of few exits from a valley that resembled a gauntlet of death. That Burne expresses such astonishment at the direction of Philip's retreat, and specifically suggests that the logical route was 'to the rear', implies that his entire analysis of the battle failed to take into account the presence and, thus, significance of the east bank of the valley, and vitally, the limitations it imposed upon the French. This is perhaps all the more remarkable when one considers that the battlefield discussed in such detail, indeed visited, by Burne and others, is the very same as that which exists today.

The Maye

Though not a part of the actual battlefield, in a medieval landscape the River Maye would have formed an effective southern limit to the comings and goings of events in the valley immediately to its north. Certainly any army approaching the English position from Abbeville would have taken some consideration of the crossing of the river, and it is interesting to note that the Chemin de l'Armée crosses the Maye immediately downstream from its source, presumably before depth and width were of too great a consequence. Having said this, unless seen in winter when it struggles to carry the run-off from the surrounding fields and frequently fails, it can appear as little more than a stream. Certainly in summer

---

[56] Burne, *The Crecy War*, p. 183 n. 1.

[57] Strangely, it is at the northern end of the valley that Burne seems to acknowledge the existence of a 'ravine', but then ignores it. *The Crecy War*, p. 191.

[58] *Jean le Bel*, ii, p. 103.

this would be a fair description. However, three pieces of evidence suggest that at the time of the battle the Maye may have been both wider and deeper. The first is perhaps no more than anecdotal, and concerns the derivation of the name of the village of Crécy-en-Ponthieu. Written originally as 'Cressy', this toponym reflects the fact that the settlement was known for the extensive water-cress beds that stretched out from either bank of the Maye as it skirted the village. Given the natural conditions favoured by water-cress, it is no hard step to imagine the river being sprawled across its valley both to the west and east of the village, just as it does to the west of the village today.

The second piece of evidence perhaps deserves more respect, and combines the discovery of a remarkable collection of pottery (dated as coincident with the battle of Crécy),[59] with evidence applicable to the River Maye. Recent excavations at the site of the medieval 'Château Fort' of Crécy revealed a concealed chamber accessible only from an entrance let into the side of the ancient and disused well. Both the base of this chamber and the well shaft beneath its entrance had been used historically as a place of disposal. During excavation work by the local archaeological society to recover the pottery, the lower section of the well shaft was also excavated of material to its natural base. On completion of excavation, an examination was made of the levels of 'tide lines' left historically by the water levels within the original well. These suggest that at the time of the battle of Crécy the water table, at least around the well, was perhaps up to one metre higher than it is today. Water tables, of course, can be notoriously individual, dictated frequently by highly localised geological conditions. However, it has been estimated that this well, being sunk into the natural chalk substrate that underlies all of Crécy, shares the same water table as that of the Maye. In support of this, and perhaps inconsistent with Oman's description of the Maye as 'an insignificant thread of water', is archaeological evidence that indicates that at least one water mill was operational just to the west of Crécy in the late thirteenth century.[60] It will be a matter of judgement as to how much water is needed to provide rotational power for an efficient mill, and for that matter how much energy is suggested by 'an insignificant thread of water'. Nevertheless, the change of level between the Maye immediately south of the battlefield and the traditional site of the water mill is little more than five metres, a sufficient fall to generate power, provided that there is a quantity of water upstream.

It seems reasonable, therefore, to imagine that in 1346 the Maye, at its point directly to the south of the battlefield, was to some degree wider than we see it today. A potential consequence of this for the dynamics of the battle is that if the French were inclined to approach the English from the mouth of the valley, the width of their advancing front would have been limited on their northern flank by the eastern bank of the valley, and on their southern flank by the Maye. It is clear, from reference to the map, that this would reduce their frontal width from the six to seven hundred yards that is indicated in traditional versions of the

---

[59] Available for inspection at the Emhisarc Museum in Crécy.

[60] The receiver of Ponthieu's account book indicates that there were two seigneurial watermills in or around Crécy in 1331. E101/166/2, fos 7r, 17r, 18r.

battle to a maximum of perhaps three hundred yards or less in an approach from the south. It can be readily seen that attempting to get even 20,000 men into the valley by what effectively would have been a bottleneck – this without its diminishment by fallen dead – would have been testing. Certainly for those who chose to flee the cauldron of arrow storm that was taking place within the adjacent valley, the lazy Maye, stretched wide to the south, could have been an hindrance to a massed and pursued retreat.

Agriculture and the battlefield

Having looked at certain specific aspects of the battlefield it may be useful to draw back and briefly consider its general appearance on the day of the battle, more than 650 years ago. Such an exercise must of necessity be one of speculation, but with that proviso, it should help to fix a better picture of the sort of terrain over which the battle may have been fought. By the early fourteenth century agriculture in northern France was well developed.[61] The clearance of land for systemised agriculture had taken place centuries before, and the sweeping countryside enclosed between the villages of Crécy, Wadicourt and Estrées lès Crécy, set back from the forest by the River Maye and overseen by windmills, would have been natural agricultural terrain. Thus the landscape viewed by both Edward and Philip would have been a chequered mixture of untouched nature and contrasting geometric systems broadly reflecting land ownership, management and contemporary diet. Occasionally, between these two will have been areas of reclamation, a process of continuing agrarian necessity driven by that of demographic expansion. Although, unlike Italy and England, France had yet to produce written work on the theories of husbandry, practices had nevertheless been refined. Respect for the efficacy of fertilisation of the soil, crop rotation and fallowing of land was well established, as was the benefit of certain crops to the productivity of soil. Almost uniquely in France in the thirteenth century, marling of the fields was practised in Picardie. (Although undoubtedly linked to geology, it is perhaps worth noting in the context of Ponthieu that the right to sink marl pits within one's own land had been granted to the English by statute in 1225.) Though involving a significantly greater capital cost, the horse (where yields of oats allowed) had replaced the ox as the means of traction and had subsequently brought new efficiencies to the processes of ploughing, harrowing and sowing. Furthermore, in what has been called the 'painification de la France', the farmer was now seen as the bread-basket not only of his family but also of the community as a whole. Consequently, we can expect much of the farmland to have been devoted to essential cereals: rye, barley, oats and wheat. In addition, from the mid-thirteenth century, the value to the land, as well as to the belly, of the cultivation of vegetables, such as peas, lentils, beans and vetch, had been appreciated. We

---

[61] For a general history, see G. Duby and A. Wallon, *Histoire de la France rurale, vol.1* (Paris, 1975).

should expect evidence of these alongside areas of fallowed land, used for the rearing of livestock.

Thus, arriving towards the battlefield in late August, we can begin to imagine a landscape chequered with ordered fields and scattered with woodland. Perhaps with the imminence of battle, there would have been an absence of people and much of the livestock. We can picture the Maye and its meandering path, over-hung by willow and widening into broad bands of shallow green and water meadow. For an army like Edward's, and indeed for that of the French arriving from Abbeville, we can safely predict the lure this presented to the thirst of both horse and man. Who can doubt that before the battle the horseflesh of both armies drank by the banks of the Maye around Crécy? Looking up the Vallée des Clercs, its floor was perhaps a patchwork of fields in post-harvest colours, their boundaries defined by discarded stones or low raised banks. And the western slope where the English gathered was perhaps striped by bands of meandering field, some recently under the plough, some in the faded green of summer, both defined by kept hedges or simply bare terracing. It seems likely that at the base of the lowest terrace, or certainly within the floor of the valley, a ditch would have directed the surface water of the upper valley and its sides down towards the Maye.[62] Protruding from both Wadicourt and Crécy, as close to homes as was practically possible, would have been enclosures for the keeping of pigs and chickens. Here also, most probably, were small orchards of fruit trees, and patches of herbs, and here and there beehives. And close to the windmill or windmills up on the ridge it seems reasonable to imagine huddles of buildings perhaps sheltering slightly downhill from the prevailing winds.

If this suggests a landscape not so very different from rural France before the First World War it should not be too surprising. The principal developments of agriculture that established the field system of land management had occurred prior to the fourteenth century, and although more land came under the plough, much of the landscape, equipment and practices before and at the turn of the twentieth century would have been instantaneously recognisable to farmers of centuries before. Indeed, if one seeks a brief but familiar image of Edward's army marching across France, one could do worse than recall the endless lines of draught and mounted horse of the Great War, moving across open countryside towards the front.

What, if anything, can this offer the historian of the battle of Crécy? It is impossible to say whether the valley floor across which the French charged was in scant stubble or already ploughed, or indeed in part fallow; only that none would have presented much difficulty to approaching cavalry. It is tempting to imagine potholes being more easily sunk in freshly ploughed ground (if we are to believe the testimony of Geoffrey Baker),[63] but the odds facing Edward's army would have equally motivated the digging of hard baked earth. Ditches may have been obstacles, and if the anecdotal stories of a heavy downpour are true, perhaps the valley drain was wet and heavy. Where lynchets occurred,

---

[62] The early plan of the battlefield indicates a ditch or stream rising beyond the head of the valley and draining into the Maye.

[63] But see below, Chapter 9, pp. 334–42.

combined with ditches or hedges, then these would have been a serious disincentive to advancement, even to accomplished horsemen blessed with great élan. The falling ground of a ditch at the base of a rearing bank would have slowed the very best horse and horseman to a near stop in order to negotiate it. And if the western slope was a terrace of fields, even in part, it would nevertheless have been a daunting prospect to attack, especially with no supporting missile cover. Perhaps a glance at the agriculture of the battlefield offers but few things. It suggests that the valley was accessible, that marl pits for the burial of the dead may well have existed, and that, harvest permitting, those fortunate enough to have survived may have supped rather better than we are led to believe.

The testimony of the chronicles

Nothing that the chronicles or other narrative sources have left us by way of a description of either the battle or battlefield can lead us to the ground. They are at best slender, anecdotal and occasionally conflicting references, some so general as to suit any battlefield, others containing suggestions of detail. Nevertheless, no look at the traditional battlefield would be complete without asking what if any light these references cast on the location of the battle.

The physical features of the field are rarely mentioned by the chroniclers of Crécy.[64] Although several of French provenance mention the reinforcement of hedges to strengthen the English position,[65] there is no explicit reference in any of our sources to the bank on the eastern side of the Vallée des Clercs. Indeed, Jean le Bel insists that the battle was fought on an open field without ditches, though this – like King Edward's report that the action took place 'en plain champ' – reads like a stock description, intended to dispel any suggestion that the victory could be attributed to the exploitation of advantageous ground.[66] With the *Chronique des quatre premiers Valois*, which notes the French arrival at 'la valée de Cressi', we may think that we catch a glimpse of the traditional battlefield,[67] but for an indication of the slope upon which the waves of French cavalry broke against the English line, it is necessary to turn to the administrative records documenting the loss of war horses in 'la bataille du mont de Cressy'.[68]

Three aspects of the role played by the Genoese crossbowmen in events on the battlefield are frequently spoken of in the chronicles: first, that their bowstrings were affected by rain;[69] second, that their aim was hampered by the

---

64 For a detailed examination of these narrative sources, see Chapter 9.

65 *Chronique Normande*, pp. 80–1; *Chronographia*, ii, p. 232; *Chronique des quatre premiers Valois*, p. 16. But perhaps we should be cautious in interpreting these 'hedges', since the short continuation of the *Chronique de Flandre* notes that the English 'firent une grande haye de leur charroy'. *Chronique de Flandre*, ii, p. 42.

66 *Jean le Bel*, ii, p. 106; also, *Récits*, p. 229.

67 *Chronique des quatre premiers Valois*, p. 16.

68 P. Contamine, *Guerre, état et société à la fin du moyen âge* (Paris, 1972), p. 105.

69 *Jean de Venette*, ed. Newhall, pp. 43, 176–7.

sun;[70] and, third, that their subsequent retreat was cruelly obstructed by an enraged French cavalry.[71] The first of these must remain obscure, but of the other two we can perhaps at least attempt some comment. In every account of the battle, at least those that accept the present site and general English position, it is assumed that the Genoese would have been shooting towards the sun. Even if no such account existed, common sense would suggest that in their choice of battle ground the English captains, being positioned on their own chosen ground, would instinctively wish their archers to have the sun if not behind them then certainly not in their eyes. Opinions may differ about how the longbow was used, and perhaps for the initial 'showers of arrows' precision was not a priority. But as the battle was pressed and range diminished, for countrymen, hunters and foresters to whom economy of ammunition, precision and personal survival would have been second nature, the advantage of light and visibility of target would have been equally instinctive. In this respect their position at Crécy was perfectly provided for.

The slaughter of (or at least attack upon) the retreating Genoese by the advancing French cavalry attracts a greater logic when one considers the 'new battlefield'. Having in all probability entered the Vallée des Clercs from the south and coming under English attack, the early retreat of the Genoese would logically have consisted of turning about and seeking escape by the same way. But if the oncoming army behind were funnelling into the valley, and with both crossbowmen and cavalry pressed close to the east to avoid missile attack, it seems hard to imagine that conflict between these two bodies of men could have been avoided. A clash would certainly have been more likely in such a confined space than in the open battlefield of traditional accounts.

The only geographical reference to the battlefield left to us by Froissart places it loosely 'between Crécy and Labroye',[72] and not, as one might expect with the privilege of modern maps, between Crécy and Estrées lès Crécy. This curiosity may be magnified when one considers that Labroye is some distance from Crécy. Thus, the description can be likened to locating one's nose between one's eyes and one's feet. Certainly at first glance Crécy and Labroye are an unlikely pair of co-ordinates to fix a battle that was fought so close to Crécy. And indeed the mention of the more remote Labroye, both as Philip's first sanctuary[73] and as the other co-ordinate, clearly struck Burne as both curious and geographically illogical. However, the logic of these co-ordinates takes on a

---

[70] *Froissart*, ed. Luce, iii, p. 176.

[71] *Froissart*, ed. Luce, iii, p. 178.

[72] *Froissart*, ed. Luce, iii, p. 181. This particular locational reference is not mentioned by Froissart's exemplar, Jean le Bel, but is probably ultimately derived from that earlier chronicler's work, since le Bel does record Philip's flight to Labroye – a simple statement that Froissart expands into a dramatic episode. Le Bel states that the battle took place 'assez prez de Cressy en Ponthyeu'. *Jean le Bel*, ii, p. 104. However, it should be noted that the anonymous Bourgeois of Valenciennes also recorded that the battle was fought 'entre Cressi et la Broye' (*Récits*, p. 232), as did the Gilles le Muisit, who wrote, within a few years of the engagement, that it took place 'in campo inter villam de La Broye et villam de Crecy en Pontiu' (*Gilles le Muisit*, p. 160).

[73] *Froissart*, ed. Luce, iii, p. 185.

clarity when one looks in greater detail at the battlefield: it recognises that the valley has no practical east–west axis. Failure to recognise this prevented Burne (and others) from perceiving the impossibility of retreat to the east, and obscured from him the fact that the singular and longitudinal north–south axis of the valley points directly towards Labroye. As soon as one accepts that the northern end of the valley provided one of only two means of escape, and that this was almost certainly the escape route of the wounded Philip, the logic of the geographical and historic reference between Crécy and Labroye establishes itself. Indeed, if one plots a line of a retreat from the northern end of the valley, the first community along such a direction of retreat and escape is Labroye. And if Froissart's placement of the battle as between Crécy and Labroye derives from Philip having taken refuge at Labroye, there is perhaps not only a consistency between fact and account, but one that is supported by a closer look at the evidence of the battlefield itself.

Although Henry Knighton's account of the battle may be at variance with standard accounts,[74] it is of interest to us here because of its unique and specific geographic reference to an area in which he states fighting took place. His 'campo de Westglyse' points directly to an area west or north-west of Wadicourt, signalled today by the presence of a remote farmstead known as Watteglise.[75] It is unclear whether Knighton intends to locate the entire battle in a field near 'Westglyse' or whether he is recording that some fighting, perhaps notably that which extended into the night, occurred there. Of the first there is no way of telling, except perhaps to observe that the ground around Watteglise is the very summit of the surrounding plain, flat and open, and a most unlikely place for an army seeking a defensive position upon which to make battle. If, however, we interpret the reference to mean that, very late in the night, fighting took place around 'Westglyse', then this is not only consistent with indicating the general direction outside Crécy that Edward's army assembled, but consistent with the battle decaying into pursuits and skirmishes late into the evening, notably close to a natural exit from the valley. Indeed, as we have seen, retreat from and towards the north of the battlefield is borne out by Philip's flight to Labroye, and the similar dispersal of thousands of troops would suggest fighting may have taken place in a wide area all about the 'formal' battlefield.

With few exceptions,[76] the site of the traditional battlefield of Crécy has been tacitly or explicitly accepted by military historians for more than 150 years. This can perhaps be explained by the simple acceptance of precedent, but also by the fact that, circumstantial though the evidence might be, on balance it points more directly to the site claimed for the battle by tradition than to any alternative. While the absence of archaeological evidence means that, technically, the jury

---

[74] *Knighton*, ed. Martin, p. 61, n. 1.

[75] 'Nam pugnauerant usque ad profundam noctem, in campo de Westglyse iuxta Cressy' ('they fought into the dead of night, in the field of Westglyse outside Crécy'): *Knighton*, ed. Martin, pp. 62–3.

[76] J. Bradbury, *The Medieval Archer* (Woodbridge, 1985), p. 105: 'we do not know precisely where the battlefield was and so cannot base our descriptions on the nature of a site that we have chosen'.

must remain out, no evidence exists to suggest that tradition has been the victim of deception. The undisputed references to 'Cressy', the accepted directions of convergence of both the English and French armies, and indeed the specific mention of 'Westglyse' by Knighton, all support the battle having been fought close by the village of Crécy-en-Ponthieu. Although beyond this, the evidence dilutes, the collective toponymic echoes, the windmill, the innocuous nature of alternative sites, and the remarkable tactical potential of the traditional site, come forward in support rather than contradiction. In the author's view, therefore, those who have based their histories on the traditional battlefield have been justified in doing so, though whether their subsequent interpretations have fully appreciated its topography and thus military value is a matter of judgement.

Among those who have accepted the traditional battlefield are some of the most eminent military historians of the period, including not a few who have been sufficiently confident of the site to have based their descriptions of the battle on an apparently detailed appraisal of the ground. Almost without exception, however, these descriptions and plans of the battle oblige the French cavalry to advance upon the English position on a wide front across a precipitous bank – much of which for the length of the valley is four or more metres in height – and then, as we have seen from Burne, for the French to retreat up it. Curious though it may be that the eastern bank has hitherto attracted no mention from a formidable array of military historians, we can be grateful to the author of the early plan of the battlefield for its virtue of economy. Indeed, a comparison of this drawing with that offered by Sir James Ramsay perhaps underlines the essential value of recording only specific features of the terrain. But if military historians' failure to observe the existence of the eastern bank of the Vallée des Clercs must remain a curiosity, of real importance is the bank's influence on the battle, specifically the manner in which it may have limited and dictated the French approach. If we accept that an influence was inevitable, and that the hitherto assumed massed wide frontal attack from the plateau of Estrées-lès-Crécy was physically unlikely, if not impossible, as would have been any retreat except by the north or the south, then it would seem that the choice of battlefield at Crécy by Edward III, his tactics, the deployment of his archers, the debate on the herce, and on lines and or wings, and the course of the battle, deserve further consideration.[77]

[77] For a discussion of the 'herce', see Bradbury, *The Medieval Archer*, pp. 95–104.

4

The Battle of Crécy[1]

MICHAEL PRESTWICH

It is impossible to reconstruct the past. The historian can, at best, do no more than present a crude outline, a sketch in which many of the details are missing. Medieval battles present particular problems. Even contemporaries would have found it impossible to gain a full picture of events that were inevitably confused and confusing. Individual participants will have had vivid stories to tell about their part in a conflict, but will not have been in a good position to know what happened overall. Communications on the battlefield were difficult, and commanders must have found it impossible to know what was happening in all sectors. To make matters worse, the chroniclers who wrote about the events were rarely present, and were unlikely to have military experience. Accounts may not only be inconsistent in different sources, but even within the same source. The generally reliable *Life of Edward II*, for example, contains two divergent accounts of the death of the earl of Gloucester at Bannockburn, which the author did not even attempt to reconcile.[2] A further problem is that medieval audiences did not want to know the same things as modern historians. Questions of strategy and tactics had little fascination for them. This helps to explain why newsletters written by those on campaign leave so much unanswered. Frequently, the problem facing medieval historians is that of a lack of evidence, but an over-abundance of potentially contradictory sources can create even more difficulties. The battle of Crécy was one of the most notable events of the fourteenth century. Its astonishing outcome reverberated around Europe, and accordingly many chroniclers described it, in England, France, Italy and elsewhere. Not surprisingly, the stories they tell are far from consistent one with another.

The chroniclers tried their best to describe the English triumph at Crécy. Jean le Bel, a Hainaulter whose work provided a basis for Jean Froissart's later narrative, obtained accounts from both sides. He recorded what he was told in person by the count of Hainault, and ten or twelve knights who had accompanied him, whose horses had been killed under them in the battle. He also put down what he was told by various English and German knights. His inclusion of the name of one of the Germans, Races Massures, suggests that he may have been an

[1] I am very grateful to Sir Philip Preston and Andrew Ayton for their advice and help in writing this chapter.
[2] *Vita Edwardi Secundi*, ed. N. Denholm-Young (London, 1957), pp. 52–3.

informant.[3] Gilles li Muisit, a French chronicler, found that the fact that some wrote about the battle from the French side, and others from the English, added to his problems. His solution was that 'I will write only those things which I have heard from certain trustworthy persons . . . not however affirming them to be totally accurate.'[4] Most chroniclers did not indicate what their sources for the battle were. They must have used some information gleaned from men who had fought at Crécy. There were also newsletters sent home to England, but these are not as good a source as might be expected, for they provide little detail of the fighting. Edward himself sent a letter to his officials in London detailing the first part of the campaign, up to the capture of Caen, and another to Thomas Lucy, once he reached Calais. Among other surviving letters there is one from Richard Wynkeley, the king's confessor, but he provides no useful details about the battle. 'The battle was fierce and long-drawn out, because the enemy bore themselves nobly,' was all that Michael Northburgh, one of Edward III's officials, had to say.[5] Historians have to amalgamate the various accounts to construct a convincing whole, but this involves a difficult process of selection. One approach, often adopted, is simply to ignore the pieces of the puzzle that do not fit, and to tell a story based on a single tradition, usually that represented by Froissart. Among English historians, Colonel Burne's account has been highly influential. He employed his theory of 'inherent military probability' to construct it; however, it is very possible that in all too many cases military events were too improbable and fortuitous for this to be a reliable method.[6]

The build-up to the battle is well described in the sources.[7] The English army succeeded in forcing a crossing of the Somme on 24 August, using the ford at Blanquetaque. The river was tidal at this point, and the ford was defended by Godemar du Fay, with a reasonable force. The English, however, were able to force the crossing by skilful use of their archers. The entire army was able to get to the north bank of the river in little more than an hour. The main French army appeared later in the day, on the southern bank. The two armies faced each other across the marshy river that evening, and most of the next day. The French, however, wisely decided not to fight there. To cross the river in the face of the English archers would have been an act of utter folly. The one action that did take place was one of those chivalric incidents that chroniclers, and no doubt those present, so much enjoyed. A French knight challenged the English to send a knight to joust three times with him, to prove his love for his lady. Thomas

---

[3]   *Jean le Bel*, ii, pp. 105–6. The section dealing with the battle is conveniently translated in *The Wars of Edward III*, ed. C.J. Rogers (Woodbridge, 1999), pp. 131–5. For 'Races Massures', see Chapter 5, pp. 175, 249.

[4]   Translation taken from K. DeVries, *Infantry Warfare in the Early Fourteenth Century* (Woodbridge, 1996), p. 160.

[5]   *Murimuth*, p. 216; *Avesbury*, p. 369. The newsletters are discussed by Fowler, 'News from the front', pp. 76–84. See also Chapter 9, pp. 292–5.

[6]   A.H. Burne, *The Crecy War* (London, 1955), p. 12. 'When in particular doubt or difficulty, I have applied the test of what I call Inherent Military Probability to the problem, and what I.M.P. tells me, I usually accept.' The most recent accounts of the battle are by DeVries, *Infantry Warfare in the Early Fourteenth Century*, pp. 155–75; C.J. Rogers, *War Cruel and Sharp* (Woodbridge, 2000), pp. 266–71; and D. Nicolle, *Crécy 1346* (Oxford, 2000).

[7]   For a detailed discussion, see Chapter 2, pp. 85–107.

Colville met the challenge. All went well in the first two exchanges, but one knight's shield was broken. The two men decided that a further joust without a shield would be too dangerous, and they became firm friends for life.[8]

Philip VI withdrew his forces from Blanquetaque to Abbeville. The English moved northwards, through the forest of Crécy, where they camped for the night near its eastern fringe.[9] On the next day, 26 August, they took up position near the village of Crécy, ready to engage the French as they marched northwards. It is clear that Edward made a deliberate decision to stand and fight. The reasons for this are debatable. The traditional argument is that Edward realised that he could no longer outrun his enemies, and that it was better to stand and fight on ground of his choice than to be pursued and caught by the French. Such opinions match modern views on other periods of medieval warfare. In the eleventh century 'Battle was a desperate business; the risks terrible; the outcome uncertain.' The wise commander tried everything before choosing battle, which was the last resort.[10] The alternative view of the 1346 campaign, strongly and persuasively argued by Clifford Rogers, is that the English king throughout intended to force Philip to fight in open battle, in the right circumstances.[11] The campaign was punctuated by challenges issued by Edward to his enemy Philip VI; it was Philip, not Edward, who was reluctant to fight. Crécy was a good place for the English to meet the French. It had two advantages as a battlefield. Firstly, the ridge between the village and Wadicourt presented an excellent site for establishing a good position from which to fight. Secondly, it was in Ponthieu, which was English territory. The county had been acquired through inheritance in 1279.[12] Fighting there, Edward would have the moral advantage of being on what was, in a sense, home ground.

A common problem with medieval sources is their failure to provide much topographical detail about precisely where battles were actually fought.[13] The sources for the battle of Crécy do not describe with any accuracy the precise site where the English drew up their line of battle. Froissart and the Valenciennes chronicler, for example, merely place the English position between Crécy and Labroye. Knighton's chronicle uniquely locates fighting around 'Westglyse', almost certainly to be identified with Watteglise, to the north or north-west of Wadicourt. This, however, was in the final stages of the battle, and reveals nothing about the initial English position. The recently rediscovered St Omer chronicle explains that the first division was drawn up facing the fields, near a windmill, with a wood behind, which fits the accepted identification for the

---

[8] *Anonimalle*, pp. 21–2. See also Chapter 2, p. 97 and n. 278.

[9] G.F. Beltz, 'The battle of Cressy', *Archaeologia*, xxviii (1840), pp. 176–7, has a full discussion of the topography and possible routes. Michael Northburgh's letter makes it clear that the route taken was through Crécy forest: *Avesbury*, p. 368. For further discussion, see Chapter 2, pp. 98–103.

[10] J. Gillingham, 'William the Bastard at war', *Anglo-Norman Warfare*, ed. M. Strickland (Woodbridge, 1992), pp. 149–50.

[11] Rogers, *War Cruel and Sharp*, pp. 230–72. See also, above, Chapter 2, *passim*.

[12] M.C. Prestwich, *Edward I* (London, 1988), p. 316.

[13] For the problems of locating another battle in 1346, see D.W. Rollason and M.C. Prestwich, eds, *The Battle of Neville's Cross 1346* (Stamford, 1998), pp. 9–10, 66–77.

battlefield.[14] Sir Philip Preston sets out the arguments for the traditional site in Chapter 3 above. It makes sense that the English occupied the high ground and the slope from which they could command the gentle bowl formed at one end of the Vallée des Clercs. It seems very likely that the windmill that stood on the site of the present-day viewing tower is the one referred to in the accounts of the battle. Terracing on the slope provided a useful defensive feature. While the topography provided considerable advantages for the English, it is relatively innocuous in appearance, and would not have deterred the French from attacking. It has, however, to be understood that there is little basis for this iden-tification of the site in the chronicles and letters of the fourteenth century. It depends on local tradition, and logical deduction from the terrain itself.

The main difficulty with the traditional interpretations of the site does not lie with the English position, but with the French advance. Most reconstructions of the battle assume that the French forces advanced straight towards the English position, coming down into the Vallée des Clercs, and then up the slope. There is, however, a major topographical problem in this. To reach the bottom of the valley it would have been necessary to descend a steep bank, vertical in places. This is not an obstacle that could have easily been surmounted. Infantry could have scrambled down it with difficulty; some horses would undoubtedly have fallen. It seems clear from the ground that the French would have had to advance into the Vallée des Clercs on quite a narrow front. Those who came from the south would have been confined by the River Maye on the one side, and the steep bank on the other, within a space of some three hundred yards. Rather than advancing straight towards the English, they would have had to wheel to face them. The French may also have advanced from the north, as is suggested by the Valenciennes chronicle, but again it would not have been possible for them to deploy their troops on a wide front.[15] They would have entered the valley at a narrow point where the bank is at its steepest. The English formed up on the slope could present a relatively narrow front to the French, which would have been hard to outflank. This meant that the advantage the French had in terms of sheer numbers was minimised. The topography meant that the French were effectively funnelled into what became a savage killing ground, from which the steep bank made it hard to escape. This was surely the 'small place' that Edward III referred to in his letter written after the battle, where a large number of knights and squires, put at 1,500, were slain.[16]

The English preparations in advance of the battle were careful. The king ordered the construction of an enclosure, made of all the carts and carriages in the army. The horses and baggage were put in it; there was only one way in and out of this temporary fortification. The army was then formed up in three main divisions or battles. The *Acta Bellicosa*, which described the campaign up to 19

---

[14] *Froissart*, ed. Luce, iii, p. 181; *Récits*, pp. 229–30; *Knighton*, ed. Martin, p. 63; St Omer chronicle (Bibliothèque Nationale, Paris, MS Fr. 693), fo. 261v. This account was discovered by Professor Clifford J. Rogers, and I am deeply grateful to him for allowing me to use his transcript of it.

[15] *Récits*, p. 230, suggests that the French advanced from Labroye.

[16] *The Wars of Edward III*, ed. Rogers, p. 131.

August, described the divisions as they were organised at the outset of the campaign. The vanguard was under the Prince of Wales, with the earls of Northampton and Warwick; the king commanded the centre, with the earl of Oxford and, among many others, Godfrey of Harcourt. The bishop of Durham headed the rearguard, with the earls of Arundel, Suffolk and Huntingdon.[17] A version of Murimuth's chronicle (Nero D. X) described the first division at the battle in the same way, specifying that Northampton and Warwick were constable and marshal respectively, but this account provides no details of the other divisions.[18] The St Omer chronicler garbled some of the names, but provided a similar picture, with the prince, Northampton and Warwick commanding the vanguard, the king with Oxford leading the second division, and the third under Arundel, Suffolk and Huntingdon. There is, however, no mention of the bishop of Durham.[19] This may demonstrate the accuracy of this account; for it may well be that the bishop did not join the army until later.[20] Jean le Bel gives a different version. His account of the first division is similar, but instead of Northampton he had the earl of Stafford (anticipating an elevation that did not occur until 1351). He also placed Godfrey of Harcourt in the vanguard. His second division is similar to the rearguard of the *Acta Bellicosa*, but the command is again slightly different, with the earls of Northampton and Suffolk, and the bishop of Durham. The king himself commanded the third.[21] It is of course possible that changes were made to the initial arrangements after the expedition landed at La Hougue, with Northampton transferred from the vanguard, and it is certainly very likely that the king's division was held in the rear at Crécy, rather than the centre. In the face of the weight of the other evidence, however, le Bel's account of the command structure of the three divisions should be dismissed.

Is Jean le Bel's version of the deployment of the three divisions also to be discounted? He suggested that they were lined up in such a way that the king's was in the centre, flanked by the other two.[22] This is how most commentators have interpreted the English battle array, but it is more likely that they were drawn up one behind the other. Rogers has put the case for this, pointing out that it is clear that the bulk of the fighting was done by the prince's battle, and that the St Omer chronicle, among others, suggests that the divisions of the English

---

[17] *Acts of War*, ed. Barber, p. 29. See Chapter 5, pp. 162–8, for a fuller discussion.

[18] *Murimuth*, p. 246.

[19] St Omer chronicle, fos 261v–262r.

[20] Hatfield was apparently still in the north on 17 July, when he attended a meeting at New-castle to discuss the state of the northern border: *Calendar of Documents relating to Scotland*, ed. J. Bain (Edinburgh, 1881–8), iii, pp. 266–7. Edward III's fleet sailed for Normandy on 11 July. I am grateful to Nicholas Barker for pointing this out. There is, however, a considerable weight of chronicle evidence for Hatfield's presence at Crécy, which is hard to dismiss. Members of his retinue had received protections for service in France in late June, which strongly suggests that at that stage Hatfield was planning to sail with the king: Wrottesley, *Crecy and Calais*, p. 101. This conflict of evidence is hard to resolve; either the note of the meeting at Newcastle is misdated, or Hatfield succeeded in the difficult task of meeting up with the English expedition in August.

[21] *Jean le Bel*, ii, pp. 105–6.

[22] *Jean le Bel*, ii, p. 106: 'et retint la tierce pour lui qui debvoit ester entre ces deux'.

army were placed one behind the other.[23] The weakness of such a plan was that the English could have occupied no more than a relatively narrow front in this way, which would have left them open to attack from the flanks. The terrain would, however, have made such attacks difficult. In addition, the flanks of the English army were well protected by archers. A further advantage of drawing up the divisions one behind the other was that the French would not see long lines of English troops opposing them. They would be likely to underestimate the size of Edward III's army, and would be more likely to be drawn into the trap he set them. It seems most probable, therefore, that the prince's division was placed in the front, with the other two in support behind.

There has been much more debate among historians about the organisation of the archers than about that of the army as a whole.[24] Geoffrey le Baker's account has the archers placed to the sides of the royal army, like wings. In this way they would not, said Baker, obstruct the men-at-arms, and would not themselves face a head-on attack by the enemy.[25] The Valenciennes account suggests that there were two groups of archers, in shield-shaped formations to the side of the main force. Most shields, of course, were triangular, and this is surely what the chronicler meant.[26] These two accounts are consistent, and make good sense, particularly if it is accepted that the English divisions were drawn up one behind the other. What has complicated the debate is a well-known passage in Froissart, where he claims that the archers were 'a manière d'une herce', in a harrow formation. The meaning of this phrase still remains uncertain. The most favoured is that it refers to a triangular formation, akin to a harrow. One relevant meaning of the word 'hearse' is 'a harrow-shaped triangular frame, designed to carry candles, and used at the service of *Tenebræ* in Holy Week'. It is much more likely that a clerk, such as Froissart, would have had this in mind, rather than an agricultural implement.[27] By the sixteenth century, the term was used for a formation of archers, 'broad in front and narrow in flank'.[28] It was assumed, notably by Colonel Burne, that the apex of the triangle would point toward the enemy, but it is more probable that the broad, straight front would face them.[29] That would maximise the shooting-power of the formation. Froissart was, of course, writing some fifty years after the battle, and there is a danger that later advances in military tactics conditioned his description. It seems safe to conclude that there were triangular formations of archers on the English flanks. Given the probable number of archers, it is unlikely that they were all positioned

---

23 Rogers, *War Cruel and Sharp*, pp. 266–7.
24 See also, Chapter 10.
25 *Baker*, pp. 83–4.
26 *Récits*, p. 231.
27 *Shorter Oxford English Dictionary* (Oxford, 3rd edn, reprinted 1959), i, p. 878. J. Bradbury, *The Medieval Archer* (Woodbridge, 1985), p. 99, argues that 'Whatever a formation like a candelabrum means, it hardly suggests anything triangular.' This is precisely what the word does suggest.
28 E.M. Lloyd, 'The "herse" of archers at Crecy', *EHR*, x (1895), p. 540.
29 Burne, *The Crecy War*, p. 172. Colonel Burne gives a remarkable piece of supporting evidence for his view; he claims that the Saxons at Mount Badon adopted a wedge formation against King Arthur's cavalry.

in this way; some may well have been placed in front of the divisions of knights and men-at-arms to screen them, and some were certainly used to defend the encampment to the rear. Robert Hardy has recently suggested that there were wedges of archers between two front-placed English divisions, with further archers on each flank, and yet more both in front and behind the men-at-arms. This would certainly have enabled the full number of archers to be deployed, but it is not likely that the English divisions were stationed as Hardy suggests.[30]

The accounts of the English formation as given by Baker and Froissart are distinct and different, but represent versions of the same or a similar scenario. The Florentine chronicler Giovanni Villani gives a very different account. His version lays emphasis on the English use of the protective circle formed by carts, which other chroniclers do not suggest played a significant part in the fighting. The carts, according to Villani, were covered with cloth, which absorbed the crossbow bolts shot at them. Guns as well as archers were used to defend this formation, which seems to have anticipated the wagon-forts later used by the Hussites in Bohemia.[31] It is tempting to dismiss Villani, a chronicler writing in a distant land. It is difficult to understand how the French could have got close enough to come within range of guns mounted in the defended laager of carts, which was surely to the rear of the three divisions. Villani's account of the battle is, however, full and circumstantial, as well as very nearly contemporary. It is possible, as Jonathan Sumption has suggested, that he obtained his information from newsletters circulated by Italian merchant houses operating in London or the Low Countries; it is less likely that he had eyewitness accounts from some of the Genoese crossbowmen who fought at the battle. One modern explanation that lays emphasis on the defensive cart formations can probably be dismissed. Sumption has interpreted the English formation as consisting of three divisions, ranged one behind the other, with the archers placed on the wings surrounded by circles of baggage carts.[32] It is much more likely that there was just one large defensive formation of carts towards the rear of the English position, and it is perfectly possible that in the course of the fighting some French cavalry succeeded in reaching it, probably by outflanking the main English divisions.

Other accounts of the way in which the English drew up their forces also stress the use of the carts. The St Omer chronicle survives in a fifteenth-century manuscript, but it appears to be derived from a contemporary source.[33] Again, there were three English divisions. The Prince of Wales commanded the first. The second was under the king, drawn up near the first, with the defensive formation of carts to its rear. The third was the rearguard, which looked after the tents and transport. No mention is made in this account of the archers, but the use of the carts tallies with Villani's narrative. In this account the king commanded the second division, not the rearguard. An account by a German

---

[30] R. Hardy, 'The longbow', *Arms, Armies and Fortifications in the Hundred Years War*, ed. A. Curry and M. Hughes (Woodbridge, 1994), p. 178.

[31] *Villani*, vii, p. 165.

[32] Sumption, *Trial by Battle*, pp. 527, 623 (n. 24).

[33] St Omer chronicle, fos 261v–262r.

chronicler, Mathias von Neuenburg, fits rather better with the English sources. He explained that the English placed all their horses, with their grooms, in a circle of carts behind the army. The king stationed the archers in front of the line of knights. It seems likely that Mathias used information from some of the Germans present at the battle. His account should not be dismissed, even though he does not refer to archers stationed on the wings of the army.[34]

The sources, then, are not sufficiently consistent for there to be any real certainty about the way the English were drawn up for battle. There is not enough evidence to make it possible to provide a reliable plan or diagram of their formation. The best guess is that towards the rear there was a circular defence formed by the many carts used for transport. This was very probably defended by some light guns as well as archers. In front of this were the three divisions. The king's was probably in the rear; the other two may have been side-by-side, or, and this is more likely, one behind the other, with the Black Prince's in the van. Archers were in wings on the flanks of the army, probably organised in triangular formations. In addition, they probably formed a screen in front of the men-at-arms. If Froissart was right, the English had the advantage that at the time of day that the battle began, the French had the low evening sun in their eyes as they advanced.[35]

Colonel Burne assumed that the English occupied the full length of the ridge between Crécy and Wadicourt, some 2,000 yards in all. Making allowance for gaps, he assumed that Edward's men occupied a front of about 1,700 yards.[36] The sources provide no indication of the overall length of the English position, but if the divisions were drawn up one behind the other, Edward's formation would have been considerably more compact than Burne thought. On that basis, the English front might have been perhaps no more than 1,000 yards long at most, concentrated towards the southern end of the ridge. Since it would have been difficult for the French to operate on a wide front, given the topography of the site with its steep bank down into the Vallée des Clercs, that would have been all that was needed.[37]

What of the French? Tradition has it that when Philip moved out from Abbeville, he first advanced towards Noyelles. Then he received information that the English were near Crécy, and redirected his advance.[38] He ordered a knight with four companions to go ahead to reconnoitre. They brought back the news that the English were formed up in three divisions. The French were in three divisions according to Villani; four according to one English account; nine

---

34 *Die Chronik des Mathias von Neuenburg*, ed. A. Hofmeister (Monumenta Germanica Historica, Scriptores Rerum Germanicum, 1936–7), ii, p. 398. I am very grateful to Dr L.E. Scales for this reference.
35 *Froissart*, ed. Luce, iii, p. 176.
36 Burne, *The Crecy War*, p. 170.
37 Evidence of the length of battle lines is scarce. At Dupplin Moor, fought in 1332, the Scots dead were said to have formed a mound some 220 yards long, and it is probable that this was the length of the English front: *Avesbury*, p. 297. The English army at Dupplin was much smaller than that at Crécy.
38 Beltz, 'The battle of Cressy', pp. 181–2, discusses the route taken by the French army.

according to another. The Valenciennes chronicler has five.[39] Philip and his advisers then discussed what to do. The Chevalier Henri le Moyne of Basel was asked for his advice. It was, he said, late in the day. They should wait overnight, then organise their forces and go against their enemies 'in the name of God and St George'. This was agreed. Chaos ensued. Those in front halted; pride demanded that those behind would not move back until the front ranks moved first. The topographical constraints of the Vallée des Clercs must have added to the difficulties; the bank would have limited movement considerably. Some of the French cavalry at the rear tried to advance; honour required that they should do so. They rode virtually aimlessly to and fro until they suddenly came up against the three English divisions. It was no longer possible to delay battle.

The English troops waited in their positions for a long while before the action began. One commonly reported preliminary of battle was a speech by the king or commander. At Poitiers, for example, the Black Prince was said to have made two addresses, one to the men-at-arms and one to the archers.[40] Edward III is not recorded as ever making major speeches in this way. Rather, his custom was to go round the army, talking to as many men as he could. Jean le Bel describes the way he did this at Crécy, cheerfully encouraging all to do their duty, making brave men of any cowards. Froissart's additional gloss was that Edward rode a small white palfrey, and that he carried a white baton. There was time for a meal, and an opportunity for the archers to dig pits so as to hamper the advance of the French cavalry.[41] At nones (mid-afternoon), news came to the English at last that Philip and his army were nearby. The trumpet was sounded, all armed themselves, and the men waited for the battle to start.[42] The wait was a long one. Both the letter written by the king (or at least written in his name) to Thomas Lucy, and Michael Northburgh in his newsletter, put the start of the fighting at a little before Vespers, which was at about six in the evening. Villani gave similar timing in his account. The fact that the engagement was fought so late, in the dusk and even dark, must have added to the normal chaos and confusion of battle.[43]

Along with the speech or words of encouragement, another normal preliminary to battle was the knighting of some of those about to fight. The account provided by the 'Monk of Malmesbury' notes that Alan la Zouche and John de Lisle were both raised to baronial status on the day of the battle (he surely meant the rank of banneret), and that fifty men were knighted.[44] Documentary evidence does not support so large a number, but seven squires in the king's

---

[39] *Villani*, vii, pp. 165, 369; *Avesbury*, p. 371; *Baker*, p. 82; *Récits*, pp. 230–1.

[40] M. Prestwich, *Armies and Warfare in the Middle Ages* (New Haven and London, 1996), pp. 312–14.

[41] For further discussion of the 'pits', see Chapter 9, pp. 340–2.

[42] *Jean le Bel*, ii, p. 106; *Froissart*, ed. Luce, iii, p. 170.

[43] *The Wars of Edward III*, ed. Rogers, pp. 130–1; *Avesbury*, p. 369; *Villani*, vii, p. 167. The Anonimalle chronicle gives earlier timings, with the French showing themselves at tierce, about eight or nine in the morning, and the fighting starting at nones, in the early afternoon (*Anonimalle*, p. 22).

[44] *Eulogium*, iii, p. 211. The chronicle places the knightings after the battle, but the normal convention was for them to take place beforehand.

household, and no doubt a fair number of others, owed their rise in social and military standing to the battle.[45]

When the battle began, the commanders of the Genoese crossbowmen, Carlo Grimaldi and Ottone Doria, ordered their men to advance, ahead of the cavalry. These Italians were professional troops, doubtless infuriated by the antics of the French cavalry. A number of accounts state that shortly before the battle there was a heavy shower of rain, the first for over six weeks according to Thomas Burton's Meaux Abbey chronicle. This, it was later claimed, soaked the strings of the crossbows, making them impossible to use. The story is surprising, for professional soldiers would surely have had some means of keeping their bowstrings dry. It was, of course, a convenient excuse for French chroniclers to use, since it laid the blame for the defeat on Italians and the weather, rather than the French. Although most early sources, such as Jean le Bel's chronicle, and the English accounts, do not mention the rain, Villani, whose account is almost contemporary, does include it, but interestingly he makes little of it, and does not link it to the failure of the crossbowmen. A better explanation for the difficulties that the latter faced is that they lacked much of their equipment, notably their large shields or *pavises*, and much of their ammunition, which had not been unloaded from the baggage carts.[46] The Genoese advanced in three stages, with a great shout each time. The English archers stayed motionless and silent; then they made one step forward and began to shoot. Their range was longer than that of the Genoese, and with their longbows they could loose their shafts far quicker than the crossbowmen could their bolts. Villani suggested that three arrows could be shot in the same space of time as one crossbow bolt. Many of the Genoese turned to flee. Behind them the French horse continued to mill around in total confusion, until they moved forward, riding down and slaying the Genoese, very possibly under orders to do so. As the hail of arrows began to fall on the cavalry, infuriated and maddened horses hurled themselves into the ranks of infantrymen, making the chaos worse still. According to Villani, the English bombards, primitive cannons, also had their effect. Their noise was deafening, and they caused many casualties, both among men and horses. Many of the French fled before they had even formed up properly for battle.[47]

The opening of the battle was disastrous for the French, whichever version of events is accepted. The succeeding stages are harder still to describe. Effectively, the conflict took the form of successive French assaults, perhaps as many as fifteen if we believe Baker's account, on the solidly established English positions. The skill of the French cavalry in wheeling and turning again and again to charge the English lines should not be underestimated. The count of Blois, however, chose to dismount to fight, courageously advancing to his death. The English held firm; the French were increasingly dispirited as the evening wore

---

45 See Chapter 5, pp. 194, 246.

46 *Melsa*, iii, p. 58; *Jean de Venette*, ed. Newhall, p. 43; *Jean le Bel*, ii, pp. 102–3; *Villani*, vii, pp. 165–6; *Chronographia*, ii, p. 232. The question of whether there was a rain shower is discussed at length by J. Viard, 'La campagne de juillet–août 1346 et la bataille de Crécy', *Le moyen âge*, 2nd ser., xxvii (1926), pp. 1–84, at p. 73 n. It should be noted that the St Omer chronicle makes no mention of the shower.

47 *Villani*, vii, pp. 165–6.

on.[48] That is the conventional view of what took place. Villani provided a very different account, and suggested that the Prince of Wales's division advanced, attacking the first French formation. The second English division under the earl of Arundel joined in, and the first two French divisions were routed. Philip VI and his men in the third division, however, forced the English to retreat back to their defensive circle of carts. King Edward's men came out from behind this, and attacked the French from the flank and from the rear. In the final stages of the fight they were victorious. The Norman chronicle provides some support for this, suggesting that the Prince of Wales advanced to attack the French.[49] If (and there are considerable doubts about this) the king of Bohemia's cross marks the site where he was killed, the English did indeed advance a long way from their original position. There is no way that these different versions of events can be reconciled, but it seems likely that as the battle continued, the fighting spread over a wide area, even reaching as far as Watteglise.

Some incidents can be isolated. At one point some of the French and their allies succeeded in breaking through into the prince's division. A knight was sent to the king, who was in the rear, near a windmill. 'Sir, the earl of Warwick, lord Stafford, lord Reginald Cobham and the others who are about your son, are vigorously attacked by the French; and they entreat that you would come to their assistance with your battalion, for, if their numbers should increase, they fear he will have too much to do.' The king refused, with the famous saying that he was determined that they should let the boy win his spurs.[50] This is splendid stuff, from Froissart of course, and it is very probably apocryphal, though there is no doubt that the Prince was put in a position of some considerable danger. He and his men fought with great courage, in the chaos of the mêlée. According to the Valenciennes account, the fighting was so fierce that the prince was brought to his knees on two occasions. His standard bearer, Richard FitzSimon, put the banner down and stood on it, so that it could not be seized. He took his sword in two hands, swinging it to defend the prince, shouting 'Edward and St George! To the king's son!' At this, Thomas Hatfield, the warlike bishop of Durham, and various knights, came to the rescue, and Richard was able to raise his banner once more. The tale might have a little more plausibility if it came from an English source, but it should not be dismissed out of hand. Documentary evidence, however, shows that it was Thomas Daniel who replanted the prince's banner in the course of the fighting.[51] Two French accounts have it that the

---

[48] *Baker*, p. 84; St Omer chronicle, fo. 262v.

[49] *Villani*, vii, pp. 166–7; *Chronique Normande*, p. 81.

[50] *Froissart*, ed. Luce, iii, pp. 182–3. This translation is from *Chronicles of England, France, Spain . . . by Sir John Froissart*, ed. T. Johnes, 2 vols (1839), i, p. 167. It is curious that in his life of the Black Prince, the Chandos Herald made no reference to this incident. The account of Crécy in the life is brief, and concentrates on the French noble casualties: *Chandos Herald*, ed. Tyson, pp. 57–8. For Reginald Cobham, see N. Saul, *Death, Art and Memory in Medieval England* (Oxford, 2001), pp. 124–30. It is surprising that Cobham is described as being with the Prince; in the *Acta Bellicosa* and the St Omer chronicle he is listed as being in the king's division.

[51] *Black Prince Register*, i, pp. 45, 48.

Black Prince was briefly captured by the count of Flanders, only to be swiftly rescued, but this tale is probably not to be believed. [52]

The most famous story about the fighting is that of the blind king of Bohemia, John of Luxembourg, who asked his knights to lead him into the battle so that he could strike one blow with his sword. They tied their horses together and rode into the mêlée; the next day all were found together, slain. This is one of the great moments of chivalry at its most pointless; the king of Bohemia's son, Charles, showed far more sense, for he left the battlefield when he saw what was happening there.[53] Chroniclers looked for the inevitable tragic stories. The St Omer chronicle has the tale of the Count of Alençon's standard-bearer, who had not put on his helmet and was ordered to do so. 'Sire, when I come to the battle, I shall put it on when it suits me, and it will never be taken off by me.' This turned out to be true, for he was killed in the fight.[54]

Philip VI himself fought bravely. It was said that two horses were killed under him; there was clearly a very real danger that he would be captured. He suffered several wounds, clear evidence that he was involved in hand-to-hand combat. John, count of Hainault took charge of him, and led him off the battlefield.[55] The sacred French war banner, the famous *Oriflamme*, was left behind, ripped and torn amid the dead and dying. No longer, noted an English writer, could it be counted among the relics of the French monarchy.[56]

The fighting had been horrific. It is likely that a significant element in it was the way that men move in crowds. Those behind tend to push forward inexorably; recent disasters at football grounds have demonstrated what can happen. The large numbers on the French side aggravated the situation. According to Geoffrey le Baker, 'many were crushed to death, without a mark on them, in the middle of the French army'.[57] Descriptions of heaps of dead suggest that suffocation, as men clambered over each other, was a real problem, just as it had been for the Scots at Dupplin Moor in 1332. As the heaps grew, so they provided new obstacles in the way of the French trying to attack the English lines.

Casualties on the French side were abnormally heavy. The king's letter to Thomas Lucy contained a grand list, starting with the king of Bohemia, the king of Majorca, the duke of Lorraine, the archbishop of Sens, the bishop of Noyon, the grand prior of the Hospitallers in France, the abbot of Corbeil, the count of Alençon, and continuing with many other names of men of high rank.[58] Jean le Bel listed in addition Louis count of Blois, the count of Salm, the count of Auxerre and the count of Sancerre. The Valenciennes chronicler included the duke of Lorraine, the count of Harcourt, the viscount of Ventadour, the count of

---

[52] *Récits*, p. 233; *Chronique Normande*, p. 81; *Chronographia*, ii, p. 233.
[53] *Froissart*, ed. Luce, iii, pp. 178–9, 420–1. Charles was wounded on the next day as he fled from Crécy; H.S. Lucas, *The Low Countries and the Hundred Years War, 1326–1347* (Ann Arbor, 1929), p. 553.
[54] St Omer chronicle, fo. 262v.
[55] *Chronique Normande*, p. 81; Rogers, *War Cruel and Sharp*, p. 269.
[56] *Murimuth*, p. 247.
[57] *Baker*, p. 84.
[58] *The Wars of Edward III*, ed. Rogers, p. 131. The Anonimalle chronicle contains a similar list, also including the king of Majorca, who in fact escaped (*Anonimalle*, p. 23).

Montbéliard, the viscount of Thouart, the count of Forest, the count of Bians-Mons, and Thibault of Bar. Jean le Bel, surely exaggerating, put the total dead at nine princes and about 12,000 knights, with 15,000 or 16,000 common soldiers. He also noted that only 300 English knights were killed.[59] Michael Northburgh gave the remarkably precise figure, perhaps derived from an official count, of 1,542 men-at-arms killed, and did not attempt to put a figure on the mortality of foot soldiers.[60] The German account by Mathias von Neuenburg took an interestingly nationalistic view of the casualties. According to him, the French fled from the battlefield, archers first and then the whole line. The Germans, however, remained to fight, suffering very heavy casualties as a result.[61]

The French casualties were a body-blow to French chivalry. For the English, they also represented a huge loss of potential income from ransoms.[62] According to the St Omer account, Edward's German allies pointed this out. 'Sire, we are astonished that you allow so much noble blood to be spilt. If you took them for ransom, you would achieve much of your war aims, and would have a very large ransom.' The king's response was curt. Orders had been given, and it had been agreed what should be done.[63] Geoffrey le Baker suggested that it was the French who made the first move in refusing to take captives. Their commanders had all asked Philip VI for specific prisoners, but he was concerned that his troops should not be distracted from the fight by the business of taking captives. Accordingly, he had the *Oriflamme* raised, the flag that testified that no quarter was to be given. The English retaliated by raising their Dragon standard. This depicted the royal arms, with the symbolic savagery of the leopards and the mildness of the lilies, brought together with the cruelty of the dragon.[64] The message was the same as that of the *Oriflamme*. There were to be no prisoners, and none were named in any of the chronicle accounts of the battle. Michael Northburgh in his newsletter states that some knights and squires were taken by Northampton, Suffolk and Warwick on the day after the battle, but there is no evidence of any substantial trade in prisoners like that which took place in the aftermath of the battle of Poitiers. Crécy provides a salutary warning against an interpretation of fourteenth-century war that over-emphasises financial profit. A later Polish chronicle makes the interesting point that Edward III treated foreign prisoners (Czechs, Germans, Spaniards and others) with great moderation, freeing them without taking ransoms.[65] Edward III was in a very

---

[59] *Jean le Bel*, ii, pp. 108–9; *Récits*, p. 233.

[60] *Avesbury*, p. 369. The letter to Thomas Lucy gives a similar figure for men-at-arms, noting that 'More than 1,500 knights and esquires perished in a small place where the first clash occurred.' *Wars of Edward III*, ed. Rogers, p. 131.

[61] *Chronik des Mathias von Neuenburg*, p. 398. Baker states that only forty dead Englishmen were found on the battlefield, and this number presumably included archers: *Baker*, p. 85.

[62] C. Given-Wilson and F. Bériac, 'Edward III's prisoners of war: the battle of Poitiers and its context', *EHR*, cxi (2001), pp. 804–5.

[63] St Omer chronicle, fos 262v–263r.

[64] *Baker*, p. 82. For the *Oriflamme* (which was lost by the French at Crécy), see P. Contamine, *Guerre, état et société à la fin du moyen âge* (Paris, 1972), pp. 671–3. See also Prestwich, *Armies and Warfare in the Middle Ages*, p. 314.

[65] *The Annals of Jan Długosz*, ed. M. Michael and P. Smith (Chichester, 1997), pp. 296–7. I am grateful to Andrew Ayton for drawing this to my attention. Długosz goes on to suggest,

tight situation before the battle took place. This was a fight for survival, and victory was far more likely if his troops were not concerned with accepting surrenders and promises of ransom in the middle of a ferocious conflict. It was important for them to maintain their station, and not to pursue potential captives. Froissart drew the obvious contrast with the battle of Poitiers, which was so profitable to the English.[66] What mattered above all to Edward was to achieve victory, and this he did in resounding fashion.

The aftermath of the battle was told by Jean le Bel. At the end of the engagement, there was no immediate pursuit and rout. It was late, and the troops must have been exhausted. Near midnight, the men were told to stand down, but not to disarm. The king dined with the great men in the army; they thanked God for the victory, given to so few against the whole power of France. The next morning some of the English went out to see what was happening. They found large numbers of common French people, who had slept in woods, ditches and hedges. They thought the approaching English were in fact French troops; and soon learned their mistake as they were slain. The scale of this engagement is not entirely clear; the Valenciennes account has it that it was a second battle, but it was surely hardly comparable to the previous day's fighting. Even so, French casualties were very heavy. The letter to Thomas Lucy put them at 4,000, much higher than in the battle proper.[67] This massacre marked the final victory for Edward's army. After the troops returned to the English camp, the king sent out Reginald de Cobham, with a herald who could recognise French coats of arms, to draw up a list of the French casualties. The corpses of the princes and great nobles were collected together. There was still some alarm lest the French should succeed in regrouping their forces, and Edward remained with his men on the battlefield on the Sunday, the day after the great victory. The remains of armour and equipment were gathered up, and on the king's orders were burned, to prevent their future use. The English were perhaps shocked by the sheer scale of their success; there are no accounts of great celebrations. The death of the king of Bohemia was mourned in a solemn ceremony, conducted by Thomas Hatfield, bishop of Durham. The death of a king was not to be treated as a triumph, and Edward's grief at the fate of a fellow-monarch was surely genuine. The advance towards Calais began on the following day.[68]

The news of the great success was swiftly reported to England. Richard Wynkeley, the king's confessor, wrote his newsletter on the campaign and the battle on 2 September, and two days later Michael Northburgh completed his account. Bartholomew Burghersh and John Darcy, both royal councillors and men of great distinction and experience, who had fought at Crécy, reported on the battle to a council of bishops at Westminster, and explained the plan to besiege Calais. The regency government in England sent out writs on 6 September, announcing the victory to the main English towns, and asking

---

contrary to the evidence, that French prisoners taken at Crécy were ransomed, and that Edward III used the money for castle-building.

66 *Froissart*, ed. Luce, iii, p. 186.
67 *The Wars of Edward III*, ed. Rogers, p. 131.
68 *Baker*, p. 85; *Jean le Bel*, ii, pp. 106–8; *Récits*, pp. 234–5; *Avesbury*, p. 369.

merchants to bring supplies and munitions for the siege of Calais.[69] The war moved into a new phase.

How can the English victory be explained? It was, after all, very much against the odds. Edward III and his army were massively outnumbered. Although it is very likely that the English king welcomed the opportunity that battle presented, he and his men must have been exhausted by their long march up the Seine, and north from Paris. Since crossing the Seine at Poissy Edward had not been in a position to control events; the strategic advantage lay with Philip's pursuing army. But when it came to the battle, it became clear that in tactical terms the English had the upper hand. Even so, the considerable duration of the fighting demonstrates that the outcome was far from certain. Crécy was no walkover for the English.

There is some merit in the traditional explanation for the English triumph, which emphasised the technological superiority of the English archers, whose role in the battle was surely vital. The effectiveness of the bow in battle was much more significant than the question of how the archers were organised in the field, 'en herce' or otherwise. A bow was not a complex piece of equipment. It was cut from a single piece of wood, usually yew. Care had to be taken to take full advantage of the way in which the heartwood could be compressed, while the sapwood provided elasticity. There was no handle, and no sighting arrangement, in contrast to modern bows. The simplicity of the weapon had one important advantage at Crécy; it could be easily strung and unstrung. If there was a shower, as there may have been before the battle, the bow strings could be quickly removed and protected from the effects of rain. The bow had a range of up to 300 yards in experienced hands, though it was more effective up to 200 yards. It was possible to shoot at an impressive rate.[70] The arrows might have different types of heads, all of which were devastating in different ways. The narrow, sharp bodkin-head was particularly effective against armoured men. Orders had been issued for the collection of 2,100 bows, and 5,550 sheaves (133,200 arrows).[71] There was of course much more weaponry available than that, for each archer would have brought his own equipment of bow and quiver containing twenty-four arrows. The effects of English archery were described by le Bel. 'The archers shot so marvellously that some of those on horseback, feeling these barbed arrows which did such wonders, would not advance, while others bucked as if enraged, others capered hideously, and others turned their backs on the enemy.'[72] It was in the initial stages of the battle that the English archery made its mark, preventing effective French cavalry charges. As the battle proceeded, no doubt archers began to run out of arrows, and to find targets increasingly hard to identify. In the mêlée it would have been hard for them to distinguish friend from foe. Their main role was to blunt the initial

---

[69] *Murimuth*, pp. 214–17; *Avesbury*, pp. 367–9; *Foedera*, III, i, pp. 89–90.

[70] For a summary of modern views on the longbow, see Hardy, 'The longbow', *Arms, Armies and Fortifications in the Hundred Years War*, ed. Curry and Hughes, pp. 171–80. A French expert, M. Renaud de Beyfettes, has confirmed in conversation that a bow with an 80 lb pull would be very effective up to 200 yards, with a maximum range of up to 300 yards.

[71] H.J. Hewitt, *The Organisation of War under Edward III* (Manchester, 1966), p. 64.

[72] *Jean le Bel*, ii, p. 103.

enemy onslaught, and this they did superbly. They were especially effective against horses; the men would have been better protected by armour. There is no evidence to show what proportion of French casualties were caused by archery, as against hand-to-hand fighting. Arrows, however, were not always fatal. Among his wounds, Philip VI suffered an injury caused when one hit him in the face, but this does not seem to have been serious. Interestingly, David II of Scotland would also be wounded in the face by archery later in the year. Like Philip, he recovered.[73]

The French missile technology was that of the crossbow. This, of course, was a much more sophisticated weapon than the longbow. It was far more complex in construction, but required much less skill and experience to aim and shoot. It was a deadly and terrifying instrument, condemned by the papacy in the twelfth century.[74] It could be far more powerful than the longbow, and shot a fearsome heavy bolt. The maximum range was greater than that of the longbow, and approached 400 yards.[75] It had two major disadvantages in the circumstances of Crécy. It was slow to reload. Unlike the longbow, it had to be lowered from the shooting position so that it could be bent. This was no disadvantage in siege warfare, but in battle it was a major problem, and provided a striking contrast with the longbow. Secondly, it could not be unstrung easily, and so, if it became wet from rain, it could slacken just like a gut-strung tennis racket, though whether this was a factor at Crécy must remain questionable. Further, the crossbowmen were highly vulnerable to the English archery, since they did not have their *pavises* with them.[76]

The English had guns at Crécy. There has been argument over this, but there is little doubt that this was the case.[77] Edward III had ordered the manufacture of a hundred 'ribalds', and evidence strongly suggests that they were made in the Tower. There is also evidence for the supply of gunpowder. The value of these guns must have been very limited. The best guess is that they were multi-barrelled weapons, using lead shot, and mounted on small carts. These weapons could probably fire a single potent volley, but the task of reloading was a very lengthy one. The one place where they could have been used was in the defence of the fortified ring of wagons in the rear of the army. What the use of guns shows more than anything else is the willingness of the English to experiment and innovate – but the technology was not yet there to make the gun an effective battlefield weapon. It was not until the late fourteenth and fifteenth centuries

---

[73] Sumption, *Trial by Battle,* p. 530; *Knighton,* ed. Martin, p. 63; *Murimuth,* p. 247; *Scotichronicon by Walter Bower,* ed. D.E.R. Watt et al., vii (Edinburgh, 1996), pp. 258–61, 464.

[74] It is still a frightening weapon today, as its use by Serbian paramilitaries demonstrates.

[75] For a full, if dated, discussion, see P. Payne-Gallwey, *The Crossbow* (London, 1903).

[76] Jean de Venette suggested that the strings shrank, so that they could not even be put on the bows. It is much more likely that they would have stretched. *Jean de Venette,* ed. Newhall, p. 43; editor's notes, pp. 176–7. See also above, n. 46.

[77] Burne, *The Crecy War,* pp. 192–202, provides a useful summary of the arguments, though he perhaps places rather too much weight on the nineteenth-century discovery of five cannon-balls on the site of the battle.

that guns began to appear regularly in battle.[78] It is most unlikely that the English use of guns at Crécy was decisive, but the smoke and noise they made surely helped to demoralise their opponents. The French were not strangers to guns. Philip VI made payments in September and October 1347 for cannons and powder, but there is no indication that they were meant for the battlefield. They were intended for the stationary warfare of the set-piece siege.[79]

There are no further technological explanations. There is nothing to suggest that English armour was superior. Indeed, at the start of Edward III's reign English armour had been regarded as thoroughly out of date, consisting largely of mail, leather and heavy great helms. By the time of Crécy, the English were better equipped. There was more plate worn, and lighter battle helmets, bascinets, had replaced the old great helms. These were curved, the better to deflect blows, and with movable visors and better eye-holes were far more convenient to wear in the confusion of the mêlée. There is nothing, however, to suggest that the French were not quite as well equipped as the English in terms of the armour they wore.[80]

Experience was surely important. Edward III himself had campaigned against the Scots in 1327, and men such as Warwick, Northampton, Arundel and Suffolk had ample understanding of command after the campaigns in Flanders and Brittany.[81] At lower levels, there would have been many seasoned veterans to provide the army with vital qualities. It is clear that fighting in war was not an activity just undertaken by young men. Military careers in the fourteenth century might be very long; John de Sully, for example, claimed to have memories of battle extending from Halidon Hill in 1333 to Nájera in 1367. Many of those at Crécy had served a hard apprenticeship in Edward III's Scottish wars. Robert de Benhale, the hero who had fought the giant Scot Turnbull in the preliminaries at Halidon Hill, fought at Crécy. Taking a list of fifty-four bannerets and knights who were paid by the crown to fight in Scotland in 1334, at least twenty-six can be shown to have campaigned in France in 1346.[82] Of course, many of Philip VI's army would have had experience fighting in Flanders and elsewhere, but it was the English who had a solid core of what amounted to professional soldiers. These were hardened men, with bonds of shared experience. As Andrew Ayton has shown, the retinues that formed the essential building-blocks of the army had coherence and continuity.[83] Taking a more short-term view, the English army had been in the field since 12 July, which gave Edward time to establish order and a measure of discipline. The campaign in Normandy had been astonishingly successful, and morale must have been high. This was a coherent and well-organised army, a contrast to the French host.

---

[78] T.F. Tout, 'Firearms in England in the fourteenth century', *Collected Papers*, ii (Manchester, 1934), pp. 238–40; K. DeVries, *Medieval Military Technology* (Ontario, 1992), p. 148.

[79] *Les journaux du trésor de Philippe VI de Valois*, ed. J. Viard (Paris, 1899), pp. 69–70.

[80] For a brief discussion, see Prestwich, *Armies and Warfare in the Middle Ages*, pp. 21–6.

[81] For further discussion of this point, see Chapter 5, pp. 200–201.

[82] Prestwich, *Armies and Warfare in the Middle Ages*, p. 54; BL, Cotton MS, Nero C. VIII, fos 233ff. Wrottesley, *Crecy and Calais, passim*.

[83] Chapter 5, pp. 204–15.

The most obvious way in which the English demonstrated their military experience at Crécy was in the tactics they adopted. The battle was a triumph for methods that the English had developed in the years following the disastrous defeat at Bannockburn in 1314. There were three key elements. Firstly, it was essential to establish a strong defensive position. Then there was the use of archers to break up an enemy advance, and finally there was the employment of dismounted men-at-arms in the mêlée. The first time that the plan was attempted was on the Stanhope campaign in 1327, but on that occasion the Scots refused to engage the dismounted English troops. Then the tactics were triumphantly successful at Dupplin Moor in 1332, and at Halidon Hill in 1333. In 1339, to the amazement of their allies, the English dismounted to fight the French at Buironfosse, but no battle took place on that occasion. Edward had arranged his troops in three divisions on foot, placed close together, with the horses and baggage hidden behind a nearby wood.[84] The parallel to Crécy is close. In 1342 at Morlaix, in Brittany, the earl of Northampton dismounted his men, forming them up in a single line of battle. The English dug ditches and pits, and formed up in a position in which they could not be outflanked or taken from the rear. Successive French charges failed to break the infantry lines. Both sides withdrew from the field of battle, but the English had won the day. The fight was on a very much smaller scale than Crécy, and there is no clear evidence that the archers were used in the same way.[85] Crécy was not, of course, a complete carbon-copy of previous English successes. In particular, the use of the strongly defended circle of carts was an innovation, which, though it appears to have been successful, was not followed up in later engagements. Apart from this, however, the tactical elements were all tried and tested.

It is surprising that the French could not cope with the English method of fighting. They were not wholly unfamiliar with it. There was a substantial body of Hainaulters present in the English army on the Stanhope campaign, and through them news might well have spread of the unusual way in which the English planned to fight, with dismounted men-at-arms. Buironfosse and Morlaix should have given the French a very clear indication of English tactics. In addition, the French had suffered defeat at the hands of infantry forces at Courtrai in 1302, and Arques in the following year. What may be much more significant, however, is the fact that at Cassel in 1328 Philip VI had won a great cavalry success. After a bold dash into the French encampment, the Flemish infantry were routed by a highly effective counter-attack.[86] It is easy with hindsight to see why the French were successful at Cassel; their opponents abandoned a good defensive position on high ground, and laid themselves open to attack in a way the English avoided. Philip and his advisers may have simply interpreted the success in terms of the power of their cavalry. We may be able

---

[84] *Jean le Bel*, i, p. 163. The abortive battle is discussed by Sumption, *Trial by Battle*, pp. 286–8.

[85] Morlaix is conveniently discussed by Tout, 'The tactics of the battles of Boroughbridge and Morlaix', *Collected Papers*, ii, pp. 223–5, and by DeVries, *Infantry Warfare in the Early Fourteenth Century*, pp. 137–44. See below, p. 337.

[86] DeVries, *Infantry Warfare in the Early Fourteenth Century*, pp. 100–11.

today to see a pattern of victories for dismounted troops in the first half of the fourteenth century, even an 'infantry revolution'; Philip is unlikely to have viewed it that way. It would take a great deal to dent the myth of the superiority of the armoured, mounted knight, bolstered as it was by a sense of social as well as military dominance.

One clear reason for the English success was the confusion among the French at the start of the battle. The French army had been hastily assembled, and had none of the coherence and sense of purpose of the English. Morale must have been very low. Earlier in the month, the French had abandoned the siege of Aiguillon in Gascony. The English had done immense damage in Normandy, notably with the sack of Caen. No battle had taken place between Philip VI and Edward III outside Paris, despite the French king's challenge to his English rival. At Crécy, if Jean le Bel is to be believed, the French decided not to fight that day, but were virtually compelled to do so by the refusal and inability of the cavalry to make an orderly withdrawal from the battlefield. Command was extremely difficult in this period; orders were hard to transmit, particularly since medieval armies had very limited organisational structures. The need that men had to prove themselves in battle, the requirements of honour and pride, could run counter to prudence and good sense, as the English had discovered at Bannockburn in 1314. Quarrels between commanders on that occasion had resulted in unco-ordinated and futile cavalry charges, and the death of the earl of Gloucester. Similarly, there was no sense of order and system underlying the attacks made by the French on the English lines at Crécy. Froissart pointed out that the late start of the battle caused particular problems for the French; with the onset of dusk it became much harder for men to identify and locate their lords.[87]

The sources reveal a great deal about the battle of Crécy. Unfortunately, they do not all tell quite the same story, and it is not possible to establish the course of events with absolute certainty. Nor can Colonel Burne's 'inherent military probability' resolve all the contradictions. What seems probable in the twentieth century may have been implausible in a fourteenth-century context. Above all, what the sources cannot bring out, for all the efforts of the chroniclers, is what the fighting was really like. This demands a leap of imagination. The noise of battle was terrifying, with drums and trumpets, the hiss of arrows in flight, the neighing of frightened horses, the clash of metal on metal, and the unexpected bangs from the English guns. The smell of fear, of frightened men and panicking animals, must have pervaded the field. Banners and coats of arms provided visual splendour as the engagement began, but in the dying light as the fight went on the colours would have become less and less evident. The dusk must have made the appalling scene of the fighting look even worse, bringing additional fear and confusion. This was not a gentlemanly fight, dominated by the conventions of chivalric culture. There was horrific carnage, and heaps of dead and dying men marked the killing ground of the battlefield. We should wonder at the bravery of men who submitted willingly to such horrors.

---

[87] *Froissart*, ed. Luce, iii, p. 181. Presumably this was less of a problem for the English, as they would not have moved far from their defensive positions.

5

The English Army at Crécy

ANDREW AYTON

The battle of Crécy was by any standards a momentous event, and it has certainly not been neglected by historians. It is, therefore, a little curious that few of those who have studied this battle have devoted much attention to the composition of the English army. While a great deal has been written about weaponry and tactics, the men who fought and won at Crécy have been left in the shadows. Until recently, the only historian to examine the army in detail and publish the results was Major General the Honourable George Wrottesley, whose *Crecy and Calais* appeared a little over a hundred years ago.[1] A considerable quantity of valuable primary source material was brought together in this volume and it has become a much-cited work. It is, therefore, all the more unfortunate that Wrottesley's collection of documents is riddled with omissions and transcription errors. Nor did the editor subject his material to the full and rigorous analysis that it deserved. We might regret that his more talented and better-qualified contemporary, J.E. Morris, the true pioneer in the field of Edwardian army studies, did not find time to do so.[2] What is perhaps surprising is that, for the better part of a hundred years, no one else tackled the job.

For an explanation of this neglect we probably need look no further than the sources, which are voluminous yet frustratingly incomplete and often infuriatingly imprecise.[3] Matters are complicated still further by the unusual length of the campaign, which lasted for over a year from the landing at La Hougue until the surrender of Calais, and by the size of the English army, which appears to have grown to gargantuan proportions during the siege of Calais. It may well be that more than one historian has toiled over these materials, only to abandon the attempt. But despite the problems, the composition of the English army demands close attention for several reasons. In a world in which politics and war were closely intertwined, in which the political and military elites were

---

[1] G. Wrottesley, *Crecy and Calais from the Original Records in the Public Record Office* (London, 1898). For a recent view of this army, and the sources relating to it, see A. Ayton, 'The English army and the Normandy campaign of 1346', *England and Normandy in the Middle Ages*, ed. D. Bates and A. Curry (London and Rio Grande, 1994), pp. 253–68.

[2] See Morris's critical review of Wrottesley's book in *EHR*, xiv (1899), pp. 766–9. For Wrottesley's response and Morris's reply, see *ibid.*, xv (1900), pp. 199–202. Several of the real weaknesses of Wrottesley's collection did not emerge during this exchange.

[3] It is, for example, frequently difficult to distinguish the men who joined the army during the siege of Calais from those who had landed at La Hougue and fought at Crécy.

composed of essentially the same men, a major Edwardian army, especially when led personally by the king, was as much a political entity as a military one. For that reason, an investigation of the men who lined up with Edward III on a hillside in Ponthieu could contribute a great deal to our understanding of that king's political world, for these men experienced first hand the carnage of the battle, the exhilaration of victory and the scale of the triumph that was achieved over the massed chivalry of the greatest kingdom in Christendom. Such an investigation would ideally take account of the wider 'public' lives of these men, as well as their social and regional origins, which needless to say would take us well beyond the scope of the present study. Our concern is with the more strictly 'military' function of the English army in July–August 1346. By investigating the men who fought on the English side, together with the underlying dynamics of the mid-fourteenth-century military community, it may be possible to add a little to our understanding of both the course and outcome of the battle, and the wider English military successes of this period. This is not as modest an aspiration as it seems, given the uncertainty surrounding much of what happened on the field of Crécy, not to mention the current differences of opinion concerning the nature – or very existence – of the Edwardian military revolution.

Investigation of the men who accompanied Edward III to Crécy in 1346, from the most celebrated of the captains to the most humble of the rank and file men-at-arms and archers, requires a close examination of the records that illuminate Edwardian military service. Such research, which may be termed 'military service prosopography', informs the discussion in the last part of this chapter. First, however, we need to take a look at the size, structure and general characteristics of Edward III's army at Crécy. The surviving sources do not make this an easy task. Our first problem is that there is no surviving pay-roll (*vadia guerre* account) for this army.[4] We know that such a document once existed and, indeed, survived the middle ages, for it was consulted by antiquaries in the sixteenth and seventeenth centuries, but it is no longer traceable. Pay-rolls illuminate many of the armies of the Edwardian period and later, allowing us to see their component units and their leaders, the numbers of men under arms, periods of service and amounts of pay (and other benefits) due.[5] Had records of this kind been available, aggregation of the data would have permitted a fairly accurate impression to be gained of the overall size and essential dimensions of the army that landed at La Hougue and marched to Crécy. But the book of foreign expenses, containing *vadia guerre* and related accounts, for Walter Wetwang's term as Keeper of the King's Wardrobe appears to have been lost. All that we have are small fragments of information from these accounts – individual entries that have been recorded elsewhere, such as the pay details for the companies led by the brothers Thomas and Otes Holand, which were copied onto a Memoranda

---

[4]   See Appendix 1 below for a more detailed discussion of this problem and full documentary references.

[5]   For *vadia guerre* accounts, see A. Ayton, *Knights and Warhorses: Military Service and the English Aristocracy under Edward III* (Woodbridge, 1994), pp. 138–55.

Roll.[6] There are other financial records generated by the pay process that have survived, such as the 'prests' made to leaders of retinues (usually advances on their wages) that are to be found on an Issue Roll and in Wetwang's book of receipts.[7] These are fairly systematic, but are usually unspecific about the size of retinues or the period of their service, and they do little more than confirm the participation of a selection (certainly not all) captains.[8] Moreover, they also throw little light on the companies of English and Welsh archers.

Although now lost, we know that Wetwang's *vadia guerre* account was accessible to antiquaries during the fifteenth, sixteenth and seventeenth centuries. Extracts from Wetwang have been found in a surprising variety of documents. Some have been published, perhaps the best known being the College of Arms manuscript that Wrottesley included in his *Crecy and Calais*. Although sometimes interpreted as a 'Calais roll', this document – and others like it – is an imperfect guide to the army that besieged that town for eleven months from September 1346 to August 1347. Somewhat more convincing is the interpretation that 'it includes everyone who served at any point over the sixteen-month expedition' (though allowing for some double-counting and omissions).[9] However, using the Wetwang abstracts to reconstruct the size and structure of the English army that landed at La Hougue in July 1346 is a task fraught with difficulties. It is true that the abstracts do convey the essential character and structure of the army, including the broad distinction between, on the one hand, the 'mixed' retinues of men-at-arms and archers, raised and led by aristocratic captains, and on the other, the companies of arrayed archers and spearmen, recruited in the English shires and Welsh lordships. But the Wetwang abstracts present major interpretative problems (for which, see Appendix 1), which arise from the fact that the original *vadia guerre* account was only partially copied, and not always accurately. The periods of service of the many contingents in the army have been omitted, as have the amounts of money that they were due to receive in wages. Figures are supplied for the personnel serving in each of the retinues, but the data relating to the arrayed troops have been so heavily summarised that the contributions of individual counties cannot be ascertained; and a comparison of the various abstracts reveals many discrepancies in the manpower numbers provided. Add to these problems the incidence of corrupt name forms and duplicate entries, not to mention the occurrence of 'double counting' in the abstracts and the fact that some contingents have been omitted altogether, and it is clear that wholly reliable figures for the size of the army, or its chief, constituent parts, cannot be calculated. The Wetwang abstracts can be used to gain an impression of the size and structure of the army (for the retinues in the army, see

---

6   Wrottesley, *Crecy and Calais*, pp. 176–7.
7   Issue Roll: E403/336. Book of receipts: E101/390/12. See Ayton, 'The English army and the Normandy campaign of 1346', p. 259 n. 42. For the surviving Wardrobe accounts, see Tout, *Chapters*, iv, pp. 115–19.
8   The earls of Arundel, Huntingdon and Suffolk are not included among the recipients of prests. Only in the case of the earl of Oxford (E403/336, m. 42) is it noted that the prest is a 'first quarter' payment.
9   Rogers, *War Cruel and Sharp*, p. 423.

Appendix 2, Table 2), but we should never forget that we are interpreting imperfect evidence.

We would not expect the narrative sources to provide the kind of systematic detail offered by a pay-roll, but do they have anything useful to contribute to our understanding of the size and structure of Edward III's army? With regard to the size, unfortunately not. For example, if we aggregate Jean le Bel's detailed manpower figures for the English army in the battle, we arrive at an overall total of 17,000 men, which conflicts with the figure of 24,000 that he had given earlier in his narrative.[10] Both estimates are implausibly high. Some of Froissart's manpower numbers are more circumspect, but they are different in each of the main versions of his chronicle.[11] Turning to the English chronicles, Adam Murimuth would have us believe that 65,000 men landed at La Hougue,[12] while most of the others side-step the issue of army size, as do the campaign newsletters.

Some of the narrative sources are more useful for the insights that they offer concerning the major sub-divisions of the army and their commanders. Several chronicles accurately report the names of the principal captains in the army at the beginning of the campaign.[13] Outstanding in this respect is the *Acta Bellicosa,* the campaign diary apparently written by a member of Edward III's army.[14] This tells how, during the early days of the expedition, the army was divided into three 'battles' or divisions (*tres acies*), and it goes on to list the names of those who 'raised their banners' in each, 48 in all (see Appendix 2, Table 1).[15] Comparison of the *Acta Bellicosa* list with other records reveals a few flaws (chiefly with regard to forenames), but what is more striking is its overall reliability.[16] Admittedly it is a not a complete roster of the bannerets in the army: perhaps a quarter are not named. However, Sir William Fitzwarin is the only banneret known to have been leading a separately paid retinue at La Hougue who is missing from the *Acta Bellicosa* list. Although nearly all of the major retinue commanders are represented, this is not simply a list of retinues, as we would find, for example, on a pay-roll. Seventeen of the bannerets named can be shown to have been serving under 'greater' captains. Rather, what we have is in some ways a more revealing guide to the operational structure of the army for the Normandy campaign, and perhaps also for the battle of Crécy itself. On the one hand, we see the fundamental fabric of retinues in the army, some serving independently, others grouped under the umbrella authority of a

---

[10] *Jean le Bel*, ii, pp. 100, 105–6.

[11] *Froissart*, ed. Luce, iii, pp. 169–70, 405–8.

[12] *Murimuth*, p. 199.

[13] *Murimuth*, p. 199; *Baker*, p. 79. Altogether less reliable are Froissart, whose lists of captains are littered with errors, omissions and corrupt name forms (*Froissart*, ed. Luce, iii, pp. 130–1, 169–70, 352, 405–8), and Chandos Herald, who was writing in the mid-1380s (*Chandos Herald*, ed. Tyson, p. 52). Both, for example, place Ralph, earl of Stafford with the army, though in July/August 1346 he was not yet an earl and actually serving in Aquitaine.

[14] See Chapter 1, p. 2 n. 4.

[15] Corpus Christi College, Cambridge, MS 370, fos 98r–98v.

[16] The only problematic entries concern 'Eble [Roger?] Straunge (centre), 'Botiller of Wemme' (centre) and John Sutton (rearguard), whose service as bannerets in July 1346 cannot be corroborated by other sources.

magnate; and, on the other, we are given some idea of how a large assembly of retinues, drawn from all corners of the realm, of widely contrasting sizes and apparently lacking the cohesion found in a permanent army, was organised and controlled in the field in order to facilitate logistical support and optimise fighting potential.

The vanguard, or first division, consisted of four large retinues, led by the Prince of Wales, the earls of Northampton and Warwick (respectively, the constable and marshal of the army), and Bartholomew Burgherssh senior. The remainder of the bannerets listed can be shown, chiefly by the evidence of letters of protection, to have been serving with either the prince or one of the earls.[17] While we may be sure that each banneret would have brought a company of men with him, this can only be demonstrated in the case of some of them, particularly those serving in the earls' retinues, which are (as we shall see) particularly well documented. The rearguard division also had a clear structure: there were five large retinues, led by the bishop of Durham, the earls of Arundel, Suffolk and Huntingdon and Hugh Despenser, and each of the remaining rearguard bannerets were actually serving under one of these five magnates. The 'centre' division, led by the king, appears at first glance to be composed of a more diverse collection of bannerets; but upon closer inspection what many have in common is that they were either members of the royal household or otherwise closely associated with Edward III. Thus, we see the earl of Oxford, who had recently recovered the office of Chamberlain of England;[18] Godfrey de Harcourt, the king's guide to Normandy and the recipient of his fees;[19] four royal clerks who carried the rank of banneret;[20] and a group of household bannerets, who included some of the king's most trusted and resourceful military lieutenants.[21] But five of the bannerets listed in the 'centre' division appear to have been drawn temporarily into the royal orbit. None was closely connected to the king in normal circumstances, though Edward Montagu was the brother of the late earl of Salisbury, Edward III's confidant early in his reign; and it was presumably under his uncle's banner that the young heir to the earldom, William, served in 1346.[22] He, like the Prince of Wales, was knighted at La Hougue; ten years hence they would share the triumph of Poitiers. For the moment, the king's close supervision of the Montagu family's contribution to

[17] Eight bannerets are named. The Wetwang abstracts suggest that 17 bannerets served in the four retinues of the first division. Clearly, most of the unnamed ones were members of the prince's retinue.
[18] *Complete Peerage*, x, Appendix F, pp. 58–9.
[19] E.g., E403/336, m. 41.
[20] Walter Wetwang, Keeper of the Wardrobe; John Thoresby, Keeper of the Privy Seal; Philip Weston, Steward of the Chamber (Tout, *Chapters*, iv, p. 268); and the formerly influential William Kildesby, 'the stormy petrel of curiality' (Tout, *Chapters*, iii, p. 161).
[21] Richard Talbot (the Steward), John Darcy (the Chamberlain) and his son, John, Reginald Cobham, Robert Ferrers, Thomas Bradeston, Maurice Berkeley, Michael Poynings and John Stryvelyn. Of the household bannerets who are known to have landed at La Hougue, only William Fitzwarin has been omitted.
[22] The protection records suggest that he headed a small retinue (C81/1738, no. 26; C76/22, m. 11), but there is no indication of this in the pay records, so we should perhaps interpret this as a company within Edward Montagu's retinue.

the war effort during this period of transition was but one dimension of a common-sense approach to managing his army, which also included the grouping together of all the relatively small, 'independent' retinues under the umbrella of royal authority.[23] Presumably this was prompted by logistical as well as tactical considerations. If we also take account of the knights bachelor and esquires of the royal household, and the small companies that many brought with them, it can be seen that the 'centre' battle was, in effect, an expanded 'household division'.

There is general agreement among the narrative sources that the army at Crécy was also arrayed in three battles or divisions.[24] Is it not likely that these were essentially the same in composition as the divisions that had begun the campaign, the divisions whose captains the author of the *Acta Bellicosa* lists so carefully?[25] There is no dispute that the Prince of Wales led the first division in the battle: this is mentioned in Richard Wynkeley's letter, dated 2 September, and even in Thomas Bradwardine's 'victory sermon', preached before the king and his lieutenants during the siege of Calais, probably in late October or early November.[26] Bradwardine's colleague at St Paul's, Adam Murimuth, who must have written his account of Crécy within months of the battle, adds that alongside the prince in the first division were the earls of Northampton, the constable, and Warwick, the marshal of the army, and this is confirmed by other chroniclers.[27] If 'Murimuth Nero D. X' may be interpreted as evidence that the three divisions had indeed remained essentially unchanged in composition from La Hougue to Crécy, we find this proposition receiving further reinforcement in other sources.[28] Most conclusive is the evidence of the 'St Omer chronicle', a

---

23 The retinues led by John Grey [of Ruthin], [Thomas] Breuse and possibly [Roger?] Straunge and [William?] Botiller of Wem. John Grey of Ruthin received advances on his retinue's wages (E403/336, mm. 41, 44), but does not appear in any of the Wetwang abstracts. 'Roger le Straunge' is listed with a retinue of 1 banneret, 1 knight, 5 esquires and 7 archers in BL, MS Harley 3968, fo. 118v (cf. Wrottesley, *Crecy and Calais*, p. 201), but this may relate to service during the siege of Calais. [William?] Botiller of Wem is not recorded in any of the pay records for the campaign.

24 Noted, for example, by Murimuth, Baker, the Meaux chronicle, John Reading, Jean le Bel (followed by Froissart) and the short continuation of the *Chronique de Flandre*.

25 A point made by R. Barber, *Edward Prince of Wales and Aquitaine* (Woodbridge, 1978), p. 64. The only unavoidable change had been the withdrawal to England of the sick earl of Huntingdon, and an indeterminate proportion of his retinue, after the capture of Caen.

26 *Murimuth*, p. 216; H.S. Offler, 'Thomas Bradwardine's "Victory Sermon" in 1346', *Church and Crown in the Fourteenth Century*, ed. A.I. Doyle (Aldershot, 2000), XIII, pp. 1–40 (at p. 25). Bradwardine had written a short newsletter to 'his friends in London' from La Hougue on 17 July: *Murimuth*, pp. 201–2.

27 *Murimuth*, p. 246 (this assumes that Murimuth himself was the author of the version of his chronicle in BL, Cotton MS, Nero D. X); *Historia Roffensis*, fo. 92r; *Anonimalle*, p. 22; *Knighton*, ed. Martin, pp. 62–3. The distribution of captains given by Jean le Bel and Froissart, with Northampton in the second division (an arrangement widely accepted by modern writers), is unreliable: *Jean le Bel*, ii, p. 105; *Froissart*, ed. Luce, iii, pp. 169–70; 405–8. Cf. *Chronique des quatre premiers Valois*, p. 16: 'le conte de Lincole et le conte de Glocestre ourent la seconde'. Equally untenable is Wrottesley's reconstruction of the English divisions: *Crecy and Calais*, pp. 31–40.

28 The Florentine chronicler Giovanni Villani (d. 1348) notes that the first of the three battles ('tre schiere') was led by the Prince of Wales, the second was under the earl of Arundel (the

valuable narrative for the period 1342 to 1347, which has recently been rediscovered by Dr Clifford Rogers.[29] This lists the names of the prominent English
captains in the three 'batailles' at Crécy,[30] and although there are some omissions, most notably in the second and third divisions, as well as a few errors and
corrupt name forms, much more striking is the degree of correspondence with
the list of bannerets in the *Acta Bellicosa*.[31] The St Omer chronicle's divisions at
Crécy are composed in essentially the same way as those of mid-July; and this is
not because one narrative source is simply a copy of the other. The names
embedded in the Latin text of the *Acta Bellicosa* are given in conventional and
immediately recognisable forms; those in the St Omer chronicle, a French text,
are distorted, sometimes to the point of obscurity, perhaps as a result of oral
transmission, and they are listed in a different order. Moreover, 'St Omer' adds
seven recognisable names – four to the first division and three to the second –
that fit perfectly into the existing scheme.[32] Particularly notable are the additions
to the king's division: William Fitzwarin, the only royal household banneret at
La Hougue to be omitted by the *Acta Bellicosa*; John Lisle, who was elevated to

most senior of the 'rearguard' captains) and the third was kept under the king's personal
direction. The order in which Villani presents the three battles may reflect battlefield deployment. *Villani*, vii, pp. 163–4.

[29] Paris, Bibliothèque nationale de France, MS Fr. 693, fos 248r–279v (I am indebted to Dr
Rogers for sending me a copy of his transcript, which I have since compared with the original
manuscript). The 'St Omer chronicle', as Dr Rogers has termed it, is closely related to a short
continuation of the *Chronique de Flandre*, covering the period 1342–7, of which one copy is
to be found in Paris, Bibliothèque nationale de France, MS 20363. This was published by
Baron Kervyn de Lettenhove in his *Istore et croniques de Flandres d'après le textes de divers
manuscrits*, 2 vols (Brussels, 1879–80), ii, pp. 27–45, 56–71 (see *ibid.*, i, pp. xxii, xxiii, for a
brief and somewhat dismissive description of the manuscript; ii, pp. 42–5, for the account of
the battle of Crécy). A second copy of the short continuation is to found in a late fifteenth-
century manuscript in the British Library (Royal MS, 16 F. III): the account of the battle of
Crécy, which differs little from that published by Lettenhove, is on fos 173r–174v. The precise
nature of the relationship between the St Omer chronicle and the short continuation of the
Chronique de Flandre is not certain. The former offers a fuller narrative, including several
lengthy passages not included in the short continuation (e.g., an account of the battle of La
Roche Derrien of 1347), but the latter does include details omitted by the St Omer manuscript, including some small points relating to the battle of Crécy. Differences in phrasing are
numerous. It seems likely that these two texts are independent versions of a common source.
[30] St Omer chronicle, fos 261v–262r. Although describing the English 'batailles' in essentially the same way as the St Omer chronicle, the short continuation of the *Chronique de
Flandre* omits the list of bannerets.
[31] Among the errors would appear to be the inclusion of Thomas Dagworth ('dachuerde') in
the first battle, John Montgomery in the second, and the earl of Huntingdon in the third. Four
of the names are obscure: in the second battle, 'Robert de Calchoune'; in the third, 'John de
Chitoune', 'Tringas' (possibly 'Hastings') and 'Baruf'. Compared with the *Acta Bellicosa*,
eight bannerets in the second division (including the four royal clerks) and nine in the third
(including the bishop of Durham) have been omitted.
[32] In the first division: William Careswell (Bartholomew Burgherssh's retinue); [Robert]
Scales (earl of Warwick); Roger Mortimer and Bartholomew Burgherssh junior (Prince of
Wales). Roger Mortimer had only received knighthood at La Hougue, yet the document
requesting protections for the men in his company proclaims his social prominence: titled
'seigneur de Wygemore', his name is followed by those of 3 knights and 10 esquires.
C81/1710, m. 26, cf. C76/23, m. 23.

that status on the day of the battle; and 'le fitz au conte de warenne', who was William Warenne, an illegitimate son of the earl. Although not, it seems, a banneret, William was the old earl's preferred heir, 'our dearest son', and doubtless he worked hard at the role of representative of an ancient comital house. His retinue was not large and, like the young William Montagu's company, found a natural place in the king's division.[33]

How could the author of the St Omer chronicle have been so well informed about the English army – indeed, so much better informed than other French commentators on the battle? The question is not made easier by the fact that we do not know the identity of the writer. In Dr Rogers's view, he 'was somehow connected to the French garrison of St Omer, and may even have been a man-at-arms himself, or perhaps a herald'.[34] That he may have been a herald, or had ready access to heraldic records, could offer a solution to our problem. There are, in fact, a couple of explanations. It is possible that his source was a roll of arms, specifically an 'occasional roll' of the arms of the magnates and bannerets in the English army at Crécy. Although no such roll is known to exist for this particular event, heraldic records of this kind have survived for other military episodes of the Edwardian period, beginning with the battle of Falkirk in 1298 and including the Scottish campaign of 1335.[35] Indeed, there is such a roll – albeit something of a curiosity – for the siege of Calais.[36] If we take, for example, the Falkirk Roll, with its focus on 'les grauntz seigneurs a Baniere', 111 in all, who are grouped into 'quatre bataillez', and if we remove the arms blazoned against each name, we are left with a list of bannerets similar in format to that preserved in the St Omer chronicle. The drawing up of a roll of arms at or after Crécy, and its subsequent dissemination, would explain how the St Omer chronicler was able to list the English captains in such detail, yet could say no more than other narrative sources about the commanders in the French army.[37] It may well be that the compilation of such a roll actually began at La Hougue, and

33 Warenne's retinue: 4 knights, 15 esquires, 15 archers, 8 Welshmen (Wrottesley, *Crecy and Calais*, p. 199). The king had a particular interest in the Warenne inheritance: F. Royston Fairbanks, 'The last earl of Warenne and Surrey and the distribution of his possessions', *Yorkshire Archaeological Journal*, xix (1907), pp. 249ff.; C. Given-Wilson, *The English Nobility in the Late Middle Ages* (London, 1987), pp. 135–6. Note Warenne's close connection with the Poynings, who were also serving in the king's division: N. Saul, *Scenes from Provincial Life: Knightly Families in Sussex, 1280–1400* (Oxford, 1986), pp. 33, 37–8.

34 C.J. Rogers, ed., *The Wars of Edward III: Sources and Interpretations* (Woodbridge, 1999), p. 117.

35 For comment on these rolls, see A.R. Wagner, *A Catalogue of English Medieval Rolls of Arms* (London, 1950), pp. xiv, 27–9, 54–6, 61; M. Prestwich, *War, Politics and Finance under Edward I* (London, 1972), pp. 68–9; N. Denholm-Young, *The County Gentry in the Fourteenth Century* (Oxford, 1969), pp. 101–5. On the role played by heralds in warfare and in the compilation of rolls of arms, see A.R. Wagner, *Heralds and Heraldry in the Middle Ages*, 2nd edn (Oxford, 1956), chapters 4 and 5.

36 A 'highly interesting fragment of what was once doubtless an extensive series of the armorial bearings of persons who distinguished themselves during . . . the siege of Calais'; it appears to have survived only because the back was used for a later heraldic compilation. J. Greenstreet, 'The "Third" Calais Roll of Arms', *Walford's Antiquarian Magazine and Bibliographer*, i (1882), pp. 92–4.

37 That the bannerets' names have been taken from another source by the writer of the St

that a heraldic source also underlies the *Acta Bellicosa* list. The army pay records are unlikely to have been the source, for they would have been organised according to different principles – hierarchically, with the focus on captains leading separately paid retinues.

The second explanation for the list of bannerets in the St Omer chronicle is also rooted in heraldry. It is possible that, before the battle, a herald attached to the French army drew up a list of the leaders in the English army based upon an on-the-spot identification of the heraldry displayed on their banners. This is not as far-fetched as it sounds. Observing that the armies were so close to each other 'Qe chescun purra veoir le roy / De l'un l'autre, et l'ordenement', Chandos Herald reveals the pre-battle preoccupations of men of his profession.[38] Among the instructions included in a fifteenth-century manual for heralds is the stipulation that before a battle they 'doivent congnoistre les gonfanons' of the enemy so that they could pass on the information to the leader of their army, or indeed to any nobleman who should ask.[39] The note-taking was to continue during the fighting, the heralds getting as near to the action as possible in order to record the armorial bearings of the most valiant knights in both armies. That our list may be based upon a visual inspection of the English army on the day is suggested by several features. The Prince of Wales's battle, which by all accounts was most exposed to the French attacks, is also the most fully documented by the St Omer chronicle, while coverage of the rearguard division, which 'gardoient les tentes et le charroy', is far less substantial. Inclusion of the earl of Huntingdon may reflect the presence of his banner on the field of Crécy, though not his person since we know that he had returned to England after the taking of Caen. That the chronicler thought that others, like Thomas Dagworth, were present may simply have arisen from heraldic misidentification.

Combining the statistical data provided by the Wetwang abstracts with the structural information in the 'banneret lists' enables us to hazard a reconstruction of the English army at La Hougue, or at least of that section of it composed of retinues (Appendix 2, Table 2). The limitations of this reconstruction need always to be borne in mind. The Wetwang abstracts offer an indication of the size of retinues led by captains whom we know from other sources to have been at La Hougue. The inclusion of some of the lesser captains is based upon a certain amount of informed guesswork, and in arriving at the manpower totals for the three divisions it has also been necessary to estimate the size of those retinues that are not included in the Wetwang abstracts and the number of men-at-arms and archers who were attached to the household but not members of one of the bannerets' or knights' retinues.[40] Consequently, it would be misleading to suggest precision in the manpower totals. As can be seen in

Omer text and inserted into his narrative is strongly suggested by the fact that they are missing from the short continuation of the *Chronique de Flandre*.

[38] *Chandos Herald*, ed. Tyson, pp. 56–7.

[39] P. Contamine, 'Batailles, bannières, compagnies: aspects de l'organisation militaire française pendant la première partie de la Guerre de Cent ans', *Les Cahiers Vernonnais*, iv (1964), p. 19.

[40] See Appendix 1 and the footnotes to Appendix 2, Table 2 for a fuller explanation of the method employed and of individual decisions.

Appendix 2, Table 2, the combined strength of the four large retinues of the vanguard division may have been about 850 men-at-arms and 820 archers (mostly mounted), together with the 500 Welsh foot who were attached to the Prince of Wales's retinue. In all, then, there were in the region of 2,200 combatants in the prince's division. The rearguard division was somewhat smaller, consisting of five retinues, which together numbered 720 men-at-arms and about 500 archers, or more than 1,200 men all told. The king's 'centre' division poses the greatest interpretative problems, but it is likely that it was the largest of the three 'battles'. Aggregating the available retinue data yields totals of about 900 men-at-arms and 950 archers, but allowing for three retinues that do not appear in the Wetwang abstracts, as well as the esquires of the royal household, the companies of men-at-arms and archers accompanying the lesser members of the household, and the king's archers, we should perhaps increase these totals to 1,150 men-at-arms and 1,400 archers.[41] Since it is likely that the contingents of foreign troops were also attached to the king's division (see below), we need to add perhaps a further 150 men, mostly men-arms, to the total.

These figures for the retinue-based manpower in the three divisions of the army, resting as they do on a combination of documentary evidence and informed guesswork, are probably fairly close to the mark. (Our real problem with regard to determining the operational structure of the army from La Hougue to Crécy concerns the companies of arrayed troops: a problem to which we shall return below.) The fact that as many as 2,800 men-at-arms, of whom about 2,700 were 'English', may have landed with the king in Normandy in July 1346 highlights the extent to which Edward III had succeeded in engaging the English nobility and gentry in his French war. For although we must allow for the presence of some 'self-made' men of sub-genteel origin among the men-at-arms, we can safely assume that the majority were knights and esquires of gentle blood. The support of the nobility and gentry had been more than respectable since the beginning of the French war. To each of the first three major campaigns they had contributed from 1,500 to 2,000 men-at-arms, but what we see in the mid-1340s is a further expansion of the gentry's military involvement.[42] Indeed, the scale of the turnout for the Normandy campaign in 1346 is all the more impressive when it is recalled that the second half of 1346 also witnessed military operations in several other theatres of war. The earl of Derby was in Aquitaine with a substantial expeditionary force; there were further detachments in Brittany, Flanders, Ireland and elsewhere; and in the north of England, a few months after Crécy, the regional military community would be mustered at short notice and would come to blows with the Scots at Neville's Cross.[43]

---

[41] Allowing 30 men-at-arms and 30 archers for the retinues of John Grey, Alan la Zousche and Edward atte Wode, and 200 men-at-arms and 400 archers for the additional household troops. Both are very much guesstimates, and conservative ones at that.

[42] A. Ayton, 'Edward III and the English aristocracy at the beginning of the Hundred Years War', *Armies, Chivalry and Warfare in Medieval Britain and France*, ed. M. Strickland (Stamford, 1998), pp. 173–206 (at pp. 179–82).

[43] For documentary references, see Chapter 1, nn. 53, 55–7.

How was it that Edward III was able to raise so large a contingent of men-at-arms for his expedition while other English armies operated simultaneously elsewhere in France? There had been enhancements to the terms of service, most notably, in 1345, the introduction of *regard* for continental campaigns, which may have benefited ordinary men-at-arms as well as captains;[44] but pressure, in the form of a novel military assessment of landowners, must also have played a part. When an obscure landholder like John Hunden felt obliged, 'par cause de ses terres en le countee de Nicole', to send his son, Robert, to Portsmouth 'bien armer et mounter', it is likely that a recruit was being provided who would not have appeared at muster in ordinary circumstances.[45] What is clear is that the community of earls shouldered a large part of the responsibility of recruitment, with the result that extensive social – and recruiting – networks were placed at the disposal of the crown. The only English earls who were not somewhere on active service in 1346 were ageing or infirm;[46] and those who were serving were in the field with large retinues. The earls' links with the gentry, based on lordship and locality, provided the crown with plentiful recruitment opportunities. Their wealth enabled them to carry the financial burden of leadership, including the cost of raising retinues and keeping them in arms. The captains' personal resources were essential to the functioning of the military machine, for it would often be necessary for them to make disbursements to sub-contractors before advances on wages had been received from the crown; and, as we see during the Crécy campaign, the king did not always have sufficient ready cash to keep his armies paid in the field.

It has been argued elsewhere that recruiting considerations played an important part in Edward III's creation of six new earls (with accompanying endowments where necessary) in the parliament of March 1337.[47] On the eve of that parliament there had been only three earls who were likely to provide a direct military contribution to the war effort: Arundel, Oxford and Warwick. Thus, the

---

[44] On *regard*, see Ayton, *Knights and Warhorses*, pp. 110–13.

[45] C81/313, no. 17722; Wrottesley, *Crecy and Calais*, p. 88. The new military assessment required landowners in shires lying south of the Trent (plus Nottinghamshire) to find, equip and send to muster a specific number of men-at-arm, hobelars or archers according to the annual value of their land. The service would be performed at the king's wages. See M. Powicke, *Military Obligation in Medieval England* (Oxford, 1962), pp. 195–8; G. Harriss, *King, Parliament and Public Finance in Medieval England to 1369* (Oxford, 1975), pp. 392–4; Ayton, 'The English army and the Normandy campaign of 1346', pp. 254–8. The government's view of the military assessment and how it should operate was neatly summarised in a response to a Commons petition in September 1346: *Rot. Parl.*, ii, p. 160.

[46] The ageing earl of Warenne provided 40 men-at-arms and 40 archers, according to the tariff of the new military assessment, and his two illegitimate sons, William and Edward, served: Wrottesley, *Crecy and Calais*, pp. 102, 149. The earl of Devon sent his son, Hugh Courtenay (a royal household knight), with a small retinue and was employed himself as chief warden of the maritime land of Devon, 'cum familia sua et toto posse suo'. He was too ill to perform service in early 1347. Wrottesley, *Crecy and Calais*, pp. 76, 125, 135, 267. The earl of Gloucester died in 1347, not having served since 1342–3. By the time of Crécy, his son in law and heir, Ralph Stafford (who had been appointed Seneschal of Aquitaine in 1345), had effectively taken his place at the table of leading captains. He was created earl in 1351.

[47] See Ayton, 'Edward III and the English aristocracy at the beginning of the Hundred Years War', pp. 187–94.

elevation of six men to earldoms represented a massive reinforcement of the team of senior captains, with one of the aims being the more effective exploitation of recruiting networks among the nobility and gentry. For example, in the case of William Bohun, earl of Northampton, this would involve reactivating the Bohun lordship networks for military purposes,[48] while Robert Ufford's elevation to the earldom of Suffolk would enable him to draw on the East Anglian recruiting grounds that had been left under-exploited since the departure from the scene of the king's uncles, the earls of Kent and Norfolk.[49] Despite unforeseen events – notably, the capture of Salisbury and Suffolk in 1340 – the policy proved to be successful. For the Breton campaign of 1342–3 the community of earls turned out in force (nine played some part in the expedition) and recruited 45 per cent of the English army's men-at-arms – nearly 900 men.[50]

Royal management of the team of senior captains – if we can think in such terms – was a continuing process: there had to be new men to replace those who left the arena. In 1344 the earl of Salisbury was killed in a tournament, leaving a young son who, as we have seen, was first armed on the sea shore at La Hougue. Consequently, the Montagu family's contribution to the army at Crécy (the retinue led by the late earl's brother, Edward) was far smaller than the earldom would normally have been expected to furnish.[51] Fortunately, new captains were emerging. The recruiting potential of the Despensers' lordship, resting as it did upon part of the Clare inheritance, had been fully reactivated in the person of Hugh Despenser, son and grandson of the men who had been executed in 1326. Hugh III had recovered some of his father's land in the spring of 1337 and his mother's later in the same year; and he had married Elizabeth, the daughter of the earl of Salisbury (who was, moreover, the widow of Giles Badlesmere, who had died in 1338) in 1341.[52] Although he had not acquired an earldom by the time of Crécy, the Brut copy of Wetwang's pay-roll suggests that he served 'as an Erle' in 1346.[53] Despenser's rise was significant, but the most striking new structural feature of Edward III's army in 1346 was the Prince of Wales's retinue. Its sheer size was breathtaking. With 378 men-at-arms, 453 archers and

---

48 John Bohun, earl of Hereford and Essex had died in 1336, and his successor, Humphrey, appears to have been an invalid. In addition to the royal grant of £1,000 *per annum* in 1337, William Bohun had benefited, in 1335, from an advantageous marriage to Elizabeth Badlesmere, who was the third of four sisters and co-heiresses of Giles Badlesmere (who died childless in 1338), and the widow of Edmund Mortimer. *CPR, 1334–8*, pp. 416–17; J.M. Parker, 'Patronage and service: the careers of William Montagu, earl of Salisbury; William Clinton, earl of Huntingdon; Robert Ufford, earl of Suffolk; and William Bohun, earl of Northampton', MA thesis, University of Durham, 1986, pp. 35–6.

49 Kent's last campaign was in 1327, Norfolk's in 1333. Ufford had served with Kent in Gascony in 1324–5 and with Norfolk at Stanhope Park in 1327. On Ufford's martial relationships in East Anglia, see R. Gorski, *The Fourteenth-Century Sheriff: English Local Administration in the Late Middle Ages* (Woodbridge, 2003), pp. 22–4.

50 Ayton, 'Edward III and the English aristocracy at the beginning of the Hundred Years War', p. 193 and references cited in n. 110.

51 For the Breton campaign of 1342–3, Salisbury's retinue had consisted of 95 men-at-arms and 80 mounted archers: E36/204, fos 106r, 108r.

52 *CPR, 1334–8*, pp. 461–2; *CIPM*, VIII, no. 132. Elizabeth's dower, following Badlesmere's death: *CIPM*, VIII, no. 185 (pp. 143–7).

53 *Brut*, ed. Brie, ii, p. 539.

over 500 Welsh foot it was composed of nearly four times more men than the next largest retinue in the army. Just how it was assembled has yet to be researched in detail, but it is clear that this was done rapidly, and that the emergence of the king's eldest son as a military figure created a powerful new magnet attracting men from all corners of the military community.[54] The appearance of the prince's retinue compensated for the absence of the earls of Derby and Pembroke, not to mention Stafford and Mauny, in Aquitaine; and the prince and the six earls who disembarked with the king at La Hougue contributed over 40 per cent of the army's men-at-arms, and approaching half of the retinue personnel. If we include Despenser (serving 'as an Erle') and the bishop of Durham as members of the comital community, as perhaps we should, each of these figures rises to over 50 per cent.[55]

That over half of the retinue-based personnel in the army were serving in nine large retinues suggests an army that was tightly and efficiently organised, an impression that is reinforced by the fact that the 'household division' – the combined retinues of the bannerets, knights and esquires of the royal household – supplied the greater part of the remainder. It must be admitted that the size of the household division at La Hougue and Crécy cannot be determined precisely, for in addition to the absence of Wetwang's original army pay-roll, we also lack a list of royal household personnel for 1346. Relying, therefore, on evidence for 1341–4 and 1347–9, and a limited amount of informed guesswork (see Appendix 2, Table 2), it can be suggested that over a third of retinue-based personnel – perhaps 1,000 men-at-arms and over 1,200 archers – were serving under the organisational umbrella of the household division. The king's household knights formed a major component of the English army at Crécy as they had under Edward III's predecessors; here was a thread of continuity that stretched back via Edward I to the Norman kings and beyond.[56] Indeed, numerically, the king's military household in 1346 was rather larger than it had been during the early campaigns of the French war.[57] Although the proportion of the army's men-at-arms that the royal household contributed was smaller than that supplied by the comital community, it needs always to be remembered that the earls' contribution involved nine retinues. The king could call on an extensive network of bannerets, knights and esquires, and through them he had access to a

---

[54] For the Prince of Wales's retinue, see D. Green, 'The household and military retinue of Edward the Black Prince', PhD thesis, University of Nottingham, 1998 – a most illuminating study, which is hardly to be criticised for not discussing the previous experience of the knights and esquires who served with the prince at Crécy. Most of these men had been drawn into his service since the abortive Sluys expedition of July 1345, for which the prince's retinue appears to have been quite modest in size: 13 men received protections in June 1345 (C76/20, m. 8), of whom five served again the following summer.

[55] The precise figures, drawing on the data in Appendix 2, Table 2, are: 42 and 46 per cent for the prince and the six earls; 54 and 56 per cent for the larger group. Given the problems involved in the calculation of the personnel totals for the English army, we should not place too much weight on these precise figures.

[56] See M. Prestwich, *Armies and Warfare in the Middle Ages: the English Experience* (New Haven and London, 1996), pp. 38–41 for a useful overview, with references.

[57] For the household division in the armies of 1338–43, see Ayton, 'Edward III and the English aristocracy at the beginning of the Hundred Years War', pp. 184–7.

pool of men-at-arms and archers drawn from all corners of the kingdom.[58] The maintenance of such a recruiting network, and its periodic replenishment, depended upon a combination of well-deployed patronage and shrewd man management. Those raised to the status of banneret or knight were provided with financial support, while men with good connections and proven ability were sought out and retained. Once the fifty or so retinues brought by household bannerets and knights had been mobilised, the administrative structures that the king took with him into the field, combined with the binding force of his personal presence, gave his household division a unity comparable with that achieved in the retinues of the earls. The cohesion of the household division was further enhanced by stability within the ranks of the household bannerets, knights and esquires. Of the twelve bannerets who received fees and robes from the king during 1341–4, ten served with Edward III in Brittany in 1342–3. Seven of these men accompanied the king in 1346 (three were deployed elsewhere),[59] and their number was supplemented by six elevations from among the ranks of the household knights, two on the day of the battle of Crécy.[60] Seven household esquires were also raised to knighthood at Crécy. They joined a group of household knights bachelor, at least three-quarters of whom had served in the king's retinue in Brittany in 1342–3.

When the royal household took the field in 1346 it brought with it not only a large contingent of men-at-arms and archers, but also a range of non-combatant, ancillary services required by the army. The loss of Wetwang's original book of foreign expenses deprives us of a detailed view of this aspect of the 'household in arms', but the Wetwang abstracts, although heavily summarised, do provide some impression of the variety and number of non-combatant personnel who travelled to Normandy with the king's household in 1346. These included three dozen clerks, a rather larger number of household officers and domestic staff, and an impressive array of musicians.[61] To be added to this are those who were engaged in such mundane but essential tasks as pavilioner, carter and groom. Beyond the royal household were the companies of military engineers, like the miners from the forest of Dean, recruited by Guy Brian;[62] Master Andrew Le

---

58 For the widely spread regional origins of household personnel at this time, see C. Shenton, 'The English court and the restoration of royal prestige, 1327–1345', DPhil thesis, University of Oxford, 1995, chapter 4.

59 Ralph Stafford and Walter Mauny were with earl of Derby in Aquitaine, and John Montgomery was in Flanders. Ralph Ufford had died in office as justiciar of Ireland in April 1346.

60 John Lisle and Alan la Zousche became bannerets on the day of the battle. Only Richard Talbot and Michael Poynings have the appearance of new recruits (the former, a soldier of great experience, became steward following Ralph Stafford's appointment as Seneschal of Aquitaine), but in truth they were not new to the royal household. Talbot had been a member early in Edward III's reign (*Calendar of Memoranda Rolls, 1326–1327* (London, 1968), pp. 373, 377), Poynings as recently as 1340–41 (E101/389/8, mm. 9, 26–7).

61 Wrottesley, *Crecy and Calais*, pp. 202–3; *A Collection of Ordinances and Regulations for the Government of the Royal Household* (London, 1790), pp. 3–4.

62 Brian was given the task of selecting 40 miners, but appears to have raised 60. Wrottesley, *Crecy and Calais*, pp. 78, 148; E372/191, m. 48d (the sheriff of Gloucester's account, which suggests, curiously, that the miners set out for Portsmouth on 2 October 1346).

Fever de la Tour and his team of a dozen smiths from London;[63] and the company of forty carpenters led by William of Winchelsea.[64] The latter were presumably the men responsible for repairing the bridges over the rivers Vire, Douve and, most notably, the Seine at Poissy. These were the unsung heroes of the earlier stages of the campaign, but of more immediate relevance to the battle itself were the army's armourers and fletchers, though in truth we catch few glimpses of them in the surviving records.[65] Even less visible are the men responsible for the guns (probably multi-barrelled ribalds mounted on carts), which, it seems certain, were fired at Crécy.[66] Perhaps Robert Aubyn and his two fellow 'artillators', who can be seen during the siege of Calais, had been in charge of the guns at Crécy.[67] If we allow for the fact that the major noble retinues would have had household establishments similar to the king's, albeit on a smaller scale, it is clear that all told there must have been hundreds, perhaps thousands, of non-combatant and support personnel in the English army. Some, indeed, may well have borne arms in some capacity on the day. Others, it may be assumed, were employed in logistical support duties, of which perhaps the most important was the conveyance of supplies of arrows to the archers in the front line – an important consideration for an army dependent upon a missile weapon.

The line-up of clerical personnel who accompanied the king to Crécy was, in its own way, as impressive as the array of military talent that fought in the battle.[68] In addition to the four high-status royal clerks who carried the rank of banneret and headed sizeable retinues (see Appendix 2, Table 2), the king was accompanied by the chief clerks of the household departments of the wardrobe and the chamber, along with those of the office of privy seal. Among the king's closest advisers on the 'council beyond seas' were John Carleton, a privy seal clerk of thirty years' experience, and Michael Northburgh, dubbed 'valens clericus' by Robert Avesbury.[69] Northburgh – together with Richard Wynkeley, Dominican friar and king's confessor, and Thomas Bradwardine, academic and future archbishop of Canterbury – wrote about the battle soon after the dust had settled, though it must be conceded that their accounts lack the immediacy of eyewitnesses, probably because the view from the baggage park could not have allowed them to be real spectators. That campaigning was not altogether without risks for the clerical personnel accompanying the army was shown at Caen when Geoffrey of Maldon, Augustinian friar and professor of theology, was employed

---

63 Wrottesley, *Crecy and Calais*, p. 79.
64 E101/390/12, fo. 8r; Wrottesley, *Crecy and Calais*, pp. 62, 65, 80.
65 Wrottesley, *Crecy and Calais*, p. 90 (Gilbert Croxby).
66 For the evidence concerning the use of guns at Crécy, see T.F. Tout, 'Firearms in England in the fourteenth century', *EHR*, xxvi (1911), pp. 666–702 (at pp. 670–3, 688–91), summarised in Tout, *Chapters*, iv, pp. 470–1; J.R. Partington, *A History of Greek Fire and Gunpowder*, new edn (Baltimore and London, 1999), pp. 106–8; and A.H. Burne, *The Crecy War* (London, 1955), pp. 192–202.
67 E404/496, no. 176. The term 'artiller' or 'artillator' was applied to those who made and used 'both the older and newer types of warlike engines. He was a craftsman, an engineer, and not a soldier.' Tout, 'Firearms in England', p. 679.
68 Tout, *Chapters*, iii, pp. 164–70; iv, pp. 114–15; v, pp. 21–3.
69 Tout, *Chapters*, iii, p. 168 n. 3; iv, p. 114 n. 3; v, p. 101.

to present surrender terms to the town. His offer was spurned and he was thrown into prison.[70] But on the day of the battle of Crécy, the most strenuous activity facing the non-combatant clerks in the army, apart from ministering to the spiritual needs of the troops, was scribal. We see royal clerks formalising the grant of annuities to the newly created household knights,[71] while those responsible for maintaining the draft records that later formed the basis of William Retford's magnificent 'kitchen journal', calmly noted down the expenses of the royal household's kitchen, which on Saturday, 26 August were lower than usual.[72] Similar routine record-keeping tasks were no doubt being performed by the secretaries and clerks in the households of the various English noblemen at Crécy.[73]

Of the non-combatants at Crécy it was surely the medical personnel who faced the greatest challenge on the day of the battle. Little enough is known about this group of men, though it seems probable that the physicians Roger Heyton and Jordan Canterbury were among them.[74] It is impossible to generalise about how effectively they were able to treat the wounded at Crécy. We merely catch glimpses of the work of the dressing stations, as with Thomas Crewe's recollection that he had accompanied his wounded brother to the hospital;[75] and here and there we find indirect evidence of successful field surgery. Sir Nicholas Burnaby, of the Prince of Wales's retinue, had been severely wounded in the foot by a quarrel, presumably at the beginning of the battle, but he apparently recovered and we later see him serving at the siege of Calais with Hugh Despenser.[76] On the other hand, it would seem that the wound received by one of Edward III's German allies, Johann von Schönfeld, posed more of a challenge to the surgeons. Over two weeks after the battle, in a letter to the bishop of Passau, Schönfeld noted that he had been wounded on the right side of his face and that an arrow, about an inch long, remained lodged in his head.[77]

As we have seen, the 'centre' battle, under the king's personal command, was in effect an expanded household division. It would seem that among the retinues brought under the organisational umbrella of the 'household in arms' were a number of foreign contingents. This is suggested by, among other pieces of evidence, the *Acta Bellicosa*, which includes Godfrey de Harcourt among the bannerets in the centre division.[78] Precisely how many men Harcourt had with

---

[70] *Acts of War*, ed. Barber, p. 31.

[71] E.g., a privy seal warrant, dated 'a Cressy le xxvi jour daugst', recorded the grant of £200 p.a. to Sir John Lisle, to support the rank of banneret, which 'il ad receu de nous'. C81/314, no. 17810.

[72] 41s 7½d on 26 August ('sub foresta de Cressy'), which jumped to 97s 8½d on the following day ('in campis sub foresta de Cressy'). E101/390/11, mm. 61d–62.

[73] Clerks were included among those receiving letters of protection: three in the earl of Arundel's retinue, for example (C76/22, mm. 11, 24).

[74] Protections and exonerations: C76/22, mm. 9, 10d, 12. Purchase of medical supplies: E403/336, m. 42.

[75] *Black Prince Register*, iii, p. 413.

[76] Wrottesley, *Crecy and Calais*, pp. 107, 125, 145.

[77] J.F. Böhmer, ed., *Acta Imperii selecta* (Innsbruck, 1870), no. 1055.

[78] Although the Bourgeois de Valenciennes places Harcourt in the vanguard during the earlier stages of the campaign, he is alongside the king at Crécy (*Récits*, pp. 217, 221, 225,

him, and how many other troops of continental origin were with Edward III at Crécy, cannot be determined, but the overall total is unlikely to have been significantly higher than 150 (see Appendix 2, Table 2). This much is certain: unlike the armies with which Edward III had fought the early campaigns of the French war, in the Low Countries, which involved a prominent role for expensive and unreliable continental allies, at Crécy '[t]here were but a few Strangers . . . with King Edward'.[79] Jean le Bel tells us that the only foreigners in the army were a handful of German archers led by a certain 'messire Races Massures'. Froissart rightly corrects this to 'German knights', and in fact the only surviving indenture of war for the English army in 1346 concerns the service to be provided by a company of about two dozen German men-at-arms headed by a certain 'Rasse Mascurel' – clearly Jean le Bel's man.[80] But, of course, Jean le Bel *was* exaggerating a little. A variety of captains of continental provenance can be found among those receiving payments for service with the English king in 1346. In addition to Godfrey de Harcourt, there were other dissident Norman lords with the English army, most notably William de Groucy, who remained loyal to Edward III after Harcourt had rejoined the Valois camp, and Hugh Calkyn, a more shadowy figure who is dubbed 'of Normandy' by the Exchequer records.[81] What is interesting is that both Groucy and Calkyn, and indeed Wulfart de Ghistelles (a Hainaulter whose role in the Crécy campaign is noted by a couple of chroniclers) appear to have been old hands in Edward III's service. A 'William de Groucy' was one of the knights attached to the count of Namur when he was captured by the Scots at Edinburgh in 1335. Calkyn had been retained by Edward III in 1340 and served at the siege of Tournai, while Ghistelles had accompanied that king to Scotland in 1335, fought with him again in France in 1339 and received the fees of a household knight in 1340–1.[82] Also recorded as serving with the English in 1346 were contingents from Burgundy, Brabant and 'Almannia', the latter involving, in addition to Rasse Maskerell and his companions in arms, several Rhenish knights and Johann von Schönfeld, who sent a report on the battle of Crécy to the bishop of Passau.[83] But none of these foreign contingents was large and it is clear that, overall, they contributed less than 2 per cent of the combatants in Edward III's army.

*   *   *

Apart from the relationship between retinue size and the rank of the captain, perhaps the most striking feature of the data presented in Appendix 2, Table 2 is

---

232). Other chronicles note that the German knights consulted the king during the battle: St Omer chronicle, fo. 262v; *Chronique de Flandre*, ii, p. 44.

[79] J. Barnes, *The History of that Most Victorious Monarch Edward III* (Cambridge, 1688), p. 340.

[80] *Jean le Bel*, ii, p. 106; *Froissart: Amiens*, iii, p. 13; E101/68/3, no. 64 (indenture). See Appendix 2, Table 2, n. 36 for details of payments made to Rasse Maskerell and his men.

[81] For Groucy, see Chapter 6, n. 18. For Calkyn: E403/336, mm. 21, 43.

[82] BL, Cotton MS, Nero C. VIII, fo. 239v (Groucy). E101/389/8, mm. 9, 12 (Calkyn). BL, Cotton MS, Nero C. VIII, fo. 238r; *Norwell*, p. 340; E101/389/8, mm. 9, 26–7 (Ghistelles).

[83] See Appendix 2, Table 2 and F. Trautz, *Die Könige von England und das Reich, 1272–1377* (Heidelberg, 1961), pp. 326–7, 332–3.

the prevalence of 'mixed' retinues, consisting of approximately equal numbers of men-at-arms and mounted archers. The emergence of mixed retinues of mounted troops, recruited directly by captains, had been one of the most important developments in English military organisation during the ten to fifteen years prior to the Crécy campaign.[84] It is unlikely to have been the result of a single policy decision, or to have been driven simply by 'military logic'. Rather like written contracts, the mixed retinue appears to have been a pragmatic response to administrative and organisational challenges. In this instance, the problems were how to raise mounted archers without imposing politically unacceptable costs on the shire communities, and how to support them in the field, financially and logistically, when the king was not personally involved and the administrative staff of the royal household not present. The answer, highly satisfactory from the crown's point of view, was for the archers to be recruited by captains who were already accustomed to raising retinues of knights and esquires, and who could be prevailed upon to shoulder these additional costs and responsibilities. We should not imagine that full 'operational' integration of men-at-arms and archers occurred overnight, and yet the military advantages of such integration had been demonstrated in Scotland before the start of the French war.[85]

By the 1370s and 1380s it was normal for even the largest English field armies to be composed almost entirely of mixed retinues, but in the summer of 1346 this was not yet a practical proposition. At Crécy, the retinues probably contributed less than half of the manpower in Edward III's army.[86] As can be seen in Appendix 2, Table 2, there was no uniformity in retinue size, and it is likely that there was much variety in composition too, this being in part a reflection of different recruiting practices. It is possible that some captains were authorised to make use of traditional, array-style selection methods to help them assemble their mounted archers; indeed, this may have been necessary in the case of magnates who had agreed to provide large numbers of men.[87] There is evidence of this approach to recruitment being employed in 1337 for the Scottish war; and in the 1340s we find the earl of Northampton seeking authorisation for Sir Robert Bourchier to select twelve archers in Essex for service in the earl's retinue in Brittany.[88] Of course, captains turned to their estates and their tenants for recruits. But when we find, for example, that at least half of the eighty men who mustered at Heighley castle in Staffordshire on 25 April 1345 for service in Sir James Audley's retinue had been 'raised among the gentry

---

[84] P. Morgan, *War and Society in Medieval Cheshire, 1277–1403* (Manchester, 1987), pp. 37–49; Ayton, *Knights and Warhorses*, chapter 1; Prestwich, *Armies and Warfare in the Middle Ages*, pp. 125, 134–5.

[85] Morgan, *War and Society in Medieval Cheshire*, pp. 41–2.

[86] On the continuing employment of county and urban levies, see Powicke, *Military Obligation in Medieval England*, pp. 184–7; K. Fowler, *The King's Lieutenant: Henry of Grosmont, First Duke of Lancaster, 1310–1361* (London, 1969), p. 222 (Aquitaine, 1345–6).

[87] For John of Gaunt's employment of such methods and his evident anxiety that sufficient archers would be raised, see A. Goodman, *John of Gaunt: the Exercise of Princely Power in Fourteenth-Century Europe* (Harlow, 1992), pp. 218–19, 222–3.

[88] *Rotuli Scotiae*, i, pp. 480, 501–2. C81/1735, no. 2.

families and tenantry close to the Audley lands', we should not assume that we are seeing reluctant conscripts rather than volunteers, willing and able to serve in the retinue of their lord.[89] Hard evidence of 'professional' archers offering their services to captains in 1346 is hard to come by (it is more plentiful by the 1370s and 1380s); but what we can see during the summer of the Crécy campaign are the individual mounted archers who were sent to muster by land-holders seeking thereby to discharge their military assessment. It seems clear that many of these bowmen had been hired to do the job. One consequence of this additional supply of manpower would have been to reduce the need for 'conscription'.

There is another respect in which the composition of the retinues at Crécy was less uniform than the pay-roll abstracts suggest, and once again it is the military assessment records that provide the clue. Landholders with land worth £10 *per annum* were required to serve as, or to provide, a hobelar, who was an armoured horsemen less heavily equipped than a man-at-arms.[90] The military assessment records suggest that there were indeed many hobelars among the troops who fought in France in 1346. Only one is specifically assigned to a retinue: Thomas Stonleye, who served under Sir William Careswell in Bartholomew Burgherssh's retinue (vanguard battle) and was killed before Meulan.[91] But we may reasonably assume that the others were also serving in retinues, for there was no real alternative. It is curious, therefore, that the various surviving abstracts from Wetwang's pay-roll make little allowance for hobelars. The seven assigned to Sir Reginald Cobham's retinue are the only combatants of this type specified among the retinue-based personnel at Crécy.[92] It would seem that the hobelars, who like mounted archers were paid 6d per day, have been included in the archer totals. To the clerks drawing up the summarised version of the *vadia guerre* account that appeared in Wetwang's book of foreign expenses, there may have seemed little point in distinguishing between these two categories of mounted men, whereas foot archers were separately itemised because they were paid 3d per day. In this way, fighting men have become accounting units in the documentary record;[93] but however indistinguishable hobelars and archers may have seemed to a clerk seeking to be economical with his parchment, to the historian of the battle of Crécy the distinction is of some importance. We may be sure that some of the 'mounted archers' were actually hobelars, and that our assessment of the projectile weapon capability of the

---

[89] E101/24/20; Morgan, *War and Society in Medieval Cheshire*, pp. 75–6.

[90] According to an order of 27 March 1335, a hobelar's arms were (in addition to his unarmoured horse): aketon or plates, bascinet or palet, gorget, iron gauntlets, sword, knife and lance. *Rotuli Scotiae*, i, pp. 328–9; Powicke, *Military Obligation in Medieval England*, p. 192; A. Prince, 'The army and navy', *The English Government at Work, 1327–1336*, ed. J.F. Willard and W.A. Morris, 3 vols (Cambridge, Mass., 1940), i, pp. 339–40. Note also, V.H. Galbraith, 'Extracts from the *Historia Aurea* and a French "Brut" (1317–47)', *EHR*, xliii (1928), p. 206 and n. 2.

[91] Wrottesley, *Crecy and Calais*, pp. 142, 145, 149, 165 (Stonleye), 174.

[92] The College of Arms manuscript printed by Wrottesley gives an overall total of 528 hobelars, of whom 362 were supplied by the towns and 97 appear in the enigmatic 'de servitio' category. Wrottesley, *Crecy and Calais*, pp. 195, 203–4.

[93] For other, more fully documented cases, see Ayton, *Knights and Warhorses*, pp. 152–5.

English army should be reduced proportionately, but by how much? As for the hobelars themselves, they should not be dismissed as fighters of little value. During the Scottish wars these lightly armed cavalrymen had demonstrated that they were ideal for reconnaissance and raiding in difficult terrain.[94] They did, therefore, have a part to play in a chevauchée, and were no doubt effectively employed during the campaign from La Hougue to Ponthieu. On the battlefield they could serve alongside the men-at-arms as dismounted spearmen. This important tactical role has long been ascribed to hobelars, and given their equipment – comparable with, or better than, that carried by the Scots who dismounted to form schiltroms – they were no less suited to fighting on foot in defensive formations than were the men-at-arms in the English army.[95]

It is tempting to regard the mixed retinue as the essential organisational underpinning for the classic English fighting methods of the Hundred Years War: the chevauchée or mounted raid, and the combined arms tactics that were employed in battles and numerous small-scale encounters throughout the war. This was, after all, exactly the kind of warfare that was being fought in 1345–6 in secondary theatres of war by Edward III's lieutenants as he prepared and finally executed his major expedition to northern France. The Normandy–Crécy campaign was *somewhat* different, but although too sedate to be termed a chevauchée, it did culminate in what was to be the perfect performance of 'English' tactics on the continental stage. So, what part did the mixed retinue play in the English victory at Crécy? We cannot give a categorical answer to this question, and we should certainly avoid jumping to conclusions, for as Anne Curry has observed, 'organisation of armies in terms of recruitment and control is not necessarily the same as organisation in the field'. The mixed retinue 'is how armies were administered and paid, not necessarily how they fought'.[96] A closer look at the internal structure of the mixed retinues may make it easier to assess whether the men-at-arms and archers in such units are likely to have fought together.

The fundamental building blocks in an English army (or at least in that part of it composed of mixed retinues) were the companies that a captain would recruit as pre-existing units and which would amalgamate to form his retinue. These basic units of recruitment are less immediately visible in the records because, from the crown's point of view, they were not 'pay units'. Retinue muster rolls, which may have revealed their existence, have not survived. Fortunately, however, it is possible to discern them in some of the 'protection warrants' that

94 C. McNamee, *The Wars of the Bruces: Scotland, England and Ireland, 1306–1328* (East Linton, 1997), pp. 23–5, 148–57.

95 For the role of 'armati' and 'lancearios' (which we may take to be hobelars) at Boroughbridge in 1322, see *Lanercost*, ed. Stevenson, p. 243; *Vita Edwardi Secundi*, ed. N. Denholm Young (London, 1957), p. 124; T.F. Tout, 'The tactics of the battles of Boroughbridge and Morlaix', *EHR*, xix (1904), pp. 711–15. However, cf. Prestwich, *Armies and Warfare in the Middle Ages*, p. 135, for the view that there is 'no evidence to suggest that hobelars dismounted to fight'.

96 A. Curry, 'Review article. Medieval warfare. England and her continental neighbours, eleventh to the fourteenth centuries', *Journal of Medieval History*, xxiv (1998), pp. 81–102 (at p. 100).

have survived for the Crécy campaign.[97] When a captain wrote to the chancellor requesting the issue of letters of protection for his men he would naturally include a list of the men concerned, a list that would normally distinguish knights, esquires and non-combatants. Such warrants also quite often reveal the company structure of the retinue. The principal problem with these records, many of which have been brought together in a series of files in the class of Chancery Warrants (C81) at the National Archives, is that they do not usually bear a precise date. However, correlation with the enrolled protections on the Treaty Rolls enables us to identify some of the warrants that relate to the retinues in the Crécy army. Some light is thrown on the structure of the Prince of Wales's retinue by a collection of the prince's warrants sent to the chancellor, John Offord, on the eve of departure for La Hougue. Here we see, among others, the company of Sir Hugh Cressy and his three named esquires, and Sir Robert Bilkemor with his two *vallets*.[98] An impression of the mosaic of small units that lay beneath the monolithic exterior of the prince's huge retinue is revealed by such documents, but their coverage is very incomplete.

More substantial are the protection warrants that survive for the earl of Warwick's retinue, which together almost amount to a muster roll. This is the nearest we get to such complete coverage for a retinue involved in the battle of Crécy. A core document provides an invaluable overall impression of the structure and composition of Warwick's retinue, laid out in two columns.[99] The first column names the earl's three bannerets and notes the number of men-at-arms in their companies: Sir Thomas Ughtred (with twenty men-at-arms); Sir Aimery St Amand (twenty men-at-arms); and Sir Robert Scales (fifteen men-at-arms). Then are listed twenty-one knights (and one unnamed companion), with the number of esquires associated with them added against each name, thirty-one in all. (These thirty-one men are listed in the second column.) The names of the men-at-arms serving in two of the bannerets' companies can be found in subsidiary documents.[100] This collection of documents offers a vivid impression of the web of connections that gave the army's large retinues an inner strength and

[97] On protection warrants, their value and limitations, with archival details, see Ayton, *Knights and Warhorses*, pp. 160–2. The presence of commanders at sub-retinue level is also suggested, somewhat less clearly, by notes of warranty associated with enrolled protections and pardons.

[98] C81/1710, nos 21 (Cressy), 28 (Bilkemor).

[99] C81/1742, no. 26.

[100] C81/1741, no. 10 (Ughtred, with 20 men); C81/1742, no. 25 (St Amand, with 18 men). Whether these documents provide a complete picture of Warwick's retinue may be doubted, for they account for only 112 men-at-arms, whereas the College of Arms abstract of Wetwang's pay-roll suggests a total of 199 men-at-arms. Perhaps we should expect some names to be missing, for protection warrants would not normally be expected to list all men-at-arms. (It must be admitted that the core document does not proclaim itself to be a request for protections; and the subsidiary roll of Ughtred's men lists 20 men-at-arms, the number given in the core document.) That the core document does not list all of the men-at-arms is suggested by the fact that none of the knights has more than two esquires associated with him, whereas the indenture of retinue (20 April 1339) made between the earl of Warwick and Sir Robert Herle (who has two esquires in C81/1742, no. 26) stipulates that he would serve with four. M. Jones and S. Walker, eds, 'Private indentures for life service in peace and war, 1278–1476', *Camden Miscellany, XXXII*, Camden Soc., 5th ser., iii (1994),

cohesion. Thus, although a mid-fourteenth-century 'contract' army appears to have an ephemeral character, close examination of the make-up of its component retinues reveals an altogether more complex situation.

Protection warrants are silent with regard to the archers and their place in the structure of retinues.[101] That they were indeed fully meshed into the fabric of retinues at company level in 1346 is suggested by the numerous small companies of men-at-arms and archers that were grouped together to form the royal household division (see Appendix 2, Table 2). It is also demonstrated in a variety of documents generated by the new military assessment of the mid-1340s. Three examples must suffice. A certificate of service bears witness that John Segrave of 'Folkestan' served in Bartholomew Burgherssh's retinue with 'deux compaignouns et deux archiers'. A similar letter, this time from Sir Maurice Berkeley, notes that Alexander Seynlo, 'moun valet', who owes the service of an archer for his land in Hampshire, was duly serving with a bowman. Another document notes that Sir Adam Everingham of 'Rokkele' arrived at Portsmouth with two men-at-arms and an unspecified number of archers, and although Sir Adam was forced by illness to withdraw, his men joined the retinue of Sir John Darcy senior.[102] A few decades later, the documentary evidence suggests that captains depended to a considerable extent upon their sub-contracting men-at-arms for the recruitment of archers and the maintenance of discipline in the field, and there is no reason to believe that this was not also the case in 1346.[103]

Given that by the mid-1340s men-at-arms and archers were often to be found serving together in mixed retinues, having in many cases been recruited together at company level, should we not consider the possibility that they also fought together – that the fundamental 'atomic' structure of the army was reflected in tactical dispositions in the field? Of course, men-at-arms and archers would often find themselves side-by-side in combat situations. The campaign from La Hougue to Crécy had involved many assaults on towns and bridges in which 'combined arms' were employed. But conventional wisdom has it that deployment for a set-piece battle involved very different dispositions. An essential feature of 'English' tactics, so the argument goes, is that a block of men-at-arms was flanked by wings of archers. This formation would either be adopted for each of the several 'battles' in an army, or the archers would be positioned on the extreme wings of the whole army. It is such a tactical formation that some of the chroniclers seem to be describing, and Crécy is no exception. The problem with this arrangement – apart from the suspiciously 'mechanical' view of generalship and battlefield conditions, including terrain, that it presupposes – is that it would

---

no. 37 (pp. 70–1). There are no more than 34 enrolled protections for men serving in Warwick's retinue during the Normandy–Crécy campaign.

[101] The same applies to the private indentures of this period, whether for life service or short periods: Jones and Walker, eds, 'Private indentures for life service in peace and war, 1278–1476'; Wrottesley, *Crecy and Calais*, p. 192.

[102] C81/1721, no. 79; SC1/39, no. 182; Wrottesley, *Crecy and Calais*, p. 166.

[103] A. Goodman, 'The military subcontracts of Sir Hugh Hastings, 1380', *EHR*, xcv (1980), pp. 114–20; S. Walker, 'Profit and loss in the Hundred Years War: the subcontracts of Sir John Strother, 1374', *BIHR*, lviii (1985), pp. 100–6.

necessitate the break-up of mixed retinues, tearing apart the fabric of the army down to company level, thereby discarding the advantages brought by retinue-based esprit de corps. In short, it does not make military sense. We shall need to look closer at this problem in the concluding chapter of this book.

* * *

It is important to recognise that Edward III's army at Crécy was something of a hybrid institution, for alongside the mixed retinues of 'horse soldiers' – the innovative element – there were large numbers of foot soldiers recruited in the shires and towns of England and Wales by means of commissions of array.[104] In 1346 mass recruitment of infantry was still necessary if Edward III were to raise an army, from his own kingdom, large enough to challenge Philip of Valois in the field. Just how many men were actually recruited is not known, for our only systematic guide to numbers is an unsatisfactory one. What we have are not the totals that were actually transported to Normandy, but the numbers that the government hoped could be raised by commissions of array. To begin with what was to be the most important recruiting ground: Wales was to supply 7,000 footmen, of whom half would be archers and half spearmen. Just over half of these troops (3,550) were to be drawn from the lands and lordships of Edward, Prince of Wales, while the remainder were to be raised by lords whose lands lay mainly in south Wales and the Marches (see Table 1).[105] The prince was also to raise a hundred Cheshire archers.[106] In England, 29 shires lying south of the River Trent were ordered to supply, in total, 3,900 foot archers. Individual county targets ranged from 280 archers for Kent to 40 for Rutland.[107] In addition, 50 mounted archers were ordered from Shropshire, Worcester and Hereford to act as a royal bodyguard.[108] Separate orders were issued, on 10 February 1346, to 142 towns in the south and midlands of England. The original combined recruiting target for these towns was a little under 2,000 men, the

---

[104] This had become common practice during the Scottish wars of the first two Edwards and continued into the French war of the third. Prestwich, *War, Politics and Finance under Edward I*, pp. 99–107; Prestwich, *Armies and Warfare in the Middle Ages*, pp. 123–5.

[105] C76/22, m. 33 (3 February 1346); Wrottesley, *Crecy and Calais*, pp. 69, 80–81. The orders required each of the contingents to consist of archers and spearmen in equal numbers. Cf. the erroneous assertion by Sir James Ramsay that 'the order to the Prince of Wales' is 'a mere repetition' of the order to the Marcher lords: *The Genesis of Lancaster, 1307–1399*, 2 vols (Oxford, 1913), i, p. 319. Somewhat earlier, on 28 August and 29 September 1345, and 20 January 1346, the prince had been required to array a total of 4,000 Welshmen, half from the north and half from the south: C76/21, mm. 2, 5, 10; Wrottesley, *Crecy and Calais*, pp. 58, 62, 63. The orders issued on 3 February 1346 represent, therefore, a significant increase in numbers.

[106] Wrottesley, *Crecy and Calais*, pp. 58, 80.

[107] C76/21, m. 9 (28 August 1345, for planned passage three weeks after Michaelmas); C76/22, m. 29 (5 March 1346, for passage on 1 May); Wrottesley, *Crecy and Calais*, pp. 58–60, 72–3. Fifteen of Cambridgeshire's 100 archers were to be supplied by the town of Cambridge, and 40 of Lincolnshire's 200 by the city of Lincoln. One hundred of the archers arrayed in Gloucestershire, and a similar number in Herefordshire, may have been sent to Carmarthen rather than Portsmouth: *ibid.*, pp. 62, 65, 78.

[108] Wrottesley, *Crecy and Calais*, p. 65.

great majority of whom were to be *armati* (hobelars).[109] Individual quotas ranged from 600 men for London to two men for Blandford.

Table 1. Targets for recruitment of infantry in England and Wales

English shires

Devon	60	Norfolk	200
Somerset	160	Suffolk	100
Dorset	100	Hampshire	60
Wiltshire	200	Kent	280
Gloucestershire	200	Essex	200
Herefordshire	160	Hertfordshire	100
Oxfordshire	160	Cambridgeshire	100
Berkshire	120	Northamptonshire	200
Bedfordshire	60	Rutland	40
Surrey	100	Buckinghamshire	100
Sussex	200	Staffordshire	160
Shropshire	200	Huntingdonshire	60
Warwickshire	160	Middlesex	60
Worcestershire	80	Lincolnshire	200
Leicestershire	80		

Welsh lordships

Edward, Prince of Wales	lands and lordships in Wales	3,550
	Cheshire	100
William Bohun, earl of Northampton	Maelienydd (Radnor)	150
Rees ap Griffith	Narberth (Pembroke)	50
Henry, earl of Lancaster	Monmouth, Grosmont & White Castle (Monmouth)	200
Joan, countess of March	Ewyas Lacy (Hereford)	40
Humphrey Bohun, earl of Hereford and Essex	Brecknock (Brecon)	300
Gilbert Talbot	Blaen-Llynfi (Brecon), *Kirkehowel* Ystrad-Towey (Cardigan)	100
Joan, countess of March	Kerry & Cydewain (Montgomery)	100
Bartholomew Burgherssh	Ewyas Lacy (Hereford)	40
John de la Ware	Ewyas Harold (Hereford)	20
Lawrence Hastings, earl of Pembroke	Gwent-Uchcoed & Abergavenny (Monmouth)	150
Elizabeth Burgh	Usk (Monmouth)	150
Hugh Audley, earl of Gloucestershire	Newport & Gwent-Iscoed (Monmouth)	200
Hugh Despenser	Glamorgan & Morgannwg (Glamorgan)	300
John Mowbray	Gower (Glamorgan)	150
Henry, earl of Lancaster	Kidwelly, Carnwallon & Is-cennen (Carmarthen)	200

[109] 1,963 men. C76/22, m. 35; Wrottesley, *Crecy and Calais*, pp. 66–8. All were to be hobelars (*armati*), except 100 of London's quota, who were to be men-at-arms.

Welsh lordships *cont.*

James Audley	Cemmaes (Pembroke) & comote of Perfedd (Carmarthen)	100
Thomas Beauchamp, earl of Warwick	Elfael (Radnor)	60
Richard Fitzalan, earl of Arundel	Oswestry & Clun (Shropshire)	200
John Cherleton	Powis (Montgomery)	500
Richard Fitzalan, earl of Arundel	Chirk (Denbigh)	100
Roger Mortimer	*Warthrymyon*, Radnor (Radnor) Wigmore (Hereford)	200
Mary, countess of Norfolk	Chepstow & Gwent-Iscoed (Monmouth)	100
Lawrence Hastings, earl of Pembroke	Coytrahen	40

In the absence of systematic muster records or pay-rolls we cannot be sure how many men were actually raised by these means,[110] but those fragmentary documentary indications that we have suggest that the numbers transported to Normandy may have fallen some way short of the array targets. On 26 May, the king expressed concern that some 'rebellious and disobedient' archers, having been selected in the shires, had failed to arrive at Portchester.[111] The contingent of archers from Norfolk, marching from London to Portsmouth, numbered only 129 men, or about two-thirds of the county quota of 200; and the company of Cheshire archers 'may have been made up of as few as seventy-one men' rather than a hundred.[112] We also know that Kesteven, a third part of Lincolnshire, supplied 40 archers, which may suggest that recruitment in the county as a whole (including the city of Lincoln's quota of forty) fell short of its target of 200 men.[113] Precise data concerning the number of Welsh infantry who actually served are also lacking. The only indications offered by the records are the lump sums issued to pay the wages of the Welshmen during their march to Portsmouth: £349 for the north Wales contingent, £230 for those from the south. Assuming a march of fifteen days and ten days respectively, and the usual daily pay rates, we find that these lump sums would have paid for two contingents each of about 2,500 men, or in other words a little over two-thirds of the personnel that had been ordered.[114] This fits tolerably well with Clifford Rogers's suggestion that the figures for Welsh troops given in the College of Arms version of Wetwang's pay-roll should be interpreted as those who began the campaign (4,572 in all), particularly since we know that some Welsh

---

[110] For a discussion of what the Wetwang abstracts reveal about the arrayed troops in the English army, see Appendix 1.

[111] C81/1332, no. 1.

[112] E403/336, m. 42; Morgan, *War and Society in Medieval Cheshire*, p. 104.

[113] E403/336, m. 42; Wrottesley, *Crecy and Calais*, p. 65. Set a target of 160 archers in May 1342, Lincolnshire actually raised 120, of whom 40 came from Kesteven: C76/17, m. 41d; E101/23/8.

[114] E403/336, m. 44. The rates of travel are based on those of similar contingents of arrayed troops raised later in 1346: e.g., E101/552/23 (Cambridge to Sandwich); E101/559/15 (Gloucester to Sandwich). The rates of pay are set out in Robert Brady's extracts from Wetwang's pay-roll: *Complete History of England*, 2 vols (London, 1685, 1700), ii, Appendix, p. 85. On marching rates of archers in England, cf. H.J. Hewitt, *The Organisation of War under Edward III* (Manchester, 1966), pp. 42, 44.

'returned home from the sea-coast without leave'.[115] But it must be emphasised that much uncertainty surrounds the Welsh contingents in 1346–7 and how they have been recorded in the Wetwang abstracts. Do the various documentary references to the recruitment of Welsh troops in April–May 1346 relate to the large companies discussed above, or to the five hundred or so men attached to the prince's personal retinue? How many additional Welshmen arrived during the siege of Calais?[116] It is easier to pose such questions than to find satisfactory answers.

It is upon such very insecure documentary foundations that any estimate of the numbers of arrayed troops taken to France must rest, and some may be inclined to doubt whether as many as two-thirds of the numbers specified in the commissions of array were actually mustered. It is certainly the case that the towns contributed far fewer men than originally ordered. Many of the February 1346 quotas were later substantially reduced or completely remitted, as a consequence of either an order by the king's council or cash payments by individual towns, or both.[117] Norwich, for example, had its quota of 120 *armati* reduced to sixty; Shrewsbury's fell from thirty to twelve, Stafford's from eight to six.[118] Seventeen towns, with a total assessment of 280 men, were ordered to employ their men for defence purposes rather than overseas service. Although some towns certainly did chose to send troops, we have reliable information for only a handful of cases: St Albans (seven hobelars), Watford (two) and Newcastle-under-Lyme (three); and we hear that one of the armed men from Cambridge returned to England grievously wounded.[119] The most optimistic estimate, which takes account of all the recorded reductions in assessment and complete remissions, would be that the urban communities sent a little over 1,100 men to the Portsmouth muster.[120] But that figure includes London's contingent, which should have consisted of six hundred men, though we have no confirmation that as many as this actually served. Nor do we know what became of the contingent

---

[115] Wrottesley, *Crecy and Calais*, pp. 203–4; Rogers, *War Cruel and Sharp*, p. 426. Cf. Oman's very similar conclusion: *A History of the Art of War in the Middle Ages*, 2nd edn, 2 vols (London, 1924), ii, p. 130. Desertion: *Black Prince Register*, i, pp. 8–9.

[116] *Calendar of Ancient Correspondence Concerning Wales*, ed. J.G. Edwards (Cardiff, 1935), pp. 235–7. Reinforcements: *Black Prince Register*, i, pp. 7, 13–14, 32, 49–53, 55–6, 63, 78; Wrottesley, *Crecy and Calais*, pp. 104, 119, 129.

[117] Orders were sent to a shorter list of towns on 5 March (C76/22, m. 30; *Foedera*, III, i, pp. 71–2) and 20 April (C76/22, m. 15). For many individual reductions and remissions, see Wrottesley, *Crecy and Calais*, pp. 65–6, 68, 70–2, 88; and (with many cases of cash payments in lieu of service) *CFR, 1337–47*, pp. 497, 500–4. For useful comment on the urban levies, see Oman, *A History of the Art of War in the Middle Ages*, ii, pp. 128–30.

[118] Wrottesley, *Crecy and Calais*, p. 71; SC1/40, nos 35, 37.

[119] Wrottesley, *Crecy and Calais*, pp. 107, 137, 170. We know that contingents of hobelars were sent to the siege of Calais from Cambridge (8), Salisbury (10), Winchester (10) and Worcester (10): E403/339, mm. 5–6.

[120] 1,117 men from 90 towns. This is almost certainly more than actually served. The enrolled records are not always consistent or clear about either the size of assessments or the extent to which they have been discharged, nor are these records complete. For example, a letter from Richard Talbot certified that the men of Hereford and Leominster had made 'fyns devaunt nous' – 40 marks and £10 respectively – to discharge their assessment (SC1/41, no. 106), yet there is no record of this in either the Treaty or Fine Rolls.

of 320 *archers* that London had been ordered to provide.[121] Remove the Londoners and we have a maximum of 517 *armati* being supplied by the other towns (their original assessment being 1,363). On a county level, the nine Dorset towns, with a total assessment of thirty-eight *armati*, cannot have provided more than eighteen and probably sent fewer.[122] It is possible, therefore, that the reference to 362 hobelars 'of diverse cities' in the College of Arms version of Wetwang's pay-roll concerns these men, though whether London's contingent was included is not clear. The problem is further complicated by the fact that in October 1346 sixteen towns were ordered to send, overall, a further 306 men to the siege of Calais.[123]

However, the limited corporeal service provided by the towns was almost certainly exceptional. Indeed, that our informed guess of a 'two-thirds' fulfilment of the shire array targets may well actually be an *underestimate* is suggested by the response to the orders for reinforcements issued on 26 July.[124] Detailed records, including a number of muster rolls, have survived for the contingents of archers that were raised and transported in response to these orders. If we compare the numbers requested with the numbers actually raised, we find a remarkable degree of congruency. All of the eight shires for which a comparison is possible raised exactly the number of archers that were required.[125] These archers had been recruited before Crécy had been fought; indeed, they were marching across England on the day of the battle. Consequently, the high turnout cannot convincingly be attributed to a sudden surge of enthusiasm for the French war. Nor, indeed, was it an unprecedented turnout. In June–July 1338, eighteen shire contingents gathering in Norwich prior to Edward III's first French expedition provided 90 per cent of the archers that had been specified in the commissions of array.[126] The pay-roll for this army suggests that, one way or another, more than three-quarters of the archers ordered by the crown from the English shires actually served in France.[127] If such comparisons serve a useful purpose, it is to suggest that the recruitment in

121 Wrottesley, *Crecy and Calais*, pp. 58, 70. In late March 1346, London was also preparing to send archers to Gascony: *Calendar of Letter Books . . . City of London, Letter Book F, c.1337–52*, ed. R.R. Sharpe (London, 1904), p. 138.
122 Wrottesley, *Crecy and Calais*, p. 68; *CFR, 1337–47*, pp. 502–3.
123 Wrottesley, *Crecy and Calais*, pp. 103, 105, 203.
124 Wrottesley, *Crecy and Calais*, pp. 101–2.
125 Essex, Norfolk, Suffolk, Rutland, Dorset, Somerset, Hampshire and Wiltshire. E101/575/15; E101/584/5, m.1; E372/191, m. 48; Hewitt, *The Organisation of War Under Edward III*, p. 44: Table II. Note that the number of archers raised in Wiltshire in August 1346 should be 60 not 50.
126 When the shire levies were inspected at Norwich, 54 men were rejected and sent home, leaving 998 archers, whereas the government's recruiting target for the 18 shires had been 1,110. (Three other contingents, not embraced by the commissions of array of 26 February, have been excluded from the calculation.) *Treaty Rolls, 1337–39*, no. 123; E101/21/21, mm. 2–3 (wage account for the archers, June–July 1338).
127 Excluding the troops sent by Cheshire (150) and London (100), the number of archers not serving in retinues was 1,465. This included the 'official' shire contingents, in most cases somewhat depleted by comparison with the 'Norwich' strength of June-July 1338. Consequently some of the contingents had been amalgamated to form units of viable size. There was also a company of 445 men from various parts of England who had joined the

the shires for the Crécy campaign may have been more successful than some historians have supposed. The only grounds for doubt would seem to be the unusually heavy manpower demands that the crown was making in 1346, and the sequence of postponements and delays owing to shipping shortages and adverse weather, which may have further affected recruitment. We know that some arrayers experienced problems fulfilling their commissions, while others were 'negligent' and 'tardy';[128] but in truth none of these problems were peculiar to 1346, and the delays may have allowed latecomers to join the army. Among those who arrived at the last minute were Thomas Crewe and his brother, who were allowed aboard the prince's cog 'Thomas' 'at the Isle of Wyght . . . as he was crossing to Hoggis'.[129]

If it is uncertain how many archers and spearmen disembarked at La Hougue and fought at Crécy, we do know a little about the internal organisation and appearance of the companies. The shire companies of archers were composed of groups of 20 men, each led by a vintenar or 'twentieth man'. Five vintenaries were led by a centenar, or (if the whole contingent) a 'leader' (*ductor*), who was often a local man-at-arms. Since the county's quota of archers would be sub-divided among its constituent hundreds, the vintenaries would be composed of men from the same district.[130] London's contingent was organised along similar lines. In the spring of 1345, the city's company of 80 archers had been raised according to its usual principle of ward quotas (there were 24 wards), and the same presumably occurred in 1346. Each alderman selected and equipped the allotted number of men from his ward (five from Vintry ward, for example), and these little companies were grouped into four troops, each commanded by a vintenar.[131] What must have given the company of Londoners a distinctive appearance was their uniform: they were clothed in coats (*courbys*) and hoods, decorated with red and white stripes.[132] We know less about the outfits worn by the English shire levies, though the commissions of array did stipulate that the men should be uniformly clothed ('de una secta vestitos').[133] On one occasion

army 'freely', which presumably included small contingents from the shires that are not otherwise recorded in the pay-roll. The government's orders in February had required the English shires to provide, all told, 1,950 archers. The orders to two counties, Sussex (100 men) and Buckinghamshire (40), were later cancelled. *Norwell*, pp. 358–60; *Treaty Rolls, 1337–39*, nos 123, 506, 509.

128 *CPR, 1345–8*, p. 113; *Calendar of Ancient Correspondence Concerning Wales*, pp. 235–7; *Black Prince Register*, i, pp. 9, 14.

129 *Black Prince Register*, iii, p. 413.

130 Prince, 'The army and navy', *The English Government at Work, 1327–1336*, i, pp. 357–8. Note, however, that some regrouping and 'weeding' could occur: Powicke, *Military Obligation in Medieval England*, p. 129.

131 *Calendar of Plea and Memoranda Rolls . . . City of London, 1323–64*, ed. A.H. Thomas (Cambridge, 1926), pp. 221–2; P. Konieczny, 'London's war effort in the fourteenth century', forthcoming. I am grateful to the author for allowing me to consult this paper in advance of publication.

132 In the 1380s, troops from Norwich were also clothed in tunics and hoods of white and red: W. Hudson, 'Norwich militia in the fourteenth century', *Norfolk Archaeology*, xiv (1901), pp. 284, 302.

133 *Treaty Rolls, 1337–39*, no. 123. Prince, 'The army and navy', *The English Government at*

the sheriff of Rutland confirms that he has met this requirement, but does not mention the colour of the outfits provided.[134] In addition to ensuring that the recruits would have adequate clothing for the campaign, a uniform provided a ready means of identification. This may have been prompted as much by disciplinary considerations as by the need for combat recognition, for we should probably imagine considerable variety in the colours and patterns adopted by the various shire and urban communities contributing troops to the army. When the dazzling array of heraldic banners and surcoats is also taken into account, it can be seen that an Edwardian army was indeed a host of many colours.

The distinctive appearance of the Welsh contingents can also be visualised: the green and white outfits of the prince's Welsh (and Cheshire) companies – short coats (*courtepy*) and hats (*chaperon*) – are frequently mentioned in the records, and we catch a glimpse of the red and white clothing supplied to the earl of Arundel's Welsh troops.[135] Also notable is the distinctive appearance of the Welsh companies in the pay-rolls, for it is usual for a chaplain, a surgeon, standard bearer and a *proclamator* to be included among those receiving the king's pay.[136] With the exception of standard bearers, such ancillary personnel are never mentioned in the pay records for either the English shire or urban levies, or the retinues of men-at-arms and archers. If Froissart is to be believed, the fighting role of the Welsh at Crécy was also distinctive. He has them despatching wounded French men-at-arms with long knives.[137] The writs ordering their recruitment seem to recognise the importance of preserving this separate identity, for it was firmly emphasised that 'Englishmen dwelling in Wales were not to be chosen among the Welsh'.[138] Perhaps, however, this merely reflects recognition of an impenetrable language barrier; indeed, it may well have been the language issue that explains the provision of paid ancillary personnel – including, sometimes, *interpretatores* – for the Welsh companies.

It is far from clear how the shire companies and the Welsh contingents were integrated into the operational structure of the army. As we have seen, the *Acta Bellicosa* reveals that the army was composed of three 'battles' or divisions, and offers sufficient information to identify the retinues in each of them. Although neither this document nor the abstracts of Wetwang's pay-roll cast any light on how the large numbers of English and Welsh infantry were incorporated into the army's tripartite structure, there can be little doubt that they were so

Work, 1327–1336, i, pp. 362–3; Hewitt, *The Organisation of War under Edward III*, p. 39; Prestwich, *Armies and Warfare in the Middle Ages*, p. 141.

134 C47/2/34, no. 2.

135 *Black Prince Register*, i, pp. 14–15, 68, 80; Morgan, *War and Society in Medieval Cheshire*, pp. 104–5; R.R. Davies, *Lordship and Society in the March of Wales, 1282–1400* (Oxford, 1978), p. 81 n. 61.

136 Wrottesley, *Crecy and Calais*, pp. 203–4; Prince, 'The army and navy', *The English Government at Work, 1327–1336*, i, pp. 342–3; Prestwich, *Armies and Warfare in the Middle Ages*, pp. 127–8; D.L. Evans, 'Some notes on the history and principality of Wales in the time of the Black Prince, 1343–76', *Transactions of the Honourable Society of Cymmrodorion*, 1925–6, pp. 25–100 (at pp. 48–61).

137 *Froissart*, ed. Luce, iii, p. 187.

138 Wrottesley, *Crecy and Calais*, p. 69; *Black Prince Register*, i, pp. 52, 55.

incorporated. Otherwise, it is difficult to see how a company of two hundred archers led by a 'ductor' of low rank and limited personal means – a company not bound to the crown by a contractual agreement – could be supplied or controlled on the march, or deployed effectively on the battlefield. In some matters the shire levies came under the authority of the constable and marshal of the army – respectively, the earls of Northampton and Warwick.[139] The author of the *Acta Bellicosa* notes that these earls had been appointed 'to check the rashness of the troops', though the narrative sources for the campaign make it clear that maintaining discipline within the army, and in particular controlling looting and burning, was a difficult if not impossible task.[140] We know that the constable and marshal, and their lieutenants (Sir Adam Swynbourne and Sir Thomas Ughtred), authorised the granting of charters of pardon, which suggests that they maintained, or had access to, muster rolls of the shire levies.[141] They also performed a supervisory role in such routine but essential aspects of army life as overnight billeting and sentry duty. Bearing in mind their organisational responsibilities, and that Northampton and Warwick were members of the king's inner circle, it is possible that they, or their lieutenants, were in overall control of the English and Welsh archer companies and issued orders directly to the leaders of individual contingents. But, on balance, it is more likely that each of the companies was assigned, individually or as part of a group, to one of the three battles, and thereby brought under the authority of the commander of that formation. An arrangement of this kind is clearly stipulated in the earliest surviving collection of ordinances for an English army, dating from 1385, and it is likely that the same applied in 1346; indeed, more than likely, given the otherwise free-floating status of the arrayed companies.[142] We might suppose that the companies would be distributed in such a way as to maximise compatibility and tactical advantage: that the contingents from the Welsh and Marcher lordships of Prince Edward, the earls of Northampton and Warwick, and Bartholomew Burgherssh would be assigned to the vanguard division, for example. Indeed, it is possible that individual companies were 'attached' to specific retinues. This is no more than conjecture, of course, but not of the idle variety. For here we are confronting one of the most important, if all too often side-stepped questions concerning the English tactical dispositions at Crécy: namely, how the two main sections of the army – the mixed retinues and the shire levies – were deployed on the battlefield, and how their very different organisational features may have

---

[139] For the functions performed by these officers, see Prestwich, *Armies and Warfare in the Middle Ages*, pp. 171–5; and M. Keen, 'Richard II's ordinances of war of 1385', *Rulers and Ruled in Late Medieval England*, ed. R. Archer and S. Walker (London and Rio Grande, 1995), pp. 33–48.

[140] *Acts of War,* ed. Barber, p. 29; Rogers, *War Cruel and Sharp*, pp. 241–2.

[141] E.g., pardons issued 'by the testimony' of Sir Adam Swynbourne, under-constable of the army: *CPR, 1345–8*, pp. 487, 494, 496–500, 502–5, 507–8, 510–13. A fourteenth-century tract concerning the rights of the constable and marshal notes that they were each 'to have a roll of all the men of arms in the army, and of all the infantry, to be the more able to appoint the watches, sentinels and scouts, for the safety of the army': F. Grose, *Military Antiquities Respecting a History of the English Army*, 2nd edn, 2 vols (London, 1812), i, p. 187.

[142] In 1385, the army was composed essentially of contracted retinues. Keen, 'Richard II's ordinances of war of 1385', pp. 38–9.

influenced English tactics. This is a subject to which we shall return in the concluding chapter of this book.

* * *

Having surveyed the size and structure of the army that landed at La Hougue, it would no doubt be helpful to summarise the conclusions that have been reached. Analysis of the available records suggests that the army probably consisted of about 14,000 fighting men. There may have been as many as 2,800 men-at-arms, the majority being knights and esquires of gentle blood, serving in the retinues of magnates, knights and royal servants. A similar number of mounted archers and hobelars were also attached to these retinues. Estimating the number of men in the companies that had been recruited in the English shires and towns and in the Welsh lordships is even more problematic, but based on the reasoning outlined above, it can be suggested that all told more than 8,000 men may have been provided from these sources. The great majority of these were foot soldiers, and perhaps 5,000 were archers.[143]

This was the largest army to be transported to France by Edward III, but the six weeks of hard campaigning prior to Crécy must have taken its toll. Although the English narrative sources play down the losses, we may be sure that during those six weeks the army suffered considerable combat casualties. The campaign involved a series of frontal assaults, most notably at Caen and at various attempted river crossings, on the Seine and the Somme, culminating in what was clearly a hard-fought encounter at Blanquetaque. The evidence tends to suggest that the archers and other foot soldiers sustained the heaviest casualties,[144] though we certainly do hear of men-at-arms being killed and wounded. Perhaps the most notable example, and certainly the most fully documented, is Sir Edward atte Wode, who during the assault on the castle of Roche Guyon was killed by 'una petra jactata de castello'.[145] In addition, the earl of Huntingdon retired sick to England after the capture of Caen, and part of his retinue, along with others who had fallen ill, accompanied him.[146] We are told that detachments

---

[143] Cf. the similar estimates of army size, based upon somewhat different but carefully thought-out methodologies, by Oman, *A History of the Art of War in the Middle Ages*, ii, pp. 127–31; and Rogers, *War Cruel and Sharp*, pp. 423–6. For calculations that gave rise to lower estimates, see Ramsay, *Genesis of Lancaster*, i, pp. 318–19; F. Lot, *L'art militaire et les armées au Moyen Age*, 2 vols (Paris, 1946), i, pp. 344–7; Sumption, *Trial by Battle*, p. 497.

[144] A point made forcefully by J. Viard, 'La campagne de juillet–août 1346 et la bataille de Crécy, *Le moyen âge*, 2nd ser., xxvii (1926), p. 67 n. 1. For example, Richard Whet, an archer, was killed during the assault on Caen: Wrottesley, *Crecy and Calais*, p. 155. Michael Northburgh noted that 'noz gentz del host . . . avoient mult affaire' at Caen (*Avesbury*, p. 359), while Froissart comments on the heavy English losses at the hands of the townspeople (*Froissart*, ed. Luce, iii, p. 145).

[145] *Eulogium*, iii, p. 208; *Acts of War*, ed. Barber, p. 35; *CIPM*, ix, no. 35.

[146] The king described the earl's illness as a 'molt forte et perillouse maladie': Fowler, 'News from the front', p. 84 (C81/314, no. 17803). William Daudele, of Sir Robert Ferrers's retinue, who had also fallen ill, was required to 'conduct certain prisoners taken at Caen' to England (Wrottesley, *Crecy and Calais*, p. 104). Those who accompanied Huntingdon to England included his *familiaris* Sir William Septvans, whose wife bore him a son, William,

were left in Normandy to man garrisons, at Carentan and Caen, though the assertion by some French chronicles that 1,500 Englishmen were left in Caen, and
subsequently massacred, is surely wishful thinking.[147] It is more likely that
Edward III's Norman allies provided the bulk of these garrisons. Lastly, we
should allow for the attrition of the march: men who died from disease, accident
or the action of the rural population. The *Acta Bellicosa* records the loss of some
archers in a burning building, for example.[148] It is clear that these men were not
replaced before 26 August, for although the despatch of reinforcements had been
ordered only a fortnight into the campaign, none as far as we know arrived
before the battle of Crécy had been fought.[149] Indeed, as he marched north from
the Seine towards Ponthieu, the king cannot have been sure that fresh troops
would arrive in time. According to the *Acta Bellicosa*, believing that he would
meet the enemy shortly, the king 'did not want to lose any men' in assaults on
fortified towns along the line of march. So, although we cannot with confidence
offer a figure for the size of the English army on 26 August, we may be sure that
hundreds of men, perhaps more than a thousand, had been lost during the six
weeks since the landing at St Vaast-la-Hougue. Jean le Bel referred to Edward's
army at Crécy as a 'little company', but we should guard against the temptation
of seeing this as a 'happy few'; comparison with Agincourt is not in any sense
apt. Edward III's men had done some hard marching and some hard fighting, but
the discomforts of the siege camp lay in the future. They were well rested before
the battle and probably well fed, exhilarated by their success at the Blanquetaque
crossing of the Somme and buoyed by the king's words of encouragement.

It is as difficult to be precise about English casualties in the battle as it is to
provide a reliable figure for the size of the army. The few English sources that
offer information all state that Edward III's losses at Crécy were light,[150] though
some of the suggestions appear improbably low. For example, Richard
Wynkeley, who was present but probably not an eyewitness to the fighting, tells
us that two knights and an esquire fell in the battle, together with a few

on 28 August. Meanwhile, the earl was staying at Poplar, near London, taking medicines
(*CIPM*, xii, no. 96). Several of the earl's archers were later arrested in Shropshire: SC1/39,
no. 190. It seems that the greater part of Huntingdon's retinue remained with the army,
perhaps commanded by one of Clinton's bannerets, John Botetourt or John Grey of
Rotherfield (the latter is most likely since he is frequently named in the notes of warranty for
the issue of pardons).

[147] *Chronique Normande*, p. 77 n. 1 and the closely related *Chronographia*, ii, pp. 225–6, an
account accepted by H. Prentout, *La prise de Caen par Edouard III, 1346* (Caen, 1904), pp.
41–2, and Viard, 'La campagne de juillet–août 1346 et la bataille de Crécy', pp. 29–30.
According to the *Grandes chroniques*, ix, p. 274, Edward burnt much of the town before
leaving.

[148] *Acts of War*, ed. Barber, p. 31.

[149] Orders for the raising of 1,240 archers in the English shires had been issued by the
regency council on 26 July, and on 29 July, Edward III, writing from Caen, commanded that
these reinforcements be sent to Le Crotoy. C76/23, m. 22; Wrottesley, *Crecy and Calais*, pp.
101–2; Fowler, 'News from the front', p. 84 (C81/314, no. 17803). But the force, commanded
by Sir Thomas Haukeston and Sir William Fraunk, could not have joined the king's army
until well after the battle had been fought (*Foedera*, III, i, p. 89; E101/390/12, fo. 8v).

[150] Cf. *Jean de Venette*, ed. Newhall, p. 44: 'Many of the English perished, but not so many
as of our men.'

Welshmen somewhat later.[151] Rather more plausibly, Geoffrey le Baker reports, with a nice touch of detail, that when the army was mustered on Sunday 27 August it was discovered that only forty men had been killed.[152] But even this figure seems low, given the hand-to-hand fighting that some accounts of the battle suggest had taken place. Remember the ferocious mêlée around the Prince of Wales and his standard; and Geoffrey le Baker's vivid description of the prince's men during a lull in the battle, 'leaning on their lances and swords, taking breath and resting quietly on mounds of corpses'. In the light of this, it is tempting to take Jean le Bel's figure of '300 English knights' slain as actually meaning 300 men of all ranks.[153] Although that may well be of the right order of magnitude, the fact remains that we know the names of only two of the English dead. After the battle, Sir James Audley reported that one his esquires, Robert Brente, a minor Somerset landowner, had been killed, while the Monk of Malmesbury recorded the death of a newly created knight, Aymer Rokesley.[154] We should note also that at least two knights, Sir Robert Tyford and Sir James Haumville, were taken prisoner by the French in the battle,[155] perhaps another indication of the fierceness of the hand-to-hand fighting. What is striking about this list of English losses, apart from its brevity, is that all four men were serving in retinues that were located in the rearguard division: the two prisoners in the earl of Suffolk's retinue, the two fatalities in the earl of Arundel's. Apart from casting further doubt on the improbably low casualty figures suggested by some English sources (note that there is not a single known fatality from the vanguard division, which bore the brunt of the fighting), this tends to confirm that the rearguard division did play some part in the battle, perhaps in a confused mêlée after nightfall, perhaps in the mopping-up operation on the following morning.

That two English knights fell into the enemy's hands at Crécy is all the more notable given that there is little reliable evidence that French prisoners were taken in the battle. The contrast with the battles of Neville's Cross and Poitiers,[156] and indeed with the earlier stages of the Normandy–Crécy campaign, could not be sharper. The capture of Caen on 26 July had yielded many

---

151 *Murimuth*, pp. 216–17 (cf. p. 247). A real eyewitness, Johann von Schönfeld, noted that 'dominus rex Anglie nisi unum solum milite perdidit in exercitu suo': J.F. Böhmer, *Acta Imperii selecta* (Innsbruck, 1870), no. 1055. Cf. *Knighton*, ed. Martin, pp. 62–5: three knights killed during the battle and one esquire before. Thomas Bradwardine suggested that 'De nostris vero nullus dominus, miles aut armiger in illo conflictu ceciderat aut grave vulnus reciperat aut captus fuerat, de quo sciam,' though the last three words reflect his detachment from the events of the battle (Offler, 'Thomas Bradwardine's "Victory Sermon" in 1346', p. 26).

152 *Baker*, p. 85. Cf. *Froissart: Amiens*, iii, p. 26: only three English knights and about twenty archers.

153 *Jean le Bel*, ii, p. 108.

154 Brente: SC1/39, no. 178; cf. Wrottesley, *Crecy and Calais*, pp. 125, 146. Rokesley: *Eulogium*, iii, p. 211. His inquisition post mortem accurately states that he died on Saturday next after St Bartholomew, i.e. 26 August: *CIPM*, viii, no. 627. Both men were serving under the earl of Arundel: C76/23, mm. 11, 24.

155 Wrottesley, *Crecy and Calais*, pp. 134, 165.

156 See C. Given-Wilson and F. Bériac, 'Edward III's prisoners of war: the battle of Poitiers and its context', *EHR*, cxvi (2001), pp. 802–33.

prisoners, including Raoul de Brienne, count of Eu and Jean de Melun, lord of Tancarville and chamberlain of Normandy, and over a hundred knights. This rich haul was highlighted by many of the narrative sources and left a number of documentary trails in the administrative records.[157] Two of the principal benefi- ciaries were Sir Thomas Holland and Sir Thomas Daniel. Holland released his prisoner, the count of Eu, to the king for 20,000 marks, an astronomical sum, payable over a three-year period from the customs duties on wool, while Daniel handed Tancarville over to the Prince of Wales, in return for an annuity of 40 marks (to be converted into a heritable grant of £20 p.a. of land).[158] But of French prisoners taken at Crécy, the administrative records reveal nothing. Admittedly, Michael Northburgh's newsletter records that the English 'pristrount de chivalers et esquiers a graunt nombre' on the morning after the main battle, while Bradwardine noted in his sermon that 'some were taken alive';[159] but the only chronicle to dwell on the subject comes from an unex- pected corner of Europe – Poland. Jan Długosz's *Annals*, written in the mid–late fifteenth century, notes that Edward III freed 'all the prisoners who [were] Czechs, Germans, Spaniards and other foreigners', but held the French prisoners to ransom.[160] But how much reliance should we place on such a late source, particularly since several chroniclers state that the commanders of both armies had decided before the battle that no quarter would be given? Indeed, the St Omer chronicle has Edward's German allies questioning the king's judgement on this matter.[161] Whether or not specific orders were issued, we should also remember that English tactics, heavily dependent on archery, ensured that many potentially ransomable knights and esquires would be killed before they had an opportunity of crossing swords with their opponents. Then, of course, there is Froissart's grisly anecdote that, at one point in the battle, the Welsh infantry were allowed to slip between the men-at-arms and archers and swarm over the disabled French men-at-arms, dispatching them without mercy with their long knives ('grandes coutilles').[162] This was, in all senses, 'guerre mortelle', and so

---

[157] English newsletters: *Murimuth*, p. 203 (Burgherssh); *Avesbury*, p. 359 (Northburgh); Fowler, 'News from the front', pp. 83–4 (Edward III). *Acts of War*, ed. Barber, p. 33; *Baker*, pp. 80, 253 (Cotton MS, Cleopatra, D. VII, fo. 179). Continental chronicles: *Chronique Normande*, p. 76; *Récits*, p. 218; St Omer chronicle, fo. 259v (cf. *Chronique de Flandre*, ii, p. 40); *Jean le Bel*, ii, pp. 82–8; *Froissart: Amiens*, ii, p. 386. Note also, comment in Rogers, *War Cruel and Sharp*, p. 251 n. 75. For prisoners taken (or acquired) at Caen by Sir William Kildesby, see *CPR, 1345–8*, p. 362; Wrottesley, *Crecy and Calais*, p. 133. *Knighton*, ed. Martin, pp. 58–9 notes that '300 and more' prisoners were sent to England.

[158] Holland: *CPR, 1345–8*, pp. 337, 538–9, 550–1. Daniel: *Black Prince Register*, i, p. 45. Tancarville was kept at Wallingford castle: *Black Prince Register*, i, pp. 28, 33, 60, 62. See also Viard, 'La campagne de juillet–août 1346 et la bataille de Crécy', p. 25 n. 1.

[159] *Avesbury*, p. 369; Offler, 'Thomas Bradwardine's "Victory Sermon" in 1346', p. 26. Northburgh's testimony on prisoners was the source for the similar comments in John of Reading's chronicle, which in turn influenced the author of the English continuation of the *Brut*. *John of Reading*, p. 101; *Brut*, ed. Brie, ii, p. 299. The words of the Anonimalle chronicle ('Les nouns de ceaux qe furent pris al iournee ne sount point yssi escript') may have been lifted from another newsletter, now lost: *Anonimalle*, pp. 23, 161.

[160] *The Annals of Jan Długosz*, trans. M. Michael (Chichester, 1997), pp. 296–7.

[161] See Chapter 4, p. 151.

[162] *Froissart*, ed. Luce, iii, p. 187, which describes the troops involved as 'Gallois et

it is perhaps not altogether surprising to find little evidence of French prisoners being taken, though it would indeed have been an extraordinary encounter had there been none.

That there was plentiful booty to be had, from the French baggage and the corpses lying on the field, may reasonably be assumed, though it cannot be documented. Unless secretly pocketed (and who can doubt that much would have been concealed), such spoils would have been divided according to the standard arrangements for continental field campaigns at this time. Half of the value would be surrendered by the captor to his retinue commander, who in turn surrendered half of his half to the king.[163] Indentures stressed that such an arrangement would apply in particular to the division of ransoms extracted from prisoners of war. Half may seem an excessively large 'portion' for the captain (and king) to take, but it should be recalled, firstly, that this was an army serving for the king's pay; and, secondly, that lubrication of the military machine often depended upon the captains' own financial resources. The standard daily pay rates (for example, 1s for a man-at-arms, 6d for a mounted archer) came as part of a package of terms of service, which included, for men-at-arms, *restauro equorum* and *regard*.[164] The former provided for the valuation of the principal warhorse brought by each man-at-arms and the payment of compensation in the event of its loss.[165] *Regard* had been introduced for continental campaigns as recently as 1345 and was generally paid to captains at a quarterly rate of 100 marks for the service of thirty men-at-arms.[166] Whether at this time the *regard* payment was passed on to the men-at-arms themselves (in which case representing a supplementary payment of about 6d per day) or retained by the captain as a contribution towards his overheads is not certain, but on balance the latter seems more likely. In general, profits were not to be made from the crown's disbursements, which were intended to cover costs rather than to offer significant rewards. In practice, they can hardly have even covered costs; and the fact that pay habitually slipped into arrears meant that junior captains could find themselves seriously out of pocket. Sir Warin Trussell had only two esquires and two archers in his company in 1346, yet a year's pay and regard for himself and his men would have amounted to £116 13s 4d. He was paid £25 6d in April as an advance, but was still owed £35 16s 10d in February 1352.[167] Elevation to knighthood during the campaign would be accompanied by a doubling of daily

---

Cornillois'. Froissart adds that Edward III 'fu depuis courouciés que on ne les avoit pris à raençon'.

163 See Ayton, *Knights and Warhorses*, pp. 127–37. The St Omer chronicle states that Edward ordered his men to bring to him the heraldically decorated surcoats of the dead, but allowed them to keep anything else they might find on the battlefield: St Omer chronicle, fo. 263r; *Chronique de Flandre*, ii, p. 44.

164 On the terms of service offered at this time: for a brief overview, see A. Ayton, 'English armies in the fourteenth century', *Arms, Armies and Fortifications in the Hundred Years War*, ed. A. Curry and M. Hughes (Woodbridge, 1994), pp. 22–5; and for a more detailed discussion, see Ayton, *Knights and Warhorses*, chapter 4.

165 No horse inventories for the Crécy army have survived, but we do know that *restor* payments were made: e.g., to Sir Thomas Bourne (E404/496, no. 86).

166 Ayton, *Knights and Warhorses*, pp. 110–13.

167 BL, Harleian MS 3968, fo. 123v; E403/336, m. 43; Wrottesley, *Crecy and Calais*, p. 173.

wages, but the new status also brought greater costs and responsibilities. The seven household esquires who were knighted by the king on the day of Crécy received annuities to support their new status;[168] but most of the men raised to knighthood on that day (the Monk of Malmesbury suggests that there were 50 elevations all told) would have received no such financial support. Indeed, at least two of them, John Colby and Ralph Shelton, may be regarded as 'knights of force', since they had been distrained to knighthood in 1344.[169]

Soon after the battle, rewards were distributed to a number of men. Within a week, Sir Richard Fitz Simon, the Prince of Wales's banner bearer, was granted £20 *per annum*, 'on account of the prince's affection towards him'; and this was followed by a gift of £100 marks 'as a reward for his labours in the prince's service' during the Crécy campaign. According to the Bourgeois of Valenciennes's chronicle, Fitz Simon had heroically defended the prince and his banner in the battle, an incident that had evidently also involved Sir Thomas Daniel, for he was later granted 40 marks per year, in part for replanting the prince's banner at Crécy.[170] On 7 September, the king conferred upon Sir Philip Buketot, a veteran who had served under Richard Talbot at Crécy, 'la baillie de garder notre foreste de Shottore'.[171] Reward for good service could come in other forms. In November the earl of Warenne's enfeoffment of Edward III was reversed because it was deemed prejudicial to the interests of the earl of Arundel, to whom Warenne's lands would naturally pass upon his death. Arundel had raised the matter with the king 'when he was on his passage, near Yarmouth, in the Isle of Wight', and after Crécy he got his way.[172] What these examples illustrate is that, apart from booty, such material rewards as arose from the battle of Crécy tended to be gained through the deployment of 'English' resources. Other forms of reward merely involved transferring responsibilities from the shoulders of favoured 'Crécy men' on to those of their stay-at-home contemporaries. This, for example, would have been the effect of the steady flow of orders granting men exemptions, in conventional form, from being appointed to a range of local administrative duties in return for their 'good service in the war in France'.[173]

It was much the same with the various recruitment incentives offered by the crown, for these too involved gains for some Englishmen at the expense of others. This is perhaps most evident in the case of charters of pardon, which were offered to criminals willing to perform a spell of military service, and

---

[168] *CPR, 1345–8*, p. 474.

[169] *Eulogium*, iii, p. 211; cf. *Knighton*, ed. Martin, pp. 64–5. Colby: E159/121, m. 228. Shelton: *CPR, 1345–8*, p. 291. Distraint returns: E198/3/22, m. 3.

[170] *Black Prince Register*, i, pp. 14, 40, 45, 48. *Récits*, p. 233. M. J. Bennett, *Community, Class and Careerism* (Cambridge, 1983), p. 186. It is worthy of note that Richard Fitz Simon appears on the muster roll for the earl of Derby's retinue in Aquitaine in 1345–6 (E101/25/9, m. 3), so he must have returned to England before July 1346.

[171] C81/314, no. 17813.

[172] *CPR, 1345–8*, pp. 221, 480. G. Holmes, *The Estates of the Higher Nobility in Fourteenth-Century England* (Cambridge, 1957), pp. 7, 41–2. As Tout noted, Arundel's succession to the Warenne estates in 1347 made him 'the strongest of the territorial magnates, if we omit the prince of Wales and the duke of Lancaster' (Tout, *Chapters*, iii, p. 190). The recruiting implications of this will not have escaped the king.

[173] *CPR, 1345–8*, pp. 474, 476–8, 481, 515.

which were regarded as a threat to public order by the political community and, indeed, society at large.[174] Of course, not all of the crimes committed were serious felonies. David Thloet ap David ap Phelipp of Flintshire, who served with the Prince of Wales, had stolen four boards in the town of Thlanelewy.[175] And many of the pardons were of a general nature, suggesting that in some cases they had been sought as a precautionary measure rather than to deal with the legal consequences of specific crimes.[176] But, as a Commons petition to king and council in 1347 expressed it, 'many murders, woundings, robberies, homicides, rapes and other felonies and misdeeds without number are done and maintained in the kingdom because the evil doers are granted charters of pardon . . . to the great destruction of the people'.[177] Although not indifferent to these problems, the government was also aware of the advantages brought by such a distinctive pool of recruits. Desperate men who had been outlawed for violent crimes might be expected to pursue the king's war in France with few inhibitions, perhaps even with relish. And from the crown's point of view, there were financial benefits too. On the one hand, it was usual for an enlisted outlaw to serve 'a ses custages propres' – that is, without receiving the king's pay; on the other, he would have to hand over a fee for the issue of his charter of pardon. Always short of ready cash in the field, the king noted in a privy seal warrant to the chancellor, dated 8 September 1346, that he wanted the pardons to be issued in the siege camp outside Calais, because he could then use the sealing fees 'en eide de paier gages a noz communes'.[178] Since, in theory at least, a charter of pardon cost the recipient 16s 4d and several thousand were issued during the course of the siege of Calais, this represented a useful addition to the king's perennially insufficient supply of cash.[179]

If as many as a thousand of Edward III's 'Crécy men' were criminals engaged in a form of rehabilitation, there were hundreds more whose service could result in disruption to the legal system back in England. An English combatant with significant property interests would usually obtain a letter of protection with clause *volumus* before his departure. This would ensure the

---

[174] In early January 1346, sheriffs were ordered to proclaim that all those holding pardons issued on the condition of further service were to hasten to the muster at Portsmouth: *Foedera*, III, i, p. 66. Many more would receive a pardon during the Crécy–Calais campaign. On service pardons, see Ayton, *Knights and Warhorses*, pp. 144–5, 163–6. For the opposition of the political community, see A. Musson and W.M. Ormrod, *The Evolution of English Justice: Law, Politics and Society in the Fourteenth Century* (Basingstoke, 1999), pp. 79–80; and Hewitt, *The Organisation of War under Edward III*, pp. 172–5.

[175] *Black Prince Register*, i, p. 125.

[176] For an example, see the pardon issued to Sir Richard Sandford on 4 September 1346, which is the only original charter of pardon known to have survived from this expedition. Shropshire Record Office, Sandford Collection, 2/63; for a translation of the document, see W.G.D. Fletcher, 'Sir Richard de Sandford, of Sandford, knight, 1306–1347', *Shropshire Archaeological and Natural History Society*, 3rd ser., vi (1906), pp. 155–66 (at p. 162).

[177] *Rot. Parl.*, ii, p. 172, cited in B.A. Hanawalt, *Crime and Conflict in English Communities, 1300–1348* (Cambridge, Mass. and London, 1979), p. 235.

[178] C81/314, no. 17816.

[179] E101/212/4 (hanaper accounts, 1347–8); N. Hurnard, *The King's Pardon for Homicide Before A.D. 1307* (Oxford, 1969), pp. 55–8.

security of his property from a range of legal actions for a specified period during his absence.[180] If he failed to do so he could leave himself open to hostile litigation. Of course, the system was open to abuse. Some men used protections to delay the legal process in cases that were likely to go against them. There must have been much frustration in the courts as protections were presented and proceedings suspended *sine die,* still more so because the king could also be persuaded to suspend assizes of novel disseisin, which were not covered by letters of protection. Thus, during the weeks leading up to embarkation in July 1346, a steady flow of royal orders provided additional legal security for those intending to serve with the king.[181] The crown's priorities were made crystal clear in the case of 19 men who had been indicted for a trespass on the River Thames. They were taken into the king's protection because he was unable to 'dispense with their services'.[182] Throughout the campaign further privileges were extended to particular individuals who were serving with the army. For example, early in the siege of Calais, Sir Herbert St Quintin found himself indicted for assault on a certain Thomas Ferthyng.[183] Since, on the day that the incident was alleged to have taken place he was already at Portsmouth, in the earl of Arundel's retinue, the king ordered the case to be suspended. Legal protection was one of the essential lubricants of the Edwardian military system, for (like enfeoffment to use) it enabled members of the landholding class to meet their military responsibilities without jeopardising their personal and property interests in England. Thus, when Philip Weston drew to the king's attention 'une assise de novelle disseisine quele Baudewyn de Langdon ad arrainez devers Wauter de Carmynowe' concerning 'tenementz en Trebrethek', Edward III had no hesitation in ordering the suspension of the case until his return to England 'en manere come est accorde par les autres qi passerunt ovesque nous'.[184] The order was issued from Freshwater on 7 July as the fleet assembled off the Isle of Wight. Whatever the rights and wrongs of the case, Carmynowe had already embarked and was now directly engaged in the king's business.

Less tangible, but no less important than the material rewards to be gained from military service, was the enhancement of the martial reputation, individually and collectively, of the English army. The men in the Prince of Wales's division, who bore the brunt of the fighting, would no doubt have carried home the most vivid tales of prowess performed and witnessed. But even those who did not actually come to blows with the enemy on the day had participated in a great set-piece chivalric event, and doubtless basked in the glory attached to 'Crécy men' in future years. For all the additional expense and the responsibilities that came with elevation to knighthood, how must John Colby have prized the king's

---

[180] On letters of protection, see Ayton, *Knights and Warhorses*, pp. 157–62.

[181] Suspension of assizes of novel disseisin (8 men in total): *CCR, 1346–9*, pp. 83, 143. It was emphasised that it was not the king's intention to protect those who having made recent disseisins had then set out in his service.

[182] *CCR, 1346–9*, p. 85

[183] C81/314, no. 17819. It is worthy of note that St Quintin had taken the precaution of securing a protection and appointing attorneys before embarking for France: C76/22, mm. 4, 7. For further cases, see *CCR, 1346–9*, pp. 155–6, 70.

[184] C81/313, no. 17776.

privy seal, which noted that he 'prist mesme lordre de nous a la bataille de Cressy'. In a real sense, the enhanced martial reputation of the English in general, and of individual Englishmen in particular, had been gained at the expense of the French and their allies. This was symbolised by the Prince of Wales's adoption of the fallen King John of Bohemia's ostrich feather crest as his own badge.[185] And the chivalric celebration did not stop there, for there is good reason to believe that the foundation of the Order of the Garter was also closely connected with the battle of Crécy. Indeed, it may well be that 'the Garter was an integral part of Edward's Norman campaign from its inception', symbolising his claim to the French throne and bearing the uncompromising motto 'Hony soit q' mal y pense'.[186] That the victory at Crécy served, in English eyes, to vindicate that claim and that the establishment of the Order was intended as a commemoration of both military and moral triumphs can hardly be doubted. As Juliet Vale has persuasively argued, in making 'the device he had adopted for the campaign the basis for an order of chivalry', we see 'an act of complex motivation: a pious act of thanksgiving; a fitting reward for those who had served him outstandingly in the battle; but also a means of enshrining in perpetuity the symbol of his vindicated claim'.[187] The majority of the founder knights were indeed veterans of the battle, including Sir Richard Fitz Simon among a cluster of men from the Black Prince's division. Furthermore, the first six successor knights were also 'Crécy men'.[188]

*   *   *

Over half a century ago, K.B. McFarlane observed that late medieval society would 'only yield its secrets to the investigator who can base his conclusions upon the study of hundreds of fragmentary biographies'.[189] The application of this method to the study of Edwardian warfare – an exercise that may be termed 'military service prosopography' – is very much in its infancy. It is, moreover, beset with methodological problems: those that are posed by the sources combined with the difficulties involved in career reconstitution. Shortage of data is not one of the problems, for what is immediately apparent from the most cursory of examinations of the sources (of the materials in Wrottesley's *Crecy and Calais*, for example) is just how many of the men who accompanied Edward III to France in 1346 can be named. The records *are* voluminous, yet they are also frustratingly incomplete. There are no surviving muster rolls or horse inventories for this army, and so for the greater part of our nominal data we must

---

[185] Barber, *Edward Prince of Wales*, pp. 68–9, drawing on John of Arderne's testimony, which was first brought to light by a sceptical Sir Nicholas Harris Nicolas in *Archaeologia*, xxxii (1847), pp. 332–4.

[186] J. Vale, *Edward III and Chivalry* (Woodbridge, 1982), chapter 5 (pp. 77, 81).

[187] Vale, *Edward III and Chivalry*, p. 82.

[188] On the choice of the founder knights, see Barber, *Edward Prince of Wales*, pp. 89–91; Vale, *Edward III and Chivalry*, pp. 86–91; D'A.J.D. Boulton, *The Knights of the Crown: The Monarchical Orders of Knighthood in Later Medieval Europe, 1325–1520* (Woodbridge, 1987), pp. 126–31. See also, H. Collins, *The Order of the Garter, 1348–1461* (Oxford, 2000), Appendix 1.

[189] K.B. McFarlane, 'Bastard feudalism', *BIHR*, xx (1945), pp. 161–81 (at p. 173).

rely on three types of source. Firstly, there are enrolled letters of protection, which yield the names of rather more than seven hundred individuals.[190] Secondly, we have the varied records generated by the novel military assessment of the mid-1340s, which contribute several hundred further names (so scattered and imperfectly calendared are these records that as yet it is difficult to offer a more precise figure).[191] Thirdly, there are charters of pardon, of which well over a thousand were authorised while the army was in Normandy or during the early days of the siege of Calais.[192]

Each of these types of source poses interpretative problems. Letters of protection record the intention to serve rather than actual service, and we occasionally catch a glimpse of a defaulter, though it is unlikely that this is a statistically significant problem.[193] Generally, protection recipients were men-at-arms; indeed, since the primary purpose of these documents was to provide legal security for landholders, the lists of those receiving them (or applying for them) show a marked bias towards knights.[194] Altogether less well represented are landless younger sons, scions of the least wealthy parish gentry families, and men with the necessary equipment to be men-at-arms but lacking a genteel background. The enrolled protections for the Crécy campaign pose further problems. There are fewer of them than we might have expected, given the number

---

[190] Letters of protection for the Crécy campaign were enrolled on the Treaty Rolls (C76/22 and C76/23) and have been imperfectly calendared in Wrottesley, *Crecy and Calais*. It would be misleading to offer a precise total since it is not always easy to distinguish duplicates and, in the case of some men receiving protections in August and September, it is unclear whether they were about to leave for France or were already with the army. About a third of protection recipients also appointed attorneys; indeed, some men made such appointments without securing an enrolled protection. Mention should also be made of 'protection warrants' (the captains' bills requesting the issue of protections for men in their retinues), the majority of which are to be found in Chancery Warrants (C81), files 1719–56. Identifying which of these lists relate to the Crécy campaign would probably add hundreds of extra names to the 'Crécy roll', but as yet the necessary work has been done for only a selection of retinues.

[191] Of the writs of exoneration on the Treaty Rolls and Memoranda Rolls, many relevant to the Crécy–Calais campaign are to be found in Wrottesley, *Crecy and Calais*. Certificates of service are dispersed among the volumes of Ancient Correspondence (SC1) and files of Chancery warrants (C81). For these sources, see Ayton, 'The English army and the Normandy campaign of 1346', pp. 254–8.

[192] Enrolled on *Rotulus Normannie* and calendared in *CPR, 1345–8*, pp. 476–8, 483–508. In fact, over 1,100 pardons are listed on these pages, but caution is necessary since it is clear that some of the recipients were not at Crécy.

[193] For example, the protection issued to William son of Alice atte Forde of Wetheresfeld (C76/23, m. 15) was revoked because the king had learnt that he 'stays in England attendant upon his own affairs': *CPR, 1345–48*, p. 190. Defaulting is unlikely in the case of charters of pardon and military assessment exonerations, but with these records it is sometimes unclear whether a man had served from the beginning of the campaign, or merely joined the army during the siege of Calais. Moreover, as the years after the campaign slipped by, inconsistencies and errors began to appear in the retrospective military assessment records: e.g., the notion that Henry, earl of Derby and Sir Ralph Stafford had been with the army at La Hougue in July 1346 (Wrottesley, *Crecy and Calais*, pp. 177, 186).

[194] Admittedly, there are also a few non-combatants (clerks, servants, surgeons), but identifiable archers are rare.

of men-at-arms in the army,[195] and they are distributed unevenly among the retinues in the army. Was this because some captains secured protections for only a
small proportion of their men? Some light may be cast on the matter by two
letters written on the eve of the army's departure. On 3 July, the earl of
Northampton complained to the chancellor that the hanaper clerk was
demanding from his men 2s for the issue of a letter of protection (the sealing
fee), which seemed to them expensive given that 'ils mettent en aventure vie et
membre' in the king's service.[196] It would appear that the earl's men were
refusing to pay, since only six have enrolled protections dated before 3 July, and
none of the 17 named on the one lengthy protection warrant to survive for
Northampton's retinue (dated 1 July) appears in the enrolled lists.[197] On the
other hand, on 6 July, in a letter to the chancellor dictated while on board ship
off the Isle of Wight, Hugh Despenser noted that two of his men had arrived so
late for the passage that it had not been possible to request protections for
them.[198] Neither man has an enrolled protection for the Crécy campaign.

The military assessment records go some way to compensate for the deficien-
cies of the protection data. Most useful for our purposes are the certificates of
service and enrolled writs of exoneration that record the actual performance of
military service, either by the assessed landowner himself or by men on his
behalf. Admittedly, to some extent the coverage is biased towards the landed
community, but what we are given is a balanced selection of landowners, less
'knightly' than that offered by letters of protection. Moreover, those serving in
fulfilment of the obligations of others include ordinary men-at-arms, hobelars
and archers who have otherwise left no mark on the records for this army. This is
also one of the strengths of the enrolled charters of pardon, for while they are
not usually explicit about military status, it is likely that most of the pardon
recipients were archers.[199]

The 'Crécy roll' that can be compiled from these sources lacks the evenness
of coverage that would be provided by muster rolls, but it is nevertheless quite
lengthy. Although precision is not yet possible, it is clear that when all of the
sources have been fully processed the names of several thousand of the 'Crécy
men' will have been recovered. This may not be comparable to the Agincourt
roll, but it is an impressive return for an Edwardian army for which the corpus of
records is very incomplete. Drawing up a list of names is only the first step. The
next is to 'identify' the men behind the names – that is, to establish convincing
links between our Crécy records and other historical data. This is the real

---

[195] Cf. the French campaigns of 1338–43: Ayton, 'Edward III and the English aristocracy at
the beginning of the Hundred Years War', pp. 182–3.

[196] C81/1734, no. 60. The earl closes by asking that the protections should be handed over,
noting that on his return he will ensure that the clerk receives 'suffisaunt garant pur la liveree
des protections avanditz'. A sealing fee of 2s was quite usual for the issue of a letter of
protection.

[197] C81/1734, no. 53.

[198] C81/1724, no. 87.

[199] The thousands of enrolled pardons issued during the Edwardian period have been very
little studied by historians and may yet yield much to a painstaking researcher. Preliminary
thoughts on the 'Crécy pardons' are offered below.

challenge facing the prosopographer of Edwardian military service.[200] Reconstituting the earlier military careers of our Crécy men is hampered by two major problems. Firstly, the records for military service are not only incomplete, but inconsistently so from campaign to campaign. Secondly, for many of our men, nominal record linkage – the bringing together of scraps of information about the same person – can never be achieved satisfactorily.[201] Reconstituting the careers of the common soldiers in Edwardian armies, the archers and the spearmen, is a particularly difficult task. The difficulties are somewhat less formidable when we turn to the men-at-arms, the knights and esquires. It is true that we tend to see knights rather than esquires, and the military activities of men once they have become established rather than their early careers. But with a richer array of sources available and a smaller pool of men involved, it is often possible to determine geographical origins, and social and retaining relationships, and to achieve some success with career reconstitution.

An investigation of the military and social backgrounds of the men who fought with Edward III at Crécy may help us to understand the course and outcome of the battle. It has often been suggested, though never demonstrated with appropriate supporting evidence, that this was an army of veterans, men who had not only fought in the previous French campaigns, but for whom the Scottish expeditions of the 1330s had been a proving ground.[202] We need to recognise that military experience can mean a number of different things. On one level, it may mean an acquaintance with the discomforts and camaraderie of campaigning life. Beyond that is combat, and even a fairly uneventful chevauchée would involve some skirmishing, or a frontal assault on a defended position. Here a man's relationships with close comrades in arms, his personal arms training and his nerve would be put to the test. Such campaign hardening was surely important. Even those who bore arms for the first time at the landing at La Hougue had experienced a good deal during the six weeks' campaign that preceded Crécy. This may have been especially valuable for the archers of the shire levies, for their domestic backgrounds can hardly have prepared them for war. But a grand set-piece affair like Crécy was, of course, on a quite different level of experience. The sight of the two armies, fully arrayed, and the sheer size of the French host, would have been an awesome spectacle for even the most hard-bitten of veterans. We might suppose that prior experience of the distinctive combined-arms tactics, among captains with command responsibilities and rank and file fighters, must have contributed to the English victory. So, how experienced were the English at Crécy?

At least with the captains we are on solid ground, for they are clearly distinguishable in the sources. The five earls at Crécy – Arundel, Northampton, Oxford, Suffolk and Warwick (plus Huntingdon, who had returned to England

---

[200] Cf. R. Gorski, 'A methodological Holy Grail: nominal record linkage in a medieval context', *Medieval Prosopography*, xvi (1996), pp. 145–79.

[201] Note, for example, the case of 'John de Lynlaye, alias John de Herdewyke': Wrottesley, *Crecy and Calais*, p. 178.

[202] E.g., Rogers, *War, Cruel and Sharp*, pp. 234–5, which provides evidence for the English leaders, though the text states that 'many of the English soldiers and captains had become experienced veterans'.

earlier in the campaign) – had all fought at Halidon Hill in 1333, or had been in the vicinity.[203] Thereafter, these men, and many who were to be bannerets in Edward's army in 1346, served regularly in Scotland, and then in the early campaigns of the French war.[204] For example, the great majority of Edward III's retinue commanders in 1346 had been similarly employed during the hard winter campaign in Brittany in 1342–3. All fifteen of the household bannerets who led retinues at Crécy had served with the king in Brittany, thirteen of them in the household division.[205] The earl of Northampton brought to the field of Crécy the gritty experience of the battle of Morlaix, as did his lieutenants on that occasion, Richard Talbot and Hugh Despenser.[206] Both Talbot and Despenser had been at Halidon Hill; Talbot, indeed, had been one of the adventurers who had triumphed against the odds at Dupplin Muir in 1332.[207] Yet there was a group among the Crécy captains whose careers in arms began during Edward II's Scottish wars. For example, Robert Morley and Bartholomew Burgherssh senior can both be found on horse inventories dating from the summer of 1315,[208] while Robert Ufford (later earl of Suffolk) led a little company to the siege of Berwick in 1319.[209] But among the English captains at Crécy, the veteran's palm would probably have been awarded to the sub-marshal of the army, Sir Thomas Ughtred. For him, the road to Crécy had begun at Bannock-burn in 1314, and had carried him through a string of further, hard-fought battles – Byland, Dupplin Muir, Halidon Hill and St Omer – in addition to less eventful chevauchées and tours of garrison duty.[210] He would have been in his fifties by 1346, an elder statesman among an impressive team of captains, veterans of a series of campaigns and pitched battles involving the combined-arms tactics that were to prove so effective at Crécy. Whenever we are tempted to think of Edwardian warfare as a young man's game we should remember the crucial role of greybeards like Sir Thomas Ughtred.

Determining how far the experience of the captains was shared by the rank and file men-at-arms in the English army at Crécy is a less straightforward task.

---

[203] All except Northampton were witnesses to the agreement to surrender Berwick, dated 15 July 1333, four days before the battle at Halidon Hill: *Rotuli Scotiae*, i, p. 253. Northampton's elder twin brother, Edward Bohun, was a witness, while William himself was a royal household knight and had been issued with a protection (C71/13, m. 24; BL, Additional MS 46350, m. 12) and so was almost certainly on campaign with Edward III.

[204] Arundel, Northampton and Warwick were at Sluys, for example. For the earls' involvement in the early French campaigns, see Ayton, 'Edward III and the English aristocracy at the beginning of the Hundred Years War', pp. 187–94.

[205] For a list of retinue commanders in 1342–3, see Ayton, *Knights and Warhorses*, Appendix 2, Table A.

[206] On Northampton's expeditionary force in Brittany in 1342, including Hugh Despenser's retinue, see Ayton, *Knights and Warhorses*, Appendix 2. Talbot served in Despenser's retinue: C61/54, m. 30; E36/204, fo. 87r.

[207] Talbot: R. Nicholson, *Edward III and the Scots* (Oxford, 1965), p. 80; *Rotuli Scotiae*, i, pp. 253–4. Despenser: C71/13, m. 20.

[208] E101/15/6, mm. 2, 3.

[209] E101/378/4, fo. 21r. Ufford was also involved in the War of St Sardos, as was Richard Talbot: BL, Additional MS 7967, fos 33v, 105r.

[210] For Ughtred's career, see A. Ayton, 'Sir Thomas Ughtred and the Edwardian military revolution', *The Age of Edward III*, ed. J.S. Bothwell (Woodbridge, 2001), pp. 107–32.

Perhaps the best starting point is provided by the records of the Court of Chivalry, and specifically by the depositions of those laymen who were called upon to give evidence in the two great armorial disputes of the 1380s.[211] Of interest to us are those men who while recalling incidents from their careers in arms mentioned that they had fought at Crécy. As a source of vivid snap-shots of individual careers, which cumulatively demonstrate the depth of experience in the English army at Crécy, the Court of Chivalry depositions can hardly be rivalled. A search of over five hundred depositions yields a total of 38 men who stated explicitly that, forty years earlier, they had fought in the campaign of July–August 1346: 23 deponents in the *Lovel* v. *Morley* case and 16 from the rather better-known *Scrope* v. *Grosvenor* case, with one man, Sir Richard Sutton, giving evidence in both armorial disputes.[212]

These depositions are of great value to the prosopographer of Edwardian military service. First, there is no reason to doubt the essential reliability of the information that they provide. Memory lapses there may have been, but deliberate falsification was surely rare.[213] Second, they offer not just isolated fragments of information but career profiles. Although often brief and skeletal, these profiles – especially if they include the precise start and (if appropriate) finish of a martial career – will often provide a reliable chronological framework that can be fleshed out with other kinds of biographical information. If not wholly removed, the problems of nominal record linkage are greatly diminished. Third, since few of the 38 deponents who recalled Crécy would have been knights in 1346,[214] we can be confident that in this case, as so often with the Court of Chivalry records, we can peer into the otherwise rather shadowy world of sub-knightly men-at-arms. Here we see young men at the outset of their careers, who would later become knights; and veterans of lesser-gentry origin who eschewed knighthood. There are, indeed, two men – Henry Hoo and Philip Warenner – who styled themselves as being of 'gentle blood' (*gentil sanc*) rather

---

211 For these records, see A. Ayton, 'Knights, esquires and military service: the evidence of armorial cases before the Court of Chivalry', *The Medieval Military Revolution*, ed. A. Ayton and J.L. Price (London, 1995), pp. 81–104. On the Court of Chivalry, see M. Keen, 'The jurisdiction and origins of the Constable's court', *War and Government in the Middle Ages*, ed. J. Gillingham and J.C. Holt (Woodbridge, 1984), pp. 159–69.

212 *Lovel* v. *Morley*: C47/6/1, nos 1, 2, 4, 5, 6, 10, 11, 13, 14, 18, 19, 25, 38, 39, 43, 92, 99, 104; PRO30/26/69, nos 167, 175, 176, 183, 186. N.H. Nicolas, ed., *The Scrope and Grosvenor Controversy*, 2 vols (London, 1832), i, pp. 74, 77–8, 124–6, 144–6, 161–2, 165, 180–1, 185–6, 189–90, 201–5, 210–13, 217–19.

213 Given that the line of questioning in the Court of Chivalry did not call for full military autobiographies from the deponents, we should not expect to be given complete career profiles. Some omissions can easily be detected; others may reasonably be assumed. Several men mention failing memories. Sir Maurice Bruyn recalled Crécy in his *Scrope* v. *Grosvenor* deposition, but omitted to mention it in the *Lovel* v. *Morley* hearings. William Montagu, earl of Salisbury, mentions only the siege of Calais, yet we know that he had been knighted soon after the landing at La Hougue. There can be no doubt, therefore, that an extrapolation from our sample would underestimate the military experience that Edward III's men-at-arms brought with them to Crécy.

214 Fewer than half had attained that status by the mid-1380s. *Scrope* v. *Grosvenor*: 12 knights and 4 esquires. *Lovel* v. *Morley*: 5 knights and 18 esquires or others.

than adopting the conventional label of 'esquire'.[215] Of course, our 38 men could not be regarded as a representative sample of the knights and esquires at Crécy. Apart from any other consideration, they must have been of below average age. But they do help to counter the strong bias towards knights that so many of our sources exhibit.

That there were virgin soldiers alongside the veterans in the English army is only to be expected. Out of our sample of 38 men, six stated explicitly that they had begun their careers in arms during the 1346 campaign, and perhaps a dozen more were also first-timers. Some, indeed, were teenagers. Even so, a man like Bernard Brocas, who had been first armed 'on the seashore at La Hougue',[216] had experienced a good deal during the six weeks of campaigning before Crécy; and there would have been many seasoned warriors on hand to guide him through his military apprenticeship. Somewhat more experienced was Hugh Coursoun of Carleton, for he had spent the summer and autumn of 1345 in Aquitaine. He had been first armed at the abortive siege of Langon, and then witnessed the dramatic taking of Bergerac and the earl of Derby's even more remarkable victory at Auberoche on 21 October, followed by the siege of La Reole. How it was that he then returned to England in time to embark with the king in July 1346 is not clear;[217] but to have fought at Bergerac, Auberoche, Caen and Crécy – perhaps the only man to have done so – represented a memorable first year of campaigning. Alongside Brocas and Coursoun were veterans of several prior tours of duty. Ten of our 38 deponents had fought at Sluys and/or the siege of Tournai in 1340. One of these was John Rithre, an esquire from Yorkshire who had been first armed at the stand-off at Buironfosse in 1339, after which he had found almost continuous military employment in the Low Countries, Scotland, Brittany and Ireland before embarking for Normandy in 1346.[218] His professionalism could hardly be doubted, yet there was a significant minority among our 38 men whose careers stretched back further, to the Scottish expeditions of the 1330s. Five had served at Halidon Hill and, it seems, regularly thereafter, although these men must have seemed comparative youngsters to William Wollaston, an esquire of ninety-six and more years in 1386, who was first armed at Bannockburn.[219] The careers of such men as Wollaston and Ughtred, straddling the period of military reforms from Bannockburn to Crécy, are examples of the essential human element in those processes of tactical and organisational change that historians have identified during this period. It is important to recognise that the baton of tactical development, which was

---

[215] The relative obscurity of our sample is indicated by the fact that few of our 38 are otherwise recorded as serving in Edward III's army in 1346, or indeed on earlier campaigns.

[216] *Scrope and Grosvenor*, i, 180–1.

[217] C47/6/1, no 99. Courson, a minor Norfolk landowner, had served in Aquitaine in Sir John Norwich's retinue: C76/22, m. 7d. Norwich was one of the earl of Derby's leading bannerets in 1345–6 (E101/25/9, m. 3) and there is no evidence that he returned to England before the Crécy campaign.

[218] *Scrope and Grosvenor*, i, 144–6. The only aspect of his early career that is otherwise recorded is his spell of duty in Ireland in 1344–6: *CPR, 1343–5*, p. 244; C260/57, m. 28.

[219] Wollaston: PRO30/26/69, no. 186. Nothing more about his military career has been found.

essential to the English success at Crécy, was carried not only at the level of command, but also within the rank and file of the army. The martial lives of William Thweyt, Henry Hoo and William Hesilrigge are emblematic of the experience of many in the wider body of ordinary men-at-arms at Crécy who had fought at Halidon Hill, Sluys and Morlaix.[220]

To understand how the weight of experience may have made the difference at Crécy, we need to look beyond individual careers to consider what might be termed 'team activity'. It is clear that English campaigning in general, and battle tactics in particular, rested upon the close co-operation of men working in groups: comrades in arms fighting alongside one another; companies meshing together in a retinue or larger tactical formation. So, to what extent were the men-at-arms at Crécy not only experienced in battle conditions, but also serving in retinues of stable composition, surrounded by men whom they knew and could trust?

It has been argued, from close examination of the records, that the early Edwardian period – the late thirteenth and early fourteenth centuries – witnessed very limited stability in the composition of campaigning retinues. Contingents were 'constantly shifting' in composition; 'men would serve with a different lord on each campaign'.[221] This is what the pioneering studies of indentured retinues had led us to expect: permanent retainers provided a stabilising influence in a contract army, but only 'a nucleus around which . . . less stable elements could collect'.[222] But had matters changed by the time of the early French campaigns? There has not been much research on this,[223] and there has been a tendency to assume that the retinues in Edward III's armies were also of shifting composition. But what if it could be shown that there had been a significant level of stability and continuity of personnel? Might this not be one of the fundamental ways in which Edward III's armies differed from those of his predecessors, an important aspect of the transformation of English armies during the 1330s and 1340s?

[220] Hoo was serving with Sir Robert Morley in the rearguard battle: C47/6/1, no. 10. Hesilrigge was in the earl of Northampton's retinue in the vanguard battle: *Scrope and Grosvenor*, i, p. 126; C76/22, mm. 2, 3. Thweyt was serving in Sir Thomas Hereford's company in the earl of Oxford's retinue in the centre battle: C47/6/1, no. 92; Wrottesley, *Crecy and Calais*, p. 188. For Thweyt's long and unusually well-documented career, see A. Ayton, 'William de Thweyt, esquire: deputy constable of Corfe Castle in the 1340s', *Notes and Queries for Somerset and Dorset*, xxxii (1989), pp. 731–8.

[221] N. Saul, *Knights and Esquires: The Gloucestershire Gentry in the Fourteenth Century* (Oxford, 1981), p. 83 (examining the retinues of the Berkeleys during first two decades of fourteenth century). Prestwich, *Armies and Warfare in the Middle Ages*, pp. 44–5, based on his own research presented in *War, Politics and Finance under Edward I*, p. 65.

[222] N.B. Lewis, 'The organisation of indentured retinues in fourteenth-century England', *TRHS*, 4th ser., xxvii (1945), pp. 33–4.

[223] See, for example, Ayton, 'Sir Thomas Ughtred and the Edwardian military revolution', pp. 122–5. Kenneth Fowler's study of the retinue of Henry of Lancaster seems to suggest limited continuity of personnel: 'the number of those who served in his retinue on several occasions, both donees and non-donees, amounted to no more than a small proportion of the total troop' (Fowler, *King's Lieutenant*, p. 183 and appendix III, table 1). However, a modified analytical method could give rise to a different result.

To investigate this problem effectively, it is necessary to shift our focus from individual combatants to individual captains and their retinues; and we must draw upon every kind of evidence available.[224] Let us take as a case study the retinue of the earl of Northampton, the constable of the English army at Crécy. As we have seen, the community of earls made a particularly important contribution to the king's war. Northampton himself was one of Edward III's most trusted and capable lieutenants. He had played an active personal role in the reshaping of English fighting methods, including the development of 'English' tactics, from Weardale to Crécy; and, if our assessment of the evidence is correct, Northampton and his men were alongside the Prince of Wales in the vanguard division at Crécy, in the forefront of the fighting. Fortunately, Northampton's campaign retinues are well documented. Of particular value is a series of protection warrants that present his knights and esquires in list form. When correlated with enrolled protections they can be precisely dated.[225]

The size of Northampton's personal retinue at Crécy cannot be established with precision. The College of Arms version of the Wetwang's pay-roll, printed by Wrottesley, suggests that the earl had with him 160 men-at-arms and 141 mounted archers, and this is probably of the right order of magnitude.[226] We can recover the names of as many as 72 of these men.[227] Although half of them are knights, our heavy dependence on the military assessment records does allow us

---

[224] The Court of Chivalry records offer inconclusive evidence. References to captains under whose banner particular spells of service were performed are patchy in the *Scrope* v. *Grosvenor* depositions, and although such detail is presented more regularly in the *Lovel* v. *Morley* records, we are usually offered only selected career highlights. Overall, the body of data is insufficiently large for a clear view to be formed.

[225] C81/1734, no. 40 (Low Countries, 1337); C81/1750, no. 12 (Low Countries, 1338–9); C81/1735, no. 15 (Sluys–Tournai, 1340); C81/1735, no. 22 (Brittany, 1342–3); C81/1735, no. 21 (Brittany, 1345); C81/1734, no. 24 (Calais, 1348). Further, shorter bills requesting protections are to be found in C81, files 1721, 1734, 1735, 1752. In addition to enrolled protections for each expedition, there is a horse inventory for Scotland, 1336 (E101/19/36, m. 5) and *restauro equorum* accounts for a diplomatic mission in 1337–8 (E101/311/31, fo. 3r) and campaigns in 1338–9 (*Norwell*, pp. 309–10) and 1342–3 (E36/204, fo. 86v).

[226] Wrottesley, *Crecy and Calais*, p. 193. It should be noted that slightly different figures are to be found in other manuscripts (e.g., Harleian MS 3968, fo. 115r: 178 men-at-arms and 161 archers; 161 archers in *Brut*, ed. Brie, ii, p. 538), but the College of Arms data agree with those supplied by Robert Brady.

[227] Enrolled letters of protection and attorney appointments, together with protection warrants, supply only 32 names: C76/22, mm. 2–4, 6, 13, 16, 22, 25, 36; C81/1734, nos 28, 31, 53–4, 60. Fortunately, the shortfall can be made up by the records connected with the military assessment of the mid-1340s, which reveal the identities of 48 individuals, sometimes confirming service suggested by protections. Wrottesley, *Crecy and Calais*, *passim*; C76/22, m. 14d; C76/23, m. 16d; C81/1734, nos 55–7, 63–4. No fewer than eight names can be garnered from the Court of Chivalry depositions of the 1380s, including six that are not provided by any other source (*Scrope and Grosvenor*, i, pp. 124–6, 144–6, 212–13; C47/6/1, no. 2). A handful of Northampton's 'Crécy men' are a little doubtful (they may only have served at the siege of Calais, or with a different captain), but their inclusion is counterbalanced by the exclusion of others for whom the evidence is not quite solid enough – a good example being Sir John Coggeshale junior, who certainly served at Crécy and had accompanied Northampton in the past. We know the names of a further eight men who appear to have joined Northampton during the siege of Calais.

to appreciate the disparities of wealth within the group of men-at-arms serving in Northampton's retinue. While Sir Roger Huse sought to discharge the obligations arising from land in Dorset, Wiltshire, Hampshire, Surrey and Essex, Northampton's valet, Thomas Lovet, owed the service of a single archer from his 'terres' in Northamptonshire.[228]

Among Northampton's 72 'Crécy men', we find six who were already serving under William Bohun's banner in Scotland in 1336, and three more who appear in 1337.[229] These men and a number of others (some of whom either did not serve at Crécy or simply cannot be found in the imperfect records)[230] provided an inner circle of longstanding comrades in arms as, gradually, others were drawn into Bohun's service following his elevation to an earldom. This core group included family members, like Edmund and Oliver Bohun; the Essex Nevilles, the brothers John and Hugh; another pair of brothers, Gerard and Roger Wyderyngton of Northumberland;[231] William Tallemache, Northampton's one known indentured retainer;[232] and Adam Swynbourne, perhaps the earl's most trusted companion, who had served with him on every opportunity since the Dunstable tournament of 1334 and was sub-constable of the army at Crécy.[233]

These men formed the stable core of Northampton's campaign retinues throughout the first ten years of the French war. Such a permanent nucleus is perhaps only to be expected; what is more notable is that it was surrounded by many individuals whose connection with the earl was far from transitory. Of the 72 men known to have been with Northampton at Crécy, over half (41) can be shown to have served with him before. Thirty-one (43 per cent) had accompanied him to Brittany in 1345, where there had been some hard fighting.[234]

---

[228] C81/1734, nos 63 and 64.

[229] 1336: Sir Oliver Bohun, Sir John Neville, Sir Hugh Neville, Sir Adam Swynbourne, Richard Whiteparish, Sir Gerard Wyderyngton. E101/19/36, m. 5. 1337: Sir Edmund Bohun, John Clopton, Sir William Trussebut. *CPR, 1334–8*, pp. 530–1.

[230] Among those whose presence at Crécy cannot be detected are Sir Richard Denton, William Gunwarton and William Ireland, all three of whom had campaigned regularly with Northampton from 1336: E101/19/36, m. 5; *CPR, 1334–8*, pp. 505, 529–31; *Treaty Rolls, 1337–39*, nos 291, 318, 654, 773; *Norwell*, p. 310; C76/15, mm. 19, 20; C76/17, m. 36; E36/204, fo. 86v; *Foedera*, III, i, pp. 38–9; C76/20, m. 21; C81/1734, m. 24; C81/1735, no. 21. William Ireland was granted half a manor in 1346: Holmes, *The Estates of the Higher Nobility in Fourteenth-Century England*, p. 70.

[231] In the fortunes of the Wyderyngton brothers we see the story of English arms in the first half of the fourteenth century: their father had been killed at Bannockburn; Gerard was at Crécy; and both he and Roger were at Neville's Cross. *CPR, 1334–38*, p. 264; C76/22, m. 2; *Rotuli Scotiae*, i, p. 678. Ayton, 'Edward III and the English aristocracy at the beginning of the Hundred Years War', pp. 174, 198.

[232] Indenture, 17 June 1340: DL25/32. He served with Northampton from 1337 until 1359, including the Crécy campaign. Ayton, 'Edward III and the English aristocracy at the beginning of the Hundred Years War', pp. 173–4; Wrottesley, *Crecy and Calais*, p. 85.

[233] 'Roll of arms of the knights at the tournament at Dunstable, in 7 Edward III', *Collectanea, Topographica et Genealogica*, iv (1837), p. 391. Although Swynbourne's name appears on a roll of Sir Thomas Dagworth's retinue serving in Brittany in 1346 (E101/25/18), it is likely that he returned to England and took ship with Northampton to Normandy since he can be seen certifying the issue of pardons as early as 4 September 1346 (e.g., *CPR, 1345–8*, pp. 486–7).

[234] Brittany: *Murimuth*, p. 189; Sumption, *Trial by Battle*, pp. 458–9, 471–3.

Twenty-five (35 per cent) had been in his retinue in 1342 and were very likely with him at the battle of Morlaix. Twenty (28 per cent) of his Crécy companions had borne arms with him at Sluys in 1340. Should we conclude from these data, incomplete as they are, that at least half of Northampton's men-at-arms at Crécy had fought with him before; and that at least a third had already come through a hard-fought battle under his banner? Such an extrapolation would appear to be warranted, particularly if we focus on the *knights* who served under Northampton and view the prosopographical evidence from different vantage points. For example, of the 46 identifiable knights serving under Northampton in Brittany in 1342, no fewer than 20 had been with him at Sluys. Given the incompleteness of military service records in general and the fact that the Crécy records for Northampton's retinue are weakened in particular by the lack of a lengthy retinue roll such as we commonly find attached to protection warrants, it may well be that we are underestimating the extent of what might be termed 'battlefield continuity' in the earl's retinue. That is certainly the impression we get from a close examination of the 36 identifiable knights who served under Northampton at Crécy (we lack names for about a dozen more). Twenty-nine of these men – four out of five of them – had served with the earl before, and nearly half of them were veterans of the 1342 campaign and therefore, in all likelihood, of the battle of Morlaix. That so large a proportion of Northampton's knights at Crécy – the company commanders – had fought together before can only have enhanced the operational effectiveness of the retinue. And this impressive level of stability was maintained for the next expedition, following the fall of Calais. At least three-quarters of the knights who accompanied Northampton to France in the autumn of 1348 had seen service with him on an earlier occasion, which is all the more remarkable given the losses through camp sickness that had been sustained during the siege of Calais.[235]

While it is clear that a sizeable group of men remained loyal to the earl from year to year, and that a notable degree of stability had been achieved in Northampton's retinue by the time of the battle of Crécy, this is not to suggest that there had been no significant changes in composition during the decade leading up to the battle. The retinue fluctuated in size from one expedition to the next, and men entered the earl's service as others died, retired from warfare or moved on to other captains. The major changes occurred early in the French war, for it was then that the size of the retinue grew substantially, the number of men-at-arms under the earl's banner more than doubling from 1338 to 1342. The prosopographical data suggest that for each of the expeditions of 1340, 1342 and 1345 about twenty knights served under Northampton for the first time;[236] and

---

[235] Of the 35 knights listed in a protection warrant, half (18) can be shown to have been at Crécy with the earl and seven more had served with him before 1346 (C81/1734, no. 24). The 20 names that appear on the Treaty Roll (C76/26, mm. 3, 6) have been 'pointed' with a cross on the protection warrant. Note also C81/1734, no. 20, which lists one knight and two esquires, all of whom appear on the Treaty Roll (C76/26, mm. 2–3).

[236] Increase in the number of men-at-arms: 56 in 1336 (BL, Cotton MS, Nero C.VIII, fo. 241); 89 in 1338–9 (*Norwell*, p. 327); 135 in 1340 (E101/389/8, m. 11); 200 in 1342–3 (E36/204, fo. 106). In 1338–9 there had been 15, rising to 25, bannerets and knights; in 1340, a maximum of 49; and in 1342, 58. There are no comparable data for the expedition to

that fifteen of these new recruits were still with the earl at Crécy.[237] One way of achieving this expansion in numbers was to engage captains who could supply 'off-the-peg' companies, and we can identify two bannerets, Nicholas de la Beche and Geoffrey Say, performing this role for Northampton in 1342.[238] Say did the same for the earl in 1345 and returned once again with his sub-retinue for the Crécy campaign, thereby contributing to the stability of the earl's personnel in that battle even though the connection that Say's men had with Northampton was indirect.[239] Perhaps most notable among the others who joined Northampton for the first time in 1342 were two members of the Scrope family, the cousins, William (of Bolton) and Henry (of Masham).[240] For Sir William Scrope it was to be a short-lived association, for he was seriously wounded at Morlaix and thereafter withdrew from military activity; but Northampton retained the services of Sir Henry, who fought at Crécy, accompanied (if we are to believe the testimony of deponents in the *Scrope* v. *Grosvenor* case in the 1380s) by his brothers, William and Stephen.[241] Other families contributed several members to the earl's retinue at Crécy. Apart from the Bohuns, the Nevilles and the Says, there were perhaps three members of the Wauton family – two seasoned campaigners who had served before under Northampton's banner, Sir John and Sir Thomas, and one first-timer, William.[242] And there were three Cloptons, two of whom, John and Thomas,

Brittany in 1345. The exact figures for knights serving with the earl for the first time are: 18 (1340), 26 (1342) and 23 (1345); but given the incompleteness of the military service records, the citing of precise numbers would be inappropriate.

[237] Three of the 'new' knights from 1340, five from 1342 and seven from 1345.

[238] The 'sub-retinues' can be identified in protection warrants and in corresponding blocks of protections entered on the Treaty Rolls. Beche with eight men: C81/1735, no. 17; C76/17, m. 38. Say with eight men: C81/1734, no. 36; C76/17, m. 25. Say was a very experienced soldier, whose career had begun in the 1320s.

[239] Brittany, 1345: C81/1735, no. 21. Geoffrey Say is second on the list, after Northampton and Dagworth; his sub-retinue appears as a block of nine names at the end. Crécy, 1346: Say and 16 men for whom Northampton requested protections (C81/1734, nos 53–4). Cf. Wrottesley, *Crecy and Calais*, pp. 127, 142, 144, 170, 180. Six of Say's men had served with him under Northampton before; indeed, two of them, Roger Say and Thomas Pympe, are to be found in the small company that Say provided for the earl of Derby's retinue in 1338 (C81/1738, no. 67; *Treaty Rolls, 1337–39*, nos 579, 580). Northampton's other banneret at Crécy, Robert Bourchier, had been serving with the earl since the first French expedition of 1338. He too must have been responsible for a company of men-at-arms and archers, but the only documentary indication of it is the service of Bourchier's valet, William Enefeld (C81/1721, no. 19; Wrottesley, *Crecy and Calais*, pp. 82, 90, 141, 161); but cf., for 1342, C81/1735, no. 2.

[240] C81/1735, no. 22. Their switch to Northampton appears to have been prompted by the death of Sir Geoffrey Scrope, with whom they had served in 1340 (C81/1738, no. 81).

[241] 'Conventional' documentary evidence for the Scropes' involvement at Crécy is limited to Sir Henry: Wrottesley, *Crecy and Calais*, p. 132. For the Court of Chivalry depositions, see *Scrope and Grosvenor*, ii, pp. 16, 18, 106, 108, 112–13 and the references cited. There is insufficient evidence to argue that Richard Scrope, cousin of the three brothers, was also at Crécy: cf. Maurice Bruyn's deposition (*ibid*., i, pp. 161–2).

[242] Some uncertainty is caused by a 'Thomas de Wauton' serving in the earl of Warwick's retinue, but this is perhaps a separate man (Wrottesley, *Crecy and Calais*, pp. 83–4, 151, 163). William Wauton was 'first armed' at Crécy, and added that 'il ad este armez par tout

were veterans. Given the operation of a common social network from which some or all of their men-at-arms and archers would also have been drawn, it is clear that the participation of family groups like the Scropes, the Wautons and the Cloptons can only have contributed to the cohesion of the earl's retinue.

The expansion of the earl of Northampton's retinue that had occurred early in the French war had stopped by 1346. Our evidence, albeit imperfect, suggests that at Crécy he had with him several dozen fewer men-at-arms than had accompanied him in 1342. It is important to appreciate this if we are to understand the composition of the retinue in 1346. The twenty-year-old William Wauton was certainly not the only man to be serving with Northampton for the first time in July 1346, but the fact that, for 29 more men, we cannot trace prior military contact with the earl should not be taken at face value, being more a product of the vagaries of documentary survival.[243] As we have seen, only seven of the 36 identifiable knights in Northampton's retinue at Crécy were new to his service. Indeed, most of these 'new' men were actually experienced warriors.[244] Of the remaining 29 knights, eight had joined Northampton for the first time in 1345; the rest had served with the earl over a longer period. In the absence of muster rolls, no comparable statistics are available for the earl's esquires (or, of course, for the archers), and there is no way of telling whether the experience of the few who are visible, either through Court of Chivalry depositions or more conventional records, was representative of the wider constituency of manpower. But if John Clopton, William Hesilrigge, John Rithre, Nicholas Sabraham and Richard Whiteparish were typical, this was indeed a formidable force, a settled team of veterans who knew each other well. That it was smaller than the team that had accompanied the earl to Brittany in 1342 (and also, probably, that of 1345) was the result of a variety of circumstances. Sir Robert Marny and Sir Walter Selby had been among Northampton's most loyal comrades in arms for ten years, yet they missed the battle of Crécy, the former having joined Sir Walter Mauny's retinue for the expedition to Aquitaine, the latter apparently remaining on the northern border where he would meet his death at the hands of the Scots shortly before the battle of Neville's Cross.[245] Others who had fought regularly with

son temps' with the earl of Northampton (*Scrope and Grosvenor*, i, pp. 212–13). William's father, William, had served under Northampton at Sluys (C81/1735, no. 15), and died during the siege of Calais in the service of the earl of Oxford (Wrottesley, *Crecy and Calais*, p. 163; *CIPM*, viii, no. 682).

[243] Twelve of these first-timers are mentioned only in the military assessment records, and no strictly comparable material exists for earlier campaigns. Nine more were serving in Geoffrey Say's sub-retinue, which appears not only to have been expanded at short notice (it may have been double the size of its 1345 counterpart) but is also by far the most fully documented section of Northampton's retinue.

[244] One of them, Sir Nicholas Peyvre, appears to be another of the men who had been in the earl of Derby's service in Aquitaine yet returned to England in time to embark with the king's army (E101/25/9, m. 3; C76/20, m. 15). He had fought in Brittany in 1342 with Sir Nigel Loring (C76/17, m. 25), who was also a member of Derby's retinue in 1345.

[245] Marny going to Aquitaine: C76/20, mm. 15, 21; *Scrope and Grosvenor*, i, pp. 170–1. For his career and relevant sources (including a second Court of Chivalry deposition, C47/6/1, no. 27), see Ayton, 'Edward III and the English aristocracy at the beginning of the Hundred Years War', p. 174 and n. 8. Selby's service with Northampton, 1337–45: E101/19/36, m. 5; *CPR, 1334–38*, p. 530; E36/204, fo. 86v; C81/1735, no. 21.

Northampton in the past were drawn into the service of the Prince of Wales, the newly emergent magnate who, during his military apprenticeship, was building a retinue from scratch and needed experienced men around him. Among those who joined the prince were the bannerets, John Fitzwalter[246] and John Verdon,[247] and the knights, Hugh Blount[248] and Thomas Wale.[249] The departure of these men, and their companies of men-at-arms and archers, removed a sizeable group from the pool of manpower available to Northampton. For example, 17 members of John Fitzwalter's sub-retinue in 1346 have enrolled protections.[250] As significant a loss to the earl were the men who had accompanied him to Brittany in 1345 and stayed on there with his erstwhile retainer and brother-in-law, Sir Thomas Dagworth, who was appointed deputy-lieutenant in the duchy in January 1346.[251] More than half a dozen knights (and an indeterminate number of others) remained in Brittany when Northampton returned to England.[252] In a sense, this was a sub-retinue of the earl's, the 'second unit', which under Dagworth's direction won the fiercely fought first battle of La Roche Derrien on 9 June 1346 while the main body of Northampton's retinue prepared for the expedition that would lead them to Crécy. That the earl maintained a close interest in those of his men, like Sir Guy Ferrers, who had remained in Brittany, is shown by a letter of 16 May 1346, which asked for the renewal of a protection that, a year earlier, he had obtained for Ferrers and which had now just expired.[253]

Such were the processes that shaped the composition of a major retinue in the English army at Crécy. There had been changes in its make-up, but they did not break its cohesion; and there was, in any case, a good deal of stability, for the 'new' men, whether experienced but new to the earl's service or 'first armed' in

---

[246] Fitzwalter's service with Northampton, 1337–43: *CPR 1334–8*, p. 530; *Treaty Rolls, 1337–39*, nos 193, 300; C76/15, m. 20; C81/1735, no. 22. After Crécy, on 20 March 1347, Fitzwalter was retained by the prince for half a year's service with 19 men-at-arms and 12 archers (*Black Prince Register*, i, p. 128), but he was back in Northampton's retinue in 1348 (C81/1734, no. 24).

[247] Verdon's service with Northampton, 1336–43: E101/19/36, m. 5; *CPR 1334–38*, p. 531; *Norwell*, p. 310; C76/17, m. 36. He also appears to be associated with Bohun in the 'Roll of arms of the knights at the tournament at Dunstable, in 7 Edward III', p. 391.

[248] *Foedera*, III, i, pp. 38–9; Wrottesley, *Crecy and Calais*, pp. 86, 99.

[249] Wale's service with Northampton, 1340–5: C76/15, m. 19; C76/17, m. 36; C81/1735, no. 22. Wale was one of the founder knights of the Order of the Garter; another, Sir Bartholomew Burgherssh junior, joined the prince, having served with Northampton in 1342 (C81/1735, no. 22).

[250] Not including a clerk. Wrottesley, *Crecy and Calais*, pp. 98–9 (C76/22, m. 12).

[251] Indenture dated 28 January 1346: E101/68/3, no. 62. On Dagworth's career, see M. Jones, 'Sir Thomas Dagworth et la guerre civile en Bretagne au XIVe siècle: quelques documents inédits', *Annales de Bretagne et des Pays de l'Ouest*, lxxxvii (1980), pp. 621–39.

[252] Five knights (excluding Sir Adam Swynbourne) are listed on Dagworth's retinue roll for 1346 (E101/25/18). A sixth, Sir Richard Totesham, whose service links with Northampton can be traced back to 1336, was entrusted with La Roche Derrien. E101/19/36, m. 5; *CPR 1334–38*, p. 531; *Treaty Rolls, 1337–39*, no. 653; C76/15, m. 20; E36/204, fo. 86v. Sumption, *Trial by Battle*, pp. 473, 495; *Grandes chroniques*, ix, pp. 265–9.

[253] C81/1734, no. 62. Earlier protection, dated 15 May 1345, and to last one year: C76/20, m. 24.

the present campaign, joined a settled team of seasoned warriors. In exhibiting so marked a degree of continuity of personnel, Northampton's retinue at Crécy was not exceptional. Upon examination, the retinues of the other long-established captains in the vanguard division, those of the earl of Warwick and Sir Bartholomew Burgherssh, display similar characteristics, as do those of the rearguard division – even a retinue like Sir Hugh Despenser's, which appears to have grown in size rapidly over a short period.[254] Of the two dozen or so men in Despenser's Crécy retinue who can be identified, at least ten had served with him before. This must be regarded as a minimum figure given the incompleteness of the military records.[255] Indeed, it is telling that seven out of Despenser's ten men with enrolled protections in 1345 rejoined his retinue the following year. It is perhaps not surprising to find that four of his Crécy comrades had been among the 14 men-at-arms who had fought with him in Scotland in 1337–8, and that at least five, probably more, had been at his side at Morlaix.[256]

What of the king's retinue, the military wing of the royal household, which formed the core component of the 'centre' division at Crécy? The stability of the group of household bannerets and knights, and their campaigning experience, have been noted already. Much the same can be said of the king's esquires: of the seven household esquires who were raised to knighthood on the day of Crécy, for example, four – all esquires of the chamber – can be seen serving together during the Roxburgh campaign of 1334–5 and frequently thereafter.[257] As for the retinues brought by individual household bannerets and knights, here too we find evidence of settled composition. Sir Michael Poynings's retinue at Crécy is particularly well documented. Twenty-two names are revealed by the protection and military assessment records, perhaps two-thirds of the men-at-arms who accompanied Poynings to France.[258] Although only six can be shown

---

254 Scotland, 1337–8: Despenser with 2 knights, 17 men-at-arms and 8 archers (E101/388/5, m. 14). Brittany, 1342: with 1 banneret, 13 knights, 58 esquires and 26 archers (E36/204, fos 106r, 108v). The Wetwang abstracts suggest that he had about twice as many men-at-arms with him in 1346.

255 Main block of enrolled protections: C76/22, m. 7. See also Wrottesley, *Crecy and Calais*, index 'Despencer'; C81/1724, nos 86, 87, 92; SC1/39, no. 195. Despenser's principal lieutenant at Crécy was Sir Robert Morley. Although a versatile warrior of thirty years' experience, we know comparatively little about the men who served with him during this period. Consequently, his sub-retinue at Crécy, evidence for which is to be found solely among the military assessment records (10 men: Wrottesley, *Crecy and Calais*, pp. 83, 149, 157, 159, 161, 163, 172, 179, 185; protections are wholly lacking), has been excluded from the Despenser retinue statistics.

256 C76/20, mm. 1, 17 (1345). E101/19/36, m. 1 (Scotland, 1336). E101/35/3, m. 1 (Scotland, 1337–8): Sir Richard Blundel, Sir Edward Kendale, Nicholas Langeleye, Roger de la Warde. Blundel, Kendale and Warde, together with John Clete and Mathew Soor, accompanied Despenser to Brittany in 1342 (C61/54, m. 30; E36/204, fo. 87r). Despenser's younger brother, Edward, was killed at Morlaix: *Murimuth*, p. 127; *CIPM*, viii, no. 395. On the close ties between Kendale and Warde, and Despenser, see Saul, *Scenes From Provincial Life*, p. 183.

257 Brian, Dengayne, Mauley and Ravensholme: BL, Cotton MS, Nero C. VIII, fos 235v, 239v, 243v–244r, 246v; E101/389/8, m. 14; E36/204, fo. 108r.

258 C76/23, m. 23 (a block of 18 enrolled protections); Wrottesley, *Crecy and Calais*, index 'Ponynges'.

to have served with Poynings before, it needs to be borne in mind that his retinue in 1346, just like Despenser's (and Northampton's earlier in the war), had probably doubled in size,[259] and an injection of 'new' men was required to make up the numbers. Half of the men who had accompanied Poynings to France in 1345 returned the following year, and four of the 13 men-at-arms who had fought with him at Sluys were in his retinue at Crécy.[260] As with Northampton's and Despenser's retinues, Poynings's 'new arrivals' in 1346 joined a stable core group.[261]

That in such circumstances the new recruits were often not only seasoned campaigners in their own right but already acquainted with one another is nicely illustrated by the largest retinue in the household division, which was led by Sir Richard Talbot. As we have seen, Talbot was a veteran of Dupplin Muir, Halidon Hill and Morlaix. Yet in 1345–6 he needed for the first time to recruit an independent retinue for the French war, and as steward of the royal household and a figure of baronial standing it had to be a substantial one.[262] Raising seventy to eighty men-at-arms, and as many archers, required him to cast his recruiting net widely, and although he was able to attract experienced men to his banner in 1346, very few – only three – of the two dozen or so of his men who are identifiable can be shown to have served with him before.[263] One of them, Sir Philip Buketot, had been a constant companion of Talbot's in the Scottish wars, in field operations and garrison commands, and the two men had also served together at Morlaix.[264] But Talbot's retinue seems to have lacked a stable core of personnel, probably because during the early years of the French war his career had focused

---

[259] 1339: Poynings with 3 knights and 11 esquires (*Norwell*, p. 330). Sluys, 1340: with 2 knights, 11 esquires and 12 archers (E101/389/8, mm. 12, 15). Brittany, 1342: with 2 knights, 10 esquires and 8 archers (E36/204, fos 106v, 109r).

[260] 1345: C76/20, m. 16. 1340: C76/15, m. 21.

[261] Particularly notable are Poynings's uncle, Michael, Sir Arnold Savage, William Lacy and Roger Dallingridge, all of whom had served with Poynings's father in the earl of Cornwall's retinue in Scotland in 1336 (E101/19/36, m.1) and then with Poynings himself after his father's death on campaign in October 1339. On the Poynings's martial role and their companions in arms, see Saul, *Scenes from Provincial Life*, pp. 37–8, 67.

[262] Talbot had served in Bartholomew Burgherssh's retinue at Halidon Hill (C71/13, m. 28), after which he was primarily concerned with his own affairs as 'lord of Mar' in Balliol's unstable regime in Scotland and was a prisoner of the Scots from September 1334 to April 1335. *Complete Peerage*, xii, part 1, pp. 612–14; Nicholson, *Edward III and the Scots*, pp. 158–61, 168–9. During the later months of 1337 he appears on the Scottish March in royal service with a retinue of 42 men-at-arms and 40 mounted archers (E101/20/18). In December 1337 he became keeper of the town of Berwick, which post he held until 20 March 1340 (E101/20/25, m. 4; E101/388/5, m. 15; E101/21/30; E101/22/9; E101/22/21; *Rotuli Scotiae*, i, pp. 517, 585). He took up the post of keeper of Southampton, holding it until 17 May 1340 (E101/22/34). His first taste of the French war came in 1342 when he served in Brittany under Hugh Despenser.

[263] Sir John Abberbury and Giles Arderne in 1345: C76/20, mm. 13, 22. The names of Talbot's Crécy men are derived, as usual, from a combination of enrolled protections and military assessment records. Three of the men who appear in Talbot's retinue during the siege of Calais may also have served with him at some time during the later 1330s; of these the most likely identification is William Hauleye or Hanleye (E101/20/18, m. 2; Wrottesley, *Crecy and Calais*, p. 131).

[264] E101/20/18, m. 2; E101/35/3, m. 2; E101/22/9, m. 1; E101/22/21, m. 2; E36/204, fo. 87r.

on garrison commands in Scotland and England. Yet, although brought together largely from scratch, there were still elements of stability within Talbot's retinue at Crécy: pre-existing ties, not necessarily between captain and man-at-arms, but between some of the retinue members. For example, Sir Edmund Toner and Sir Richard Turbeville were landholders with neighbouring manors in Dorset who had fought together in Brittany in 1342 under the banner of the formidable Thomas Hatfield (later, bishop of Durham). For the Crécy campaign they both joined Talbot's retinue, accompanied by two further members of the Turbeville family, John and Andrew – and several additional Dorset men. These included Sir John Mautravers, with whom Sir Edmund Toner had recently served in Ireland, and William Martyn, whose family's land, like the Toners', lay principally in the valley of the River Piddle.[265]

Clusters of men drawn from a particular locality were, of course, not unusual in the large retinues of the magnates. It was natural, indeed expected, that Northampton would recruit heavily in the Bohun landholding strongholds; a sizeable slice of the Essex gentry were with him at Crécy, for example, just as they had fought with his father and grandfather, the earls of Hereford and Essex.[266] And as the redoubtable J.H. Round noted, it is 'not surprising' to find a cluster of Sussex men in the retinue of Sir Michael Poynings, whose chief seat was at Poynings in that county.[267] But no shrewd captain would miss an opportunity to make a new 'connection' that could provide access to a regional pool of manpower. Take, for example, the earl of Warwick's retinue at Crécy. Of course, he was accompanied by men of longstanding loyalty, men like Sir William Lucy and Sir Robert Herle, who had fought with the earl on every opportunity during the previous ten years.[268] Yet it is clear that Warwick's right-hand man at Crécy, the sub-marshal of the army, was Sir Thomas Ughtred. Their association appears to have been formed only during the previous summer, when Ughtred joined the earl for the abortive expedition to Sluys. What Warwick acquired when he engaged Ughtred in 1345 was a company of Yorkshiremen. We know the names of 21 of them; and two-thirds of these men rejoined Ughtred for service with Warwick the following year, along with others from the same region. Some were Ughtred's trusted military companions; many hailed from those areas of the East Riding and the neighbourhood of York where Ughtred's principal landholdings lay.[269]

---

[265] Talbot's retinue members from Dorset, 1346: C76/22, m. 12; Wrottesley, *Crecy and Calais*, p. 106. Brittany, 1342: C76/17, m. 21. Ireland, 1344–6: C260/57, m. 28. Dorset landholding in 1346: *Feudal Aids*, ii, pp. 45–61.

[266] J.C. Ward, *The Essex Gentry and the County Community in the Fourteenth Century* (Essex Record Office, 1991), p. 18; Ayton, 'Edward III and the English aristocracy at the beginning of the Hundred Years War', pp. 174, 192. G. Jones, 'The Bohun Earls of Hereford and Essex, 1270–1322', MLitt thesis, University of Oxford, 1984, p. 76.

[267] J.H. Round, 'The lords Poynings and St John', *Sussex Archaeological Collections*, lxii (1921), pp. 18–19.

[268] 1336: E101/19/36, m. 7d. 1337: E101/20/17, m. 7. 1340: C76/15, mm. 25, 27. 1342: C76/17, mm. 20, 39; E36/204, fo. 88r. 1345: C76/20, m. 11. For Herle's indenture of retinue (20 April 1339) with the earl of Warwick, see Jones and Walker, eds, 'Private indentures for life service in peace and war, 1278–1476', *Camden Miscellany XXXII*, no. 37 (pp. 70–1).

[269] C81/1741, nos 10 (1346) and 21 (1345). For Ughtred's career and retinue, see Ayton, 'Sir

What these examples – the retinues of Talbot, Warwick and Northampton – suggest is that when a campaign retinue has the appearance of being newly formed, or when considerable changes appear to be taking place in established retinues, with the men apparently lacking prior 'vertical' links with the captain, it may nevertheless have been held together internally, 'horizontally' so to speak, by a complex pattern of associations, based on family, tenure, friendship and shared locality, as well as prior service. Close scrutiny reveals such a web of connections in the case of the Prince of Wales's retinue, which had the distinction of being by far the largest in the army, while having been assembled almost from scratch during the months leading up to the campaign. Of course, there were plenty of veterans in the retinue, and their prior service had not infrequently brought them into contact with each other. That military associations forged during the past played some part in the recruiting process can be seen clearly in the case of Sir John Orreby's company. What all except one of his men-at-arms had in common was that at some point over a period of ten years, and under three different captains, they had served alongside him.[270] Orreby and Robert Wyclif had been esquires in Sir Ralph Neville's retinue in Scotland in 1336–7; he had served with Roger Sturdy under Geoffrey Scrope in Flanders in 1338–9; and with Sir William Synythwait and John Bussy in Sir Nicholas Cantilupe's retinue in Brittany in 1342–3.[271]

It would also appear that the composition of the prince's retinue was influenced by the senior captains who fought alongside him in the vanguard division. We have noted how the prince's retinue benefited from the transfer of experienced knights from the service of the earl of Northampton: the bannerets Sir John Fitzwalter and Sir John Verdon, for example. It is probable that the greatest influence on the formation of the prince's retinue had been Bartholomew Burgherssh senior, who was master of the prince's household and 'the most conspicuous member of the prince's council'.[272] Two of the young prince's bannerets were Burgherssh's own son, Bartholomew, and his son-in-law, Sir John Mohun, both of whom had served their military apprenticeship with Burgherssh senior.[273] Moreover, men-at-arms who had fought with Burgherssh in the past were to be found scattered throughout the companies that made up the prince's huge retinue: Sir Robert Geddyng in Fitzwalter's;[274] William Soty in

Thomas Ughtred and the Edwardian military revolution', *The Age of Edward III*, ed. Bothwell.

[270] Protection warrant for Orreby's company: C81/1710, no. 33. By May 1347, Orreby was a banneret: *Black Prince Register*, i, pp. 80–1.

[271] Neville: E101/19/36, mm. 3d, 4; E101/20/17, mm. 6, 8. Scrope: *Treaty Rolls, 1337–39*, no. 371; *Norwell*, pp. 314, 317. Cantilupe: C76/17, m. 24.

[272] Tout, *Chapters*, iv, pp. 319, 321, 433. It is notable that Burgherssh had also served the prince's uncle, John of Eltham, the earl of Cornwall.

[273] Burgherssh junior: *Treaty Rolls, 1337–39*, no. 428 (Flanders, 1338–9); C71/21, m. 2 (Scotland, 1341); C76/17, m. 20 (Brittany, 1342). John Mohun: C71/21, m. 2 (Scotland, 1341); C76/17, m. 26 (Brittany, 1342); C76/20, m. 13 (France, 1345).

[274] With Fitzwalter: C76/22, m. 12. With Burgherssh in Flanders, 1338–9: *Treaty Rolls, 1337–39*, no. 428. Geddyng served under Northampton at Sluys and Tournai: C76/15, m. 20.

Mohun's;[275] and perhaps most significant of all, Sir Ralph Spigurnel and William Haclut in Roger Mortimer's company.[276] Mortimer, a freshman to the military arena, was surrounded by men who had seen it all before. Spigurnel had served on every available opportunity since 1334, and in Mortimer's company he was reunited with William Hilton, with whom he ridden in Scotland and France under Sir John Tibetot's banner in the 1330s.[277] If we fancy that we can detect Burgherssh's managerial hand in Spigurnel's placement as Mortimer's mentor, as elsewhere in the building of the prince's retinue, then we should also recognise that the grander conception of the army's structure, with the prince's retinue in the vanguard division buttressed by those of Northampton, Warwick and Burgherssh, was probably the king's. However, we should not forget the role played by the young prince himself. That he was actively engaged in the important tasks of reinforcing existing connections and forging new ones is suggested, for example, by his lavish distribution of warhorses to knights during the Normandy campaign, and by his subsequent retaining of further men by indenture.[278]

*   *   *

If 'military service prosopography' is to a degree possible with knights and esquires, when we turn to the archers, whether mounted or on foot, and the hobelars, we are faced by altogether more challenging problems. Our sources are far from helpful. As we have seen, in the absence of pay-rolls for the Crécy campaign, we have only an approximate idea of the numbers of archers, hobelars and spearmen in the English army. Nor without muster rolls do we have a systematic record of the names of these men. What we have are the names of over a thousand men who received charters of pardons during the march across Normandy or in the weeks immediately after Crécy. In all likelihood the great majority of them were English archers (Welshmen are not common), but in only one case – William Dun of Ocle, 'archer' – can we be certain.[279] For the rest, we can but suggest that the notes of warranty that accompany the enrolled pardons may provide a clue. We know that in the case of retinue-based combatants, pardons were certified by captains, at retinue or sub-retinue level. This still leaves the problem of distinguishing archers from men-at-arms, though at least we know that William Dun of Ocle, who was serving under Sir Bartholomew Burgherssh senior, was one of the archers in the vanguard division whose efforts were so decisive to the outcome of the battle. As for the arrayed archers, as we have seen, it is probable that their pardons were certified by either the marshal or

---

275 With Mohun: C81/1710, no. 25. With Burgherssh in Brittany in 1342–3: E36/204, fo. 87v.

276 With Mortimer: C81/1710, no. 26. Spigurnel with Burgherssh in France, 1341, 1345: C76/16, m. 13; C76/20, m. 17. Haclut with Burgherssh in Brittany, 1342–3: C76/17, m. 29.

277 C71/14, m. 11 (1334); E101/19/36, m. 5d (1336); *Treaty Rolls, 1337–39,* no. 438 (1338).

278 *Black Prince Register,* iv, pp. 67–9, 71; i, pp. 83, 127–9.

279 *CPR, 1345–8,* p. 506. Note also Richard son of Henry Flechere of Arndale, and John Kyng 'fleccher' of Bouenheth (*ibid.,* pp. 485, 498). For a couple of Welshmen, see *Black Prince Register,* i, p. 125.

the constable, or their immediate lieutenants. One or other of the names of these four men appear on a large proportion of the notes of warranty.

More specific references to named archers and hobelars are to be found in the military assessment records. Here we see men who have been selected by land-holders to discharge their military assessment. For example, William Warde served as an archer on behalf of William Charnels; and Richard Whet did the same for Robert Lynham, though he was killed in the assault on Caen.[280] It is safe to assume that most of these 'proffered' archers served in retinues rather than in the shire contingents, and sometimes they are indeed precisely 'located' within the army structure, as with Ralph Trutthfeld, who served as an archer in the company of Sir Warin Trussell, and Thomas Stonleye, a hobelar in Sir William Careswell's sub-retinue.[281] This is the most reliable nominal evidence that we have for the archers and hobelars at Crécy, but unfortunately there is no more than a sprinkling of such cases – tens rather than hundreds – which is hardly sufficient for prosopographical analysis of a section of the army that consisted of thousands of men.

In the absence of a substantial body of explicit nominal data, what can be said about the English and Welsh archers and spearmen at Crécy? The commissions of array offer some idea of their regional origins. As can be seen in Table 1 above, it was only the shires south of the River Trent (excluding Cornwall) that were required to contribute companies of archers to the king's army. There certainly were northerners serving in the retinues of such captains as Sir John Stryvelyn (see below) and Sir Thomas Ughtred, but on the whole the principal military duty expected of the northern counties, including Derbyshire and Nottinghamshire, was defence, and it was a duty that they were called upon to perform in October 1346.[282] It would appear that the Welsh Marches, including both Welsh lordships and English shires, contributed more manpower to the army at Crécy than any other region of comparable extent in King Edward's realm. This is all the more striking given the sparseness of the population (and, relatively, movable wealth) in this region.[283] That this was a particularly valuable

---

[280] SC1/39, no. 180; Wrottesley, *Crecy and Calais*, p. 155. The service of both men is confirmed by the marshal, the earl of Warwick.

[281] C81/1740, no. 21. Presumably one of the two archers in Trussell's little company: BL, Harleian MS 3968, fo. 123v. Stonleye (who was killed at Meulan): Wrottesley, *Crecy and Calais*, p. 165.

[282] M. Prestwich, 'The English at the battle of Neville's Cross', *The Battle of Neville's Cross 1346*, ed. D.W. Rollason and M.C. Prestwich (Stamford, 1998).

[283] If the 1346 shire array targets are correlated with the population figures for 1377, as calculated from the poll tax returns of that year (imperfect data, but the best we have), the heaviest demands were being made on Hereford and Shropshire (followed by Rutland); and this does not include the recruitment of Welsh troops in these counties. Devon, Hampshire and Suffolk were shouldering the lightest burden. J.C. Russell, *British Medieval Population* (Albuquerque, 1948), chapter 6 (pp. 132–3); H.C. Darby, *A New Historical Geography of England* (Cambridge, 1973), Figures 35 ('The 1334 Lay Subsidy') and 42 ('Poll Tax Population, 1377'). How consistently the Crown's manpower demands were related to population density and/or wealth has never been researched in detail. H.J. Hewitt noted that it cannot be assumed that 'the proportion of men to be raised was the same in different counties' (*The Organisation of War Under Edward III*, pp. 36–7). Cf. J.R. Maddicott, 'The English

recruiting ground may be attributed in part to the military obligations owed to a lord by his Welsh tenants, obligations that created a pool of potential manpower that was at once jealously guarded by the lord, providing him with his 'proprietary army', and yet exploited by the crown. Here was 'military lordship in action'.[284] As for the English shires of the Welsh Marches that sent contingents to the Portsmouth muster in 1346, they could claim a continuous military tradition longer than that of any other part of England, a tradition stretching back to the first Welsh war of 1277 and maintained throughout the subsequent Scottish wars.[285] The southern and midland shires of England had contributed companies to Edward I's wars only very occasionally, but they were called upon more frequently under Edward II and became involved in Edward III's French war from the outset.[286] Consequently, it is quite possible that the men recruited in the English shires in 1346 included a good many veterans: we may be sure that the arrayers would have selected seasoned soldiers if they were available. Much the same can be said of the English towns – or at least some of them. While it would probably be fair to conclude that the towns 'made a comparatively small contribution' to the king's armies, one that was hardly commensurate to their wealth and population,[287] London at least did send a sizeable company of men to a series of Edward III's expeditions, and, as Peter Konieczny has shown, there would be a core, and sometimes a clear majority, of experienced soldiers in these contingents.[288]

Another source for the geographical origins of the archers at Crécy is the toponymic evidence provided by the names of many of the recipients of pardons.[289] There is great potential here for the exploration of local recruiting patterns, though as yet little detailed research has been done. Consequently, no

---

peasantry and the demands of the Crown, 1294–1341'. *Past and Present*, Supplement 1 (1975), p. 37.

[284] Davies, *Lordship and Society in the March of Wales, 1282–1400*, chapter 3, especially pp. 80–5. For the collective military obligations owed by free Welshmen, as adapted for post-1300 conditions involving English lords and foreign wars, see F.C. Suppe, *Military Institutions on the Welsh March: Shropshire, AD 1066–1300* (Woodbridge, 1994), chapter 5.

[285] J.E. Morris, *The Welsh Wars of Edward I* (Oxford, 1901), pp. 93–9; Prestwich, *War, Politics and Finance Under Edward I*, pp. 103–4; Morgan, *War and Society in Medieval Cheshire*, pp. 31–3.

[286] J.E. Morris, 'Mounted infantry in medieval warfare', *TRHS*, 3rd ser., viii (1914), p. 96; *Norwell*, pp. 358–60.

[287] W.M. Ormrod, *The Reign of Edward III* (New Haven and London, 1990), p. 180. In the early fourteenth century the urban sector probably accounted for about 15 per cent of the population of England: R.H. Britnell, *The Commercialisation of English Society, 1000–1500*, 2nd edn (Manchester, 1996), p. 115.

[288] P. Konieczny, 'London's war effort in the fourteenth century', forthcoming.

[289] Given the widespread emergence of hereditary surnames among the sub-genteel sections of society during the first half of the fourteenth century (at least in the south, the midlands and East Anglia), locative surnames may not always be a perfect guide to an individual's immediate origins; but according to R.A. McKinley, 'dispersion' of most names of this type was limited prior to the Industrial Revolution. Identification of place-names is not always a straightforward task, though it is made somewhat easier when 'of the county of' is added to a pardon recipient's name. For an illuminating discussion, see R.A. McKinley, *A History of British Surnames* (Harlow, 1990), pp. 10, 20–3, 29–39, chapter 2.

more than illustrative examples can be offered here. A particularly striking case involves a group of men contributed to the Crécy–Calais expedition by a cluster of Northamptonshire villages. It was reported to the sheriff that William Draper of West Haddon, one of the archers serving in the county's arrayed contingent who had been 'grievously wounded' in France, had been allowed to return home. Meanwhile, Roger Andreu of Winwick by West Haddon (it is barely a mile away) received a pardon for service in France, as did Richard, son of Andrew of Lilbourne (a nearby village), whom we are told had killed a man from Winwick. If there is a strong possibility that Roger and Richard were involved in the same criminal deed, we may be sure that the two brothers, John and Robert Geffray, had also worked together. They were from Yelvertoft, which lies on the road between Lilbourne and Winwick.[290]

Such toponymic evidence may also be used to examine the recruitment of retinue-based archers, who as we have seen may be distinguished by reference to the notes of warranty that accompany enrolled pardons. We would expect to find captains recruiting their mounted archers from the areas in which their landholdings lay. This seems to be the case with Sir Robert Morley, for the names of the great majority of the 15 men whose pardons Morley certified suggest that they hailed from his family's home territory of East Anglia.[291] But in other cases it would seem that captains looked further afield, perhaps because they lacked a long-established landholding base, or perhaps in order to secure the services of 'professional' archers from other corners of the kingdom. Take, for example, Sir John Stryvelyn's retinue. In the immediate aftermath of Crécy, Stryvelyn certified the issue of pardons to 41 men, a striking fact in itself, since according to the Wetwang abstracts there were only 50 combatants in the retinue (including 26 archers) and only one of them, Peter Heleye, had an enrolled protection.[292] The toponymic evidence indicates a cluster of men from the region of Stryvelyn's *caput* at Belsay in Northumberland, as well as others drawn from a little further south in county Durham, and from (among other places) Yorkshire, Lincolnshire, Norfolk and Northamptonshire.[293] Stryvelyn, apparently a Scot by origin, had acquired Belsay in 1335, and the diverse origins of his men may partly be the consequence of his recently established lordship in the region, though it does not necessarily indicate that Stryvelyn's retinue was composed of a miscellaneous assembly of *individuals*. The clearest example of a coherent *group* among these pardon recipients concerns the three brothers, Adam, John and William, sons of Robert Chernely.[294] They had evidently been engaged in crime together; now, at Crécy, they fought together.

What do we know of the social and economic standing of the archers at Crécy? Some clues are offered by Edward III's re-enactments and extensions of

---

[290] Wrottesley, *Crecy and Calais*, pp. 109, 269; *CPR, 1345–8*, pp. 499, 501. Although only one, William Draper, is described as an 'archer', it is likely that the others were too.

[291] *CPR, 1345–8*, pp. 486, 492–3. For Morley's Norfolk roots and the military community of the region, see Ayton, 'Knights, esquires and military service: the evidence of armorial cases before the Court of Chivalry'.

[292] *CPR, 1345–8*, pp. 485–508 (one of them is styled 'chaplain'). Heleye: C76/22, m. 4.

[293] Belsay: *Complete Peerage*, xii, part 1, pp. 407–8.

[294] *CPR, 1345–8*, pp. 485, 489.

the Statute of Winchester (1285). Itself based on earlier assizes of arms, the statute had required every free man between the ages of 15 (later 16) and 60 to possess military equipment appropriate to his means, as determined by the value of his land or chattels; and to appear at a 'view of arms' in his hundred twice a year.[295] According to Edward III's promulgations of the statute during the 1330s, those with land worth from £2 to £5 *per annum* were to be equipped with a bow and arrows, a sword and a knife.[296] This definition of the section of society that would be expected to yield foot archers was very much that of the earlier Edwardian kings.[297] What occurred in the years immediately prior to Crécy was the crown's identification of the socio-economic group that would be called upon to provide mounted archers. This was not done by altering the politically sensitive 'customary' scale of wealth-specific categories defined by the Statute of Winchester, the maintenance of which had prompted petitioning (and a statute) in the first parliament of Edward III's reign.[298] Rather, it was the novel military assessment of the mid-1340s (itself 'highly contentious') that laid down that a landowner whose property was worth £5 *per annum* was to be, or to provide, a mounted archer, while the income threshold for a hobelar was £10, and for a man-at-arms, £25.[299] There was, therefore, at least in principle, a clear separation in economic and social terms between archers, whether mounted or on foot, and mounted, armoured warriors – the hobelars and men-at-arms. However, the archers were not themselves a homogeneous group any more than the 'peasantry' was; and those who served in the king's armies cannot have been drawn exclusively from the comparatively narrow socio-economic bands specified in royal proclamations. Indeed, the original Statute of Winchester, and its re-enactments under Edward II and Edward III, appear to cast the net much more widely, by inviting 'all others' (that is, those not included in the lowest specifically identified groups, which were 'less than 40s of land' and 'less than 20 marks of chattels') to have bows and arrows, if living outside the forest and bows and bolts (presumably crossbows), if within.[300] Thus, the very poorest freemen were encouraged to possess a bow, if nothing else; and this aspect of the Statute of Winchester may have proved useful when the heavy recruiting demands of the Edwardian wars began in the mid-1290s. The crown's initiatives to maintain the pool of available bowmen and their regular recruitment in large numbers, combined with (among other things) the emergence of the mounted archer and of opportunities for freelance service throughout Europe, make this a

---

[295] *Statutes of the Realm*, ed. A. Luders et al., 11 vols (London, 1810–28), i, pp. 96–8.

[296] *Foedera*, II, ii, pp. 900–1 (30 December 1334); *Rotuli Scotiae*, i, p. 422 (6 May 1336).

[297] *Parliamentary Writs and Writs of Military Summons*, ed. F. Palgrave, 2 vols in 4 (London, 1827–34), II, ii, p. 661 (1 August 1324); Appendix, p. 94 (8 August 1315). Powicke, *Military Obligation in Medieval England*, pp. 88–9, 119–20.

[298] Prince, 'The army and navy', *The English Government at Work, 1327–1336*, i, p. 362.

[299] Powicke, *Military Obligation in Medieval England*, pp. 190, 192, 195–8.

[300] 'omnes alii, qui habere possunt, habeant arcus et sagittas extra forestam, et infra forestam arcus et pilos': *Foedera*, II, ii, p. 901. The 'less than 40s of land' class were required to have gisarme (poleaxe), knife, and lesser arms; the 'less than 20 marks of chattels' group, sword, knife and lesser arms.

period of pivotal importance, and dynamic change, in the social history of the English archer.

About two-thirds of the archers at Crécy – the foot archers – had been recruited by commissioners of array in the English shires, or by the 'stewards or bailiffs' of the Welsh lordships. While we know that, in England, the local communities provided the archers' equipment and the first instalment of their pay, it is less easy to generalise about how the men were actually selected,[301] how easy it was to find willing – and capable – recruits, and from which sections of the peasantry they were drawn. It seems that the village communities often decided themselves who would be sent, choosing local men or hiring outsiders. It was then the responsibility of the commissioners of array or their deputies to review the recruits, including presumably their archery skills, and to weed out those who were unsuitable. This is what appears to be happening at Norwich in July 1338, for example.[302] The size of the pool of potential recruits must have varied a good deal from region to region. Although the population as a whole was probably declining during the 1340s, prior to the first plague visitation, it is clear that there was much local variation in economic conditions,[303] just as there was in the burden of recruitment. As to how far the local quotas were met by members of the '£2 to £5 class' of landholders, we can as yet offer only informed guesswork. For while these men should have possessed the equipment, and presumably the skills, of an archer, they also had domestic responsibilities, not least their landholdings, to consider; and given the risk of 'land unsown or corn unharvested', who could blame them for being reluctant to enlist for a campaign of uncertain duration?[304] If the foot archer's rate of pay, 2d or 3d a day, would not have impressed a wealthy freeholder or skilled artisan, it would have been altogether more appealing to a labourer with little or no land, or to a household servant,[305] just as it would to those who were surplus to local requirements – the younger sons and the 'marginal' elements of society, Langland's 'thieves and wasters'.[306] It would seem, therefore, that if we are to imagine the social make-up of the companies of archers raised in the English shires, we should probably envisage not only husbandmen, possessors of a plough-team and a respectable landholding, but also, perhaps in greater numbers, landless wage-

---

[301] Maddicott, 'The English peasantry and the demands of the Crown', pp. 37–8, 42–3.

[302] Prince, 'The army and navy', *The English Government at Work, 1327–1336*, i, pp. 357–8; but cf. pp. 359–60. E101/21/21.

[303] B.M.S. Campbell, *Before the Black Death: Studies in the 'Crisis' of the Early Fourteenth Century* (Manchester, 1991).

[304] Maddicott, 'The English peasantry and the demands of the Crown', pp. 44–5. Might we not assume, however, that a husbandman's holding would be managed in his absence by the village community who had chosen him to serve in the army on their behalf?

[305] Foot archers were paid 3d per day in 1346–7, as they had been for the French campaigns of 1338–9 and 1340 (but 2d in Brittany in 1342–3), with mounted archers receiving 6d per day: Robert Brady, *Complete History of England*, ii, p. 243; *Norwell*, pp. 358–61; E101/389/8, mm. 14–16; E36/204, fos 108v–110v. Civilian wages: Maddicott, 'The English peasantry and the demands of the Crown', p. 41.

[306] Cf. B. Geremek, *The Margins of Society in Late Medieval Paris* (Cambridge, 1987), pp. 113–16, for the 'marginal' life of Jehan Le Brun.

labourers, cottagers and *famuli* – men who could be more easily spared by the village community and had little to lose from being away from home.

The social composition of the corps of mounted archers, who contributed about a third of the bowmen at Crécy, is even more difficult to characterise. Receiving 6d per day, twice the rate paid to foot archers, the mounted archer also cost much more to equip,[307] the principal expense being his horse, which although only a hackney could easily cost 20 shillings. Mounted archers for the French war were not normally recruited by commissions of array, probably in part because of the financial burden that would have been imposed upon the shires. Most served in mixed retinues, with the cost of horse and harness being borne by themselves, their captain or a sponsor.[308] Much would depend upon individual circumstances, and consequently it is not easy to generalise about the social origins of the retinue-based archers. In 1346, some of them had been equipped and sent to muster by £5 *per annum* landholders seeking to discharge their military assessment. This would often have been kept in the family. For example, John Longedon of Warwickshire sent his son, Ralph.[309] Such cases as this have prompted historians to characterise mounted archers as men of yeoman stock, drawn from 'the elite of village society', as Michael Prestwich has put it.[310] There is much to be said for this characterisation, as long as it is recognised that the Crécy campaign represents an early stage in the development of the mounted archer. For in the 1340s, as we have seen, we may find a captain like the earl of Northampton employing traditional, array-style selection methods in his home territory of Essex in order to assemble at least a proportion of his mounted archers.[311] It must also be emphasised that the social background of many of the men employed by £5 landholders to discharge their military assessment cannot be determined. If it is tempting to think of Chaucer's Knight's Yeoman from the *General Prologue* of the *Canterbury Tales* as a typical mounted archer, it needs always to be borne in mind that this pen-portrait dates from half a century after Crécy.[312]

Whatever the social standing of an archer, whether he was serving in a mixed retinue or a shire company, the characteristic that all presumably had in common was competence with the longbow. It would be natural to assume that proficiency with the bow was widespread among the peasantry of England and Wales in the 1340s. Is this not the implication of one of the most famous of the vivid scenes of peasant life depicted in the Luttrell Psalter (c. late 1330s), which

[307] As much as eight times more, if the costs of the 1290s are compared with those of the 1330s: Maddicott, 'The English peasantry and the demands of the Crown', p. 41. For the price of hackneys, see Ayton, *Knights and Warhorses*, p. 57.

[308] For an example, from 1420, of archers being 'at the horsing' of their captain, see J.M.W. Bean, *From Lord to Patron. Lordship in Medieval England* (Manchester, 1989), p. 239.

[309] Wrottesley, *Crecy and Calais*, p. 150.

[310] Prestwich, *Armies and Warfare in the Middle Ages*, p. 143; Morgan, *War and Society in Medieval Cheshire*, p. 41.

[311] C81/1735, no. 2. We may assume that the archers would have been horsed and equipped at the earl's expense.

[312] F.N. Robinson, ed., *The Complete Works of Geoffrey Chaucer*, 2nd edn (London, 1957), p. 18.

shows a group of men practising their archery skills at the butts? The problem with this assumption is that documentary records suggest that skilled archers may not have been quite so numerous in 1346. Take, for example, the order for Welsh reinforcements for the siege of Calais, which noted that each man was to be issued with a *lancea penselata* 'unless he was a competent archer'.[313] As we have seen, the re-enacted Statute of Winchester *required* only a narrow social band, the £2 to £5 class, to possess the equipment of an archer. That the poorest freemen were also encouraged to have bows and arrows at their disposal, and presumably be able to use them, may have been more in hope than expectation. As Michael Powicke notes, the Statute of Winchester was 'manifestly concerned with police duties, not war', and was likely to give rise to 'masses of stick-armed villeins fit for little but the hue and cry'.[314] Just how apposite this judgement is can be seen when the surviving records of 'views of arms' held during the 1330s and 1340s are examined. In Norfolk in 1336, the great majority of the arrayed manpower had a staff or axe, and a knife, the archers being 'a small, select body apart', consisting mostly of £2 to £5 landholders.[315] A similar situation, with only a handful of bowmen, may be observed in views of arms in Middlesex in 1338 (though here swords were much more common), in Suffolk in 1346 and in Norwich in 1355.[316] Perhaps men simply left their bows at home on such occasions. It should, however, be observed that that few peasants would have had any reason to become competent archers. Their daily lives did not require such skills; archery, therefore, would have been a pastime for those who had the desire and the opportunity to pursue it. Bows were not even the usual weapon of the peasant deer poacher: he preferred traps, snares or a sling.[317] This is not to suggest that either the archers at Crécy or their equipment was deficient (the latter being provided by the shires and replenished by the crown); merely that the supply of bowmen with the necessary level of competence may not have been as plentiful as is sometimes supposed.

In the light of this, it is hardly surprising that the crown was particularly keen to secure the services of those among the civilian population who might be regarded as 'professional' archers. Time and again we find the orders to commissioners of array stressing the importance of selecting foresters and parkers for service in the king's army. For example, a few weeks after Crécy, the Prince of Wales instructed each of his chief parkers at Berkhamsted, Byfleet and Watlington to choose 'six good companion-archers, the best [they] can find' for

---

313 Wrottesley, *Crecy and Calais*, p. 104.

314 Powicke, *Military Obligation in Medieval England*, pp. 95, 119.

315 E101/19/37; Powicke, *Military Obligation in Medieval England*, p. 193.

316 J.R. Alban, 'National defence in England, 1337–89', PhD thesis, University of Liverpool, 1977, Appendix 5(a), pp. 412–15; Prestwich, *Armies and Warfare in the Middle Ages*, p. 139 (C47/2/58). In the leet of Conesford in Norwich only 8 out of 191 men were armed as bowmen: W. Hudson, 'Norwich militia in the fourteenth century', *Norfolk Archaeology*, xiv (1901), pp. 271, 274–5, 295–301.

317 'Bows and arrows seem not to have been particularly favoured by peasant poachers': J. Birrell, 'Peasant deer poachers in the medieval forest', *Progress and Problems in Medieval England*, ed. R. Britnell and J. Hatcher (Cambridge, 1996), pp. 68–88 (at p. 75).

service in France.[318] What such men brought to the army was a level of skill with the bow, a capacity for marksmanship, beyond that which might be expected from an ordinary villager. Our sources suggest that they were not particularly numerous in the army: few of the pardon recipients are specifically designated 'parkers' or 'foresters', though, of course, the onomastic evidence may not be a wholly reliable guide in this respect.[319] This much is clear: such men as the father and son, William and John Smart, parkers from St Osyth in Essex, who received pardons for service under Sir Robert Morley, or Henry Parker, who headed a company of ten archers raised from Rutland in October 1346,[320] were elite practitioners with the longbow, much sought after by captains and commissioners of array wishing to stiffen their companies with toxophilite expertise. Perhaps we should regard such men as the 'Robin Hoods' of mid-fourteenth-century England, their life experiences almost certainly fuelling the tales of the forest-bound, outlaw hero that were gaining popularity at this time.[321] It would seem that there is indeed an affinity between some at least of our Crécy archers and Chaucer's Knight's Yeoman, for as the great writer noted of his subject: 'A forster was he, soothly, as I gesse.'

It may be possible to indicate the approximate numbers of archers in service, to have some idea of regional distribution of recruits and to attempt a characterisation of the social groups from which they were drawn; but it is not so easy to 'identify' them, which is an essential prerequisite for prosopography. We may know the names of a good many of these common soldiers, but knowing a name does not get us very far, for unless the named man can be linked securely to appearances in other documents, the name remains no more than a label for a faceless man without an identity. There are two major problems. The first is the sheer numbers of men involved, for this is not a small world like that of the gentry. The second arises from the fact that the patchiness of the Crécy records is repeated for other major expeditions. The armies of the second quarter of the fourteenth century are not well served by muster rolls; those that we have for the archer reinforcements sent by several counties after Crécy are rare survivals. The implication of all this is that military service prosopography is not possible with Edwardian archers in the way that it is with the men-at-arms. The present state of research would suggest that, with the exception of some specialised groups, few English archers can be 'identified'.[322]

As a consequence of these methodological problems, however much we

---

318 *Black Prince Register*, i, p. 18. Royal orders to select foresters and parkers: C61/49, m. 23 (1337); *Rotuli Scotiae*, i, p. 501 (1337); *Treaty Rolls, 1337–39*, no. 123 (1338); C76/15, mm. 27d, 29d (1340). Cf. Goodman, *John of Gaunt: The Exercise of Princely Power*, p. 218.
319 *CPR, 1345–8*, pp. 492 and 505 (parkers); 487, 497 and 505 (foresters).
320 E101/584/5, m. 2.
321 A. Ayton, 'Military service and the development of the Robin Hood Legend in the Fourteenth Century', *Nottingham Medieval Studies*, xxxvi (1992), pp. 126–47.
322 The 'specialised groups' would include those employed in the English garrisons in Scotland during the 1330s and 1340s, for which muster rolls do allow a degree of rudimentary career reconstitution to be carried out. For references, see Ayton, *Knights and Warhorses*, pp. 167–8. For analysis, see P. Leaver, 'A long way from home? English garrisons in Scotland, 1335–42', MA thesis, University of Hull, 2001.

might suspect that many of the archers and hobelars at Crécy, particularly those serving in retinues, were quite as experienced as the men-at-arms, aware of the demands that would be made of them and acquainted with the men around them, we are, by and large, unable to prove it. If a more complete range of Wetwang's Wardrobe accounts had survived for the period of the Crécy–Calais expedition, an exception to this might have been possible with regard to Edward III's bodyguard of archers. As it is, all that have are a few suggestive documentary fragments. Earlier records show that of the 20 archers serving the king in this capacity as members of his household in 1334–5, three were still occupying the same position ten years later.[323] At least one of them, John Pulford, drew wages as an archer of the king's household for the Crécy–Calais campaign, and there may well have been others.[324] John Ward, another of the king's archers from the time of the Roxburgh campaign (indeed the leader of the augmented bodyguard on that occasion and frequently thereafter until the Breton campaign of 1342–3), was also at Crécy. But in his case a military career had been accompanied by social elevation, for by 1346–7 he was a knight leading a small company of three esquires and two mounted archers.[325]

Apart from the elite group of the king's bodyguard, all that we can do with regard to the archers in 1346 is offer evidence of clusters of men from the same area, who must have known each other, serving together in the same retinue or company. Take, for example, the six men from Worfield, near Bridgnorth in Shropshire, all tenants of the earl of Huntingdon, who served as archers in that earl's retinue until the capture of Caen, after which they left with the earl for England. We know about them because when they arrived home in Worfield they were arrested by the sheriff for returning 'sanz garraunt', in other words as deserters, and the earl's letter requesting their release has survived.[326] As we have seen, clusters of men from the same locality can also be detected in the military assessment records and among the recipients of charters of pardon. So, although we are unable to demonstrate continuity of service and stability of retinue composition among the archers, as we can with the men-at-arms, we can at least suggest that a bowman, whether serving in a retinue or as part of a shire contingent, was likely to be fighting alongside men whom he knew.

*   *   *

The army with which Edward III fought the battle of Crécy was a large, socially diverse community of men. In its size and social mix it could be likened to a town on the move, although at this time there were actually few English towns as populous as the Crécy army and none offered a more representative sample of the male population of King Edward's realm. Recruiting had taken place in all corners of England and Wales and had drawn on all levels of the social

---

[323] John Chester, Nicholas Holford, John Pulford. BL, Cotton MS, Nero C. VIII, fo. 219r; E36/204, fo. 91v.

[324] E404/496, no. 24.

[325] Morgan, *War and Society in Medieval Cheshire*, pp. 44–7, 52–4.

[326] The men were William Gravenore, Richard Gravenore, Henry Gold, Richard Smyth, William Hockoumbe, John Tybynton: 'nos archiers et nos tenaunz de Worfeld'. SC1/39, no. 190; Wrottesley, *Crecy and Calais*, p. 104.

hierarchy. Consequently, although there were few 'strangers' with the army, there would have been much cultural and linguistic diversity, and much scope for misunderstanding and rivalry.[327] The particular distinctiveness of the Welsh has already been discussed; the potential for north–south tensions can easily be imagined. Another consequence of kingdom-wide mobilisation was the armorial disputes that flared up when noblemen from different families appeared at muster bearing the same heraldic arms. We know that this happened during the Crécy campaign, and that Edward III ordered the 'chalenges darmes' to cease, no doubt because they were disrupting the cohesion of the army and distracting from the military objectives of the campaign.[328] However, at least one armorial dispute – between Robert, Lord Morley and Nicholas Burnell – was settled during the siege of Calais.[329] The Court of Chivalry proceedings were held in St Peter's church, in the siege lines outside Calais, and excited great interest in the army. The building was packed to the rafters for the verdict, as knights and esquires crowded in to witness the leaders of the political elite pass judgment on matters central to the honour and social standing of two of its members.

The scene in St Peter's church serves as a reminder that an Edwardian army was a political organism as well as a military machine. It is perhaps not altogether surprising that the politics of military service have not received the attention that they deserve. This was, after all, the period in which the Commons in the king's parliament was emerging as a force to be reckoned with; and by comparison with the formal proceedings of parliament, it is far more difficult to determine the *nature* of the political interaction that occurred on campaign. But we would be unwise to ignore this dimension of an Edwardian army simply because it is obscure, for this was a world in which politics and war were closely intertwined, in which the political and military elites were composed of essentially the same men. To mobilise a major royal army, like that which fought the battle of Crécy, was to convene a gathering of the political community, which in terms of size could not be rivalled by any other event. Among the 2,500 to 3,000 men-at-arms were the king and many of the most prominent lay magnates, while the knights and esquires who served in the magnates' retinues were themselves a more than representative sample of the 'community of the realm'. That, at the time of Edward III's landing at La Hougue, part of the aristocracy was similarly engaged elsewhere in France serves only to underline the fact that military service involved a larger proportion of the political community than any other form of 'public' activity.[330]

It was not only the involvement of such large numbers simultaneously that

[327] Particularly while awaiting embarkation: see Hewitt, *The Organisation of War under Edward III*, p. 46.

[328] PRO30/26/69, nos 176, 183.

[329] According to William Wollaston, esquire, Burnell had challenged Morley 'sur les champs' in Normandy, though he could not remember precisely where: PRO30/26/69, no. 186. For the *Burnell* v. *Morley* dispute, see Ayton, 'Knights, esquires and military service: the evidence of the armorial cases before the Court of Chivalry', *The Medieval Military Revolution*, ed. Ayton and Price, pp. 81–104.

[330] Cf., for example, July 1338: Ayton, 'Edward III and the English aristocracy at the beginning of the Hundred Years War', pp. 200–1.

made military service such an important activity for the nobility and gentry. Campaigning brought these men together for an extended period, usually months rather than the few weeks that an average Edwardian parliament lasted;[331] and during this time they would be collectively engaged in a martial adventure that combined personal support for the king's 'just quarrel' with the performance of their inherited martial role. Viewed in this way, the Crécy campaign represented six weeks of concentrated, collective endeavour for the political elite of England: a period during which longstanding relationships would be tested in the harsh arena of war, and new associations forged; a period of unrivalled opportunity for young, ambitious knights and esquires, and for magnates seeking men of outstanding talent. Above all, it was a period for discussion and the exchange of ideas on all manner of subjects. In the unusually intense conditions created by service in the king's army, the social network of the political elite became a 'small world' around which ideas and opinions flowed rapidly. Indeed, the army as a whole can be viewed in these terms. Over a quarter of a century ago, J.R. Maddicott argued that the regular raising of contingents of infantry from among the rural peasantry is likely to have broadened their political consciousness, 'taking them from their villages, bringing them into the presence of great men and great events, and breeding news, gossip and scandal'.[332] It would be difficult to imagine an event greater than the battle of Crécy. Not only would it have been the defining moment in the lives of most of those present, it would have been an experience carried home, and relived, in countless manor houses and village taverns across the land.

As we have seen, Edward III's senior captains at Crécy were drawn from the political elite of his realm. That this did not in itself guarantee unity of purpose had been shown only too clearly during the reign of Edward II. But the rivalries and jealousies that had been manifest at Bannockburn, and indeed Stanhope Park, were far less evident in the armies of Edward III's maturity. His lieutenants were team players. They had shared the experience of the Scottish and French wars, as well as such key political events as the Nottingham castle coup in 1330 and the reshaping of the political order thereafter. At the very least they knew each other well, having met regularly in parliament and the council chamber, on the hunting field and in the king's campaign pavilion. Some became close friends, as we see, for example, with Sir Maurice Berkeley and Sir Thomas Bradeston.[333] If we visualise the English army as consisting of a network of relationships, captains like Berkeley and Bradeston – and, still more, the magnates like Northampton and Warwick – were the principal 'hubs' in the network.[334]

---

331 For the duration of sessions, see Ormrod, *The Reign of Edward III*, Table 5 (p. 208).

332 Maddicott, 'The English peasantry and the demands of the Crown', p. 45.

333 Saul, *Knights and Esquires*, pp. 76–7. Note also C81/1749, no. 12, a protection warrant, which shows Bradeston, still an esquire, serving alongside Berkeley prior to the death of the latter's father in 1326. Both men had close ties with Edward III. Berkeley had been retained for life in June 1330 (*CPR, 1327–30*, p. 530), while Bradeston was also 'one of the king's closest friends': Vale, *Edward III and Chivalry*, p. 61.

334 Dominated by a small number of major hubs, this is known as a 'scale-free' or 'aristocratic' network. See A.-L. Barabasi, *Linked: The New Science of Networks* (Cambridge, Mass., 2002);

While being connected to each other by bonds of amity and shared status,[335] the 'hubs' were themselves the foci around which the men in the army clustered. Seen in this way, these 'clusters' (retinues) were not discrete entities. When men switched from one captain to another, as they might do from one campaign to the next, they were often moving between closely associated retinues. Thus, it would be misleading to present a mid-fourteenth-century English army as a sea of shifting relationships. Men moved between the retinues raised in a particular region; they moved with comrades in arms, as a company; they moved at the recommendation of captains. Indeed, as we have seen, during the 1340s there was far less movement between retinues than has sometimes been supposed. Many of the seasoned warriors at Crécy were serving under captains, and along-side other knights and esquires, with whom they had campaigned on earlier occasions. Retinues exhibited a striking degree of cohesion, based upon conti-nuity of service and networks of individual relationships. Although the bulk of the evidence concerns knights and esquires, we can assume that such relation-ships extended to the archers, many of whom were recruited in 'mixed' compa-nies and probably served alongside men-at-arms in the field.[336]

Was the stability of retinue composition, which was so striking a feature of the English armies of the 1340s, a distinctive development of Edward III's reign? If so, what part did this play in the success of English armies during this period? Only tentative answers can be given to these questions. Before a secure response to the first can be offered, a great deal more work needs to be done on the personnel of Edward II's armies. As for the second, here too more prosopographical analysis is needed; but even when we have established as complete a picture as the sources allow, much will still depend upon the inter-pretation of the evidence. Of this much we can be sure: conditions during the 1330s and 1340s certainly favoured continuity of service within retinues. During the second decade of Edward III's reign, a team of senior commanders, serving regularly with large retinues, performed an increasingly important recruiting role. Indeed, from the comital creations of March 1337 through to the emergence of the Prince of Wales as a war leader in 1346, the king's manage-ment of the aristocratic elite for recruiting purposes can be counted as one of his particular successes. At Crécy, retinue-based combatants were more numerous than on any previous campaign, and three-quarters of these men were serving in 14 large, mixed retinues (consisting of 100 or more combatants). If we regard the companies brought by the royal household bannerets and knights as a single unit (the 'household division'), the proportion rises to over 95 per cent of reti-nue-based personnel located in only 11 'retinues'.[337] The contrast with the highly fragmented structure of early Edwardian armies is striking, as is the fact

M. Buchanan, *Nexus: Small Worlds and the Groundbreaking Science of Networks* (New York and London, 2002).

[335] What the major captains at Crécy had in common was membership of that still fluid group, the parliamentary peerage.

[336] The likelihood of close tactical co-operation between men-at-arms and archers, perhaps in the manner of a 'lance', is discussed in Chapter 10, pp. 353–9.

[337] These figures exclude the foreign contingents and companies led by men of sub-knightly rank. See Appendix 2, Table 2.

that all of the Crécy retinues were 'mixed', combining men-at-arms and archers. This process of consolidation within the military community, driven by the recruiting needs of a small team of senior captains, was fuelled by the traditions of martial service that had been established within gentry families during the Scottish wars of three successive reigns. The king's lieutenants drew heavily on this pool of available manpower, a pool that had been supplemented as a consequence of the military assessment of the mid-1340s. The regional basis of much of this recruitment and the attractions of serving under a magnate rather than a lesser figure were no doubt important in enabling the earls, and others of similar status, to retain the services of knights, esquires and archers from one campaign to the next. That major expeditions were almost annual events between Halidon Hill and Crécy would also have helped to strengthen ties within retinues, both between the captain and his men, and between the men themselves.

Looking back from the vantage point of Crécy, we can see that the leading captains carried with them a 'core group' of personnel from the Scottish to the French wars, and that stability of retinue manpower became particularly evident as campaign followed campaign during the early years of the French conflict. It is worth remembering this when we are tempted to dismiss these early expeditions as expensive failures. Moreover, esprit de corps established on active service was reinforced by warlike activities in England, for the core of a magnate's campaign retinue would also accompany him on to the tourney field.[338] Following a lengthy ban during Edward II's reign, tournaments flourished during the first twenty years of his son's rule.[339] Well over forty can be documented during these two decades, with a heavy concentration during the early 1340s,[340] and this is undoubtedly only the tip of the iceberg. Some were large-scale events, like the Dunstable meeting of February 1342, which was attended by six earls, many barons and over 250 knights – 'almost all the young fighting men of England' – but no foreigners.[341] The Windsor tournament, held during the early weeks of 1344, is remembered most for being the occasion of the foundation of Edward III's Round Table, but it was also important in bringing together the aristocracy during a lengthy truce in the French war.[342] Such attention to collective martial endeavour away from the battlefield reinforced team spirit among captains and no doubt also among the men in their retinues.

It is easier to draw attention to the cohesion within Edward III's army at Crécy, based as it was upon continuity of service and networks of individual relationships, than it is to demonstrate the impact that it had on the battle. But that it would have strengthened the combat effectiveness of both individual

---

[338] J. Barker, *The Tournament in England, 1100–1400* (Woodbridge, 1986), pp. 27–9, 120–3.
[339] Vale, *Edward III and Chivalry*, chapter 4.
[340] Juliet Vale's 'Provisional List of the Tournaments of Edward III, 1327–55' (*Edward III and Chivalry*, Appendix 12, pp. 172–3) can be supplemented. See, for example, C. Shenton, 'The English court and the restoration of royal prestige, 1327–1345', PhD thesis, University of Oxford, 1995, p. 238.
[341] *Murimuth*, pp. 123–4; cf. *Baker*, p. 75.
[342] *Murimuth*, pp. 155–6; 231–2.

retinues and the army as a whole can hardly be doubted. We should imagine men-at-arms fighting together co-operatively, in pairs or small groups, if necessary back to back, rather as we see a few years later with the English mercenary companies in Italy.[343] In the stressful conditions of the mêlée, what counted was not only skill and experience, but also bonds of mutual trust, a sense that you could rely on the men around you. We find only hints of this micro-level tactical co-operation in the narrative sources, but then so much about the battle of Crécy remains obscure if we rely only on the chronicles. Indeed, the case of Crécy serves as a particularly forceful reminder that narrative sources can tell only part of the story; that, where possible, medieval battles should be studied by reference to a wider a range of sources. Exercise of the historical imagination is crucial here, though in truth the suggestion that we may better understand a battle by examining in detail the organisation and personnel of the armies that fought it could hardly be described as radical. This, in any case, has been the underlying aim of this chapter. For while casting new light on the English army at Crécy, and beyond that on the social and political relationships of the mid-fourteenth-century military community, it is hoped that the close study of the administrative records, and the prosopographical analysis that has stemmed from that study, has contributed a little to our understanding of the course and outcome of the battle.

---

[343] M. Mallett, *Mercenaries and their Masters: Warfare in Renaissance Italy* (London, 1974), p. 37; K. Fowler, 'Sir John Hawkwood and the English condottieri in Trecento Italy', *Renaissance Studies*, xii (1998), pp. 131–48 (at p. 137).

Appendix 1

Reconstructing Walter Wetwang's lost
vadia guerre accounts for the Crécy–Calais campaign

It is known that a separate book of foreign expenses, containing *vadia guerre* and related accounts, was drawn up for the period during which Walter Wetwang was keeper of the king's wardrobe,[1] but it has been lost. We have some idea of the form that the army 'pay-roll' took, because such documents have survived elsewhere, and because extracts from the original have been preserved in other, near contemporary records. The most explicit instance concerns a Memoranda Roll entry dating from 1353, which notes that the book of Walter Wetwang, late keeper of king's wardrobe, had been examined, specifically the section entitled 'de vadiis guerre in partibus Normannie, Francie et coram Calesio', in order to determine the wages owing to the Holand brothers, Thomas and Otes, for the Crécy–Calais campaign. The search revealed the size of their companies, the period of service and the wages due.[2] In another Memoranda Roll entry from the same year, this time detailing the size and period of service of Sir Thomas Haukeston's retinue, the information also appears to have been taken from Wetwang's pay-roll, or a related document, though there is no explicit mention of it.[3] Somewhat tantalising as these extracts may be, they do serve a useful purpose, namely to confirm the authenticity of other, more substantial documents, dating from the fifteenth to the eighteenth centuries, which appear to be partial transcripts of Wetwang's lost *vadia guerre* accounts.[4] Some of these

---

1 Tout, *Chapters*, iv, p. 115. These *vadia guerre* accounts will be referred to as 'Wetwang's', though in fact he died in November 1347 and his final accounts were drawn up by others.
2 Sir Thomas had served (at 2s per day) with four esquires (12d) and four mounted archers (6d) from 4 June 1346 until 31 January 1347, that is, for 242 days, costing in all £62 11s. Sir Otes, with three esquires, serving for the same period, was owed £60 10s in wages. Those conducting the search were concerned that the original account offered no guidance on the period of service after 31 January; nor was it clear to them whether debts still owed to the Holands, recorded in Wetwang's book of debts, were related to the above wage bills. What they seem to have missed is that the wages total owed to Thomas Holand should have been £96 16s! Wrottesley, *Crecy and Calais*, pp. 176–7.
3 Wrottesley, *Crecy and Calais*, p. 176. A third instance is concerned with the payment of expenses to Irish contingents arriving in England before joining the army camped outside Calais: *ibid.*, p. 183. Apart from these examples, precise information concerning the number of paid troops in retinues is to be found in only a very few contemporary records: occasionally on the Issue Rolls (e.g., E403/336, m. 49: Sir Giles Beauchamp's company) or in Wardrobe Debentures (e.g., E404/496, nos 100, 178).
4 What follows is an expanded reworking of the discussion of these 'Wetwang abstracts' in A. Ayton, 'The English army and the Normandy campaign of 1346', *England and Normandy*

'Wetwang abstracts' have been wholly or partially published. Perhaps the best known is the College of Arms MS 2 M 16 (fos 82–97), which was printed over a century ago by George Wrottesley;[5] but this publication was by no means the first,[6] nor, indeed, was it to be the last.[7] No other collection of medieval army records have received this amount of attention. It is unfortunate, therefore, that the only attempt to compile a catalogue of available Wetwang abstracts is Anthony Wagner's classification of those versions that record the arms of the captains listed.[8] Nevertheless, as a consequence of the widespread dissemination of the Wetwang abstracts, these documents have exerted a powerful influence upon modern interpretations of Edward III's army in 1346–7, and upon Edwardian military studies in general.

It needs to be borne in mind that these early modern documents represent very incomplete transcripts of Wetwang's original *vadia guerre* accounts. The incompleteness has several distinctive aspects. First, the data concerning the arrayed troops in the army (the shire levies and Welsh contingents) have been heavily summarised. The original pay accounts would have provided separate entries for each of the contingents of archers, spearmen and hobelars, but what we find in the various abstracts are aggregated manpower figures, with no indications of periods of service.[9] The fact that the different scribes have adopted different principles for their summaries does help a little. The Brut abstract distinguishes a contingent led by Sir Thomas Haukeston, for example, which is presumably part or all of the force of reinforcements of which he was appointed marshal in August 1346. The various abstracts also agree with regard to the

---

in the Middle Ages, ed. D. Bates and A. Curry (London and Rio Grande, 1994), pp. 253–68, prompted by an interesting discussion in C.J. Rogers's *War Cruel and Sharp* and by further reflection on the subject.

5 Wrottesley, *Crecy and Calais*, pp. 191–204. The manuscript, which includes the arms of the captains tricked against their names (certainly not in Wetwang's original pay-roll and omitted by Wrottesley), is described in *Catalogue of English Medieval Rolls of Arms*, ed. A.R. Wagner, Society of Antiquaries, *Aspilogia*, I (London, 1950), pp. 158–9.

6 Robert Brady, *Complete History of England*, 2 vols (London, 1685, 1700), ii, appendix, pp. 86–8. Edward Rowe Mores, *Nomina et insignia gentilitia nobilium equitumque sub Edoardo primo regi militantium. Accedunt classes exercitus Edoardi tertii regis Caletem obsidentis* (Oxford, 1749), pp. 89–101 (using a copy 'ex rotulo pergameno penes Virum cl. Jacobum West, armigerum', which is very similar to the version in BL, Harleian MS 3968, fos 114r–129r). *Collection of Ordinances and Regulations for the Government of the Royal Household* (London, 1790), pp. 1–12. Francis Grose, *Military Antiquities Respecting a History of the English Army*, 2nd edn, 2 vols (London, 1812), i, pp. 265–7. J.J. Champollion-Figeac, ed., *Lettres de rois, reines, et autres personnages des cours de France et d'Angleterre*, 2 vols (Paris, 1847), ii, pp. 82–5 (an abbreviated version, with many misreadings, of BL, Harleian MS 3968, fos 114r–129r). J. Gairdner, ed., *Three Fifteenth-Century Chronicles*, Camden Soc., new ser., xxviii (1880), pp. 81–5 (a fifteenth-century text in London, Lambeth Library, MS 306).

7 *Brut*, ed. Brie, ii, pp. 538–41 (a summary of Wetwang embedded in a fifteenth-century version of the English Brut: BL, Harleian MS 53).

8 *Catalogue of English Medieval Rolls of Arms*, ed. Wagner, pp. 158–60. Among British Library MSS, see, for example: Stowe MS 574, fos 28r–42v; Additional MS 38823, fos 59r–69r; Harleian MS 246, fos 9v–17v.

9 E.g., Wrottesley, *Crecy and Calais*, pp. 203–4; *Collection of Ordinances and Regulations for the Government of the Royal Household*, pp. 5–6; *Brut*, ed. Brie, pp. 540–1.

general scale of the mobilisation that was achieved (that there were as many as 15,000 infantry archers, for example) during the course of the long Crécy–Calais campaign, from July 1346 to August 1347. But whether it is possible to tease out of these summaries reliable figures for the numbers of arrayed troops, English and Welsh, serving at any particular stage in the campaign may be doubted.

The material relating to the retinues in the English army is less heavily summarised in the Wetwang abstracts and is consequently of more use to the historian. Admittedly, the transcripts do not retain the appearance of a pay-roll. Omitted are the detailed indications of duration of service or the amounts of money owed in wages that would have been included on the original pay-roll. What we are offered are merely the names of captains and the number of men, of different personnel categories, in their retinues. That, of course, is useful enough; and where it is possible to compare the figures given in the transcripts with those recorded in reliable contemporary extracts from the original accounts – as we can with the Holand brothers and Sir Thomas Haukeston (noted above) – we find an exact match.[10] If such instances provide further grounds for discounting the idea that the Wetwang abstracts are merely 'a Tudor forgery',[11] we should not forget that these incomplete transcripts do nevertheless present many interpretative problems. Corrupt name forms and duplicate entries suggest incompetence or at least lapses in concentration on the part of the copyists. If the more substantial versions are compared, we find differences in the order of entries, and most perplexing of all, many inconsistencies in the manpower numbers attributed to particular retinues. When Sir John Darcy senior has 48 esquires according to one manuscript, but 68 in another, and when a third gives him 80 archers rather than 60, which abstract is to be regarded as the most reliable?[12] Such disparities are commonplace with the larger retinues and not infrequently to be found with the smaller ones. It may well be that each of the abstracts is essentially accurate, and that the various scribes adopted different 'principles' for their transcriptions, choosing different figures from a pay-roll that charted fluctuations in retinue numbers in considerable detail. This may be the case, but there is no way of telling.

There is a more significant problem. It is clear that no single version provides a complete picture of the retinues that were included in Wetwang's original accounts. This is obvious in the case of the shorter abstracts, which either summarise Wetwang's accounts or include only selected extracts from them.[13] But comparison of the more substantial abstracts, the ones that have the appearance of completeness, reveals significant omissions. The most widely used of

---

[10] Holands: Wrottesley, *Crecy and Calais*, pp. 176–7; BL, Harleian MS 3968, fo. 120r. Haukeston: Wrottesley, *Crecy and Calais*, pp. 176, 201; BL, Harleian MS 3968, fo. 128v.

[11] *Anonimalle*, p. 161.

[12] Ayton, 'The English army and the Normandy campaign of 1346', p. 265. Edward Rowe Mores drew attention to this problem in his 1749 edition of two Wetwang abstracts: a copy owned by James West, which Mores correlated with a manuscript in the Ashmolean Museum (the manpower figures from these two manuscripts are given in roman and arabic numerals respectively). Mores, *Nomina et insignia*, pp. xxxvii, 89–101.

[13] E.g., BL, Harleian MS 53 (summary); Lambeth Palace, MS 306 (extracts).

the 'long' versions, the sixteenth-century College of Arms manuscript published in Wrottesley's *Crecy and Calais*, which was the basis of J.E. Morris's calculations (and, more recently, Clifford Rogers's), certainly exudes an air of completeness. But compare the College of Arms manuscript with another Wetwang abstract (indeed, what is probably the oldest of them, the version that is embedded in a fifteenth-century manuscript of the Brut), which has also long been in print, and doubts begin to arise. For while their treatment of the earls' and bannerets' retinues is essentially the same,[14] the manpower figures in the summarised section of the Brut abstract, which begins 'Sir William Warenne, knight, with another ninety-five knights', do not match those in the corresponding part of the College of Arms manuscript, which has only fifty-five knights.[15] Both documents are clearly based squarely on Wetwang's original *vadia guerre* account – the sequence and scope of the material make this abundantly clear – and yet the Brut copyist appears to have included some retinues, led by knights, that the College of Arms scribe has for some reason omitted.

Fortunately, we can recover these missing retinues by reference to another of the Wetwang abstracts, a later sixteenth- or early seventeenth-century manuscript, BL, Harleian MS 3968.[16] As indicated by its title, 'Nomina et Insignia principalium Praefectum, qui Calisiae obsidioni adfuerunt', this is only a partial transcript of Wetwang's *vadia guerre* account, being a list of the captains and their retinues, embellished with the captains' arms tricked. The arrayed troops are omitted. In only 12 of its 29 pages does the sequence of captains in Harleian MS 3968 follow that in the College of Arms manuscript; the rest of the sequence is jumbled, and this, combined with a number of evident transcription errors, may incline us to doubt the value of the document as a whole. Yet it includes 22 retinues (in all, 34 knights, 132 esquires and 155 archers), mostly led by royal household knights, that have been omitted by the College of Arms manuscript.[17] Once we are aware of these additional captains, the gap in the College of Arms's coverage, particularly of the household division, becomes all too evident. How this section of the original document, summarised as it was by the scribe responsible for the Brut abstract, came to be omitted by the scribe producing the College of Arms text will remain a mystery. In fact both were capable of error.

---

[14] Although there are some minor disparities in the manpower figures, the match is very close. The sequence of retinues is the same in each and although the Brut abstract summarises most of the bannerets' retinues ('Walter de Mauny with another 25 bannerets, with their retinues, i.e., 124 knights, 593 men-at-arms, 592 mounted archers, hobelars and 'paunsers', and 119 foot archers), if we turn to the corresponding point in the College of Arms manuscript and aggregate the bannerets' retinues we arrive at the same number of bannerets and very similar figures for their retinues.

[15] Brut does not give a figure for men-at-arms, only '[mounted archers], pavisers and hobelers on horsebakke', and 'archers on foote'.

[16] BL, Harleian MS 3968, fos 114r–129r. This manuscript and other related items are described in *Catalogue of English Medieval Rolls of Arms*, ed. Wagner, pp. 159–60. A document that preserved the same material as BL, Harleian MS 3968, though ordered slightly differently, was published by Edward Rowe Mores in 1749: *Nomina et insignia*, pp. 89–101.

[17] BL, Harleian MS 3968 also assigns more knights to several retinues than the College of Arms MS, so the Brut's total of 95 is comfortably reached.

Each manuscript includes an important 'banneret clerk' omitted by the other,[18] and there are other captains who certainly received advances on their retinue's wages but who are not to be found in any of the Wetwang abstracts.

That the Wetwang abstracts have been interpreted in several different ways is hardly surprising given the number of versions that exist. They have been quite widely referred to as a 'Calais roll'. They record 'the Calais army' according to Wrottesley,[19] while J.E. Morris concurred, adding that 'the date is certainly late in July [1347]'.[20] In an article published in 1994, I argued that the Wetwang transcripts could not be interpreted as offering a snap-shot of the army at a single point during the siege of Calais, because it can be shown that some of the captains listed on the roll were not serving in the army at the same time.[21] That these documents did indeed provide a 'Calais roll' was not disputed: the point was that the roll listed all the retinues that served at any point during the long siege, rather than at a single moment. More recently, Clifford Rogers has offered an interpretation that represents the next logical step, that the Wetwang transcripts in fact include 'everyone who served at any point over the sixteen-month expedition'.[22]

It must be conceded that Rogers's suggestion has much to commend it, though it is necessary to register a couple of reservations. First, it should be noted that the opening rubric of some of the Wetwang abstracts does suggest that what follows is a list of the army that besieged Calais.[23] Indeed, it may well be that an attempt was made by some of the copyists to select information from the pay-rolls that related specifically to the siege of Calais, and that this focus on the siege may provide some explanation for the differences (in personnel numbers and the omission of retinues) that are evident when different versions of Wetwang are compared. The other qualification that needs to be made is that some of the Crécy captains do not appear on any version of the roll, and so we cannot reconstruct a complete pay-roll from the transcripts that have come down to us. Limiting ourselves to captains of banneret status, the retinues led by Sir Alan la Zousche and John Grey of Ruthin are missing from the Wetwang abstracts, as are those of several foreign captains, most notably Godfrey de Harcourt (see Appendix 2, Table 2).

Yet despite these qualifications, Rogers's interpretation is compelling, and, beyond his own arguments, there is further strong evidence to suggest that his may be the most satisfactory suggestion yet made about the Wetwang abstracts. The extract that Robert Brady published as an appendix to the second volume of

---

[18] The College of Arms manuscript has John Thoresby and his retinue of 69 men, while the Brut has Philip Weston with 60 men.

[19] Wrottesley, *Crecy and Calais*, pp. 4, 191.

[20] J.E. Morris's review of *Crecy and Calais*: *EHR*, xiv (1899), pp. 766–9, at p. 768; also, J.E. Morris, 'Mounted infantry in medieval warfare', *TRHS*, 3rd ser., viii (1914), p. 97.

[21] Indeed, some men appear twice on the roll – as members of retinues and as independent captains: Ayton, 'The English army and the Normandy campaign of 1346', pp. 266–7.

[22] Rogers, *War Cruel and Sharp*, Appendix: The Strength of the Army at La Hougue, 1346, p. 423.

[23] E.g., BL, Harleian MSS 246 and 3968; Mores, *Nomina et insignia*, p. 89.

his *Complete History of England* in 1700 casts particularly interesting light on this problem.[24] It is very short and has two sections. The first consists of a list of categories of personnel, with manpower numbers and pay rates, plus the total amount of money paid in wages (including to mariners) for the whole campaign, from 4 June 1346 until 12 October 1347, that is one year and 131 days. Then, there is a sequence of extracts, intended as exemplars, from the *vadia guerre* section of Wetwang's accounts, consisting of the retinue details of the Prince of Wales, the earls of Lancaster and Northampton, the bishop of Durham and Ralph, Baron Stafford, and rounded off by some summary statistics for the retinues led by knights.

Brady's extract is brief, selective and there has been much aggregation to acquire the manpower statistics for the army. A small sample of the retinues has been included and there is no indication of periods of service. While the original accounts would have specified wage rates, army personnel totals were not a feature of such records. And yet this Wetwang extract is valuable in that it preserves the starting date for the 'pay period' of the army (4 June: over a month before the landing at La Hougue), which, it will be recalled, is confirmed by the Memoranda Roll entry that records the pay details for the Holand brothers. There is also an air of authenticity about it, which stems in large part from the presentation of the pay-roll extracts as continuous text, thereby apparently preserving some of the formulae of Wetwang's account. Thus the Prince of Wales served 'in partibus Normanniae, Franciae, et coram Cales', while the earl of Lancaster served merely 'coram Cales'. Such distinctions are not to be found in the numerous other sets of abstracts from Wetwang, which tend to present an undifferentiated list of retinues, leaving it to the modern historian to distinguish the Crécy captains from those who arrived during the siege.

It would seem that Brady's details were taken directly from the 'Book of particulars of the Account of Walter Wetwange' – that he (or those working on his behalf) had consulted the original document. He was certainly in a position to do so, since as a staunch royalist he was a privileged scholar with full access to the records in the Tower of London.[25] The chief clerk there, Lawrence Halstead, acted as Brady's research assistant, copying records for him. Indeed, in July 1686 Brady was granted a salary of £300 'for his care and paines in and about the records in the Tower of London'. Moreover, as Peter le Neve recalled later, during the 1680s Brady himself had 'sat all morning long many mornings one after the other' in the Treasury of Receipt, Tally Court, examining the records there.[26] However, this close association with the public records lasted only until March 1689, when the new regime appointed the whig scholar William Petyt as keeper of the Tower Record Office.

Publication in 1700, the year of Brady's death, of the Wetwang extracts in the second volume of the *Complete History* appears to provide the latest evidence

---

[24] Brady, *Complete History of England*, ii, Appendix, pp. 86–8.
[25] J.G.A. Pocock, 'Robert Brady, 1627–1700. A Cambridge historian of the Restoration', *Cambridge Historical Journal*, x (1951), pp. 186–204.
[26] SP 46/139, mm. 81–2, quoted in E. Hallam, *Domesday Book Through Nine Centuries* (London, 1986), p. 126.

for the existence of Wetwang's account book, since subsequent copies and publications seem to be based on earlier transcripts rather than direct access to the original. We must assume that the original was removed from the Tower or fell victim to the appalling conditions in which many of the records were kept. There is plentiful evidence for the appropriation of some of the more attractive medieval records (a number of important account books are to be found among the various collections now held by the British Library), and it is likely that Wetwang's account book was also removed.[27] And since no more copies of it appear to have been made after 1700, the finger of suspicion must point to Brady, who after all recorded, in a marginal note to his Wetwang extracts, that he was quoting from a document that was in his possession.[28] As a postscript to this speculation, it may be worth adding that Brady's papers were 'lost through the mischance of an executor's senility' – that is, they were burnt.[29] It may well be that Wetwang's book was among the materials that were consigned to the flames.

A further point should be made about Brady's Wetwang extracts. It is notable that the entries that he prints, in the order in which they appear and the personnel figures that they give, match those in the College of Arms manuscript *almost* exactly. In the five entries – concerning the Prince of Wales, Lancaster, Northampton, the bishop of Durham and Ralph Stafford – only one statistic differs from the details printed in Wrottesley's College of Arms edition, and then, only very slightly. Given that the sequence of entries in the College of Arms manuscript also corresponds to the order of material in what is probably the earliest (albeit heavily summarised) Wetwang transcript (that which is embedded in a fifteenth-century copy of the Brut),[30] it would seem that we may have in the College of Arms figures a good starting point for the reconstruction of the structure and content of Wetwang's lost *vadia guerre* account. Of course, as we have seen, these data do differ to some degree from those given in the other abstracts, and some retinues have been omitted. So our best approach to reconstructing Wetwang's original accounts would be to use the College of Arms text as a 'base', to which we can add the retinues and other information supplied by the other versions and by other records, with the whole process 'informed' by the extracts from Wetwang that have been preserved in contemporary documents.

Accepting Rogers's argument, that the Wetwang transcripts when taken together show the great majority of the retinues that served as separately accounting entities at some point during the 16-month accounting period of the Crécy–Calais campaign, we may now be able to deduce the format of Wetwang's

---

[27] Cf. the removal of the collection of indentures from the Exchequer records in 1719. They were kept in private hands until 1770, when they were returned to the State Paper Office, but some had been lost during the interval. A. Curry, *The Battle of Agincourt: Sources and Interpretations* (Woodbridge, 2000), p. 410 and n. 10.

[28] 'e veteroi Rotula hujusce Temporis penes meipsum'. A point noted by J.E. Morris, *EHR*, xiv (1899), p. 766.

[29] Pocock, 'Robert Brady', p. 186.

[30] *Brut*, ed. Brie, ii, pp. 538–41.

lost pay-roll.[31] It may well have been of the thoroughly reorganised and heavily summarised variety, like the *vadia guerre* accounts for the Reims campaign, for example.[32] This is certainly the impression given by Robert Brady's extracts, though the disparities in manpower numbers that we find when different abstracts are compared may suggest that the original pay-roll had a more complex format. We will never know, but we may be sure that there once existed a voluminous collection of draft accounts in which fluctuations in numbers in individual retinues were minutely documented and to which newly arrived retinues were appended where necessary. But when the final, digested version of the account was being compiled, the various draft documents would have been brought together and their contents summarised to some degree. In the process there would also have been much reorganisation of the material, so that (as we see in the surviving transcripts) the retinues would now be presented according to the rank of captains, regardless of the periods served by their retinues – regardless, that is, of whether the retinues were serving in the king's army at the same time. In this way, the Prince of Wales, a Crécy veteran, would be followed by Henry, earl of Lancaster, who was far away in Aquitaine at the time of the battle. We cannot be sure how summarised the final version of Wetwang's pay-roll was, but given the length of the expedition, it is likely that some indication of manpower fluctuations at retinue level was retained. This is what we find in the pay-roll for the 1338–40 expedition, for example.[33] It may well be an echo of these fluctuations that we see in the disparities between our various versions of Wetwang: where two manuscripts record different manpower figures for a retinue, this may be the result of two copyists choosing different numbers from a sequence for that retinue rather than transcription error.

Wetwang's *vadia guerre* account began with the large retinues of the Prince of Wales and Henry, earl of Lancaster, followed by those of the other earls. According to precedence, Northampton and Warwick, the constable and marshal, appeared at the beginning of the sequence of earls, and Pembroke and Kildare at the end. Then came the bishop of Durham and Hugh Despenser, who the Brut copy says served 'as an erle' (there is some indication elsewhere that he served at a higher pay rate than normal for a banneret),[34] followed by the bannerets (several of whom can be added from Harleian MS 3968). These would have been headed by five senior household bannerets – Stafford, Talbot, Darcy senior, Burgherssh and Mauny – the first four of whom were current or former stewards or chamberlains. Although serving in Flanders during the summer of 1346, only joining the king's army after the siege of Calais had begun, Sir Hugh

---

31 For a discussion of Edwardian *vadia guerre* accounts, see Ayton, *Knights and Warhorses*, pp. 138–55.
32 Included in the account book of William Farley, Keeper of the Wardrobe: E101/393/11, fos 79r–116v.
33 Included in the account book of William Norwell, Keeper of the Wardrobe: E36/203. Published as *The Wardrobe Book of William de Norwell, 12 July 1338 to 27 May 1340*, ed. M. Lyon, B. Lyon, H.S. Lucas and J. de Sturler (Brussels, 1983), pp. 325–62.
34 *Brut*, ed. Brie, ii, p. 539. Despenser is termed 'earl of Glostre' in BL, Harleian MS 3968, fo. 116r and Mores, *Nomina et insignia*, p. 90.

Hastings and Sir John Montgomery were inserted into the sequence of bannerets, as was Sir John Mautravers, now reconciled with the king following a long period of exile in the Low Countries.[35] The remaining bannerets either established independent retinues during the siege of Calais (Ughtred, Morley and probably Howard) or were foreign captains, though it should be noted that only a proportion of the latter known to be serving with the army appear on the pay-roll. After 'Sir Henry of Flanders' came the sequence of retinues led by knights bachelor, beginning with Sir William Warenne (the bastard son of the earl of Warenne).[36] At this point we need to insert a substantial block of household knights from Harleian MS 3968. The College of Arms manuscript lists only a proportion of these lesser captains (and they are not grouped together either), but it does suggest that the group of household knights who received the accolade on the day of Crécy formed a separate block of entries in the pay-roll, perhaps beginning with Sir Guy Brian (see Appendix 2, Table 2). Some knightly retinues were formed during the siege of Calais, following the arrival of a new captain (for example, Sir Nigel Loring) or the death or departure of a major captain and the fragmentation of his retinue. These would no doubt have constituted a separate block in Wetwang's pay-roll, as to some extent they do in the College of Arms manuscript. The last of the significant retinues in the pay-roll are those that were led by the 'banneret clerks'. Five can be identified in the Wetwang abstracts, four of whom served from the outset of the expedition.

At this point it would be appropriate to take stock and calculate the size of the contribution made by the retinues to Edward III's army at La Hougue.[37] The first step is to identify the captains who certainly served from the beginning of the expedition, by reference to the records of wage advances (prests) and the notes of warranty associated with enrolled letters of protection, service pardons and writs of exoneration. Those captains, mentioned above, who arrived during the siege or, having served from the outset under another captain, later established an independent retinue need to be excluded (there is a danger that the latter would otherwise be counted twice).[38] Equally, we must make allowance for retinues that appear to be missing from the Wetwang abstracts. Owing to the imperfect nature of our records, a certain amount of informed guesswork is required in deciding which of the minor Wetwang captains to include and which to exclude, and also how many extra men to allow for the missing retinues. Having established our list of 'La Hougue captains', how are we to interpret the manpower data assigned to them in the Wetwang abstracts? There are two issues here. First, given that there are discrepancies between the data provided by the various Wetwang abstracts, discrepancies that are usually irresolvable, the most

[35] For Hastings and the other English captains serving with him in Flanders, see *Foedera*, III, i, pp. 83, 86; *Knighton*, ed. Martin, pp. 58–9. There is a separate pay account for Hastings's retinue in Flanders: E372/191, m. 49.

[36] Somewhat mysterious is the next captain, 'Sir Amyan de Brett'.

[37] The method proposed here combines the approaches employed by J.E. Morris, *EHR*, xiv (1899), p. 767; Morris, 'Mounted Infantry in Medieval Warfare', pp. 97–8; Ayton, 'The English Army and the Normandy Campaign of 1346', pp. 263–8; and Rogers, *War Cruel and Sharp*, pp. 423–6.

[38] Ayton, 'The English Army and the Normandy Campaign of 1346', pp. 265–7.

substantial and reliable version, the College of Arms manuscript, has been regarded as the 'core' text. Second, while we cannot be sure that the scribe was consistent in his selection of data, Rogers's working assumption, 'that the retinues were at their maximum strength at the start of their service, and that is the number listed in the Wetwang abstracts' has also been followed here.[39] The results of this process of selection are presented in Appendix 2, Table 2, where the retinues judged to have been present at La Hougue have been further grouped into the divisions suggested by the *Acta Bellicosa* and St Omer chronicle.

After the last of the retinues included in the more substantial of the Wetwang abstracts (Sir William Kildesby's), we encounter material that has evidently been heavily abbreviated by the copyist. In the College of Arms text, the section that enumerates the sub-knightly personnel of the royal household lacks names; but in content it is nevertheless essentially comparable with other Edwardian pay-rolls.[40] Just how many of these men were accompanying the king when the army landed at La Hougue, and how many arrived later, is unclear, but we would probably be justified in assuming that the majority were with the king from the outset. This is of some relevance to our discussion of 'strenuous' personnel, since as well as several dozen clerks and household staff, and several hundred workmen and artisans, this section of the College of Arms text includes over 200 men-at-arms and over 400 archers (mostly mounted) – a substantial contribution to the manpower of the 'household division'.[41] Half of the men-at-arms (101) were actually household esquires, some of whom would have had other fighting men associated with them, as individuals or in small companies, as would have at least a proportion of the clerks. Doubtless Wetwang's original pay-roll supplied their names; we must make do with knowing the identity of the few who received prests.[42]

With regard to the remainder of the army, the arrayed troops, the contents of the original pay-rolls have been so heavily summarised in the surviving abstracts that they are very difficult to use. The problem, outlined earlier in this Appendix, is that there is no reliable method of disentangling the troops who landed at La Hougue and marched to Crécy from the reinforcements that arrived during the siege of Calais. Admittedly, the Brut abstract does distinguish a contingent led by Sir Thomas Haukeston: a substantial force of 161 men-at-arms, 313 mounted archers and 241 foot archers, which we may assume was part or all of the contingent of reinforcements for which he was appointed marshal

[39] Rogers, *War Cruel and Sharp*, p. 423.
[40] Wrottesley, *Crecy and Calais*, pp. 202–3. Cf. *Collection of Ordinances and Regulations for the Government of the Royal Household,* pp. 1–12, which prints an abstract that, having omitted the retinues, begins with the sub-knightly household personnel, providing information that is similar, but not identical, to that found in the College of Arms text. The Brut abstract (p. 540) supplies several names, but the personnel figures are more heavily summarised and total numbers are smaller than those given in the College of Arms text.
[41] In addition to the 230 men-at-arms, there were 67 sergeants-at-arms. Of the 427 archers, 55 were foot soldiers, and 121 were designated 'king's archers'.
[42] E.g., Philip Barton, clerk; Aymer Atheles, a long-serving esquire of the chamber and Henry Baa, an experienced sergeant-at-arms: E403/336, mm. 41, 44; E101/390/12, fo. 6v.

on 21 August 1346.[43] But it is not clear how these data relate either to the summarised material at the end of the College of Arms abstract, where Haukeston's force is not distinguished, or to the information that is supplied elsewhere: the retinues of Haukeston, Sir William Fraunk and Sir Miles Stapleton, as separately recorded among the main sequence of captains in the Wetwang abstracts,[44] or the fairly plentiful evidence that we have for the companies of arrayed archers that were raised during the late summer and autumn of 1346.[45] The College of Arms and Brut texts both provide details of the Welsh troops in the Crécy–Calais army, but their numbers do not agree. The Brut abstract summaries the rest of the arrayed troops very simply. There are more sub-divisions in the corresponding part of the College of Arms text, but interpreting them rests heavily on guesswork. The 364 'hobelars and archers of divers cities' could well represent the total number of men that were raised by the towns for the army that sailed in July (nearly 2,000 had originally been asked for); but what of the two sections labelled 'Other English souldiers/Archers' (totalling 5,443 men) and 'Archers from counties' (10,806)? How many of these men were at La Hougue and Crécy? Clifford Rogers offers an ingenious method for answering this question,[46] but in truth it is really no less speculative than the method that has been employed by the present author, which involves extrapolation from the patchy available data on the troops that were actually recruited.[47] It is noteworthy, and perhaps significant, that these two methods produce similar results.

Some of the Wetwang abstracts end with a summary list totalling each of the categories of personnel in the army.[48] These aggregations are certainly the work of the copyists, summarisation on an original Edwardian pay-roll being confined to totalling the money accounted for in wages. (We should always remember that a pay-roll was intended first and foremost to be a financial account, not an order of battle for the benefit of posterity.) Indeed, just such a wages total (£127,201 2s 9½d) is included among Robert Brady's extracts from Wetwang and can be used to gain some indication of the size of the army.[49] Sir James Ramsey, and recently Clifford Rogers, have shown that this amount of money could have paid for an army with an average strength of about 10,000 to

---

[43] *The Brut*, ed. Brie, ii, p. 540. Haukeston was marshal, while Sir William Fraunk was appointed constable: *Foedera*, III, i, p. 89.

[44] Wrottesley, *Crecy and Calais*, pp. 199, 201; BL, Harleian MS 3968, fo. 123v (Fraunk).

[45] E101/575/15; E101/584/5, m.1; E372/191, m. 48; Hewitt, *The Organisation of War Under Edward III*, p. 44, Table II; E403/339, mm. 5–6.

[46] Rogers, *War Cruel and Sharp*, pp. 425 n. 12, 426.

[47] See above, pp. 181–6; and Ayton, 'The English Army and the Normandy Campaign of 1346', pp. 261–3.

[48] For three versions, each differing slightly from the others, see Wrottesley, *Crecy and Calais*, p. 204; Brady, *Complete History of England*, ii, p. 86; *Collection of Ordinances and Regulations for the Government of the Royal Household*, p. 8.

[49] Brady, *Complete History of England*, ii. p. 86; see also, apparently derived from a different abstract, Grose, *Military Antiquities*, i, p. 266. The summarised enrolment of Wetwang's accounts for the period from 11 April 1344 to 24 November 1347 (1,323 days) show that *vadia guerre* amounted to £149,991 14s 11½d, not including £1,027 10s 8d spent on garrisoning Calais (Tout, *Chapters*, iv, pp. 118–19).

11,000 men.[50] There are, however, problems with this calculation. The wages total, as provided by Brady, actually includes the wages of 16,000 mariners, though this may not be a large amount of money because the periods of paid service were probably short. It is also clear that the total includes not just *pay,* but also *regard* and almost certainly *restauro equorum* as well. We know that these two elements of the financial package were offered to captains in 1346–7, and it is quite possible that both were included in the *vadia guerre* section of Wetwang's accounts under each captain, along with his retinue's wages. This, for example, is what we find in the pay records for the Reims campaign in William Farley's Wardrobe Book. Wherever they were located in Wetwang's book of particulars, it is certain that at least the *regard* payments have been included in the 'wages' total. *Regard* was calculated according to a formula – usually 100 marks for 30 men-at-arms for a quarter of a year's service – and as a consequence it is not unusual to generate total amounts of money that include halfpennies and farthings. Since all the pay rates included in Brady's schedule involve whole pennies, to produce an overall total that includes a halfpenny, *regard* payments must have been included in the 'wages' total; and since mariners' wages have been incorporated, it is likely that *restauro equorum* has been too. How large are these payments likely to have been? Using the standard *regard* formula and drawing on data for warhorse losses during other mid-fourteenth-century expeditions[51] (and assuming that the transport fleet was employed for only short periods), we should perhaps allow in the region of £20,000 to £30,000 for these costs, thereby reducing the amount available for wages to about £100,000. As a consequence, it is necessary to scale down the average army size suggested by Ramsey and Rogers by a fifth. The implications of this are significant. It may be that the army was somewhat smaller at the outset than we have thought; but perhaps more likely is that it shrank in size rapidly during the early stages of the investment of Calais (there are plentiful documentary indications that this actually happened) and that it only grew to substantial proportions once again towards the end of the siege.

---

[50] Dividing what the notional army of 32,000 would have cost had it served throughout the campaign (496 days) by the actual wages bill for the campaign: J. Ramsey, *Genesis of Lancaster*, 2 vols (Oxford, 1913), i, p. 352; Rogers, *War Cruel and Sharp*, p. 423 n. 3.
[51] See Ayton, *Knights and Warhorses*, p. 121.

Appendix 2

Table 1. The bannerets in the three 'battles' of the English army, July/August 1346, according to the *Acta Bellicosa* and the St Omer chronicle[1]

Vanguard
Edward, Prince of Wales
* Bartholomew Burgherssh, junior
John Fitzwalter
William Kerdeston
John Mohun
* Roger Mortimer
John Verdon

William Bohun, earl of Northampton
Robert Bourchier
[Geoffrey][2] Say

Thomas Beauchamp, earl of Warwick
[Aimery][3] St Amand
* [Robert][4] Scales
Thomas Ughtred

Bartholomew Burgherssh, senior
* William Careswell

Centre [with Edward III]
John Vere, earl of Oxford
John Chevereston

Godfrey de Harcourt

Bannerets of the royal household
Richard Talbot
John [Darcy],[5] senior
Maurice Berkeley
Thomas Bradeston
Reginald Cobham
John Darcy, junior

---

[1] Captains of major retinues are in bold type; bannerets leading sub-retinues are indented; * denotes additions to the *Acta Bellicosa* list (Cambridge, Corpus Christi College, MS 370, fos 98r–98v) from the St Omer chronicle (Paris, Bibliothèque Nationale, MS Fr. 693, fos 248r–279v, at fos 261v–262r).

[2] 'Roger' in source, apparently in error for Geoffrey.

[3] 'William' in source, apparently in error for Aimery.

[4] Source unspecific, but must be 'Robert'.

[5] Source omits surname, but sense makes clear that it is 'Darcy'.

Robert Ferrers
* William Fitzwarin
* John Lisle[6]
Michael Poynings
John Stryvelyn

William Kildesby, clerk
Walter Wetwang, clerk
John Thoresby, clerk
Philip Weston, clerk

[William?][7] Botiller of Wem
[Thomas][8] Breuse
John Grey [of Ruthin][9]
Edward Montagu
[Roger?][10] Straunge
* [William][11] Warenne

Rearguard

Thomas Hatfield, bishop of Durham
Thomas Astley
William Cantilupe[12]

Richard Fitzalan, earl of Arundel
James Audley
Gerard Lisle
John Straunge [of Blaunkmonster][13]

---

6   Elevated to the status of banneret on the day of Crécy: *Eulogium*, iii, p. 211; C81/314, no. 17810; *CPR, 1345–8*, p. 194.

7   No forename in source, but this is presumably intended to be 'William' (*Complete Peerage*, ii, p. 232), who would have been in his late forties in 1346. However, while his son, William, undoubtedly served (with the earl of Huntingdon), whether the father was at Crécy may be doubted, since in October 1346 he was summoned to join the king at the siege of Calais (Wrottesley, *Crecy and Calais*, p. 103) and he does not appear in any of the pay records. As far as we can tell, he had last served (with Reginald Cobham) during the summer of 1340: C76/15, m. 20.

8   'Peter' in source, but must be 'Thomas', since Peter only became a knight at Crécy.

9   'John de Grey' in source; probably 'of Ruthin', who did serve with a retinue in July–August 1346 (E403/336, m. 41). See *Complete Peerage*, vi, p. 154.

10   'Eble' in source, though not recorded as serving in this army. Probably this is the 'Roger le Straunge' [of Knokyn] who appears at the head of a retinue in the Wetwang abstracts. He was in his mid-forties at the time of Crécy and had been a banneret since 1326–7 (E101/382/7 m. 2). It is curious to note that in 1335 Roger had inherited his uncle, Eble le Straunge's land: *Complete Peerage*, xii, part 1, pp. 340–1, 353–4. Although it is certain that Roger served during the siege of Calais, there is some doubt whether he was with the army in July–August 1346. A 'Roger Lestraunge' provided warranty for pardons issued in September 1346 (*CPR, 1345–8*, pp. 502, 504), but a document, dating from 1351, suggests that 'being detained by grievous infirmity, [he] had sent his son, Roger le Straunge the younger': Wrottesley, *Crecy and Calais*, p. 169.

11   'The son of the earl of Warenne' in source.

12   Placed in the vanguard battle by the St Omer chronicle.

13   'John de Straunge' in source; probably 'of Blaunkmonster', who served with the earl of Arundel.

Robert Ufford, earl of Suffolk
Robert Colville [of Bitham][14]

William Clinton, earl of Huntingdon[15]

John Botetourt[16]
John Grey [of Rotherfeld][17]

Hugh Despenser
Robert Morley

John Sutton [of Holderness?][18]

---

[14] 'Robert de Colvill' in source; probably 'of Bitham', who served with the earl of Suffolk.
[15] Returned to England after the capture of Caen.
[16] Probably remained with the army following the earl of Huntingdon's return to England.
[17] 'John Grey' in source; probably 'of Rotherfield', who led a sub-retinue under the earl of Huntingdon (John's son, John, served in the Prince of Wales's retinue). Probably remained with the army following Huntingdon's return to England. See *Complete Peerage*, vi, pp. 145–7.
[18] This is presumably 'John de Sutton of Holderness' (*Complete Peerage*, xii, part 1, pp. 574–5), but there is no further, conclusive documentary evidence for his service in July–August 1346. Note, however, that in September 1346 a 'John de Sutton, knight' is named providing warranty for pardons issued to men, some of whom, perhaps significantly, were from the East Riding of Yorkshire: *CPR, 1345–8*, pp. 488, 490, 492.

Table 2: The retinues in the three 'battles' of the English army, July/August 1346[1]

Vanguard	Earls[2]	Bnts	Knts	Esqs	Total M/a	M/Arc[3]	F/Arc	Others	Retinue Total
Edward, Prince of Wales	1	11	102	264	378	384	69	513[4]	1344
William Bohun, earl of Northampton	1	2	46	112	161	141	0	0	302
Thomas Beauchamp, earl of Warwick	1	3	64	131	199	149	0	0	348
Bartholomew Burgherssh, senior	0	2	26	82	110	58	19	0	187
	3	18	238	589	848	732	88	513	2181

1 The structure of the three 'battles' is based essentially on the lists in the *Acta Bellicosa* (Cambridge, Corpus Christi College, MS 370, fos 98r–98v) and the St Omer chronicle (Paris, Bibliothèque Nationale, MS Fr. 693, fos 248–279r, at fos 261v–262r). Retinue information, including personnel data, has been taken from the various 'Wetwang abstracts' (see Appendix 1). These data have been correlated with other records to ensure the inclusion of all captains who can reliably be placed with the army in July–August 1346 and the exclusion of those who joined Edward III after the battle of Crécy. The College of Arms copy of Wetwang (Crecy and Calais, pp. 193–204) has been regarded as the core version, and its data have been preferred in (the all too frequent) cases where the various abstracts do not agree. Those captains and retinues that appear in BL, Harleian MS 3968, but not the College of Arms manuscript, are tagged with an asterisk (*). Also included in this table are captains who do not appear in the Wetwang pay-roll abstracts, but whose service can be demonstrated by reference to other sources (usually wage advances recorded on the Issue Rolls or in Wetwang's book of receipts). On the other hand, men below the rank of knight receiving prests (including clerks) have not been separately named. In most cases they were attached to the royal household, and many were serving as individuals or with only a modest military escort (e.g., William Boulton, a privy seal clerk who was accompanied by one archer: E404/496, no. 178). In presenting the retinue personnel data, some categories have been grouped together in order to achieve a compact table (details in footnotes). In the 'Others' column, 'h' denotes 'hobelars', and 'p' indicates 'paunsers'. It cannot be over-emphasised that the data presented in this table are based not upon the original army pay-roll, but upon copies of it that omit crucial information (e.g., periods of service) and that frequently disagree with each other over details. As a consequence, this reconstruction of part of Edward III's army in July–August 1346 should be regarded as providing an essentially reliable list of retinues (there may be some doubt about the minor retinues in the king's division), but only an indication – albeit probably of the right order of magnitude – of the numbers of men serving in them.

2 The prince and the bishop of Durham have been included among the 'earls'. While it is possible that Despenser was paid 'as an erle' (as suggested by *Brut*, ed. Brie, ii, p. 538) he has been included among the bannerets.

3 Where the Wetwang abstracts specify simply 'archers', they have been regarded as 'mounted archers' in this table.

4 A Welsh contingent, including 1 chaplain, 1 *medicus*, 1 *proclamator*, 5 standard bearers, 25 vintenars and 480 foot. Clifford Rogers argues that these men were 'probably later reinforcements' on the strength of an entry on the Treaty Roll (Wrottesley, *Crecy and Calais*, p. 129), which concerns an order to find shipping for 700 Welshmen in June 1347.

	Earls	Bnts	Knts	Esqs	Total M/a	M/Arc	F/Arc	Others	Retinue Total
Centre [Edward III]	1	1	22	44	68	63	0	0	131
John Vere, earl of Oxford									
Royal household: bannerets and knights, and their retinues⁵									
Richard Talbot, bnt	0	1	14	60	75	82	0	0	157
John Darcy, senior, bnt	0	1	11	48	60	80	0	0	140
John Beauchamp, of Warwick, bnt*6	0	1	1	13	15	13	0	0	28
Giles Beauchamp, bnt*7	0	1	1	5	7	6	0	0	13
Roger Beauchamp, of Somerset, bnt*	0	1	2	5	8	9	0	0	17
Maurice Berkeley, bnt	0	1	6	32	39	29	2	0	70
Thomas Bradeston, bnt	0	1	6	24	31	30	0	0	61
Reginald Cobham, bnt	0	1	6	42	49	24	32	0	112
John Darcy, junior, bnt8	0	1	8	20	29	24	0	7	53
Robert Ferrers, bnt	0	1	3	25	29	32	0	0	64
William Fitzwarin, bnt	0	1	1	10	12	9	0	0	21

5   There are no surviving lists of household bannerets and knights for the period of the Crécy campaign, merely a heavily summarised abstract from Wetwang's accounts, which record that 16 bannerets and 66 knights received robes in 21 Edward III (only 13 bannerets and 36 knights received fees): *A Collection of Ordinances and Regulations for the Government of the Royal Household* (London, 1790), p. 10. Consequently, this section of Table 2 is, in part at least, somewhat conjectural, being based in most cases on evidence for 1341–4 and 1347–9: E36/204, fos 89r–92r; N.H. Nicolas, 'Observations on the institution of the most noble Order of the Garter', *Archaeologia*, xxxi (1846), pp. 1–163 [which prints the accounts of the Great Wardrobe, December 1345–January 1349]. In the case of three men (Alan Clavering, Michael Poynings and Warin Trussell), explicit evidence for household membership extends only to 1340–1 (E101/389/8, mm. 9, 26–7), but indirect evidence suggests that they should be included in the household division in 1346. The most conjectural of the inclusions among the household knights is John Berkeley. In determining the size of the 'household division', allowance should also be made for the esquires of the royal household; the companies of men-at-arms and archers that accompanied some of the lesser members of the household; and the king's archers. According to the College of Arms abstract of Wetwang, these may have contributed over 200 men-at-arms and over 400 archers, mostly mounted, to the household division, and it is likely that most accompanied the king to La Hougue and Crécy.

6   King's standard bearer: E101/390/12, fo. 13v.

7   Sir Giles, 6 men-at-arms and 30 archers were transported by sea from the Thames to Portsmouth prior to the departure of the expedition: E403/336, m. 46.

8   Elevated to status of banneret on 15 July 1346: C81/313, no. 1779?; *CPR, 1345–8*, p. 473.

				Total				Retinue
Earls	Bnts	Knts	Esqs	M/a	M/Arc	F/Arc	Others	Total
John Lisle, bnt[9]	0	1	6	11	18	23	0	0	41
Michael Poynings, bnt[10]	0	2	8	23	33	12	0	0	45
John Stryvelyn, bnt	0	1	1	22	24	26	0	0	50
Alan la Zouche of Ashby, bnt[11]	0								
Simon Basset, knt	0	0	1	2	3	3	0	0	6
Thomas Beaumont, knt	0	0	1	7	8	5	2	0	15
[John Berkeley, knt[12]	0	0	1	2	3	0	0	0	3]
John Borhunt, knt	0	0	1	1	2	2	0	0	4
Thomas Bourne, knt*	0	0	1	4	5	6	0	0	11
John Brocas, knt*	0	0	1	14	15	24	0	0	39
Alan Clavering, knt	0	0	1	3	4	3	0	0	7
Gawain Corder, knt*	0	0	1	4	5	4	0	0	9
Hugh Courtenay, knt	0	0	2	8	10	8	0	0	18
Robert Dalton, knt*	0	0	1	4	5	8	0	0	13
Richard Damory, knt*	0	0	1	6	7	6	0	0	13
Aymer Darcy, knt	0	0	1	2	3	4	0	0	7
John Deyncourt, knt*[13]	0	0	1	2	3	3	0	0	6

9 Elevated to status of banneret on the day of Crécy: *Eulogium*, iii, p. 211; C81/314, no. 17810; *CPR, 1345–8*, p. 194.

10 BL, Harleian MS 3968, fo. 119r suggests, plausibly, that Poynings was the only banneret in this retinue, and that he had 13 archers.

11 Elevated to status of banneret on the day of Crécy (*Eulogium*, iii, p. 211), but died during the siege of Calais (*CIPM*, viii, nos 662, 715). Not included in the Wetwang abstracts, but received an advance on his wages on 10 April (E403/336, m. 41) and on 21 November a further payment was ordered for Sir Alan, now styled 'banneret', for the wages of his men-at-arms and archers (E404/496, no. 28), five of whom had been issued with protections (C76/22, mm. 7, 10) and nine, including one protection recipient, with pardons (*CPR, 1345–8*, pp. 485, 493, 495, 498).

12 Perhaps a royal household knight (Wrottesley, *Crecy and Calais*, pp. 88, 143), but the wording of these documents is by no means conclusive. BL, Harleian MS 3968, fo. 124v, assigns 3 esquires and 4 archers to Berkeley's retinue. This is probably the John Berkeley, esq, who served in Scotland with the earl of Salisbury in 1338 (E101/35/3, m. 2d).

13 'Henry' Deyncourt in BL, Harleian MS 3968, fo. 116r, but this must be a transcription error, as is surely the 'one banneret' that is assigned to this very small retinue. John Deyncourt, knt, received a prest on 10 April: E403/336, fo. 43.

	Earls	Bnts	Knts	Esqs	Total M/a	M/Arc	F/Arc	Others	Retinue Total
Ivo Fitzwarin, knt	0	0	1	2	3	4	0	0	7
Otes Holand, knt*[14]	0	0	1	3	4	0	0	0	4
Thomas Holand, knt*	0	0	1	4	5	4	0	0	9
Nicholas Langford*	0	0	1	2	3	3	0	0	6
John Shirbourn, knt*	0	0	1	3	4	3	0	0	7
Thomas Swinnerton, knt*	0	0	2	2	4	4	0	0	8
Warin Trussell, knt*	0	0	1	2	3	2	0	0	5
William Trussell of Cublesdon, knt	0	0	3	9	12	18	0	0	30
Gilbert Turbeville, knt*	0	0	1	8	9	8	0	0	17
Henry Tyes, knt	0	0	1	2	3	4	0	0	7
Richard de la Vache, knt*	0	0	1	4	5	5	0	0	10
Stephen Waleys, knt	0	0	2	4	6	13	0	0	19
John Warde, knt	0	0	1	3	4	2	0	0	6
Edward atte Wode, knt[15]									
John Beauchamp, son of Giles, knt[16]	0	0	1	5	6	4	0	0	10
Peter Breuse, knt	0	0	1	2	3	10	0	0	13
Guy Brian, knt	0	0	1	6	7	6	0	0	13
Henry Dengayne, knt[17]	0	0	1	0	1	0	0	0	1
Thomas Lancaster, knt	0	0	1	2	3	5	0	0	8
Robert Mauley, knt*[18]	0	0	1	9	10	25	0	0	35
John Ravensholme, knt	0	0	1	2	3	0	0	0	3

14 Entries in BL, Harleian MS 3968, fo. 120r for Otes and Thomas Holand are confirmed by an extract from Wetwang's original account book preserved on a Memoranda Roll: Wrottesley, *Crecy and Calais*, pp. 176–7.

15 A newly created knight (perhaps at La Hougue), he was killed in the assault on Roche Guyon: *Eulogium*, iii, p. 208; *CIPM*, ix, no. 35.

16 Beauchamp and the following six knights were granted annuities to support knighthood on the day of Crécy: *CPR, 1345–8*, p. 474.

17 A wholly different retinue is suggested in BL, Harleian MS 3968, fo. 118r: 1 banneret, 2 knights, 4 esquires and 8 mounted archers.

18 The copyist has confused the names of 'Mauley' and 'Morley': BL, Harleian MS 3968, fos 118r, 119v.

	Earls	Bnts	Knts	Esqs	Total M/a	M/Arc	F/Arc	Others	Retinue Total
William Kildesby, clerk[19]	0	1	3	73	77	68	11	0	156
Walter Wetwang, clerk	0	1	3	25	29	35	0	0	64
John Thoresby, clerk	0	1	2	30	33	36	0	0	69
Philip Weston, clerk[20]	0	1	3	27	31	30	0	0	61
Other retinues in king's division[21]									
Thomas Breuse, bnt	0	1	6	13	20	20	0	0	40
John Grey [of Ruthin], bnt[22]									
Thomas Lathum, bnt[23]	0	1	1	8	10	23	0	0	33
Edward Montagu, bnt	0	1	9	15	25	20	0	0	45
William Warenne, knt	0	0	4	15	19	15	0	8[24]	42
	1	25[25]	166[26]	723	915	905	50	15	1885

19 John Leukenore secured a letter of protection for service in Kildesby's retinue (C76/22, m. 8). However, he also received an individual prest on 10 April 1346 (E403/336, m. 41) and appears as a captain in BL, Harleian MS 3968, fo. 124r. It is possible that he served with a separate retinue from La Hougue, though it is more likely that this occurred only after Kildesby's death during the siege. However, it would seem that John had also died before the middle of October 1346, when his father, John, was excused taking up knighthood on account of the son's service: *CPR, 1345–8*, p. 223; Wrottesley, *Crecy and Calais*, p. 136 (but cf. pp. 184, 207).

20 *Brut*, ed. Brie, ii, p. 540.

21 Although listed in the *Acta Bellicosa*, [William?] le Botiller of Wem and [Roger] le Straunge have been excluded because it is doubtful whether they served in July–August 1346. For details, see notes to Table 1.

22 Not included in the Wetwang abstracts, but 'John de Grey' and 'John de Grey of Ruthin' received wage advances: E403/336, mm. 41, 44. He may have been a household banneret: cf. the 'John de Grey' who was a chamber knight and one of the king's close companions in 1347–9: Nicolas, 'Observations on the institution of the most noble Order of the Garter', pp. 24–6, 41–2, 46. That, however, may have been John de Grey of Rotherfield.

23 Lathum is a somewhat enigmatic figure, partly because he is not included in the *Acta Bellicosa* list, but there can be little doubt that he served in July–August 1346. He received wage advances in April (E403/336, mm. 41–2), a letter of protection in June (C76/22, m. 10) and provided warranty for pardons issued in September (*CPR, 1345–8*, pp. 486, 498, 500, 502). His inclusion in the king's division is conjectural, but the most likely of options. Clifford Rogers suggests that he may have served with Hastings's force in Flanders (*War Cruel and Sharp*, p. 424 and n. 8).

24 Eight Welshmen.

25 Total includes Alan la Zouche and John de Grey of Ruthin, as well as the four 'banneret clerks'.

26 Total includes Edward atte Wode.

	Earls	Bnts	Knts	Esqs	Total M/a	M/Arc	F/Arc	Others	Retinue Total
Foreign contingents[27]									
William de Groucy, bnt[28]	0	1	3	15	19	0	0	0	19
Godfrey de Harcourt, bnt[29]									
John de Levedale [of Brabant], bnt[30]	0	1	4	12	17	0	0	16 p	33
Hugh Calkyn of Normandy, knt[31]	0	0	1	4	5	0	0	0	5
Konrad von Dyck; Ernald von Esch, knts,[32]	0	0	2	?	?	0	0	0	?
Wulfart de Ghistelles, knt*[33]	0	0	1	4	5	5	0	0	10
William Graunsone of Burgundy, knt[34]	0	0	1	7	8	0	0	8 p	16

27 In addition to Godfrey de Harcourt, a number of other foreign knights and their followers are recorded in the Wetwang abstracts, among recipients of wage advances and in other sources. Our problem is how to decide which of them accompanied Edward III to La Hougue and fought at Crécy. Those listed here received prests before the departure from England or are substantiated by other reliable sources. Excluded are those in the Wetwang abstracts who cannot be shown to have served before the beginning of the siege of Calais and those who appear to be connected with either Sir Hugh Hastings's campaign in Flanders (e.g., Flemish valets: E403/336, m. 42) or Sir Thomas Dagworth's operations in Brittany (e.g., a company of Scotsmen: Sir Patrick Macolagh, with 2 men-at-arms and 5 valets, two of whom were also of the Macolagh family: E403/336, m. 42; E403/339, m. 6; E404/496, no. 203).

28 For evidence of Groucy's service throughout the campaign, see Chapter 6, p. 259 n. 18. Pay-roll: Wrottesley, *Crecy and Calais*, p. 198.

29 Harcourt is not included in the Wetwang abstracts, but he did receive advance payments of wages and *regard*, totalling £668 13s 4d: E403/336, mm. 41, 42, 43.

30 Prests: E403/336, mm. 41, 43; E101/390/12, fo. 8. Wrottesley, *Crecy and Calais*, p. 198. It should be noted that Calkyn is designated 'of Flanders' in early modern transcripts of the army pay-roll: Wrottesley, *Crecy and Calais*, p. 201; BL, Harleian MS 3968, fo. 129r.

31 Prests to Hugh and his men: E403/336, m. 43. On 1 June 1346 he was granted 100 marks p.a. for life: *CPR, 1345–8*, p. 123.

32 Payment (10 April) of *regard* and war wages to these Rhenish knights and 'their men'. Note also the war wages payment to William Malherb', 'valletti de parte Juliacensi'. E403/336, m. 43; E101/390/12, fo. 6v. F. Trautz, *Die Könige von England und das Reich, 1272–1377* (Heidelberg, 1961), p. 326 n. 504.

33 Prest (10 April) to Wulfart and his men-at-arms and archers: E403/336, m. 43. Although from Hainault, he appears as 'William Wolford', Gascon knight, in BL, Harleian MS 3968, fo. 129r. His role in the campaign is noted in *Récits*, pp. 225–6, and in *Froissart*, ed. Luce, iii, p. 406 (Amiens MS).

34 Prest for William and his men-at-arms: E403/336, m. 42. Wrottesley, *Crecy and Calais*, p. 201.

	Earls	Bnts	Knts	Esqs	Total M/a	M/Arc	F/Arc	Others	Retinue Total
Rasse Maskerel, knt, et al.[35]	0	0	3	10	13	0	0	10 p	23
Tilmann von Rodenburgh, knt, et al.[36]	0	0	2	?	?	0	0	0	?
Johann von Schönfeld, knt, et al.[37]	0	2	17	52+	67+	5	0	34	106+
Rearguard[38]									
Thomas Hatfield, bishop of Durham	1	3	48	162	214	81	0	0	295
Richard Fitzalan, earl of Arundel	1	3	41	105	150	154	0	0	304
Robert Ufford, earl of Suffolk	1	1	36	58	96	63	0	0	159
William Clinton, earl of Huntingdon[39]	1	2	30	98	131	93	0	0	224
Hugh Despenser, bnt[40]	0	3	40	86	129	105	0	0	234
	4	12	195	509	720	496	0	0	1216

35 Advances on war wages to Rasse Maskerel, Adam von Ederein and Gerhard von Wendendorp, knights, and 'their men' (£25 4s and £162 14s: E403/336, mm. 42–3), followed by an order (Portchester, 6 July) for a further payment of £40: *Foedera*, III, i, p. 85. On 2 May these three German knights had sealed an indenture with Edward III to serve in the coming campaign with 10 'healmes' ('Helme'; men-at-arms) and 10 'paunsers' ('Gepanzerte'; armoured men, perhaps comparable with hobelars), the former paid 12d per day, the latter, 6d. E101/68/3, no. 64. Trautz, *Die Könige von England und das Reich, 1272–1377*, pp. 326 n. 504, 332 n. 541. For the presence of 'messire Races Massures' at Crécy, see *Jean le Bel*, ii, p. 106.

36 This Rhenish knight, together with Otto von Illyngburgh, received payments for themselves and 'socii sui' in mid-June and early July: E101/390/12, fo. 8; *Foedera*, III, i, p. 85. Trautz, *Die Könige von England und das Reich, 1272–1377*, p. 332 and n. 539.

37 Payment (10 April) to this knight and 'sociorum suorum militum de Almannia': E403/336, m. 44. On 12 September 1346, Schönfeld reported on the battle of Crécy to the bishop of Passau. J.F. Böhmer, ed., *Acta Imperii selecta* (Innsbruck, 1870), no. 1055.

38 Although listed in the *Acta Bellicosa*, John Sutton has been excluded since there is no conclusive evidence for his service as a captain in July–August 1346. For details, see notes to Appendix 2, Table 1.

39 Returned to England after capture of Caen.

40 Gilbert Despenser, knt, received an individual prest on 10 April (E403/336, m. 43), but there is no other evidence of an independent retinue (he appointed attorneys on 6 June: C76/22, m. 9). He had served in Hugh Despenser's retinue in Brittany in 1342 (C61/54, m. 30), and it is probable that he did so again in 1346. The other possibility is that he was a royal household knight.

6

The Nobility of Normandy and the English Campaign of 1346

CHRISTOPHE PIEL

The great battles of the middle ages have often been viewed by traditional histo-riography as formative moments in the emergence of the first national identities in western Europe.[1] Thus the two greatest engagements of the Hundred Years War, Crécy and Agincourt, have been construed not essentially in terms of dynastic rivalries, but as confrontations between two new-born nations. More recently, political history has sought to reassess the claim that national feeling existed at the end of the Middle Ages,[2] and in this respect, this chapter, which will examine the political behaviour of the Norman nobility at the time of Edward III's campaign in 1346, aims to contribute to a better understanding of the functioning of political society of that time.[3] Can the political choices of the Norman nobility be accounted for by reference to 'national' considerations, or should we look for an explanation at a less elevated, more local level, where personal interests were at stake?

In 1346, Normandy had been under French domination for almost one and a half centuries, having been removed from the Plantagenet empire by Philip Augustus in 1204. Thanks to the political astuteness of the king of France, who respected the former institutional systems of the province, such as the Exchequer of Rouen, Capetian rule was readily accepted and Normandy remained a duchy separate from the other, older royal lands.

One of the most difficult tasks facing the king of France was to establish the loyalty of a nobility whose eyes were focused not only on their Norman posses-sions, but also towards England and their estates on that side of the channel. Royal caution prevailed, and though under the Treaty of Paris of 1259 (in which the English king had waived his rights to the duchy of Normandy) some of the Norman estates were seized and granted to French vassals of the Capetians, several families managed to retain both their English and Norman possessions.

---

[1] One notable example of this can be found in G. Duby, *Le Dimanche de Bouvines* (Paris, 1973).

[2] See, for example, C. Beaune, *Naissance de la nation France* (Paris, 1985).

[3] Cf. the recent study of the Norman nobility at the time of King John's loss of the duchy in 1204: D. Power, 'King John and the Norman aristocracy', *King John: New Interpretations*, ed. S.D. Church (Woodbridge, 1999), pp. 117–36.

A prime example is that of the pre-eminent Estouteville family from eastern Normandy who, despite the English line becoming separated from the original Norman branch, retained ownership of estates on both sides of the channel into the fourteenth century.[4] But this was a rare exception. In the vast majority of cases the separation of Normandy from England resulted in a radical split of noble 'cross-channel empires' into distinct, individual and autonomous Norman and English estates. Typical of such division were the estates of the Harcourt family and those of the counts of Eu.[5]

Despite the political rupture of 1204 and the cyclical outbursts of war during the thirteenth century, economic relations continued, and we can observe the retention of perennial ties between the two nobilities, founded on a common mental and ideological background.[6] But with the passing of the years, as attacks on the Norman coastline from across the channel increased, mistrust grew and finally thrived, leading eventually to widespread hostility. The maritime war at the end of the thirteenth century was a fundamental cause of the strong and growing belief in the Norman nation that the English were definitely the enemies of the duchy,[7] and it is apparent that by the beginning of the fourteenth century in Normandy a complete break with England had been achieved.[8] The dream of a return to the English crown had completely vanished; indeed, such an idea was no longer welcome.

This state of affairs was, needless to say, welcomed by the last Capetians, as it contributed greatly to the reinforcement of the king of France's power. Normandy was the most valuable of Philip Augustus's 'Plantagenet conquests'. Indeed, yielding as it did one quarter of the fiscal income of the state from only one-eighth of the area of the kingdom, Normandy was the jewel of the royal domain. Moreover, an anti-English Normandy had strategic significance. Located as it was immediately between England and France, the duchy potentially provided an excellent security buffer for the heart of the kingdom, making the king of France appreciably less vulnerable as compared to the time of Henry II and his sons.

From the very beginning, therefore, the kings of France displayed a real interest in the duchy. They refused to alienate this most precious holding as an apanage for the youngest of the royal family, making only a rare exception for the heir to the throne, two such heirs being crowned dukes of Normandy in Rouen during the fourteenth century (the future kings John II and Charles V).

---

4   E.M. Hallam, *Capetian France 987–1328* (London, 1980), p. 254.
5   R. Cazelles, *La société politique et la crise de la royauté sous Philippe de Valois* (Paris, 1958), pp. 138 and 145.
6   Cf. the view that among the local aristocracies in England and Normandy 'a clear orientation to one realm or other had developed long before 1204': D. Crouch, 'Normans and Anglo-Normans: a divided aristocracy?', *England and Normandy in the Middle Ages*, ed. D. Bates and A. Curry (London and Rio Grande, 1994), pp. 51–67.
7   On the maritime war, which began in 1292, and its wider implications for Anglo-French relations, see M. Prestwich, *Edward I* (London, 1988), pp. 377ff.
8   On Anglo-Norman relations during this period, see W.M. Ormrod, 'England, Normandy and the beginnings of the Hundred Years War, 1259–1360', *England and Normandy in the Middle Ages*, ed. D. Bates and A. Curry (London and Rio Grande, 1994), pp. 197–213 (esp. pp. 199–201, and sources cited there).

Prince John, who became duke in 1332, ruled the province only after the defeat of Crécy, his father Philip holding the reins of power until then.[9] Even after their accession to the royal throne the former dukes did not forget the special links that bound them to Normandy. In his will of October 1374, for example, Charles V commanded that on his death his heart should be buried in Rouen cathedral. After 1364 (if we discount the somewhat forced if ephemeral grant of the title to the ambitious younger brother of Louis XI in 1465), the only bearer of the honorary title of duke of Normandy was to be the last Dauphin of France, Louis XVI's second son. By contrast, the resurrection of the ducal title from 1332 to 1364 highlights the specific political context of the time, reviving for the Normans an important symbol of their identity. In fact, what we see in the fourteenth century is a conspicuous backlash in the form of demands for autonomy.

The growth of autonomy in Normandy

The vital importance of Normandy for the Capetian monarchy accounts for their initial and studied respect for the privileges of the duchy, and more specifically for those of the nobility. But this was a wait-and-see policy, determined by the actual strength of royal power. Behind it lay the ultimate goal of the kings and their councillors: to subdue the province entirely to the will of the French crown. With the strengthening of the state, especially under the last direct Capetians, Philip the Fair and his sons, the political centre of the kingdom became increasingly eager to have control over the 'periphery'. This resulted in an increase in fiscal burden owing to the near continuous wars of the period – wars that in many respects can be regarded as the genuine melting pot of the modern state. Gradually the Norman institutions were neutralised by the substitution in political office of men from Paris who were wholly devoted to the king. This policy of stealthy reinforcement of an executive primarily loyal to the interests of Paris generated a backlash reaction that gave rise, at the beginning of the fourteenth century, to new claims for autonomy throughout the duchy. This led to the formation of the noble League of 1315, and to the subsequent grant of the 'Charte aux Normands' by King Louis XI.[10]

Although such developments were not unique to Normandy, none of the concessions in the several other similar charters went as far as those enshrined in the 'Charte aux Normands'. Indeed, it conferred such provincial liberties that until the fall of the *Ancien Régime* the Charter was to be regarded as the foundation of Norman identity. According to the provisions of the Charter, Normans received assurances that no taxes would be levied within the duchy without the consent of the people of the province. Furthermore, it established that the

---

9   J. Tricart, 'Jean, duc de Normandie et héritier de France: un double échec ?', *Annales de Normandie*, xxix (1980), pp. 23–44.

10   On the 'Charte aux Normands' of 1315 and its subsequent history, see P. Contamine, 'The Norman "nation" and the French "nation" in the fourteenth and fifteenth centuries', *England and Normandy in the Middle Ages*, ed. D. Bates and A. Curry (London and Rio Grande, 1994), pp. 215–34 (esp. pp. 223–7).

authority of the royal officers was no longer supreme, and that they and their actions were to become accountable before the Exchequer, which at the same time became a court of appeal against violations of the Charter.

Although this Charter, which had been obtained by the nobility, was supposed to correspond with the interests of a large majority of the Norman population, in reality it reflected more precisely an expression of the paramount influence of the nobility. They were virtually the only interlocutors of the king in the political sphere, leading the French historian Raymond Cazelles to refer to this social group as the political society – *société politique* – of the time.[11] As a consequence, the nobility, their influence confirmed, emerged as the genuine protectors of Norman identity, making the major contribution to the establishment of the so-called *États de Normandie* – the institution in which the political dialogue between prince and subjects took place. The taxes issue united the opposition against royal authority at the very time when the crown was compelled to raise additional monies in order to meet the tremendous increase of expenditure brought about by the conflict with England. Indeed, at the beginning of the Hundred Years War in 1337, at the expense of acknowledging his weakened formal influence in Normandy, Philip VI was only successful in raising war monies by giving in return a solemn confirmation of the Charter. Likewise, two years later in 1339, it was only in return for a similar affirmation that he was able to obtain the nobility's promise of an expeditionary force to invade England.[12]

During these fundamental years in the formation of the Estates of Normandy, the members of the Norman high aristocracy, together with the major prelates of the province, formed a formidable and resolute council with whom the king was obliged to negotiate. They included the count of Eu, the count of Harcourt, his brother, the well-known Godfrey de Harcourt, Marshal Robert Bertran, and the lord of Graville.

Defence, organisation and noble involvement

If, at the beginning of the Crécy campaign, we can characterise the political relationship between the king and the duchy as being mutually pragmatic, what can be said of it at the outbreak of hostilities, and what in particular can be said of the defensive measures taken by Philip VI of Valois and his council? Can, for example, these measures be interpreted as proving the king's mistrust of the Normans, or did Philip truly rely on the Norman nobility to secure the province? And given the Norman failure to prevent the advance of the English beyond Normandy, does this conspicuous failure of defence suggest a lack of strategic and political astuteness on the king's part, or was the Norman commitment to

---

[11] See Cazelles, *La société politique et la crise de la royauté sous Philippe de Valois*, and *Société politique, noblesse et couronne sous les règnes de Jean II le Bon et Charles V* (Paris and Geneva, 1982).

[12] For a fuller discussion of this, see Contamine, 'The Norman "nation" and the French "nation" in the fourteenth and fifteenth centuries', pp. 227–8.

such a defence always lukewarm? To find answers to these questions we must, of course, look at the security measures adopted by Philip VI of Valois.

In order to gain the advantage of surprise against his adversary, Edward III took drastic steps in an effort to ensure the secrecy of his military preparations.[13] Despite this, such a huge undertaking could never have escaped the attention of numerous spies distributed around English harbours, and although their reports may not have been able to provide a precise destination, the government in Paris was certainly warned that an expeditionary force against France was being prepared. During the last days of June 1346, a sudden panic was clearly noticeable within the French royal entourage. This, of course, was lamentably late when one considers that the disembarkation of the English army would begin on the following 12 July. Orders were given to the *baillis*, who were invested with particularly extensive powers. Artillery and other military supplies were urgently sent to the garrisons of Leurre, Étretat and Chef-de-Caux, suggesting that the French expected the English to reach mainland France in northern Normandy.[14] But in addition to this, more general precautionary measures were taken, aimed at securing the Norman coastline as a whole. Every male of sufficient age to bear arms was called upon to do so, although the *arrière-ban* was much too belated to provide the king of France with an efficient army before August.

When the English disembarked at Saint-Vaast-la-Hougue on 12 July they faced little resistance. The core of the Norman army was assembled north of the Seine. In Cotentin, Marshal Robert Bertran, delegated by the king as captain of the 'maritime border' of this part of the duchy, and with the assistance of the officers of the *bailliages* of Cotentin and Caen, could only muster a small body of soldiers, compelling him, after a brief skirmish with the enemy, to retreat towards the southern city of Carentan. Other Norman troops wandering in the neighbourhood hurried to seek shelter behind the fortified walls of towns scattered about the countryside – a countryside that was consequently left unprotected against the brutality of the English troops. During the second half of July, the marshal's efforts focused on delaying the advance of the enemy, while two other prominent leaders of the French royal host, Constable Raoul of Brienne, count of Eu (appointed to the defence of Harfleur) and Chamberlain John of Melun, count of Tancarville, set about preparing the major city of Caen for a siege, which would impede the progress of Edward's army. However, on 26 July, Caen was stormed and, with the exception of the castle, taken. The counts of Eu and Tancarville were both captured and sent to England as prisoners. Little help was forthcoming from the army that had been gathered by Philip VI himself in Rouen, where he arrived in person on the day of the downfall of Caen.

After crossing the River Seine and marching deliberately westwards to engage Edward, Philip effected a sudden retreat to Rouen, preventing the English from reaching the city by pulling down the bridge over the Seine. Edward decided against a siege of the Norman capital and headed upstream towards Paris, followed closely by the French army on the other bank of the

13 Sumption, *Trial by Battle*, pp. 493, 499.
14 Sumption, *Trial by Battle*, p. 499.

Seine. The clash between the two kings was destined to take place outside the duchy of Normandy, and for the king of France the events of late July provided clear evidence that Normandy's defences had failed, and that the campaign had begun disastrously.

If the course of events had not proceeded well for the king of France, how were they regarded by the Norman nobility? With the exception of Godfrey de Harcourt, who paid homage to Edward III as the rightful king of France, there is no evidence that the Norman nobility provided substantial support for the English.[15] Thus, if the defence of Normandy had gone badly at the outset, the nobility cannot be charged with unwillingness to stand by the Valois king. The relative weakness of Normandy can perhaps best be explained by the fact that a large number of barons and knights of the duchy were busy fighting the English in Gascony in an army commanded by the duke of Normandy. Indeed, at the very moment of the arrival of Edward III, this army was besieging the town of Aiguillon. This was known by Godfrey de Harcourt, who according to Froissart, actually pressed Edward to land in Normandy with these words: 'In Normandy there are only people who were never armed. And the flower of knighthood, who could be there, is now before Aiguillon with the duke.'[16] It is interesting to observe that the words that Froissart puts in Harcourt's mouth suggest that the vast majority of Normans held the English to be a genuine enemy.

As soon as the royal council became aware of the imminent English attack in Normandy, the first emergency step was hurriedly to recall some of the captains of the army in Gascony, and especially those whose status was appropriate to the defence of the province. Typically these were men who were not only royal officers, but also leaders of the nobility in the duchy. Indeed, the latter position entitled them, in their position at the apex of the feudal pyramid, to gather the whole nobility into the king's service. Thus, for example, the constable, the count of Eu, headed back hastily from Aiguillon and was placed in command of the defence of Harfleur, before going to Caen to assist the count of Tancarville. The marshals seem to have flown to the rescue of the troops in Normandy at the same time, since Philip de Valois considered Robert Bertran, lord of the nearby land of Bricquebec, as 'captain of the maritime border'. This appointment by the

---

[15] Evidence in English administrative records for the period prior to the Crécy campaign suggests that Norman support for Edward involved a small group of dissidents. Godfrey de Harcourt, accompanied by a retinue of five knights and 24 men-at-arms, had participated in the English expedition to Guernsey during the summer of 1345. M.H. Marett Godfray, 'Documents relatifs aux attaques sur les Iles de la Manche, 1338–1345', *La société Jersiaise pour l'étude de l'histoire*, Bulletin, iii (1877), pp. 11–53 (at pp. 47–53). Also in the English king's pay on this occasion were two members of the Groucy family (William and Nicholas), Roland de Verdon and a group of esquires and valets. Harcourt, William de Groucy and Hugh Calkyn, and several *vallets* ('Odard Darrentyn' and two companions; and 'Peter de Hassely') can be seen drawing funds in December 1345: E403/336, m. 21. Harcourt and Calkyn are recorded as receiving disbursements from the paymaster of the English army prior to the campaign (E403/336, mm. 41, 43; E101/390/12, fos 5v, 6r, 6v, 7r); for Groucy, see below n. 18. For Harcourt's supporters in Normandy, see Rogers, *War Cruel and Sharp*, p. 226 and n. 39.

[16] 'ce sont gens en Normendie qui oncques ne furent armé. Et toute la fleur de le chevalerie, qui y poest estre, gist maintenant devant Aguillon avoech le duch': *Froissart*, ed. Luce, iii, p. 131.

Valois king appears to have been an attempt to counterbalance the support offered to Edward III by the 'disloyal' Godfrey de Harcourt, who was a seigneurial neighbour of Robert Bertran, his estates at Saint-Sauveur-le-Vicomte being located about ten kilometres or so from Bertran's fief of Bricquebec. Bertran's effectiveness originated from his delegated royal powers combined with his social prestige as a leading lord of the territory where he was to fight.

In many ways the fight between the two kings paralleled the smaller-scale rivalry between their two clienteles. Jean de Melun, count of Tancarville, was not only one of the most powerful lords of eastern Normandy, with a corresponding clientele, but he could also draw on a peculiar legitimacy within the nobility of the duchy, for he was the hereditary Chamberlain of Normandy as well as being appointed Chamberlain of France by King Philip VI. An analysis of the retinue of the constable, Raoul de Brienne, count of Eu, as it existed in Harfleur in 1346, casts light on the intricate relationship between royal offices held by members of the higher aristocracy and their own feudal and local power base. In the 'bataille' of the constable of France, 168 persons are designated 'men-at-arms', and one can readily discern a close link between the geographical origins of these men and the location of the count of Eu's seigneurial holdings in Flanders, Picardy and eastern Normandy.[17]

However, the fact that the vast majority of Norman nobles, following the political attitudes of their patrons, remained faithful to the French crown should not necessarily imply a consistent determination to stand in the way of the king of England. In Cotentin, immediately after the English landing, and at the start of their advance inland, the towns rapidly surrendered. We now know that the parts played in that episode by Roland de Verdon and Nicolas de Grouchy were probably decisive.[18] These two knights actually belonged to the clientele of

---

17 For the roll of the count of Eu's retinue of men-at-arms at Harfleur and Caen (Paris, Bibliothèque Nationale, De Camps, vol. 83, fo. 472), see H. Prentout, *La prise de Caen par Edouard III, 1346* (Caen, 1904), Documents inédits, VIII, pp. 69–72. See also, editorial discussion in *Jean le Bel*, ii, p. 79 n. 2; and R. Cazelles, *Catalogue de comptes royaux des règnes de Philippe VI et Jean II (1328–1364)*, Recueil des historiens de la France (Paris, 1984), which provides a detailed list of the existing manuscripts at the Bibliothèque Nationale in Paris and at the municipal library in Rouen. The constable of France's landed possessions were extensive. Not only was he count of Eu, but he inherited from his father some considerable estates in Higher Normandy, Poitou, Saintonge and on the borders of Burgundy. His grandmother bequeathed to him the county of Guines, and Philip VI granted him lands in Ponthieu. He also married a rich heiress, Catherine, Louis of Savoy's daughter, which event brought with it a vast demesne for which he did not have to pay homage to the king of France. His seigneurial power even extended beyond the borders of the kingdom, since he possessed lands in England and Ireland: they had been seized by Edward III at the outbreak of hostilities, but the count might reasonably hope to recover them when peace was restored. See Cazelles, *La société politique et la crise de la royauté sous Philippe de Valois*, p. 247.

18 *Chronique Normande*, p. 75; cf. *Grandes chroniques*, ix, p. 271 and Rogers, *War Cruel and Sharp*, p. 244 and n. 35. It interesting to note that at Caen on 30 July 1346 Edward III granted an annuity of £100 to William de Groucy in recompense for 'les damages et pertes qil ad endurez en notre service': PRO, C81/314, no. 17804; *CPR, 1345–8*, pp. 168–9. William remained in the English army, with a retinue, throughout the siege of Calais: *CPR, 1345–8*, p. 228; PRO, E404/496, no. 543; Wrottesley, *Crecy and Calais*, pp. 148, 198. Groucy's property, together with that of Roland de Verdon, had been confiscated and granted to Robert Bertran's

Godfrey de Harcourt, suggesting that in this case the clientele relationship worked in favour of the English undertaking.[19] Nevertheless, the basic fact remains that the key role played by client–patron relations in the political functioning of that time dictated that, by a comfortable majority, the Norman higher aristocracy would choose to be faithful to their Valois sovereign, encouraging most of the lesser nobility to act in the same way. Godfrey de Harcourt, when advising Edward III to launch an attack in Normandy, may have deliberately overestimated the number of his partisans, since as a younger brother of the count of Harcourt he could not possibly have controlled the whole clientele of that household. Indeed, the count of Harcourt joined the army that his parent, Godfrey, had chosen – that of Philip VI of France – and died in his king's service on the battlefield of Crécy. Thus in seeking to understand the failure of the early defensive campaign in Normandy in 1346, it cannot be argued that the nobility were responsible for the French king's worsening situation. A more plausible explanation for the relative ease with which Edward's army crossed through the province should be sought in the decisions of the French king and his advisers.

As far as the particular behaviour of Godfrey de Harcourt is concerned, might this have been due to a volatile personality, or could it have been that his position was actually consistent with the attitudes of the Norman nobility as a whole? In other words, if we take a closer look at the political behaviour of the nobles who were faithful to the Valois king, is it possible to discern attitudes that might be considered somewhat similar to those adopted by the younger Harcourt in 1346? Such a question inevitably leads us to look in more detail at the political motivations of the Norman nobility with specific regard to its relationship with the king and the emerging state.

The high level of support given to Philip VI by the leading members of the Norman aristocracy is not surprising if it is recalled that all of these lords were in the service of the king and dependent upon him for a variable but not insignificant amount of their income. By the beginning of the fourteenth century, in addition to holding the highest offices in the duchy, the Norman nobility were lured, in a steady and increasing stream, by the proximity of Paris, the royal court and the government to the central institutions of the monarchy. Enguerrand de Marigny was the first and most famous of a long line of Norman counsellors.[20] During the reign of Philip of Valois, the large number of the duchy's nobles in the king's entourage inspired Raymond Cazelles to talk of a 'Norman party', from which stood out the prominent families of Vienne and Bertran.[21] Under John II it was the turn of the Melun clan to acquire a paramount position.[22] In the wake of these leaders, Norman clientelism thrived. Indeed, at the

daughter, Jeannette: *Registres du Trésor des Chartes*, ed. J. Viard and A. Vallée (Paris, 1979), III, ii, no. 5906.

[19] Tricart, 'Jean, duc de Normandie et héritier de France: un double échec?', pp. 23–4.

[20] J. Favier, *Un conseiller de Philippe le Bel : Enguerran de Marigny* (Paris, 1963).

[21] Cazelles, *La société politique et la crise de la royauté sous Philippe de Valois*.

[22] Cazelles, *Société politique, noblesse et couronne sous les règnes de Jean II le Bon et Charles V*, chapter 38, pp. 402–19, and Françoise Autrand, *Charles V* (Paris, 1994), pp. 193–4.

end of the fourteenth century the continuing migration of the nobility towards the institutions of the royal state was a popular means of supplementing the diminished income from noble estates. Politics, therefore, was becoming a basic struggle between the different aristocratic clans for access to the fiscal manna of the state.

Thus, for a better understanding of the behaviour of the Norman nobility in the face of English aggression in 1346, it is necessary to regard the circumstances less in terms of a national rift than in terms of tensions running through the noble classes, tensions that to a great extent explain the nature of the relationships between the Norman nobility and the monarchy. This tension is well illustrated by looking again at the so-called 'betrayal' of Godfrey de Harcourt. Traditional historians judged his behaviour sternly, having little reluctance to label him a 'traitor'. Eugène Déprez, for example, writing in 1908, referred to Harcourt as a 'double traitor'.[23] However, it can be argued that behind an apparent objectivity consistent with the emerging concept of modern scientific history, Déprez, along with others of the 'positivist' French school at the beginning of the twentieth century, was influenced by an ideology driven by a rising nationalism in the pre-First World war era.

It seems that in 1346 Harcourt was somewhat isolated in his alliance with the king of England. But his rebellion had its roots in 1341, in a conflict with his rival and neighbour Robert Bertran, lord of Bricquebec, a staunch servant of Philip VI. Bertran resented Harcourt because of his attitude during the war of succession in Brittany, when Harcourt let down the king's favourite Charles de Blois in favour of the pretender Montfort, who was supported by the king of England. This position led Harcourt to be charged with plotting to become the duke of Normandy. His subsequent banishment and the seizure of his lands resulted in his recognition of Edward III as the king of France and his guiding of the English army through Normandy to Calais. However, during the years immediately prior to 1346, Godfrey appears to have been fully integrated into Norman noble society, even occupying a position of prominence. In 1339 he was among the few lords of the highest rank, representing the noble class, who negotiated with the king of France the reinforcement of the 'Charte aux Normands'. Here again, this local power derived from control over a clientele. This somewhat blurred social configuration, based on the patron–client relationship, together with feudal ties and other social links, is referred to as 'bastard feudalism' in English historiography.[24] Among this wide range of different social links, vassalage appears to have remained the core element of the social cohesion binding the aristocracy. This relationship, and even dependency, is demonstrated by the trial of a squire for his participation in one of Godfrey d'Harcourt's plots. The squire's defence was to claim that he had no choice but to join the

---

[23] E. Déprez, 'La double trahison de Geoffroy d'Harcourt', *Revue Historique*, xcix (1908), pp. 32–4.
[24] K.B. McFarlane, 'Bastard feudalism', *BIHR*, xx (1945); and, for a reassessment of McFarlane's theory, P. Coss, 'Bastard feudalism revised', *Past and Present*, no. 125 (1989), pp. 27–64, and D. Crouch, D.A. Carpenter and P. Coss, 'Debate. Bastard feudalism revised', *Past and Present*, no. 131 (1991), pp. 165–203.

conspiracy because he was the vassal of the lord of Saint-Sauveur-le-Vicomte, the ancestral seat of Godfrey d'Harcourt. Certainly Edward III had in mind Harcourt's network of influence over the local nobility when he ordered the royal fleet to sail towards the coast of the Cotentin peninsula.

In spite of the severity of the retaliatory measures taken against Godfrey and his companions (three were executed in Paris on 3 April 1344), he was easily forgiven when he decided to return to the Valois camp during the siege of Calais.[25] Not only did Philip VI return his lands, he appointed Harcourt 'Sovereign captain of the bailliages of Rouen, Outre-Seine and Caen' – a command of the highest rank.[26] Had Philip simply forgotten Harcourt's so-called betrayal? Here we must remind ourselves that power derived from a constant process of negotiation between king and nobility, providing both with mutual benefits. For the king's authority to have substance and recognition, and above all for it to be diffused and respected at a local level, he was entirely reliant upon the local nobility. And in return for supporting the crown, a noble who received delegated royal authority could use this to achieve pre-eminence over his rival noble competitors. Thus, the relationship between the king and his nobility was an essential and constant struggle for power, in which pragmatism necessarily had a respected place. In such a context, the political attitudes of Godfrey de Harcourt should perhaps be seen not as those of a curious individual personality, but as being typical of the nobility and their endless and compulsive jostling for political advantage. Indeed at the beginning of the Hundred Years War, 'rebellion' or protest by the nobility was by no means restricted to Godfrey de Harcourt. The count of Eu, who as constable of France had sided with Philip VI, was captured at Caen and taken prisoner to England. On his return he was immediately put to death on the orders of the new king of France (and former duke of Normandy), John II. The reason for this apparent brutality appears to be that, while in England, Eu had paid homage to Edward as king of France and he may even have granted his land in Guines to the English king.[27]

Whatever the reason, the execution of a man of such elevated social rank provoked ill-feeling in the nobility against the new French king, especially in Normandy where the House of Brienne had a strong clientele network. With the assassination of the king's favourite, Charles of Spain, in 1354, Charles of Évreux-Navarre, who had a claim to the throne, openly revolted against his Valois cousin. This was undoubtedly the most serious challenge to the

[25] Lettres de rémission from Philip VI were issued on 21 December 1346: printed in L. Delisle, *Histoire du château et des sires de Saint-Sauveur-le-Vicomte* (Valognes, 1867), Pièces Justificatives, no. 79 (pp. 109–11). Within days, orders were being issued for the seizure of Harcourt's property, and the arrest of his men, in England, especially in Dorset and on the Isle of Wight: *CFR, 1337–47*, pp. 490, 495. Some of his property was delivered to John le Nuiz, the Prince of Wales's armourer, in repayment of debts that Harcourt had run up prior to his departure from England: *CCR, 1346–9*, p. 189.

[26] Delisle, *Histoire du château et des sires de Saint-Sauveur-le-Vicomte*, Pièces Justificatives, no. 82. For Philip VI's usually severe treatment of traitors, see S.H. Cuttler, *The Law of Treason and Treason Trials in Later Medieval France* (Cambridge, 1981), pp. 145–54.

[27] Cazelles, *La société politique et la crise de la royauté sous Philippe de Valois*, pp. 247–52; cf. Cuttler, *Law of Treason and Treason Trials in Later Medieval France*, p. 154.

established king, as the House of Évreux-Navarre was from the same Capetian origins as the Valois, and consequently a viable pretender to the crown of France. This rebel was not to be underestimated since he ran a constellation of powerful territories, including not only the southern kingdom of Navarre, but also a major seigneurial complex that had been built up around its core, the county of Évreux. Charles was, therefore, ruling a clientele that was not only impressive, but also increasing in numbers thanks to the king's aggression against the nobility in 1356. In that year, barely six years after the execution of the count of Eu, John II, taking advantage of a banquet in Rouen castle, arrested the king of Navarre and had two of the most important Norman nobles, Count Jean de Harcourt, nephew of Godfrey, and Jean Malet, lord of Graville, summarily executed. After this veritable coup d'état, the majority of the nobility of Lower Normandy joined the party of the House of Navarre, led by the Charles's brother, Philip, and Godfrey de Harcourt, eager to avenge his nephew's death. In a letter to Edward III, written soon after the murder of Charles of Spain, Charles of Navarre wrote that 'all the nobles are now with me until death',[28] a view that if overstated in early 1354 was perhaps not so in 1356.

Beneath and beyond the complexities of the relationship between the crown and the nobility lay deeper, fundamental motives that influenced and finally decided the political choices made by noble individuals. Looking for these at the time of the Normandy stage of the Crécy campaign, the decisive factors and the nobility's consequent attitudes cannot be rationalised by focusing solely on the confrontation between the monarchies of France and England. The reason for this is that the risks at stake, which remain invisible at the level of the kingdom, only become discernible and influential when we look closer at the local and domestic political level. When Jean IV de Harcourt remained faithful to the Valois king and was killed at the battle of Crécy, his younger brother carried off at least part of the Harcourt clientele to the opposing party. And the events in Rouen castle in 1356, when Jean V de Harcourt was put to death and his younger brothers Louis and Guillaume were imprisoned, clearly showed that the lineage as a whole was tempted to stand against the Valois. That discontent and opposition might have remained obscure if a parallel conflict between the houses of Harcourt and Bertran had not come to light. What was at stake at this humbler, though essential, level was the leadership of local noble society and the power and influence that went with it. To defeat the English invasion of 1346 and with it Godfrey of Harcourt, Philip VI appointed Bertran de Bricquebec to defend the coastline of the Cotentin peninsula, in which were located both the Harcourt and the Bertran estates. This suited Bertran de Bricquebec, because he had a personal interest in bettering his local rival.

As well as the management of seigneurial interests and social pre-eminence within the local elite, kinship played a major part in the global strategy of the nobility. Behind the Harcourt–Bertran conflict was a private war of some decades standing between the Houses of Harcourt and Tancarville. Bertran's grandmother was the daughter of Alix de Tancarville, and he had consequently

---

[28] 'Tous les nobles de Normandie sont passés ovesque moi à mort et à vie': *Froissart*, ed. Lettenhove, lviii, p. 356. Cf. Autrand, *Charles V,* pp. 107–8.

inherited and maintained an animosity towards the Harcourt. Equally conspicuous as a conflict of kinship was the Harcourt–Valois confrontation. Before
ordering the execution of the count of Harcourt in 1356, the French king bitterly
reproached the count by saying: 'you belong to the lineage of the count of
Guines'.[29] This reminder of the count's kinship to the count of Eu, the constable
of France, also executed six years before, demonstrates only too well the degree
to which kinship was an inseparable part of the complexities of politics. This
rivalry within the duchy exemplifies how local and 'national' interests were
inexorably entwined, and how, finally, local domestic interests became a
compelling factor in determining the political decisions taken by the nobility.

The revival of Norman identity at the beginning of the fourteenth century coin-
cides with the integration of the duchy into the kingdom of France. At the time
of the Crécy campaign its nobility were loyal to the king, this fidelity being
demonstrated by the fact that many members of the high Norman aristocracy
fought and died on the battlefield of Crécy. Thus the explanation for Edward's
early success in Normandy in 1346 should not be attributed to any failure of
commitment by the Norman nobility, but rather to a lack of support for the
duchy from central government and to strategic mistakes by Philip VI and his
entourage. The rebellion of some members of the Norman aristocracy, notably
Godfrey de Harcourt, during the first decades of the Hundred Years War
occurred during a period of dynastic crisis for the monarchy. However, this
dissension by some among the Norman nobility reflects only the competitive
dynamics of politics, which involved constant negotiation and the struggle for
power. Because of the weakness of the state, royal government at 'the centre'
had no choice but to collaborate with the local elite when attempting to enforce
its authority within the province. At the same time, the nobility was clinging to
its feudal liberties, yet, in order to maintain their social pre-eminence, seeking
influence and recognition in the emerging state.[30]

At the time of Crécy, nationhood was in the process of forming, and consequently the battle was not what we would now regard as a confrontation between
two 'nations'. While it is clear that the future of the two kingdoms was at stake,
uppermost in the minds of those Norman nobles who entered the battlefield was
perhaps their feudal responsibilities and the power play of domestic politics in
Normandy.

---

[29] Autrand, *Charles V,* p. 178.
[30] P.S. Lewis, 'The centre, the periphery and the problem of power distribution in fifteenth-century France', *The Crown and Local Communities in England and France in the Fifteenth Century* (London, 1981), pp. 33–50; G.E. Aylmer, 'Centre et périphérie: définition des
élites du pouvoir', *Les élites du pouvoir et la construction de l'État en Europe*, ed. W.
Reinhard (Paris, 1996), pp. 77–102.

7

Vassals, Allies and Mercenaries:
the French Army before and after 1346

BERTRAND SCHNERB

The celebration of our great defeats is one of the oldest traditions in French historiography. And the battle of Crécy – as well as those of Poitiers and Agincourt – is one of the disasters that is deeply etched on our national memory. For a long time, French scholars have tried to explain this sad event. All too often they have contrasted the high quality of English military organisation with the disorder of a French 'feudal army', and in explaining the outcome of the battle have given precedence to political and social considerations over tactical and purely military ones. Typical of this is the following description from Lavisse and Rambaud's classic work, *Histoire générale*:[1]

> [At the time of Crécy] the military burden of war was entirely supported by an arrogant and romantic nobility, scorning the 'piétaille' – that is to say infantry – ignoring tactics, fighting just like in tournaments, unable to use scouts or to stop when marching. This nobility was ready for defeat.

While being suffused with historical hindsight, this sentence also seems to over-look the fact that the English nobility of the fourteenth century was no less arro-gant and romantic than its French counterpart. So, what kind of army did the French have at the battle of Crécy, and how was it organised? And what changes in French military structures and mentality were brought about by the battle? Let us look first at how the French troops were recruited.

Philip VI's army has frequently been described as being 'feudal', meaning that the king's vassals were the nucleus of his army. The military feudal system was indeed one of the bases of French military organisation, because, by virtue of their feudal obligations, vassals were obliged to serve, customarily for forty days, in the royal army at their own cost. But by the end of the thirteenth century, the king of France often paid for the 'service d'ost', that is to say 'feudal mili-tary service', and from the beginning of the fourteenth century there existed a special financial administration to collect money and use it for the prosecution

---

[1] '[Au moment de la bataille de Crécy] tout le poids de la guerre retombe sur une noblesse prétentieuse, romanesque, méprisant la "piétaille", c'est-à-dire l'infanterie, répugnant à toute tactique. Elle combat à la guerre comme en champs clos; elle ne sait ni s'éclairer, ni s'arrêter. Elle est marquée pour la défaite.' E. Lavisse and A. Rambaud, ed., *Histoire générale*, 12 vols (Paris, 1893–1901), iii, pp. 76–7.

of the king's war.[2] This service involved the nobility of the whole kingdom. When the king of France thought it necessary, he convoked or summoned all his 'vassaux' and 'arrière vassaux' (vassals of his vassals). This summons concerned not only the minor landlords of the royal 'domaine', who held their fiefs directly from the king, but all other noble tenants as well. When the king issued a 'mandement de gens de guerre', a 'call to arms', territorial princes such as the duke of Burgundy, the count of Flanders, the count of Alençon and the count of Blois were obliged to come in person, bringing their own feudal contingents with them.

Moreover, in cases of the greatest danger, the king could summon the 'arrière ban', commanding 'all men, noble or not, between the age of eighteen and the age of sixty, able to take arms and to fight, on horseback or on foot' to defend the kingdom and the crown. With the *arrière ban* system, military obligation extended to everybody. Urban communities sent their militias, and rural communities sent carriages and carters. However, a few territorial principalities – the duchy of Brittany, the county of Flanders and, of course, the duchy of Guyenne, held by the king of England – were exempt from the *arrière ban*.[3]

Theoretically, the combination of these two systems, the 'feudal ban' and the *arrière ban*, should have been very efficient. With the feudal contingents alone, the king of France could gather a great army, stronger than any other western army of the time, while the *arrière ban* would provide him with numerous infantry and carriage transport. But, in practice, mobilisation was neither so easy nor so efficient. The feudal army was always assembled slowly and with great difficulty. It was, of course, straightforward enough to obtain the service of troops who were resident close to the area coming under direct enemy attack; but, by contrast, troops raised in distant provinces, far removed from an immediate threat, would be slow to arrive for a battle, frequently doing so after the dust of combat had settled. Furthermore, French commanders awaiting the arrival of contingents could not predict how large they would be, since many of the king's vassals and *arrière vassaux* did not obey when they were summoned, despite the fact that royal bailiffs and other justice officers could impose fines or even confiscate their fiefs to punish their disobedience. Needless to say, this uncertainty made military planning either difficult or impossible, and severely hampered rapid reaction to an attack. An additional limitation of what in theory was an efficient system of military recruitment was the poor quality of the common infantry provided by urban communities in response to the proclamation of the *arrière ban*. Ill-trained and quickly scared on the battlefield, they were an unreliable part of the army.

As a system of military recruitment, feudal organisation may not have been wholly inefficient; but its unpredictable, deceptive character meant that it could not be relied upon by the French high command, and as a consequence it was necessary to find other ways to recruit troops of high quality. One of these was

2   B. Schnerb, 'De l'armée féodale à l'armée permanente', *Le miracle capétien*, ed. S. Rials (Paris, 1987), pp. 123–32.
3   P. Contamine, *Guerre, état et société à la fin du Moyen Age. Études sur les armées des rois de France, 1337–1494* (Paris and Den Haag, 1972), pp. 26–55.

the recruitment of volunteers by contract – men who were not bound to the king by ties of feudal obligation.[4] Military contracts appeared early in France. Documentary evidence of such agreements can be found in Burgundian records from the end of the thirteenth century. In 1299, for example, Robert II, duke of Burgundy, on behalf of the French king, Philip IV, engaged Geoffroy d'Osselle, a Burgundian knight from the county of Burgundy. In return for 600 livres, this nobleman was contracted to serve for a period of 24 weeks with 20 men-at-arms under his command. The contract, known as a 'lettre de convenances', listed all the conditions of service, and various points concerning the reimbursement of the costs of war, prisoners, ransoms, etc.[5]

Other Burgundian documents, dating from 1336, ten years before the battle of Crécy, show how common this kind of contract was. At this time, Odo IV, duke of Burgundy, engaged many knights to make war against the rebellious nobility of his county of Burgundy. For example, Guillaume d'Antigny, lord of Sainte-Croix, promised to serve the duke for one year with 40 men-at-arms. According to this agreement, d'Antigny had to post garrisons in various towns and to open his own castles for ducal troops. In return, the duke paid him 4,000 livres. At the same time, three lords from Beaujolais – Edouard, lord of Beaujeu, Guillaume de Molon and Mitier de Laye – were also engaged by contract. They promised to serve for one year with 100 men-at-arms (50 under the command of the lord of Beaujeu, 25 under Guillaume de Molon, and 25 under Mitier de Laye). The lord of Beaujeu received 1,500 livres, Guillaume and Mitier 600 livres each. Moreover, the duke had to pay daily wages for the service of these three knights and promised to reimburse their losses of horses and other things.[6]

In the same way as the duke of Burgundy, the king of France also engaged lords, knights, captains and other men-at-arms by contract. These contracts were called 'lettres de retenue'. In a military contract drawn up in July 1339, Jean de Marigny, bishop of Beauvais, royal lieutenant in Languedoc, on behalf of King Philip VI, engaged the count of Foix, with 300 men-at-arms and 1,800 infantrymen. In the same year, this bishop also engaged Pierre de La Palu, lord of Varambon, a knight from Savoy, with 330 men-at-arms and 300 sergeants.[7] Frequently, these noble volunteers were foreigners. The accounts of the royal treasurers of war show that, at the time of Crécy, the French armies had among their ranks many noblemen from Savoy, from Dauphiné (which at this time did not belong to the royal family) and even from northern Italy.[8]

Contracts were also used for the recruitment of foreign mercenaries. Such troops had been engaged by French kings since at least the end of the twelfth century.[9] In the fourteenth century, mercenaries were recruited for their military speciality. They served the king in large units under the command of their own

---

4 Contamine, *Guerre, état et société*, pp. 55ff.
5 Dijon, Arch. dép. Côte-d'Or, B11 721.
6 Dijon, Arch. dép. Côte-d'Or, B11 721.
7 Contamine, *Guerre, état et société*, p. 58.
8 Paris, Bibliothèque nationale de France, Nouv. acq. fr. 9241, fos 102ff.
9 P. Contamine, 'L'armée de Philippe Auguste', *La France de Philippe Auguste. Le temps des mutations.* Actes du colloque du CNRS (Paris, 29 sept.–4 oct. 1980), ed. R.-H. Bautier (Paris, 1982), pp. 577–93 (at pp. 586–7).

captains. The famous Genoese crossbowmen who fought at Crécy were soldiers of good reputation and were recruited because there were very few bowmen and crossbowmen in France.

Another part of the French forces was provided by allied princes, who were under French influence or bound to the royal family by marriage or other family links. We know that in the 1340s King Philip could secure the help of, among others, the king of Bohemia, the duke of Lorraine, the prince-bishop of Liège, the count of Savoy, the count of Saarbrücken, the count of Namur and the count of Geneva. These princes were very active supporters of the French monarchy. In 1332, for example, the king of Bohemia promised to help the king of France against his enemy, providing him with 500 men-at-arms; and this he actually did on three occasions – in 1339, 1340 and 1346.[10]

What, therefore, can be said of the French army at the beginning of the Crécy campaign? First, it should be pointed out that the feudal system of recruitment had worked quite well during the years 1339–46, providing Philip VI with a large army. During this period, the royal summons extended over a huge area, and it would seem that the vassals of the king obeyed with good will. According to the accounts of the treasurers of war, in September 1340 Philip VI was able to mobilise 28,000 men-at-arms for the defence of his whole kingdom. Of these men, 20,000 came from the different provinces of the kingdom (Brittany and Guyenne excepted) and 8,000 were foreigners (28.5 per cent).[11] In this year, 1340, for example, during the campaign in Flanders, the duke of Burgundy, who was also count of Artois, had under his command 1,683 men-at-arms, comprising 1,188 from the duchy and county of Burgundy, and 495 from the counties of Artois and Boulogne.[12] At the same time (September 1340), 16,700 foot soldiers were in the king's service, of whom about 2,000 (12 per cent) were crossbowmen.[13] It should be emphasised, however, that this strength was not concentrated in a single place, but was distributed across four areas, the largest number of men being in Flanders, the remainder in Normandy, Poitou and the Languedoc.

Unfortunately, the total strength of the French army on the battlefield of Crécy is unknown because the financial accounts are lost. However, we know that contingents came from Flanders, Picardy, Normandy, Paris, northern Burgundy and the valley of the River Loire. It seems, therefore, that at this time the military feudal system, recruitment by contract and the *arrière ban* were very efficient, especially in the northern half of the kingdom. During the Crécy campaign, Philip VI convoked the *arrière ban* and many cities and towns responded, providing his army with strong contingents of infantry. At the same time, the allied princes provided troops of high quality. At Crécy we know that the king of Bohemia and his son, Charles, the king of Germany, the duke of

10 P. Contamine, 'Politique, culture et sentiment dans l'Occident de la fin du Moyen Âge: Jean l'Aveugle et la royauté française' and A. Atten, 'Die Luxemburger in der Schlacht von Crécy', *Johann der Blinde, Graf von Luxemburg, König von Böhmen 1296–1346*, ed. M. Pauly (Luxembourg, 1997), pp. 343–61, 567–96.
11 Contamine, *Guerre, état et société*, p. 70.
12 Paris, Bibliothèque nationale de France, Nouv. acq. fr. 9239, fos 201–10.
13 Contamine, *Guerre, état et société*, p. 70.

Lorraine, the count of Namur, the count of Salm and the count of Saarbrücken were present with large contingents under their command. The count of Savoy and his brother, Louis of Savoy, with at least 500 men-at-arms, were marching to join the king of France, but arrived the day after the battle.[14]

A contingent of Genoese crossbowmen was also present on the field, reportedly under the command of two captains, Carlo Grimaldi and Antonio Doria. Unfortunately, there are no surviving accounts to provide the exact number of these mercenary troops; and it seems that the number of French foot soldiers was greatly exaggerated by chroniclers. For example, according to Jean Froissart, there were 20,000 men-at-arms, 60,000 common foot soldiers and 15,000 to 20,000 Genoese crossbowmen on the field. According to Richard Wynkeley the French force consisted of 12,000 men-at-arms, 60,000 foot soldiers and 6,000 Genoese crossbowmen, while Giovanni Villani also estimated that the Genoese mercenaries were 6,000 strong.[15] If we compare these figures with information available in the accounts of the treasurers of war for 1340, we find that the French manpower numbers suggested by the chroniclers are clearly unacceptable. In the summer of 1340, according to the records, the part of the French army campaigning in Flanders or garrisoned in towns and castles in the area included 22,500 men-at-arms, 2,500 foot sergeants and only 200 crossbowmen. At this time, for the defence of the whole kingdom, there were about 12,700 foot soldiers and 2,000 crossbowmen.[16] Even if we accept that the contingent of crossbowmen was greatly reinforced in 1346 – and there is no proof that it was – it would seem improbable that the king of France could gather, for the Crécy campaign alone, between three and ten times more crossbowmen than the number he had assembled throughout his whole kingdom in 1340. Moreover, there must be some doubt whether the city of Genoa, or even the whole of northern Italy, would have been able to provide so large a contingent of mercenaries and send it abroad.

In conclusion, it is clear that the men-at-arms were the most potent and most important part of the French army at Crécy; and it is doubtful that 6,000 crossbowmen were actually present on the battlefield on the French side.

How was the French army organised on the battlefield of Crécy? The structure of command reflected the prevailing social and military conceptions of war. As the 'natural' leader of the nobility, and of the people of his kingdom, the king was at the head of the army, and as such, had to be personally present on the field.[17] But, of course, he was not alone. His military counsellors were about him. First, there were his relations, the 'princes of the royal blood'. At Crécy, Philip VI was attended by his brother, Charles, count of Alençon, his nephew, Louis, count of Blois, and his cousin, Louis of Nevers, count of Flanders. Also present, and also members of the French royal family through marriage, were

---

[14] *Froissart*, ed. Luce, iii, pp. xlviii–lxiii and 171ff.; A. Atten, 'Die Luxemburger in der Schlacht von Crécy', *Johann der Blinde*, ed. Pauly, pp. 567–96.

[15] Atten, 'Die Luxemburger', p. 577 ; *Froissart*, ed. Luce, iii, p. 175.

[16] See nn. 11 and 13 above.

[17] Jean Barbey, *Etre roi* (Paris, 1992), pp. 229–34.

John of Luxembourg, king of Bohemia,[18] and his son, Charles, king of Germany, later to become Emperor Charles IV. And, of course, in war the king could seek the advice of other councillors. Among them were the great officers of the crown who held military offices – the constable, the marshals, and the 'maître des arbalétriers' (master of crossbowmen). Of these, it seems that the constable of France was not present at Crécy, but the two marshals and the master of crossbowmen were.[19] The marshals of France were perhaps Charles of Montmorency and Robert of Wavrin, lord of Saint-Venant.[20] The master of crossbowmen was perhaps le Galois de la Baume, a nobleman of Savoy, who already held this office in 1338–40.[21]

During the campaign, the princes and great lords, whether vassals or allies, along with the great military officers of the crown, were leaders of large units called 'batailles'.[22] In 1340, the leading commanders of Philip VI's army were the king himself; his son John, duke of Normandy; Raoul, count of Eu, constable of France; the king of Bohemia; the duke of Brittany; the prince-bishop of Liège; the count of Savoy; the count of Flanders; the count of Armagnac; the count of Foix; the count of Alençon; the duke of Burgundy; the king of Navarre; both of the marshals of France, Robert Bertran, lord of Bricquebec, and Mahieu of Trie, lord of Araines; and le Galois de La Baume, master of crossbowmen. Thus, there were 15 'batailles', and these great units were themselves divided into 'bannières' (banners) and companies, under the command of knights banneret and other captains.[23]

This tactical organisation still existed in 1346, and chroniclers who describe the battle of Crécy mention the 'batailles' of the king of Bohemia (left wing); Charles of Luxembourg (right wing); the Genoese crossbowmen (first line); the count of Alençon, the duke of Lorraine, the count of Blois, the count of Harcourt and the count of Flanders (second line); the king of France, the lord of Beaujeu, and the marshals (rearguard).[24]

It is very hard to re-enact a battle like Crécy, or to reconstruct it. Neverthe-less, what appears to have happened is that the king of France and his military councillors, informed by their scouts that the English army held a strong posi-tion, decided to delay the attack until the following day. The French troops were tired after a long march (19 km), and were in need of rest. Moreover it was necessary to rally the whole army in order to attack with the greatest possible

---

[18] Bonne of Luxembourg, King John's daughter, was married to John, duke of Normandy, son of Philip VI, and later King John II.

[19] *Froissart*, ed. Luce, iii, pp. 171ff.

[20] *Dictionnaire des maréchaux de France du Moyen Age à nos jours* (Paris, 1988), pp. 310–11 and 451.

[21] Contamine, *Guerre, état et société*, pp. 70 and 159–60.

[22] J.-F. Verbruggen, 'La tactique de la chevalerie française de 1340 à 1415', *Publications de l'Université de l'État à Elisabethville*, i (July 1961), pp. 39–48; Ph. Contamine, 'Batailles, bannières et compagnies: aspects de l'organisation militaire française pendant la première partie de la guerre de Cent ans', *Actes du colloque international de Cocherel. Les cahiers vernonnais*, iv (1964), pp. 19–32.

[23] Contamine, *Guerre, état et société*, p. 79.

[24] A. Atten, 'Die Luxemburger in der Schlacht von Crécy', *Johann der Blinde*, ed. Pauly, p. 577 and map, p. 575.

strength, and we know, for example, that at this time the contingent of the count
of Savoy was still marching to join the king. However, the fight began in unfavourable circumstances for the French: firstly, because of the indiscipline of
those men-at-arms who disobeyed the marshals' orders to stop; and secondly,
because King Philip and his noblemen felt such hatred for the English that they
could not delay the attack. 'When King Philip came to the place where the
English stood and saw them, his blood was up. He hated them so much that he
could not renounce to fight. He said to his marshals, "Send our Genoese
crossbowmen ahead and let's begin the battle, in the name of God and of my
lord saint Denis!" '[25] The French attack began with improvisation, and ended in
the greatest confusion. The combination of indiscipline and imprudence led the
French army to defeat. A French chronicler wrote: 'Par hastiveté et desarroy
furent les François desconfis.'[26] In this defeat, the tactical circumstances were
more important than any weaknesses in military organisation.

In what respects did the battle of Crécy bring about changes in French military organisation and mentality? According to the records, very few changes
were made to the French military system until the reign of Charles V. After
Crécy, the military feudal system, the recruitment of volunteers, the help of
allied princes, and the engagement of mercenaries all continued. The Genoese
crossbowmen, for example, maintained their good reputation, in spite of their
poor performance in 1346. The accounts of the treasurers of war show that
Genoese crossbowmen were still serving in French armies during the second
half of the fourteenth century and the first half of the fifteenth. In the final analysis, they do not seem to have been held responsible for the defeat. In contrast,
the common troops provided by the cities and towns, who had proved wholly
ineffective on the battlefield, were no longer summoned in large numbers. In the
following years, the king preferred to ask the towns to provide small contingents
of well-equipped and well-trained sergeants and crossbowmen, rather than large
numbers of infantry who were ill-disciplined and useless in a fight against professional soldiers.[27]

Important changes did, however, appear in tactics. As we know, at Crécy,
French mounted troops were defeated by archers and men-at-arms fighting on
foot. After this battle, the main troops of the French army fought on foot.
Mounted troops were only used to attack the rear or the flanks of the enemy, as
at Poitiers, West Roosebeke and Agincourt.[28] Furthermore, French captains tried
to increase the number of archers and crossbowmen in their armies, in order to

---

[25] 'Quant li rois Phelippes vint jusques sus la place où li Englès estoient priès de là arresté et
ordonné, et il les vei, se li mua li sans, car trop les haioit. Et ne se fust à ce donc nullement
refrenés ne astrains d'yaus combatre, et dist à ses mareschaus: "Faites passer nos Genevois
devant et commencier la bataille, ou nom de Dieu et de monsigneur saint Denis!" ' *Froissart*,
ed. Luce, iii, p. 175.
[26] 'Hastiness and disorder were the causes of French defeat.' *Chronique des quatre premiers
Valois*, p. 16.
[27] P. Contamine, *Histoire militaire de la France*, vol. I: *Des origines à 1715* (Paris, 1992), p.
135.
[28] Verbruggen, 'La tactique de la chevalerie française de 1340 à 1415', pp. 39–48.

challenge English archery.[29] But, by contrast, the noble mentality did not change at this time. After the battle of Crécy, the heroic attitude of French and allied knights and squires, who preferred to die than to take flight (exemplified by the sacrifice of John the Blind, king of Bohemia) was magnified. Indeed, those who took flight were regarded as guilty of a dishonourable deed. In 1351, King John II, in creating the 'ordre de l'Étoile' (the Order of the Star) in response to the creation of the Order of the Garter by Edward III, forbade the members of his new order to take flight, or even retreat, during battle. It was better for them to be killed or captured in action, than to escape and lose their honour. The statutes of the 'Order of the Star' were a pure expression of chivalric mentality. The capture of the French king during the battle of Poitiers, ten years after Crécy, was a direct consequence of his fidelity to these statutes.[30]

Crécy was a great defeat, but did not serve as a lesson. French leaders did not understand at that time what was wrong with their chosen tactics. Without doubt, they considered the battle of Crécy to have been an accident. But, this event, followed immediately by the siege and fall of Calais, was the beginning of profound troubles for the French monarchy. The military failure was followed by other difficulties: monetary and financial problems, political dissension, the weakening of royal authority, and – not least – the Black Death. After 1348, French military power was considerably diminished by comparison with what it had been during the 1339–46 period. Troops were irregularly paid and ill-controlled, recruitment became more difficult and indiscipline increased. A great reform of institutions, tactics and even military mentality would be necessary – a task that would be carried out by King Charles V.[31]

---

[29] For the example of Burgundian captains, see B. Schnerb, *Bulgnéville (1431)* (Paris, 1993), p. 62.

[30] *Froissart*, ed. Luce, iv, pp. 126–7; Y. Renouard, 'L'ordre de la Jarretière et l'ordre de l'Étoile. Étude sur la genèse des ordres laïcs de chevalerie et sur le développement progressif de leur caractère national', *Le Moyen Age*, iii–iv (1949), pp. 281–300; D'A.J.D. Boulton, *The Knights of the Crown. The Monarchical Orders of Knighthood in Later Medieval Europe, 1325–1520* (Woodbridge, 1987), chapter 5.

[31] F. Autrand, *Charles V* (Paris, 1994), pp. 568–612.

8

The Battle of Crécy:
A Hard Blow for the Monarchy of France

FRANÇOISE AUTRAND

The 'déconfiture de Crécy', which opens a series of three black years – Crécy in 1346, Calais in 1347 and the Black Death of 1348 – holds bitter memories for the French. The disaster of the following year, the fall of Calais, at least had its heroes – the burghers of Calais. Very early on, even before the 'History of France' of the Third Republic, and the sculptures of Rodin, Eustache de Saint Pierre and his five companions had a place of honour in the national memory. From the Ancien Régime, a school book, *l'Instruction sur l'histoire de France*, by Le Ragois,[1] devoted more than a quarter of the chapter on Philip VI to the six burghers. 'Renown will never forget the name of Eustache de Saint Pierre, the most noble burgher of that time, and his heroic generosity in saving his fellow citizens.'[2] Nothing like this happened at Crécy, which left only the odious images of knights charging in disorder to gain the first place and the greatest share of glory and spoils, trampling on the Genoese crossbowmen whose wet bowstrings could no longer shoot their deadly quarrels; and, finally, the pitiful image of King Philip VI of Valois, fleeing into the pitch-black night to the closed doors of the 'château de La Broye', crying out: 'Ouvrés, ouvrés, chastelain! C'est l'infortunés rois de France'.[3]

The moral shock

If Crécy remains such an unfortunate memory, it is because at the time France failed to face up to the defeat. Crécy was neither the first nor the last military disaster of the fourteenth and fifteenth centuries, but no other caused such a moral shock.

One has only to read the chronicles of the time, and the pages devoted to the 'déconfitures',[4] whether they are written in French or in Latin, by a clerk or a

---

[1] Abbé Cl. Le Ragois, *Instruction sur l'histoire de France et sur l'histoire romaine*, 1st edn (Paris, 1687). The twenty-first edition had been re-edited eighteen times before 1877.
[2] The 'Bourgeois de Calais', having passed into legend, made their grand re-entry into history thanks to an article by J.-M. Mœglin: 'Édouard III et les six bourgeois de Calais', *Revue historique*, ccxcii (1994), pp. 229–67.
[3] *Froissart*, ed. Luce, iii, p. 185.
[4] F. Autrand, 'La déconfiture. La bataille de Poitiers (1356) à travers quelques textes

monk, in Normandy or in Flanders, or even in Paris, whether they are recounting events at Courtrai, Crécy, Poitiers, Nicopolis or Agincourt, their story is constructed according to the same scheme. There were worrying omens, a flock of crows or a mouse running under the tent. On the eve of the fatal day, the future victor made peace offerings, which were imprudently rejected. At the council, consisting of the wise and the foolhardy, it was the latter's bad advice that was followed. The victors had prepared with seriousness of purpose and humility, while the preparations of the vanquished had been undertaken light-heartedly and with bravado. In the engagement, the French knights threw themselves into the attack in a disorderly fashion, jostling with the men on foot. They broke up against the line of English archers. On the evening of the battle there was the glorious return of the victor and the roll call of the dead, and the story finishes with an exposition explaining the unexpected but not undeserved defeat of the powerful beaten army by reference to the intervention of fortune and providence. From one chronicle to another, from one defeat to another, the same words reappear: 'the knights fell *à tas*' without having been able to strike a single blow. 'La fleur de chevalerie a chu'. God punished the proud and raised the humble: 'deposuit potentes de sede et exaltavit humiles'.

Nevertheless, each account ends with a note of hope or consolation for the defeated, a note of honour for their wretched courage! But Crécy was an exception, for there was not a word of excuse for the vanquished king: 'La fu le roy Philippe trop hastif et ne voult croire conseil',[5] the severity of this judgement deriving from his leaving the battlefield before the fighting was over. Indeed, the chroniclers are unanimous in depicting this departure not as a strategic retreat, but as a shameful flight: 'rex fuga lapsus evasit',[6] 'turpiter campum deserens'.[7] Conscious of this, Philip entered Paris 'indutus confusione',[8] 'ultra modum tristis et dolens',[9] bringing shame and confusion to his kingdom. All the chroniclers are agreed in their appreciation of the consequences of the defeat, whether it be the author of the *Grandes chroniques de France*, who was close to the king and wrote for him, or Froissart the Hainaulter, who in the name of Prouesse declared his neutrality. 'Toute France ot confusion telle qu'elle n'avoit onques mais par le roy d'Angleterre souffert don't il soit memoire à present,' writes the former,[10] while in the latter, Froissart deplores the 'déconfiture' and

---

français des XIV° et XV° siècles', in P. Contamine, Ch. Giry-Deloison and M.H. Keen, *Guerre et société en France, en Angleterre et en Bourgogne XIV°–XV° siècle* (Lille, 1991), pp. 93–121.

5 *Chronique des quatre premiers Valois*, p. 16. The same rebuke is evident in the chronicle of Gilles de Muisit: Philip VI does not listen to wise counsel but issues a cry to arms 'motu proprio'. He carries along his faithful subjects by shouting 'Qui tantum me diligit me sequatur!', that is to say 'Qui m'aime me suive!': *Gilles le Muisit*, pp. 161–2. The abbot of Tournai regards this as the explanation of the disaster, which came about 'casu fortuito ut ex improviso, et quia rex Franchie consilio sibi dato non acquievit', *ibid.*, p. 163.

6 *Chronique de Richard Lescot religieux de Saint-Denis (1328–1344) suivi de la continuation de cette chronique (1344–1364)*, ed. J. Lemoine (Paris, 1896), p. 72.

7 *Chronographia*, p. 233.

8 *Chronique de Richard Lescot*, p. 73.

9 *Chronographia*, p. 234.

10 *Grandes chroniques*, ix, p. 283.

loss of so many valiant men 'par lesquelz li royaumes de France fut moult depuis afoiblis d'onneur, de puissance et de conseil'.[11]

Among those who fell in the battle, the fine figure of the king of Bohemia stands out conspicuously, but none of his glory reflected on the camp of the French. His son, Charles, then king of the Romans and future Emperor Charles IV, astutely understood how to turn the situation to his advantage. He came to the battle, but as Froissart, who did not much like the Germans, puts it, 'quant il vei que la cause aloit mal pour yaus, il s'en parti'.[12] And one variant adds, 'fist la voller l'aigle d'Alemaigne car il s'en parti'.[13] All in all, Charles had taken a reasonable stand, and even wiser was his decision to erect a monument to the dead of Crécy, which was original enough for the *Grandes chroniques de France* to mention it: 'En ce meismes temps le roy de Boesme fu porté a Lucembourg et yleques meismes fu noblement enseveli. Et oultre, les armes ou escuz de L chevaliers esleuz qui aveques li moururent a Crécy, sont environ sa sepulture noblement et autentiquement peintes.'[14] Indeed, the political genius of Charles IV is demonstrated by his choice of burial place for his father. To preserve both the remains and the glory of the king of Bohemia, he chose the Benedictine abbey of Notre Dame in the capital of the county of Luxembourg, the heartland of the patrimonial lands of the dynasty.[15]

Even though he had spent a great part of his career in the service of the king of France – at some expense to himself – and was linked to the French throne by several marriage alliances, the 'good king of Bohemia' had remained his own man and a symbol of international chivalry.[16] It is hardly a paradox, therefore, that the eldest son of Edward III, who had taken part in the battle, should have wanted something for himself from this chivalric king who had fallen on the opposing side. And so henceforth the dead king's heraldic device, *Ich Dien*, was borne by the Princes of Wales.

In France, neither Philip VI, nor later his son King John, were able to take advantage of the prestige and reputation of John of Luxembourg. On the contrary, in the political crisis of the years 1355–60, the king of Bohemia became an emblematic figure for the opposition to the French monarchy. After Crécy, the poet, Guillaume de Machaut, who had been the king of Bohemia's secretary, entered the service of the king's daughter, Bonne de Luxembourg. She

---

11 *Froissart*, ed. Luce, iii, p. 186. See also, 'l'Ancien poème sur la bataille de Crécy écrit par un familier de Jean de Hainaut, seigneur de Beaumont', J.A.B. Buchon, *Collection de Chroniques nationales françaises* . . ., xiv (Paris, 1826), pp. 279–300.

12 *Froissart*, ed. Luce, iii, p. 179.

13 *Froissart*, ed. Luce, iii, p. 422.

14 *Grandes chroniques*, ix, p. 287.

15 Around the king's tomb were sculptured figures representing the fifty companions who fell with him at Crécy: M. Margue, ' "Fecit Carolus ducere patrem suum in patriam suam". Die Überlieferung zu Bestattung und Gran Johans des Blinden', *Grabmäler der Luxemburger. Image und Memoria eines Kaiserhauses*, ed. M.V. Schwarz (Luxembourg, 1997), pp. 79–96; and M. Margue, ' "Regum de stirpe". Le prince et son image: Donations, fondations et sépultures des Luxembourg dans leurs terres d'origine (première moitié du XIV° siècle)', *King John of Luxembourg (1296–1346) and the Art of his Era*, ed. K. Benešovská (Prague, 1998), pp. 105–6.

16 R. Cazelles, *Jean l'Aveugle, comte de Luxembourg et roi de Bohême* (Bourges, 1947).

was the wife of the duke of Normandy, and, after her death, Machaut maintained a close relationship with her family. But in this divided court, he was on the side of the young king of Navarre, before beginning to write for the king of France's sons – the dauphin, Charles, the duke of Normandy, and John duke of Berry. In *Le Confort d'ami*, which Machaut wrote in 1357, the king of Bohemia is portrayed as a model for the other princes.[17] The 'good king of Bohemia' was generous; indeed, he was something of a spendthrift.[18] He would grant lands to those who had been loyal to him, and felt no shame in abandoning it to victors:

> Et terre aussi qu'est despendue
> Vaut trop mieux que terre perdue.[19]

Furthermore, he sought only the love of his subjects, which alone brings victory and power. For, as the well-known proverb says, 'il n'est pas sire en son pays, qui de ses hommes est hai'.[20] It is not difficult to recognise in this idealised figure, an anti-portrait of the king of France – Jean le Bon. The king of Bohemia used to give generously,[21] while by contrast the king of France burdened his subjects with taxes, with no regard for 'leur droit et franchise';[22] the king of Bohemia sought advice from well-informed people, while the king of France, instead of respecting the social order, was surrounded by irresponsible favourites and encouraged upstarts; the king of Bohemia went from victory to victory while the king of France was routed 'tout au milieu de son pays';[23] John of Luxembourg, if he ever suffered a military reverse, never treated with the enemy, while the king of France was always ready to consent to a shameful peace. The king of Bohemia raised his son to the dignity of emperor,[24] while John le Bon was only able to disinherit his son and son-in-law, and give up their lands to the English. We have to wait another generation, for the sons of John le Bon and Bonne de Luxembourg, before the princes of the 'fleur de lys' can rekindle the glory of their grandfather, the king of Bohemia.

The disastrous psychological effect produced by the flight of the king was not forgotten during the years that followed Crécy; indeed, it is not impossible that it had some influence on the foundation of the 'Order of the Star'.[25] In 1351, King John who had just succeeded to the throne, and wanting to draw the ranks of the

---

[17] *Le Confort d'ami, Œuvres de Guillaume de Machaut*, ed. E. Hœpffner, vol. 3 (Paris, 1921).
[18] 'De l'argent il n'avoit cure, Ni rien qu'honneur ne desiroit': *Le Confort d'ami*, v. 2950–1.
[19] Balade XXVIII, Donnez, signeurs, donnez à toutes mains . . ., *Poésies lyriques*, ed. V. Chichmaref (Paris, 1909), pp. 554–5. This ballad formed part of a series of works composed by Machaut with the intention of ridiculing the treaty concluded in London between Edward III and King John in 1359 and known by the name of 'la grande endenture'. This treaty was rejected by the three estates of the realm meeting in Paris on 25 June. Françoise Autrand, *Charles V* (Paris, 1994), pp. 364–8.
[20] *Le Confort d'ami*, v. 3216–24.
[21] *Le Confort d'ami*, v. 2923–33.
[22] *Le Confort d'ami*, v. 3821.
[23] *Le Confort d'ami*, v. 2981.
[24] *Le Confort d'ami*, v. 3075–7.
[25] L. Pannier, *La Noble Maison de Saint-Ouen et l'ordre de l'Étoile* (Paris, 1872). For the Order of the Star, see also, D'A.J.D. Boulton, *The Knights of the Crown: the Monarchical Orders of Knighthood in Later Medieval Europe, 1325–1520* (Woodbridge, 1987), chapter 5.

French chivalric community more closely around the crown, instituted the Order of the 'chevaliers de Notre-Dame de la Noble Maison', whose emblem had to be the star that guided the magi: 'Monstrant regibus astra viam.' The new Order finds its place in the series of orders of chivalry that were then appearing in western Christendom. Its statutes had what was needed, in terms of images and colour, to capture the spirit of the knights of the times, but one of the articles in the founding charter is original: 'Should anyone be so shameful in the eyes of God or Our Lady as to flee a battlefield or refuse an ordained task, he will be suspended from the Order.'[26]

This disposition was astonishing. Froissart refers to it in the chapter that he devotes to the creation of the Order, but mentions it only to show why the Order failed. He says that 'it was decided that they would never flee from a battle further than four acres, but would rather die or be taken prisoner'.[27] Then, a few lines further on, he tells of an obscure skirmish that took place not long after in Brittany between the English and the French,[28] the latter including knights of the Order of the Star: 'Guy de Nesle, sire d'Aufemont en Vermandois was left dead on the battlefield, and it was a shame because he was a valiant knight; and with him were more than ninety knights of the Order of the Star, who fell because they had sworn never to flee, for had they not taken an oath they would have fled. That is how the company of the Star dissolved.'[29]

It would not be wrong to conclude that on the battlefield of Poitiers, both King John and his bearer of the *Oriflamme*, Geoffroy de Charny (who had inspired the Order of the Star), must have remembered the oath that they had taken on the eve of the Epiphany in 1352.[30] This is why Geoffroy de Charny, 'le plus preudomme et le plus vaillant de tous les autres', fell with the *Oriflamme* in his hands, while the king was taken prisoner.

The political crisis

Following the disaster of Crécy, Philip VI did not return straight to Paris. He dared not face the mockery of the Parisians, who during the preceding month had taken up arms to prevent the demolition of shacks that were leaning against

[26] 'Et se il y aucun qui honteusement, que Diex ne Notre-Dame ne veillent, se parte de bataille, ou de besoigne ordenée, il sera souspendus de la compaigne.' *Ordonnances des roys de France de la troisième race*, vol. 2 (Paris, 1729), pp. 465–6.
[27] 'Et leur couvenoit jurer que jamais il ne fuiroient en bataille plus lonch que de quatre arpens à leur avis, ainçois morroient ou se renderoient pris': *Froissart*, ed. Luce, iv, p. 128.
[28] The battle of Mauron, 14 August 1352, for which, see J. Sumption, *The Hundred Years War*, vol. II : *Trial by Fire* (London, 1999), pp. 94–5.
[29] 'Et y demora mors sus le place messires Guis de Neelle, sires d'Aufemont en Vermendois, dont ce fu damages, car il estoit vaillans chevaliers et preus durement. Et avoecques lui demorèrent plus de quatre vingt et dix chevaliers de l'Estoille pour tant qu'ils avoient juret que jamais ne fuiroient; car si le sieremens n'euist esté, ils se fuissent retret et sauvet. Ensi se desrompi ceste noble compaignie de l'Estoille': *Froissart*, ed. Luce, iv, p. 128.
[30] P. Contamine, 'Geoffrey de Charny (début du XIV° s.–1356) "le plus preudomme et le plus vaillant de tous les autres" ', *Histoire et société. Mélanges Duby*, vol. 2 : *Le tenancier, le fidèle et le citoyen* (Aix-en-Provence, 1992), pp. 107–21.

the walls of the city and threatening its defence.[31] The military defeat had thoroughly exposed the incapacity of the government to defend the country. Artois, which was especially vulnerable, was in open revolt. To this can be added a general unease regarding taxes. With what was one to pay an army that had been torn to pieces by an adversary of such inferior numbers?[32] Facing the immediate political consequences of the defeat, clearly measures had to be taken. However, those that were taken would prove insufficient to calm the political tensions aroused by the defeat.

Political responsibility for the defeat was borne by the king's council, which for the past ten years had been controlled by the same group of men: Eudes, duke of Burgundy, the queen's brother; the Bourguignon clan; and the presidents of the *Chambre des Comptes*.[33] Very quickly, in the winter of 1346, the leadership changed. The duke of Burgundy, who was engaged in a struggle with his Artésien subjects, was dropped by the king, who supported the rebels. The Bourguignons were removed from the council. Even the king's eldest son, John, duke of Normandy, who was close to his uncle, the duke of Burgundy, had to step aside. The connection between the government and the *Chambre des Comptes* was completely dissolved.[34]

As is so often the case after a defeat, it was believed that both guilty men and saviours could be found. The guilty were those who managed the kingdom's financial affairs – taxation, the coinage and war finance. Three among them – Pierre des Essars, Martin des Essars and Jean Poilevilain – were arrested, imprisoned, tortured and finally freed without trial, though fined a considerable sum (50,000 livres for Pierre des Essars), which served to replenish royal coffers that were more empty than ever. Other measures had the same aim: the arrest of Italian usurers, their expulsion and the confiscation of their assets, with debts owed to them becoming repayable to the Treasury; and the seizure of the revenues of clergy dwelling outside the kingdom. These woeful measures, intended to satisfy public opinion, also made it possible to avoid summoning the assembly of the *États* of the kingdom, which would have demanded a role in government and in the shaping of reforms as a condition of consenting to taxation.

The saviours were three persons of distinction, who were relatively independent and experienced in the management of large estates. They were the

---

31 For the political consequences of Crécy, see R. Cazelles, *La société politique et la crise de la royauté sous Philippe de Valois* (Paris, 1958).

32 The Carmelite Jean de Venette echoes the discontent: 'Sed revera quanto plures nummi in Francia per tales extorquebantur, tanto magis dominus rex depauperabatur, et nulla prosperitas, imo omnia infortunia in regno, proh dolor! sequebantur. Officiales ditabantur princeps depauperabatu. Pecuniæ multis militibus et nobilibus, ut patriam et regnum juvarent et defensarent, contribuebantur; sed omnia ad usus inutiles ludorum, as taxillos et alios indecentes jocos contumaciter exponebantur.' *Chronique de Guillaume de Nangis et de ses continuateurs*, ed. H. Géraud, vol. 2 (Paris, 1843), p. 205.

33 Cazelles, *La société politique et la crise de la royauté sous Philippe de Valois*, pp. 173–91.

34 Cazelles, *La société politique et la crise de la royauté sous Philippe de Valois*, pp. 186–7. By contrast, the *Parlement*, which in 1345 had been granted a statute guaranteeing them a certain independence with regard to their power, found that this was reinforced in practice by co-operation. Guillois, *Recherches sur les maîtres de l'hôtel des origines à 1350* (Paris, 1909), p. 279.

abbots of three of the principal Benedictine abbeys of the kingdom, namely Saint Denis, Marmoutier and Corbie. The first task of the abbots was to introduce a clear separation of powers between the king's council and the *Chambre des Comptes*. The confusion between management and decision, administration and policy, had the worst possible consequences with respect to the removal of all controls on the royal finances, sheltering their agents from the king's justice, which was exercised through the *Parlement*.[35] Elsewhere the abbots kept a watchful eye on royal expenditure. Controlling and reducing royal expenditure was certainly necessary. But how were the coffers of the *Trésor* to be filled without taxes and loans – that is to say, without reassembling the *États* or having recourse to financiers, the usual moneylenders, who for the moment were excluded from consideration? The only solution was to extract as much revenue as possible from the royal demesne, which included the minting of coins, escheats, the salt tax (*gabelle*) and the farming out of provostships. The promises made to the *États* in 1346, namely that the salt tax would be suppressed and the provosts brought under control, were consequently a dead letter.

The measures taken during the period of the abbots' ascendancy had no future. They brought no solution to the recurring problem of royal finance, and did not provide a structure for political debate, which had been demanded in vain by the three *États*. But they allowed the storm to blow over – a storm that was not of long duration. From April 1347 the duke of Normandy, who had been kept out of the way since the previous October, made his return to the political scene. He presided over an assembly of towns in Picardy, and supervised the fortification of Amiens. It was he, moreover, who negotiated an alliance with the duke of Brabant, concluded at the beginning of June 1347.[36]

The return of the duke of Normandy coincided with the abbots' withdrawal from politics. The embezzling financiers, those indispensable money-lenders, came back into favour. Dialogue with the representative assemblies resumed. On 30 November 1347, the representatives of the three *États* met in Paris.[37] They did not mince their words: 'O powerful Lords, you should know how and by which counsel led you to war and how, being badly advised, you have lost all, and gained nothing.'[38] Of their discussions and resolutions we know nothing. Without doubt they invited the king to negotiate with the local assemblies, for in the early months of 1348 such meetings, to organise the defence of the country, took place in Paris, Normandy and Vermandois, and in the *sénéchaussées* of

---

[35] The *ordonnance* of Vivier-en-Brie, in providing the *Chambre des Comptes* with a rational organisation, had created the cutting edge of the modern state: H. Jassemin, *La Chambre des Comptes de Paris au XIV° siècle* (Paris, 1933), vol. 1, p. 703. P. Lehugeur, *Philippe le long, roi de France. Le mécanisme du gouvernement* (Paris, 1931), pp. 222–43.

[36] Cazelles, *La société politique et la crise de la royauté sous Philippe de Valois*, pp. 193–212.

[37] Cazelles, *La société politique et la crise de la royauté sous Philippe de Valois*, pp. 213–29.

[38] 'Très poissons sire, vous devés savoir comment et par quel consel vous avés vos guerres demenees et comment vous, par malvais consel, avés toudis perdu et nient ganiet'. A. Guesnon, 'Documents inédits sur l'invasion anglaise et les états au temps de Philippe VI et Jean le Bon', *Bulletin philologique et historique du CTHS* (1897), pp. 208–59, at p. 242.

Beaucaire and Toulouse. Taxes, intended for paying the local militia for a fixed number of weeks or months, were granted in exchange for reforms.

Shortly afterwards, the Black Death cut short the war, and consequently tax revenue as well. In August 1350, Philip VI died, and the duke of Normandy became King John II. In reality the new king had already been in power, together with his followers. Once the few years of grace that accompanied the new reign had passed, the old problems returned: a dynastic challenge, the threat of war and plans for peace that were worse than war. The ruling group retired within itself as a hermetically sealed royal party.[39] Attacks against the royal council; resistance to taxation; assembly of the *États*, which demanded reforms but could not be forced to consent to taxation: the situation in 1356 repeated that of 1346. On 18 September, the royal army was defeated, and this time the king did not flee, but was taken prisoner. The political crisis that followed this defeat and the king's capture was more serious and deeper than that which had followed Crécy, and it was to last until 1360. It was impossible on this occasion to avoid the fundamental problems posed by the political tensions of the time.

This defeat brought to light the fragility and instability of the dynasty. Philip VI, Philip the Fair's nephew and first cousin to the last three direct Capetians – Louis X, Philip V and Charles IV, all three sons of Philip the Fair – had close blood ties to the direct line of Hugues Capet. Yet the fact remains that his accession to the throne was felt as a change of dynasty, disturbing the equilibrium of the kingdom. In reality, the chances of the other pretenders – the young Edward III, and Philip, count of Évreux, who was marred to Louis X's daughter, Jeanne, queen of Navarre – were slim as compared with those of Philip, count of Valois. The latter was the closest nephew to Philip the Fair and a prince who at thirty-five years of age was in the prime of life. He was, moreover, 'born of the kingdom'.[40] But in lieu of a crown, Philip of Valois's rivals expected territorial compensation. Edward III's frustration was one of the origins of the Hundred Years War. The king of France's military defeats gave strength to arguments against the dynasty.

After Crécy, John, duke of Normandy, the eldest son of Philip VI, seems to have been afraid of being displaced from the succession to the throne, and the sources make it certain that he had disappeared from the court from October 1346 to April 1347.[41] Froissart reports a quarrel between the king and his son: 'There were then, between the king of France and the duke of Normandy, great

[39] Autrand, *Charles V,* p. 189.
[40] 'Nee du realme': *Scalacronica*, cited by J. Calmette, *L'élaboration du monde moderne* (Paris, 1934), p. 39. On the succession to the crown, see A.W. Lewis, *Royal Succession in Capetian France. Studies on Familial Order and the State* (Cambridge, Mass. and London, 1981). On the exclusion of females from the succession to the crown, see P. Viollet, 'Comment les femmes ont été exclues, en droit, de la succession à la couronne', *Mémoires de l'Institut national de France, Académie des Inscriptions et Belles-Lettres*, xxxiv, part 2 (1895), pp. 125–78. P. Contamine, ' "La royaume de France ne peut tomber en fille". Fondement, formulation et implication d'une théorie politique à la fin du Moyen Age', *Perspectives médiévales*, xiii (1987), pp. 67–81. On the succession of 1328, see J. Viard, 'Philippe de Valois. La succession à la couronne de France', *Le Moyen Age*, xxiii (1921), pp. 219–22.
[41] Cazelles, *La société politique et la crise de la royauté sous Philippe de Valois*, p. 201.

words and they thence parted company due to a misunderstanding.'[42] Raymond Cazelles linked this rupture – which kept the father and son apart for six months – to an agreement concluded between the duke of Normandy and Charles of Luxembourg, king of the Romans.[43] In January 1347, the future emperor surrendered the land that his father, killed at Crécy, had possessed in France; land that had been inherited by Charles's sister, Bonne, and that would later pass to Jean de Berry. On the following 7 May, Charles IV promised to bring help to his brother-in-law and nephews in the event of their being ousted from the succession to the throne: 'Et si acciderit, quod Deus avertat, quod dictus frater noster vel alter ipsorum nepotum nostrorum in successione regni Francie, velut avi, quovismodo in personis seu rebus ipsorum impedirentur, nos modis omnibus quibus poterimus ipsos juvabimus.'[44] That the duke of Normandy had real worries is proved by the tenor of the treaty, for no other act of the same type contains an article similar to this.

It is possible that the duke of Normandy did not take lightly the efforts made by Edward III to convince the inhabitants of the kingdom of France that he was their legitimate king, efforts that were well received and not only by the Flemings and the barons. It is possible that he took seriously the 'revelations' of Saint Brigit of Sweden, which suggested to the two kings a solution that would bring the conflict to an end. Deriving his legitimacy from a conventional election, Philip VI would keep the crown for life, bequeathing it thereafter to Edward III, whom he would adopt as his eldest son.[45] Some people may have been won over by such an arrangement, which, after all, was to be embodied in the Treaty of Troyes of 1420.

In 1350 when Philip VI died, succession by his eldest son was not assured. The abbot of St Martin of Tournai, Gilles le Muisit, reports that many were astonished that Edward III had not tried to prevent the coronation of King John, and attributed this to the indecisive naval battle of Winchelsea on 29 August, during which the English vanquished a Spanish armada but suffered heavy losses.[46]

From 1353 the dynastic contest acquired a new vigour when Charles, count of Évreux and king of Navarre, called 'the bad' by a sixteenth-century Spanish chronicler (a pejorative epithet immediately adopted in French historiography),

---

[42] 'Et eut adonc entre le roy de France et le duch de Normandie grosses paroles et s'en parti li dus par mautalent.' *Froissart*, ed. Luce, iv, pp. 8, 21.

[43] Cazelles, *La société politique et la crise de la royauté sous Philippe de Valois*, pp. 202–3.

[44] Cited by Cazelles, *La société politique et la crise de la royauté sous Philippe de Valois*. Text published by Du Mont, *Corps diplomatique universel du droit des gens*, vol. 1, part 2 (Amsterdam, 1726), p. 238.

[45] Cazelles, *La société politique et la crise de la royauté sous Philippe de Valois*, p. 204. The seriousness of such a proposition could be doubted had it not been for the fact that the English recalled 'la prophetie de saincte Brigide' in diplomatic negotiations. In 1439 the French responded by evoking the prophesies 'd'ung saint hermite nomme Johannes'. The English cardinal then suggested 'que ce seroit ung bon mariage dudit hermite et de saincte Brigide'. *Anglo-French Negotiations of 1439*, ed. C.T. Allmand, Camden Miscellany 14, Camden Soc., 4th ser. (London, 1972), p. 116.

[46] R. Cazelles, *Société politique, noblesse et couronne sous Jean le Bon et Charles V* (Geneva and Paris, 1982), pp. 128–9.

entered the political scene. The grandson of Louis X through his mother, Jeanne, and cleverly deprived not only of the French crown but also of the county of Champagne, Charles married the eldest daughter of King John in 1352. Robbed of most of his inheritance and rigorously excluded from the king's council by members of the royal party, Charles became the head of the powerful opposition movement, which then began to win over the greater part of political society in France. The political programme of the 'Navarrese party' did not overlook the dynastic dimension of the contest. The text known as the 'articles contre Robert le Coq',[47] an indictment drawn up by the 'parti des officiers' against the bishop of Laon, one of the Navarrese leaders, reported the 'périlleuse langue'[48] used by the bishop in his pronouncement against the king. Great emphasis was placed on lineage: 'The king's blood is bad and rotten';[49] his line is not the equal of 'this true and good blood of Navarre'.[50] He had 'murdered his wife'; the dauphin is merely a 'bastardiaux'.[51]

After the defeat of Poitiers, in the wave of strife that swept over King John and his government, and without the agreement of the Dauphin, Charles duke of Normandy, the *États généraux* hastened to liberate the king of Navarre from the prison in which he had been incarcerated since 5 April 1356. In November 1357 the king of Navarre returned to the political stage. The failure of the *États généraux* and of the Parisian revolution was a failure for him as well. In his downfall, Etienne Marcel took Charles 'the bad' with him. The defeat at Cocherel in 1364 of the Navarrese army, which had wanted to 'oppose and break the crown'[52] of Charles V, was a fatal blow to the king of Navarre's ambitions. Ruptured reconciliations and planned treachery notwithstanding, the struggle of the Valois against Navarre was ended only with the death of the latter.

It is possible that the royal rancour, born out of the Navarrese dynastic struggle, played a part over the centuries in the animosity shown against not only the memory of the kings of Navarre, but also against the duke of Nemours, who was heir to their French lordships.[53]

The question of the unity of the kingdom, which formed the root cause of the conflict between the Valois king and the other pretenders to the French throne,

---

[47] Text edited by L. Douët d'Arcq, 'Acte d'accusation contre Robert le Coq, évêque de Laon', *Bibliothèque de l'École des chartes*, ii (1841), pp. 350–88.

[48] *Ibid.*, article nos 6 and 9.

[49] 'Le roi est de très mauvais sang et pourri': *ibid.*, article no. 18.

[50] 'ce vray et bon sanc de Navarre': *ibid.*, article no. 30.

[51] Just like his father: *ibid.*, article nos 30 and 31.

[52] Christine de Pisan, *Le Livre des fais et bonnes meurs du sage roy Charles V,* ed. S. Solente, vol. 1 (Paris, 1936), pp. 121–2: Viewing the king of France's decisive victory, Christine de Pisan wrote that 'Fortune au double visage volt à France commencier à demoustrer et faire luire le ray du soleil de sa riant et belle face.'

[53] A simple manual of the *Chambre des Comptes*, written in the fifteenth century by the clerk Jean le Bègue, in supplying the references to the records concerning 'Navarre et Nemoux', denigrates the kings of Navarre along the way: 'Charles premier de ce nom qui fist moult de contraversies au roy Charles Vme'; regarding his successor, there is evidence 'du serment de feaulté que fist le roy de Navarre au roy angloys'. Similarly, it is noted that 'monseigneur de Nemoux qui fut decapité'. Paris, Bibliothèque nationale de France, ms latin 12 815, fo. 40v.

also divided the political community. If in 1328 the great men of the kingdom had chosen unity, during the years from 1340 to 1360 quite a few had moved over to the idea of partition, which would satisfy the wronged descendants of the last Capetians. This current of opinion was altogether stronger than the idea of the territorial integrity of the kingdom, which though held dear by lawyers could not outweigh regional solidarity. The defeat at Crécy underlined the difficulty of defending a country crossed by divisions that threatened to break it up.

The Midi had reluctantly to co-operate with the capital, with its investigations and its would-be reforms, which were expressed in the despatch of rapacious commissioners. From the time of his accession to the throne, Philip VI had endeavoured to renew the links with the pays de Languedoc, which had been reluctant to endure the Capetian yoke. He had some success in this respect, but the benefits of this policy were lost because of the war and the taxation that it entailed.[54] Soon Languedoc, a land of towns, of written law and land registers, stood alone in the face of the demands for defence and taxation.[55]

The towns of the Midi were not alone in appreciating the necessity of self-reliance where their defence was concerned. During the years after Crécy and Poitiers, the threat posed by English chevauchées and the Free Companies forced towns from one end of the kingdom to the other to repair their defensive walls. The crown approved of such work and authorised the levying of taxes to finance it. There was some resistance, especially from the clergy, and there were suits and appeals in the *Parlement*, but the towns held their own. Their budgets, hitherto quite modest, increased in size considerably. It was necessary to keep accounts, to satisfy suspicious taxpayers, and to organise meetings for the examination of plans, contracts and accounts. From all this, a local policy emerged.[56]

In the 1340s, a new schism appeared in the structure of the kingdom, separating west from east. From Flanders to Gascony, the population of the coastal regions of France felt a certain economic and political unity, which they did not share with the inhabitants of the French heartland, the Burgundians and the peoples of the eastern part of the kingdom, whose inclination was towards the empire. These tensions surfaced at the king's council, where groups united by their local origins opposed one another: for example, the Burgundians against the men of the west, as Cazelles has shown. Such tensions could also stir the nation. The fate of Artois, after Crécy, illustrates both the problem and the solution found by the crown. During the early fourteenth century, Artois was one of the most sensitive spots in the kingdom. Barons, towns and communities quickly

---

[54] 'Gravantur omni tempore bellorum et pacis: temporis bellorum propter diversas impositiones, subsidias et gabellas; pacis tempore propter diversos commissarios per majestatem regiam missos super pluribus et diversis populo impositis ad extorquendum pecunias jure vel injuria.' Dom Devic et Dom Vaissète, *Histoire générale du Languedoc*, new edn, vol. 10 (Toulouse, 1885), c. 996.

[55] J.B. Henneman, *Royal Taxation in Fourteenth-Century France: the Ransom of John II, 1356–1370* (Philadelphia, 1976), pp. 123–205.

[56] See Albert Rigaudière, *Gouverner la ville au Moyen Age* (Paris, 1993), especially chapter 10, 'Le financement des fortifications urbaines en France du milieu du XIV° siècle à la fin du XV° siècle'.

banded together and protested. At the time of Crécy, Artois had a count, the duke of Burgundy, Eudes IV, the queen's brother, on whom the responsibility for the defeat rested. Eudes was count of Artois and Burgundy 'by his wife', which made the Artésians say in anger 'that there was hardly a lord in Artois, that being a woman; that the duke was *mesiaux* and rotten, and should not be duke of Burgundy; and that he was a traitor to the king'.[57] It is understandable that the duke of Burgundy, as count of Artois, had been unable to guarantee the defence of Artois, which had taken the full force of Edward III's chevauchée and the depredations of the English troops besieging Calais. What the Artésians were demanding was to be 'taken into the king's hands', which Philip VI conceded to them at the end of 1346. The duchess of Burgundy died in 1347, and Duke Eudes followed her to the grave in April 1349. Their heir was Philip de Rouvres, their grandson, a young child whose father had died in 1346 and who was in the guardianship of his mother, Jeanne de Boulogne. A widower since September 1349, the duke of Normandy was able to marry Jeanne on 9 February 1350. Artois, along with the duchy of Burgundy, remained in the hands of John, who became king, while the problem of the succession in Burgundy was not settled. However, King John and especially his son, Charles V, did strive to establish a 'fleur de lys prince' in the inheritance of the wealthy Burgundy, and this was to be Philip the Bold.

In order to ensure the defence of the kingdom and especially its cohesion, the idea of bringing together the greatest fiefs of the royal family was established. Helped by the war and the insecurity created by the Companies, Charles V put forward a policy of apanage, which can be regarded as an early effort of decentralisation, preserving the diversity of the vast French kingdom.[58]

The cost of war, and of fighting men's wages in particular, required forms of taxation that served also (ever since Philip the Fair's attempts to introduce them) to meet the expenses involved in the development of a modern state. Now, at the time of Crécy, those who demanded taxes had to seek consent for them, which meant consulting the representatives of the three *États* of the kingdom. Summoned in 1347, the *États* were again assembled in 1351 and 1355, before the great crisis that required them to sit almost continuously from 1356 until 1358. The towns of Languedoc regularly attached themselves to these general meetings between 1356 and 1362; indeed, so frequently that such attendance took on an institutional character. There still existed local assemblies, such as the *États* of Normandy.[59] During the sometimes violent debates that were held there, as elsewhere in speeches, diplomatic negotiations and theoretical writings, two opposing currents of thought met head on. The first, which was by far the

---

[57] 'qu'il n'avoit point de seigneur en Arthois, mais une dame; que messire le duc estoit mesiaux, pouris, qu'il n'avoit onques eu duc en Bourgoigne qu'il n'eut esté traître au roi': Guesnon, 'Documents inédits sur l'invasion anglaise et les états au temps de Philippe VI et Jean le Bon', p. 6. One notices once again the personal insult concerning the prince's rightful ancestry. On the Artois affair, see Cazelles, *La société politique et la crise de la royauté sous Philippe de Valois*, pp. 196–200.

[58] Autrand, *Charles V,* pp. 664–8.

[59] A. Coville, *Les États de Normandie. Leur origine et leur développement au XIV° siècle* (Paris, 1914).

most potent, advocated a traditional view – that of a feudal monarchy, ancient and vibrant, in which the king was obliged to extend justice and favour to all, and where royal power respected customs and privilege scrupulously. The second was that which advanced the modern state, espousing such notions as the 'crown', the common good of the commonwealth, and sovereignty. Its ultimate weapon was rationality and efficiency, while the magic word of the others was 'reforms'. In the representative assemblies during the period 1340 to 1360, the *États* party tirelessly demanded the abolition of those evil 'novelties' that had been introduced by the king's all too numerous agents, in return for the raising of a tax, the assessment, collection and use of which the *États* proposed to control. As for the result that might be expected from this tax, consented to and administered by the *États*, the 'parti des officiers' declared not surprisingly that it would yield nothing.[60] The tax demands of the *États* were wholly unrealistic. Other negotiating structures were put into place to prevent the *États généraux* becoming the political mouthpiece for the community of the realm.

Political debate survived the defeat of the *États généraux* and the rallying of the 'reformers' of the monarchy. This was for the personnel of the intellectual entourage of Charles V ('the Wise'), namely 'the Charles V club',[61] among whom two groups opposed one another in dialogue that was on occasion lively. On one side were the philosophers, or 'artistes', whose leader was the translator of, and commentator on, Aristotle's 'Politics', the great Nicolas Oresme.[62] It was he who defended the community's right to take part in the government of the kingdom. Opposing the 'artistes' were the 'légistes', whose study of Roman law made them more royal than the king. The philosophers regarded them as 'idiots politiques' for the emphasis that they placed on practicalities rather than on the principles of power.[63] Among them, men like Évrart de Trémaugon, very probably the author of *Songe du vergier*,[64] were theoreticians of the all powerful state and of the concept of the king as 'empereur en son royaume'.

The battle of Crécy brought with it the destruction of the French army and a political crisis that prevented an effective military retaliation, with the result that the English were able to establish a lasting presence in Calais. With a bridgehead on the continent, the king of England found himself in a strong position, and all at once France's strategic predicament was weakened, but not its diplomatic situation. Somewhat disquieted, the duke of Brabant, the count of Flanders and

---

60 At the *États généraux* of October 1356, this is the argument brought forward by the 'parti des officiers' to reject the offer of the *États*: 'Lesquelles offres sont mout petites, ne n'estoient à accepter pour pluseurs causes . . . la tierce car en verité l'execution en est aussi comme impossible, ou au moins si fort, que elle en vaudroit peu ou nient. Et ce appert assez par le moïen et le darrenier subside, de quoy l'en n'a pas peu lever le vintisme.' Acte d'accusation, article no. 72.

61 Autrand, *Charles V*, pp. 728–31.

62 *Maistre Nicole Oresme. Le Livre de Politiques d'Aristote*, ed. A.M. Menut (Philadelphia, 1970).

63 J. Krynen, 'Les légistes "idiots politiques". Sur l'hostilité des théologiens à l'égard des juristes, en France, au temps de Charles V', *Théologie et droit dans la science politique moderne* (Rome, 1991), pp. 171–98.

64 *Le Songe de vergier*, ed. M. Schnerb-Lièvre, 2 vols (Paris, 1982).

the emperor became reconciled with France, which had become stronger on its eastern frontier with the acquisition of the Dauphiné in 1349. The defeat at Crécy would not have been the 'hard blow' that it was for the monarchy were it not for the fact that it served to reveal a profound political malaise, which marked a stage in the development of the modern state.

9

Crécy and the Chroniclers

ANDREW AYTON

Three questions were posed in the opening chapter of this volume. The third –
'how significant an event was the battle of Crécy'? – was explored in that
chapter; indeed, it is perhaps the central theme of the book. In Chapter 2, the
discussion turned to the first question: 'why did the battle of Crécy take place?'
Having reviewed the evidence, a new interpretation was offered that suggested
that the battle of Crécy can perhaps best be understood in the context of its
geographical location in the county of Ponthieu; that one of the strategic options
that Edward had in mind at the outset of the campaign, an option that had
become central by the time that his army had reached Caen, was to provoke
Philip VI into battle in Ponthieu, on a site that had been pre-planned.

In the concluding part of this book we shall return to the second question that
was posed in the opening chapter: 'how was it that the English won the battle?'
Addressing this very issue in a sermon to the English high command a few
weeks after the battle, the eminent churchman, Thomas Bradwardine, who had
been present on 26 August but probably not a real eyewitness to the fighting,
had a clear view of the subject. The English had triumphed not because of military skill, good fortune or fate, but because it was God's will.[1] Naturally,
Bradwardine was not alone in expressing this view. The author of the *Grandes
chroniques*, writing at Saint-Denis soon after the battle, considered the outcome,
including the heavy casualties sustained by Philip VI's army, to be divine
punishment for the sins of the French – their pride, greed and vanity. In his
opinion, it was small wonder that God had wished to correct 'les excès des
François par son flael le roy d'Angleterre'.[2]

A modern historian will seek a more earth-bound explanation for the
outcome of the battle. But the search will not be easy, for as Michael Prestwich
noted in Chapter 4, it is notoriously difficult to establish, from the narrative
sources, a clear picture of what happened on a medieval battlefield. We may be
offered glimpses of a few individual incidents (often the chivalric deeds of
particular aristocratic warriors), perhaps a vivid characterisation of the heat of
the fray, but rarely a clear outline of the main sequence of events. Crécy is no
exception. An historian seeking to understand how it was that the English won

---

1 H.S. Offler, 'Thomas Bradwardine's "victory sermon" in 1346', *Church and Crown in the
Fourteenth Century*, ed. A.I. Doyle (Aldershot, 2000), XIII, pp. 1–40.
2 *Grandes chroniques*, ix, pp. 284–5. See also Rogers, *War Cruel and Sharp*, p. 271.

the battle will find that the fourteenth-century accounts written by contemporaries, or based in part on contemporary testimony, do not of themselves, individually or collectively, provide sufficiently clear evidence for a wholly satisfactory answer to be formulated. Indeed, when the numerous narrative sources are scrutinised, what we find are confident statements that flatly contradict the views of other, equally confident commentators; imprecision or even complete silence on fundamentally important aspects of the battle; and the use of descriptive terminology that may well have conveyed an unambiguous meaning to a fourteenth-century reader, but which remains elusive to us.

Most post-medieval commentators on the events of 26 August 1346 have focused, on the one hand, on English superiority in weaponry and tactics, and, on the other, on French weaknesses and mistakes. The latter include serious errors of judgement by the commanders and the lack of effective command and control, which allowed the impetuosity of the French knights to determine events, with disastrous results. Of course, some secondary accounts of the battle are 'coloured more than a little by an anachronistic nationalism';[3] but even allowing for such bias, the variety of modern interpretations is largely the consequence of the variety of fourteenth-century sources for the battle. Whether English strengths or French weaknesses are given greater emphasis – and whether other 'factors', such as the torrential downpour shortly before the attack by the Genoese crossbowmen, are regarded as significant – has depended upon judgements concerning the relative reliability of the many and varied contemporary or near contemporary narrative sources that offer an account of the battle.

In returning to this problem in the concluding section of this book, the intention is not to present a detailed account of the battle based essentially upon evidence derived from the chronicles and other narrative sources, for Michael Prestwich's reconstruction in Chapter 4 takes us as far as such sources allow. The approach in this chapter and the next will be rather different. This chapter offers a critical evaluation of the narrative sources for the battle – both the chronicles and, as far as possible, the sources upon which they rely – the aim being to assess how much they can contribute to an explanation of the English victory. Chapter 10 investigates the possibilities offered by other kinds of evidence, principally the topography of the battlefield and the composition of the two armies. It also takes a closer look at the role played by archery in determining the outcome of the battle.

In re-examining the narrative sources we must consider the relationships between the various accounts of the battle that were written during the half century or so after it was fought. We need also to take a closer, comparative look at those chronicles and their authors that have been most influential in shaping modern interpretations of English tactics.[4] Given that 'the value of these, as of

---

3   M. Bennett, 'The development of battle tactics in the Hundred Years War', *Arms, Armies and Fortifications in the Hundred Years War*, ed. A. Curry and M. Hughes (Woodbridge, 1994), pp. 3–4: on the influence of the belief in the 'superiority of English firepower "throughout the ages" '.

4   For the English and Hainaulter chroniclers discussed below, see A. Gransden, *Historical*

other chronicles, is the value of their sources',[5] we must try to establish what evidence, oral and documentary, was available to our authors and what use they made of it.

It should be noted at the outset that fourteenth-century accounts of the battle written from the French perspective have contributed little to the debate on English tactics – an historiographical neglect that is unfortunate, since the French chroniclers do throw some light on this subject.[6] However, it cannot be denied that the tactical dispositions of the English are not the primary concern of these writers, who in explaining the outcome of the battle place the greatest emphasis on the imprudently hasty and consequently ill-prepared and disorganised way in which the French army began their attack. 'Par hastiveté et desarroy furent les François desconfiz,' as one of these chroniclers observed.[7] There is a general consensus among the earliest French accounts that Philip VI rejected the advice of those of his advisers who suggested postponement of the battle until the next day.[8] The Genoese crossbowmen were at a grave disadvantage because their large protective shields (*pavises*) and most of their ammunition were packed onto carts that had not yet reached the battlefield.[9] For some French chroniclers, the heavy shower of rain also played a crucial part in disabling the missile-weapon capability of Philip VI's army.[10] What is more, the French

---

Writing in England, vol. 2: *c. 1307 to the Early Sixteenth Century* (London and Henley, 1982); and J. Taylor, *English Historical Literature in the Fourteenth Century* (Oxford, 1987).

[5] V.H. Galbraith, 'The battle of Poitiers', *EHR*, liv (1939), p. 475.

[6] Several of the accounts that view the proceedings from the French perspective appear to have been written within a year or two of the battle: the chronicle of the blind, septuagenarian abbé of Saint-Martin of Tournai, Gilles le Muisit (d. 1352); the relevant section of the *Grandes chroniques*, the semi-official history written at the monastery of Saint-Denis, near Paris; and the narrative, apparently written at St Omer, upon which were based the short continuation of the *Chronique de Flandre* and the 'St Omer Chronicle' (for fuller discussion of the various St Omer texts, see Chapter 5, n. 29). The account of the Crécy campaign in the chronicle of Jean de Venette, the head of the Carmelite order's French province, was probably written in 1359–60, though he (like the author of the corresponding section of the *Grandes chroniques*) had been a witness to the damage wreaked by Edward III's troops near Paris in 1346. The *Chronique Normande* was compiled about a decade later, probably by a lesser nobleman. The *Chronique des quatre premiers Valois*, dating from the last twenty or so years of the fourteenth century, appears to be the work of a cleric based in Rouen. The account of the battle in the *Chronographia regum Francorum*, written in the early fifteenth century at St Denis, has a number striking similarities with that in the *Chronique Normande*, presumably as a result of shared sources.

[7] *Chronique des quatre premiers Valois*, p. 16.

[8] *Gilles le Muisit*, pp. 161, 163–7; *Grandes chroniques*, ix, p. 282; *Chronique de Flandre*, ii, p. 43; St Omer chronicle, fo. 262r. Also *Jean de Venette*, p. 43; *Chronique des quatre premiers Valois*, p. 16. Rogers, *War Cruel and Sharp*, p. 267 and n. 166.

[9] *Gilles le Muisit*, pp. 161–2; *Chronique Normande*, p. 80; *Chronographia*, ii, p. 232.

[10] *Grandes chroniques*, ix, p. 282 (crossbow strings softened by the rain); *Jean de Venette*, p. 43 (rain caused the strings to shrink); *Chronographia*, ii, p. 232 (French stunned by the storm). R.A. Newhall argues that if the rain had any effect on the crossbow strings it would probably have been to cause them to stretch (*Jean de Venette*, pp. 176–7 n. 63), while Jules Viard, in an exhaustive discussion of the subject, doubts whether the rain contributed significantly to the French defeat. 'La campagne de juillet-août 1346 et la bataille de Crécy', *Le moyen âge*, 2nd ser., xxvii (1926), pp. 1–84 (at p. 73 n. 2).

cavalry then became entangled with the remnants of the fleeing Genoese, and the confusion, or 'triboul', that ensued provided great encouragement to the English.[11] Lastly, the French chronicles place great emphasis on the role played by the English (or 'Welsh' as some insist) archers in Edward III's victory.[12] The flower of the French nobility were cut down by 'par pou de gent et gent de nulle value, c'est assavoir archiers', as the *Grandes chroniques* expressed it.[13] Indeed, reading some of the French accounts, we may be forgiven for wondering whether Edward III's army was composed entirely of archers.[14] Presumably it was inconceivable to these authors that the massed power of French chivalry could have been defeated by their English counterparts. But for all their stress on the part played by the archers, what the French chroniclers have to say about English tactics in the battle has been overshadowed, in modern secondary accounts, by the evidence of several writers of English or 'neutral' provenance – namely, Geoffrey le Baker, Jean le Bel, the Bourgeois of Valenciennes and Jean Froissart. These influential, if problematic, accounts of English tactics will be re-examined below; but it would be as well to note here that more attention should be paid to what other chronicles, notably those of French or Italian provenance, have to say about the deployment and fighting methods of the English army.

Eyewitness accounts of the battle of Crécy

For all the thousands of men who were on, or near to, the field of Crécy on 26 August 1346, only a handful wrote accounts of the battle that have survived to this day. The recollections of many more combatants and witnesses are preserved in the work of the chroniclers. We need to be aware of the limitations of such eyewitness testimony, whether it be from the pens or the mouths of men who witnessed the events first hand. A medieval battle was an inherently complex event, with much taking place simultaneously, perhaps over a wide area. No one person would have had a clear view of everything happening in a single moment, let alone during the whole course of the action. Even if weighty testimony from several witnesses were available it would not be 'easy for anyone to write up a narrative dealing with simultaneous actions'.[15] Of course, the testimony would not be consistently reliable. The restricted viewpoint of some

---

[11] *Chronique de Flandre*, ii, p. 43; St Omer chronicle, fo. 262v; *Chronique Normande*, p. 81; *Jean de Venette*, p. 43.

[12] *Gilles le Muisit*, p. 162; *Grandes chroniques*, ix, p. 283; *Chronique de Flandre*, ii, p. 43; St Omer chronicle, fo. 262v; *Chronique Normande*, p. 81; *Chronique des quatre premiers Valois*, p. 16; *Chronographia*, ii, p. 232.

[13] *Grandes chroniques*, ix, p. 283.

[14] E.g., *Jean de Venette*, p. 43: '[Philip VI] boldly attacked the English drawn up facing them and their great multitude of archers in battle array'.

[15] A. Curry, *The Battle of Agincourt: Sources and Interpretations* (Woodbridge, 2000), pp. 16–18. See also the perceptive discussion in R.C. Smail, *Crusading Warfare (1097–1193)* (Cambridge, repr., 1976), pp. 165–8. For a more positive view of eyewitness testimony, see J.F. Verbruggen, *The Art of Warfare in Western Europe During the Middle Ages*, English trans., 2nd edn (Woodbridge, 1997), pp. 16–18.

eyewitnesses would have been acquired under conditions of considerable stress. Eyewitnesses might not understand what they had seen or chroniclers what they were told. In all sorts of ways the passage of time could affect the recollections of both witnesses and writers. It would be natural for either participants or authors to support 'their arguments with things which they could not know with certainty',[16] and it is often difficult to distinguish the authentic detail from that which has been embroidered or even invented. Such problems need to be borne in mind when evaluating the accounts of those chroniclers, like Jean le Bel, who are explicit in their reliance on the testimony of participants in the battle, and of those, like Geoffrey le Baker, who are not, but who almost certainly did gather evidence from eyewitnesses. This has a particular bearing on the interpretation of those enigmatic descriptions of English archer deployment that we find in the chronicles and to which historians have devoted so much attention. None of the authors had actually seen how the archers were deployed at Crécy: at best, they were trying to make sense of what they had been told by someone who had.

Reading Gilles le Muisit's account of Crécy helps us to appreciate the frustrations that chroniclers in search of hard facts from eyewitnesses must commonly have experienced. The septuagenarian abbé's work also serves as an illustration of how, in the absence of such evidence, even the most scrupulous authors were prone to judgements coloured by partisan bias or other preconceived notions. Le Muisit was only too well aware that 'those fighting cannot consider anything going on away from them, nor are able to judge well even those things which are happening to them'; and that after a battle rumour and speculation are rife. Consequently, he assures the reader that 'I will write only those things which I have heard from certain trustworthy persons . . . not however affirming them to be completely what happened'. How does this affect his narrative of the battle? He states that he could find no one to provide reliable information on the actions of either the French or the English kings in the battle, yet immediately adds that 'some say' that Philip VI remained with his men on the field for a long time (eventually retiring to Labroye), while the English withdrew because it was late and they were unable to see anything. Then, the following morning, the English returned to the field and gathered the spoils of the battle, and on account of this they were judged to have been victorious.[17] He also notes that he had difficulty ascertaining the truth about English casualties in the battle, but concludes that they must have been heavy, given the losses that had been sustained by the French army. A few lines later, this has become fact: 'On the side of the king of England were killed numerous princes and nobles, whose names I do not know, and a great many other Englishmen and archers.'[18]

Shaped by personal experience and often influenced by an aristocratic view of warfare, the sharpness of focus brought by eyewitness testimony is both its strength and its principal limitation. These qualities are especially evident in the

---

16 A chronicler's perspective: *Gilles le Muisit*, pp. 160–1. This passage is translated in K. DeVries, *Infantry Warfare in the Early Fourteenth Century* (Woodbridge, 1996), p. 160.
17 This version of the French 'defeat' and the English 'victory' was repeated several decades later in the *Chronique des quatre premiers Valois*, p. 17.
18 *Gilles le Muisit*, pp. 160–4.

work of those professional spectators of medieval battles, the heralds of arms. War correspondents with very specialised interests, the heralds were encouraged to get as close to the action as possible. They brought a degree of detachment to their work, but were very selective in what they recorded, their particular interest being the valiant deeds of knights. They were, as Maurice Keen has put it, 'the general registrars of prowess'.[19] There are a number of episodes in the chronicle accounts of Crécy that can probably be traced to the heralds' notes. The sequence of heroic vignettes that we find in the related texts of the short continuation of the *Chronique de Flandre* and the St Omer chronicle reads very much like a memoir drawn from a herald's battlefield notebook. One by one the counts of Blois, Flanders and Alençon (and his banner bearer, Jacques de Stralles), and the King of Bohemia and Henri le Moine de Bale, go down fighting.[20] 'De toutes pars se venoient faire tuer les grans seigneurs car peu de deffense avoit en eulx,' the chronicler adds poignantly. Given their preoccupations we should not be surprised that the heralds, and therefore the chroniclers who relied upon them for evidence, were unable to offer anything more than a patchy, episodic narrative of the battle itself. Yet the heralds have preserved some vivid snap-shots of combat. It is, for example, instructive to learn that the count of Blois dismounted and fought on foot; and it is to be conveyed to the heart of the chivalric mentality, founded as it was upon honour, when we hear the blind king of Bohemia, seeking a guiding hand for his bridle, remind Henri le Moine that he had fled from the field at Laupen in 1339. Both men must have known that the king himself had departed hastily from a battle, at Vottem, only a few weeks before Crécy.[21]

Despite the limitations of eyewitness testimony, we may regret that Sir Thomas Gray, who possessed that rare combination of martial experience and literary skill, was not present at Crécy.[22] As we shall see, it is likely that at least one detailed account of the battle was written by a participant on the English side. Although this text has not survived in its original form, we can snatch glimpses of its character and content from the imprint that it seems to have left on the chroniclers' accounts of Crécy. It is probable that other eyewitness accounts have been lost, but fortunately four despatches, each produced within days the battle, have survived.[23] Three of these bulletins form part of a larger

[19] M. Keen, *Chivalry* (New Haven and London, 1984), pp. 134, 138–9. P. Contamine, 'Batailles, bannières, compagnies: aspects de l'organisation militaire française pendant la première partie de la Guerre de Cent ans', *Les Cahiers Vernonnais*, iv (1964), p. 19.

[20] *Chronique de Flandre*, ii, pp. 43–4; St Omer chronicle, fo. 262v.

[21] J. Viard, 'Henri le Moine de Bale à la bataille de Crécy', *Bibliothèque de l'École des chartes*, lxvii (1906), pp. 489–96; see pp. 493–4 for this version of the story of the king of Bohemia, derived from Conrad Justinger's *Berner chronik* (1421).

[22] He was at Neville's Cross, although the loss of that part of his *Scalacronica* that covers the mid 1340s robs us of his account of the great English victories of 1346. All that we have is Leland's abbreviated abstract of Gray's original text: *Scalacronica*, ed. H. Maxwell (Glasgow, 1907), pp. 112–20 (pp. 114–15 for 1346).

[23] Essex Record Office, MS D/DBa T1/8, an undated latter to Lady Alice Rokele from, it seems, a member of Queen Isabella's household, has been identified as a 'letter giving news of the battle of Crécy' (Essex Record Office Transcripts, no. 109). In fact, it makes no specific reference to that battle and the internal evidence suggests that it was written after the

corpus of campaign newsletters addressed to individuals, institutions or the royal council in England, with the king's letters – or parts of them – intended for wider circulation.[24] If some at least of these letters 'appear to have been sent as straight, unadulterated news',[25] this is assuredly news viewed from the English perspective, with losses and difficulties minimised and divine favour abundantly displayed. The king's bulletins are notably laconic where military matters are concerned, but the other newsletters offer clear descriptions of the assault on Caen and much detail on smaller engagements. It is, therefore, disappointing to find that coverage of the battle of Crécy itself is so insubstantial. We would willingly exchange the duplicated lists of French casualties for a description of the battlefield, a narrative of the fighting or anything approaching an explanation of the English victory.

If anyone was in a position to recall the overall shape of the battle of Crécy it was Edward III himself, for he had planned the engagement and his reputed command centre on the mound of a windmill would have given him a fine view of much of the 'traditional' battlefield.[26] It is, therefore, all the more frustrating that his newsletter (dated 3 September) remains tight-lipped on the subject of how his army achieved its victory.[27] Apart from noting that the English fought on foot, the letter reveals nothing about tactical formations, and archery is not even mentioned. This reticence concerning tactical detail is very much the norm with Edward III's newsletters;[28] but at Crécy even he may have found it difficult to provide a blow-by-blow account of the battle, and not just because the closing stages were fought in fading light or even darkness. For as another spectator of battles, the duke of Wellington, put it, 'to write the history of a battle is as difficult as it is to write the history of a ball'.[29] Nevertheless, Edward's letter is not wholly lacking in clues about the nature of the battle. Firstly, he notes that it was a long and hard-fought action, which began in the late afternoon or early evening and continued into the night, with the French fighting nobly and frequently rallying.[30] However damaging the rout of the Genoese was to French

---

capture of Calais in August 1347. I am grateful to Miss Shelley Davis for drawing this document to my attention.

[24] For these newsletters, see Chapter 1, n. 2.

[25] Fowler, 'News from the front', p. 77.

[26] According to Froissart, Edward 'se tenoit plus amont, sus le mote d'un moulin à vent', *Froissart*, ed. Luce, iii, p. 182. The windmill, which is traditionally believed to have been on the site now called *Moulin Édouard III*, is also mentioned in the narratives originating from St Omer: the first English 'battle' 'se traist amont vers les champs pres dun moulin et par derriere avoit ung boys' (St Omer chronicle, fo. 262r; the wording in *Chronique de Flandre*, ii, p. 42, is slightly different).

[27] Edward III to 'son chier et feal chevalier Thomas Lucy': Oxford, Bodleian Library, MS Ashmole 789, fos 148r–148v; printed in *Le Prince Noir*, ed. Michel, pp. 308–11.

[28] As in his bulletins following the stand-off at Buironfosse in 1339 (*Avesbury*, pp. 305–6) and the battle of Sluys in 1340 (Sir N.H. Nicolas, *A History of the Royal Navy*, 2 vols (London, 1847), ii, pp. 501–2).

[29] Quoted by Anne Curry, 'Review article. Medieval warfare. England and her continental neighbours, eleventh to the fourteenth centuries', *Journal of Medieval History*, xxiv (1998), p. 96.

[30] 'Et estoient le bataillez trop fort et longement duraunt, quar il dura de devant hour de

prospects in the battle, it is clear that Philip VI's army did not abandon the fight without a protracted and heroic struggle. Secondly, after listing the notable casualties in the French army, Edward's letter conjures up a vivid image of the battlefield: 'In a small area where the first onslaught occurred more than 1500 knights and esquires died, quite apart from those who died later elsewhere on the field.'[31] What the king appears to be describing is a 'killing ground', a confined space in which the advancing French cavalry were cut down in large numbers, presumably by archery. This is a passage to which we shall return when considering some of the other chronicle accounts, particularly in the light of the topography of the 'traditional' battlefield. However, even if we think that we can identify the location of this 'petit place', we should remember too that the king's letter continues by referring to those who were killed 'après de tout pars du champ', suggesting that after 'la primer assemblée' the battle ranged more widely.

In addition to the king's letter of 3 September, we have two by clerics who were close to the sovereign, Richard Wynkeley (2 September) and Michael Northburgh (4 September).[32] They, like Thomas Bradwardine, whose victory sermon made brief reference to the battle, were probably safely ensconced in the baggage park during the fighting, only emerging the following morning to survey the scene of carnage. Consequently, they have little to say about the course of the battle, which in the case of Northburgh at least is a pity, since his two campaign letters reveal a man with an acute eye for detail and a vivid descriptive turn of phrase.[33] Wynkeley does, however, imply that the brunt of the fighting – three major French attacks – was sustained by the Prince of Wales's division. Northburgh's few words on the battle are clearly based on those in the king's letter; but he does offer an independent view of the renewed fighting on the Sunday morning,[34] and both he and Wynkeley provide specific information about the casualties. They list the great men who had been killed in the French army, but while the king's letter includes the king of Majorca among the slain, Wynkeley is less certain about whether he had been killed,[35] and Northburgh omits him altogether. Northburgh also notes that 1,542 'bones gentz darmes' had

---

vespre tant que à soir, et lez ennemiz se porteront moult noblement, et moult sovent se ralierent.'

[31] 'Et moururent en ung petit place où la primer assemblée estoiet, plus de mille et v^c. chivalers et esquiers, estre tout plain dez aultres, si que moururent après de tout pars du champ.'

[32] *Murimuth*, pp. 214–17; *Avesbury*, pp. 367–9.

[33] *Avesbury*, pp. 358–60, 367–9. Particularly striking are the comparisons that he draws between specific French and English towns, and the detail that he offers about the many smaller engagements that occurred during the campaign.

[34] He states that the earls of Northampton, 'Northfolk' (presumably a transcription error for 'Suffolk') and Warwick defeated 'un autre bataille' of French troops, which arrived 'devaunt le solail leve' on the Sunday morning, adding that they 'pristrount de chivalers et esquiers a graunt nombre, et tueront M^lM^l et pluis'.

[35] 'de quo communiter et verisimiliter opinatur'. James II, the exiled king of Majorca, survived the battle. See G. Martin, 'John the Blind: the English narrative sources', *Johann der Blinde, Graf von Luxemburg, König von Böhmen 1296–1346*, ed. M. Pauly (Luxembourg, 1997), pp. 83–92 (at p. 89).

been killed in the fighting on Saturday evening – an exact figure that may well be based upon the close inspection of the French corpses, or more precisely their heraldic insignia, which (according to several chroniclers) took place on Sunday morning. As we have seen, the king's letter gives a similar figure for the French losses in the 'small area where the first onslaught occurred'. Wynkeley prefers to stress the lightness of the English casualties, though he also adds that Philip VI had reportedly been 'wounded in the face by an arrow' – the only reference to archery in any of the English battlefield bulletins.

Although neither of the 'clerical' newsletters offers a narrative of the battle, nor indeed any tactical detail, both were to have a considerable influence on those in England who later came to write about Crécy. A fourth letter (dated Bruges, 12 September), sent by Johann von Schönfeld to the bishop of Passau, has had no such impact on historiography.[36] Schönfeld was a German knight serving in the English army and there can be no doubt that he was involved in the fighting, for he notes that he had been wounded by an arrow on the right side of his face.[37] Yet – or perhaps indeed because of this wound – his letter casts no light on the fighting, except for mentioning that the battle took place 'iuxta unam dietam sancti Georii iuxta villam, que vocatur Kersy' – an intriguing if as yet unidentified topographical reference. While noting that Edward III 'non perdidit nisi unum solum militum', Schönfeld summarises the notable casualties on the French side (which, he says, included the king of Majorca) and repeats the figure of 1,500 'barones, milites and nobiles' killed fighting for Philip VI. He adds that the names of the slain are to be found on a schedule ('cedula') enclosed with his letter. In fact, the *cedula* is an intriguing document, taking the form of a 'neutral' communiqué announcing the result of the battle, but quite obviously drawn up by the English or their allies, and probably intended for circulation around Europe.[38]

The English newsletters and the chronicles

Whatever their immediate purpose, and despite their limitations, the English newsletters from the Crécy campaign were to be highly influential with those in England who wrote about the battle during the mid to late fourteenth century. The character of the despatches shaped the character of the chronicle accounts that were compiled, and when the letters of Wynkeley and Northburgh were

---

[36] J.F. Böhmer, ed., *Acta Imperii selecta* (Innsbruck, 1870), no. 1055. The letter receives a passing mention by Fritz Trautz, *Die Könige von England und das Reich, 1272–1377* (Heidelberg, 1961), p. 333.

[37] He tells the bishop that he had come to Bruges from France 'vulneratus in dextra parte faciei mee, et adhuc longitudo quasi unius digiti sagitte est in capite meo residens, sed spero per dei gratiam bene curari'.

[38] It begins: 'Anno domini m.ccc.xlvi., indictione xiv., pontificatus domini Clementis pape sexti anno quinto, mensis augusti die xxvi., prelium fuit inmensum inter duos reges, videlicet Anglie et Francie, in quo idem dominus rex Anglie illustris victoriam dei gratia obtinuit et triumphum. Idem bellum fuit in Francia iuxta quandam villam, que dicitur Kersy, quinque miliaribus iuxta Monstruel in Poncien.'

most readily to hand, a chronicle would offer what in effect was a 'view from
the baggage park'. But it is clear that Wynkeley and Northburgh were not the
only eyewitness texts to be in circulation. Traces of other newsletters or similar
eyewitness testimony, for which complete texts are lacking and the author
unknown, can be detected in a large proportion of English chronicles. It is
impossible to say how many separate despatch-like documents or campaign
diaries were circulating in England – or, indeed, throughout continental Europe
– after Crécy; and any conclusions that may be offered about individual 'lost'
documents and their influence on particular chronicles must necessarily be
tentative. But such is the shadow that these missing documentary materials have
cast over the historiography of Crécy that we simply cannot ignore them.

With regard to that which is almost certainly the most substantial 'lost' narrative of Crécy – the missing concluding section of the *Acta Bellicosa* – we are at
least on reasonably solid ground: we can be confident that it once existed. As we
have seen, the *Acta Bellicosa* is a detailed campaign diary, apparently written by
a member of Edward III's army, which survives in a single, tantalisingly incomplete fourteenth-century copy.[39] Four leaves in the centre of the manuscript are
missing (between fos 100v and 101r, covering the period from 29 July to 10
August), and the text breaks off suddenly in mid-sentence (and mid-page) when
the narrative reaches 20 August. The volume, of which this unfinished copy
forms the last of three parts, may have originated in Norwich,[40] but the provenance of the campaign diary itself is uncertain. Internal evidence suggests that
the writer was connected in some way with the Prince of Wales's division. There
is a noticeable focus on the actions of men associated with that part of the
army;[41] and, as Richard Barber has noted, the inclusion of the text of the king's
letter to Philip VI, dated Auteuil, 17 August, 'would point to someone attached
to the prince's council, with access to such documents'.[42]

Assuming that the original text extended to the end of the campaign, the
closing folios 'might well have given us a vivid and first-hand account of the
battle itself'. Is there any evidence that this lost, eyewitness account was used by
later chroniclers, from whose work it may be possible to form an impression of
the original text? Richard Barber has suggested that copies of the complete *Acta
Bellicosa* may been have available to, and summarised by, the anonymous Monk
of Malmesbury abbey who completed his *Eulogium historiarum* during the

---

[39] Cambridge, Corpus Christi College, MS 370, fos 97r–103v. See Chapter 1, n. 4.
[40] The second part, in a different hand, concerns, firstly, a visitation made by Bishop William
Bateman of Norwich in 1347; and, secondly, an itinerary of three English travellers to the
Holy Land in 1344–5.
[41] The deeds of the earls of Warwick and Northampton, and in particular of the Prince of
Wales's men, take centre stage. For example, apart from William Montagu, all of the men
named as being knighted at La Hougue (Roger Mortimer; William Roos; Roger de la Warre;
Richard de la Bere) were serving in the prince's retinue. C76/22, m. 8; *Black Prince Register*,
i, pp. 80, 127–8; Wrottesley, *Crecy and Calais*, p. 86; R. Barber, *Edward Prince of Wales and
Aquitaine* (Woodbridge, 1978), p. 49.
[42] *Acts of War*, ed. Barber, p. 26. The copy of the king's letter is dated 'Autel', 17 August, in
Acta Bellicosa (Cambridge, Corpus Christi College, MS 370, fos 102v–103r), whereas the
enrolled copy bears the date 'Autes', 15 August (*CPR, 1345–48*, pp. 516–17). The *Acta*
version contains a number of scribal variations that suggest that the document was dictated.

1360s;[43] and Thomas Burton, who wrote his chronicle at Meaux abbey, in the East Riding of Yorkshire, during the 1390s.[44] At first glance, these may not appear to be chronicles likely to yield detailed accounts of the Anglo-French wars, for both were large-scale historical enterprises that were, in the main, concerned with other matters: in the case of the *Eulogium*, with 'universal history', whereas the Meaux chronicle was primarily a history of a Cistercian abbey. But both chroniclers included sections on fourteenth-century English history and both were interested in Edward III's wars. Moreover, they both display a capacity for handling documentary sources. Particularly pertinent is the Monk of Malmesbury's use of a detailed campaign diary as the source for his account of the Poitiers campaign of 1356.[45] Thomas Burton claimed that 'I have only included what I have found written in other works or in a variety of documents, or have heard from reliable witnesses, or have myself seen,' and the result was indeed a chronicle of great historical value.[46] Consequently, if the *Acta Bellicosa* were available to these chroniclers, we should expect them to make use of it.

Dr Barber's argument that they did indeed make use of it rests on the 'many details' that these three texts are said to have in common. It must be admitted that the evidence is far from conclusive.[47] The accounts of Crécy by the Meaux and Malmesbury writers are actually not at all alike. Just about the only similarities are references to the pre-battle appearance of a flock of crows, the wounding of the French king, and the rout of the newly arrived French troops on the Sunday morning.[48] Otherwise, Malmesbury can be characterised as a curiously structured compilation consisting of a number of distinctive points of detail, but without a clear narrative, while Meaux is more tightly structured, has more to

[43] One of the universal histories 'compiled under the influence of the Polychronicon' of Ranulf Higden, the *Eulogium historiarum* was a chronicle written (so the author says) 'to escape the tedium of monastic life . . . no doubt mainly with the inmates of his own monastic house in mind'. Taylor, *English Historical Literature*, pp. 105–6. For the Crécy campaign, see *Eulogium*, iii, pp. 206–11.

[44] For Burton and his chronicle, see Gransden, *Historical Writing in England*, ii, pp. 355–71. For the Crécy campaign, see *Melsa,* iii, pp. 55–60.

[45] Chapter 185, 'Itinerarium Edwardi Quarti': *Eulogium*, iii, pp. 215–26. For a valuable discussion of this campaign diary, see F.S. Haydon's editorial introduction: *ibid.*, pp. xxix–xxxvi. Drawing attention to the detail concerning individual combatants in the Monk of Malmesbury's narrative of the Crécy campaign, Haydon considered it likely that an eyewitness account had been used for this as well, but it seems that he was not aware of the *Acta Bellicosa* (*ibid.*, pp. xxv–xxvi).

[46] Burton's was 'a work of scholarship unrivalled in depth and scope by any other chronicle written in England in his time' in the opinion of Gransden, *Historical Writing in England*, ii, p. 361.

[47] Barber, *Edward Prince of Wales*, p. 61 n. 19; *Acts of War*, ed. Barber, p. 26. There are some similarities between the campaign accounts offered by these three texts, but if there is a relationship between them it is complex. For example, the capture of the castle of La Roche Guyon is noted in all three texts, but each has details omitted by the others.

[48] Even in these respects the emphasis is different. For example, the Malmesbury chronicler states that the French regarded the crows as an ill-omen, while Burton is more interested in the storm that followed. He notes that it was the first rain since the English had landed, that is, for six weeks and three days. Of course, both chroniclers include lists of the notable casualties on the French side, but they are not identical.

say about the organisation of the English army and offers a fuller account of the battle itself. Thus, Thomas Burton tells us that, having sent his horses and carts to the rear, Edward III deployed his army in three divisions between the town and forest of Crécy.[49] The battle lasted from the hour of vespers into the night, with the French attacking the Prince of Wales's division. After the crows had made their appearance and the storm had passed, the French assaults were repeatedly repulsed, the chronicler adding that at one point the bishop of Durham reinforced the prince's division. Burton's narrative continues with the French flight, the desultory skirmishing that continued through the night and the more substantial fight that occurred the following morning. The Monk of Malmesbury offers little of this material in his account. He prefers to record the creation of two (named) bannerets and 50 knights before the battle, and the subsequent death of one of the newly elevated men, Aymer Rokesley, who impetuously threw himself into the fray on the Sunday morning. But of these two chroniclers, it is the Malmesbury writer who stresses the part played by archery, noting that there was 'a heap of over a thousand destriers, along with their riders, killed and wounded by arrows'; and that the archers used up most of their ammunition in the battle.[50]

If the Monk of Malmesbury and Thomas Burton did indeed have access to the *Acta Bellicosa*, it would appear that they each made a distinctively personal selection of material from the text and that they supplemented it with evidence drawn from other sources. For his opening words on the campaign, and some details on the battle itself, the Monk of Malmesbury drew on Higden's *Polychronicon*.[51] Being a late composition, the Meaux chronicle may have been influenced by the gradual accumulation of tradition on the great events of Edward III's reign, as well as by distinctive 'local' material from the East Riding of Yorkshire.[52] But Richard Barber's suggestion that both chronicles made use of the campaign diary is not to be lightly set aside. Indeed, if we were to combine the material on Crécy in these two, very different chronicles what we would have is an account of the battle that could indeed have come from the *Acta Bellicosa*. It would be an account that includes a coherent narrative of events from the perspective of the Prince of Wales's division, plausible observations on organisational, tactical and logistical matters, and detail on the fortunes of individual English knights – such detail, it should be noted, being recorded in

---

[49] 'rex Edwardus, equis suis et cariagiis post tergum dimissis, ne sui liberius ad fugam convolarent, exercituque suo in tres acies divisio, inter villam et forestam de Cressy campum præelegit'. Burton had already noted that this was 'home ground' for Edward: 'ad solum proprium jure hereditario sibi debitum ab antiquo'. He adds that there were merely 3,000 men-at-arms in Edward's army, plus archers, and that they were pitted against Philip VI's 30,000 armoured men and countless common soldiery. *Melsa*, iii, p. 58.

[50] 'uno cumulo mille dextrariis et eo amplius cum assessoribus suis sagittis occisis et vulneratis'; 'sagittarii pro magna parte suas sagittas expendissent'. *Eulogium*, iii, p. 211.

[51] *Polychronicon Ranulphi Higden*, ed. J.R. Lumby, Rolls Ser., 9 vols (London, 1882), viii, pp. 340–2. Battle details: 2,000 French knights and 'vulgus innumerabile' killed; Philip VI wounded 'in femore et in gutture'.

[52] Antonia Gransden suggested that Burton may have used 'some lost monastic chronicle written at Meaux in the mid-fourteenth century': *Historical Writing in England*, ii, pp. 359–61.

no other narrative sources for the battle. The occasional mismatches can be attributed to the reworking of their material by our chroniclers. They are also unlikely to have had before them identical texts of the *Acta Bellicosa*. Altogether more probable is that the single surviving manuscript of this diary fragment was itself a variant of a fuller original text, which was widely circulated and copied, and from which a number of chronicles independently took extracts and compiled summaries. As we shall see, several other chronicles include distinctive pieces of information about the battle that cannot be traced to a known original source but which *could* have been found in the *Acta Bellicosa*. Consequently, it may be necessary to add the Nero D.X manuscript of Murimuth's chronicle, the *Historia Roffensis*, the *Historia Aurea*, the Anonimalle chronicle and that written by Henry Knighton to the list of works whose account of Crécy may have been based to a greater or lesser degree on this enigmatic campaign diary, whether its ur-text or a variant copy.

The problem of establishing the extent of the influence of this lost narrative is actually more complicated still, for we know that there were other, independently written diaries for this campaign. Over a hundred years ago, E.M. Thompson printed from Cotton MS, Cleopatra, D. VII 'a contemporary itinerary, copied in a hand of the fifteenth century'.[53] A similar document must lie behind Geoffrey le Baker's detailed account of the march from La Hougue to Crécy and, in all probability, the campaign narrative written by the Bourgeois of Valenciennes as well. That there is a basic underlying similarity between these itineraries and, indeed, the *Acta Bellicosa* is hardly surprising. The 'discrepancies' in detail that may be found are no doubt largely the result of the texts having been 'written independently by persons marching with different divisions of the army'.[54] But of this particular type of document, it is evident that the *Acta Bellicosa* stood out as unusually detailed. It is far more substantial than either the Cleopatra D. VII text or Baker's chronicle, and consequently we should imagine the lost section on the battle to have been a good deal more informative than the colourless summary that we find in Cleopatra D. VII. Baker's campaign diary may have been similar, since for the battle he appears to have found and digested a variety of sources, including oral testimony and documents, one of which (as we shall see) seems also to have come to the attention of Giovanni Villani in Florence.

We must turn now from the lost eyewitness narratives of the battle to those that have survived. The influence that these accounts have had on the chronicles can be more easily established. Of the three surviving English newsletters from Crécy, that which was issued under the name of the king has left fewest traces in fourteenth-century English chronicles. Brief extracts – sometimes merely faint echoes – of the king's account of the campaign and battle can be detected here

---

[53] Included among the valuable notes to his edition of Geoffrey le Baker's chronicle: *Baker*, pp. 252–5.

[54] *Baker*, p. 255. By comparison with the *Acta Bellicosa*, Cleopatra D. VII is more concise, with a tighter journal structure. Discrepancies: e.g., in the former, La Roche Guyon was taken on 10 August; in the later, 'le chastel de la Roche et le chastel de Gyonne sour Seyne' fell on 7 August.

and there,[55] but only the Anonimalle chronicle can be shown to be heavily reliant on material from the king's despatch. The apparently limited circulation of the king's letter is but one of several puzzling features of this enigmatic document. It appears to have been the third letter to be sent from France under the king's name during the Crécy–Calais campaign. The second, dated at Caen on 29 July, survives both in its original state, a privy seal letter 'to the chancellor, treasurer and others of our council remaining in London', and in an edited form, as distributed by the council on 3 August.[56] Three copies of the latter are known to exist: in the city of London records; in the register of Bishop Trillek of Hereford; and in the Lanercost chronicle, the author of which had access to the copy sent to Archbishop Zouche of York.[57] That this was indeed the second letter that the king had sent – that he had already reported on his arrival at La Hougue – is made clear near the beginning of the 29 July bulletin.[58] The king's third newsletter, dated 3 September and covering the whole campaign from La Hougue to the beginning of the siege of Calais, survives in a single copy addressed to 'son chier et feal chevalier Thomas Lucy'.[59] This document prompts several questions.

---

[55] For example, in the Meaux chronicle (the English crossed the Somme at Blanquetaque a thousand men abreast in only an hour; Philip VI had many Gascon crossbowmen put to death after the battle of Crécy): *Melsa*, iii, pp. 57, 59–60. Note also the similarity between the king's account of the stand-off at Blanquetaque and versions of the event in Knighton and Baker. However, such fragments may have been obtained from the campaign diaries that were almost certainly in circulation after the battle. There is some resemblance between the list of casualties in the king's letter and those that are to be found in various chronicles (e.g., *Knighton*, ed. Martin, p. 63; *Lanercost*, ed. Stevenson, p. 344; *Melsa*, iii, p. 59), but this is more likely to be a consequence of the general circulation of casualty lists, such as the 'cedula' attached to Johann von Schönfeld's letter.

[56] Privy seal letter: C81/314, no. 17803; printed in Fowler, 'News from the front', pp. 83–4. Despatch of edited copies to archbishops, bishops and sheriffs: *Foedera*, III, i, p. 88; *Calendar of Letter Book F*, ed. R.R. Sharpe (London, 1904), pp. 142–3.

[57] Jules Delpit, ed., *Collection générale des documents français qui se trouvent en Angleterre* (Paris, 1847), no. 145 (pp. 71–2); *Registrum Johannis de Trillek, episcopi Herefordensis, 1344–1361*, ed. J.H. Parry (London, 1912), pp. 279–81; *Lanercost*, ed. Stevenson, pp. 342–3. The copies are not identical. The version received by the city of London and the bishop of Hereford is closely based on the king's privy seal letter of 29 July, though changed from the first to the third person and with the logistical and strategic orders to the council cut out. It takes the form of a *cedula* attached to a covering letter. The version sent to the archbishop of York, as preserved in the Lanercost chronicle (itself a copy of a lost Franciscan chronicle), is somewhat different. Dated 30 July (perhaps a transcription error), it is in the form of a privy seal letter from the king addressed directly to the primate. (At the end of his 29 July despatch, the king had ordered the forwarding of letters to the archbishop of York and 'the other lords of the north'.) It assumes no prior knowledge of the campaign, beginning with the landing and disembarkation at La Hougue (this is not included in the other versions of the letter and may include material from the king's first bulletin), and inserts a passage emphasising the need to remain vigilant against the threat of 'noz ennemys Descoce'.

[58] The 29 July letter is concerned with the period 'puis le temps que nous arrivasmes a la Hoge pres de Barflu *dont nous vous feismes autrefoiz signifier la manere de nostre arivailler*' [my italics]. The italicised part of this quotation was edited out of the version of the letter distributed by the council. No copies of the first letter survive, unless it is Burgherssh's 17 July despatch to Archbishop Stratford that is being referred to.

[59] A seventeenth-century copy, included in a volume of transcripts: Bodleian Library, MS Ashmole 789, fos 148r–148v. Printed (inaccurately) in *Le Prince Noir*, ed. Michel, pp.

Why, as seems likely, was this post-Crécy newsletter circulated far less exten-sively than the king's earlier bulletin? Why is the only surviving copy addressed to a northern banneret with whom the king does not appear to have had particu-larly close connections?[60]

The most likely explanation for the limited circulation of the king's letter is that, with parliament due to meet within a fortnight or so of the battle, it was considered unnecessary to distribute a battlefield communiqué to the great men of the realm, since they would be fully briefed on recent events in France when they assembled at Westminster.[61] And on 13 September the king's envoys, headed by Bartholomew Burgherssh, duly reported to parliament. Edward III's despatch of 3 September may well have been used by Burgherssh in his presen-tation, but there is no evidence that it was distributed to the ecclesiastical and lay magnates who had gathered at Westminster.[62] Rather, it seems to have been sent to those lords, both lay and ecclesiastical, who had not been there to hear Burgherssh's report; or, to be more precise, to those who, by an order dated 30 July, had been excused attendance to allow them to concentrate their attention on the defence of the north of England.[63] Among the eleven lay lords, who would normally have been summoned to parliament and were now excused, was Sir Thomas Lucy, the head of a leading noble family of the western March, which had long been actively engaged in defending the Scottish border.[64] That it was indeed prudent to excuse these northern lords from attending parliament was underlined a little over a month after Burgherssh had made his speech before the assembly at Westminster. For among the leaders of the English army that triumphed over the Scots at Neville's Cross on 17 October were at least half a dozen of the lords who had been allowed to remain in the north. Hastening from the western Marches with a large number of men, Sir Thomas Lucy missed the

308–11. This letter and the archbishop of York's newsletter in the Lanercost chronicle begin in exactly the same way, suggesting that the text of the latter was simply reused for the first section of the former.

[60] For Sir Thomas Lucy (d. 1365), see *Complete Peerage*, viii, pp. 252–3. It should be con-ceded that Lucy had been a banneret of the royal household during the earlier 1340s (E36/204, fo. 89r), and that a month before leaving for France the king had granted him 700 marks *per annum*, albeit from the issues of Cumberland, in return for two Scottish prisoners of war, Sir Dugal Magdowell and his eldest son (*CCR, 1346–49*, p. 81).

[61] The writs of parliamentary summons were issued on 30 July: *RDP*, iv, pp. 558–60.

[62] The rolls of parliament indicate that nine bishops, four abbots or priors, but only three lay magnates, plus the justices and the representatives of the Commons, attended this session. *Rot. Parl.*, ii, p. 158. Fourteen of the lay peers who had been summoned, including five earls, did not attend, but such poor attendance was not unusual: J.S. Roskell, 'The problem of the attendance of the lords in medieval parliaments', *BIHR*, xxix (1956), pp. 153–204 (p. 168 for this parliament).

[63] The archbishop of York, the bishops of Carlisle and Durham (or his vicar general), the abbots of St Mary's York and Selby abbey, and 11 lay lords. *RDP*, iv, pp. 560–1. One of those excused, Sir Thomas Wake of Liddel, chose to attend parliament.

[64] Thomas had taken over this role from his father, Anthony, who had died in 1343 (*Com-plete Peerage*, viii, pp. 250–2). It is interesting to note that in 1339 the men of Cumberland had petitioned the king's council to excuse Sir Anthony from attending parliament, so that he could 'stay with them to do his best for the safety of the country'. *Northern Petitions*, ed. C.M. Fraser, Surtees Society, cxciv (1981), no. 111.

battle itself, but did good service pursuing the fleeing Scottish army to the border.[65]

The proposed connection between the recipients of the king's 3 September newsletter and the list of those excused attendance at parliament is reinforced by a further piece of evidence. Only one fourteenth-century English chronicle has an account of the campaign and battle of Crécy that can be shown to have drawn heavily on Edward III's newsletter: the Anonimalle chronicle.[66] The provenance of this work has not been proven to the satisfaction of all scholars, but the overwhelming thrust of the evidence suggests that it was 'copied in its final version at St Mary's abbey, York'.[67] For the section covering the period from 1333 to 1346 the Anonimalle chronicler's principal source was a lost northern Franciscan chronicle (which was also the basis of the Lanercost chronicle),[68] into the narrative of which was woven evidence from other sources, including Edward III's newsletter of 3 September. This section of the chronicle 'appears to be the work of a York author' of 'the middle years of the fourteenth century'.[69] That the king's battlefield bulletin was available to a chronicler based at St Mary's abbey in York can be explained by the fact that the abbot was one of five northern churchmen who had been excused attendance of the September 1346 parliament. We may assume, therefore, that he, like Sir Thomas Lucy, would have received a copy of the 3 September letter and that it remained among the records of the abbey until the Anonimalle chronicler made use of it later in the century. What use did this author make of it?

The account of the campaign and battle of Crécy in the Anonimalle chronicle is based squarely on the king's despatch of 3 September. The opening words on the campaign, which this chronicle shares with the Lanercost text, would appear to have been taken from the lost Franciscan chronicle; but while Lanercost then presents a transcript of the archbishop of York's copy of the king's 29 July letter, the Anonimalle writer turns to Edward III's 3 September letter, presumably because he recognised that it would provide a solid basis for his narrative for the whole campaign.[70] For long stretches of that narrative, this letter has been

---

[65] Thomas Sampson's newsletter on the battle of Neville's Cross: *Froissart*, ed. Lettenhove, v, p. 491.

[66] *Anonimalle*, pp. 19–23.

[67] Taylor, *English Historical Literature*, chapter 7 (at p. 133). Cf. Gransden, *Historical Writing in England*, ii, p. 111.

[68] Like the Anonimalle chronicle, the text that originates from the Augustinian priory of Lanercost in Cumberland survives in a single manuscript of the second half of the fourteenth century. H.S. Offler, 'A note on the northern Franciscan chronicle', *Nottingham Medieval Studies*, xxviii (1984), pp. 45–59, examines the relationship between these chronicles (and a third, a Latin Brut chronicle: Dean and Chapter Library, Durham: MS B. ii. 35, fos 1–35) and the lost chronicle that they each used, apparently independently, for information about the period 1338 to 1347.

[69] Taylor, *English Historical Literature*, pp. 139–41, 143. V.H. Galbraith dated this section to 'before 1382': *Anonimalle*, pp. xxiii–xxx, xxxiv–xxxvi.

[70] *Lanercost*, ed. Stevenson, pp. 341–2. The 'Durham version' of the lost Franciscan chronicle omits the 29/30 July letter: Offler, 'A note on the northern Franciscan chronicle', p. 49. V.H. Galbraith argued that the Anonimalle writer based his account of the Crécy campaign successively on the two surviving letters that were sent in the king's name (*Anonimalle*, pp.

reproduced verbatim by the Anonimalle writer, apart from the necessary change from the first to the third person, and occasional amplification.[71] However, at several points, material derived from other sources has been inserted into the narrative. Whereas the king's letter notes simply that he stayed in Poissy for three days, the Anonimalle chronicler adds that it was in a 'tresbeale nonerye bien a quatre lews de parys iiii jours'. He continues: 'En quel temps fuist prist le beal chastelle de roi de Fraunce qe sappella Moun Ioye.' The source of this additional information is not certain, but it may be significant that the material can be found in the *Acta Bellicosa*. That this campaign diary, or at least one of its variants, was indeed the source, is given some support when it is noted that the most lengthy of the Anonimalle writer's insertions into King Edward's letter – the tale of Sir Thomas Colville's chivalrous exploit at Blanquetaque – also appears, in a more condensed version, in the Monk of Malmesbury's chronicle.[72]

V.H. Galbraith observed that the Anonimalle text 'follows that of the letter to Sir Thomas Lucy . . . up to, but not including the account of Crécy'.[73] Comparison of the two texts suggests that this statement is a little too categorical. For while it is undoubtedly the case that the chronicler breaks away from Edward III's meagre treatment of the battle, the influence of the king's letter – in both phrasing and factual content – can be found at a number of points in the Anonimalle narrative.[74] The one important passage that the Anonimalle author omitted was the king's enigmatic reference to 'ung petit place ou la primer assemblée estoiet'. On the other hand, he did incorporate material into his account from at least one other, unidentified source.[75] We find nothing about the ominous appearance of crows or the pre-battle storm, nor are we given a clear impression of English dispositions or tactics, or the sequence of events in the battle. There is also no mention of archery.[76] Yet the Anonimalle compiler had

xxxiv–xxxv, 160), but it is altogether more likely that he used only the 3 September letter. There is no trace of the 3 September despatch in the narrative of the Lanercost chronicle, which for the march from Caen to Crécy appears to be based on Richard Wynkeley's newsletter.

[71] Such as locating La Hougue 'en Normandie' and adding that 'son adversaire' was 'de Fraunce'; and, more substantially, adding a passage that emphasised the damage that was done to settlements and the countryside during the march up the Seine.

[72] *Anonimalle*, pp. 22, 160. *Eulogium*, iii, p. 210. In these versions of the story, Colville jousts with a French knight and they part as friends. In Thomas Walsingham's retelling of the tale, the French knight had shouted insults against Edward III across the river, and Colville killed him: *Gesta Abbatum Monasterii Sancti Albani*, ed. H.T. Riley, Rolls Ser. (London, 1867), ii, p. 376.

[73] *Anonimalle*, p. 160.

[74] For example: of the French king's army, 'il avoyt pluis de xii m^l homms darms, des queux viii m^l furrent des gentiles gentz et des communes graunt noumbre'; the battle was 'fort et longement enduraunt'; the French lost 'bien de md.' killed. In terms of content and the order of names, the list of notable French casualties has more than a little in common with that in the king's letter.

[75] Galbraith pointed put that 'the official tone of the concluding sentences, "les nouns de ceaux qe furent pris al journee ne sount point yssi escriptz", suggests that the source was a newsletter with a list of casualties attached'. *Anonimalle*, pp. xxxv, 161.

[76] The 'alblasters' in the French army are mentioned in passing, but neither their actions nor those of the English bowmen are described.

before him a text that revealed that the 'lavaunt garde' was led by the Prince of
Wales, with the constable (Northampton) and marshal (Warwick), and that this
part of the English army was so hard-pressed during the battle that they had to
be relieved by the bishop of Durham, and the earls of Suffolk and Huntingdon.
Despite the erroneous inclusion of Huntingdon, this is an important passage,
which is both plausible (the bishop of Durham and the earl of Suffolk were
leading captains in the rearguard or reserve division) and finds echoes in a
variety of other accounts of the battle, including – as we have seen – the Meaux
chronicle, which in turn suggests a connection with the lost account in the *Acta
Bellicosa*.

If Edward III's Crécy newsletter had only limited influence on chronicle
writers, this can certainly not be said of Michael Northburgh's. The letter
survives as an attributed transcript in Robert Avesbury's chronicle, which was
compiled between 1356 and 1359 (the year of his death).[77] In fact, the section on
the battle of Crécy consists of nothing more than Northburgh's letter, which
Avesbury clearly preferred to Wynkeley's for the climax of the campaign.[78]
Although Avesbury's work now exists only in fifteenth-century copies, we know
that it was an important source for a chronicle that was written by a Westminster
monk, John of Reading, during the last years of his life (he died in 1368/9).
Reading's chronicle covers the years 1346 to 1367, and for the first half of it he
draws quite heavily on Avesbury's text. Consequently, his brief account of the
battle of Crécy consists of an abbreviated version of Northburgh's newsletter,
with no more than minor additions.[79] Lifted straight from Northburgh are the list
of principal French casualties, together with the newsletter's distinctive figure of
1,542 noble men-at-arms killed, and the details of the bloody action that was
fought on Sunday morning.[80] He takes Northburgh's figure of 'iiii grosses
batailles' for the French army and adds that the English had 'tres acies' and that
the battle took place 'in campo juxta Cressy'. These additional details, though
(as we shall see) reminiscent of Murimuth Nero D. X, may have been taken
directly from another, now lost newsletter. The only original feature in John of
Reading's account is the observation that the French army's withdrawal from the
field was commonly referred to as 'Noster beal retreit'. This sounds like the
kind of word-of-mouth story, 'common talk', that Reading mentions in the

---

[77] Avesbury was registrar of the court of the archbishop of Canterbury, at Lambeth.
[78] Avesbury included the first part of Wynkeley's 2 September letter, but turned to
Northburgh for the story from Poissy to Crécy. Northburgh's earlier letter, on the first stage of
the campaign, also appears in Adam Murimuth's chronicle, but his second is preserved only
by Avesbury. See Martin, 'John the Blind: the English narrative sources', pp. 88–9. It is quite
possible that Avesbury used the same texts as Murimuth, since he had access to the archive of
St Paul's: Gransden, *Historical Writing in England*, ii, p. 69.
[79] *John of Reading*, pp. 100–1. Reading also used Ranulf Higden's *Polychronicon*, in its continuation down to 1348, but there is no sign of this influence in Reading's account of Crécy.
James Tait in *John of Reading*, pp. 26–7; *Polychronicon Ranulphi Higden*, ed. Lumby, viii, pp.
340–2.
[80] In suggesting, erroneously, that the earl of 'Northfolke' was involved in this action, he preserves what must have been a transcription error by Robert Avesbury, since it is inconceivable
that Northburgh himself could have made such a mistake.

preface to his chronicle.[81] Very much reflecting the content of Northburgh's original letter, Reading tells us nothing about the sequence of events in the main battle on Saturday evening.

It is hardly surprising, therefore, that John of Reading's slight and derivative account of Crécy has played no part in modern discussions of the battle. Overall, the chronicle is an undistinguished piece of work, which, according to its editor, 'possesses no literary and but moderate historical value';[82] yet it proved to be an influential text in the last decades of the fourteenth century. The thin coverage of English affairs from 1347 to 1367 in the easily accessible historical literature 'led to a more general use of Reading's chronicle by later compilers than his intrinsic worth would justify'.[83] Thus, we find Thomas Walsingham at St Albans abbey turning to Reading as one of his sources for the retrospective sections of his large-scale historical works.[84] In fact, Walsingham's colourful but insubstantial account of Crécy in the *Chronica Maiora*, which was probably written during the 1390s, owes nothing to Reading (and, therefore, Northburgh's newsletter);[85] but his *Ypodigma Neustriae* (1419–22), 'The Symbol of Normandy', dedicated to Henry V, offers a completely different, though still brief, narrative of the battle, into which several distinctive extracts from John of Reading's account have been inserted.[86]

More significant in ensuring the enduring influence of Northburgh's newsletter on later medieval perceptions of Crécy was the use of John of Reading's text by the compilers of the English-language continuations of the Brut. The 'Edward III continuation', written during the last quarter of the fourteenth century, relies heavily on John of Reading, being no more than an abbreviated

---

[81] *John of Reading*, p. 99.

[82] Tait in *John of Reading*, p. 8. It also survives in only a single, fifteenth-century copy, which does not include the whole of Reading's original text.

[83] Tait in *John of Reading*, p. 8.

[84] Tait in *John of Reading*, pp. 57–62.

[85] The account of the Crécy campaign (but not the brief treatment of the battle) in the St Albans continuation of Higden's *Polychronicon* (1343–77), which may also have been written by Walsingham, does depend on Northburgh's newsletter, presumably through the agency of John of Reading: *Adam Murimuthensis Chronica*, ed. T. Hogg (English Historical Society, 1846), p. 176. For the account in *Chronica Maiora*, see Thomas Walsingham, *Historia Anglicana, 1272–1422*, ed. H.T. Riley, Rolls Ser., 2 vols (London, 1863–4), i, pp. 268–9; *Chronicon Angliae, 1328–1388*, ed. E.M. Thompson, Rolls Ser. (London, 1874), pp. 22–3. This is partly derived from the St Albans continuation of *Polychronicon* (the French casualties and Philip VI's wounds to throat and thigh), but is distinctive for its focus on the blind King John of Bohemia. The latter asks for a report on the English position and is told that they are finely deployed for battle and have positioned all their baggage in the rear. When the crows fly over the French army, King John interprets it as an ill-omen: 'Prodigium . . . est hoc, et dirum signum; significat nempe exercitum fore mactandum.' He has himself led into the fray in order to fight with the Prince of Wales.

[86] Thomas Walsingham, *Ypodigma Neustriae*, ed. H.T. Riley, Rolls Ser. (London, 1876), p. 287. Little remains from the account of Crécy that appeared in *Chronica Maiora*: only the extracts from the St Albans continuation of the *Polychronicon*, including the assertion that the king of Majorca was among the slain. The new account has a somewhat different list of French casualties, and the material on John of Bohemia has been replaced by sizeable extracts from John of Reading. It is noticeable that Reading's (and Avesbury's) erroneous reference to the earl of Norfolk has been corrected by Walsingham to 'Suffolk'.

translation of it for the period 1346 to 1361. Consequently, the most popular chronicle in late fourteenth- and fifteenth-century England offered a short account of Crécy that was, in effect, a trimmed version of Northburgh's news-letter, combined with Reading's minor additions.[87] Nothing has been added to Reading's text. Given that 120 medieval copies of the English Brut have survived, a great many people will have read or heard the story of Crécy as recorded by this chronicle, yet they can have gained no clearer idea of *how* the English had won the battle than had those who read the newsletters circulating immediately after it had been fought.[88]

The impact of Richard Wynkeley's Crécy newsletter on historiography is more complex as it appears to have been used directly by several chroniclers. The letter survives as a copy in one of the manuscripts of Adam Murimuth's chronicle.[89] As with Avesbury's use of Northburgh's despatch, Murimuth's account of Crécy consists of an attributed transcript of Wynkeley's Latin letter; but unlike Avesbury, Murimuth must have inserted this document into his chron-icle within months of the battle, since he died during the course of 1347.[90] Wynkeley's letter offers an independent view of events on 26 August: its date suggests that it was written shortly before the king's and Northburgh's despatches. But it has very little to say about the battle, and so – in contrast to John of Reading's use of Northburgh – when we can detect Wynkeley's influ-ence on later chroniclers, in every instance the letter has been digested and supplemented.[91] For example, no more than faint traces of Wynkeley's words can be found in the *Eulogium historiarum*, where the Monk of Malmesbury embroidered the correspondent's hearsay report of the French king being wounded in the face by an arrow. As we have seen, the Malmesbury author was able to base his account of the battle on a much more substantial source.

Much the same can be said of the influence of Wynkeley's despatch on the *Historia Aurea*, another work of 'universal history', in this case stretching from the Creation to 1347, which was probably compiled by a secular clerk, John, vicar of Tynemouth in the mid-fourteenth century.[92] Clear echoes of Wynkeley's

---

87 *Brut*, ed. Brie, ii, pp. 298–9; Tait in *John of Reading*, pp. 47–52; Taylor, *English Historical Literature*, pp. 127–32.

88 No more illumination was to be gained from Ranulf Higden's *Polychronicon*, which was the only other historical work with a national audience, at least among educated readers. The accounts of Crécy that appear among the *Polychronicon* continuations are very thin. See, for example, *Polychronicon Ranulphi Higden*, ed. Lumby, viii, pp. 340–3 (Latin text and two medieval English translations); and the version in the St Albans continuation: *Adam Murimuthensis Chronica*, ed. Hogg, p. 176.

89 BL, Harleian MS 3836. As we have seen, Avesbury included only the first part of Wynkeley's letter in his chronicle. There must have been other copies in circulation.

90 *Murimuth*, pp. 214–17. Adam Murimuth, a canon of St Paul's, London, who had pursued an active career as an ecclesiastical lawyer and diplomat, was in his 72nd year when he died during the first half of 1347.

91 It should noted that the Lanercost chronicle summarises Wynkeley's despatch of 2 Sep-tember for the march from Caen to Crécy, but passes over the battle with hardly a word, apart from listing the notable casualties on the French side. *Lanercost*, ed. Stevenson, pp. 343–4.

92 The 'three chief manuscripts' of the *Historia Aurea* 'are incomplete texts which descend from an *Historia Aurea* even more vast than any of those surviving': V.H. Galbraith, 'The *His-toria Aurea* of John, vicar of Tynemouth, and the sources of the St Albans Chronicle

letter can be found in the account of the Blanquetaque crossing in the *Historia Aurea*, but the narrative of the campaign as a whole cannot be traced to this source, nor can more than a single phrase in that of the battle of Crécy itself.[93] The concluding part of this 'battle piece' was published by V.H. Galbraith in 1928.[94] It includes the storm and the portentous crows, and closes by mentioning the arrival of a large French force on the Sunday morning, which was put to flight, with heavy losses, by the Prince of Wales and the earl of Warwick. Galbraith argued that the account of the battle proper, which he did not include in the printed extract, is an abridged version of Wynkeley's letter. However, while following Wynkeley's emphasis on the attacks repulsed by the Prince of Wales's division, the *Historia Aurea* also relates that the army's second division was led by the king and the third by the bishop of Durham. This is not noted by Wynkeley; indeed, the structure of the English army is presented in this way in only one known English source – the *Acta Bellicosa*.

The contribution of Wynkeley's despatch to Henry Knighton's narrative of the battle was somewhat more substantial. Knighton, a canon at the Augustinian abbey of St Mary of the Meadows, Leicester, wrote his chronicle during the last quarter of the fourteenth century. The section that includes the campaign and battle of Crécy rests squarely on Adam Murimuth's chronicle, and specifically on the newsletters that Murimuth copied into his text.[95] The account of the campaign from La Hougue to the capture of Caen is based principally on Burgherssh's newsletter of 29 July, with points of detail added from Murimuth's connecting text and Michael Northburgh's despatch from Caen.[96] Then, after summarising the document outlining the French invasion plans of 1338–9, which is also included in Murimuth's chronicle, Knighton continues with the march from Caen to Crécy. For this he makes use of Richard Wynkeley's 2 September newsletter, but also draws on at least one other, unidentifiable source, which was probably a campaign diary, perhaps one of the variants of the *Acta Bellicosa*.[97]

(1327–1377)', *Essays in History Presented to Reginald Lane Poole*, ed. H.W.C. Davis (Oxford, 1927), pp. 379–98 (at pp. 385–8). See also V.H. Galbraith, 'Extracts from the *Historia Aurea* and a French "Brut" (1317–47)', *EHR*, xliii (1928), pp. 203–17; Taylor, *English Historical Literature*, pp. 103–5. Dating: the *Historia Aurea* was available to Sir Thomas Gray, who completed his *Scalacronica* during the 1360s.

93 Oxford, Bodleian Library, Bodl. MS 240, p. 579; cf. *Murimuth*, pp. 214–17. Galbraith, 'Extracts from the *Historia Aurea*', pp. 206, 212–13. Galbraith points out that 'a much altered version [of the *Historia Aurea*] of the years 1327–46 is in print as a continuation of the chronicle of Walter of Hemingburgh': *Chronicon domini Walteri de Hemingburgh*, ed. H.C. Hamilton, English Historical Society, ii, pp. 297–426. This edition stops short of the Crécy campaign, but does include the documents that immediately precede it in the *Historia Aurea*. These include Philip VI's challenge to Edward III (14 August) and the latter's reply (15 August): *ibid.*, pp. 423–6; Bodl. MS 240, pp. 578–9.

94 Galbraith, 'Extracts from the *Historia Aurea*', pp. 212–13.

95 *Knighton*, ed., Martin, pp. 54–65. Geoffrey Martin's valuable discussion of Knighton's sources (*ibid.*, pp. xxix–xli) makes it clear that the chronicler made use of many documents, including newsletters, which no longer survive in their original form.

96 *Murimuth*, pp. 199, 202–5, 212–14.

97 *Murimuth*, pp. 205–11, 214–17. Meulan (*Mellenty*), which Knighton says, mistakenly, was reached on 14 August, is mentioned in none of the surviving newsletters and, of the English

The same combination of sources appears to lie behind Knighton's narrative of the battle itself. Geoffrey Martin has observed that it 'is not closely related to any of the standard accounts of Crécy';[98] it is, quite simply, a mélange. From Wynkeley's letter the chronicler took the size of the French army and Philip VI's face wound; but his details of the small English losses differ slightly from Wynkeley's and his more elaborate description of the repulse of the three major French assaults also suggest a different, more detailed source. Indeed, the less than wholly successful organisation and abbreviated character of parts of Knighton's narrative seem to indicate that he had some difficulty synthesising material that had been gathered from several sources.[99] The 'rich archival resources' that Geoffrey Martin has noted at St Mary of the Meadows could be a mixed blessing.[100] We might wish that Knighton had simply reproduced his sources verbatim – as, for example, he did to great effect in his description of Sir Walter Mauny's attack on Trégarantec in Brittany in 1342[101] – but for Crécy we must be content with tantalising fragments of information. Some of them appear to have been taken from sources that were more widely available. That he can supply the names of the principal captains in the Prince of Wales's division suggests a documentary affinity with several other chronicles (that is, they used the same sources), including the late version of Murimuth's chronicle in Cotton MS, Nero D. X.[102] His apparently curious statement that 'many of the poorest Englishmen were made knights' should probably be related to the monk of Malmesbury's more precise comments about the creation of knights before the battle, an event that is well attested by administrative records and which was accompanied by the granting of annuities.[103] However, when Knighton notes in passing that 'they fought into the dead of night, in the field of Westglyse near to Crécy', he provides a topographical reference that is to be found nowhere else.[104] Knighton's source for this information was probably a newsletter, perhaps a 'private' one like Johann von Schönfeld's to the bishop of Passau, which as we have seen also includes an enigmatic topographical reference. Unfortunately, as with Schönfeld's words, it is not easy to interpret Knighton's 'campo de Westglyse iuxta Cressy'. The location may be connected in some way with Watteglise, a farmstead standing 1½ km to the north-west of Wadicourt, though of course the 'field' of Westglyse may have been rather closer to Crécy.

narrative sources, only the *Acta Bellicosa*. As Geoffrey Martin notes, Knighton adds the earl of Warwick to Northampton and Sir Reginald Cobham, who according to Wynkeley, led the crossing of the Somme at Blanquetaque.

98 *Knighton*, ed. Martin, p. 61 n. 2.

99 For example: the French army is described as being 'ready and arrayed in three lines of battle' before the English have taken up position at Crécy; the casualties are discussed several times and the fighting into the night twice; there were three assaults or sixteen all told.

100 Martin, 'John the Blind: the English narrative sources', p. 91.

101 *Knighton*, ed. Martin, pp. 38–41.

102 In addition to what both texts have drawn from Wynkeley's newsletter, Knighton and Murimuth D. X have a few other features in common, suggesting that they had shared at least one other source.

103 See above, pp. 193–4.

104 'Nam pugnauerant usque ad profundam noctem, in campo de Westglyse iuxta Cressy.' *Knighton*, ed. Martin, pp. 62–3.

Moreover, it is not clear from Knighton's words how much fighting actually took place on this particular site: the main battle, or the more dispersed closing stages, which the chronicler says were illuminated by moonlight.[105]

Richard Wynkeley's testimony was not always so fully digested by chroniclers. His words stand out most obviously from the chronicle of the anonymous monk of Christ Church priory, Canterbury, a text that was apparently being written contemporaneously during the later 1350s and 1360s. For the first twenty years of Edward III's reign, the Canterbury monk drew heavily on Adam Murimuth's chronicle and so it is not surprising to find that his account of Crécy is based substantially on Wynkeley's newsletter. But, as James Tait pointed out, it was also in 1346 that the Canterbury text 'introduces one or two passages of some length from other sources'.[106] The description of French military preparations in the Cotentin peninsula prior to Edward III's landing cannot be traced to any known English source, but its resemblance to material in the *Acta Bellicosa* suggests that the Canterbury chronicler had before him a different campaign diary or a newsletter.[107] But for the remainder of the campaign, unidentifiable sources add only occasional points of detail to a narrative that appears largely to have been composed from the newsletters in Murimuth's chronicle:[108] for the march from La Hougue to Caen, the despatch that Northburgh wrote at Caen; and for the period from Caen to Crécy, Wynkeley's 2 September newsletter. The Canterbury account of the battle sticks closely to Wynkeley's text up to his listing of the French casualties, adding words only for emphasis or amplification.[109] But at that point the monk puts aside the newsletter and opts for an alternative ending. After stating that the English pursued the enemy, he recalls the appearance, before battle was joined, of 'black birds' in the sky above the French army, a portent of the carnage that was to follow. Bearing in mind the 'unique information' that the Canterbury chronicle offers for several episodes of the French wars of the 1350s and 1360s,[110] the supplementary material for Crecy is disappointing. He is not even the first English chronicler to mention the ominous crows.[111]

---

[105] 'Nam luna clare lucebat, sicut Deus voluit, per .iii. partes noctis'.

[106] *Canterbury*, pp. 63–75 (at p. 69); 187–92 (account of the campaign and battle).

[107] *Canterbury*, notes, pp. 356–6. The French preparations are mentioned in several continental chronicles (see Rogers, *War Cruel and Sharp*, pp. 218–19). That the landing was resisted by Marshal Bertran is noted in Chandos Herald's verse life of Edward, Prince of Wales (*Chandos Herald*, ed. Tyson, p. 53), which was apparently the source for *Froissart: Amiens*, ii, pp. 372–4.

[108] For the additions, see Tait's notes: *Canterbury*, pp. 357–8

[109] For example, the 'gladio apud Cressi' was fought 'in campo *magno*': *Canterbury*, pp. 191–2.

[110] Gransden, *Historical Writing in England*, ii, p. 109.

[111] The first was probably the *Historia Roffensis*: BL, Cotton MS, Faustina, B. V, fo. 92v. In addition to the Canterbury chronicle, the crows featured in a number of later accounts of the battle from monastic authors, including the Monk of Malmesbury and Thomas Burton at Meaux abbey, as well as the author (probably a secular clerk) of the *Historia Aurea*. By the time that Thomas Walsingham came to write about the 'black birds' of Crécy, they had been transformed into the entire *corvidae* genus: 'scilicet corvi, corvices et monedulae, et aliae cadaverum sectatrices': *Chronicon Angliæ*, ed. Thompson, p. 22; *Historia Anglicana*, ed. Riley, i, p. 268.

That Wynkeley's letter should also have been a source for the variant of Murimuth's chronicle in BL, Cotton MS Nero D. X, a text written either shortly before or after Murimuth's death in 1347, is not altogether surprising.[112] That said, the author of this text omits all of the newsletter transcripts and opts instead for continuous prose. The narrative of the seven-week campaign is brief and generally lacking in specific detail, though a few features suggest a documentary affinity with other chronicles, including Knighton and the Anonimalle text.[113] As for the account of Crécy itself, a framework of material has clearly been derived from Wynkeley's letter: the numerical strength of the French army; the three French attacks on the Prince of Wales's division; the wounding of Philip VI in the face by an arrow and the tearing to shreds of the French royal banner; and the minimal English casualties. But Wynkeley's material was replaced if the chronicler preferred the testimony of another document, as is evident with the list of notable French casualties.[114] And Wynkeley's meagre account of the fighting has been vividly embellished in Murimuth Nero D. X, with the image of lances and arrows seeking out the entrails of men and horses, whatever the armour that was borne by them.[115] This may be no more than a literary flourish; but there are other aspects of this early account of the battle that have clearly come from concrete sources. When Nero D. X tells us that Edward selected a spacious field suitable for battle and awaited the arrival of the enemy on foot,[116] we may fancy that we hear echoes of the king's newsletter; but the chronicle then continues with distinctive material on the structure of the two armies. The French army, we are told, consisted of seven 'acies', while the English were formed up in three divisions ('tres acies'), the first under the command of the Prince of Wales, the earl of Northampton (the constable) and the earl of Warwick (the marshal).

Exactly the same information about the structure of the French and English armies is supplied by the *Historia Roffensis*, a chronicle that has been attributed to William of Dene, a clerk in the service of Hamo of Hythe, bishop of Rochester.[117] The narrative of the battle offered by the *Historia Roffensis*, like that in

---

[112] *Murimuth*, pp. 246–8. This variant text may have been written by Murimuth himself, though he would have had only a few months to complete the task before his death. The editor, E.M. Thompson, suggests that 'the date of the writing is probably not much later than the middle of the fourteenth century' (*Murimuth*, p. xviii). There is a later, less full copy of this manuscript in BL, Cotton MS, Otho C. II.

[113] E.g., size of fleet: *Knighton*, ed. Martin, pp. 54–5; *Anonimalle*, p. 19. The similarities with Knighton, suggesting shared sources, become clearer when we reach the battle of Crécy.

[114] Murimuth Nero D. X made use of a different casualty list, distinctive for its inclusion of 'dominus Russingburgh qui fuit maximus Franciæ præter regem' and the closing summary: 'et de aliis militibus et armigeris plus quam duo millia, ac de hominibus de communi sine numero'. Cf. *Knighton*, ed. Martin, pp. 62–3; and the *Polychronicon* continuations: *Polychronicon Ranulphi Higden*, ed. Lumby, viii, p. 340; *Adami Murimuthensis Chronica*, ed. Hogg, p. 176.

[115] 'lanceis et sagittis densissime intervenientibus, quæ non minus hominum quam equorum viscera sunt scrutatæ, armatura qualicumque raro prohibente'.

[116] 'juxta villam de Cressy, circa horam primam, dominus rex Angliæ cum suis elegit sibi campum spatiosum et bello convenientem, quo ipsemet cum omnibus suis descendit in pedes, equis suis amotis, exspectando adventum inimicorum'.

[117] BL, Cotton MS, Faustina B. V (fos 92r–92v for Crécy). For useful, brief comments on

Murimuth Nero D. X, was written within a few years of the events described, and there can be little doubt that the source that, independently, both chroniclers used was an eyewitness account.[118] It no longer survives in an undigested form, but we may be able to detect its influence in chronicles written later in the fourteenth century. As we have seen, the Meaux chronicle states that the army was deployed in three battles ('tres acies'), with the Prince of Wales at the head of the first;[119] but since no mention is made of Northampton or Warwick, we should not on this evidence alone assume a documentary affinity with Murimuth Nero D. X or the *Historia Roffensis*.[120] Two other chronicles omit to mention the three divisions, but do notice the commanders of the first. The Anonimalle chronicle observes that the 'lavaunt garde' was led by the Prince of Wales, accompanied by the constable and marshal, while Knighton's chronicle actually names the two earls who were with the prince in the first division.[121] Lastly, a somewhat different perspective is provided by the *Historia Aurea*. In addition to having the prince at the head of the first division, this chronicle assigns the king to the second and the bishop of Durham to the third.[122] This arrangement can be traced only to the *Acta Bellicosa*, though (significantly) it is also implied by the story, as related by the Anonimalle and Meaux chronicles, of the employment of the bishop of Durham's men-at-arms to relieve the prince's division at a crisis point in the battle.

Would it stretch the evidence too far to suggest that each of these chroniclers, and probably others besides, made use of the same lost eyewitness source for part, perhaps a substantial part, of their account of the battle of Crécy? Naturally, their battle narratives are not identical, but there are sufficient similarities (beyond those noted above) to suggest the imprint on all of them of a widely circulated source. The plausibility of this proposition gains some reinforcement if we consider the implications of our examination of the three known English newsletters from Crécy and how they were used by chroniclers. We have seen how a range of chronicle compilers relied, to a greater or lesser degree, on

this chronicle, see C.J. Rogers, 'The Scottish invasion of 1346', *Northern History*, xxxiv (1998), pp. 53, 70. An edition is being prepared by Mark Buck for Oxford Medieval Texts.

[118] It is unlikely that one of these chronicles was the source for the other since in other respects their accounts of the battle do not resemble one another. There is no trace of Wynkeley's newsletter in the Rochester chronicle, which (as we shall see) contains a good deal of material not found in any other early English account of Crécy.

[119] *Melsa*, iii, p. 58.

[120] It is notable that the 'tres acies' are not to be found in the surviving newsletters from the battle, though Thomas Bradwardine does refer to them in his 'victory sermon' of late October or early November 1346 (Offler, 'Thomas Bradwardine's "victory sermon" in 1346', p. 25). Given that it was common, perhaps usual, to divide a large army into three units for the march and the battlefield, it is possible that the three English divisions at Crécy became common currency without specific documentary input. This would explain one of John of Reading's additions to Northburgh's newsletter (*John of Reading*, p. 100). Geoffrey le Baker also mentions three divisions, but, as we shall see, his chronicle may lie at the end of a different branch of the complex tree of documents arising from this battle.

[121] *Anonimalle*, p. 22; *Knighton*, ed. Martin, pp. 62–3.

[122] Warwick is associated with the Prince of Wales in the fighting on the Sunday morning. Oxford, Bodleian Library, Bodl. MS 240, p. 579.

Wynkeley's despatch; but had Murimuth not included a complete transcript of the newsletter in his chronicle, we could only have suspected the existence of a widely used source. How such a document was actually used by chroniclers is also instructive. It might be partially disguised when combined with other materials; indeed, when two compilers have taken different extracts from it (as we have suggested may have happened with Thomas Burton and the Monk of Malmesbury), its presence may not even be suspected. Close correlation of the three newsletters with the chronicles has also shown just how much material originated in other, unknown sources. So, even allowing for the role of oral testimony, which some chroniclers mention, it is clear that there must have been other eyewitness accounts that have not survived the intervening centuries. But how many, what were they like, and who wrote them?

The first question is impossible to answer, and it is in any case complicated by the likelihood of variant texts. However, with regard to the second question, some characteristics can be ascertained from the imprint that the source or sources (whether newsletter or longer 'diary' account) have left on the chronicles. It has been noted already that the lost source provided distinctive information not mentioned by any of the known eyewitness accounts. Apart from the three divisions of the army (perhaps not in itself significant) and the captains of the first, we are given some impression of what may have been the 'crisis point' in the battle, when the 'rearguard' reinforced the hard-pressed men of the Prince of Wales's division. This episode appears in the Anonimalle and Meaux chronicles, both of which make reference to the involvement of the bishop of Durham's men.[123] More broadly, it can be seen that the chronicles, and thus their source or sources, focused mainly on the Prince of Wales's division, an emphasis that is admittedly present in Wynkeley's letter but not in Northburgh's or the king's. Moreover, we are given very much an aristocratic view of the battle. For example, we are told about the newly created knights and we see the fighting through the eyes of men with swords and battle-axes in their hands. Very little is said about missile weapons: the role played by the English archers is hardly mentioned and the Genoese crossbowmen are practically invisible.[124] In short, the English chronicles that we have examined so far, and presumably the source or sources upon which they were based, do not explain the English victory by reference to tactics. Rather, the triumph is presented as a feat of endurance and a mark of God's grace. The essence of Knighton's account, for example, is that the English won despite being hungry and wet from the storm; they withstood a series of attacks from an enemy who had arrived on the battlefield in an orderly manner; and they continued fighting long into the moonlit night, and were ready to start again early the next morning.[125] Knighton's narrative is a composite and was influenced no doubt by his own response to his sources. Yet when viewed alongside those other chronicles with which his account appears to have a documentary affinity, it is clear that he did not change

---

[123] *Anonimalle*, p. 22; *Melsa*, iii, p. 58. Cf. *Baker*, p. 84.
[124] The presence of the 'alblasters' is mentioned in passing in *Anonimalle*, p. 22.
[125] *Knighton*, ed. Martin, pp. 60–3.

the essential thrust of his sources. If the English chronicles fail to explain the English victory, this is largely because their sources failed to do so.

If we were allowed an educated guess at the identity of the mastermind behind the lost despatch or diary that has left an imprint on our chronicles, we would suggest Bartholomew Burgherssh senior. He had been responsible for at least two newsletters early in the campaign, written on 17 and 29 July, and the second of these includes a well-observed account of the assault on Caen.[126] Moreover, while leading one of the four large retinues in the prince's division, he is the only front-rank captain in that division *not* to be mentioned in any of our chronicles – Murimuth Nero D. X, the *Historia Roffensis*, the *Historia Aurea*, Henry Knighton or the Anonimalle chronicle. This is precisely the impression that we would expect to find in a letter 'written' by Burgherssh in the first person. Since he was the leader of the four-man team sent by the king to address parliament, a fortnight or so after the battle, what perhaps we may have detected is not so much a newsletter that had been sent back to England, as the report that Burgherssh presented to the assembly at Westminster.[127]

Indeed, it is quite possible that Burgherssh was responsible for something rather more substantial than a newsletter. As we have seen, there are good grounds for thinking that the lost eyewitness source for Crécy may well be the missing concluding section of the *Acta Bellicosa*;[128] and there is some evidence to suggest that it was Burgherssh who directed the drawing up of this campaign diary. There is more than a passing resemblance between Burgherssh's two campaign newsletters and the text of the *Acta Bellicosa*, but with the latter offering a fuller account that has benefited from further reflection on the events described.[129] Also tending to suggest Burgherssh's editorial control of the campaign diary is the omission of his own name (apart from among the four dozen bannerets listed near the beginning of the narrative), but the inclusion of two members of the Burgherssh family: Bartholomew junior, as one of those involved in the repair of the bridge over the River Douve (19–20 August); and

---

126 *Murimuth*, pp. 200, 202–3. Note the attention that Burgherssh gives in these letters to the actions of his colleague in the first division, the earl of Warwick. Note also that the second letter acknowledges the important mobile, offensive role played by the archers in the capture of Caen: they attacked those defending the bridge with volleys of arrows and then engaged in fierce hand-to-hand fighting.

127 As we have seen, the rolls of parliament include only a summary of Burgherssh's speech: *Rot. Parl.*, ii, p. 158.

128 Of course, the principal captains of the prince's division were known to the author of the *Acta Bellicosa*: he had provided lists of bannerets in each of the army's divisions early in his narrative.

129 The suggestion in the 17 July letter that the king had not planned to land in Normandy, but was taken there by a providential wind, is elaborated upon in the *Acta Bellicosa* version, although it is no longer claimed that the original destination was Gascony. The list of men knighted at La Hougue is in the same order in the two texts; and both texts mention Warwick's chivalric escapade after the landing as well as the raid on Barfleur. As compared with the 29 July letter, the *Acta* version of the assault on Caen suggests a less spontaneous and undisciplined affair. However, the two texts offer similar figures for the number of notable captives; they both tell us that the lord of Tancarville was captured by one of the prince's knights (named in the *Acta*); and they both state that over a hundred ships were destroyed by the English fleet from the Cotentin to the mouth of the River Orne.

Henry, who was knighted by the Prince of Wales on 22 August.[130] Whoever suggested the drawing up of the campaign diary, Burgherssh was the natural choice for overseeing the project. He was closely connected with both the king and the Prince of Wales: he was the king's spokesman in parliament in September 1346, and was master of the prince's household and the dominant figure on his council. If anyone was responsible for the two Edwards' public relations, it was Burgherssh. Moreover, as a former seneschal of Ponthieu, he had almost certainly played a crucial role during the closing stages of the Crécy campaign, if not in the planning of it. Burgherssh would surely have known about the Blanquetaque ford and he may even have drawn attention to the potential offered by the Crécy battlefield. As much as anyone, he had a personal interest in celebrating 'the acts of war of the most illustrious prince lord Edward, by grace of God king of England and France and of Edward the eldest son of that king, Prince of Wales' during the summer of 1346. And what better reward for Burgherssh senior's role in the triumph at Crécy than for his son, Bartholomew, to be included among the founder knights of the Order of the Garter (the father was probably by this time too old for jousting)?

Giovanni Villani and the English *carrino*

In addition to the English eyewitness accounts of Crécy that have been examined so far – those that have survived and those whose existence can be detected through their imprint on later chronicles – there appears to have been another source, or group of sources, which have left a mark on a smaller number of chronicles. Of particular significance in this respect is the unpublished *Historia Roffensis*. This, as we have seen, is an early secondary account of the battle, which has a documentary affinity with several chronicles, particularly Murimuth D. X. But in other respects, the Rochester chronicle is strikingly different from other English chronicles. It offers a narrative of the campaign that is not closely related to any known eyewitness account. Like the *Acta Bellicosa*, it provides details of the king's 13 July proclamation prohibiting damage to persons and property in Normandy, but that is where the close resemblance between these texts ends.[131] The Rochester chronicle also has features in common with Edward III's 3 September despatch (for example, noting the king's desire for battle and his frustration at the breaking of the Seine bridges); but it adds details of Philip VI's challenge and Edward III's verbal response to the French king's messenger, which suggests the influence of an additional source.[132] Turning to the battle, we find a similar situation. What the *Historia Roffensis* and Murimuth Nero D. X have in common is the information on the two armies that we have already noted; but apart from this they do not resemble

---

130 *Acta Bellicosa*, ed. Moisant, pp. 162–3.

131 *Historia Roffensis*, fo. 91r; Rogers, *War Cruel and Sharp*, p. 240 n. 6. For example, *Historia Roffensis* lacks the wealth of detail about men and places that is such a distinctive feature of the anonymous campaign diary.

132 *Historia Roffensis*, fo. 91v; Rogers, *War Cruel and Sharp*, p. 257.

each other. Moreover, the *Historia Roffensis* owes no discernible debt to Wynkeley's newsletter, and offers a number of distinctive points of its own on the battle. If it has been correctly dated, it is the first known English narrative source to notice the ominous appearance of 'crows and black birds'; and rather in the same vein, a parallel is drawn, somewhat laboriously, between the victory of Judas Maccabeus over the Syrian general Nicanor and the English triumph at Crécy. But from the point of view of understanding what took place on the battlefield, of greater importance are the comments on English dispositions. Having noted the three principal commanders of the first division, the chronicler adds that they 'primo congredi disposuerunt, qui mox stationes suas componentes et carectas suas anteponentes, strenue et viriliter oppugnaverunt'.[133]

What is immediately striking about this statement (if we set aside the apparent confusion of simultaneous defence and attack) is the suggestion that carts were an integral part of the Prince of Wales's defensive position, with the troops positioned behind them. Such a suggestion is not to be found in Murimuth Nero D. X, nor indeed in any other early English account of the battle. It is, however, a central feature of the highly individual and very early account written by the Florentine chronicler, Giovanni Villani (d. 1348).[134] The value of this chronicle has been assessed in Chapter 4 by Michael Prestwich, but such is its significance that it is necessary to examine it further here. Villani offers a coherent and well-crafted narrative of the battle, the essence of which is, firstly, that the English employed a protective enclosure of carts – a 'campo di carri', or 'carrino' as he terms it; and, secondly, that the fighting was less static than many accounts suggest, with the English counter-attacking at crucial moments in the battle. According to Villani, the *carrino* was constructed from the many carts that the English had with them, combined with those taken from the countryside. This was not merely a baggage park at the rear of the English army, but a kind of field work *within* ('dentro') which the three divisions of the army were deployed on foot, with archers on or near the carts and guns incorporated into the defensive perimeter (he says 'under' the carts).[135] Villani notes further that the English left an opening in the *carrino*, not wishing to avoid battle, and that the fighting was concentrated in this restricted area ('il luogo stretto da combattare').[136] Once the first French division, consisting of crossbowmen and a few hundred cavalry, had been routed, the prince's division mounted their horses and attacked the French cavalry of the first and second divisions. The mêlée was hard-fought and long, but the balance was tipped by the arrival of the second English division, led by the earl of Arundel, and the first two French divisions were routed. This prompted Philip VI to lead the third division – effectively the remainder of the French army – into the fray. Under this pressure the English retired to their *carrino*; but Edward III's third division left the wagon

---

133 *Historia Roffensis*, fo. 92r.
134 *Villani*, vii, pp. 163–70.
135 'E ordinò il re d'Inghilterra i suoi arceri, che n'avea grande quantità su per le carra, e tali di sotto con bombarde': *Villani*, vii, p. 163.
136 *Villani*, vii, pp. 163, 165.

enclosure by another way, opened up for the purpose, and attacked the French in the flank and rear, the English archers and Welsh spearmen targeting in particular their adversaries' horses.

Villani offers a detailed account of the battle that in a number of important respects is different from most of the others that are available, whether of English, French or Low Countries provenance. The one exception among the English sources is the *Historia Roffensis*, which presents what may perhaps be interpreted as a much compressed version of Villani's story. Thus, the defensive use of carts and the prince's division attacking the French have been combined by the Rochester chronicler in a single statement. And it is striking that another distinctive feature of the *Historia Roffensis*, the appearance of 'crows and black birds' before the battle, is also to be found in Villani. The latter notes, without any trace of portentous overtone, that before the battle there appeared above the armies 'two great crows crying and croaking, and then a little rain fell'.[137] It seems likely that the Rochester chronicler had access to documentation, perhaps a newsletter, that has left no trace on any other English chronicle,[138] but which in some form found its way to Florence. If this is the case, he and Villani responded to it very differently.[139]

Apart from the *Historia Roffensis*, there is no sign of Villani's *carrino* in the English sources, from the newsletters onwards.[140] Nor is there any suggestion that sections of Edward III's army counter-attacked during the battle on the Saturday evening. To read the English accounts is to gain the impression that this was fought as a static, defensive action, with King Edward's men remaining rooted to their starting positions. This impression arises from the fact that most English accounts of the battle make no attempt to trace a clear sequence of events after the failure of the first cavalry attack. After that, the rest of the battle is lost in a blur of generalisation, with one or two isolated, spotlighted episodes. We probably have the newsletters to blame for this: those that we have do not offer a real narrative of the battle; those that have been lost may not have been very much more informative. According to the English chronicles, the only movement involving Edward III's army was the relief of the hard-pressed men of the prince's division by a detachment of the bishop of Durham's men-at-arms. As we have seen, this appears in the Anonimalle and Meaux chronicles, and presumably originated in the lost eyewitness account – perhaps the *Acta Bellicosa* 'ur-text' – that has been discussed already. Since the bishop was one of the captains in the rearguard division, of which the earl of Arundel could be

---

137 'due grandi corbi gridando e gracchiando; e poi piovve una piccola acqua'.

138 This should not occasion surprise: the *Historia Roffensis* also includes a transcript of an otherwise unknown newsletter from the siege of Tournai: see C.J. Rogers, 'An unknown news bulletin from the siege of Tournai in 1340', *War in History*, v (1998), pp. 358–66.

139 Apart from their descriptions of Edward III's landing in Normandy, which are phrased similarly and in which both display confusion over the date, the campaign narratives of Villani and the Rochester chronicler do not resemble each other. Villani's is longer and used sources of French provenance.

140 Walsingham's late fourteenth-century *Chronica maiora* noted that all the baggage had been positioned in the rear (*Chronicon Angliae, 1328–1388*, ed. Thompson, p. 22; *Historia Anglicana*, ed. Riley, p. 268); and we find the same point in *Melsa*, iii, p. 58.

counted the senior military commander, it is likely that the 'relief episode' and Arundel's attack in support of the prince's division as narrated by Villani are different descriptions of essentially the same event. That event has also left a mark on other accounts of the battle. Geoffrey le Baker tells us that the king sent twenty knights to assist his son. It is notable that the chronicler did not know the identity of the leader of this contingent and left a blank space in the text, presumably intending to insert a name in due course.[141] In Froissart's accounts of Crécy, the reader's attention is naturally drawn to Edward III's refusal to send aid to his son, in order to 'let the boy win his spurs' – an episode that may be dismissed as a product of the author's fertile literary imagination. But it should be recalled that Froissart also states that the second division, which was positioned on the prince's wing, 'vinrent rafreschir la bataille dou dit Prince'.[142] In the Amiens MS, Froissart notes that the bishop of Durham (with Northampton) was involved in the 'relief'; in a later version, it was the earl of Arundel.

If echoes of particular moments in Villani's story can be heard in the Anonimalle and Meaux chronicles, as well as in the works of Geoffrey le Baker and Jean Froissart, the Florentine chronicler's overall conception of the battle receives substantial support in several French chronicles, most notably the *Chronique Normande.* Although the identity of the author is not known, internal evidence suggests that he was a militarily experienced lesser nobleman of Norman origin. The text as we have it was written in about 1370, but it is possible that some sections had been drafted earlier.[143] The chronicle includes valuable accounts of several of the smaller engagements of the French war, in some of which our author fought. Although in all likelihood on active service during the summer of 1346,[144] he does not appear to have been present at Crécy. Presumably his brief but distinctive account of events on that day was derived from eyewitnesses in the French army; and given his own military experience, he is unlikely to have misunderstood the story that he heard. He tells us that Edward III surrounded his army with carts,[145] so that when the Genoese advanced against them, the English were shielded from their enemies' crossbow bolts by their carts and by substantial hedges.[146] The flight of the Genoese and the subsequent confusion within the ranks of the French cavalry prompted the English to sally forth from their carts and launch a counter attack. What followed is narrated with less precision than we find in Villani's account; but it is clear that the archers targeted the vulnerable horses of the French, contributing significantly thereby to the break-up and flight of Philip VI's army.[147]

---

141 'unde missus [blank] cum xx. militibus in principis succursum': *Baker*, p. 84.
142 *Froissart*, ed. Luce, iii, pp. 182–3, 423–5; Barber, *Edward Prince of Wales*, pp. 246–8.
143 For the author and the surviving, imperfect copies (of a copy) of the original text of the chronicle, see the editors' Introduction to *Chronique Normande* (pp. i–lxxv). For Crécy, see pp. 80–2.
144 Auguste and Emile Molinier suggest that he served under the count of Eu at Aiguillon and Caen, and then in a garrison in north-eastern France during the siege of Calais. *Chronique Normande*, pp. x–xiii.
145 'fist son ost clorre de son charroy'.
146 'les Anglois furent bien targiez de leur charroy et de fortes haies et d'autre targement'.
147 'Et quant les Anglois virent ce triboul, ilz saillirent hors de leur charroy et coururent seure

Aspects of the *Chronique Normande*'s narrative of the battle can also be found in other chronicles written from the French perspective. Jean de Venette has the English attack 'our ill-ordered French lines' after King Philip's men-at-arms had turned on the Genoese, while the Rouen-based author of the *Chronique des quatre premiers Valois* supports his fellow Norman chronicler's reference to hedges playing a part in the English defences: 'Les Anglois archiers furent du premier embuschiés de les haies et par leur trait occistrent moult de chevaulx et de gens.'[148] A more complete concordance with the *Chronique Normande* is to be found in the early fifteenth-century *Chronographia regum Francorum*,[149] which states that the English 'made an enclosure from carts and wooded hedges', from which they emerged to exploit the confusion in the French army following the flight of the Genoese. Once again, the implication is that the archers were potent and mobile.[150]

Echoes of the *Chronique Normande* are also to be found in the two related narratives from St Omer – the short continuation of the *Chronique de Flandre* and the St Omer chronicle – though here the points of close textual similarity amount to no more than a few distinctive phrases. Indeed, the overall impression conveyed by the St Omer texts is that their view of the English dispositions is based upon independent testimony. They offer a valuable description of the English position prior to the start of the battle.[151] Indeed, they are notable among chronicles written from the French perspective in that they display detailed

aux François et mout les greverent et plus de trait que d'autre chose, car les chevaulx des François, qui se sentirent feruz des saiettes, se prindrent à desroier et en chay mors pluseurs. Et lors se prindrent François à desconfire et grant partie enfouy sanz assembler.'

[148] *Jean de Venette*, p. 43; *Chronique des quatre premiers Valois*, p. 16.

[149] Indeed, these texts have so much in common, including specific detail and the order in which the material is presented, that we must suspect that either the *Chronographia* drew heavily on the *Chronique Normande* as one of its sources or, as seems more likely, their authors had access to a common source, which has since been lost. The similarities include: that there were 2,000 crossbowmen, and that they ran out of ammunition; the inclusion of the same, partly erroneous list of English captains; and the statements that the Prince of Wales was temporarily taken prisoner by the count of Flanders, and that Philip VI was unhorsed and led from the field by Jean of Hainault, his itinerary being Labroye, Doullens and Amiens. For the *Chronographia*, which was compiled at St Denis between 1415 and 1422, see J.F. Verbruggen, *The Battle of the Golden Spurs: Courtrai, 11 July 1302*, ed. K. DeVries, trans. D.R. Ferguson (Woodbridge, 2002), p. 70 and references cited in footnotes.

[150] 'Anglici vero sagittabant fortiter contra eos et fecerunt clausurum de curribus et sepibus nemorum . . . Franci ergo videntes eos fugere, estimantes eos traditores esse, multos ex eis occiderunt; quod videntes Anglici, statim egressi de clausura, aggressi sunt Francos et plures ex eis occiderunt sagittis quam alio modo.' *Chronographia*, ii, p. 232.

[151] St Omer chronicle, fos 261v–262r; *Chronique de Flandre*, ii, pp. 42–3. The significance of the St Omer texts' account of Crécy has been discussed for the first time in a modern work of scholarship by C.J. Rogers, *War Cruel and Sharp*, pp. 266–71. It is worth noting, however, that F.-C. Louandre made use of the St Omer texts in his account of Crécy (*Histoire d'Abbeville et du comté de Ponthieu jusqu'en 1789*, 3rd edn, 2 vols (Abbeville, 1883), i, pp. 201–18), as did the French cavalry officer, Joachim Ambert: 'Mémoire sur l'expédition anglaise de 1346, et sur la bataille de Crécy', *Le Spectateur Militaire*, xxxix (April–September 1845). Quoting a passage that only appears in the unpublished version of the St Omer chronicle, Ambert notes that his source was 'Chronique manuscrite qui appartient á la famille de Tramecourt' (*ibid.*, p. 131 n. 2).

knowledge of the workings and structure of the English army.[152] As we saw in Chapter 5, the lists of bannerets included in the St Omer chronicle (BN, MS Fr. 693) correspond well with the evidence provided by the *Acta Bellicosa* and other sources. According to the St Omer texts, the first division, under the nominal command of the Prince of Wales, 'se traist amont vers les champs pres dun moulin et par derriere avoit ung bois'. The second division, commanded by the king, was near to ('empres') the first, and both were protected by a defensive enclosure of carts. The extent of this enclosure is not absolutely clear. The unpublished text of the St Omer chronicle (BN, MS Fr. 693) states that they 'firent une deffense de leur charroy par derriere eulx'; but the short continuation of the *Chronique de Flandre* puts it somewhat differently, noting that they 'firent une grande haye de leur charroy, par quoy on ne les peust sourprendre'. One implication of the second version is that the enclosure of carts may have covered more than just the rear of the army, extending perhaps to the flanks and, indeed, to vulnerable points in the front of the English position. Bearing in mind that these two texts are probably variants of an original that has been lost, it is possible, perhaps likely, that the more elaborate wording of the second is more faithful to the original text. The other notable feature of the second version is the use of 'grande haye' to mean a fence or form of palisade, rather than a hedge. Indeed, we should be aware that this particular word was sometimes employed in a figurative rather than literal sense. For example, Froissart refers on several occasions to 'un grande haie' of men-at-arms or even archers.[153]

The St Omer texts state that the men of the third division 'tenoient l'arrière-garde et gardoient les tentes et le charroy'. Under the leadership of the earl of Arundel and the bishop of Durham, this section of the army would have been positioned behind the other two divisions – as a reserve, ready to intervene in the front-line fighting as well as watching the rear of the 'wagon fort'. In the event, as we have seen, at least part of this reserve was deployed during the battle in support of the prince's division. The St Omer texts' treatment of the English army's tactical movements during the battle lacks the clarity that we find in some of the other chronicles, especially Villani. However, St Omer does have the English advance from their positions to take advantage of the confusion when the French cavalry and the Genoese became entangled with each other:

> Et ainsi que la chose estoit en tel triboul, passèrent les Anglois à toute leur battaille et allèrent aux haches et aux espées. Là commença l'estour moult crueuls, mais les Genevois se tournèrent tous en fuitte. Quant ce veirent les Anglois, ils prindrent cuer en eulx. Si trairent tant espessement que nul ne le povoit endurer.[154]

---

152 Apart from St Omer, the only other 'French' chronicle to comment on the three English battles and their commanders is the *Chronique des quatre premiers Valois*, p. 16. One apparent error in the St Omer texts is the suggestion that Sir Reginald Cobham was marshal of the English army. It is interesting to note that Froissart has him accompanying Warwick and Harcourt in their pre-battle survey of the ground at Crécy: *Froissart*, ed. Luce, iii, pp. 166, 402.

153 *Froissart*, ed. Luce, iii, pp. 177, 180.

154 *Chronique de Flandre*, ii, p. 43. The St Omer chronicle, fo. 262v, has 'sur eulx assemblerent a haches et maches' instead of 'allèrent aux haches et aux espées'.

It is clear from this review of a variety of chronicles that Giovanni Villani's narrative of the battle is by no means wholly isolated. Surely it deserves more than the peremptory dismissal that it received from T.F. Tout.[155] Indeed, there is much about the Florentine's account that rings true. He shows how each of the three divisions of the French army was made up of mixed arms, as would be dictated by sound tactical sense. The first battle was composed of crossbowmen and 300 mounted men-at-arms under the command of King John of Bohemia. The second, led by the count of Alençon, consisted of 4,000 cavalry and many 'sergenti a piè'. In the third, King Philip led the remainder of the army, horse and foot. Villani's account of the uneven contest between archer and crossbowman is succinctly explained in terms of rates of shooting: the archers could unleash three shafts for each of the crossbowmen's quarrels.[156] The arrows, he adds, appeared in the sky like a cloud ('nuvola') – a nice variant on a frequently evoked image. The English guns added further to the pressure on the advancing French troops: their impact on the battle was more than merely psychological, since they caused many casualties among both men and horses.[157] This is very much in line with French narratives of the battle, for while they all stress the crucial role played by archery, the *Grandes chroniques*, a contemporary account, also notes that the English 'gitterent trois canons', with the result that the Genoese crossbowmen 'tournerent les dos et laissierent à traire'.[158] That the English chronicles, including the most detailed accounts, like Baker's, make no reference to the guns should not cause us to doubt Villani. Guns are not mentioned in the newsletters that have survived, but then neither is the effect of archery.

As for Villani's *carrino*, this again is entirely plausible. Such a 'wagon fort' would not have been a wholly unprecedented feature of European warfare. For example, the Flemings created such a structure to protect their rear and flanks before the battle of Mons-en-Pévèle in 1304. As the *Annales Gandenses* noted, the Flemings 'made a sort of fortification out of the wagons in their rear of their own line, connecting one with another, but taking off one wheel from each, so that the French, if they wished to encircle them, should not be able to attack them from the rear'.[159] At Crécy it would have made good tactical sense for the English to use carts to reinforce a defensive position that also included natural

---

[155] That 'the English [were] entrenched behind a laager of wagons . . . was plainly not the case, even though some French chronicles . . . share in the error of the Italians': T.F. Tout, 'Firearms in England in the fourteenth century', *EHR*, xxvi (1911), p. 672. Cf. F.-C. Louandre (*Histoire d'Abbeville*, i, p. 201), who accepted the testimony of these chronicles. In his view, Edward 'entoura son armée de chariots, tant des siens que de ceux qu'on trouva dans le pays laissant néanmoins une ouverture pour sortir et rentrer quand il serait temps, et il fit ainsi un vaste camp retranché'.

[156] By contrast, the *Chronique Normande* tells us that the crossbowmen quickly ran out of ammunition, their supply carts being far in the rear. When the English noticed their opponents' shooting slackening they quickened the pace of theirs: *Chronique Normande*, pp. 80–1.

[157] 'grande uccisione di gente e sfondamento di cavalli': *Villani*, vii, p. 165.

[158] *Grandes chroniques*, ix, p. 282.

[159] Quoted by DeVries, *Infantry Warfare in the Early Fourteenth Century*, p. 36. Cf. Verbruggen, *The Art of Warfare in Western Europe during the Middle Ages*, p. 198.

topographical features, the '*rideaux*' or '*radillons*', and which may, by necessity, have stretched over an extended area. Indeed, as we have seen, several French chronicles emphasise the protection afforded by the combination of carts and 'fortes haies' in the English position. This, combined with the fact that, according to Villani, the carts were covered with *sargane* and cloth, as protection against crossbow bolts, also helps to explain the low English casualties in the battle. On the other hand, we would perhaps expect those casualties to have been higher as a consequence of the mêlées ('aspra e dura') that Villani describes.

What were the sources for Villani's vivid account of the battle? Clearly, he had access to first-hand testimony, and it has often been suggested that he must have spoken to survivors from the contingent of Genoese crossbowmen. This finds support in the extended attention that Villani gives to the miserable fate of the 'balestrieri genovesi e altri Italiani'. Moreover, as we have seen, he also offers a plausible picture of the structure of the French army. Yet Villani's Crécy narrative is told from more than one perspective. For the English view of the battle, as Jonathan Sumption has argued, it is likely that Villani had access to 'Florentine newsletters from London and Bruges, in turn based on newsletters from the English army'.[160] Traces of such documents are to be detected in his narrative. He states, accurately, that the English army consisted of three battles ('tre schiere'), with the first led by the Prince of Wales, the second under the earl of Arundel ('Rondello') and the third kept under the king's personal direction.[161] Not only does this correspond with the structure of the army described by *Acta Bellicosa* and the St Omer chronicle,[162] but Villani's text bears an uncanny resemblance to a passage in Geoffrey le Baker's chronicle – except that Baker omits Arundel's name.[163] The suspicion that, at this point in their narratives, Villani and Baker were using essentially the same source is reinforced by examination of how the two texts proceed:

> Villani: 'e chi era cavallo iscese a piè co' cavalli a destro per prender lena e confortarsi di mangiare e bere'
> Baker: [of the king]: 'observato quod sui omnes pedites insultum hostilem expectabant, dextrariis et cursariis cum victualibus venacioni hostium fugitivorum reservatis'

If in this case, the underlying source has been lost, elsewhere in Villani's account it may perhaps be identified. When the Florentine chronicler states that Philip VI had 'bene da dodicimila cavalieri', we are reminded of both Richard Wynkeley's letter ('hominum xii millia galeatorum') and Edward III's ('plus de xii mille dez hommes–darmes').[164] Similarly in Villani's identification of 'il

160 Sumption, *Trial by Battle*, p. 623 (n. 24).
161 *Villani*, vii, pp. 163–4. It is worth noting here that Villani does not appear to have had access to the document that supplied the names of the three principal captains of the first division.
162 That is, the structure of three divisions, with their principal captains. Whether Arundel's division would be regarded as the 'second' or 'rearguard' formation was a matter of perception.
163 *Baker*, p. 82.
164 *Murimuth*, p. 216; *Le Prince Noir*, ed. Michel, p. 310. When Villani notes that 'tutte le

conte d'Orbi e quello di Chiarentana' as the earls commanded by the king to deal with the remaining French forces on the Sunday morning after the battle proper, we should perhaps look for distorted versions of the names supplied by Michael Northburgh's letter: 'Northamtone', 'Northfolk' and 'Warewyk'.[165]

Since Villani was a victim of the Black Death in 1348, his account of Crécy must have been written within months of the battle. If his information was derived from newsletters, they can hardly have gathered much dust on his desk. His, therefore, is an account that has not become distorted through the passage of time; it has not been influenced by knowledge of later tactical or technological developments. Indeed, this makes all the more telling his comments on the employment by the English of 'bombarde che saettano pallotte di ferro con fuoco, per impaurire e disertare i cavalli de' Franceschi'.[166] Villani's account of the battle is not, however, wholly impartial. Although not directly interested in the outcome of the Anglo-French war, Villani does consider the French defeat to be the result of divine judgement. Allied with the Papacy, the French monarchy had become the pre-eminent power in Europe, but pride and greed ensured its decline, and 'divine disfavour, revealed in the extinction of the [Capetian] dynasty, further manifested itself in the reverses of its successors'.[167] So, following his account of the battle, Villani notes that the defeat was due to the French king's sins, specifically the injustice of his treatment of the king of England and his failure to fulfil a crusading vow.[168] However, whether Villani's providential view of history has significantly affected his narrative of events in the battle may be doubted. It is perhaps more likely that distortion has arisen from source misinterpretation, whether by Villani himself or by intermediaries from whom he derived his information. We cannot comment on the intermediaries, but Villani himself was a widely travelled man of the world, active in business and civic politics. His chronicle, upon which he had been working for two decades by 1346, shows him to be preoccupied, to an unusual degree for his time, with precise information concerning the population and economy of his home city;[169] and it also shows him to be an experienced commentator on warfare.[170] That said, we must admit the possibility that Crécy has been unconsciously reinterpreted according to the norms of Italian warfare. For example, when he tells us that the Prince of Wales's men mounted their warhorses before advancing from the *carrino* it may be because it would be inconceivable for

---

sue bandierè e pennoni reali erano rimasi al camp abbattuti', we hear an echo of Wynkeley. When he adds that Philip VI fled by night to Amiens, he may have been following Edward III's letter.

[165] *Avesbury*, p. 369. As we have seen, 'Norfolk' was written in error for 'Suffolk'.

[166] *Villani*, vii, p. 163.

[167] For an excellent discussion of Villani's perception of an 'historical mechanism that bore earthly powers up to success, and then down to failure', see L. Green, *Chronicle into History: an Essay on the Interpretation of History in Florentine Fourteenth-Century Chronicles* (Cambridge, 1972), chapter 1 (quotations, pp. 23, 25).

[168] *Villani*, vii, p. 170.

[169] 'Such a social and economic profile of the city in exact, statistical terms is unique for the period': Green, *Chronicle into History*, pp. 41–2.

[170] See L. Green, *Castruccio Castracani* (Oxford, 1986), *passim*; Verbruggen, *The Battle of the Golden Spurs: Courtrai, 11 July 1302*, pp. 63–9.

Italian knights, willingly, to fight on foot. However, the fact remains that Villani offers a version of events that is neither implausible as a whole, nor completely isolated among the narrative accounts of the battle. Indeed, in its essentials the Florentine historian's narrative agrees with several French accounts, including one that was written by a man with direct personal experience of warfare. When two 'battle pieces', written independently by well-informed laymen, narrate events in essentially the same way we must take what they say seriously. The argument in their favour becomes still stronger when their accounts find support, on individual points, in a range of other chronicles. As we shall see, that list of chronicles includes those written by Jean le Bel and Jean Froissart.

Jean le Bel, Jean Froissart and the Bourgeois of Valenciennes

The accounts of the battle of Crécy that have been reviewed thus far, both the surviving primary sources and the chronicles that were strongly influenced by them, have played comparatively little part in modern discussions of the battle. Whether the focus has been on English tactics and dispositions, or more broadly on the sequence of events in the battle, there has been a tendency to rely primarily on a different group of texts, and it is to these that we must now turn. The focal point of the investigation will be Geoffrey le Baker's chronicle, which has been the most influential account in modern discussions of English tactical deployment in the battle. Alongside it will be considered a group of chronicles of Low Countries provenance: those of Jean le Bel, Jean Froissart and the Bourgeois of Valenciennes

Jean le Bel, a wealthy and worldly secular clerk from Liège, began writing his chronicle in 1352, apparently in response to a request from his friend, Jean of Hainault.[171] Le Bel's account of Crécy, written in 1358, is often regarded as one of the most substantial and balanced narratives of the battle. His credentials are certainly promising. He had personal experience of campaigning and of the English court, having accompanied Jean of Hainault to England to take part in the Weardale expedition of 1327. Yet at the time of Crécy his friend was serving the king of France, and le Bel notes that he was able to draw on the eyewitness testimony of: 'my lord and friend John of Hainault . . . from his own mouth, and ten or twelve knights and companions of his household, who were in the press with the valiant and noble king of Bohemia, and had their horses killed under them'. He adds that 'I have also heard it told in such a way by several English and German knights who were there, on the other side.'[172] Although he makes

---

171 For Jean le Bel, see: Jules Viard's 'Introduction' to *Jean le Bel*, ii, pp. i–xlv (see pp. 101–10 for le Bel's account of the battle); Gransden, *Historical Writing in England*, ii, pp. 83–9; D.B. Tyson, 'Jean le Bel: portrait of a chronicler', *Journal of Medieval History*, xii (1986), pp. 315–32; D.B. Tyson, 'Jean le Bel, annalist or artist? A literary appraisal', *Studies in Medieval French Language and Literature presented to Brian Woledge*, ed. S. Burch North and M.A. Screech (Geneva, 1988), pp. 217–26; and N. Chareyron, *Jean le Bel* (Brussels, 1996). That Jean of Hainault had prompted Jean le Bel to write is not revealed by the author, but by his friend, Jean d'Outremeuse.

172 'Je l'ay escript au plus prez de la verité, ainsy que je l'ay ouy recorder à mon seigneur et

no mention of documentary sources (which may actually have contributed little to his chronicle), Jean le Bel was potentially as well-informed as any chronicler of the battle of Crécy.

Le Bel's professed aim, here as elsewhere in his chronicle, was to write an account 'as close as possible to the truth'. Yet accompanying this striving for factual accuracy was the exploration of themes that could assume such importance that they determined the structure and content of his narrative. Edward III is the central chivalric figure of his chronicle: a valiant and noble king, whose wisdom, conduct, generosity and reliance on good counsel put him head and shoulders above his Valois rival.[173] Le Bel's account of the battle of Crécy is essentially a set-piece demonstration of the difference in stature between these two kings. There is hardly a detail that does not contribute to this end. A cursory examination of the text suggests that the story of the battle is simply being told twice, first from the French viewpoint and then from the English (the latter dealing only with the preparations and aftermath); but a closer reading reveals that le Bel's Crécy is a tale of two kings and of two armies.[174] Philip VI lacked the authority to control his army. Thus, at the start of the battle, inflamed by 'pride and envy', the French nobility ignored the order to halt, and then became hopelessly entangled with the fleeing crossbowmen, their attack disordered, their horses tumbling over 'like pigs in a heap'.[175] After Philip VI's withdrawal from the battle, the remainder of his army were left leaderless and hungry, wandering the field in small groups in the dark. By contrast, the English king was confident from the outset and in complete control of his army, which before the battle was carefully deployed and well-provisioned. Edward's disciplinary regime was severe. For example, there was to be no breaking ranks for pillaging, on pain of death. But he also mingled with his men, encouraging them in person, so that 'a coward would thereby have been made brave'. 'Each so loved and feared him that none dared to violate his commands.'[176] After the battle the tight discipline was maintained, and the following day Edward ordered the drawing up of a list of the noble dead, which (needless to say) was a task that was performed efficiently.

Given that just about every detail in le Bel's account of Crécy has a part to play in his 'tale of two kings', we should approach what he says with caution. In

amy messire Jehan de Haynau, que Dieu absoulle, de sa propre bouche, et à X ou à XII chevaliers et compaignons de son hostel, qui furent en la presse avecques le prœux et gentil roy de Boheme, auxquelz les chevaulx furent tuez dessoubs eulx; et si l'ay aussy ouy recorder en telle maniere à pluseurs chevaliers anglès et d'Alemaigne qui furent là, de l'autre partie' (*Jean le Bel*, ii, p. 105). As Nicole Chareyron points out, it was unusual for le Bel to be so explicit about his sources of information: Chareyron, *Jean le Bel*, p. 57. Note that Jean of Hainault died in March 1356, so his testimony must have been gathered some time before le Bel began working on the narrative of Crécy.

173 Tyson, 'Jean le Bel: portrait of a chronicler', pp. 318–19, 321–2.
174 'portraits parallèles des rois de France et d'Angleterre, lesquels illustrent deux politiques, deux théories, deux attitudes dans l'exercise du pouvoir': Chareyron, *Jean le Bel*, p. 114.
175 'coururent tous desordonnez et entremellez sans ordre quelconques'; 'cheoient l'ung sur l'autre comme pourcheaulx à tas'. *Jean le Bel*, ii, p. 103.
176 'si doucement les prioit et amonnestoit que ung couard en fut devenu hardi'. 'Chascun l'amoit tant et doubtoit que nul n'osast son commandement trespasser.' *Jean le Bel*, ii, p. 106.

fact, his narrative of the battle proper is selective and quite brief. The defeat of the Genoese crossbowmen by the English archers is passed over swiftly: le Bel is more concerned with the fate of the French cavalry. His most memorable passage describes the impact of archery on horseflesh:

> the archers performed so marvellously that those on horseback sensed the impact of these barbed arrows [on their horses], some of which would not go forwards, others reared up as if maddened, others kicked out horribly, while others turned their rumps towards the enemy, regardless of their masters, because of the arrows they felt. Some, unable to avoid it, let themselves fall.[177]

But the next sentence is perhaps more significant, for in words reminiscent of Giovanni Villani and the other chroniclers discussed earlier, le Bel tells us that the English, taking advantage of the chaos in the French ranks, counter-attacked: 'The English lords, who were on foot, advanced and put these men to the sword, for they could not help themselves, by their own efforts or by their horses.'[178] But having reached what appears to have been a critical point in the battle on the Saturday evening, le Bel brings his account of the fighting to an abrupt close, and turns his attention to the French king's departure from the field. Since his Crécy battle piece had been conceived as a vehicle for contrasting the fortunes of a masterful king with those of an ineffective one, there was no need for further detail; indeed, it would have blurred the message. What Diana Tyson has called 'Jean le Bel's hallmarks'[179] – his 'intelligence, clarity and order' – are nowhere better displayed than in his account of Crécy; but six hundred and fifty years on, we would have been grateful for a looser rein and a little more of the testimony of Jean de Hainault and his companions in arms. It is perhaps fortunate for posterity that le Bel's account of Crécy was given a complete overhaul by Jean Froissart, an all-round man-of-letters from Valenciennes who had a gift for pure narrative.

For the period down to 1361, Book I of Froissart's *Chronicles* relies heavily on Jean le Bel's work. Consequently the Liègeois chronicler's influence can be seen in each of the versions of Froissart's Crécy 'battle piece' that we find in the three major editions of Book I: the A/B group of MSS, the Amiens MS and the Rome MS.[180] Of these, the Rome MS, which survives in a single, unfinished text, is certainly the latest (begun after 1399), but whether the A and B manuscripts represent Froissart's 'first edition' and the Amiens MS his 'second', or

---

[177] 'les archiers tiroient si merveilleusement que ceulx à cheval, sentans ces flesches barbelées [qui] faisoient merveilles, l'ung ne vouloit avant aler, l'aultre sailloit contremont si comme arragié, l'aultre regimboit hydeusement, l'aultre retournoit le cul par devers les anemis, malgré son maistre, pour les settes qu'il sentoit, et les aultres se laissoient cheoir, car il ne le poyoient amender'. *Jean le Bel*, ii, p. 103.

[178] 'ces seigneurs anglès estans à pyé s'avanchoient et feroient parmi ces gens, qui ne se poyoient aydier d'eulx ne de leurs chevaulx'. *Jean le Bel*, ii, p. 103.

[179] Tyson, 'Jean le Bel, annalist or artist?', p. 225.

[180] In Siméon Luce's edition of Froissart, the B MSS are presented as the basic text, with Amiens and Rome as variant readings (Crécy: *Froissart*, ed. Luce, iii, pp. 165–91; 401–36). The Amiens and Rome texts are now more conveniently approached through George Diller's editions: for the sections on Crécy, see *Froissart: Amiens*, iii, pp. 9–26; and *Froissart: Rome*, pp. 713–41.

vice versa, remains a hotly debated matter.[181] Indeed, as John Palmer has argued, given the complex textual relationship between the major versions of Froissart's Book I, 'there is no first or second edition of Book I at all in any meaningful sense of those terms, only a large number of MSS which combine elements of the two editions in different manners and different proportions' – a view that has received wide support.[182] However, if we confine our attention to Froissart's three accounts of Crécy, the order of composition is quite clear. The Amiens text has the closest textual affinity with Jean le Bel's exemplar, and when compared with the other versions, it looks very much like a first draft, the work 'of a fledgling historian'.[183] The A and B MSS add much new material on the battle, and the result is a weighty, thoughtful account. The character of the Rome MS is somewhat different. There is certainly some new material, but the structure is simpler and there is less analysis. The overall impression is of a less cluttered and more polished narrative, which has broken free from the words, if not the factual content, of Jean le Bel's original text. Taken together, Froissart's later accounts of the battle are the most substantial and balanced to be written by a fourteenth-century author. Perhaps even Froissart – ever critical of his own work – was satisfied with them.

In the Amiens MS we can see how Froissart set about reorganising and amplifying le Bel's account of Crécy. Le Bel's 'double narrative' of the battle is abandoned in favour of a single narrative line, which swings smoothly to and fro between the camps of the protagonists. The build-up to the battle sticks closely to le Bel's version of events, with Froissart 'improving' his source here and there. For example, he ensures that 'les Genevois arbalestriers' are at the head of the column leaving Abbeville; he notes that Philip VI kept Jean de Hainault by his side as an expert adviser on the English; and describes how suitable ground for the battle was selected by some of Edward III's senior lieutenants. Froissart follows le Bel's story that the French nobility, 'par orgoeil et par envie',

---

[181] Luce's view, that the A and B MSS represented the first edition of Book I and the Amiens MS the second, was long accepted. However, in 1981, John Palmer argued that although Froissart had probably begun work on the material in Book I during the later 1350s, neither the 'A/B' nor the Amiens version, 'in the form in which we have them', could have been finished before 1390. Palmer also pointed out (p. 17) that 'something like half of le Bel's text is incorporated verbatim or very nearly so in the Amiens MS, and only a fraction of this resurfaces in the A, B and Rome MSS, which are usually rewritten and often expanded as well'. The Amiens MS could not simply be regarded as the 'second edition' of Book I: parts of it were clearly 'the first efforts of a fledgling historian', but overall it is a 'mishmash of "first" and "second" edition elements'. It is even possible that it is 'not . . . the work of Froissart at all'. J.J.N. Palmer, 'Book I (1325–78) and its sources', *Froissart: Historian*, ed. J.J.N. Palmer (Woodbridge, 1981), pp. 7–24. George Diller has since proposed that the original version of the Amiens MS, apparently Froissart's first attempt at prose history, could have been complete by 1380, and that the second redaction of Book 1 (A and B MSS), of which there are many manuscripts, was the version that Froissart intended for publication. G. Diller, *Attitudes chevaleresques et réalités politiques chez Froissart* (Geneva, 1984), p. 158; *Froissart: Amiens*, pp. ix–xxiii.

[182] Palmer, 'Book I (1325–78) and its sources', p. 18; Taylor, *English Historical Literature*, p. 160; Peter Ainsworth, *Jean Froissart and the Fabric of History* (Oxford, 1990), pp. 219–24.

[183] Palmer, 'Book I (1325–78) and its sources', pp. 15–17.

blundered into the battle, but makes the beginning of the action more dramatic, with the Genoese crossbowmen enduring the storm and the fire of 'kanons', and finally being routed by English archery. The destruction of the French cavalry and the English counter-attack on foot are taken straight from le Bel's narrative, but when Froissart reaches what we have termed the 'abrupt close' of le Bel's battle piece, he simply appends more material.[184] Much of this consists of chivalric tales: John of Bohemia's heroic death;[185] Edward III's refusal to reinforce his son's hard-pressed division; and the rescue of Count William of Namur. But Froissart also adds a list of reasons for the French defeat, which focus principally on their mistakes and disadvantages.[186] Froissart the historian is seeking an explanation for the English victory but has yet to formulate a clear idea of how Edward III's tactics may have contributed to it.

Turning to Froissart's battle piece in the A and B MSS, and the closely related version in the Rome MS, we find that the basic structure of the Amiens MS has been retained. Some of his earlier insertions – including the English cannons – have been dropped,[187] as have some details that the Amiens MS had retained from le Bel's text.[188] Other passages, including the reasons for the French defeat, have been integrated more effectively into the narrative. But the overwhelming impression of Froissart's later versions – and especially of the A and B manuscripts – is of expansion, as episodes in the Amiens text are elaborated and supplemented. While repeating le Bel's story of a battle precipitated by the indiscipline of the French nobility, with neither the king nor his marshals able 'to be master of their men', Froissart also suggests that Philip VI lost all self-control when he saw the English and ordered the attack to begin. This, as we have seen, was the opinion of several French chroniclers. Froissart's battle is now a more complex event than before. Although noting that owing to the late start 'too few great feats of arms' were performed, he is actually able to relate a sequence of new tales of chivalric prowess. These include the attack of the counts of Alençon and Flanders on the prince's division, and the vain attempt of Philip VI to join them (the latter is not included in the Rome MS); the adventure of Jean de Hainault's standard bearer, Thierri de Senzeilles, who was riding a black courser given to his master on the morning of the battle; and the heroic last stand of several French captains, 'each under his banner and among his men'.

Froissart's later versions pay much more attention to English tactics. Most notable, of course, is the author's enigmatic description of the English archers'

---

184 In the A and B MSS, Froissart observes: 'Ensi se commenca li bataille . . .': *Froissart*, ed. Luce, iii, p. 177.

185 Jean le Bel had touched on this episode when listing the French casualties, and when Froissart reaches this point in the narrative he simply repeats the story, though erroneously referring to King 'Charles'. The A and B MSS offer an expanded version of the tale.

186 Above all, the arrogance of the French nobility, who had fought 'sans arroy, sans ordonnanche' and against the king's wishes. This disorganisation was made worse by the clash with their own crossbowmen and by the rapid onset of night. The army was also hungry and tired, and before nightfall had fought with the sun in its eyes.

187 The guns have been replaced by the appearance of a 'grant fuison de corbaus que sans nombre', a portent of the blood that would be spilt in the battle.

188 For example, the interesting passage on the homogeneous nature of the English army, apart from a few German knights, appears only in le Bel's text and the Amiens MS.

deployment. The famous 'herce' makes its appearance in the A and B manu-scripts, according to which the English 'se rengièrent en leurs batailles, ceste dou prince tout devant, mis leurs arciers à manière d'une herce, et les gens d'armes ou fons de leur bataille'.[189] This passage is the veritable Gordian knot of Crécy studies, and for over a century attempts to untie it have produced no shortage of theories as to what Froissart intended to convey to his readership by describing archers deployed 'in the form of a *herce*'.[190] The theories tend to give rise to further questions. If, for example, Froissart was referring to an agricul-tural harrow, as some have suggested, does this mean that it was the overall shape of the archer formation that was being recalled, or the positioning of indi-vidual bowmen, 'like the tines of a harrow, spaced in checkerboard fashion in a formation longer than deep'?[191] Indeed, it is possible that it was the 'bristling' character of the *herce* that was the essence of the simile: that the archers were deployed 'like a hedgehog' (*hérisson*), which implies the involvement of pikemen in support or perhaps the utilisation of fixed defences.[192]

Unfortunately, the remainder of Froissart's later accounts do little to elucidate the matter. At one point he refers to 'une si grande haie d'arciers et de gens d'armes au devant que jamès ne fust passés', which may suggest that the archers and men-at-arms fought in the same tactical formation. But two other passages in the A and B MSS imply that it was necessary for the French men-at-arms to get past the archers before they could cross swords with the prince's division. Thus we read that the conrois of the counts of Alençon and Flanders, 'en costiant les arciers, s'en vinrent jusques à le bataille dou prince', while another contingent 'par force d'armes rompirent les arciers de le bataille dou Prince et vinrent jusques as gens d'armes combatre as espées, main à main, moult vaillamment'.[193] Lastly, it should be pointed out that in the Rome MS, Froissart made a slight, but significant change to the wording of the '*herce* passage'. Here we find the English 'missent les archiers *tout devant* en fourme de une erce, et les gens d'armes ou fons', suggesting that the archers were positioned *in front* of the men-at-arms.[194]

If Froissart's description of the archers' deployment remains the subject of

---

[189] *Froissart*, ed. Luce, iii, p. 175. The second division was deployed on the wing of the prince's battle, ready to offer support if necessary.

[190] For a useful discussion of the problem and some of the theories, see J. Bradbury, *The Medieval Archer* (Woodbridge, 1985), pp. 95–104 and the literature cited there. Note, however, that Bradbury regards the A and B MSS of Froissart as 'the earliest version of his chronicle'. David Nicolle has drawn attention to the 'similarity between Froissart's herce and a formation called El Haz, "the closely packed bundle", in a fourteenth-century Spanish military treatise by Don Juan Manuel': *Crécy 1346* (Oxford, 2000), p. 53.

[191] Rogers, *War Cruel and Sharp*, p. 267 (n. 162).

[192] Bradbury, *The Medieval Archer*, pp. 99, 104. For the initial discussion of this possibility, see E.M. Lloyd, 'The "herse" of archers at Crecy', *EHR*, x (1895), pp. 538–41 (at pp. 540–1).

[193] *Froissart*, ed. Luce, iii, pp. 180, 182.

[194] *Froissart: Rome*, pp. 726–7. Froissart describes the English archers at Poitiers in the same terms ('les archiers tous devant yaux à mannierre d'une herce'): *Froissart: Amiens*, p. 104. Assuming that Froissart intended comparison with the agricultural tool, Sir Philip Preston points out to me that the simile is particularly apt, since a harrow is typically formed of two elements: the thin pole of the implement bar (the archers), forward of a deeper framework supporting the tines (the men-at-arms).

debate, at least he leaves us in no doubt that the bowmen had a decisive impact on the battle. The defeat of the Genoese crossbowmen by massed archery is described more vividly. The arrows fell like snow and the Genoese, who had never experienced such an onslaught before, fled. Then, building still further on le Bel's original story, Froissart claims that the French nobility did not merely become entangled with the fleeing Genoese, they actually turned on them with their swords. And all the time, the English were pouring arrows into the chaotic crowd before them.[195] For Froissart, the archers' rout of the Genoese was the turning point in the battle. The missile weapon capability of the French was neutralised and the flight of the Genoese proved disastrous to the men-at-arms behind them.[196] As the king of Bohemia is made to say, with more than a little understatement, 'c'est uns povres commencemens pour nous'.[197] When Froissart concludes that the French nobility were 'unable to resist the power of the English', it is clear that he is referring principally to their archers, for, as he notes, 'ce jour li arcier d'Engleterre portèrent grant confort à leur partie'.[198]

Perhaps more significant, from the point of view of modern perceptions of the battle, is that Froissart's later versions present it as a wholly defensive battle for the English. In the Amiens MS, he had noted that the disciplined English army remained rooted to their positions, with the men-at-arms not moving in front of their archers,[199] and in his later accounts he adds that they did not pursue the French. Although none of Froissart's accounts make any reference to the English using carts and hedges to reinforce their position, it is clear that in this respect his narrative is heavily dependent upon Jean le Bel; and the Liègeois chronicler's 'grand parc' that was formed from 'tous les chars et charrettes de l'ost' does not appear to have a defensive purpose (the army's horses were kept in it).[200] However, we must remember the 'agenda' underlying le Bel's account of Crécy. His wagon park was a reflection of the sound organisation of the English army; it is not a wagon fort. For him the battle was fought on 'ung beau champ où il n'y avoit fosse ne fossé',[201] the outcome being the direct result of the contrasting leadership skills of Edward III and Philip VI. This, then, is the view of the English wagon enclosure that Froissart lifted practically word for word from le Bel's chronicle. He used it in all three of his Crécy narratives, adding only that the park was 'derrière' the English army, which appears to be a matter of routine clarification rather than the result of information from another source. But, Froissart departs from his source in one important respect in his later versions of the battle (A and B MSS; Rome MS). As we have seen, Jean le Bel, like Villani and several French chronicles, tells us that the English

---

195 *Froissart*, ed. Luce, iii, pp. 176–7; *Froissart: Rome*, pp. 728–9.
196 *Froissart*, ed. Luce, iii, pp. 186–7. This extra emphasis on the crucial role played by the archers does not appear in the Rome MS.
197 *Froissart*, ed. Luce, iii, p. 178.
198 *Froissart*, ed. Luce, iii, pp. 184, 186.
199 'Toutteffois, li Englés ne se mouvoient de leur place ne dou lieu où il estoient ordounné ne nulx hommes d'armes de leur costet ne se metoit devant leur tret car il peuuissent bien foliier'. *Froissart: Amiens*, iii, p. 21.
200 *Jean le Bel*, ii, p. 105.
201 *Jean le Bel*, ii, p. 106.

men-at-arms advanced to exploit the confusion in the disordered French ranks
after the rout of the Genoese. This counter-attack was included in the Amiens
MS of Froissart's chronicle, but cut from the later versions. Instead, in the A and
B MSS, we are offered the unchivalrous spectacle of Welsh and Cornish infantrymen slipping through the ranks to dispatch French noblemen with their long
knives.[202] Since this tactically static version of Crécy has always been the most
widely disseminated of Froissart's accounts of the battle (for example, in
Johnes's English translation), the story of Edward III fighting a wholly defensive battle, which is after all suggested by other English accounts, is the story
that has been generally accepted. Nevertheless, it should be noted here that
Froissart does offer indications, even in the A and B MSS, that there was in fact
more movement in English tactics. Apart from the second division's relief of the
Prince of Wales, we hear of groups of French men-at-arms being *surrounded* by
the English and Welsh.[203]

Froissart's three versions of his Crécy battle piece, viewed individually or as
an evolving sequence, are balanced, richly textured and confident, but how far
should we be prepared to rely on them? The core of Froissart's narrative was
derived from Jean le Bel; and, as has been shown, the Liègeois chronicler's
account of Crécy was strongly influenced by his overriding theme of contrasted
noble and incompetent kingship. As for Froissart's additions to Jean le Bel, there
will always be the suspicion that his smooth and assured prose draws rather
more on his vivid, if well-informed, imagination than on solid factual knowledge of the battle. Froissart brought to his historical writing the sensibilities, as
well as the literary skill, of a poet. The image, in the A and B MSS, of Edward
III touring the ranks of his army mounted on 'un petit palefroi blanch, un blanc
baston en sa main',[204] may well be based on the recollection of an eyewitness.
But, as Richard Barber has noted, the pathetic scene of King Philip's arrival at
Labroye castle after the battle is 'straight out of Meliador'.[205] However, the
inclusion of such literary effects should not prompt us to dismiss Froissart's
work as historically worthless. Their purpose is to accentuate the drama, and
they frequently do so brilliantly. Take, for example, the rhetorical touches that
Froissart added to his story of Crécy in the Rome MS. Witnessing the disorderly
arrival of the French, experienced English knights proclaim: 'Ces gens sont
nostre.' In a phrase, Froissart conveys the mixed feelings of relief, anticipation
and self-confidence that had no doubt been recalled to him at length by eyewitnesses from the English side.[206]

Froissart's genuine concern to explain how it was that the English won the
battle, without recourse to providence, sets him apart from many of the authors
whose work we have reviewed. But like all historians he was reliant on his
sources. Apart from his intelligent reorganisation and amplification of Jean le

---

202 *Froissart*, ed. Luce, iii, p. 187.
203 *Froissart*, ed. Luce, iii, pp. 182, 184.
204 *Froissart*, ed. Luce, iii, p. 170 (A and B MSS); cf. *Froissart: Rome*, p. 719.
205 Barber, *Edward Prince of Wales*, pp. 245–6.
206 Note also the pathos of Jean de Hainault's consoling words to Philip VI: 'Vous perderés
celle fois, et vous gagnerés une autre. Ensi vont les pareçons d'armes et les fortunes en ce
monde.' *Froissart: Rome*, pp. 726, 732.

Bel's account, we can but guess how far his Crécy narrative rests squarely on his informants' words. He states in the A and B MSS that his information about the battle had been derived from eyewitnesses who served in the English army and in Jean de Hainault's company. This is really no more than a variation on Jean le Bel's words, though in the Rome MS Froissart mentions the names of John Chandos and Bartholomew Burgherssh on the English side.[207] In addition, as Froissart acknowledges at the beginning of his chronicle, he also drew on the testimony of heralds ('aucuns rois d'armes et leur mareschaus').[208] The imprint of their testimony is abundantly clear in his account of Crécy, and not only in the chivalric tales that he includes. In his remark, made several times, that because of the late start of the battle many feats of arms could not be witnessed, we can surely hear the words of the heralds who would have found their spectator role particularly difficult in the twilight of a late August evening.[209] And we also hear their testimony in the much-expanded account of the searching of the French dead in the Rome MS.[210] This unsavoury task was performed by five knights, four clerks and 'tout li hiraut de l'oost', accompanied by more than 400 men 'pour aidier a tourner et a retourner les mors'. The work was no doubt made easier by the presence of 'many heralds of French lords' who were also on the field searching for the bodies of their dead masters. In describing the aftermath of the battle, Froissart once again offers distinctive testimony.

If Froissart would have had little difficulty with the testimony of the heralds, the recollections of combatants may have posed greater interpretative problems. It must always be borne in mind that in describing archers deployed 'à manière d'une herce' Froissart was not recalling a scene that he had witnessed himself. He either invented a term that he felt summed up what had been described to him, or passed on to his readers an expression that one or more of his informants had used, perhaps not even about the battle of Crécy. In the latter case, Froissart may not have been altogether clear what was meant by the simile, and this would explain the apparent inconsistencies in his various descriptions of archer deployment. Moreover, since his later accounts of Crécy were written several decades after the events had taken place, there is a real possibility that his discussion of tactics in general, and of the *herce* in particular, were influenced by knowledge of later events and practices – his informants' knowledge as well as his own. There is a strong scent of anachronism and literary contrivance surrounding Froissart's description of English tactics at the battle of Sluys (e.g., 'between two ships of archers was a ship of men-at-arms'),[211] and we should be equally suspicious of the *herce* at Crécy.

It has been suggested by Jim Bradbury that the origins of Froissart's *herce*

---

[207] *Froissart*, iii, ed. Luce, p. 174; *Jean le Bel*, ii, p. 105; *Froissart: Rome*, pp. 726–7.

[208] *Froissart: Amiens*, i, p. 1. He certainly consulted Chandos Herald's work for the Iberian expedition of 1366–7; but that writer, who apparently wrote up his verse life of the Prince of Wales in the mid-1380s, was not a witness to the Crécy campaign and his account of the battle is brief: *Chandos Herald*, ed. Tyson, pp. 56–8.

[209] *Froissart*, ed. Luce, iii, pp. 181, 183; *Froissart: Rome*, pp. 734–5.

[210] *Froissart: Rome*, pp. 739–40. In describing the process of counting the French dead, Froissart was following Jean le Bel, but his account becomes progressively more elaborate.

[211] *Froissart: Rome*, p. 404.

may perhaps be traced to a written source, the *Récits* of the Bourgeois of Valenciennes.[212] Nothing is known of the author of this chronicle, apart from his locational roots and the social milieu in which he moved. Nor can we be sure when the chronicle was written, for the single, early fifteenth-century manuscript, which stops in 1366, is probably incomplete.[213] These uncertainties are all the more unfortunate since the *Récits* offers a valuable narrative of the events of July–August 1346, written from the English perspective. The author makes no attempt to conceal his sympathies: Edward III is the honourable party in the conflict, seeking to bring the French to battle. In character, the narrative of the campaign resembles the *Acta Bellicosa* in that it combines a clear itinerary with tales of chivalric prowess, and it also assumes an English army structured exactly as the *Acta* stipulates.[214] But a series of distinctive episodes – concerning the repair of the bridge at Poissy, the attack on Poix-en-Beauvaisis and the discovery of the ford at Blanquetaque – suggest that the author took a campaign dairy as his basic text and added to it information from one or more eyewitnesses serving in the English army. Since two of the inserted episodes concern a knight from Hainault who was serving with King Edward, Wulfard de Ghistelles, he may well have been the Valenciennes chronicler's source.[215]

In character and content, the Bourgeois of Valenciennes's account of the battle of Crécy is quite different from those penned by Jean le Bel and Jean Froissart. There is a detailed discussion of the organisation and deployment of both armies, but the narrative of the main battle on Saturday evening is brief and, like so many other accounts, does not explain how the English won. The storm breaks, the Genoese advance noisily, but their fate is not revealed. Indeed, apart from a description of their deployment (see below), the English archers are hardly mentioned. As we find with many of the English narratives, Crécy is presented by the Valenciennes chronicler as a knightly battle, with the Prince of Wales's division at the centre of it. The young prince is defended by his standard bearer, Sir Richard Fitz Simon, and further men-at-arms are brought in support by the bishop of Durham.[216] Although, as we have seen, the reinforcement of the prince's division at the crisis point of the battle is mentioned in several English accounts, and had probably featured in the *Acta Bellicosa*'s lost description of the battle, Sir Richard's exploit does not appear in any English narrative source, though it does receive some confirmation in the administrative records. On the other hand, none of the chivalric tales related by Froissart – not even the

---

[212] Bradbury, *The Medieval Archer*, p. 99.

[213] See Baron Kervyn de Lettenhove's introduction to his edition of this chronicle: *Récits*, pp. v–x. The account of the campaign and battle of Crécy occupies pp. 214–36.

[214] Some of the knightly adventures are foolhardy, such the escapade of Richard de la Marche and Thomas Holand at the bridge over the Seine at Rouen: *Récits*, p. 220. For the army, composed of advance guard, main body and rearguard, see *ibid.*, p. 225.

[215] *Récits*, pp. 225–6. Ghistelles's involvement in the assault on Poix is not mentioned in the lengthy account in the *Acta Bellicosa*, nor is the story that it was one of Ghistelles's esquires who knew the whereabouts of the ford at Blanquetaque to be found anywhere else. Ghistelles had been a military companion of Edward III's since at least the mid 1330s: see Chapter 5, p. 175 and n. 82.

[216] Sir Richard, taking his sword in both hands, cries 'Édouart à saint Jorge, au fils du roy!' *Récits*, p. 233.

circumstances of King John of Bohemia's death – are included by the Bourgeois of Valenciennes. His Crécy is a darker tale, in which there are no heroic deaths and few feats of arms. Even Fitz Simon's exploit serves primarily to emphasise that the young prince was, as yet, out of his depth in the arena of war (he was twice forced to his knees in the mêlée). For our author, it seems, there was little glory to be found on such a bloody field. Indeed, he lingers more than most writers over the distasteful aftermath of the battle. The killing continued after nightfall, as disorientated French men-at-arms seeking their lords' bodies 'before they were stripped of their arms' (i.e., heraldic identification) stumbled into the English lines and were dealt with mercilessly. A search of the battlefield led to the recovery of over 2,200 heraldic surcoats from the fallen French nobility, which were displayed like trophies in the king's pavilion, and a large quantity of arms and armour. A bonfire was made of the remaining French equipment, 'vièses et nouvelles, bonnes et mauvaises'.[217] Perhaps most tellingly, the Valenciennes chronicler recounts a scene in which the king asked his son whether, having now experienced battle, he considered it 'good sport'. The prince, notes the chronicler, 'said nothing and was ashamed'.[218] That other writer from Valenciennes, Jean Froissart, interprets this episode rather differently: in his version, the king heartily congratulated the prince, who responded by modestly bowing low in honour of his father.[219] As much as with the key events of the battle, the interpretation of the aftermath is strongly influenced by the mindset of the chronicler.

The most memorable passage in the Valenciennes chronicler's account of Crécy, and perhaps the most pertinent to our investigation of the battle, concerns the deployment of the English archers. The chronicler tells us that they were placed in two formations, one on each side of the front line of the army, 'in the manner of a shield'.[220] As with Froissart's *herce*, the meaning that the Valenciennes chronicler intended to convey is uncertain. Was he describing the shape of a tactical formation, which may therefore have resembled the physical concavity or convexity of a shield as seen in cross-section, or a body of archers arranged en masse in the triangular shape of a shield as seen from above? Was the author's intention figurative, in the sense of archers 'shielding' the rest of the army? Or, as Jim Bradbury has suggested, was the particular merit of this term that it conveyed a dual meaning – 'shape [and] shelter'? With no amplification by the Valenciennes chronicler by which the case for one of these being more plausible than the others might be strengthened, an argument can be made for each. Jim Bradbury has suggested that the 'striking similarity of phrasing' between the Valenciennes chronicler's 'shield' simile and the *herce* may suggest

---

[217] *Récits*, p. 234.

[218] 'Et demanda le roy Édouart d'Engleterre au prince de Galles, son fils, ce que luy sambloit d'entrer et estre en bataille et se c'estoit beau jeu. Et le prince se teult et fut honteux.' *Récits*, p. 234.

[219] *Froissart*, ed. Luce, iii, pp. 187–8; *Froissart: Rome*, p. 736.

[220] Edward III 'ne fist que II batailles d'archiers à II costés en la manière d'un escut. Et au milieu de eulx seroit le prince de Galles . . . et grant plenté de grans chevaliers et de gens d'armes à l'eslitte, tous à pied.' Behind them were deployed the men-at-arms and archers of the king's division. *Récits*, p. 231.

that Froissart was aware of the *Récits* and 'tried to improve' on it. There is no conclusive evidence that Froissart was aware of the Valenciennes chronicle, though there is a passage in Froissart's narrative of the channel crossing in July 1346 that may well have been borrowed from this source.[221] However, as we have seen, their accounts of the battle are distinctively different. Another possibility, perhaps more likely, is that they both had access to the same Crécy eyewitness. It may be significant that Wulfard de Ghistelles is mentioned not only by the Valenciennes chronicler, but also by Froissart, who notes that he was one of the few foreign knights in the English army (Amiens MS) and was among the knights selected to search the French dead (Rome MS).[222]

Geoffrey le Baker

The last fourteenth-century account of Crécy to be considered here was compiled by Geoffrey le Baker, a secular clerk from Swinbrook, near Burford in Oxfordshire. It has been described as the 'fullest account of the battle of Crécy produced by a contemporary'.[223] His material may have been gathered soon after the battle, but the final version of the text was written during the later 1350s, after the battle of Poitiers.[224] Baker reveals nothing about his sources for Crécy, and apart from the obvious use of one of the casualty lists that were circulating after the battle, it is difficult to find more than faint traces of known documentary sources in his account. There is no very secure evidence that he used the surviving English newsletters, which may be because, unlike those other secular clerks, Adam Murimuth and Robert Avesbury, Baker was not based in London. Nor does he seem to have relied upon the *Acta Bellicosa*. His description of the fierce fighting around the Prince of Wales and the king's despatch of reinforcements to assist his son appears to be based on a different source. However, a documentary affinity with Knighton's chronicle is suggested by Baker's summary of the battle. He notes that it continued 'until the third quarter of the night', and that 'the French raised a general war-cry three times and launched fifteen attacks',[225] followed by a sixteenth, involving a fresh contingent of troops, on Sunday morning. As we have seen, Knighton offers essentially the same information, albeit in a more confused manner. Lastly, there is the real

---

[221] See Chapter 2, p. 45 and n. 43.

[222] *Froissart: Amiens*, iii, p. 13; *Froissart: Rome*, p. 739.

[223] Martin, 'John the Blind: the English narrative sources', p. 89. Baker's account: *Baker*, pp. 82–5.

[224] Poitiers forms the climax of the chronicle, the prince's victory having been anticipated at the time of his birth in 1330 (*Baker*, p. 48.). For Baker and his chronicle, see E.M. Thomson's Preface to *Baker*, pp. v–xvii; and Gransden, *Historical Writing in England*, ii, pp. 37–42, 77–80.

[225] 'Sic a solis occasu usque ad terciam noctis quadrantem fuerat vicissim orrida Martis facie ostensa, in quanto tempore ter Gallici nostros exclamaverunt hostiliter, quindecies nostris insultum dederunt, set tandem victi abfugerunt.' *Baker*, p. 84. Cf. *Knighton*, ed. Martin, pp. 62–3.

possibility, considered earlier, that Baker used a document that also came to the attention of Giovanni Villani in Florence.[226]

It is unlikely that Baker relied solely on documentary material. He claims to have used oral testimony elsewhere in his chronicle, and given his social connections with Sir Thomas de la More of Northmoor (for whom Baker had earlier written a *Chroniculum*) and the comital Bohun family, it is probable that the chronicler acquired information from members of these families who were present at the battle. William, son of William de la More served in the Prince of Wales's retinue at Crécy,[227] while the Bohun contingent in the prince's division included Edmund and Oliver as well as the earl of Northampton himself.[228] Such eyewitness testimony would explain the vivid descriptive touches in Baker's narrative, yet also its narrow scope. For although Baker's account of the battle conveys an impression of substance, its focus is resolutely on what happened immediately in front of the Prince of Wales's division. In this respect, therefore, Baker's text supplements that of the Bourgeois of Valenciennes and, for that matter, the lost battle narrative of the *Acta Bellicosa*. But Baker's battle piece seems to be derived from an independent view of events. Thus, uniquely in an early English account, we are given a clear description of the rout of the Genoese crossbowmen. Their quarrels fell short of the English line, they were mown down by withering archery and then ridden down by reckless French men-at-arms. Baker succeeds in conveying the carnage that unfolded on this part of the battlefield. Horses stumbled and fell, the air filled with shrieks of pain, and mounds of corpses accumulated in front of the English position. As with Edward III's despatch and Villani's chronicle, we are given a clear impression of a desperate struggle in a confined space. The men in the rear of the French army, hearing the noise of battle ahead of them, but unsighted, pressed forward behind those who had already spurred their mounts towards the English. But their formations were disrupted by falling horses, their way was barred by the Prince of Wales's men and 'many were crushed to death, without a mark on them, in the middle of the French army, because the press was so great'.[229] The wounding of warhorses by arrows is mentioned in passing; but for Baker, as for other English narrators of the battle, the story of Crécy is primarily one of noble prowess displayed in close quarters combat. The French 'were cut down with swords and spears' rather than by archery. Of course, the spotlight falls primarily on the young prince, who is portrayed as displaying great courage and prodigious skill with arms. When a detachment of twenty knights arrived to reinforce his

---

[226] In addition to the evidence examined above, both chroniclers place John of Bohemia at the head of the first French division; both describe the rout of the crossbowmen (omitted by most English accounts); and both appear to be describing a battle in which the fiercest fighting occurred in a confined area.

[227] In Mortimer's company: C81/1710, no. 26; C76/23, m. 23. The de la More family were also militarily connected with the earl of Northampton: John de la More fought with the earl in 1340 (C81/1735, no. 15; C76/15, m. 19) and Sir William de la More did so in 1348 (C81/1734, no. 24; C76/26, m. 3).

[228] C76/22, m. 2; Wrottesley, *Crecy and Calais*, pp. 86, 138, 147, 157.

[229] 'in medio exercitu Francorum multi compressi a multitudine honerosa sine wlnere opprimuntur'. *Baker*, p. 84.

beleaguered troops, they 'found him and his men leaning on their lances and swords, taking deep breaths and quietly resting on mounds of corpses'.[230] This is the real strength of Baker's account: the graphic images of almost cinematic immediacy that probably came from the mouths of eyewitnesses. But we should not be surprised that these same participants could tell him very little about the rest of the battle, for apart from adding that many attacks were repulsed throughout the night, Baker writes nothing more about the fighting on 26 August. If the whole battle was indeed fought in front of the prince's division, this would suggest either an incredible lack of tactical flexibility on the part of the French, or – and this is more likely – that the topography of the battlefield allowed the English to present a comparatively short front line to their opponents. Other sources, including the king's despatch, offer hints about fighting elsewhere on the field, but of this Baker seems to have been unaware.

Baker's chronicle provides the most precise description of the tactical deployment of Edward III's army to appear in any English narrative source. He states that all of Edward III's men awaited the French on foot (which the king noted in his despatch). Then, after describing the defeat of the crossbowmen, he tells us that pits were dug in front of the prince's division (not noted by any other source),[231] and that:

> The archers were also assigned to their positions so that they did not stand together with [or 'in front of'] the men-at-arms, but at the sides of the army like wings; and in this way they would not impede the men-at-arms, nor clash with the enemy head on, but could unleash arrows from the flanks.[232]

Given that no other chronicler described the archers' deployment with such precision, it is hardly surprising that Baker's words have been eagerly seized upon by historians. That what he says appears to agree with the 'classic' English tactical deployment, as perceived on other battlefields, serves only to reinforce the plausibility of his testimony. Indeed, the deployment of archers in massed formations on the wings of the whole army, quite separate from the men-at-arms, has now become the orthodox view of English battlefield tactics in the French war.[233] The evidence, however, is far from consistent,[234] and it should be

---

230 'invenit ipsum et suos lanceis et gladiis appodiatos, super montes mortuorum longos respiracioni et quieti inclinatos'. *Baker*, p. 84.
231 'effodierunt in parvo tempore multa foramina in terra coram acie prima'. *Baker*, p. 83.
232 'Sagittariis eciam sua loca designarunt, ut, non coram armatis, set a lateribus regis exercitus quasi ale astarent, et sic non impedirent armatos neque inimicis occurrerent in fronte, set in latera sagittas fulminarent.' *Baker*, pp. 83–4.
233 This is very much the view of Jim Bradbury, *The Medieval Archer*, and Kelly DeVries, *Infantry Warfare in the Early Fourteenth Century*.
234 Take, for example, the battle of Mauron, fought in Brittany in August 1352. According to the *Chronique Normande*, the English dismounted and positioned themselves in front of a hedge with their archers on the flanks (*Chronique Normande*, p. 105). However, the despatch written by the English commander in the battle, Sir Walter Bentley, states that the fighting took place in 'open fields, without woods, ditches or other defences' and makes no mention of archer deployment. Indeed, he makes no reference at all to his archers! (*Avesbury*, pp. 416–17.) Nor does Baker record the positioning of the archers: *Baker*, p. 120. Similarly, there is no unanimity in the sources concerning archer deployment at Poitiers (see Bradbury, *The*

emphasised that captains did not simply work to a predetermined tactical blue-print. Thus, with regard to the battle of Morlaix in September 1342, none of the chronicles mentions the deployment of archers (though we know from the pay-rolls that they were present at the battle), preferring instead to relate how the earl of Northampton made improvisatory use of the ground upon which the action was fought. Knighton, probably drawing on a newsletter, states that the earl dug pits and ditches to hinder his opponent's cavalry and eventually fell back to the cover of a wood 'because of the great numbers of the enemy, who were swarming all around'.[235] Baker does not place Northampton's archers on the flanks of his army at Morlaix, yet because of the uncompromising clarity of his testimony regarding Crécy his chronicle has played an important role in the formation of the 'wings of archers' view of English tactics. Moreover, Baker's testimony appears all the more compelling because his chronicle offers a clear line of development for English tactics from Bannockburn to Poitiers. Yet for that very reason it should perhaps be regarded with suspicion.

To what extent should we be prepared to rely upon Baker's Crécy narrative and in particular his description of English deployment? Let us consider first how it compares with the other narrative sources for the battle. As we have seen, none of the primary sources – none of the newsletters – casts any light on this problem. Of the authors who, like Baker, were writing contemporary or recent history, the closest support for Baker comes from the *Récits* of the Bourgeois of Valenciennes, for as we have seen he states that 'battles' of archers were deployed 'in the manner of a shield' on each flank of a main body of men-at-arms. Judging by the captains mentioned in the *Récits* by name (and using the *Acta Bellicosa* as our guide), the main body consisted of two divisions, the advance guard and the rearguard, deployed side by side or in column, supported by the king's division, composed of mixed arms, behind. Turning to Froissart (and setting aside the *herce* as capable of just about any interpretation), we find that he – following Jean le Bel – tells us that *each* of the English 'battles' was composed of 'mixed' personnel, men-at-arms and archers, which is as we would expect. This is not irreconcilable with Baker's testimony if we interpret the latter as a description not of the whole army but rather of that part of it (the first divi-sion) in which his eyewitness informants had been serving.

Another way of reconciling Baker's testimony with these other accounts is to suppose that the three English divisions were arranged in column, one behind

---

Medieval Archer, p. 113). According to the *Chronique Normande* (p. 114), the English 'avoient fait deux ailes de leurs archiers sur les costez de leur bataille', but this is suspiciously similar to his description of Mauron.

[235] *Knighton*, ed. Martin, pp. 42–3; *Murimuth*, pp. 127, 227; *Baker*, pp. 76–7. T.F. Tout, 'The tactics of the battles of Boroughbridge and Morlaix', *EHR*, xix (1904), pp. 711–15. Bradbury's assertion that 'dismounted men-at-arms took the centre, with archers on each flank' cannot be substantiated from the chronicles (*The Medieval Archer*, pp. 103–4) any more than can DeVries's confident statement that Northampton 'included the archers among the other troops in the line of infantry, using weapons other than their longbows' (*Infantry Warfare in the Early Fourteenth Century*, p. 144). The archers may well have been intermingled with the men-at-arms, but is it conceivable that they would have been ordered to set aside their bows unless their supply of arrows had been expended?

the other, with the archers deployed on the wings of a block of men-at-arms.[236] This hypothesis assumes that the army's frontage was quite narrow, yet does not consider how the features of the battle site may have allowed the English to deploy on such a narrow front. It could also be observed that strict deployment in column would limit tactical flexibility. In any case, several chronicles appear to be describing a different arrangement. The A and B MSS of Froissart (independent of Jean le Bel) place the second English 'battle' on the flank of the prince's division. The related texts from St Omer, the short continuation of the *Chronique de Flandre* and the St Omer chronicle, locate the second (king's) division 'near' the first, with the third in the rear. Most at variance with Baker's deployment are Giovanni Villani and several of the French chronicles. These, as we have seen, position the archers within a defensive enclosure of carts and hedges. Also to be considered is the intriguing testimony of a German chronicler, Mathias von Neuenburg, which was brought to light for the first time in Michael Prestwich's chapter in this book.[237] Like Jean le Bel, Mathias speaks of an enclosure of carts for the English horses, but more distinctively he states that the archers were deployed *in front* of the men-at-arms.[238] Although he exaggerates the number of archers involved (30,000), Mathias's testimony is not to be lightly dismissed. It is probably based on an eyewitness report from one of the handful of 'Germans' serving in the English army, and there are corroborative hints elsewhere (including in Froissart's work) that at least some of the English archers were positioned in the manner suggested by Mathias. Deployment of archers 'in front', perhaps as a screen of skirmishers, would make tactical sense; but Baker explicitly rules out this possibility. His archers are on the wings of the army, not serving with (or in front of) the men-at-arms.[239]

It can be seen that Baker's description of archer deployment does not rest altogether comfortably alongside the testimony of most of the other chronicles. Moreover, when examined on its own terms it presents further interpretative problems. In order to post the archers, unsupported, in two large blocks on the wings of the whole host, it would have been necessary to remove the retinue-based bowmen from the units in which they had been recruited, thereby

---

[236] Rogers, *War Cruel and Sharp*, p. 266 n. 162. As he notes, other chronicles may also be suggesting deployment in column: e.g., the early fifteenth-century account in the *Chronicon comitum Flandriae*, which states that the prince's battle was composed of 500 men-at-arms and 5,000 archers, with two further battles of unspecified composition in support. *Corpus chronicorum Flandriae*, ed. J.J. de Smet (Brussels, 1937), i, p. 218.

[237] *Die Chronik des Mathias von Neuenburg*, ed. A. Hofmeister, Monumenta Germaniae Historica, Scriptores Rerum Germanicarum, nova series, IV (Berlin, 1955), pp. 204–6. Mathias notes that the Germans in Philip VI's army suffered heavy casualties as a consequence of fighting on after the rest of the French 'battles' had fled.

[238] 'Anglus enim omnes equos suos cum garcionibus a se iuxta silvam recondens pedestribus se commisit, curribus se circumdans, ne equites Franci alibi quam in cornu anteriori invadere eum possent, ante se et milites suos premittens XXX milia sagittariorum.' *Die Chronik des Mathias von Neuenburg*, p. 205.

[239] They also appear to be rooted to the spot, for unlike continental accounts of the battle (including Jean le Bel and Froissart's Amiens MS), Baker's Crécy is a static, defensive battle for the English, the only movement being the despatch of a contingent of men-at-arms to relieve the Prince of Wales.

disrupting the settled organisational fabric of at least part of the army – the mixed retinues. Not 'stiffened' with men-at-arms or spearmen, the archers would have been left vulnerable, unless protected by natural or improvised defences. Now, as we have seen, several of the continental chronicles tell us that at Crécy the English did indeed make use of hedges reinforced with carts, and it is not difficult to connect these descriptions with suitable features on the traditional battle site: the famous *rideaux* or *radillons*. Baker makes no reference to such fixed defences, apart from his hastily dug 'pits'. That in itself does not constitute grounds for dismissing his testimony, for silence on the topography of the site is a feature of many of the chronicles, not least those that discuss archer deployment, like the Bourgeois of Valenciennes and Jean Froissart. But there are other reasons for thinking that the 'wings' of archers at Crécy may have been a figment of Baker's imagination.

The reliability of Baker's Crécy battle piece may also be gauged by taking a closer look at the text of his chronicle, and in particular by attempting a reconstruction of the process by which he compiled his account of the events of July–August 1346. It is probable that Baker made use of a campaign diary (rather like Cotton MS, Cleopatra, D. VII), which provided a sound itinerary for the English campaign from La Hougue to Crécy but no real sense of the character of the campaign, nothing on the movements of the main French army, and little detail on the battle itself. A lack-lustre account of the campaign might be acceptable to Baker; but for the battle itself he could not settle for anything less than a big set-piece event. Consequently, he gathered oral testimony and found one or two documents, probably newsletters, and constructed his colourful account from these materials. It has been said of Baker, with justification, that 'he loved good stories, many of which probably display his talent as a raconteur more than his integrity as an historian'.[240] For evidence of this we need only recall his account of the persecution and murder of Edward II. Given his predilection for highly coloured anecdotes and his fiercely patriotic outlook, we should not imagine his Crécy narrative to be wholly rooted in documentary evidence, even were such evidence plentiful. Faced by decidedly patchy documentation, we must suspect that Baker simply filled in the gaps from his imagination and from his knowledge of military events both prior to and after Crécy. One problem that Baker faced was that his sources provided little concrete information about the French. Until the confrontation on the Somme (which, erroneously, is assigned to 25 August), Philip VI and the main French army are absent from his account of the campaign. Philip then appears, the next day, at Crécy. Although the steady build-up of the French army is indicated, there is no sense of a disorderly arrival. It is interesting that Baker places John of Bohemia at the head of the first French battle, as this tallies with Villani's account; but much of Baker's treatment of the French before the battle smacks of invention or over-elaboration.[241]

---

[240] Gransden, *Historical Writing in England*, ii, p. 78.
[241] For example, the French magnates lay claim to particular English noble prisoners; the French king responds by raising the *Oriflamme*; and the English king unfurls the dragon standard. Philip VI certainly brought the *Oriflamme* to Crécy, but the rest is probably pure invention.

Baker's account of the battle itself is not as substantial as it might appear at first glance. It does describe the defeat of the Genoese crossbowmen, which is unusual in English chronicles; and, as we have seen, it offers a vivid account of the mêlée in front of the prince's division. This, however, includes a conventional description of knightly combat that could relate to just about any battle, and very little is said about the role played by archery. Compare this with Baker's account of the battle of Poitiers, and the sharp contrast is immediately apparent.[242] Baker's Poitiers was a battle dominated by the topography of the site (which he describes very precisely), it was a battle of movement and it was a battle in which archery played a key role. The archers took advantage of the natural features of the site – hedges, ditches and a marsh. Far from being rooted in their starting positions, sections of the English army moved around the field when required. Much of this would not be out of place in the continental chroniclers' accounts of the battle of Crécy. Even the Captal de Buch's dramatic surprise attack into the rear of the French army has a striking resemblance to the tactics employed by Edward III at the climax of Crécy in Villani's account. Now, it could be argued that Baker's narratives of Crécy and Poitiers are different because the battles were indeed different in character. But we must surely consider the possibility that Baker was simply much better informed about Poitiers. To have had at his disposal so little concrete information about the battle of Crécy must have been deeply frustrating, and the temptation to fill the gaps from his imagination and his knowledge of contemporary warfare would have been difficult to resist.

There is evidence that Baker did indeed 'fill the gaps' in this way. The one really notable section of Baker's account – concerning the pits that were dug in front of the prince's division, followed by the description of archer deployment – sits uncomfortably with the rest of the narrative, and is clearly a later, rather clumsy addition to the text. (The reader's suspicions are aroused by the implausible implication that the pits were dug 'quickly' between the defeat of the crossbowmen and the attack of the French cavalry.) It is uncertain when Baker wrote the first version of his Crécy battle piece, but we know that he revisited it during the later 1350s, because he says of the Prince of Wales at Crécy that 'he learnt that knightly skill which he later put to excellent use at the battle of Poitiers'. Indeed, it seems that having completed a draft of the chronicle, Baker then proceeded to revise the whole text, or at least that part of it covering Edward III's reign.[243] For example, his description of the battle of Morlaix makes reference to both Crécy and Poitiers.[244] Compared with his account of Poitiers, his original Crécy narrative may well now have seemed unsatisfactory, lacking in particular a tactical explanation for the English victory. So he inserted a new paragraph into the text describing the digging of pits and the archers' deployment, an interpolation which, once recognised, is obvious since the original flow of the narrative has clearly been interrupted.[245]

---

[242] *Baker*, pp. 146–53.
[243] See E.M. Thompson's comments: *Baker*, pp. xvi–xvii.
[244] *Baker*, p. 76.
[245] *Baker*, pp. 83–4.

Baker's new paragraph on the archers at Crécy may have been based upon information that had come to his attention since writing the first draft of his chronicle. Yet it is equally likely, given what we know of Baker's working methods and imaginative powers, that it is of his own invention. Although 'wings of archers' deployed in the fashion described for Crécy are not to be found in Baker's other battle narratives, they were to make an appearance in other chronicles during this period, most notably in descriptions of the battle of Halidon Hill.[246] Moreover, we find archers operating against the flanks of individual French contingents in Baker's own description of Poitiers. So Baker's new paragraph is as likely to have sprung from a general awareness of tactical possibilities as from fresh eyewitness testimony. Yet it seems that Baker was also seeking, from the vantage point of the later 1350s, to present the period of warfare from Bannockburn to Poitiers as the story of England's military renaissance under Edward III. For Baker, the English victory in 1346 was not an isolated event but an important landmark in a sequence of battles in which (among other things) a clear line of tactical development could be traced.

Baker makes it clear that there had been a major advance from Bannockburn to Halidon Hill. In the débâcle of 1314 'the chivalry of England still fought on horseback', while in 1333 the nobility dismounted 'contrary to the ancient tradition of their fathers' and were deployed in a defensive position with archers.[247] The contrast with the events of 23–24 June 1314 was also clearly in Baker's mind when he was revising his Crécy battle piece. Indeed, Baker's Crécy can be read as a kind of 're-run' of Bannockburn, with the French playing the part that Edward II's 'overweening array of chivalry' had performed in 1314. At Bannockburn, he writes, the English archers had been deployed incompetently:

> Many were killed by the archers of their own army, who were not placed in a suitable position, but stood behind the men-at-arms, whereas nowadays it is usual to post them on the flanks.[248]

While in 1314 'many English' were shot 'in the back', according to Baker's revised text, the archers at Crécy were positioned in such a way as not to hinder the men-at-arms. Lessons had been learnt, and not just about archer deployment. Baker's statement that the English dug pits at Crécy, which is not corroborated by any other source, appears quite simply to have been inspired by his mistaken belief (founded upon a misinterpretation of Robert Baston's poem) that the Scots' pitfalls had played a prominent part in their victory at Bannockburn. In fact, they had played no part at all in the second day of the battle on 24 June 1314.[249] If we may only suspect that the Crécy pits were a figment of Baker's

---

246 Though at Halidon the wings were apparently positioned on the flanks of each of the three 'battles' in the English army: R. Nicholson, *Edward III and the Scots* (Oxford, 1965), pp. 132–3; Rogers, *War Cruel and Sharp*, pp. 68–9.

247 *Baker*, pp. 7, 51.

248 *Baker*, pp. 8–9. It is interesting to note that neither Sir Thomas Gray nor the author of *Vita Edwardi Secundi* mention the role played the archers at Bannockburn.

249 *Baker*, pp. 7–8, 185–8. J.E. Morris, *Bannockburn* (Cambridge, 1914), pp. 82–6; G.W.S. Barrow, *Robert Bruce and the Community of the Realm of Scotland* (3rd edn, Edinburgh, 1988), p. 217. Matthew Bennett has pointed out that after six weeks of drought, digging pits

fertile imagination, invented in the interests of reinforcing his theme of English tactical development rooted in the experience of the Scottish wars, we can see that process at work more explicitly in his Poitiers narrative. Baker relates a scene in which Sir William Douglas, a Scottish noblemen with extensive military experience, persuades King John of France to dismount most of his men-at-arms because this is how the English customarily fought, in imitation of the Scots 'ever since their disaster at [the battle of] Stirling'. King John 'foolishly agreed to the counsel of this busybody'.[250] The idea that Scottish mercenaries influenced French tactics at Poitiers may seem plausible enough; but it is unlikely to have been what happened, for, as was demonstrated nearly a hundred years ago by T.F. Tout, 'in several fights preceding the battle of Poitiers the French had already made a series of experiments in dismounting their men-at-arms'.[251] Perhaps Baker was unaware of French tactics in earlier battles – including Taillebourg, Ardres (both in 1351) and Mauron (1352) – but it hardly matters since in order to bring his story to a satisfying conclusion, it served his purpose at the climactic point of his chronicle to have the Scots play a decisive part in the downfall of their allies, the French, at the hands of the English.

It would seem that Baker's battle narratives were fuelled as much by his story-telling instincts as by accurate factual information, and that he was prepared to invent dramatic situations in order to accommodate the larger themes that he wished his chronicle to convey. This is not to suggest that Baker's testimony on the battle of Crécy is completely worthless. There may well be an essential truth in what he has to say. The deployment of wings of archers on suitable ground or supported by spearmen or men-at-arms is not an implausible idea. But it is clear that Baker's Crécy narrative can only be understood in context – that is, by reference to the remainder of his chronicle and to the story of England's military fortunes from Bannockburn to Poitiers that is one of its underlying themes. In short, this most respected of commentators on Edwardian military matters should be approached with the same combination of appreciation and scepticism as has become customary for those engaged in the interpretation of Froissart's work.

Crécy and the chroniclers: Conclusions

A reader of the chroniclers of Crécy may well be left with the impression that there are almost as many versions of the battle as there are fourteenth-century narrators of it. There are many disparities or lacunae in their testimony. The reasons for this are clear enough. A chronicler is only as good as his sources, and in many cases these were far from plentiful. Time and again we find evidence of source failure. Gilles le Muisit bemoans his lack of reliable

would have been difficult: 'Crécy, 26 August 1346', in *The Hutchinson Atlas of Battle Plans* (Oxford, 1998), pp. 41–52 (at p. 45).

[250] *Baker*, p. 143.

[251] T.F. Tout, 'Some neglected fights between Crécy and Poitiers', *EHR*, xx (1905), pp. 726–30; Bradbury, *The Medieval Archer*, pp. 91, 103.

eyewitnesses. Baker's informants were so directly involved in the thick of the fighting that they had no idea of what was happening elsewhere on the field. Jean le Bel's eyewitnesses were obviously traumatised by the appalling scenes that had occurred before their eyes. Documentary sources may be no more helpful. For example, the narrowness of English chronicle accounts appears to have arisen from their dependence upon battlefield despatches and similar documents, which for the most part were written with the intention simply of reporting the victory rather than explaining it. It should be recognised too that our authors' 'sources' might include the Bible, the Apocrypha and classical texts. As Anne Curry has noted, 'a thorough assessment of classical influences on chroniclers' treatment of battles' would probably reveal that 'many points derived more from classical *topoi* than from actual incidents'.[252]

A chronicler's narrative would often be shaped not only by his sources, but also by his preoccupations, his likely audience and his wider interpretative agenda. For some of our authors, Crécy was but a passing episode in their 'universal' histories of the world. For others, it served as a vehicle for emphasising a more general political message. We are not speaking merely of 'national' bias here, though that can certainly be detected in some of our sources, sometimes taking unexpected forms. It is notable, for example, that archery was the key to Edward III's success according to the French chronicles, yet is mentioned more sparingly by English writers. Yet this is easily explained by reference to the aristocratic bias of both eyewitnesses and chroniclers. When the author of the *Grandes chroniques* expressed disgust that so many noblemen, headed by the king of Bohemia, had been killed by archers, 'gent de nulle value', he was articulating the feelings of survivors and readers alike.[253] This had not been a chivalric event: had it been, it was inconceivable that the English would have won. On the other hand, English chroniclers were unwilling to suggest that victories like Crécy were not due primarily to the efforts of the knightly class.

Lastly, we must bear in mind that the chroniclers of Crécy were, almost without exception, prone to embroider the story that they found in their sources and to fill in 'gaps' from a mixture of imagination and wider knowledge. We have seen how Baker and Villani may well have had access to a similar account of the battle. Even allowing for the likelihood that they each had further, different sources at their disposal, it is striking that the pictures of the battle that they paint are so very different. The assumption in the past has been that Baker's is the more reliable of the two accounts; but although we may suspect that Villani created his vivid narrative by drawing on his imagination and his knowledge of Italian warfare to fill in the gaps in his sources, it should by now be clear that there is quite as much evidence that Baker did exactly the same thing.

Embroidery and supplementation of sources in order to create a distinctive narrative that served a particular purpose was a common working method among chroniclers of this period. The Crécy texts provide many examples. The night of the battle was brightly moonlit (Knighton) or profoundly dark (le Bel); the English were hungry at the start of the battle (Knighton; Villani) or well-fed

---

[252] Curry, *The Battle of Agincourt*, p. 20.
[253] *Grandes chroniques*, ix, p. 283.

(le Bel). In each case, it would be natural to conclude that one of the statements must be 'wrong', but at the same time each is valid within the context of the version of events that the author sets before us. In their eagerness to dismiss the testimony of chroniclers on grounds of factual inaccuracy, as judged by comparison with other sources, historians are in danger of missing how internally consistent these narratives often are. This, then, is the key problem facing those who seek to make use of chronicles for the reconstruction of such an event as the battle of Crécy. Regarding them, above all, as repositories of factual information that can be picked over for pieces of evidence that can then be woven together into a larger narrative runs the dual risk of overlooking the true merits of these literary works while, in all likelihood, combining data that are simply incompatible.

A single highly complex event involving a cast of thousands has given rise to a bewildering variety of accounts. Tempted as we might be to ask which are the most 'reliable', it is clear that such a question could not elicit a satisfactory answer. Let us therefore ask a somewhat simpler question. Do the narrative sources allow us to draw *any* conclusions about the battle, and specifically about how the English emerged victorious? There is no escaping the fact that the English sources are decidedly meagre. None of the surviving 'primary' sources and few of the secondary narratives have much to say about the role played by archery. There is some recognition, here and there, of the impact of bowmen on the battle,[254] but little indication of how that impact was achieved. The English sources also give the impression of a tactically static, defensive battle, the only 'movement' being the relief of the Prince of Wales's division. There is no explanation of how Edward III's tactics may have contributed to the victory. The small group of English eyewitness accounts reveal nothing on this subject: we can see this from those that have survived and deduce it from the imprint left by those (like the *Acta Bellicosa*) that have been lost. Since the secondary narratives relied heavily on these battlefield reports, adding only small points of detail from oral testimony, it is not surprising that the chronicles can tell us so little. Indeed, as we have seen, it is likely that the first version of Baker's chronicle shared this characteristic, hardly mentioning archery, and that he inserted the 'pits and wings of archers' passage in order to rectify this weakness. It was this addition that has made his chronicle appear so important among the fourteenth-century English sources for the battle. Nevertheless, even here much has been left to the imagination of the reader. We are not told how the wings of archers are supposed to have functioned, nor whether they were decisive in securing the victory for King Edward.

For fuller recognition of the impact of archery on the battle, we must turn to the chronicles of continental provenance, though they do not offer a consistent picture. Giovanni Villani and several of the French chronicles present a story very different from that sketched by Jean le Bel or the two chroniclers from Valenciennes (or, indeed, by those of English provenance), with Edward III occupying a defensive position reinforced by carts and hedges, which protected the rear and flanks and bolstered the front line as well. There is no sign of

---

[254] For example, *Murimuth*, p. 247; *Eulogium*, iii, p. 211.

Villani's *carrino* in the English chronicles, merely a brief mention of carts in the *Historia Roffensis*. (Jean le Bel's baggage camp serves a different purpose.) Presumably all but one of the battlefield despatches were silent on this subject. But what the continental chronicles have in common is a recognition that the archers' role was decisive. Most of the vivid descriptions of the chaos and carnage caused by the longbow come from the pens of these writers. They also suggest that the archers' role, as part of English tactics in general, was far from static. The advance to exploit the rout of the Genoese and the subsequent confusion among the French cavalry is recorded in many of the continental chronicles, including Jean le Bel and the Amiens MS of Froissart.

Villani's highly individual account of the battle, consisting of a sequence of attacks and counter-attacks in front of the English *carrino,* has left little imprint on a century or more of English-language writing on Crécy. That corpus of historical literature, from the flurry of publications in the late nineteenth and early twentieth centuries to the present, has preferred the testimony of Baker, Jean le Bel, Froissart and the Bourgeois of Valenciennes to that of Villani and the 'pro-French' chronicles.[255] As Charles Oman noted dismissively, 'It is certain that the two or three foreign chronicles who speak of the waggon park as a part of the English line (e.g. Villani) are wholly wrong. None of the good authorities place it anywhere save in the rear.'[256] Of course, the chronicles that were 'wholly wrong' on this score were also more explicit about the impact of English archery than their English counterparts; but for the English school it was Baker who 'can be depended upon'.[257] And it was not just English-language authors who relied upon Baker. It is true that the pioneering account of the battle by the early–mid nineteenth-century historian of Ponthieu, F.-C. Louandre, which drew heavily on Villani and the St Omer/*Chronique de Flandre* group of texts (as well as Froissart) was disseminated in England by G.F. Beltz and was used approvingly by Simeon Luce in his edition of Froissart.[258] But this thread

---

[255] Lloyd, 'The "herse" of archers at Crecy', *EHR*, x (1895), pp. 538–41; H.B. George, 'The archers at Crécy', *EHR*, x (1895), pp. 733–8; J.E. Morris, 'The archers at Crecy', *EHR*, xii (1897), pp. 427–36; J. Ramsay, *The Genesis of Lancaster, 1307–99*, 2 vols (Oxford, 1913), i, pp. 328–36; C. Oman, *A History of the Art of War in the Middle Ages*, 2nd edn, 2 vols (London, 1924), pp. 134–47; A.H. Burne, *The Crecy War* (London, 1955), chap. 7. The more recent accounts often make use of a wider variety of sources and offer different interpretations on points of detail, but the overall emphasis remains similar: Barber, *Edward Prince of Wales*, pp. 62–72; Bradbury, *The Medieval Archer*, pp. 105–8; Sumption, *Trial by Battle*, pp. 526–31; DeVries, *Infantry Warfare in the Early Fourteenth Century*, chap. 13; Rogers, *War Cruel and Sharp*, pp. 266–71; Nicolle, *Crécy 1346*.

[256] Oman, *A History of the Art of War in the Middle Ages*, ii, p. 138 n. 2; see also p. 142 n. 2. Cf. T.F. Tout: 'The two Tuscan writers . . . describe the French attack as made on the English entrenched behind a laager of wagons. This was plainly not the case, even though some French chronicles . . . share in the error of the Italians.' 'Firearms in England in the fourteenth century', *EHR*, xxvi (1911), p. 672.

[257] Burne, *The Crecy War*, p. 189.

[258] Louandre, *Histoire d'Abbeville*, i, pp. 201–20. G.F. Beltz, 'An inquiry into the existing narratives of the battle of Cressy with some account of its localities, traditions and remains', *Archaeologia*, xxviii (1840), pp. 171–92. Beltz summarised, to the point of plagiarism, the work of Louandre and Baron Seymour de Constant: 'Bataille de Cressy', *France Littéraire*, 1832, pp. 559–75. *Froissart*, ed. Luce, iii, p. xlviii n. 2. Louandre was used by Henri de

in the historiography became much less prominent following the publication of E.M. Thompson's excellent edition of Baker's chronicle in 1889. The writings of the Oxfordshire secular clerk were soon to influence French studies of the battle,[259] while providing the *locus classicus* for English-language analyses of archery tactics.

The marked preference in late nineteenth- and early twentieth-century English historiography for a small group of chronicles, and the peremptory dismissal of those that told a different story, has allowed historians to present Crécy as a very simple battle. Edward III's men waited on an open hillside, with no fixed defences apart from the *rideaux*, and the French attacked them repeatedly, but were repulsed with heavy loss. The 'phlegmatic and well-disciplined' English had seen off the 'excitable and uncontrolled' French. That, as Matthew Bennett has noted, is how it 'seemed to Victorian English gentlemen at least'.[260] From Charles Oman, through A.H. Burne to (it must be admitted) some modern accounts, discussions of how English tactics worked in practice have been 'coloured more than a little by an anachronistic nationalism and affected by [a] belief in the superiority of English firepower "throughout the ages" '. We have noticed that most fourteenth-century English sources for Crécy, both primary and secondary, hardly mention archery – a tendency that was maintained into the eighteenth century.[261] But the Victorian age witnessed the emergence of the yeoman archer as a popular military hero,[262] and so in a work dedicated to HRH Albert Edward, Prince of Wales in 1862, Charles Knight was able to describe Crécy as the

> day on which the steady courage that was the result of the comparatively free condition of the yeomen of England, was first asserted on a great scale. From that time the feudal pretensions of the iron-clad knights to be the only soldiers was practically at an end. The battles of England were thenceforth to be won by bow and bill. . . . [T]he same spirit which made every yeoman in that field of Cressy stir not one foot, whilst the great plain before them was filled with ten times their number of men at arms, has carried their descendants through many a desperate struggle, and showed from age to age 'the majesty with which the British soldier fights'.[263]

Wailly: *Crécy 1346: Anatomy of a Battle* (Poole, 1987), but this author's emphasis on the role played by Edward III's archers owes a greater debt to the English school of writing on the battle.

[259] For example, Henri Denifle's brief account is essentially a summary of Baker: H. Denifle, *La désolation des églises, monastères et hôpitaux en France pendant la guerre de cent ans* (Paris, 1899), pp. 43–4. J. Viard wove Baker into a weighty and balanced narrative alongside the French and Low Countries chronicles: 'La campagne de juillet–août 1346 et la bataille de Crécy', *Le Moyen Âge*, 2nd ser., 27 (1926), pp. 1–84.

[260] Bennett, 'The development of battle tactics in the Hundred Years War', *Arms, Armies and Fortifications in the Hundred Years War*, ed. Curry and Hughes, pp. 3–4.

[261] For example, Rapin de Thoyras, *The History of England*, trans. N. Tindal, 2nd edn, 2 vols (London, 1732), i, pp. 424–5: apart from the duel between the archers and the crossbowmen (taken from Froissart), Crécy is presented as an aristocratic mêlée.

[262] 'The picture of the gallant but socially humble English archer pitted against the debauched and scornful French gentleman was one which appealed to the rising bourgeoisie of Victorian Britain.' Curry, *The Battle of Agincourt*, p. 404.

[263] C. Knight, *A History of England*, 2 vols (London, 1862), i, pp. 463–4. Like Rapin de

This was a view that can only have been reinforced by conscription during the First World War. Moreover, late Victorian historians were influenced not only by the rise of the archer in popular esteem, but also by the techniques of modern warfare, including the preoccupation among early twentieth-century theorists with 'cross-fire'.[264] This they had in common, despite there being no general agreement about how exactly the archers were deployed: in 'wedges', on the wings of 'battles' or of the whole army, in front of the men-at-arms or intermingled with them.

Turn, however, to Hans Delbrück, and we find a view of Crécy that is not influenced by the 'firepower myth'. He argued that 'on relatively accessible terrain, marksmen, operating on their own, could not compete with a similar number of knights', so it was essential that they be backed up by men-at-arms. At Crécy, Edward III,

> by placing his dismounted knights among the archers, succeeded in utilising the volleys of arrows in a very different way from other knightly battles. The marksmen continued shooting until the last moment, with the full certainty that, if the enemy knight still succeeded in approaching him, he would be able to move a few paces to the rear, and the dismounted knight beside him would necessarily take up the fight.[265]

Moreover, Edward deployed his army in such as way as to 'lure the enemy into piecemeal attacks' up a slope. Consequently, only a few of the French knights reached their adversaries, where 'they were struck down by the English knights and spearmen'. But 'if there had first been an orderly deployment and the entire mass had then charged simultaneously against the English, the English arrows would hardly have been able to stop the assault'. There are problems with Delbrück's analysis. If the terrain has been interpreted correctly, it would never have been possible for the French to mount an effective attack on a wide front. And however 'massed' the charge, the bringing down of the front ranks by archery would have stopped the whole assault in its tracks. Nevertheless, that Delbrück's argument represents such a refreshing change serves to underline how profoundly modern perceptions of the battle of Crécy have been influenced by the viewpoint of late Victorian and early twentieth-century English historians. If we are to establish what happened on that August evening, such anachronistic accretions will need to be stripped away.

Many of our problems concerning the sources and how they have been interpreted by historians would be familiar to those who have studied the battle of Agincourt, but in at least one important respect Crécy poses an even greater challenge. For while the site of Henry V's triumph is agreed by all, no such certainty exists with regard to the battleground of Crécy. Part of the problem is that the chronicles offer comparatively little guidance on the matter. It is true

---

Thoyras, Knight's narrative of the battle is based squarely on Froissart, but the interpretation is very different.

264 M. Bennett, 'The battle', *Agincourt, 1415*, ed. A. Curry (Stroud, 2000), p. 28.

265 H. Delbrück, *History of the Art of War within the Framework of Political History*, trans. W.J. Renfroe (London, 1982), iii, pp. 454–62. He doubts the existence of Villani's *carrino* (p. 461).

that if we combine all the various locational references in these sources we are left with the area of the traditional battlefield (see Chapter 3). But the chronicles are frustratingly unspecific about the nature of the ground upon which the battle was fought. Indeed, they leave us with the distinct impression that the events unfolded on a level playing field. To some extent it was the English newsletters that were responsible for this. Edward III's despatch states that the battle was fought 'en plain champ' – a stock phrase – and there is no explicit mention of topographical features. That, of course, is hardly surprising since he would not have wished to suggest that the English had gained an advantage from the ground, even though exploiting the advantages offered by topography was exactly what he would have tried to do. Edward's letter does in fact provide a hint (the 'killing ground' where the first onslaught took place) that the battle-ground of Crécy was not wholly flat and featureless. However, it was the explicit message of Edward's report that was to have a lasting effect on English historiography, for Edward's 'plain champ' was repeated by Michael Northburgh and adopted by English chroniclers. This is also the description that we find in the 'neutral' Low Countries chronicles.[266] Jean le Bel is very clear that the action took place 'en ung beau camp où il n'y avoit fosse ne fossé', though this sounds like a battleground designed to fit the overall message of his Crécy battle piece. Indeed, Froissart's instincts told him that it must have been otherwise, for he inserts into his narrative the story of the English marshals' search for an advantageous site.[267]

We might expect to find some indication of what those advantages may have been in the chronicles written from the French perspective. Although several of them emphasise the role played by reinforced hedges in the English defensive position, they too have little to say about the physical appearance of the site. The most specific reference is provided by the *Chronique des quatre premiers Valois*, which states that the French arrived 'a la valée de Cressi'.[268] It is curious that not a single writer mentions either the steep bank on the eastern side of the Vallée des Clercs or the slope on the western side, up which modern historians have supposed the French must have advanced.[269] But turn to French administrative records and we find our hillside battle. One document orders the payment of 42 sergeants-at-arms who had served with Philip VI at the 'mont de Crécy'.[270] More telling still, we find a record of warhorses lost 'a la bataille du mont de Cressy' by knights and esquires in the company of Guillaume Flotte, sire de Revel, chancellor of France. That other documents tell of horse losses in the 'besoigne devant Cressy en Ponthieu' adds still further to the weight of evidence supporting the traditional battlefield.[271] It seems that 'la bataille du mont de

---

[266] For the Bourgeois of Valenciennes, it was 'une belle plaine': *Récits*, p. 229.

[267] *Jean le Bel*, ii, p. 106. *Froissart*, ed. Luce, iii, pp. 166, 402.

[268] *Chronique de quatre premiers Valois*, p. 16.

[269] Exceptionally, Villani speaks of a 'colletto'.

[270] H. Moranvillé, 'Philippe VI à la bataille de Crécy', *Bibliothèque de l'École des chartes*, l (1889), pp. 295–7.

[271] P. Contamine, *Guerre, état et société à la find du moyen âge* (Paris, 1972), p. 105. The sire de Revel's horse losses were for the period from 6 August to 5 September, including the battle of Crécy.

Cressy' was how the events of 26 August became known within French administrative circles, recalling perhaps how the slope rising from the floor of the
Vallée des Clercs to the English position would have appeared to King Philip's
army as it entered the mouth of the valley. Not for the first time, guileless
administrative records prove to be more revealing than sources that purport to
tell a story.

Faced by so many accounts of the battle of Crécy, with no single text dominant
and such a meagre crop of 'primary' material, an historian attempting to write a
narrative of the confrontation on that fateful evening, which includes the
sequence of principal events and some explanation of the outcome, could be
forgiven for building a composite picture from fragments of information
extracted from a range of narrative sources. Such an approach may indeed be
unavoidable. However, the problems that it involves are too rarely discussed. Of
course, constructing such a 'battle piece' would not be easy, given the ambigu-
ities and contradictions, not to mention the partial viewpoints and the yawning
lacunae, in the narrative sources. Any battle piece that failed to make allowance
for these problems would be presenting an incomplete, indeed distorted, view of
its subject. But how should we make allowance, in particular, for the evident
gaps in our knowledge? To what extent is it permissible to fill them by resorting
to speculation, however solidly founded upon well-informed leaps of historical
imagination? And how far can the problems raised by ambiguous or conflicting
evidence be resolved? However carefully the data are sifted, however critical the
assessment of the sources to find the most 'reliable' ones, the fact remains that
the character of the resulting battle piece would assuredly be shaped by the
historian's personality, as well as by his preoccupations.

Indeed, the problems arising from a 'cherry-picking' approach to the narrative sources extend beyond the effects of the modern historian's involuntary or
conscious subjectivity. For, as we have seen, the selected fragments would be
taken from narratives, each of which was itself shaped by its author's responses
to his sources, by his strengths, limitations and preoccupations as a writer of
contemporary or recent history, by his patron's wishes and by the underlying
themes of his work. Some of the narrative accounts for Crécy are little more than
straight copies of other chronicles, while others are compilations, assemblages
of information, though not without principles determining the selection. Some,
however, are distinctive and individual accounts with a coherent view, an interpretative agenda, which is of interest in its own right. If what the author of the
chronicle was seeking to achieve can be determined, it may be possible to appreciate its value as a work of historical literature, while more effectively evaluating
it as a 'source' for our purposes. For example, as we have seen, Jean le Bel's
narrative of Crécy has emerged from a mould determined by his desire to
contrast the effectiveness of Edward III's leadership, and the consequent efficient organisation of the English army, with the weakness of Philip VI and the
undisciplined state of his host.

Here, then, is perhaps the greatest problem facing an historian seeking to
'reconstruct' the sequence of events in a medieval battle from a collection of
chronicle accounts. Unless the chronicles are used in a way that is consistent

with their purpose and sensitive to the circumstances that gave rise to them, there is a real risk that they will be misinterpreted and undervalued. The narrative sources are not simply repositories of facts, which can be sampled selectively, the passages that suit a particular purpose being utilised while others are rejected. Apart from the obvious inconsistency that this involves, when an historian extracts a passage from a narrative source, he removes it from the interpretative context that has shaped its existence and without which it may lose much of its meaning. Moreover, it is evident that the 'facts' about a battle that are to be found in the many and varied sources may well be incompatible if juxtaposed or interwoven in a composite account. And this is not simply because they are of uneven quality: it is not simply that doubtful evidence is being combined with more reliable data. Each of the fourteenth-century accounts of Crécy are different to a greater or lesser degree, serving different purposes, offering different interpretations. To create a composite from passages of such varied provenance would be like making up a jigsaw picture by fitting together the pieces from a number of different, incomplete puzzles. The result is unlikely to be a valid representation of anything.

10

Topography and Archery:
Further Reflections on the Battle of Crécy

ANDREW AYTON and SIR PHILIP PRESTON Bart.

Given the problems that are attendant upon reconstructing the battle of Crécy from the narrative sources, it is small wonder that there has been so much inconclusive debate about the battle. In particular, no consensus has emerged concerning English tactical deployment, the role played by archery and the combat relationship between the archers and the men-at-arms in Edward III's army. Yet these appear to be precisely the issues that are central to an understanding of how the English brought off their remarkable victory in a battle in which so many of the aristocracy of the greatest military power in Europe were lost at the expense of so very few of her adversary. Consequently, we cannot simply sidestep these issues in the concluding part of this book. But if the chronicles deny us a clear picture of how the English army, and the archer contingent in particular, were disposed, how are we to understand and explain the English victory at Crécy? One approach would be to acknowledge and accept the limitations, even distractions, of the chroniclers' terms, and to approach the problem from a different direction, making more explicit use of evidence concerning the armies of the protagonists and the distinctive topography of the 'traditional' battlefield. With regard to the role of the archers – the crucial issue – we must consider how the strengths and limitations of these potent, mobile missile troops, having played a major part in the choice of battleground, would have dictated their deployment and the way they fought on the chosen site. This is not to turn one's back on the chroniclers, but to look with a greater resolution at a question that was not perhaps their primary concern and to which they have not themselves offered a consistent answer. It is our hope that an understanding of the composition and attributes of the English army may contribute to an understanding of both the course and outcome of the battle; and it is our conviction that any serious interpretation of the battle must take account of the ground upon which it was fought.

The longbow and Edwardian warfare

The place of the longbow in English medieval history is on the podium of weaponry. Indeed, it has become a commonplace in historical works to argue that it was the massed deployment of archers that was the principal reason for the astounding English victories of the Hundred Years War. Their numerical preponderance in the English armies of the period suggests that theirs was indeed a crucial role; but just how they achieved these victories remains the subject of debate – a debate that all too often has been fuelled by conjecture presented as fact. Much has been written about the power and range of the longbow; the great draw weights demanded of the bowman and yet his rapid rate of shooting; the dense showers of arrows that could be unleashed; and the efficiency, or lack of, with which an arrow might penetrate armour, whether mail or plate.[1] And, of course, a great deal of attention has been given to how the archer may have been deployed on the battlefield. These issues should not be ignored, of course; but a proper understanding of archery and the archer demands the adoption of a broader approach to the problem. Firstly, more attention needs to be given to the archer himself. With the emphasis principally on the longbow, the weapon and what in theory could be achieved with it, there is a danger that the man wielding the bow stave will be taken for granted. Secondly, we need to consider how the mid-fourteenth-century archer fitted into the organisational structure of the army on the march and on the battlefield. This investigation may well cast some much-needed light on English tactical deployment at Crécy and elsewhere. Very much linked to this is a third subject deserving of attention, namely how the archer, and those who directed his efforts on the battlefield, sought to maximise his fighting potential while minimising his limitations.

It must be stressed at this point that 'those who directed' the archers in the field knew exactly what they were doing. It should not be imagined that the aristocracy regarded the bow as a weapon beneath their dignity, fit only for their social inferiors. On the hunting field they would often have had a bow in their hands themselves, and their passion for field sports brought them into contact with those expert bowmen, the foresters and parkers who managed their hunting grounds.[2] Indeed, we learn from the royal household records that in July 1334 Edward III paid an archer, Walter Daly, the considerable sum of 10s as compensation for having broken his bow, presumably in the context of hunting or recreational archery.[3] We are reminded here of the shooting match between the king and the outlaw hero in the *Gest of Robyn Hode*.[4]

From senior commanders down to the captains of the smallest mixed retinues,

[1]   For contrasting views, see R. Hardy, *Longbow. A Social and Military History*, 3rd edn (Sparkford, 1998), esp. pp. 53–6, and chap. 11 and appendices; and K. DeVries, *Medieval Military Technology* (Peterborough, Ontario, 1992), pp. 37–8, which draws on J. Keegan, *The Face of Battle* (Harmondsworth, 1978), pp. 92–8, and C. Gaier, 'L'invincibilité anglaise et le grande arc après la guerre de cent ans: un mythe tenace', in C. Gaier, *Armes et combats dans l'univers mediéval* (Brussels, 1995), pp. 327–35. For a recent debate, see K. DeVries, 'Catapults are not atom bombs: towards a re-definition of "effectiveness" in pre-modern military technology', *War in History*, iv (1997), pp. 454–70, esp. pp. 460–4, which prompted a withering response from Clifford Rogers: 'The efficacy of the English longbow: a reply to Kelly DeVries', *War in History*, v (1998), pp. 233–42.

[2]   N. Saul, *Scenes from Provincial Life* (Oxford, 1986), pp. 187–92; J.C. Holt, *Robin Hood*, revised edn (London, 1989), pp. 142–5.

[3]   BL, Add. MS 46350, m. 8.

[4]   R.B. Dobson and J. Taylor, *Rymes of Robyn Hood*, revised edn (Stroud, 1997), p. 110.

there would have been a keen appreciation of the potential of the longbow; and practical campaigning experience would have taught Edward's captains how best to make the most of that potential on the battlefield. Among the senior captains in the prince's 'battle' at Crécy were the earl of Northampton, who had improvised a tactically effective deployment at Morlaix in 1342, and the army's sub-marshal, Sir Thomas Ughtred, who had led archer contingents earlier in the war.[5] The king and his lieutenants decided upon the deployment of the archers, and would have issued instructions before the battle about when shooting should commence and for how long. We may further assume that orders were conveyed around the field, to the commanders of individual battles, by gallopers. But altogether less clear is how instructions were relayed to bowmen during the battle. How was the shooting of the archers synchronised, for example? By trumpet blast, perhaps?[6] We can only speculate whether Sir Thomas Ughtred performed a role at Crécy similar to that undertaken at Agincourt by Sir Thomas Erpingham.[7] Our only guide to the 'local' chain of command is the well-documented structure of the army: much, presumably, was left to retinue captains, to centenars and vintenars, to groups of archers and indeed individuals. 'This', as Matthew Bennett has noted, 'only goes to strengthen their reputation as individuals of great military worth.'[8]

This brings the spotlight onto the Edwardian archer himself. What kind of man was he and how proficient with the bow?[9] As was shown in Chapter 5, we have as yet comparatively little 'hard' data on the archers at Crécy, and far less than has been assembled for the knights and esquires in King Edward's army. The 'mid-fourteenth-century English archer' is a major and potentially very rewarding research project awaiting its historian. Beyond their regional origins, and the broadest of socio-economic characterisations, little can be said about most of the archers. Nor can we be sure how skilled the majority of them were with the bow. It would be safe to assume that they were all competent, but we should not perhaps expect them all to have been 'Robin Hoods'. All that we can be certain of is that there were highly proficient archers among them, the foresters and parkers; and it is also likely that there were more 'professionals' serving as retinue-based mounted archers than there were in the arrayed shire companies.

We turn now to a second subject deserving more attention than it has hitherto received, namely how the mid-fourteenth-century archer fitted into the organisational structure of the army on the march and on the battlefield. Although the *tactical* relationship between archers and men-at-arms is of particular concern to us here, this is not simply to revisit the sterile debate on 'wings' or 'wedges' of

---

5 *Murimuth*, p. 108.
6 We know that trumpet blasts were used to regulate the functioning of English armies in the camp: *Jean le Bel*, i, p. 55; ii, p. 106. Using banners for synchronisation had the disadvantage of requiring visual contact, though this may have been the function of local commanders (e.g., vintenars), who could pass on an order to their men by word of mouth.
7 M. Bennett, 'The battle', *Agincourt 1415*, ed. A. Curry (Stroud, 2000), pp. 30–2.
8 *Ibid.*, p. 32. Cf. J. Keegan, *The Face of Battle*, pp. 91–3.
9 Robert Hardy offers some thoughts on his likely physical stature: *Longbow. A Social and Military History*, pp. 217–19.

archers. That debate is usually conducted without reference to the organisational structure of the army, but this is precisely the context with which we are centrally concerned: how army organisation on a retinue and company level may have influenced tactical deployment. With regard to the battle of Crécy, the problem is complicated by the fact that about a third of the archers had been recruited for service in mixed retinues alongside men-at-arms, while the remainder were serving in the companies raised in the English shires and Welsh lordships. In Chapter 5 it was suggested that the archer companies would in all likelihood have been distributed among the three 'battles' of the army. But how exactly these arrayed archers operated in the field, in relation to their retinue-based counterparts (and, indeed, the retinue-based men-at-arms) remains unresolved. It was also argued in Chapter 5 that the fundamental logic of the 'mixed retinue' was the operational – including tactical – co-operation of its personnel. It was not just that the mixed retinue happened to be composed of two types of military personnel with complementary skills. The delegation of archer recruitment to the captains of retinues may have begun as a pragmatic response to an administrative and organisational challenge, but by the 1340s recruitment of bowmen and men-at-arms had become closely connected at company level. Thus, the mixed retinue was actually composed of mixed companies: the atomic structure of this section of the army consisted of units which, in a continental European context, would be termed 'lances'.

The 'lance' is not generally considered to be an English phenomenon, yet its existence has been documented in the English mercenary companies in Italy,[10] and the small 'mixed' companies that we see there, and in various continental states, are not dissimilar to those that we find in the records of the mid-1340s in England. There has been some disagreement about the tactical function of the continental lance. In fifteenth-century France, according to Philippe Contamine, it was primarily of administrative, disciplinary and social significance, for although it allowed for more contact between men-at-arms and footmen, 'on the field of battle, the groupings were different; the men-at-arms fought on one side, the archers on the other'.[11] But, as Malcolm Vale has argued, 'members of the Flemish and Burgundian nobility often dismounted and stood among the archers in battle', and the Burgundian 'lance' of 1473 'could clearly be a tactical, as well as an administrative reality'.[12] We should give serious consideration to the possibility that a similar close relationship had developed in English armies by the time of the battle of Crécy: that the fundamental 'atomic' structure of the mixed retinues in English armies was reflected in tactical dispositions in the field, and that archers fought in close co-operation with (perhaps even alongside) the men-at-arms with whom they had been recruited and had served throughout the campaign.

---

[10] For example, in a brigade raised in 1379, each lance consisted of two men-at-arms, one archer and a page: K. Fowler, 'Sir John Hawkwood and the English condottieri in Trecento Italy', *Renaissance Studies*, xii (1998), pp. 131–48 (at p. 137).

[11] P. Contamine, *Guerre, état et société à la fin du moyen âge* (Paris, 1972), pp. 278–9, 482. Cf. M. Mallett, *Mercenaries and their Masters* (London, 1974), pp. 148–50.

[12] M. Vale, *War and Chivalry* (London, 1981), pp. 101, 124–5.

Now, as Anne Curry notes, 'if mixed retinues did stick together in the mêlée, then this would mean that archers formed groups within the lines of men-at-arms', which (she adds in parenthesis) is 'one of the possible interpretations of the controversial word *herce* in the English deployment at Crécy'.[13] This image is also reminiscent of the famous description of archer deployment at Agincourt in the *Gesta Henrici Quinti,* which states that Henry V 'mixed troops of archers in his battle lines'.[14] This was no doubt based upon recognition that the long-bow's destructive potential could be most effectively realised at relatively close range – say, within 100 yards. Distributing the archers throughout the division would, therefore, ensure a more even spread of archery and a greater variety of angles of shooting than could be achieved by positioning all of the archers on the wings of the army or 'battle'. There would be no part of the army's frontage that would not be covered, and the men-at-arms would be more effectively protected against the threat of the enemy's archery. That threat was very real. We should not forget that the Genoese crossbowmen could have inflicted heavy losses on the English at Crécy had they not been outclassed by King Edward's bowmen. It was in order to counter just such a threat (though the context concerned a Christian army facing Turkish archery) that Bertrandon de la Broquière argued in a memorandum of 1439 that 'a large part of the archers and crossbowmen should be sewn among the men-at-arms, [that is,] stationed among the men-at-arms or a little in front if necessary'.[15] This would have been no less prudent a deployment in 1346.

Moreover, the 'sticking together' of the members of mixed retinues in the mêlée raises the possibility that Froissart's 'herce' was indeed intended to recall a 'hedgehog'. An attacking force would be met by a combination of lance-points and bodkin-headed arrows, as men-at-arms and archers provided mutual protec-tion. Thomas Gray, a north country knight with extensive personal experience of warfare, describes just such a bristling defensive formation as an Anglo-Gascon force resisted French cavalry at the battle of Lunelonge in 1349.[16] Particularly revealing descriptions of such tactics can be found in fifteenth-century works. Jean de Waurin, writing of the role performed by Flemish pikemen in the

---

[13] A. Curry, 'Review article. Medieval warfare. England and her continental neighbours, eleventh to the fourteenth centuries', *Journal of Medieval History*, xxiv (1998), p. 100.

[14] 'intermisisset cuneos sagittariorum suorum cuilibet aciei'. The translation of this phrase has provoked much discussion: see Bennett, 'The battle', *Agincourt 1415*, ed. Curry, p. 28. It is interesting to note how Thomas Elmham interpreted the *Gesta*'s phrase in his *Liber Metricus de Henrico Quinto*: 'hic intermisit turmas simul architenentium' ('amongst them he intermingled troops of archers'). See A. Curry, *The Battle of Agincourt – Sources and Inter-pretations* (Woodbridge, 2000), pp. 24–5, 34, 46.

[15] For an extended quotation, see Vale, *War and Chivalry*, p. 112.

[16] 'The advanced guard of the French avoided the lance points at the first encounter, moving round the ranks of the English, who had dismounted, [but] coming so close that every Eng-lishman who chose to strike slew a horse with his lance, the Frenchmen being thrown out of their saddles to the ground': *Scalacronica*, ed. H. Maxwell (Glasgow, 1907), pp. 136–7. Cf. *Chronique Normande*, pp. 94–5. Although Gray's account does not mention archers, we may safely assume that they were present. Like other English writers of the time, Gray is apt to overlook the work of the bowmen, and it is inconceivable that they would not be included in a substantial field force in the late 1340s.

Burgundian army in 1471, notes that 'these pikes make very useful poles for placing a spike between two archers against the fearful effects of cavalry trying to break their ranks'. Charles the Bold's ordinance of 1473 required that pikemen would 'kneel while holding their pikes as low as the height of a horse's hind quarters so that the archers can fire over the said pikemen as if over a wall'.[17] Edward III and his captains can hardly have been unaware of the advantages brought by close co-operation between archers and men-at-arms. Mixed retinues offered the ideal organisational framework for such tactical co-operation, for there can be no doubt that fighting effectiveness would benefit from the social and disciplinary cohesion provided by the company structure within retinues, as well as from the camaraderie engendered by shared local origins and campaign experience. Linguistic and cultural homogeneity would also have been a binding agent within the companies of arrayed archers from England and Wales, for these shire- or lordship-based contingents were composed of vintenaries recruited at a local level. How these archer companies were combined with other units in tactical formations is unclear, but it would have made sense when attaching the shire levies to the 'battles' of mixed retinues to bring together contingents recruited from the same region of the kingdom.

It could, of course, be objected that the 'organisation of armies in terms of recruitment and control is not necessarily the same as organisation in the field'.[18] The army of the pay-roll *may not* be a reliable guide to the army as deployed on the battlefield. But what is the alternative to the close tactical co-operation of men-at-arms and archers? The conventional wisdom places wings of archers on the flanks of the army, or at least on the flanks of individual 'battles'. Archer and man-at-arms are kept apart. Now, as was shown in Chapter 9, one of the principal documentary buttresses for this view of English tactics, Geoffrey le Baker's chronicle, cannot really bear the weight that has been placed on it. But, in any case, positioning all the archers on the wings of the army simply does not make sense. It would necessitate the break-up of mixed retinues, tearing apart the fabric of the army down to company level, thereby discarding the advantages brought by retinue-based esprit de corps. And it is unlikely that the 'wings of archers' would be composed solely of men from the shire levies. Apart from the command and control problems that would result, no commander worth his salt would be prepared to leave conscripted archers exposed and unsupported on the flanks of his army. He would do what Jean de Bueil recommended on his treatise, *Le Jouvencel*, in the 1460s: position archers on the wings by all means, but protect them 'by placing men-at-arms at either end of these wings'.[19]

It is important to recognise that for all his potential as a 'battle winner', the archer, as a lightly armed combatant, could be vulnerable if deployed in the open

---

17 Vale, *War and Chivalry*, pp. 114, 124–5.
18 Curry, 'Review article. Medieval warfare', p. 100.
19 M. Bennett, 'The development of battle tactics in the Hundred Years War', *Arms, Armies and Fortifications in the Hundred Years War*, ed. A. Curry and M. Hughes (Woodbridge, 1994), p. 8. See also, Bennett, 'The battle', *Agincourt 1415*, ed. Curry, pp. 28–30.

and lacking the support of men-at-arms or spearmen. Instances of English archers being dispersed by well-timed cavalry charges are not hard to find. John Barbour describes such events at Bannockburn and Stanhope (1327), while the *Chronique Normande* (and Geoffrey le Baker) imply that something similar happened at Mauron in 1352.[20] Edward III and his lieutenants would have been well aware of this potential hazard at Crécy. Indeed, according to Bartholomew Burgherssh's despatch, during the assault on Caen, the king had become concerned that his archers would be cut up if they became involved in a mêlée unsupported, and he consequently ordered their recall.[21] In the absence of men-at-arms in close support, an archer would seek natural or improvised cover. It is well known that at Agincourt pointed stakes were used to provide greater security for archers deployed in an open field. There is no evidence for the use of this form of improvised barrier during the early stages of the Hundred Years War, but as Matthew Bennett notes, the 'defensive belt' of stakes 'was a mobile version of the woods and hedges which the English archers had previously sought on the battlefield'.[22] At Roche Derrien in June 1347, Sir Thomas Dagworth had hoped to use all the available cover during his early morning attack on Charles of Blois's camp. As he notes in his battlefield despatch, the 'lord Charles . . . had caused to be levelled and razed . . . all manner of ditches and hedges, whereby my archers might not find their advantage over him and his people, but they were obliged in the end to fight in the open fields'.[23] Taking advantage of every feature of the ground may have been even more pressing in the case of defensive positions. This is a particularly notable feature of Baker's account of the battle of Poitiers, for example. We may be certain, therefore, that any advantage offered by topographical features (hedges, ditches, walls, woods and so on) would have been exploited as the English took up position at Crécy. Yet, as we have seen, the English and 'neutral' narrative sources make no mention of hedges, banks or ditches playing a part in Edward III's defensive position, a shortcoming that is highlighted by the crucial role played by carts and hedges in the accounts of Giovanni Villani and several of the French chroniclers. Indeed, Baker's invention of the pits may have been prompted in part by the realisation that the English were unlikely to have accepted battle on an open, flat field.

In stressing the importance of cover, we are not suggesting that archers would be deployed in fixed positions, for surely another central concern of commanders and bowmen alike was how best to exploit the tactical flexibility that a highly *mobile* missile capability provided for the English army. This mobility was most obviously displayed in offensive operations, as with the archers' contribution to Henry, earl of Derby's victory at Auberoche in 1345 and Sir Thomas Dagworth's at La Roche Derrien in 1347. But the potential for

---

[20] John Barbour, *The Bruce*, ed. A.A.M. Duncan (Edinburgh, 1997), pp. 482–5, 716–19. Mauron: *Chronique Normande*, pp. 105–6; cf. *Baker*, p. 120, who relates that 30 archers who had fled from the battle were beheaded for cowardice.
[21] *Murimuth*, pp. 202–3.
[22] Bennett, 'The development of battle tactics', pp. 15–16.
[23] *Avesbury*, pp. 488–9.

tactical flexibility that mobility provided was also important in defensive situations. Bowmen would not be rooted to the spot; they were not mere 'animated dummies'.[24] At Poitiers, while some archers were 'positioned in safe trenches along the ditch and beyond the hedge', another group 'were safely positioned in the marsh, where cavalry could not reach them'. But the latter's arrows made no impression on the heavily armoured forequarters of the French cavalry and so they were speedily deployed by the earl of Oxford 'to one side . . . to shoot at the horses' [unprotected] rearquarters'.[25] At Neville's Cross, 'five hundred English archers ran on in advance, and with their missiles forced the Scots to abandon the place they had occupied, and provoked them to seek battle'.[26]

Is it not likely that such flexibility was also shown at Crécy? Some at least of the archers would have been deployed, early in the battle, in front of the main defensive line, as suggested by Mathias von Neuenburg and others.[27] This has been likened to the light infantry skirmishing screen of a later period,[28] which moreover is a particularly apt description of the archer deployment at the Blanquetaque crossing, as reported by the Bourgeois of Valenciennes. Archers led the way into the shallow waters of the Somme, closely followed by Welsh spearmen, with a large contingent of men-at-arms behind them.[29] Here was a classic combined arms operation. The archers would inflict damage on the ranks of the enemy, secure in the knowledge that they could withdraw to the security of a thicket of spearmen in the (likely) event of a counter-attack. The elegance of this deployment is the simplicity with which such a transition between offence and defence could be achieved, only requiring the highly mobile archers to fall back through the ranks of the spearmen. The Valenciennes chronicler's account of the dramatic events on the Somme two days before Crécy offers an authentic glimpse of Edwardian tactics, highlighting the co-operation between the distinctive elements of the army that was essential to their success. It is not difficult to see how the 'Blanquetaque deployment' could be adapted to a defensive battle, and this is surely what happened at Crécy, with Edward employing a proportion of his archers in a mobile, skirmishing role at the outset, backed up by 'hedges' of spearmen and men-at-arms, as well as by 'natural' cover. And, as at Poitiers, there would also have been local tactical redeployments during the course of the battle. There may even have been marksmen with 'roving commissions'.

Although English chroniclers of Crécy are silent on such matters, their continental counterparts offer plentiful evidence of movement by both archers and

---

[24] Bennett, 'The development of battle tactics', p. 8.

[25] *Baker*, pp. 147–8.

[26] D. Rollason and M. Prestwich, *The Battle of Neville's Cross 1346* (Stamford, 1998), p. 147 (Meaux chronicle); note also p. 135 (Thomas Sampson's letter).

[27] Deployment 'in front' has been suggested by Robert Hardy, who argues vigorously against the positioning of all archers on 'the wings of the entire battle array' since long stretches of the battle line would be 'unswept by the fall of arrows': R. Hardy, 'The longbow', *Arms, Armies and Fortifications in the Hundred Years War*, ed. Curry and Hughes, p. 180. For mobile deployment on the flanks, see J. Bradbury, *The Medieval Archer* (Woodbridge, 1985), p. 115.

[28] Bennett, 'The development of battle tactics', p. 8; also, Hardy, 'The longbow', p. 180.

[29] *Récits*, pp. 227–8.

men-at-arms during the battle; and the way that King Edward's army was organised may provide an additional clue. The intermingling of archers and men-at-arms at retinue – and, indeed, company – level could well have provided the practical, organisational basis for such finely judged combined arms tactics. Thus, we can easily visualise the retinue-based archers acting as skirmishers, and then falling back to rejoin their comrades in the main battle line as the enemy closed.[30] If the situation demanded it, the archer would then wield sword or club in the mêlée alongside his more heavily armoured comrades; and we should not imagine that he would be any less effective in this role than his counterparts were to be at Agincourt. Among these all-round fighting men would have been many of the most experienced combatants in the army: men who were effectively professional soldiers, who were serving in retinues whose members shared an esprit de corps founded upon regional origins and accumulated military experience. Shifting our focus in this way from the big picture, from the general layout of 'battles' on the field, to the fine texturing in the army's fabric – to the rank and file personnel and their relationships – is crucially important if we are understand a medieval battle like Crécy. For as the big tactical plan was implemented, there would, of course, have been much on-the-spot improvisation, much decision-making by small groups of men-at-arms and archers – 'micro-tactics', whereby individuals and small groups left their mark on the day.

In both defensive and offensive contexts the archer had the potential to cause great damage to an enemy *at a distance.* An attacking formation would either be stopped dead in its tracks or thinned out, its cohesion disrupted to such a degree that the English men-at-arms would have the advantage in any mêlée that occurred. But how destructive the archers could be would depend, of course, on their supply of arrows. This dependence was the archers' greatest limitation, for exhaustion of their ammunition could leave them, and the men-at-arms with whom they were fighting, dangerously exposed. We may assume that the earl of Suffolk's reputed concern that 'the archers did not waste arrows' during the battle of Poitiers was typical of the close interest that senior commanders maintained in what was an issue of fundamental importance.[31] And we can be sure that the archers themselves would be acutely aware of the need to make the best use of their ammunition.

At Crécy, as at La Flamengrie in October 1339, reserve supplies of arrows, as well as bows and strings, would have been distributed to the archers on the eve of the battle.[32] Our understanding of English tactics at Crécy and elsewhere would greatly benefit from knowing how many arrows the army had at its disposal at the start of the battle and how effectively they were distributed during

---

30 This, it should be noted, is very much the method proposed by *Vegetius: Epitome of Military Science*, trans. and ed. N.P. Milner (Liverpool, 1993), pp. 20–1, 49, 90.

31 *Baker*, p. 148. For an engagement fought near Coutances in 1356 in which the archers did indeed exhaust their arrow supply, see M. Prestwich, *Armies and Warfare in the Middle Ages* (New Haven and London, 1996), p. 322.

32 The Wardrobe Book covering the period of the Cambrésis–Thiérache campaign notes that 620 bows, 680 sheaves of arrows and over 2,000 bowstrings were distributed to archers at la Flamengrie on 23 October. *Norwell*, p. 413.

the course of it, for these factors would surely have affected how the archers were employed and, consequently, the dynamics of the battle. Unfortunately, concrete information on the English arrow supply at Crécy is lacking, and we can do no more than make tentative deductions from the available evidence. The archers serving in the shire levies would have been provided with their basic equipment by their home communities. Thus, the sheriff of Rutland noted in a return of c. 1346 that he had supplied each of the ten men who had been raised in his shire with a bow, arrows, a sword, a knife and 'uniform' clothing.[33] The retinue-based archers would also have brought their own equipment or that which had been provided by their captain. Further supplies would have been distributed from the crown's stocks, though we do not know how large these stocks were at the start of the campaign or how they were managed in the field.[34] One indication of the number of arrows per archer that the government deemed appropriate is to be found in the ratio of bows to sheaves of arrows ordered by the crown. Using this method (and data from 1338), Robert Hardy has tentatively suggested that 'an archer on campaign could count on 100 shafts, more or less, presumably replenished as often as necessary and possible'.[35] The royal orders from 1345–6 suggest a less generous provision: 50 to 70 arrows per man, in addition to supplies that the men carried themselves. If we assume the upper end of that range and a total of 7,500 archers in the army, we have a figure of half a million arrows, which (allowing 4 oz per arrow) would weigh a manageable 55 tons.[36] Manageability was crucial, of course, since these supplies and much other equipment besides had to be shipped to La Hougue and then carried in carts or on packhorses across Normandy.

A reserve stock of only half a million arrows, carried in 50 to 60 carts, may seem implausibly small, but some confirmation that these figures are indeed of the right order of magnitude is provided by the records for the small expeditionary force that Sir Hugh Hastings led to Flanders during the summer of 1346. Here we learn that two carts, with ten horses, had been hired to carry the (spare) bows and arrows required by a force of about 250 archers.[37] Not only would two one-ton carts be able to carry a reserve stock of arrows that would allow about

---

[33] C47/2/34, m. 2.

[34] Beginning in March 1345, a sequence of orders had been issued to sheriffs to collect large quantities of archery munitions for dispatch to the Tower of London. The initial order was for a total of 3,000 bows, 8,400 sheaves of arrows and 20,000 bowstrings, and this was followed up by further requests for smaller quantities (C76/20, mm. 25, 26, 31; Wrottesley, *Crecy and Calais*, pp. 61, 66). Demands on these supplies would have been made by the several expeditions that left England in 1345.

[35] Hardy, 'The Longbow', *Arms, Armies and Fortifications in the Hundred Years War*, ed. Curry and Hughes, p. 162.

[36] We have intentionally opted for an arrow weight that is at the heavy end of the spectrum since our calculations make no allowance for the carriage of spare bow staves and bowstrings. Cf. the figures for Henry VIII's invasion of France in 1513: one of the army's three 'wards' (which was of the same order of magnitude as the whole of Edward III's host in 1346) brought with it 10,000 sheaves of arrows (240,000 shafts), which were carried in 26 wagons, suggesting that about a ton of arrows was carried by each wagon. C. Cruickshank, *Henry VIII and the Invasion of France* (Stroud, 1990), p. 71.

[37] E372/191, m. 49.

70 arrows per man, but extrapolating from a ratio of 2 carts to 250 archers, we find that 60 would be needed for a force of 7,500. An additional indication that the English began the Crécy campaign with adequate rather than abundant stocks of arrows is to be found in the letter that the king wrote to his council in London from Caen on 29 July. Among the orders contained in the letter is a request for further supplies of bows, arrows and bowstrings, which (along with men and money) were to be despatched to Le Crotoy in Ponthieu. The letter is unspecific about quantities, but on 1 August orders were issued from Windsor to 15 sheriffs to acquire a total of 2,280 bows and 5,550 sheaves of arrows (or 133,200 shafts) for the king's army in France.[38] We can only speculate as to why Edward felt such a request was necessary so early in the campaign. Expenditure at Caen may have been unexpectedly high, to a degree that could not be offset by the manufacture of arrows during his march. Or the order may simply have been precautionary, for an army seeking a battle and dependent upon archery could not have too many arrows. Whatever lay behind the order, it is worthy of note that the quantities required were not huge. No doubt intended to be realistic from the point of view of acquisition and transportation, they were also of an order of magnitude commensurate with an initial reserve stock of half a million arrows.

As telling as Edward III's request for fresh supplies only a fortnight into the campaign is the fact that they do not appear to have arrived in time for the battle of Crécy. Immediately after the Somme was crossed at Blanquetaque on 24 August, a flying column under Hugh Despenser made a dash for Le Crotoy. After a stiff fight he was able to take possession of a valuable store of provisions in the town, but the sources make no mention of supply ships waiting offshore. So it seems that the English entered the battle on 26 August with what remained of the stock of arrows that had been brought to France six weeks earlier, plus those which had been manufactured on the march. It is crucial to bear this in mind if we are to understand how the archers may have been employed at Crécy, and consequently the dynamics of the battle.

Compulsive as the image of the 'arrow storm' may be, given the limited supply of ammunition, it would seem unlikely that such prolonged dense expenditure of arrows would have been advisable or even possible at Crécy. Although spells of rapid and massed shooting are certainly suggested by several of the chronicles, the speed with which such a tactic would exhaust ammunition supplies deserves attention. It is generally agreed that, even with a bow of extraordinary draw weight, an experienced archer could comfortably unleash between six and twelve arrows a minute (and might have been able to manage twenty). At this rate of shooting a thousand archers would launch 10,000 arrows into the sky within sixty seconds – a staggering sight that would justify the variety of vivid similes coined by contemporary commentators, particularly if such a sight, and its effects, had not been witnessed before. However, such rapid shooting if sustained over any length of time would demand not only remarkable skill, intensity and stamina, but also a huge store of arrows and an efficient

---

38 'Et vous mandons aussint que vous facez pourvoier tantz des arcs et des seces et cordes pour arcs come vous purrez': C81/314, no. 17803; *Foedera*, III, i, pp. 87–9.

system of battlefield distribution. Continuous shooting by five thousand archers at a rate of ten shafts per minute for just twenty minutes would have required a mobile stockpile of 1 million arrows! (Indeed, under such conditions, each archer would need to carry, or be supplied with, 50 lb of arrows.) This, as we have seen, is twice the size of the stockpile that the English probably had at their disposal at the start of the campaign. No chronicle suggests that they ran out of ammunition so quickly; indeed, what we read, in the *Eulogium historiarum*, is that by the end of the battle the archers had almost expended their arrows.[39]

In fact, it is not just logistical constraints that argue against a prolonged arrow storm, but also the mentalité of the archer himself. As was shown in Chapter 5, among the archers at Crécy were men for whom the bow was neither merely a standard issue weapon nor one intended for mass shooting. For these men it was a weapon of great precision, on the hunting field as well as in the arena of war, so that for them surely the idea of shooting blindly into the sky, even if experience told them much about direction and range, was counter-instinctive. And above all, in the case of an army reliant upon missile defence, the exhaustion of ammunition would be catastrophic. It would result in the archer becoming a relatively impotent force, and the army left with no deterrent missile defence to prevent the enemy from closing.

The battlefield and the deployment of the English army

One approach to reconstructing the battle of Crécy has been to ignore the ground altogether, either by passing over it without comment or by explicitly excluding it from consideration because, as Jim Bradbury explained, 'we do not know precisely where the battlefield was and so cannot base our descriptions on the nature of a site that we have chosen.'[40] 'We must', he notes in relation to Poitiers, 'rely only on the contemporary evidence'.[41] At first glance this may appear the prudent, scholarly approach to take; and, indeed, it would be if we were seeking to establish why one team emerged triumphant in the tournament arena. Battles, however, are rarely fought on level playing fields, and English tactics at Crécy, as in other battles and skirmishes, can *only* be understood in the context of the ground upon which they were applied. Remove the topography and there is a real danger that the discussion will become little more than an academic exercise. Since the traditional site at Crécy is by far the most likely of the battlefield candidates, we have accepted it in the argument that unfolds below. While the reader should be aware of the element of uncertainty in our approach, reassurance may be gained from the fact that the degree of uncertainty involved is no greater than that which attends the chronicle accounts for the

---

[39] *Eulogium*, iii, p. 211.
[40] Bradbury, *The Medieval Archer*, p. 105. However, the next paragraph states that the English took up position 'on ground that sloped down towards the River Maie', so the author is clearly thinking in terms of the traditional battlefield. Clifford Rogers's recent account of the battle makes no specific remarks about the site, noting only that 'the English position was strong, but far from impossibly so': *War Cruel and Sharp*, p. 265.
[41] Bradbury, *The Medieval Archer*, p. 109.

battle, upon which it is customary to place so much reliance. What we offer below are ideas concerning some aspects of the battle, which while occasionally going beyond what is strictly sustainable by the documentary evidence, may serve to stimulate further debate and deeper research into one of the most familiar, yet enigmatic, of medieval battles.[42]

It was concluded in Chapter 3 that there is little reason for doubting that the 'traditional' battlefield is indeed the site on which the battle of Crécy was fought. Moreover, this battleground includes topographical features, hitherto unnoticed in published work, that cast new light on the character and course of the battle. That the significance, in particular, of the steep bank on the eastern side of the valley has never before been recognised is perhaps the most striking weakness of Crécy historiography to date. Without exception, those interpretations of the battle that accept the traditional site have assumed that the Vallée des Clercs was a shallow dip in the landscape that presented no real obstacle in itself to the French, whose cavalry, according to these accounts, advanced across the valley and up the slope to the English position on the ridge between Crécy and Wadicourt.[43] Once the existence of the bank is recognised and its significance grasped, many points in the narrative sources begin to make sense. Since the bank makes an advance across the Vallée des Clercs impossible, the French approach to the English position must have been on a narrow front, from the southern end of the valley (and possibly also from the northern end). Once through this bottleneck, there would have been little room for Philip VI's army to manoeuvre, or even deploy in an orderly fashion, before advancing up the slope towards the English immediately to their front.

This, then, would appear to be the topographical context for so many of the chroniclers' comments about the battle, even though few say anything specific about the lie of the ground. Some authors note that the contingents at the front of the French army halted but were pushed forward by those arriving from behind – a situation that is consistent with ground that does not allow the leading contingents to spread out.[44] As Froissart noted, it would be difficult for those who were not there to appreciate the chaotic state of the French army, the 'povre arroy et ordenance en leurs conrois', before the battle began.[45] The same impression of a narrow approach and limited room for deployment is suggested by the descriptions of the crossbowmen trapped between the English archery to their front and the French cavalry behind them;[46] and, later in the battle, by

---

[42] Our approach is not, of course, original: a quarter of a century ago, something similar was attempted for Agincourt by Keegan: *The Face of Battle*, pp. 86–116. See also V. Fiorato, A. Boylston and C. Knüsel, eds, *Blood Red Roses: the Archaeology of a Mass Grave from the Battle of Towton AD 1461* (Oxford, 2000). It should be noted that, here and there, we differ from the interpretation presented by Michael Prestwich in Chapter 4.

[43] Limiting ourselves to publications of the last ten years or so, see the battle-plans in Sumption, *Trial by Battle*, p. 527; K. DeVries, *Infantry Warfare in the Early Fourteenth Century* (Woodbridge, 1996), p. 165; Bennett, 'The development of battle tactics', p. 9; D. Nicolle, *Crécy 1346* (Oxford, 2000), pp. 66–7, 74–5.

[44] *Jean le Bel*, ii, p. 102.

[45] *Froissart*, ed. Luce, iii, pp. 174, 413–14.

[46] *Villani*, vii, p. 166.

Philip VI's inability to take part in the fighting, his way blocked by the mass of men ahead of him.[47] These descriptions come from continental chroniclers, but similar imagery is offered by Geoffrey le Baker, who was presumably passing on eyewitness testimony from the Prince of Wales's battle. Unsighted contingents in the rear of the French army, fired up by the noise of battle ahead of them, pressed forward recklessly, thereby contributing to the chaotic pile-up in the confined space in front of the Prince of Wales's division: 'many were crushed to death, without a mark on them, in the middle of the French army, because the press was so great'. We are reminded here of the 'killing ground' alluded to in Edward III's newsletter – the 'small area where the first onslaught occurred [where] more than 1,500 knights and esquires died'. And we are reminded too of Villani's more explicit description of 'il luogo stretto da combattere'. All of these remarks point to a battle, or at least its early stages, that was fought in a confined area, which greatly restricted the deployment of the French army – first the crossbowmen and then, more decisively still, the massed contingents of heavily armoured mounted men-at-arms.

The ground that the English had chosen did not allow Philip VI to bring his vastly superior numbers to bear; indeed, the sheer size of his army contributed to its downfall. There would have been those among King Edward's captains, like Sir Thomas Ughtred, who would have recalled the similar advantage that well-chosen ground had conferred on Edward Balliol's small army at Dupplin Muir in 1332.[48] This was but one of the features of the site that would have made it particularly attractive to Edward and his lieutenants. Indeed, as was argued in Chapter 2, so suited was this ground to the implementation of English combined arms tactics that we must consider the possibility that it had been noticed as a potential battle site long before the summer of 1346, and that as the likelihood of a confrontation in Ponthieu became a certainty, arrangements for making the most of the site were set in motion. Historical parallels are not difficult to find. For example, we know that for some time before June 1815 the duke of Wellington had been aware of the merits of the ground at Mont-St-Jean, a few kilometres south of Waterloo, regarding it as the ideal spot for blocking a French advance on Brussels. The only factor that makes the earmarking of the Crécy battlefield less plausible is the period of time, over a decade, that had elapsed since Ponthieu had been administered by English officials. But Crécy was not an obscure backwater in Ponthieu. As one of the count's principal residences, we know that this location would have been familiar to some of Edward III's closest advisers. Indeed, we know that the king had visited Crécy himself during his youth.

Whether the site had been pre-planned – or whether we believe Froissart's tale of the marshals' search for advantageous ground on the eve of the battle – it is clear that the battlefield that was chosen was neither an open field nor an innocuous valley. It was ideally suited to the army that Edward had at his disposal and to the tactics that he wished to employ. For the ground met all of the requirements that he and his experienced lieutenants would have known were

---

[47] *Grandes chroniques*, ix, p. 283.
[48] For the circumstances at Dupplin Moor, see Rogers, *War Cruel and Sharp*, pp. 38–46.

necessary if they were to challenge Philip VI in the field with a good prospect of success. Firstly, the lie of the ground must allow him to deploy his entire army on foot in a secure defensive position, yet not inhibit offensive movement should the opportunity arise. Secondly, it must provide optimum conditions for his archers. And thirdly, it should as far as possible dictate the approach and deployment of the enemy.

The battlefield that Edward chose to fight on met all of these requirements. The slope on the western side of the Vallée des Clercs was sufficiently gentle to encourage the French to approach: indeed, from the base of the valley the gradient is deceptively gentle. Yet it also provided banks and hedges for a defending army, against or behind which the archers and the men at arms could anchor themselves. These *rideaux*, which next to Crécy formed a series of steps in the hillside, one above the other, would present serious obstacles to horses. This much is clear, but to what extent was the English position reinforced by improvised defences? Were the *rideaux* bolstered and supplemented by carts and tree trunks, thereby creating cover and a shooting platform for archers, as several French chronicles suggest? Was there in effect a wagon fort, as Villani states; or were only the rear and flanks protected in this fashion (as suggested by the short continuation of the *Chronique de Flandre* and St Omer chronicle), leaving the front of the position invitingly open to an attacker? Our review of the evidence has led us to conclude that Baker's 'pits' should be set aside as the product of his imagination; but for the rest, it depends upon which version of the battle, as presented in the fourteenth-century sources, we are inclined to accept.

In the past, some French historians envisaged 'un vaste camp retranché' between Crécy and Wadicourt,[49] whereas their English counterparts dismissed such notions as untenable. The strongest argument against the existence of such a reinforced defensive position is not the silence of the English chronicles but that it would have been difficult to construct, given the time and resources available. If enclosing a large area, Villani's *carrino* would have required a considerable number of carts, or much tree felling and carrying of timber. Would sufficient carts and other materials have been available at comparatively short notice, even allowing (as the Florentine author argues) for the utilisation of wagons drawn from the locality as well as those brought by the army itself? Perhaps we should envisage a partial enclosure, covering, firstly, the rear and flanks of the army, thus reducing the risk of surprise attack by a mounted force sweeping around the left flank of the English position north of Wadicourt; and, secondly, those lengths of the valley slope between Crécy and Wadicourt that were not occupied by formations of troops. If *rideaux* were incorporated into the English defensive line facing the valley, it may well have been possible to make use of similar landscape features to the rear. For example, less than 200 metres to the west of the windmill site is the opening to a roughly rectangular enclosure bounded by substantial hedgebanks and covering about 6 hectares. It is named

---

[49] F-C. Louandre, *Histoire d'Abbeville et du comté de Ponthieu jusqu'en 1789*, 3rd edn, 2 vols (Abbeville, 1883), i, p. 201. Seymour de Constant took a different view, but Simeon Luce followed Louandre: 'Dans cette position, l'armée anglaise était retranchée sur sa droite, sur sa gauche et sur ses derrières'. *Froissart*, ed. Luce, iii, p. xlviii n. 2.

'le Guidon' on modern maps and appears so named on cadastral plans from the Napoleonic period.[50] If it existed at the time of the battle (and the name, meaning 'knightly pennon' is certainly suggestive), it would have made an ideal, secure enclosure for horses, baggage and tents; and its perimeter bank could have formed part of 'une grande haye de leur charroy, par quoy on ne les peust sourprendre'.[51] If we allow for the utilisation of such topographical features, Villani's *carrino* may well have been a practical possibility. It is worth adding that Villani does allow for an opening in his wagon fort facing the French; for, as he notes, the English did not wish to avoid battle. This certainly makes sense, since a defensive position that had been too heavily reinforced would have discouraged an assault, whereas provoking such an attack was essential to the success of Edward III's tactical planning. Given that Jean le Bel's much-quoted description of the English cart enclosure (embroidered somewhat by Froissart) was also said to have had a single entrance, perhaps what we have in these two fourteenth-century narratives are descriptions of the same phenomenon seen from different perspectives by chroniclers with distinctive interpretative agendas.

As well as allowing for secure defensive deployment on foot, the English position on the higher ground above the valley floor also provided the archer with his preferred fighting conditions. An archer shooting at a target beneath him has better visual contact with his quarry and would need to give his arrows a minimal climbing trajectory. By shooting flat and avoiding the loss of flight energy expended in a rising trajectory, he could shoot further and with greater precision and impact. And in the valley below the archers, the approach and deployment of the enemy were, as we have seen, dictated by the ground. Entry into the Vallée des Clercs by large formations of mounted troops was restricted to either the northern or (the more likely approach) the southern end, the steep bank on the eastern side prohibiting a wide and frontal attack. Once beyond the bottleneck entrances, there was insufficient space on the valley floor for the French army to be effectively deployed. It is difficult to avoid the conclusion that the English plan would have been to occupy the ground that dominates both of these approaches, and indeed the ground between them, and by doing so trap the French cavalry on the valley floor over which the archers would have dominance.

Surveying the battlefield today, and particularly the ground above the southern entrance to the Vallée des Clercs, the logical position for a defensive line, dominating the bowl at the mouth of the valley, is immediately apparent. This crescent-shaped position is almost immediately forward of the traditional windmill site, and is secured at both ends by lengths of banking (*rideaux* or *tallus*). It is difficult to imagine a commander who had chosen to fight a defensive battle in this locality not holding this ground. We would suggest, therefore, that it was occupied by one of Edward's three 'battles'. Given that it would have borne the brunt of the initial attacks, this must have been the Prince of Wales's division. It

---

[50] We are much indebted to M. Emmanuel Tonetti for bringing this intriguing topographical feature to our attention.
[51] *Chronique de Flandre*, ii, p. 42.

commands the Abbeville approach into the Vallée des Clercs, and if success-
fully held, the constraints imposed by the steep bank on the eastern side of the
valley would have obliged an attacker to funnel onwards up the valley to the
north. If, as would have been logical, archers were positioned on the western
slopes within bowshot of the valley floor, the Vallée des Clercs, which for much
of its length is less than 200 metres across at its base, would have become, in
effect, a shooting gallery.

The positioning of the first English battle suggests itself immediately, but it is
more difficult to visualise the deployment of the second and third. As we have
seen, it would have made sense for the second to cover the length of the western
slopes of the valley from the hedgebank anchoring the left flank of the prince's
battle as far as Wadicourt. This, however, is a distance of 1,000 metres, which to
be defended securely (particularly given the importance of holding the northern
entry to the valley) may have required additional manpower from the third battle
or the utilisation of fixed defences for part of the length of the valley. Unfortunately, the chronicles do not allow us to resolve the matter conclusively, since
the few that refer to the spatial relationship between the three English battles,
either directly or indirectly, do not provide wholly consistent evidence. However,
it may be significant that the battle narrative that offers by far the most detailed
information about the captains serving in each of the battles may also be the
most reliable guide to the relative positions of these battles on the field.

Thus, the related texts of the short continuation of the *Chronique de Flandre*
and the St Omer chronicle state that the Prince of Wales's battle was deployed in
the vicinity of a windmill, and near to this was positioned the king's battle.[52] The
latter consisted essentially of the expanded household division, plus those shire
levies that had been attached to it. If deployed on the left flank of the prince's
battle, as seems likely, the household division would have covered the long
stretch of hillside as far as Wadicourt. (Available evidence suggests that it was
the strongest of the three battles, at least as far as men-at-arms are concerned.)
The king himself would have been stationed away from the front line; indeed, he
was probably at the windmill, as Froissart tells us. (The *Chronique de Flandre*
notes that that he was attired in 'ung tornicle de vert vellours à lettres d'or'.) The
third (rearguard) battle, numerically the weakest, consisting of the retinues of
Arundel, Suffolk, Despenser and the bishop of Durham, was kept in reserve,
ready to be deployed when and where needed. Although our location of the
king's battle along the western slopes of the Vallée des Clercs is conjectural, it
may be significant that the St Omer chronicler, or his source, was able to identify many of the bannerets serving in this and the prince's battle with a considerable degree of accuracy, while at the same time being far less well informed
about the composition of the reserve battle. As was discussed in Chapter 5, it is
likely that, before the battle began, the bannerets were identified from the
heraldry displayed on their banners by a herald attached to the French army. If
deployed as we have suggested, the banners of the first and second battles would
have been clearly visible, but those of the reserve battle far less so.

52 Paris, Bibliothèque Nationale, MS Fr. 693, fos 261v–262r; *Chronique de Flandre*, ii, pp.
42–3.

Although a somewhat different arrangement of battles is suggested by the Bourgeois of Valenciennes,[53] the testimony of the St Omer texts fits quite well with both the topography of the traditional battlefield and details offered by other chroniclers. It is surely significant, for example, that when we hear of reinforcements for the Prince of Wales's division, the captains involved are those known to have been serving in the reserve (rearguard) battle. Several chronicles state that it was a contingent of the bishop of Durham's retinue that was sent to relieve the prince, and one of them (the Anonimalle chronicle) adds the names of the earls of Suffolk and Huntingdon (the latter, of course, was not at Crécy, but part of his retinue did participate in the battle).[54] Moreover, a major intervention by the earl of Arundel's battle forms part of Villani's narrative.

Archery and the battle of Crécy

Let us return now to the question posed at the beginning of the concluding section of this book: 'how was it that the English won the battle?' Our investigation thus far has considered the testimony of the fourteenth-century narrative sources, the battlefield itself and the role of the archer in Edwardian warfare. We shall end by offering some thoughts on the dynamics of the battle. It is not our intention here to present a fresh blow-by-blow account of the events on that late August evening. Indeed, as will be clear by now, given the paucity of the primary sources and the interpretative problems posed by the secondary ones, we doubt whether constructing such an account with a single narrative line is actually possible. (Preferable in our view would be to accept the fuller fourteenth-century narratives as alternative versions of events.) Our approach will be to focus on the key features of the battle, which determined its character and outcome, with a view in particular to determining the nature of the archers' contribution to the English victory.[55]

The English position at Crécy had been well chosen and the contingents of

---

[53] Using the *Acta Bellicosa* as our guide to the composition of the English battles, we can interpret the Valenciennes chronicler's account as suggesting that the front line consisted of the first (advance guard) and third (rearguard) battles, with the second (centre) battle, including the king, the bishop of Durham and Harcourt in reserve 'sitting on their shields' (*Récits*, pp. 231–2). Applying this to the ground, it could be concluded that it was the third battle, under Arundel, Suffolk and Despenser, that was deployed on the left flank of the prince's battle, covering the valley slope as far as Wadicourt. In support of this arrangement, Froissart (A and B MSS) places Arundel's battle (to which, erroneously, he also assigns Northampton) on the flank of the prince.

[54] *Melsa*, iii, p. 58; *Récits*, pp. 232–3; *Anonimalle*, p. 22.

[55] There is much about the battle that remains uncertain. Many of the narrative sources focus principally on the events that unfolded in front of the Prince of Wales's division, but it is unclear how far this reflects the particular viewpoint of *their* sources rather than what actually happened. Given that, in our view, the prince's battle was deployed on the ridge above the 'bowl' at the southern entrance to the Vallée des Clercs, this leaves a substantial question mark over the remainder of the traditional battlefield, including the long stretch of hillside to Wadicourt and the rear of the English position. King Edward's despatch refers to French casualties on 'tout pars du champ', but it is unclear how extensive this was. The difficulty that we

archers effectively deployed, but there remained the problem of how best to utilise the limited supply of arrows. A high priority was the engagement and early destruction of the French missile capability. That the French would open their account by sending forward the crossbowmen would have been antici- pated. Engaging the Genoese at maximum range with the aim of eliminating them from the battle would necessitate a heavy expenditure of arrows early in the battle. But if successful, such a tactic would be decisive, since at a stroke would be destroyed the only missile force at Philip VI's disposal. With this threat removed, what remained of the arrow supply could be used against the mounted men-at-arms – but used very differently. Supported by well-chosen topography, the English archers would now benefit from optimum longbow conditions: controlled and economical target shooting at the lethal range of one hundred yards and closing. If we examine the battle, we can see that the employ- ment of archery in these two very different ways – long-range engagement, followed by tighter and closer controlled shooting – was eminently effective.

It is easy to overlook the fact that Philip VI also had a battle plan of sorts. The Genoese crossbowmen would be sent forward first, to engage and neutralise the English archers and weaken the line of men-at-arms, and this would be followed up by a massed assault by heavily armoured horsemen. These were classic 'com- bined arms' tactics; indeed, something similar had been employed at Courtrai.[56] If we believe Villani's statement that 300 horsemen accompanied the Genoese advance, there was clearly a keen awareness among the French commanders that rapid exploitation of the missile barrage was essential to the success of these tactics. Moreover, subsequent events also suggest that the first of the 'batailles' of heavy cavalry, the count of Alençon's, was positioned well forward, ready to take advantage of a breach in the English line. (This 'battle', according to Villani, was accompanied by foot sergeants.)

Unfortunately for the French, the execution of their plan left much to be desired. The crossbowmen advanced into the valley without their pavises, which along with the bulk of their ammunition were on carts that had not yet reached the battlefield. They were tired from the march and reluctant to fight that evening. A reasonable picture, therefore, is of a troop of men, herded forward into a hurried and disorganised formation, perhaps bunched too close, and prob- ably from the English perspective, perceivably disorganised. Whether or not their weapons were weakened by rain, we can assume that as professional soldiers, they were not without knowledge of what the longbow could do. There was no doubt a collective air of reluctance derived from some appreciation of what lay before them. Although probably not as numerous as contemporary writers suggest,[57] the crossbowmen nevertheless posed a serious threat to the English. King Edward, who had reputedly been wounded in the thigh by a

---

have interpreting Henry Knighton's enigmatic reference to the fighting (going on into the night) 'in the field of Westglyse near to Crécy' is illustrative of our problems.

[56] J.F. Verbruggen, *The Battle of the Golden Spurs: Courtrai, 11 July 1302*, ed. K. DeVries, trans. D.R. Ferguson (Woodbridge, 2002), pp. 231–2.

[57] Cf. Chapter 7, where Bertrand Schnerb argues against there being as many as 6,000 crossbowmen.

quarrel at Sluys, would have recognised the need to neutralise them. Here was an occasion for an 'arrow storm': a limited, pre-emptive long range archery strike, of massed shooting into a massed target.

We need at this point to look again at the battlefield and remind ourselves that a French army advancing from Abbeville would have had as their most likely, and certainly their most direct approach the southern mouth of the Vallée des Clercs where it sweeps down towards the River Maye. Above this point, and forward of the site of the windmill, the crescent ridge, which dominates the bowl-shaped mouth of the valley, would have been occupied by the Prince of Wales's division. Under the experienced command of the earls of Northampton and Warwick, and their lieutenants, Sir Thomas Ughtred and Sir Bartholomew Burgherssh, there may have been a thousand archers deployed along this ridge.[58] The precise number is uncertain, but we may be sure that they were deployed to best advantage, probably forward of the men-at-arms in open order but ready, if necessary, to withdraw to the protective cover of the 'haies', whether 'natural' (the *rideaux* on the wings of the prince's battle) or composed of men-at-arms and spearmen.[59]

As the Genoese moved forward into the bowl of the valley, and began to shoot ineffectively towards the English position,[60] an order would have been issued to the bowmen to commence a series of volleys – let us say half a dozen. Rising up from the higher ground of the crescent ridge, and descending into the valley, a series of controlled volleys, each of a thousand arrows, would have concentrated on a relatively compact target of men on the valley floor. The appearance and sound of such volleys have been evoked by the chroniclers, but we can hardly imagine the horror felt by the crossbowmen as they watched the cloud of arrows flying inexorably towards them. These men would have been almost static, so let us suppose an interval of ten or even twenty seconds between each volley: time enough for the crossbowmen if they felt inclined, or even if driven, to shuffle forward a few yards. Ten lingering seconds – sufficient for disorder to rise, yet not be calmed, and wholly insufficient for a crossbowman to rearm. And after this volley, another, and another. Under such disciplined shooting, and supposing that the deadly storm would continue to rain down on them, panic is not hard to imagine, nor the stark impossibility of advance or relief. And if the initial volleys had not broken their ranks, no doubt the English commanders were prepared to risk using more to do so, for while they had to conserve ammunition to deal with the anticipated massed attack by horsemen, breaking the Genoese was of critical importance.

---

[58] This is a guess, and deliberately a conservative one. See Chapter 5, Table 2: the numbers of archers serving in the first division *at the outset* of the campaign are difficult to determine. Uncertainty surrounds a contingent of Welsh archers attached to the prince's retinue in the Wetwang abstracts, and we cannot be sure how many of the arrayed archers from Wales and England were added to the prince's division.

[59] It may be pointed out in passing that the deployment of the archers on this crescent-shaped position may have prompted an eyewitness to compare it to the shape (and function) of a 'shield'.

[60] Recent weapons tests on the Crécy battlefield have demonstrated the inferiority of the crossbow to the longbow, in terms of range, just as *Baker* reports (p. 83).

The rout of the crossbowmen left Philip VI's battle plan in tatters. With hindsight, we know that he should have called off the battle for the evening and reconsidered his options. But his blood was up, and in any case effective control of his army had probably passed to his lieutenants, including his brother, the count of Alençon. Heavily armoured horsemen were to be called upon to achieve victory on their own. For all the reported confusion in their ranks, the sheer numbers of knightly warriors at Philip's disposal would have made for an awe-inspiring sight: 'Toute la fleur de Crestienneté estoit illec assemblée montée en armes si richement que merveilles.'[61] But in all senses his men faced an uphill task. Success would depend upon closing with the English and forcing them to break ranks, either by the 'shock' (moral as much as physical) of a massed charge or by overwhelming them in hand-to-hand combat. But their approach would by necessity be made on unfavourable ground, without missile weapon support and in the teeth of archery, whose potency had already been demonstrated.

In fact, the archery that awaited the French cavalry was to be different from that meted out to the crossbowmen. Rather than being engaged at long range, they would feel the impact of the bowmen's shafts at barely a stone's throw from the English line. There were several reasons why the English would have set aside long-range archery in favour of close-range shooting and, for the most competent of the bowmen, marksmanship. Firstly, unlike the Genoese, the heavy cavalry did not pose a long-distance threat to the English. Secondly, their greater numbers meant that sustained long-range archery, while no doubt having some effect, could have led to the exhaustion of ammunition well before the threat had been neutralised. Thirdly, given their numbers and greater dispersal, had the English employed an 'arrow storm' too many of their opponents would have remained out of range, allowing – if not obliging – them to rethink their approach, and perhaps form up at a distance for an outflanking manoeuvre. By withholding their missiles until the horsemen were almost upon them, the English ensured that, at the moment of engagement, the attacking force would be denied the opportunity of an alternative approach. These were important tactical considerations, yet the shift in tactics was also founded upon a keen understanding of the mentalité of the archer himself. He was by natural inclination a marksman, his bow a precision weapon, his arrows his preferred means of survival. King Edward and his lieutenants would have been well aware of the archer's instincts and where his particular strengths lay.

So, faced by the prospect of concerted attacks by heavy cavalry, the response is unlikely to have been a long-range engagement of the 'arrow storm' variety, but rather one that optimised the longbow by engaging the enemy at a distance that maximised both accuracy and impact. There will be differing opinions as to when this occurs, but for the sake of argument let us take this distance to be approximately 80 to 100 metres. A body of horsemen advancing uphill in line

---

[61] *Chronique de Flandre*, ii, p. 43. This is an apt phrase since Philip VI's army was cosmopolitan in composition. For convenience, we shall speak of 'French' men-at-arms; but for a celebration of the courageous contribution of John of Bohemia's men, see L. Leger, 'Un poème tchèque sur la bataille de Crécy', *Journal des Savants*, 1902, pp. 323–31.

abreast at 10 km per hour, or 166 metres per minute, would at 100 metres permit an archer perhaps four or five shots from his bow before his target was upon him. To set against the likelihood that the horsemen would accelerate over the last 100 metres is the certainty that as the range closed so the probability of a strike, and the potential damage of its impact, would increase. One hundred yards for the longbow is bread and butter. The target is clearly visible, the trajectory is flattening, and the hardened bodkin tip of a battle arrow would arrive reasonably perpendicular to its target. At such close range we should not doubt the nervousness of the archer. But the greater his danger, the greater became his target; and, as we have seen, the steadiness of the archer's aim would have no doubt been improved by the knowledge that he stood amid the spear points of his comrades or a physical barrier, or at least that such security was close at hand.

The effect that the first close-range volleys of arrows had on the approaching French horsemen would have depended to some extent upon whether the warhorses in the front line were equipped with head and chest armour (as was the case, for example, at Poitiers),[62] and probably also upon how tightly bunched together the horsemen were as they approached the English position. In theory, they would have reached the English line in a compact formation, with the men in each 'banner' or 'conroi' drawn up in serried ranks, arranged in several lines, and with the conrois deployed next to each other to form a 'battle' with a wide front.[63] That this ideal arrangement was carried forward into practice at Crécy must be doubted. There are no systematic pay records for the French army in 1346, but for 'l'host de Bouvines' of 1340 we know that the count of Alençon's 'battle' consisted of over 1,200 men-at-arms.[64] In the confined space at the mouth of the Vallée des Clercs, a large division of cavalry like Alençon's would, by necessity, have been split into several parts, presumably arranged in column. Moreover, it is unlikely that the leading formations were in good order as they began their approach to the English line. The 'triboul' that occurred as the fleeing Genoese clashed with the oncoming heavy cavalry can only have served to break up the latter's ranks. Restoring good order in such circumstances would have been difficult, if not impossible, and the steady uphill slope must have added to the problem of maintaining a tight formation. With the man-at-arm's first allegiance being to his 'bannière', we should visualise the 'bataille' disintegrating into its constituent units, of which there would have been a great many. The count of Alencon's 'battle' in 1340 was composed of no fewer than 134 companies. Twenty-three of these, ranging in size from 14 to 60 men-at-arms, were led by bannerets.[65]

---

[62] *Baker*, pp. 143, 148.

[63] J.F. Verbruggen, *The Art of Warfare in Western Europe During the Middle Ages*, English trans., 2nd edn (Woodbridge, 1997), pp. 73–7; P. Contamine, *War in the Middle Ages* (London, 1985), pp. 229–30.

[64] J.F. Verbruggen, 'La tactique de la chevalerie française de 1340 à 1415', *Publications de l'Université de l'Etat à Elisabethville*, I (1961), pp. 39–48 (at p. 41); P. Contamine, *Guerre, état et société*, p. 81.

[65] Contamine, *Guerre, état et société*, p. 81. The count's household company consisted of 73 men-at-arms.

It is unlikely to have been a single, well-formed, wide-fronted block of horsemen that approached the English line, but something more irregular, tightly packed in parts, more ragged elsewhere, the irregularity corresponding to variations in 'local' command and control. Ideally, the approach would have begun slowly with lances carried upright, only being levelled when, at the agreed distance from the enemy and at the command 'spur on' ('poignez'), the speed of advance increased to a quick trot or a gallop.[66] It was perhaps only after this change of pace had occurred that the English unleashed their first volley of arrows. We cannot be sure whether the initial volley was released simultaneously along the line, or whether it was withheld at certain points until the approaching horsemen reached a predetermined distance. The impact in detail of the first volley would have depended on a number of variables, as has been said; but there can be no doubt that overall it would have produced an immediate collapse of wounded horses, followed by the fall of unwounded mounts, brought down by collision with those in front or around them. The tighter the formation, the more extensive this 'collateral' damage would have been. Other horses, as Jean le Bel relates so vividly, threw their riders or became uncontrollable. Further volleys would have brought down sufficient men and mounts to create a barrier wholly impassable to those advancing behind, bringing the attack to a halt before it had even closed with the English line. We need not rely solely on the narrative sources for an impression of the heavy warhorse losses that were sustained so rapidly on that August evening. Turning to the *restauro equorum* records, we find, for example, that seventeen of the men-at-arms serving under the banner of the viscomte de Meleun lost their mounts in the 'besoigne devant Cressy en Ponthieu'.[67]

The dynamics of the battle had begun in earnest, fuelled not least by the English tactic of drawing the French onto their lines. Concentrated, close-range archery had produced a grisly new feature on the battlefield: long mounds of fallen warhorses and men forming what could be described as 'hedges' on the hillside. These obstacles added significantly to the difficulties facing fresh formations of mounted warriors as they sought to approach the English position. The 'hedges' would have fast become 'stock proof', since it would have been unrealistic to expect warhorses to trample through or leap over a writhing bank of wounded and trapped men and their disabled mounts. We should pause for a moment to consider the appalling plight of the wounded. Not only does an arrow cause internal damage, but any wound in which the arrow remained would be worked excruciatingly around the lesion by the random cantilever of the external shaft. To both man and horse, any movement that disturbed the shaft would be sheer torture. And those arrows that shattered in the confined spaces within the turmoil would have sprayed splinters about like grapeshot. Thus, these were not passive piles of men and horses, but mixed accumulations of dead and living, the

---

[66] Verbruggen, *The Art of Warfare*, p. 108. See also M. Bennett, 'La Regle du Temple as a military manual or how to deliver a cavalry charge', *Studies in Medieval History Presented to R. Allen-Brown*, ed. C. Harper-Bill et al. (Woodbridge, 1989), pp. 7–19 (esp. pp. 15–17).

[67] Contamine, *Guerre, état et société*, p. 105. On average, 28 men-at-arms were serving under each banner in the count of Alençon's battle in 1340.

wounded struggling in agony, their cries rising above the tumult of the battle-field. If we are to believe Froissart, many were dispatched where they lay by Welshman wielding long knives.

When Geoffrey le Baker speaks of many Frenchmen, though unwounded, being smothered to death in the press,[68] he is presumably referring to those who were trapped amid these heaps of fallen horses. It would have been a fortunate knight who was pulled out by his squire. (Thierri de Senzeilles was lucky that his horse collapsed at some distance from the action.) However, there was a more general crush of men and horses on the slopes below the 'hedges' of horse carcasses, as fresh contingents, spurred on by the noise of battle ahead of them, poured through the bottleneck opening of the valley and found little or no room to manoeuvre in the confined area of the 'bowl' beneath the English position. There could be no turning back for a body of horse or foot once it had entered the Vallée des Clercs, and the steep bank on the eastern side prevented easy movement in that direction. The only options were to advance up the obsta-cle-strewn slope into the teeth of the English archery, or to try further along the valley, in all likelihood running the gauntlet of archers lining the western slopes. Indeed, the route up the valley, which we have likened to a 'shooting gallery', would have been the natural escape route for fugitives from the fighting. Since this is the direction to Labroye (and flight in any other direction would have been impossible), it is surely the route that Philip VI took when he was led from the 'press' by Jean de Hainault.

Thus, from the French perspective, the battle had acquired a remorseless momentum that carried them to disaster. Command and control had completely broken down. Not only was Philip VI unable to influence events personally, but to judge from the extraordinarily long list of prominent French noblemen who lost their lives, many of the key figures of the army's command network were removed during the course of the battle. It seems that captains leading from the front fell victim to archery or were smothered in the 'press'. One of the particu-larly striking features of the battle of Crécy is that no notable Frenchmen were taken prisoner. Even if we accept the testimony of some chroniclers that this was a battle in which no quarter was offered, the lack of prisoners, by comparison with Poitiers and Agincourt, demands explanation.[69] In fact, the explanation is not difficult to find, for while archery played an important part in all three engagements, Crécy was different from the others in that the French nobility fought as *mounted* warriors. Close-range archery was particularly devastating against horsemen in massed formations. For not only were the mounts especially vulnerable, but when they fell they took their riders with them and, as the author of the *Chronique des quatre premiers Valois* wrote of Crécy, 'on this day men were killed by their horses'.[70] In this chaos we must assume that banners fell as frequently as captains: a few seconds of precision archery and retinues were left

[68] *Baker*, p. 84.

[69] C. Given-Wilson and F. Bériac, 'Edward III's prisoners of war: the battle of Poitiers and its context', *EHR*, cxvi (2001), pp. 802–33 (at pp. 804–5).

[70] 'Et en ce jour fut l'occision des gens par les chevaulx. Car comme les François se cuidoient rengier, leurs chevaulx cheoient mors.' *Chronique des quatre premiers Valois*, p. 16.

leaderless and without the crucial rallying point that the banner provided.[71] If the survivors made further approaches to the English line it would have been as individuals or in small groups. Order and optimism would have been replaced by a turmoil of desperation, fuelled only by blind courage. We are reminded here of the words of King Edward's despatch: 'lez ennemiz se porterount moult noblement, et moult sovent se ralierent'.[72]

The steadily extending 'hedges' of dead and wounded warhorses and men, accumulating parallel to the English line, must have had a profound effect on the dynamics of the battle. They would have represented a major obstacle to fresh formations of French horsemen, who would have been obliged to seek a way around their fallen comrades. This would not have been a rehearsed manoeuvre and would have rapidly deteriorated into a chaotic jumble of collisions, as individuals jostled among themselves to find a way forward. Brought practically to a standstill and exposing the vulnerable flanks of their mounts to the English line as they sought a way around the obstacles in their path, the horsemen presented comfortable targets to archers who were keen to ensure that each and every shaft found its mark. Those individuals and small groups who emerged from the tangle would now be within point blank range, their fate sealed. There was improvisation, as when the count of Blois dismounted his men and advanced on foot, but all to no avail.[73] It seems, therefore, that the fighting would quickly have become a fragmented affair, particularly in front of the prince's division. For the French, avenues of approach became fewer and narrower, against which the English could concentrate their archery. We can imagine areas of the battle-field changing from combat zones to neutralised ground. In the latter, there would have been little to prevent the English advancing, perhaps to recover ammunition, perhaps to take up better shooting positions in order to apply still more pressure on the already compressed and disordered crowd – no longer really an army – below them in the Vallée des Clercs. In this way, English tactics responded to the dynamics of the battle. There was more mobility than has often been recognised, and it seems that it was this aspect of the battle – the advances to the 'hedges' – that attracted the attention of continental chroniclers, from Italy, France and the Low Countries.

It would be difficult to exaggerate the effect that archery had on the course and outcome of the battle of Crécy. The bowmen sustained a form of precision shooting that for the crucial early stages of the engagement, and perhaps for the better part it, prevented their opponents from closing on the English line. Yet it is clear that some contingents of the French army did manage to engage in hand-to-hand combat: one of the few aspects of the battle that chroniclers of all backgrounds agree upon is that such close-quarters combat did take place. On at least one occasion, the Prince of Wales's division was put under such pressure that his banner, and perhaps his person, were threatened. As we have seen, this episode was interpreted in a variety of ways by the chroniclers, but its essential

---

71 On the important role played by banners as rallying points, see Verbruggen, *The Art of Warfare*, pp. 89–91.
72 *Le Prince Noir*, ed. Michel, p. 310.
73 *Chronique de Flandre*, ii, p. 43.

truth cannot be doubted since it is also attested by the administrative records. In February 1347, Sir Thomas Daniel was granted an annuity of 40 marks per annum, in part for his good service in replanting ('relevaill') the prince's banner in the battle.[74] All this points to a serious incident, which could have had a damaging psychological effect on the army had the situation not been rapidly restored. No wonder the king sent a contingent of men-at-arms (probably the bishop of Durham's men) to reinforce the young prince's division.

The mêlée around the prince's banner and the likelihood of further hand-to-hand fighting elsewhere on the field raises two questions. Firstly, how did it happen, given the apparent overwhelming dominance of English archery? Secondly, how was it that such close-quarters combat did not give rise to heavier English casualties? The first question is the easier of the two to answer. An archer is reliant on ammunition and he needs to be able to see his target. As we have seen, the supply of arrows was not unlimited, and it is possible that, locally at least, ammunition was indeed exhausted at certain stages in a battle that (to quote Edward III again) was 'trop fort et longement duraunt', from the hour of vespers into the night. In the fading light of a late August evening it would also have become increasingly difficult to pick individual targets. (A fifteenth-century Norman source tells us that Edward set a timber-filled windmill alight in order to illuminate the battlefield.[75]) Close-quarters combat was also more likely when the English advanced from their starting positions. We have argued that such redeployment probably took place several times at various points along the line, and it is not difficult to find echoes of this in the continental chronicles, which describe the English switching to the offensive to take advantage of confusion in the French army.

Some of the English sources report that Edward III's army suffered very low casualties. While the continental chroniclers offer a somewhat different impression (for example, '300 knights' killed, according to Jean le Bel), the balance of evidence points to the death of no more than a handful of men-at-arms. It is actually not difficult to reconcile this with a view of the battle that involves close-quarters combat, since the English would surely have fought with a considerable advantage. The tightness of their formations and the mutual support provided by experienced and dependable comrades-in-arms would have given them the edge against the individuals and small groups that had managed to close with the English lines.[76] A more substantial body of attackers may have been responsible for the crisis around the prince's banner, which as the command centre of the vanguard division would have attracted the most concentrated attention. But it is clear that this threat was soon neutralised. Mounted men had the advantage of height, but their horses were vulnerable to lance thrusts from dismounted men-at-arms, and they presented point-blank targets

---

[74] *Black Prince Register*, i, p. 45.
[75] Pierre Cochon, *Chronique Normande*, noted in R. Barber, *Edward Prince of Wales and Aquitaine* (Woodbridge, 1978), p. 68.
[76] The importance of such cohesion should not be underestimated: English losses appear to have been light in all of the successful 'defensive' battles of the Edwardian period, including those (like Morlaix) that were undoubtedly hard-fought affairs.

for archers intermingled among the bristling ranks of men-at-arms and spearmen. In offensive mode, these 'hedgehogs' would have been irresistible: just like the Scots at Bannockburn, 'they [would have] advanced like a thickset hedge, and such a phalanx could not easily be broken'.[77] Only when a man broke ranks would he be vulnerable, and it is significant that one of the few known English casualties at Crécy, the newly created knight, Sir Aymer Rokesle, was killed when he 'threw himself impetuously into the [French] battle formation'.[78]

It will be evident from this discussion that the outcome of the battle of Crécy had been decided at an early stage of the engagement. This was a battle very different from Poitiers, where (according to the Monk of Malmesbury) the result was still in the balance after each archer had unleashed a hundred arrows. This, he noted, was exceptional, since it was usually clear which side in a battle would emerge victorious after the third, fourth or at most sixth pull of the bow.[79] In this respect, its seems that Crécy was a more conventional engagement. A few volleys of long-range archery had dealt with the Genoese; then the first assault of heavily armoured horsemen was efficiently and abruptly halted at close range. By this time the French army was set on a disastrous course, which had been determined by the topography of the battlefield and the English tactic of drawing their opponents onto their lines. The rapid accumulation of long mounds of fallen horses and men profoundly affected the dynamics of the battle, which became a fragmented affair involving 'local' advances by the English as well as repeated attempts by groups of French horsemen to close with their adversaries. Some succeeded and there was a limited amount of close-quarters combat, but knightly heroism was no substitute for leadership, discipline and missile-weapon troops capable of challenging the English archers. So completely had King Edward been able to control the course of the battle that he needed to commit only a proportion of his reserves. But, while some among the knights and esquires in his army may not even have unsheathed their swords, his archers had almost exhausted their supply of arrows. Their role had been decisive, though their success cannot be understood simply by reference to technological issues (for example, the power of the bow) or the implementation of a tactical blueprint. Crécy was a triumph for the archer because the army leadership recognised how best to exploit his particular skills, given the opportunities offered by the ground but also the limitations imposed by the available ammunition supply. We would add that the location of many of the archers within mixed retinues (almost certainly on the battlefield as well as for administrative purposes) provided the ideal organisational framework for the exploitation of their potential.

---

[77] *Vita Edwardi Secundi*, ed. N. Denholm-Young (London, 1957), p. 52.
[78] 'impetuose se in aciem transmisit': *Eulogium*, iii, p. 211.
[79] *Eulogium*, iii, p. 225.

INDEX

Warfare in History

The Battle of Hastings: Sources and Interpretations, *edited and introduced by Stephen Morillo*

Infantry Warfare in the Early Fourteenth Century: Discipline, Tactics, and Technology, *Kelly DeVries*

The Art of Warfare in Western Europe during the Middle Ages, from the Eighth Century to 1340, *J.F. Verbruggen*

Knights and Peasants: The Hundred Years War in the French Countryside, *Nicholas Wright*

Society at War: The Experience of England and France during the Hundred Years War, *edited by Christopher Allmand*

The Circle of War in the Middle Ages: Essays on Medieval Military and Naval History, *edited by Donald J. Kagay and L.J. Andrew Villalon*

The Anglo-Scots Wars, 1513–1550: A Military History, *Gervase Phillips*

The Norwegian Invasion of England in 1066, *Kelly DeVries*

The Wars of Edward III: Sources and Interpretations, *edited by Clifford J. Rogers*

The Battle of Agincourt: Sources and Interpretations, *Anne Curry*

War Cruel and Sharp: English Strategy under Edward III, 1327–1360, *Clifford J. Rogers*

The Normans and their Adversaries at War: Essays in Memory of C. Warren Hollister, *edited by Richard P. Abels and Bernard S. Bachrach*

The Battle of the Golden Spurs (Courtrai, 11 July 1302): A Contribution to the History of Flanders' War of Liberation, 1297–1305, *J.F. Verbruggen*

War at Sea in the Middle Ages and Renaissance, *edited by John B. Hattendorf and Richard W. Unger*

Swein Forkbeard's Invasions and the Danish Conquest of England, 991–1017, *Ian Howard*

Religion and the Conduct of War, c. 300–1017, *David S. Bachrach*

Warfare in Medieval Brabant, 1356–1406, *Sergio Boffa*

Renaissance Military Memoirs: War, History and Identity, 1450–1600, *Yuval Noah Harari*

The Place of War in English History, 1066–1214, *J.O. Prestwich, edited by Michael Prestwich*

War and the Soldier in the Fourteenth Century, *Adrian R. Bell*